Wrongful Patent Assertion

Wrongful Patent Assertion

A Comparative Law and Economics Analysis

THOMAS F. COTTER

Taft Stettinius & Hollister Professor of Law,
University of Minnesota Law School

OXFORD
UNIVERSITY PRESS

OXFORD
UNIVERSITY PRESS

Great Clarendon Street, Oxford, OX2 6DP,
United Kingdom

Oxford University Press is a department of the University of Oxford.
It furthers the University's objective of excellence in research, scholarship,
and education by publishing worldwide. Oxford is a registered trade mark of
Oxford University Press in the UK and in certain other countries.

Published in the United States of America by Oxford University Press
198 Madison Avenue, New York, NY 10016, United States of America.

British Library Cataloguing in Publication Data
Data available

Library of Congress Control Number: 2025950604

ISBN 9780198885634

DOI: 10.1093/9780191994104.001.0001

Printed and bound by
CPI Group (UK) Ltd., Croydon, CR0 4YY

The manufacturer's authorised representative in the EU for product safety is
Oxford University Press España S.A. of El Parque Empresarial San Fernando de Henares,
Avenida de Castilla, 2 – 28830 Madrid (www.oup.es/en or product.safety@oup.com).
OUP España S.A. also acts as importer into Spain of products made by the manufacturer.

MIX
Paper | Supporting responsible forestry
FSC® C013604
FSC www.fsc.org

Contents

Preface

This book has been many years in the making, and would not exist were it not for the contributions of many people and many institutions. In particular, I thank the University of Minnesota for summer research grants and sabbatical funding, and the Max Planck Institute for Innovation and Competition for allowing me to use its world-class facilities. For their advice, assistance, comments, conversation, and/or provision of materials, I am especially thankful to Jorge Contreras, Léon Dijkman, Sarah Fackrell, Erik Habich, Christopher Heath, Erik Hovenkamp, Mark Lemley, Amandine Léonard, Kung-Chung Liu, Brian Love, Roderick McConnell, Peter Picht, Krista Rantasaari, Hubertus Schacht, Chung-Lun Shen, Norman Siebrasse, and Peter Teunissen. I also benefited from research assistance provided by the following individuals over the past few years: Eun Bee Cho, Mengmeng Du, Xinyue (Riley) Ji, Isabella Jurcisin, Henry Lee, Hanhui Li, River Lord, Jake Polinsky, Madi Rubin, Katja Schickl, Maxwell Terry, and Vivian Wood. I am especially grateful to the library staff at the University of Minnesota Law School, in particular Loren Turner and David Zopfi-Jordan.

Some portions of the book are adapted from my previously published works, as noted in the text.

Finally, a note on translations. For the Chinese Patent Act, I used the translation available on the China National Intellectual Property Administration's website.[1] For the Japan Anti-Monopoly Act, I used the unofficial translation available from Japanese Law Translation,[2] a website managed by the Japanese Ministry of Justice; and for the South Korea Monopoly Regulation and Fair Trade Act, I used the unofficial translation.[3] Most other translations are noted in the text.

[1] https://english.cnipa.gov.cn/col/col3068/index.html.
[2] https://www.japaneselawtranslation.go.jp/en.
[3] Available at elaw.klri.re.kr/eng_service/lawView.do?hseq=64980&lang=ENG.

1

Defining Wrongful Patent Assertion

Suppose that Company *A* files a patent infringement action against its competitor, Company *B*; and that Company *A* succeeds in obtaining a preliminary injunction excluding Company *B* from making, using, and selling products that Company *A* alleges incorporate the patented technology. As a result, Company *B* pulls the accused products from the market pending trial, while it works to "design around," that is, to develop some alternative to the patented technology that it can deploy on at least a temporary basis. Meanwhile, the infringement litigation proceeds to trial and concludes with the entry of a final judgment in favor of Company *B*, on the ground that the patent claims in suit were either invalid or not infringed (or both). Should Company *A* suffer any adverse consequences for having caused Company *B* temporarily to exit the market and design around—or for that matter, for having prosecuted an action for the infringement of what turned out to be, ex post, an invalid or noninfringed patent—and if so, what should those consequences be? Should courts be obligated to award *B* its attorneys' fees, for example, or should fee awards be available, if at all, only in extreme cases? Should *A* be required to compensate *B* for the losses *B* suffered as a result of the preliminary injunction, even if *A* acted in good faith in obtaining it? If compensation should be awarded, should it be awarded in full or in part, or perhaps capped by the amount of the bond *A* was required to post? Should it matter whether *A* is a practicing or a nonpracticing entity? Should there be any additional consequences, if *B*'s temporary exclusion from the market enabled *A* to enjoy temporary monopoly power, or if *A* obtained the patent by withholding information from (or misrepresenting information to) the Patent Office? Alternatively, even if the patent in suit is valid and infringed, should that mean that *A* is entitled to exclude *B* from the market, or should courts stay or deny injunctive relief under some circumstances? For that matter, might there be some circumstances under which *A*'s conduct prior to, during, or even independent of the litigation, should affect *A*'s entitlement to any sort of redress?

Legal systems around the world address issues like these every day, in a variety of settings and in accordance with a variety of legal doctrines. Sometimes

Wrongful Patent Assertion. Thomas F. Cotter, Oxford University Press.
DOI: 10.1093/9780191994104.003.0001

those legal doctrines are internal to patent law itself, as with the United States Patent Act's limitation on fee awards to "exceptional cases."[1] In other cases, the doctrines courts apply may be transsubstantive, as in countries that generally award fees to prevailing parties, without any special rules for patent cases. Or they might be a little of each, as with the civil-law countries' abuse of right doctrine or the common-law countries' equitable defenses, which though generally applicable may form some recurring patterns when directed at patent litigation—or even morph into patent-specific defenses, as with the U.S. equitable doctrines of inequitable conduct, patent misuse, and prosecution laches. Other relevant bodies of law may include both competition (antitrust) law—which, generally speaking, penalizes efforts to distort the competitive process—as well as *unfair* competition law, which forbids unfair or deceptive practices that impair the integrity of the market. These various bodies of law, in turn, often can be viewed as utilitarian efforts to improve social or consumer welfare, albeit by different means. Patent law itself is, by most accounts, intended to advance the utilitarian goal of encouraging investment in the creation and dissemination of useful knowledge. For this reason, doctrines internal to patent law that impose constraints upon or penalize the assertion of patent rights can be viewed as efforts to ensure that the social benefits of the patent system—its contributions to long-term, or dynamic, social welfare—do not outweigh the social costs, that is, the static and (potentially) dynamic social welfare losses that also can result from the exercise of patent rights. Similarly, competition law is often viewed as premised on the notion that consumer welfare will be maximized if firms generally are prevented from acquiring or expanding the power to control aggregate prices and output. Even unfair competition law, though arguably grounded to some extent in nonutilitarian fairness norms, can be viewed through a similar lens, insofar as deceptive conduct, if unchecked, threatens to reduce social welfare, by discouraging producers from making productive investments and impeding consumers from making informed purchasing decisions.[2] Given the different policies served by these different bodies of law, however, all of which in one way or another may regulate the assertion of patent rights, the question arises whether the various legal and equitable doctrines cohere, by providing specialized tools for addressing specific harms arising from a range of patentee behaviors—or whether they might, in some instances, be duplicative or redundant, or even

[1] 35 U.S.C. § 285.

[2] There are other policies that inform some bodies of law, such as trade secrets, that often are grouped within the rubric of unfair competition law. The bodies of unfair competition law most relevant to the topic of this book, however, are those that target deceptive conduct.

mutually contradictory. From a policy standpoint, moreover, another question is whether the doctrines focus on the right set of factors for discouraging social welfare-reducing behavior; and, to the extent different countries apply different rules to similar phenomena, whether one approach is superior to another in promoting the underlying social policies, or if instead different approaches simply fit certain legal environments better than others.

To date, there has been no comparative, book-length treatment of the above topics taken as a whole—and this is surprising, for a number of reasons. First, the number of patents annually granted throughout the world has increased substantially over the past thirty years, with China alone issuing over a million patents for new inventions annually, and the U.S. over 300,000.[3] Second, patent litigation can be enormously expensive. Fees and costs in the U.S., for example, for even a small-stakes (under $1 million) dispute, can be hundreds of thousands of dollars;[4] and while U.S. costs are, to some degree, a function of features unique to the U.S. system, including extensive pretrial discovery and the availability of jury trials, patent litigation in any country can be costly due to, among other things, the complexity of the subject matter or the need for retaining technical experts or advisers. Third, although most patents do not confer substantial market power, let alone full-blown monopoly power, some of them certainly do; indeed, the conferral of temporary monopoly power that firms may try to exploit for the purpose of recouping their research and development costs is largely the point of having a patent system in the first place. Fourth, because (1) patent infringement is (for all practical purposes) a strict liability tort, (2) much—perhaps most—patent infringement is the result of independent invention, not direct copying, and (3) liability extends down the chain of distribution, from infringing manufacturer to distributor to retailer and even, in some countries, to the end consumer, patent owners sometimes can extract royalties, ex post, that exceed the economic value of the patented technology, ex ante—a phenomenon often referred to as "patent

[3] *See* World Intellectual Property Organization (WIPO), *Intellectual Property Statistical Country Profile 2024: China*, https://www.wipo.int/edocs/statistics-country-profile/en/cn.pdf (reporting 1,044,777 patent grants in 2024 and 649,048 registered design rights); WIPO, *Intellectual Property Statistical Country Profile 2024: United States*, https://www.wipo.int/edocs/statistics-country-profile/en/us.pdf (reporting 319,815 patent grants of all types in 2024). WIPO's IP Statistics Data Center https://www3.wipo.int/ipstats/keyindex.htm, also reports that China registered over 2,000,000 utility models in 2024 (a decrease, however, from the over 3,000,000 registered in 2021).

[4] According to the American Intellectual Property Law Association, the median cost of litigating even a small-stakes (less than $1 million at risk) patent infringement action, just through discovery and claim construction, is $250,000; the median cost of litigating all the way through appeal, when applicable, is $450,000. *See* Am. Intell. Prop. L. Ass'n, 2025 Report of the Economic Survey 33 (2025).

holdup."[5] Fifth, although the majority of patent infringement lawsuits settle before trial, patent owners lose a substantial plurality, and in some countries a majority, of those cases that proceed to judgment.[6] As a result, while it may well be that a majority of patent assertions throughout the world are brought in good faith, given the sheer numbers involved even if only a small fraction of patent assertion is, by some definition, wrongful, these assertions can do considerable damage, in terms of overcharging consumers, inhibiting innovation, and impeding the integrity of the marketplace.

This book, then, seeks to provide that comprehensive, comparative treatment of how the nations of the world—primarily those that encounter a substantial amount of patent infringement litigation[7]—employ doctrines such as those mentioned above to regulate *wrongful patent assertion*, which for

[5] "Holdup" is a concept I will return to throughout, though especially in chapter 6. For extended discussion of what it means in the context of patent enforcement, see Thomas F. Cotter, Erik Hovenkamp & Norman Siebrasse, *Demystifying Patent Holdup*, 76 Wash. & Lee L. Rev. 1501 (2019); Thomas F. Cotter, *On the Economics of Injunctions in Patent Cases*, 2019 ZGE 293, 298–99. As for the question of how much patent infringement is the result of independent invention, as opposed to copying, *see* Christopher A. Cotropia & Mark A. Lemley, *Copying in Patent Law*, 87 N.C. L. Rev. 1421, 1422 (2008) (reporting, based on analysis of complaints and opinions in U.S. patent cases, that "a surprisingly small percentage of patent cases involve even allegations of copying, much less proof of copying," and that "[c]opying in patent law seems to be very much the exception, not the rule, except in the pharmaceutical industry").

[6] In a 2013 review of studies of patentee win rates in Australia and the United States, Weatherall and Webster note that "data on outcomes must be interpreted with care," in part because results "seem to vary depending on the population of cases chosen for study," and in part because wins sometimes can be "pyrrhic" or the result of better lawyering. *See* Kimberlee Weatherall & Elizabeth Webster, *Patent Enforcement: A Review of the Literature* 35–40 (2013), https://papers.ssrn.com/sol3/papers.cfm?abstract_id=2284519. That said, using a database consisting of "all substantive decisions rendered by any court in every patent case filed in 2008 and 2009—decisions made between 2009 and 2013," Allison, Lemley, and Schwartz reported that, although U.S. patentees win a majority of cases that proceed to trial, their overall success rate once dispositive pretrial motions are taken into account was only 26%, *see* John R. Allison et al., *Understanding the Realities of Modern Patent Litigation*, 97 Tex. L. Rev. 1769, 1787–90 (2014), and that the overall invalidation rate was about 40%, *see* John R. Allison et al., *Our Divided Patent System*, 82 U. Chi. L. Rev. 1073, 1080, 1099–1100, 1124–26 (2015). Contributors to the country studies included in Global Patent Litigation: How and Where to Win (Michael C. Elmer & C. Gregory Gramenopolous eds. 2021) (ebook) [hereinafter Global Patent Litigation], report outcomes, derived from Darts-IP or other databases, that vary considerably from country to country. For example, the "win rate" in Japan from 2006 to 2018 is reported as 27% for patents, though the author cautions that defendants have an incentive to settle cases that patentees are likely to win, to avoid having to pay costs. *See* Shinichi Murata, *Japan, in* Global Patent Litigation, *supra*. In countries with bifurcated liability and validity determinations, such as Germany and China, liability determinations tend to favor plaintiffs, *see* Jian Chen & Yunfeng Geng, *China, in* Global Patent Litigation, *supra*; Roland Küppers & Nora Wessendorf, *Germany, in* Global Patent Litigation, *supra*; but invalidation proceedings are more likely than infringement actions to be decided against patentees (though there are methodological choices that must be made about how to classify a case in which only some claims are invalidated. Win rates in the U.K. and France are reported to be below 50%. *See* Sabine Agé & Lonni Bas, *France, in* Global Patent Litigation, *supra*; Christopher Thornham & Paul England, *England and Wales, in* Global Patent Litigation, *supra*. Appeals, in these or other countries, can further complicate the statistical comparisons.

[7] This book will primarily be concerned with the laws of the United States; the countries comprising the Commonwealth of Nations, primarily the United Kingdom, Canada, and India; the European Union and its member states; China; and Japan.

purposes of this book I define to encompass an *assertion* of patent rights that may (or should) result in the owner suffering *adverse consequences*, by reason of having harmed or threatened to harm a *cognizable interest* without *sufficient justification*. I will devote considerable attention to these italicized terms throughout the book, but in this introductory chapter I wish to be especially clear about what I mean by "assertion," "wrongful," and the combination "wrongful patent assertion." I will then explain how the other italicized terms fit into my overall analytic framework, before closing with a brief overview of the remaining six chapters.

First off, then, the book is about doctrines relating to patent *assertion*, in the sense of either actual or (depending on the doctrine under consideration) threatened enforcement of patent rights. Since threats can be express or implicit, however, and implicitness is more a matter of degree than a binary concept, to the extent threatened enforcement matters the line between "assertion" in the preceding sense and other conduct—some but not all of which may involve assertion in the *everyday* sense of "communication," without necessarily conveying a threat to sue—is not always sharp. Both an offer to license one's patent, for example, or conversely a refusal to license it, *might* be understood to convey an implicit threat to the recipient of the offer or the refusal.[8] Nevertheless, to keep the current project focused and manageable, for the most part I will not be discussing the legality of licenses or other agreements, or of refusals to deal, except insofar as these matters bear a close relationship to patent litigation; the principal examples that I *will* address, therefore, are pay-for-delay settlements of pharmaceutical patent litigation, where the emphasis is on the legality of agreements to *settle* infringement litigation, and the U.S. defense of patent misuse, which when applicable renders litigated patents unenforceable, typically by reason of preexisting licensing terms that courts perceive as contravening public policy. I also will be omitting other forms of what might be viewed as patent abuse, such as false representations that one's products are patented,[9] or are safer or better *because* they are

[8] Mark A. Lemley & Christopher R. Leslie, *Categorical Analysis in Antitrust Jurisprudence*, 93 Iowa L. Rev. 1207, 1242 (2008) (stating that licensees generally don't need licenses "were it not for at least an implicit threat of patent suit").

[9] The United States at one time permitted any person to assert a claim for false patent marking and, if successful, to obtain half of the statutory penalty of up to $250 per act of infringement. For discussion, see Thomas F. Cotter, *Optimal Fines for False Patent Marking*, 17 Mich. Telecomms. & Tech. L. Rev. 181 (2010) (discussing then-recent case law adopting an expansive interpretation of the U.S. false patent marking statute). Since 2013, however, private litigants asserting false marking claims must prove competitive harm, thus roughly aligning false marking claims with the general law of false advertising. *See* 35 U.S.C. § 292(b). For citations to cases and scholarship discussing false marking as actionable false advertising, see Cotter, *supra*, at 187 n.28. Another example might be the incorrect listing of patents on

patented,[10] to the extent these are not coupled with an express or implicit threat to sue; conduct such as product hopping[11] or patent aggregation[12] which might have antitrust consequences but is not necessarily tied to actual or threatened patent litigation (or at least no more so than licensing or refusals to deal generally); and other activities that some would include within a broad definition of patent abuse, such as the patenting of inventions based on traditional knowledge and opposition to the compulsory licensing of essential medicines.[13] On the other hand, I *will* address false accusations of infringement—which may implicate, among other things, competition or unfair competition law, depending on the facts—because these frequently do communicate, at least implicitly, a threat of enforcement against either the recipient of the accusation or someone in the recipient's distribution chain, such as a supplier.

Second, I will refer to such conduct as "wrongful" insofar as it arguably generates net negative social consequences (by harming or threatening to harm protected interests, as discussed below), and therefore subjects or should subject the patent owner to adverse consequences of one sort or another (again, as discussed below). Please note, however, that my use of the word "wrongful" does not necessarily imply any moral judgment. To be sure, sometimes the governing legal standards condemn the conduct at issue only if it is undertaken in bad faith, or is deceitful, fraudulent, or malicious, etc. But this will not always be the case; sometimes it may be desirable for the law to impose adverse consequences even when the patent owner's conduct was well within the boundaries of good faith, from an ex ante perspective. Examples, at least as many countries see it, would include fee awards to the prevailing defendant, as well as awards

government pharmaceutical registries to delay generic competition, which however I will briefly note in chapter 3 insofar as it relates to the enforcement of drug patents.

[10] *See* Greg Reilly, *Misleading Patent Signals*, 38 Harv. J. L. & Tech. 107 (2024) (arguing that consumers may believe, falsely, that patented products are safer, of higher quality, or endorsed by the government, even when patent owners do not expressly misrepresent these attributes); *see also* Sean B. Seymore, *Patent Forfeiture*, 72 Duke L.J. 1019 (2023) (discussing other ways in which patent owners may obtain competitive advantages, not necessarily dependent on actual or threatened enforcement, by means of false statements).

[11] Product hopping occurs when a drug company may delist and remove from the market an older drug, while promoting a newer formulation or dosage to physicians and patients. In some though not all instances, such conduct can be anticompetitive, particularly if physicians respond by moving patients to the newer formulation for which generic substitutes cannot quickly be developed or marketed. *See* Thomas F. Cotter, Patent Wars: How Patents Impact Our Everyday Lives 163–65 (2018).

[12] In rare cases, an entity's acquisition of a bundle of patents might enable it to monopolize a market. *See* Alan Devlin, *Antitrust Limits on Targeted Patent Aggregation*, 67 Fla. L. Rev. 775 (2016).

[13] *See, e.g.*, Anan K. Gebru, *Biopiracy as an Abuse of the Patent System*, *in* Intellectual Property Excesses: Exploring the Boundaries of IP Protection 111 (Enrico Bonadio & Aislinn O'Connell eds. 2022); Caroline Ncube, *Limiting Access to Life-Saving Medications: Three South African Case Studies*, *in* Intellectual Property Excesses, *supra*, at 163. I take no position on either of these topics in this book.

of compensation following the lifting of what is revealed ex post to have been a wrongly issued preliminary injunction.

Third, I will use the combined term "wrongful patent assertion" broadly, to encompass not only patent enforcement the initiation or prosecution of which is or would be wrongful, in the above sense, but also circumstances in which the initiation or prosecution *as such* isn't or wouldn't be wrongful, but rather *something else* results in the patent owner suffering adverse consequences during the course of, or subsequent to, infringement litigation. That something else might be the relief sought (as, for example, when the owner requests an injunction that would cause disproportionate harm to the infringer); or conduct occurring independently of the litigation (for example, when the owner engages in patent misuse which, under U.S. law, renders the patent in suit unenforceable); or conduct for which enforcement or threatened enforcement is an antecedent (as in the pay-for-delay context, where the owner uses patent enforcement as a tool for extracting, through the subsequent settlement, unwarranted benefits).

To summarize, the phrase "wrongful patent assertion" as used in this book means the actual or threatened enforcement of patent rights, where the initiation or prosecution of litigation, or the relief sought in litigation, or conduct occurring independently of litigation, or conduct for which the litigation would be an antecedent, generate net negative social consequences, and therefore subjects or should subject the patent owner to adverse consequences of some sort. That's a mouthful, which is why I prefer the three-word phrase instead. But the definition is not arbitrary: all of the claims, defenses, and doctrines which fit within its confines and are discussed within this book are united insofar as they impose consequences upon patent litigants (or would-be litigants) for using their rights in some, on net, arguably unjustifiable manner.

Put another way, an abstract, universal definition of wrongful patent assertion would be something like this: "the *assertion* of patent rights, *wrongfully/without sufficient justification*, which causes another to suffer *cognizable harm* for which the patent owner should be subject to *adverse consequences*." Defining wrongful patent assertion in this way, in my view, can illuminate a range of legal and equitable doctrines, by focusing attention on a small number of subsidiary questions to determine what specific types of patentee conduct merit consequences, and why. Since I've already indicated that, for present purposes, "assertion" might include both actual and threatened enforcement, the relevant subsidiary questions with regard to that element are whether, within a given context, "threatened enforcement" *should* qualify as a potentially sanctionable assertion, and if so how to evaluate whether a communication is, in fact, implicitly threatening; and more fundamentally, whether "assertion" should be an element *at all* for purposes of a particular claim, defense, or doctrine. (Sometimes assertion is relevant simply by definition, as with antitrust claims premised on sham litigation; but not always.) Moving on, the remaining questions are: what sorts of "harms" resulting from the assertion of patent rights are or should be legally cognizable; what assertions of patent rights lack, or should be deemed to lack, "sufficient justification" (or to put it another way, should be considered "wrongful" under the lengthy definition above), and why; and what sort of adverse consequences, if any, should follow, to compensate victims or deter owners. To be sure, these questions are themselves interrelated. Decisionmakers cannot determine what a "sufficient justification" is, for example, until they first determine what types of harms should be cognizable, given the underlying purposes and assumptions of patent and other relevant bodies of law. Nevertheless, one has to start somewhere; and mapping out the various ways in which patent assertion can be justified or not, can provide a fruitful method for thinking about what should, and shouldn't, count as wrongful assertion, more so perhaps than to approach the problem simply through a narrow doctrinal or remedial lens. More specifically, I will show that sometimes patent assertion should be deemed unjustified precisely because, subject to other qualifying conditions, the patent in suit is adjudicated invalid or not infringed,[14] while on other occasions it may be sufficient to apply some sort of probabilistic analysis—such as whether the patent *would have been* declared invalid or noninfringed, had the issue been litigated to judgment, or what term of protection, probabilistically, was to be expected ex ante—in which case the difficult question is how confident a court should have to be, before making such a determination. In yet other circumstances, however, patent assertion may be unjustified even when the asserted patent is both valid and infringed. I describe each of these three categories below.[15]

[14] Or subject to some other impediment to relief, such as the owner's lack of standing to sue or the patent in suit being exhausted. For concision, and unless the context suggests otherwise, I will use the term "invalid or not infringed" throughout as a shorthand term that includes these other impediments as well.

[15] The project is, therefore, in some respects the reverse of the type of project undertaken by scholars such as Patrick Goold, who applies an analytic jurisprudential methodology to "unbundle" the tort of copyright infringement into a group of "copy-torts." *See* Patrick Goold, *Unbundling the "Tort" of Copyright Infringement*, 102 Va. L. Rev. 1833, 1838 (2016) (arguing that, just as "[t]here is no 'tort of land infringement'" and "no 'tort of chattel infringement,'" but rather groups of real and personal property torts, "likewise it is better to think not of a 'tort of copyright infringement' but instead a group of copyright-based torts," each of which "reflects the different *interests* underlying that right and the different ways copyright may *injure* those interests"). In the present context, I take it as a starting point that there is no unified "tort of wrongful patent assertion," and will not be arguing that there *should* be one patterned after the all-embracing civil-law norm "that one person is subject to liability to another for wrongfully injuring that person," Goold, *supra*, at 1856 n.164 (citations omitted) (contrasting this

First, in many cases it may be appropriate to conclude that an assertion is wrongful, precisely because the patent in suit is adjudicated invalid or not infringed. Most obviously, when a patent owner asserts a claim for the infringement of a patent that is ultimately concluded to be invalid or not infringed, the party against whom the claim is asserted incurs private harms including attorneys' fees and other related litigation costs; opportunity costs attributable to having to devote time to the litigation, as opposed to other more productive activities; potentially, injury to its reputation; and, in the event a preliminary injunction is entered, losses resulting from the temporary exclusion from the market. In addition, third parties may refrain from entering the market, or may agree to take a license, to avoid a similar fate. In theory, a legal system could choose from among a variety of responses to these harms—ranging from *no* liability (absolute immunity), to conditional liability, to strict liability—and, if it chooses either of the latter two options the variety of possible sanctions to deploy include awards of attorneys' fees and costs to the prevailing defendant; other compensatory damages such as lost profits or disgorgement of the patentee's profits, as a remedy for temporary exclusion; damages enhancements; patent unenforceability; fines; or attorney sanctions. In practice, as we will see, many legal systems hold the unsuccessful patent owner strictly liable for the prevailing party's fees and costs, though often these awards are not fully compensatory; and in some countries liability is conditional, not strict. Similarly, in some countries patentees are strictly liable for commercial injuries resulting from the enforcement of a preliminary injunction against the infringement of (what later turns out to be) an invalid or noninfringed patent—though again, the rule is not universally followed, and in some jurisdictions liability is capped by the amount of an injunction bond. Liability for lost profits or reputational harm in addition to the preceding ones, by contrast, if available at all, will almost always be conditioned on proof of other elements in addition to invalidity/noninfringement and harm. Claims arising under unfair competition law, for example, which may arise when a patent owner falsely accuses someone of infringing, typically require proof of at least negligence

tradition to the common-law "gallery of wrongs" framework). Instead, this project takes the already-unbundled wrongful patent assertion torts, claims, and defenses—some of which, as noted above, are specific applications of more general common or civil law norms to the assertion of patent rights—and attempts to clarify the interests served by each of them, the better to understand whether the *ways* in which they are unbundled are coherent, consistent, and social-welfare enhancing (and if not, how they might be improved). Put another way, even if there is no universal principle or set of principles that animates all of the various wrongful assertion doctrines, for purposes of evaluating the merits of possible legal reforms it is useful to understand whether, or under what specific circumstances, a given wrongful assertion tort, claim, or defense complements, duplicates, or perhaps even undermines the interests served by another wrongful assertion tort, claim, or defense.

or, alternatively, "bad faith" (though by contrast, the law of unjustified threats as applied in the U.K. and some other common-law countries applies a strict liability standard). Some antitrust claims as well, including monopolization claims based on the assertion of fraudulently obtained patents or sham litigation, may require the claimant to prove that the IP owner's misconduct was intentional or baseless (though as we shall see, for sham litigation claims both the U.S. and the E.U. focus most of their attention on objective baselessness or unreasonableness, as opposed to subjective motivation). Resort to these and other bodies of law, moreover, is often constrained by countervailing concerns. In the United States, for example, courts have interpreted the constitutional right to petition the government as providing IP owners with immunity from antitrust and unfair competition claims premised on the assertion of "sham" infringement claims, absent proof that such assertions are both objectively and subjectively baseless (the so-called *Noerr-Pennington* doctrine). Other countries impose analogous limitations on sham litigation claims, premised on the understanding that citizens enjoy a fundamental right of access to the courts. Yet another consideration is how much weight to accord to the finality of judgments, in situations in which a patent is invalidated in some subsequent independent proceeding; as we will see, this concern is most acute in nations such as Germany, in which infringement and validity determinations are bifurcated, that is, decided in separate proceedings.

Second, there may be circumstances in which, despite there being no final adjudication of invalidity or noninfringement, it is appropriate to find the owner liable based upon, *inter alia*, some sort of probabilistic evidence of how matters would have played out, but for the patent owner's alleged misconduct. The principal example here is in pay-for-delay antitrust cases arising from the settlement of patent infringement litigation between a brand name and generic drug company, whereby the latter agrees to delay entry into the market as a condition of settlement. Here the key question is whether courts should find such settlements unlawful only if they confer greater exclusivity than would have been warranted by the *potential* ex ante scope of the patent, or instead its *probable* ex ante scope; and if the latter, how one goes about determining that probability.

Third, sometimes an actual or threatened assertion may be wrongful even if the patent at issue is both valid and infringed. Probably the most common example arises when the owner uses the threat of patent assertion to extract some benefit beyond the patent's scope—hardly a self-defining concept, to be sure, since the appropriate scope of a patent is itself dependent on some underlying normative theory. In any event, antitrust law sometimes provides some means for regulating this type of assertion—under the "abuse of dominant position" doctrine, for example, or other types of monopolization claims—as do, on occasion, the civil law abuse of right doctrine and the patent misuse doctrine in the United States. Alternatively, sometimes an assertion may be sanctionable because something about the way in which the patent was obtained or is being enforced impugns the integrity of the administrative or judicial system. Examples would include the U.S. defense of inequitable conduct, which when proven renders a patent unenforceable (though not necessarily invalid) as a result of the patent applicant's breach of its duty of candor toward the Patent Office. Yet another possibility arises in connection with domestic or international forum shopping. Like other litigants, patent litigants have an incentive to seek out the court they believe will be most likely to provide them with a favorable ruling. This incentive is especially strong in the contemporary high-stakes world of standard-essential telecommunications patent litigation, and in recent years has sometimes emboldened opposing parties to seek "antisuit" injunctions, from courts within their own favored jurisdictions, to avoid the allegedly vexatious, oppressive, or jurisdiction-defeating effect of litigating in the other side's chosen forum; requests for such antisuit injunctions, in turn, sometimes provoke the counterparty to seek an "anti-antisuit" injunction, and on and on. The practice of seeking anti- (or anti-anti)suit injunctions nonetheless appears to some observers as potentially inconsistent with the parties' obligations to act in good faith, and with the aforementioned fundamental right of access to the courts.

Returning to the proposed universal definition of wrongful patent assertion—"the assertion of patent rights, wrongfully/without sufficient justification, which causes another to suffer cognizable harm for which the patent owner should be subject to adverse consequences"—I propose that legal systems should aspire to define the relevant terms in such a way as to maximize the surplus of social benefits over social costs. This is, to be sure, easier to state than to accomplish, but it is possible nonetheless to make some reasoned judgments about how to approximate this goal. First off, it should be clear that if the terms are defined broadly—so that it is relatively easy to state a claim or defense premised on wrongful assertion—the expected benefits would include (1) discouraging patent owners from extracting rents to which they are not entitled, and thus from imposing unnecessary social costs; (2) encouraging lawful conduct on the part of potential defendants; and (3) possibly, some reduction in adjudication costs attributable to greater deterrence against wrongful assertion. At the same time, however, broad definitions also pose risks of (1) discouraging patentees from engaging in conduct to which they are entitled as a matter of substantive law, and thus, at least potentially, harming innovation incentives; and (2) encouraging potential wrongful assertion plaintiffs themselves to engage in opportunistic litigation or other rent-seeking behavior (for example, the sham assertion of sham-litigation claims). Second, the magnitude of these benefits and costs depends on several factors, among them whether the legal standard adopted for evaluating a particular form of alleged wrongful assertion is simple (e.g., a per se rule) or complex (a "rule of reason"), and what the applicable remedy or sanction for the misconduct would be. Third, even though it may be impossible to quantify the resulting benefits and costs, it is feasible in many instances to make an educated guess about their relative magnitudes, and thus to reach a reasoned (albeit potentially revisable) judgment as to the optimal standard for addressing a particular species of alleged wrongful assertion.

Following from the above, I hope to show, first, that the various doctrines this book addresses can be viewed, at least aspirationally, as promoting the public interest in innovation, competition, the integrity of the marketplace, and the integrity of the judicial system; and although the lack of a *single* unifying principle to regulate the alleged wrongful assertion of patent rights might seem to risk creating unnecessary (or even conflicting) legal rights and duties, in fact there is little reason to fret about these tools turning out to be redundant, duplicative, or mutually conflicting. Having a clear idea about what each doctrine or body of law is best adapted to achieve nevertheless should help to reduce whatever risks may exist that, for example, the tools internal to patent law will produce obligations inconsistent with competition or unfair competition law, and vice versa—and, in the (one would hope, rare) cases in which such conflicts cannot be avoided, can assist decisionmakers in choosing which body of law to prioritize, and the tradeoffs resulting from their choice. Second, I will argue throughout that the optimal standards for various types of assertion may vary from one country to another, depending on other procedural and substantive features of the legal system—patent quality, jury trials, bifurcation, the availability of class actions, the extent to which liability extends to customers and end users, and so on—as well as on the unquantifiable value different legal systems place on matters such as the right of access to the courts, the sanctity of private property, and fairness to accused infringers.[16] Subject

[16] At least in Europe, human rights law plays a role in delineating the scope of the right of access to courts, procedural fairness, and the right to private property. For discussion, see, e.g., Jonathan Griffiths, *Enforcement of Intellectual Property Rights and the Right to a Fair Trial*, *in* RESEARCH HANDBOOK ON HUMAN RIGHTS AND INTELLECTUAL PROPERTY 438, 444 (Christophe Geiger ed. 2015). In the present context, this can be relevant in regard to, among other things, antitrust claims premised on the assertion of IP rights.

to these constraints, however, I will make some specific recommendations for reform, among them that policymakers should require substantial but not necessarily full compensation for attorneys' fees and costs, and for losses suffered as a result of a wrongly issued preliminary injunction; that antitrust law should be more receptive than it currently is in the United States and the European Union to claims premised on sham infringement litigation; that U.S. antitrust law nevertheless rightly limits claims based on the fraudulent procurement of patents to cases involving actual or threatened enforcement of those patents, as opposed to the mere possession of them; that the U.K.'s law of unjustified threats rightly channels patent owners to litigate against "primary" infringers, wherever possible, to prevent owners from obtaining the equivalent of a do-it-yourself preliminary injunction; that courts can apply a probabilistic assessment to pay-for-delay cases, though perhaps not so easily to other types of claims (e.g., antipatent troll cases under U.S. state law) where similar issues might arise; that the abuse of right doctrine has a legitimate role to play in regulating patent abuses, albeit one that should be limited, to the extent possible, to certain foreseeable types of abuse; and that various doctrines, including some applications of abuse of dominant position, proportionality, equitable discretion, and equitable defenses, can be viewed as efforts to rein in the risk of patent holdup.

Organizationally, the book proceeds as follows. Chapter 2 elaborates on the concept of "cognizable harm" by arguing that the relevant harms with which legal systems ought to concern themselves in the present context include harms to innovation, market distortion, and harms to the integrity of the marketplace and to the legal system itself. These harms may include, as warranted, injury to reputation, though not other noneconomic or "moral prejudice" harms. Chapter 3 then focuses on "assertion," with the principal issues being whether assertion should be a necessary element to antitrust claims premised on the fraudulent procurement of patent rights, and whether it makes sense to penalize threatened assertion against secondary but not primary infringers as under the U.K.'s law of unjustified threats.

Chapters 4, 5, and 6 discuss the various ways in which patent assertion could, in principle, be "wrongful/without justification." Chapter 4 addresses the most obvious candidate for inclusion within this category, namely wrongful assertion claims that *depend on an adjudication that the patent in suit is invalid or not infringed*. It addresses, among other topics, whether fee shifting should be mandatory; whether damages resulting from a (with the benefit of hindsight) wrongly issued injunction should be awarded in all cases, and whether such damages should be capped by the amount of an injunction bond; antitrust claims premised on sham litigation; the relevant mental state, if any, for claims arising under the laws of unfair competition and unjustified threats; and countervailing considerations including rights of access to the courts and to petition the government, as well as the social interest in the finality of judgments. Chapter 5, in turn, addresses wrongful assertion claims that can be understood as *depending on a probabilistic assessment of validity and infringement, or the probabilistic term of protection*. As above, the principal example will be pay-for-delay antitrust claims. Chapter 6 then takes up the question of whether wrongful patent assertion can sometimes be *independent of validity and infringement*. Its principal doctrinal focus will be on antitrust claims for abuse of dominant position (in the E.U. and other jurisdictions) and monopolization claims in the U.S.; the doctrines of abuse of right and abuse of economic dependence; the proportionality concept; equitable discretion to deny injunctive relief; equitable defenses, including estoppel, laches, unclean hands, inequitable conduct, and misuse; and the recent resurgence of antisuit injunctions and related remedies. A policy dilemma common to many of these topics is how to maintain sufficient flexibility to address serious risks of harm, without rendering the relative legal doctrine vague and unpredictable. Chapter 7 then concludes with a summary of the book, and (very briefly) suggests some ways in which policymakers might reform other aspects of the patent system that currently enable wrongful assertion.

My hope is that the analysis provided in this book will prove useful to courts, legislatures, litigants, academics, and other analysts and decisionmakers, to better understand how the various bodies of law addressing wrongful assertion fit together (or not, as the case may be), and how they might be improved. For as patent litigation adapts to the opportunities and challenges presented by developments in commerce and technology, so too does wrongful patent assertion, each fused to the other as parts of a never-ending work in progress.

2
Cognizable Harm

It stands to reason that when patent owners file suit, or threaten to file suit, against alleged infringers, those alleged infringers are worse off than they otherwise would have been. At the very least, the alleged infringer can expect to incur expenses in evaluating the seriousness of the claims; these expenses may include not only attorneys' fees, but also expenses paid to other financial or technical advisers, and the opportunity cost of having to devote time and resources, which could have been used for other purposes, to engage in such evaluation. Depending on the circumstances, the alleged infringer may decide to abandon the use of the allegedly infringing technology, and thus potentially to lose whatever value would have been derived from that use, and to incur costs of design-around. It may instead decide to settle, in which case it may incur costs—once again, fees paid to attorneys or other advisers, along with opportunity costs—to negotiate the terms of settlement; and then to comply with the terms of the settlement, which could involve abandonment or design-around, if no further use of the allegedly infringing technology is contemplated, or alternatively the payment of royalties, either lump-sum or ongoing. Or, if the alleged infringer's understanding of the law and facts so warrant, it may decide to fight. As noted in chapter 1, patent litigation is financially costly, particularly though not exclusively in the United States. Patent disputes are complicated; often a good deal of money is at stake; and the accused may need to retain experts, both technical and economic, to put on its best case (though the use of experts, and the availability and cost of pretrial discovery, is much more limited in many countries than in the United States).[1] All of this expense can add up; and this accumulation of expenses affects not only the alleged infringer, but also others (including suppliers, customers, and ultimately the general public) who may be impacted by sales disruptions, higher prices, reduced competition, and (as discussed below) under some circumstances a reduction in innovation.

[1] Of course, patent owners may have to incur some or all of these costs as well, to enforce their patents, although these costs may be distributed symmetrically or asymmetrically, depending on the context.

Wrongful Patent Assertion. Thomas F. Cotter, Oxford University Press. © Oxford University Press 2026.
DOI: 10.1093/9780191994104.003.0002

To be sure, if we take it as a given that the patent system is, on balance, a desirable social institution, because of the incentive it provides to invent, disclose, commercialize, or signal value,[2] then even in the presence of these private and social costs the system, on balance, enhances social welfare. Put another way, in the short term consumers may pay more if patent infringement litigation succeeds in putting an infringing competitor out of business, or causes a (former) infringer/current licensee to pass on to them its costs of licensing the technology; but if the prospect of obtaining the patent in suit accelerated the creation of a useful invention, or generated any of the other social benefits associated with the patent incentive scheme, consumers too are better off in the long run. Or so, at least, governments and other policymakers must assume to be the case, for otherwise the patent system in its present form would not exist.

The question nevertheless arises whether *all* of the costs incurred by alleged infringers are necessary to the functioning of the patent system; and the answer to this question must be no, unless patents, uniquely among all human institutions, somehow manage to fulfill their intended purpose without imperfection. Surely there must be cases in which the risk of finding oneself on the wrong side of infringement litigation causes firms to change course or to settle, even though they would have prevailed on liability, had the matter made its way through to final adjudication; or to incur substantial, but otherwise unnecessary, expenses to prove that the patent claims at issue are, in fact, invalid. The issue then becomes whether the legal system succeeds in keeping these otherwise unnecessary, and thus socially wasteful, expenses as low as reasonably possible. For again, all legal institutions are imperfect; a system that penalizes patent owners too harshly for filing or threatening to file claims that are or would be unsuccessful will deter not only the cases that never should have been brought, but probably some class of cases that, rightly, should have been.

Ideally, policymakers would craft legal rules and standards in such a way as to achieve the maximum surplus of social benefits over costs; and while it may be impossible to achieve this goal in the real world (or even to know, with confidence, that one *has* achieved it), I have long argued that theoretical and empirical economics can provide sufficient warrant for concluding that adoption of a given policy is likely to move the world closer to or farther from this goal.[3] In the present context, that translates into using these tools to assist policymakers in addressing the questions I posed in chapter 1: what sort of harms to alleged

[2] For discussion of the various proposed rationales for the patent system, *see* THOMAS F. COTTER, PATENT WARS: HOW PATENTS IMPACT OUR DAILY LIVES 37–42, 51–54 (2018).

[3] *See id.* at 45–47.

infringers should be cognizable (and which, instead, should be *damnum absque injuria*); what should count as patent "assertion" (and whether proof of an assertion should be required at all); and what sort of reasons should patentees be able to rely upon as justification for causing these harms?

This chapter will address the first of these: with what sorts of alleged harms caused by an assertion of patent rights should we, even potentially, concern ourselves?

Harms to Innovation

Perhaps the most obvious way in which patent assertion could cause harm that policymakers should care about is when an assertion threatens to discourage rather than to encourage innovation, on net. Because "every new invention necessarily builds on that which came before it,"[4] the ideal patent system would be one in which policymakers designed rules and standards to maximize the surplus of benefits, as described above, over the social costs that patent rights may generate.[5] Thus, while patent rights that are too weak may fail to generate the optimal level of invention, disclosure, and innovation, patent rights that are too strong—that last too long, for example, or that read on too many follow-up innovations or too many minor improvements over the state of the art—can wind up stifling more innovation than they promote (or, more generally, result in a net loss to long-run social welfare).

From this perspective, one would hope that policymakers, primarily legislatures, would craft patent law's rules and standards so that assertions of patent rights would generally align with the public interest. And in fact, many standard patent-law doctrines can be understood as efforts to achieve this goal. Inventions that are obvious (lack an inventive step) over the prior art, for example, are unpatentable;[6] patent applications must disclose sufficient

[4] *Id.* at xvii.

[5] These social costs would include not only the administrative costs of having a patent system in the first place, but also the transaction costs resulting from, for example, negotiating patent licenses (though these costs may be lower than the corresponding costs of licensing nonpatented, trade secret information); and, in those instances in which there are no adequate substitutes for the patented technology, the static efficiency losses (deadweight loss, in economic terminology) associated with monopoly pricing. *See* COTTER, *supra* note 2, at 45–47. As discussed below, most patents do not enable their owners to exercise meaningful market power, due to the presence of substitutes, but for the minority that do the potential for generating unnecessary deadweight loss and other social costs should be an important consideration in formulating legal doctrine.

[6] *See* KSR Int'l Co. v. Telefex Inc., 550 U.S. 398, 427 (2007) (stating that "the results of ordinary innovation are not the subject of exclusive rights under the patent laws," because if it were "otherwise patents might stifle, rather than promote, the progress of useful arts").

information to enable persons skilled in the art to practice the claimed subject matter;[7] and patents are granted for a limited term, expiring twenty years from the date of application.[8] Restrictions on the scope of patentable subject matter also are sometimes viewed as a means for ensuring that the "basic tools" of future innovation remain in the public domain, although the appropriate scope of these restrictions can be a hotly contested issue, particularly in the United States.[9] In all of these examples, the doctrine to a large extent reflects a judgment that, absent constraints such as these, innovation would be hindered (and, in addition, other social costs for which there is insufficient corresponding social benefit, incurred).

As the above discussion suggests, harms to innovation that could potentially flow from the assertion of patent rights are mostly addressed by generally applicable doctrines that are internal to patent law itself. If empirical evidence were to show that these harms are either greater or lesser than current doctrine implicitly presupposes, it would make sense for policymakers (principally legislatures, not courts)[10] to amend the relevant rules, standards, and other practices[11]—for example, by further tightening or loosening the nonobviousness or enablement standards—to better align the assertion of

[7] *See* Amgen Inc. v. Sanofi, 143 S. Ct. 1243, 1257 (2023) (stating that "Congress has included an enablement mandate as one feature among many designed to achieve the balance it wishes," between "incentivizing inventors and ensuring the public receives the full benefit of their innovations").

[8] *See* Agreement on Trade-Related Aspects of Intellectual Property Rights, Apr. 15, 1994, Marrakesh Agreement Establishing the World Trade Organization, Annex 1C, Legal Instruments-Results of the Uruguay Round vol. 31, 33 I.L.M. 1197 (1994) [hereinafter TRIPS], art. 33 (requiring a minimum term ending twenty years from the date of application). A valid patent may expire before this period, however, if the owner fails to pay maintenance fees; and domestic laws in many countries may allow for the extension of the patent term, or a further period of market exclusivity, under some limited circumstances. For discussion, *see* COTTER, *supra* note 2, at 7.

[9] *See, e.g.*, Alice Corp. Pty. Ltd. v. CLS Bank Int'l, 573 U.S. 208, 216–17 (2014).

[10] Though there may be situations where other decisionmakers, such as courts, are better poised to make the necessary adjustments. Burk and Lemley have argued, for example, that courts sometimes have made industry-specific adjustments when applying patent law doctrines such as nonobviousness and enablement. *See* DAN L. BURK & MARK A. LEMLEY, THE PATENT CRISIS AND HOW COURTS CAN SOLVE IT 59–63 (2009). Others have argued that, in awarding damages for patent infringement, courts could adjust compensation to reflect the R&D costs actually incurred to produce a given invention, though I have cautioned against such proposals. *See* Thomas F. Cotter, *Make No Little Plans: Response to Ted Sichelman,* Purging Patent Law of Private Law Remedies, 92 TEX. L. REV. *See Also* 25, 30–32 (2014). The TRIPS Agreement also may impose some limits on the extent to which member states can make technology-specific adjustments. *See* TRIPS, *supra* note 8, art. 27(1) (stating that, subject to some exceptions, "patents shall be available and patent rights enjoyable without discrimination as to . . . the field of technology").

[11] In the present context, "other practices" that might contribute to the socially dysfunctional assertion of patent rights might include devoting insufficient resources to the patent examination process, the consequence being an abundance of low-quality (that is, of dubious validity) patents; or other rules and standards, found for example in associated bodies of regulatory law, which may enable patent owners to "game" the system in various ways. *See, e.g.*, Reto M. Hilty, *Legal Remedies Against Abuse, Misuse, and Other Forms of Inappropriate Conduct of IP Right Holders, in* COMPULSORY LICENSING: PRACTICAL EXPERIENCES AND WAYS FORWARD 377, 382 (R.M. Hilty & K.-C. Liu eds. 2015).

patent rights with the public interest. For our purposes, however, the question to be addressed is whether there are *other* doctrines, internal or external to patent law, that can minimize the risk of harm to innovation resulting from patent assertion. The answer to this question is a qualified yes.

First, it has been argued that the U.S. doctrine of "patent misuse"—an equitable defense which, as discussed in chapter 6,[12] when successful renders the patent in suit temporarily unenforceable—can be used to penalize some assertions of patent rights that threaten harm to innovation.[13] Although the doctrine's contours are hardly crystal-clear, typically the defense works to penalize patent owners for imposing licensing conditions that "impermissibly broaden the 'physical or temporal scope' of the patent grant with anticompetitive effect,"[14] even if those conditions do not violate substantive antitrust law. This additional flexibility leads commentators such as Christina Bohannan to argue that misuse can play a positive role by penalizing patent owners for imposing conditions that harm innovation, but which conventional antitrust analysis fails (for reasons discussed below) adequately to address.[15] For reasons discussed later in the book, I remain somewhat skeptical of this argument; but if Bohannan is right, then misuse would appear to be the prime example of an internal patent law doctrine to discourage innovation harm, by imposing an adverse consequence upon the patent owner within the context of infringement litigation.

Second, the manner in which other bodies of law regulate patent owners' conduct can have an impact—positive or negative, intended or incidental—on innovation. Probably the most important of these is antitrust, which—because it principally targets conduct that reduces static (short-term) consumer welfare by distorting the operation of the competitive market[16]—is the subject of its own subsection, below. For now, however, it is important to note that some applications of antitrust law are intended to prevent harm to innovation as well; and in principle, this dual focus makes sense. As others have noted, because the long-term gains from innovation drive economic growth over time, conduct

[12] *See infra* ch. 6 notes 190–246 and accompanying text.

[13] *See* Christina Bohannan, *IP Misuse as Foreclosure*, 96 Iowa L. Rev. 475, 479 (2011) (arguing that courts should focus misuse law "on three wrongs that can be summed up in the term 'foreclosure'": "anticompetitive market exclusion, restraints on innovation, and preventing access to the public domain").

[14] Windsurfing Int'l, Inc. v. AMF, Inc., 782 F.2d 995, 1001 (Fed. Cir. 1986) (quoting Blonder-Tongue Labs., Inc. v. Univ. of Ill. Found., 402 U.S. 313, 343 (1971)).

[15] *See* Bohannan, *supra* note 13, at 514–15 (arguing that, for example, in cases in which the patent owner prevents a licensee from using a "nascent" technology, "such conduct constitutes misuse, provided that a court finds that some appreciable harm to innovation is possible and that the conduct is not justified by offsetting efficiencies").

[16] *See, e.g.*, Atlantic Richfield Co. v. USA Petroleum Co., 495 U.S. 328, 339 n.8 (1990) ("Every antitrust violation can be assumed to 'distort' or 'disrupt' competition").

that impedes innovation is likely to have a far greater negative impact on social welfare than is conduct that merely reduces static efficiency.[17] Unfortunately, the standard tools of economics make it much easier to predict and track the effects of conduct on static than on dynamic efficiency, which explains why antitrust tends to emphasize the former over the latter.[18] Nevertheless, there are some discrete circumstances in which antitrust enforcers consider the probable effect of present-day conduct or transactions on dynamic efficiency, for example when evaluating whether a joint venture or a merger will result in the monopolization of a nascent technology.[19] Christina Bohannan and Herbert Hovenkamp have argued, moreover, that "antitrust should play an aggressive role in policing practices that restrain the innovation of others without a serious and provable efficiency-related explanation," precisely because innovation restraints not only result in higher prices, but also can impede new technologies from coming into existence.[20] Finally, IP-related misconduct, such as the enforcement of fraudulently procured patents, potentially impacts both static

[17] *See, e.g.*, Herbert Hovenkamp, *Antitrust and the Patent System: A Reexamination*, 76 Ohio St. L.J. 467, 505–508 (2015) (citing some of the relevant economic literature). Roughly speaking, static efficiency focuses on the short term, while dynamic efficiency focuses on the longer term. *See, e.g.*, Pierre Régibeau & Katharine Rockett, *The Relationship Between Intellectual Property Law and Competition Law: An Economic Approach*, *in* The Interface Between Intellectual Property Rights and Competition Policy 505, 507 (Steven D. Anderman ed. 2007) (stating that "[s]tatic efficiency is attained when consumers and producers make their decisions taking into account the true opportunity cost of the resources involved"; and that while "[t]here is no universally accepted definition of dynamic efficiency," in general the concept requires that an investment be undertaken only if "its social benefits exceed the opportunity costs of the resource invested. In other words, inefficient investment decisions can occur when the stream of private revenues generated by the investment is not equal to its social benefits").

[18] *See* Herbert Hovenkamp, *Restraints on Innovation*, 29 Cardozo L. Rev. 247, 255–57 (2007). For further discussion, *see* Thomas F. Cotter, *Antitrust, Intellectual Property, and Dynamic Efficiency: An Essay in Honor of Herbert Hovenkamp*, Concurrences 3-2020, at 2 n.14 (citing sources).

[19] *See, e.g.*, U.S. Dep't of Justice & Fed. Trade Comm'n, Merger Guidelines, 20–21 (Dec. 18, 2023) (addressing how a dominant firm may seek to eliminate nascent competitive threats), https://www.ftc.gov/system/files/ftc_gov/pdf/2023_merger_guidelines_final_12.18.2023.pdf; U.S. Dep't of Justice & Fed. Trade Comm'n, Antitrust Guidelines for the Licensing of Intellectual Property, § 3.2 (Jan. 12, 2017) [hereinafter IP Guidelines], https://www.justice.gov/atr/IPguidelines/download (discussing the relevance of markets for goods, technology, and research and development, in evaluation of competitive effects of IP licensing). For discussion in the scholarly literature, *see, e.g.*, C. Scott Hemphill & Tim Wu, *Nascent Competitors*, 168 U. Penn. L. Rev. 1879 (2020); A. Douglas Melamed, *Mergers Involving Nascent Competition*, *in* Judging Big Tech: Insights on Applying U.S. Antitrust Laws to Digital Markets 38 (Erika M. Douglas et al. eds. 2022).

[20] Christina Bohannan & Herbert Hovenkamp, Creation Without Restraint: Promoting Liberty and Rivalry in Innovation 145–47 (2012). Without wishing to put words in the authors' mouths, one might conclude that they would agree that there could be cases in which concerns over a practice's potential to cause innovation harm would tip the balance in favor of antitrust enforcement (or, barring that, condemnation under the misuse doctrine), while a more conventional antitrust analysis would not.

and dynamic efficiency,[21] even if the dominant emphasis of antitrust remains the former, and the latter remains more difficult to quantify or predict.

Thus, whether intended or incidental, the use of antitrust (and other bodies of law) to constrain the assertion of patent rights is likely to impact innovation—ideally, for the better, by reducing innovation harm.

Harms to the Market (Market Distortion)

As indicated above, the more commonly-invoked rationale for antitrust enforcement is not to achieve dynamic efficiency, but rather to prevent or remedy conduct that distorts the operation of the competitive market.[22] The reason for caring about the working of the competitive market, in turn, is the idea that competitive markets generally make consumers better off, by discouraging or penalizing conduct or transactions by which firms acquire or maintain, without sufficient offsetting justification, the power to set prices and output in a given market—that is, "market power," sometimes culminating in full-blown monopoly.[23] In the United States and the E.U., agreements or practices that have no cognizable offsetting procompetitive justification—horizontal

[21] *See id.* at 146 (noting that "the social harm caused by an improper infringement action can reach far beyond monopoly pricing," because "[s]uch suits can also serve to delay superior rival technologies, or perhaps to keep them off the market altogether").

[22] As reflected, for example, in the following statement that until recently was available on website of the Antitrust Division of the U.S. Department of Justice, under the heading *Antitrust Enforcement and the Consumer*: "When competitors agree to fix prices, rig bids, or allocate (divide up) customers, consumers lose the benefits of competition. The prices that result when competitors agree in these ways are artificially high; such prices do not accurately reflect cost and therefore distort the allocation of society's resources. The result is a loss not only to U.S. consumers and taxpayers, but also the U.S. economy."

[23] Beginning in the 1970s, courts within the United States have largely come to accept the consumer welfare standard as antitrust's guiding principle, due in part (though hardly exclusively) to the influence of scholars and judges associated with the so-called Chicago School of law and economics. In recent years, that standard has been challenged by, among others, adherents of the "neo-Brandeisian" School, who argue that antitrust should return to what they see as its original concern about promoting fair competition, small business, and the deconcentration of political and economic power. For succinct descriptions of the neo-Brandeisian position, *see* TIM WU, THE CURSE OF BIGNESS: ANTITRUST IN THE NEW GILDED AGE (2018); Lina Khan, *The New Brandeis Movement: America's Antimonopoly Debate*, 9 J. EUR. COMP. L. & PRAC. 131 (2018). Whether neo-Brandeisianism will remain a force within the antitrust enforcement agencies, following Khan's departure as chair of the FTC during the Biden Administration, remains to be seen. (The abuse of economic dependence doctrine, as recognized in some European and Asian states, also embodies a sort of neo-Brandeisian policy in favor of small and medium-sized enterprises. For discussion of a recent patent infringement action considering application of the doctrine, *see infra* ch. 6 notes 117–42 and accompanying text.) Elsewhere, antitrust enforcers are sometimes accused, rightly or wrongly, of manipulating antitrust law to protect domestic industries from foreign competition, rather than to protect consumers.

price-fixing between competitors is the paradigm example—are likely to be condemned as "per se" illegal (unlawful "by object").[24] Other conduct is often evaluated under some version of what is referred to as the "Rule of Reason" in the United States, or counterpart legal standards (e.g., unlawful "by effect") elsewhere, meaning, roughly, that the proposed offsetting justifications are at least plausible enough to merit further scrutiny, with the degree and depth of scrutiny varying depending on the circumstances.[25] Either way, the overarching policy is to condemn policies that, on balance, threaten consumer welfare, typically by forcing consumers to pay higher prices for fewer units of output than would be the case in a more competitive market: essentially, the static welfare criterion mentioned in the preceding subsection.

Although casual observation might cause one to perceive antitrust and IP law as pursuing contradictory ends—antitrust concerning itself with the elimination of monopolies, and IP law with granting them—antitrust scholars and practitioners have long understood this view to be misguided, for several reasons. First, IP rights do not always or even typically result in their owner obtaining meaningful monopoly power. Most patents are never commercialized, much less commercially successful; and even for those that are, there often will be a range of acceptable substitutes, the presence of which constrains or

[24] *See, e.g.*, Leegin Creative Leather Prods., Inc. v. PSKS, Inc., 551 U.S. 877, 886 (2007) (stating that "[r]estraints that are per se unlawful include horizontal agreements among competitors to fix prices . . . or to divide markets") (citations omitted). In the E.U., agreements between competitors to fix prices would be illegal "by object." *See, e.g.*, Groupement des cartes bancaires (CB) v. European Commission, Case C 67/13 P, ¶ 51 (CJEU 2009) (stating that "certain collusive behaviour, such as that leading to horizontal price-fixing by cartels, may be considered so likely to have negative effects, in particular on the price, quantity or quality of the goods and services, that it may be considered redundant . . . to prove that they have actual effects on the market"). Although it is likely that a naked price-fixing agreement between competitors would be unlawful in other countries as well, some, such as China and Japan, do not apply the "per se" illegality concept. *See, e.g.*, Thomas Weck & Masako Wakui, Comparative Competition Law (2024) 57 (stating that article 2(6) of Japan's Anti-Monopoly Act, which defines "unreasonable restraints of trade," "does *not* have a *per se* concept, and the [Japan Fair Trade Commission] must demonstrate the effect of substantial restriction of competition in a particular field of trade in every case"); Simon Vande Walle & Tadashi Shiraishi, *Competition Law in Japan*, *in* Comparative Competition Law 415, 418 (John Duns, Arlen Duke & Brendan Sweeney eds. 2015) (same); Wenton Zheng, *Competition Law in China: An Overview*, *in* Comparative Competition Law, *supra*, at 443, 450–51 (stating that "Chinese courts have . . . clarified that the competitive consequences of horizontal agreements . . . may be taken into account in determining the legality of the agreements," and that "[t]his practice departs from the antitrust jurisprudence in the US and European Union").

[25] *See, e.g.*, NCAA v. Alston, 141 S. Ct. 2141, 2155 (2021) (stating that "[m]ost restraints challenged under the Sherman Act—including most joint venture restrictions—are subject to the rule of reason, which . . . we have described as 'a fact-specific assessment of market power and market structure' aimed at assessing the challenged restraint's 'actual effect on competition'—especially its capacity to reduce output and increase price") (citations omitted); GlaxoSmithKline Servs. Unltd. v. Comm'n of the European Communities, Cases C-501/06 P, C-501/06 P, C-513/06 P, C-515/06 P and C-519/06 P, ECLI:EU:C:2009:610, ¶ 55 (CJEU 2009) ("Where . . . the analysis of the content of the agreement does not reveal a sufficient degree of harm to competition, the consequences of the agreement should then be considered and for it to be caught by the prohibition it is necessary to find that those factors are present which show that competition has in fact been prevented, restricted or distorted to an appreciable extent").

eliminates the patent owner's ability to exercise market power.[26] Second, antitrust laws do not generally condemn the mere possession of monopoly power, but rather are principally concerned with abuses of that power.[27] Consistent with this view, the U.S. enforcement agencies have stated that "for the purpose of antitrust analysis, the Agencies apply the same analysis to conduct involving intellectual property as to conduct involving other forms of property, taking into account the specific characteristics of a particular property right."[28] The exercise and enforcement of IP rights is therefore neither presumptively illegal nor immune from antitrust scrutiny.[29]

That said, there can be borderline cases, in which it is unclear whether the IP owner's conduct falls within the lawful scope of its grant; in subsequent chapters, we shall come upon examples in which courts sometimes may have to choose between favoring competition or IP owners' exclusive rights. For now, it suffices to note that patent assertion can sometimes give rise to viable antitrust claims or defenses. These may include claims arising from the assertion of patents that were fraudulently procured; claims premised on the IP owner's prosecution of "sham" litigation; or, in the E.U., certain other claims involving an alleged abuse of dominant position. Further, as discussed at length in chapter 5, the assertion and subsequent settlement of a claim for patent infringement can sometimes mask an anticompetitive market allocation scheme. In these cases, the principal difficulty lies in applying a standard that can evaluate whether the terms of the settlement are consistent with the patent owner's ex ante probability of success.

Harms to the Integrity of the Marketplace

A third type of harm that may be at issue in some cases involving the assertion of patent rights is harm to the integrity of the marketplace. This type of harm is a principal focus of those bodies of law that are often grouped together under

[26] *See* Thomas F. Cotter, Comparative Patent Remedies: A Legal and Economic Analysis 26 (2013).

[27] For discussion of the concept of abuse of dominant position, principally under E.U. law, *see* ch. 3 notes 13–20, 29–33 and accompanying text, and ch. 6 notes 19–44 and accompanying text. U.S. law lacks an abuse of dominant position doctrine, but condemns the "willful acquisition or maintenance of monopoly power . . . as distinguished from growth or development as a consequence of a superior product, business acumen, or historic accident." United States v. Grinnell Corp., 384 U.S. 563, 570–71 (1966). The U.S. also differs from the E.U. and other countries in that, while monopoly acquisition or maintenance is actionable, the mere exploitation of monopoly power, as such, is not. *See* ch. 6 notes 45–46 and accompanying text.

[28] IP Guidelines, *supra* note 19, § 2.0.

[29] Subject to a handful of statutory exceptions, here and there. *See* Cotter, *supra* note 18, at 4 n.26. The exceptions are not relevant for present purposes.

the heading of "unfair competition law"—and in particular those branches of unfair competition law that regulate deceptive behavior, including the law of false advertising and commercial disparagement. As suggested in chapter 1, although one might view these bodies of law as, to some extent, grounded in nonutilitarian fairness norms, from an economic perspective they work (ideally) to enhance social welfare in two related ways. First, by penalizing the actual or potential diversion of custom from truthful to untruthful sellers, these bodies of law make it easier for purchasers to rely on advertising and other forms of commercial speech to obtain products and services that possess desired features. Second, they enable sellers to protect their commercial reputation or goodwill, which in turn provides them with an incentive to invest in developing a reputation for satisfying consumer expectations.[30]

The law of unfair competition intersects with the assertion of patent rights primarily when patent owners mispresent the scope or value of their rights. When a patent owner falsely asserts that its patent covers a competitor's product, for example, the statement (like any materially false statement) may divert trade away from the competitor and toward the speaker. Alternatively, the statement may take the form of a demand letter threatening an infringement action, unless the recipient agrees to pay royalties—for the use of a patent that the recipient is not, in fact, infringing, or that is invalid. Rationally, the recipient of such a demand may choose to give in rather than fight, given the high cost of patent litigation. Concerns over the proliferation of such demands, targeting primarily small and medium-size businesses, has led many U.S. states to enact anti-troll statutes.[31]

In these types of cases, it's easy to see how wrongful assertion harms its victims—by causing them to forgo the purchase of products or services they would have preferred, or to pay money they do not really owe to the asserting party. The reason the law recognizes these as cognizable harms seems fairly obvious as well. Not only is the conduct at issue, when it takes the form described above, morally offensive, but also if it were to become widespread it would impair the ability of consumers and other actors to rely upon market information when making purchasing decisions. In this sense, making false assertions concerning patent rights, like conduct in violation of antitrust laws as discussed above, threatens to distort the operation of the competitive market—though typically to a lesser degree than the sort of conduct that violates antitrust law.

[30] *See, e.g.*, Barton Beebe et al., Trademarks, Unfair Competition, and Business Torts 4–5 (2d ed. 2016).

[31] *See infra* chapter 5.

Proof of an antitrust offense typically requires proof of, or at least reason to infer the threat of, market distortion, in the sense that the agreement or practice at issue would enable the defendant to exercise power over aggregate price and output in some definable market.[32] Proof of an unfair competition offense does not require evidence of such extensive, market-wide harm (though sometimes the commission of an unfair competition offense can contribute to an antitrust violation, by assisting a firm in maintaining its preexisting monopoly power).[33] As with antitrust offenses, however, or with other claims or defenses such as patent misuse, decisionmakers need to employ manageable standards for distinguishing lawful from unlawful conduct. If courts erroneously find cognizable harm where it does not, or should not be found to, exist, they risk *causing* harm to innovation and market distortion. Much of the rest of this book will be devoted to evaluating whether, or how, courts can succeed in making such distinctions within a tolerable risk of error.

Harms to the Legal System

Fourth, there are numerous bodies of law, intended primarily to safeguard the integrity of the judicial and/or patent system, which under some circumstances may regulate the assertion of patent rights. Examples would include the U.S. doctrine of inequitable conduct, discussed in chapter 6,[34] under which an applicant's intentional failure to disclose material information during the course of patent prosecution can result in the subsequently-issued patent being rendered unenforceable; claims such as abuse of process and malicious prosecution, discussed in chapters 3 and 4, intended to prevent the misuse of the judicial system for purposes of harassment; and other rules and standards, independent of the patent system, obligating litigants and their representatives to exercise candor in the course of judicial proceedings, and to avoid using the judicial system for purposes of harassment. Depending on the circumstances, of course, deceptive conduct in these contexts may implicate other legal doctrines as well, including misuse, antitrust, or unfair competition claims. Although each of these claims or defenses is primarily focused on a different harm or interest, and requires proof of different elements and (for some

[32] *See, e.g.*, Atlantic Richfield Co. v. USA Petroleum Co., 495 U.S. 328, 339 n.8 (1990) ("Every antitrust violation can be assumed to 'distort' or 'disrupt' competition"; *GlaxoSmithKline*, *supra* note 25, ¶ 55.

[33] *See, e.g.*, Michael Carrier & Rebecca Tushnet, *An Antitrust Framework for False Advertising*, 106 Iowa L. Rev. 1841 (2021).

[34] *See infra* ch. 6 notes 149–89 and accompanying text.

of them) satisfaction of different evidentiary burdens, they may converge (or not) in condemning a specific act of misconduct in relation to the assertion of patent rights.

Other Social Welfare Losses

Finally, there are various legal doctrines, relevant to certain types of wrongful patent assertion, that are not easy to pigeonhole into any of the above categories—in that they are not (necessarily) patent-specific or intended to remedy innovation harm, do not necessarily implicate antitrust concerns, and may not be clearly related to preserving the integrity of the marketplace or the legal system—but which (ideally) work to reduce social welfare losses that would otherwise result from the conduct at issue. These include the following.

First, nations follow a variety of practices concerning the compensation, if any, that is due to a defendant who is preliminarily enjoined from practicing a patent that is subsequently invalidated or found to be noninfringed. I will discuss this issue in greater detail in chapter 4,[35] pausing here to note only that a rule requiring the patent owner to provide full compensation—in other words, one that recognizes the defendant's entire lost profit, during the interim period of exclusion, as a cognizable harm—would require patent owners to internalize that external cost, and thus might reduce the likelihood that patentees will file (ultimately) losing suits. On the other hand, it is sometimes alleged that a rule requiring only partial compensation, or perhaps no compensation at all, provides patent owners with some margin of error and thus better preserves the patent incentive scheme—though for reasons discussed later in the book, I find the former view much more persuasive than the latter.[36]

Second, the question sometimes arises whether a defendant is entitled to recover compensation for any losses it has incurred as a result of a final adjudication of liability, if subsequent to that adjudication the patent in suit is invalidated.[37] The answer to this question can be complicated, though there are a few more-or-less standard practices across countries. First, once there has been a final judgment of invalidity, many countries would hold that the

[35] *See infra* ch. 4 notes 58–125 and accompanying text.
[36] *See id.* notes 126–61 and accompanying text.
[37] For a short discussion of the related question of how courts respond when a first instance judgment in favor of the patentee is provisionally enforced and then reversed on appeal, *see infra* ch. 4 note 57.

patent in suit is invalid *erga omnes*.[38] In Japan, however, which has a "bifurcated" system (meaning that infringement and validity are determined in different proceedings), only an invalidation decision by the Japanese Patent Office has this result. Although infringement courts may consider invalidity as a defense to patent infringement, in Japan a judicial determination of invalidity applies only *inter partes*.[39] Until recently, China—another bifurcated system—followed an analogous, albeit more limited version, of this practice,[40] although a 2022 decision of the Supreme People's Court may herald more widespread use of an invalidity defense.[41] (In a somewhat analogous vein, in 2025 the Court of Justice for the European Union held in *BSH Hausgeräte GmbH v. Electrolux AB*,[42] that where a patent owner sues a defendant in the E.U. member state in which the latter is domiciled, the court of that state may adjudicate the defendant's alleged infringement of corresponding foreign patents—and that, if the corresponding country is a non-E.U. member, also may adjudicate patent validity, although the validity decision would be binding only in that action, and would not result in the cancellation of the foreign patent.) Second, if there *is* a final, *erga omnes* decision of invalidity, whether judicial or administrative, then logically this decision should relieve

[38] *See, e.g.*, Blonder-Tongue Lab., Inc. v. University of Ill. Found., 402 U.S. 313 (1971); Marketa Trimble, *The Extraterritorial Enforcement of Patent Rights*, *in* PATENT ENFORCEMENT WORLDWIDE: WRITINGS IN HONOUR OF DIETER STAUDER 569, 573 (Christopher Heath ed., 3d ed. 2015) [hereinafter PATENT ENFORCEMENT WORLDWIDE] (stating that "in non-bifurcated systems a trial court's decision of patent invalidity is an adjudication of validity with *erga omnes* effects," such that "the decision leads to a cancellation of the patent and the decision has preclusive effects in subsequent litigation").

[39] *See* Christopher Heath, *Patent Enforcement in Japan*, *in* PATENT ENFORCEMENT WORLDWIDE, *supra* note 38, at 383, 408–11 (noting, *inter alia*, that in such a case "if there are obvious reasons for holding the patent invalid," then "the exercise of the patent is deemed an abuse of right"); Mineko Mōri & Christopher Heath, *Comment on Decision of the Supreme Court, April 11, 2000—Case No. Hei 10 (O) 364, Texas Instruments v. Fujitsu ("Kilby III")*, 35 IIC 91, 97 (2004) (stating that the cited decision "in effect has given the courts a parallel jurisdiction over patent invalidation matters, albeit limited to an *inter partes* effect"); *see also* Trimble, *supra* note 38, at 573 (noting that in a bifurcated system, a trial court's decision on validity in the context of, e.g., a motion for a preliminary injunction "does not lead to a cancellation of the patent at issue . . . has no preclusive effects . . . and, at least formally . . . no *erga omnes* effects").

[40] *See* Thomas Pattloch, *Patent Enforcement in China*, *in* PATENT ENFORCEMENT WORLDWIDE, *supra* note 38, at 315, 319–20, 345 (stating that infringement courts will consider a "prior art" defense, but that it is raised "mostly without success"; and that even when successful, "it will not have the legal effect of confirming invalidity of the plaintiff's patent").

[41] For discussion of the decision, *Zudian Intelligent Technology Co., Ltd. v. Simsukian Electronic Technology Co., Ltd.*, (2022) 高法知民终124号, *see* Fang Ye & Shi Shuwen, *SPC Allowed Invalidity Defense In A Patent Infringement Action*, MONDAQ, Nov. 8, 2022, https://www.mondaq.com/china/patent/1248642/spc-allowed-invalidity-defense-in-a-patent-infringement-action (reporting that the decision permits dismissal where "there is a 'substantial likelihood' of invalidity of the asserted claims," and the dismissal would not "unduly prejudice the plaintiff"); *see also* Aaron Wininger, *China's Supreme People's Court Releases Summaries of 43 Legal Application Issues from 2022 Intellectual Property Cases*, CHINA IP LAW UPDATE, Apr. 27, 2023, https://www.chinaiplawupdate.com/2023/04/chinas-supreme-peoples-court-releases-summaries-of-43-legal-application-issues-from-2022-intellectual-property-cases/ (also discussing this case).

[42] Case C-339/22, ECLI:EU:C:2025:108 (CJEU 2025).

an adjudicated infringer of the obligation prospectively to continue abiding by the terms of an injunction,[43] or to pay any damages arising from a nonfinal infringement decision.[44] Some countries, including the United States, also would relieve a licensee of its obligation to continue paying royalties, if the patent is invalidated,[45] while others would not recognize invalidity as a defense to a contractual obligation to continue paying royalties.[46] Third, however, in view of the principle of res judicata, once the judgment is final and the case concluded it is doubtful that the adjudicated infringer would be able to recover any damages it had already paid,[47] much less compensation for any additional

[43] *See, e.g.*, Virgin Atlantic Airways Ltd. v. Zodiac Seats UK Ltd. [2013] UKSC 46, [59] (Eng.) (opinion of Neuberger, L.); Jacques Raynard & Privat Vigand, *Incidence d'une decision d'annulation d'un brevet sur une decision irrevocable de condemnation pour contrefaçon rendue antérieurement*, PROPRIÉTÉ INDUSTRIELLE, April 2012, at 36, 37–38 (discussing possible doctrinal routes to this conclusion); *but see* Heath, *supra* note 39, at 412–13 (noting that "[s]ince an order for injunctive relief does not automatically become ineffective once the patent has been revoked, a retrial to discharge the injunctive relief is still possible"). For an example of the latter, see Flexiteek Ams., Inc. v. PlasTEAK, Inc., No. 08-60996-CIV-COHN/SELTZER, 2012 WL 5364247, at *2 (S.D. Fla. Oct. 31, 2012).

[44] *See Virgin Atlantic*, [2013] UKSC 46, [35]–[36] (holding that "where judgment is given in an English court that a patent (whether English or European) is valid and infringed, and the patent is subsequently revoked or amended (whether in England or at the EPO), the defendant is entitled to rely on the revocation or amendment on the enquiry as to damages"); Scherer v. Newmat, Cour de Cassation, June 12, 2007 (Fr.), *English language translation published in* 39 IIC 354 (2008). In the United States, the Federal Circuit applies this rule with respect to administrative determinations of invalidity only if there is a final *nonappealable* determination of invalidity. *See* United Therapeutics Corp. v. Liquidia Techs., Inc., 74 F.4th 1360, 1372 (Fed. Cir. 2023), *cert. denied*, 144 S. Ct. 873 (2024); Fresenius USA Inc. v. Baxter Int'l, Inc., 721 F.3d 1330 (Fed. Cir. 2013). For discussion of *Fresenius* and other relevant U.S. cases, *see* Greg Reilly, *The Justiciability of Cancelled Patents*, 79 WASH. & LEE L. REV. 253 (2022).

[45] *See* Lear, Inc. v. Adkins, 395 U.S. 653 (1969).

[46] For an extensive analysis of the issue. and variations of the same, under Anglo-Canadian jurisprudence, *see* Norman V. Siebrasse's three-part series *No-Challenge Clause in Settlement Is Enforceable*, SUFFICIENT DESCRIPTION BLOG, Jan. 4, 2021, http://www.sufficientdescription.com/2021/01/no-challenge-clause-in-settlement-is.html; *There Is No Such Thing as Licensee Estoppel*, SUFFICIENT DESCRIPTION BLOG, Jan. 5, 2021, http://www.sufficientdescription.com/2021/01/there-is-no-such-thing-as-licensee.html; and Lear v. Adkins *Should Not Be Followed*, SUFFICIENT DESCRIPTION BLOG, Jan. 6, 2021, http://www.sufficientdescription.com/2021/01/lear-v-adkins-should-not-be-followed.html. As Siebrasse notes, the U.S. federal courts are split on the question of whether no-challenge clauses are enforceable after *Lear*. Several commentators have expressed the view that principles of licensee estoppel, as well as no-challenge clauses, may be unenforceable under E.U. law, *see* COTTER, *supra* note 26, at 281–84 (citing sources), though to my knowledge there is no recent case law addressing the issue. No-challenge clauses appear to be generally enforceable in Japan, but unenforceable in China. For discussion, *see* Guan Bing & Wang Ziqian, *Unknowns of 'no-challenge clause' in IP licence contracts*, CHINA BUS. L.J., May 25, 2022, https://law.asia/ip-licence-no-challenge-clause-unknowns/.

[47] *See* Wehrkamp-Richter v. Guitay, Cour de Cassation, Feb. 17, 2012 (Fr.); WesternGeco LLC v. ION Geophysical Corp., 913 F.3d 1067, 1071–72 (Fed. Cir. 2019) (stating that a "satisfied and unappealable final judgment" awarding damages cannot be reopened); *Virgin Atlantic*, [2013] UKSC 46, [35]–[36] (stating that "[o]nce the enquiry [on damages] is concluded" and there is "a final judgment for a liquidated sum," "[a]t common law, that judgment could be challenged only by way of appeal, and then only if an appeal is still open"; and expressing doubt whether "an implied statutory right to reopen [the judgment] could be derived from the scheme of the Patents Act 1977," while leaving the issue unresolved); *id.* ¶ 67 (opinion of Neuberger, L.) ("Once the damages had been paid, it seems to me that an alleged infringer would have to try and raise a restitutionary claim if it wished to recover the damages on the ground that the patent had been revoked or varied. I express no view on the strength of such a claim, which may well be highly dependent on the facts of the particular case."). For discussion of

harm suffered during the period of exclusion.[48] The principal exception to this third rule appears to be Germany, which like Japan and China, has a bifurcated system.[49] Unlike in those two countries, however, there is little scope for German infringement courts to consider validity at all;[50] and the German Patent Court's resolution of a corresponding action to invalidate the patent in suit often has not been resolved until long after the infringement litigation has terminated and the defendant has either abandoned use of the contested

Wehrkamp-Richter, *see* Sabine Agé & Marta Mendes Moreira, *Reginald Wehrkamp-Richter v Louis Paul Guitay, LPG Systems*, INTELL. PROP. MAGAZINE, May 2012, at 89; Raynard & Vigand, *supra* note 43.

[48] Heath is probably correct in stating that "most national laws would not extend the effects" of retroactive invalidation "to contracts about the use of the patent, as the latter's potential invalidity is part of the equation when the contract is concluded." Christopher Heath, *Wrongful Patent Enforcement—Threats and Post-Infringement Invalidity in Comparative Perspective*, 39 IIC 307, 319 (2008). In the U.S., the licensee would not be able to recover royalties already paid, *see* Mizuki Hashiguchi, *Unraveling the Conundrums Of Running Royalties in Cross-Border Patent License Agreements*, LES NOUVELLES, Mar. 2017, at 13, 18–19 (citing cases, and concluding that Japanese courts would probably follow the same rule), and the same result would obtain under Anglo-Canadian law, *see* Siebrasse, *There Is No Such Thing as Licensee Estoppel*, *supra* note 46. At least under some circumstances, some European countries might require the licensor to reimburse the licensee for any royalties the latter has already paid, if the patent is subsequently invalidated, but this does not appear to be the common practice. *See* Richard Binns & Nicola Walles, *Royalties for Unpatented Technology*, LES NOUVELLES, Mar. 2017, at 27, 29); *see also* Alain B. v. Thiérart SARL, PIBD No. 1068, III, 202, 203–04, Trib. de la grande instance de Paris, Jan. 12, 2017 (Fr.) (citing SA New Holland France v. SA Greenland France, Cour de cassation, Jan. 28, 2003 (Fr.)) (stating the general rule that the licensee does not recover royalties already paid); Stephan Altmeyer & Christopher Weber, *Rückzahlung von Linzenzgebühren bei rückwirkender Vernichtung eines SEP?*, 2017 GRUR 1182 (arguing that, although the general rule in Germany is that licensees are not entitled to recover the fees they have paid to license a patent that is later declared invalid, the rationale for the rule should not apply in the case of FRAND-committed SEPs); Jacques Raynard, *Anéantissement du brevet et sort des redevances de license: efficacité de la clause prévoyant la non-restitution des redevances acquitées*, PROPRIÉTÉ INDUSTRIELLE, July–Aug. 2017, at 27–30 (critiquing the rule that the licensor keeps the royalties, even in the absence of a contractual provision specifically permitting this). As for prospective royalties, EU competition law permits licenses under which the licensee agrees "to pay a royalty for the use of a patented technology for the entire period in which that agreement was in effect, in the event of the revocation or non-infringement of a licenced patent, provided that the licensee was able freely to terminate that agreement by giving reasonable notice." Genentech Inc. v. Hoechst GmbH, Case C-567/14, ECLI:EU:C:2016:526, ¶ 43 (CJEU 2017).

[49] Cf. Patent Act art. 47 (China) (stating that although "[a]ny patent right that has been declared invalid is deemed to be non-existent from the beginning," such a decision generally "shall have no retroactive effect on any judgment or mediation statement on patent infringement which has been made and enforced by the people's court, on any decision concerning the handling of a dispute over patent infringement which has been performed or compulsorily executed, or on any patent exploitation licensing contract or patent right transfer contract which has been performed—prior to the declaration of the invalidation of the patent right," but that "the damage caused to other persons in bad faith by the patentee shall be compensated" and "[w]here the monetary damage for patent infringement, the royalties for patent exploitation or the fees for the transfer of the patent right is not refunded pursuant to the provisions of the preceding paragraph, but such non-refund is obviously contrary to the principle of fairness, refund shall be made fully or partly").

[50] Infringement courts may consider the likelihood of validity when deciding a motion for a preliminary injunction, as well as a "prior art" defense which, however, applies only in connection with the doctrine of equivalents. *See* Christian Osterrieth, *Patent Enforcement in Germany*, *in* PATENT ENFORCEMENT WORLDWIDE, *supra* note 38, at 111, 137.

technology or agreed to a license.[51] In such a system, it may well make sense for res judicata to take a back seat, even if the policies behind recognizing the finality of judgments are otherwise compelling. As a consequence, in the event of invalidation, German law would permit the infringement defendant to recover the costs of the first suit and any damages paid prior to patent invalidation, under a theory of unjust enrichment.[52]

A third practice that does not clearly fall in any of the earlier-mentioned categories is the issuance of antisuit injunctions (ASIs). As discussed in greater detail in chapter 6,[53] the interest protected by an ASI is, ostensibly, the movant's interest in avoiding "vexatious" or "oppressive" parallel litigation in another forum, as well as the interest of the forum granting the ASI to preserve its own jurisdiction; at the same time, however, the view long prevalent in civil law countries (until recently, at any rate) has been that ASIs wrongly interfere with the counterparty's right of access to the courts, and with the other forum's right to exercise its lawful jurisdiction: that, in a word, such injunctions offend the principal of comity.[54] As we shall see, however, whether it is the issuance of the ASI—or the counterresponse of an anti-antisuit injunction (AASI) forbidding the seeking or enforcement of an ASI—that is the greater affront to comity is a question that admits of no hard-and-fast answer.[55]

Fourth, there is the civil law's abuse of right doctrine. Though subject to different formulations and criteria for application, as discussed in greater detail in chapter 6,[56] in general the abuse of right doctrine prohibits the unreasonable assertion of one's legal rights, *e.g.*, for a purpose that is contrary to the purpose

[51] This is referred to as the "injunction gap." Legislation enacted in 2021 was intended to reduce the problem, by requiring the Patent Court (which decides invalidation matters) to issue, upon request, a preliminary nonbinding appraisal of validity within six months. Whether it will succeed remains to be seen, though some early reports have been promising. For discussion of the legislation, *see, e.g.*, Ansgar Ohly & Martin Stierle, *Unverhältnismäßigkeit, Injunction Gap and Geheimnisschutz im Prozess: Das Zweite Patentrechtsmodernisierungsgesetz im Überblick*, 2021 GRUR 1229.

[52] For discussion, *see* Klaus Bacher, *Vernichtung des Patents nach rechtskräftigem Abschluss des Verletzungsprozesses*, 2009 GRUR 216; Heath, *supra* note 48, at 320, 322; Christian Osterrieth, *Patent Enforcement in Germany*, *in* Patent Enforcement Worldwide, *supra* note 38, at 111, 141. (Doctrinally, the recovery rests on a theory of unjust enrichment. The former plaintiff would not be liable in tort for have filed the infringement action, except in the rare case in which it filed the action in bad faith. *See* Christof Karl, Björn Kalbfus, Hubertus Schacht & Michael Schneider, *Unjustified Allegations of Infringement of Intellectual Property Rights from a German Perspective*, 74 GRUR Int. 950, 953 (2025) (discussing the procedural privilege under German law).) A 2012 amendment to Japan's Patent Act precludes this possibility in that country, *see* Heath, *supra* note 39, at 412–13 (citing Japan Patent Act, art. 104quater).

[53] *See infra* ch. 6 notes 321–23 and accompanying text.

[54] *See, e.g.*, Hilton v. Guyot, 159 U.S. 113, 163–64 (1895) (defining comity as "the recognition which one nation allows within its territory to the legislative, executive or judicial acts of another nation, having due regard both to international duty and convenience, and to the rights of its own citizens, or of other persons who are under the protection of its laws").

[55] *See infra* ch. 6 notes 326–38 and accompanying text.

[56] *See id.* notes 86–115 and accompanying text.

of the right, such as to cause unjustified harm to another or to gain an improper advantage. As applied to patent assertion in particular, courts in civil law jurisdictions have sometimes applied the doctrine in response to, among other things, frivolous or vexatious litigation; the abuse of the judicial or administrative process to harm competitors; and requests for excessive remedies, including (in a few cases) the request for injunctive relief against an implementer who is willing to license a FRAND-committed SEP on FRAND terms.[57] Given the various possible uses of the doctrine, it may be viewed, depending on the circumstances, as responding to allegations of harm to any or all of the interests noted above, as well as to promoting general social welfare. As with the (arguably analogous) U.S. doctrine of patent misuse, however, the danger lies in the doctrine's potential for being applied in unpredictable or inconsistent ways, or (erroneously) in cases in which the asserted harm to social welfare is lacking.[58]

Remedies for These Harms

When a litigant succeeds in advancing a claim or defense of wrongful assertion under one or more of the preceding headings, a final question concerns the appropriate remedy for the harm. As indicated in the immediately preceding subsection, in countries that recognize the abuse of rights doctrine, proof that the patent owner has abused its rights can result in the unenforceability of the abusive condition, and in some cases an award of damages or a fine.[59] For violations of other legal norms that regulate wrongful patent assertion, the available remedies can take a surprisingly wide variety of forms.

First off, a violation of one or more of the *patent-specific* doctrines that regulate wrongful assertion usually results in a finding of either invalidity or unenforceability. In the U.S., for example, both patent misuse and inequitable conduct are defenses to liability, not claims for relief, and thus do not entitle the infringement defendant to any further relief other than, in exceptional cases,

[57] As applied to patent assertion, a successful claim of abuse of right does not result in invalidation, but rather deprives the owner of the ability to enforce its patent under the circumstances at issue, or to obtain the requested relief against infringement—and, at least in some cases, in an award of damages to the victim, or the imposition of a civil fine. *See* Amandine Léonard, *"Abuse of Rights" in Belgian and French Patent Law – A Case Law Analysis*, 7 JIPITEC 30, 35, 48 (2016).

[58] Other claims that may fall into this "other social welfare losses" category, or may in some cases transcend more than one category, including the U.K.'s doctrine of unjustified threats, *see infra* ch. 3 notes 54–63 and accompanying text; U.S. state laws targeting patent trolls, *see infra* ch. 3 notes 64–70 and accompanying text, ch. 5 notes 131–44 and accompanying text; and the abuse of economic dependence doctrine, *see infra* ch. 6 notes 116–42 and accompanying text.

[59] *See supra* note 57.

an award of attorneys' fees.[60] Thus, only to the extent the patent owner conduct at issue violates some other legal norm would additional damages or injunctive relief be on the table.

That said, injunctive relief, damages, and partial loss of enforceability certainly are available remedies for violations of these other legal norms, though the specifics differ from one country to another. In the U.S., violations of antitrust law can result in injunctive relief[61] and treble damages[62] (except where the complaining party is the Federal Trade Commission, which can seek only injunctive relief and more limited monetary awards[63]). Damages are limited, however, to financial losses resulting from the violation,[64] and can be difficult to quantify in cases where, for example, the claim is one for enforcement of a fraudulently procured patent. Other countries do not award treble damages for antitrust violations;[65] but where a patent owner's claim for injunctive relief for the infringement of a FRAND-committed SEP amounts to an abuse of dominant position, the result is typically the loss of the right to an injunction

[60] *See* 35 U.S.C. § 285 ("The court in exceptional cases may award reasonable attorney fees to the prevailing party").

[61] Most commonly, this means a decree forbidding certain conduct, or (in the case of, for example, mergers) permitting the conduct to go forward subject to conditions; much less commonly, it can mean structural relief, such as an order for the breakup of an existing monopoly. In some cases involving IP rights, however, courts have ordered the IP owner to offer licenses on a royalty-free or FRAND basis. For discussion, *see* Jorge L. Contreras, *A Brief History of FRAND*, 80 Antitrust L.J. 39 (2015).

[62] *See* 15 U.S.C. §§ 15(a), 15a, 15c(a)(2).

[63] *See* AMC Capital Mgt., LLC v. Fed. Trade Comm'n, 141 S. Ct. 1341 (2021) (discussing the remedies available in actions commenced by the Federal Trade Commission).

[64] *See* Thomas F. Cotter, *Damages for Noneconomic Harm in Intellectual Property Law*, 72 Hastings L.J. 1055, 1104–05 (2021) (stating that "courts have interpreted § 4 of the Clayton Act, which authorizes a civil action by 'any person who shall be injured in his business or property by reason of anything forbidden in the antitrust laws,' as precluding the recovery of damages for emotional distress, on the textual ground that this type of harm is not an injury to 'business or property'") (citations omitted).

[65] The maximum fine potentially available in the E.U. for violations of articles 101 or 102 of the Treaty on the Functioning of the European Union (TFEU) is 10% of a company's "total turnover in the preceding business year." Council Regulation (EC) No 1/2003 of 16 December 2002 on the implementation of the rules on competition laid down in Articles 81 and 82 of the Treaty, O.J. L 001, 04/01/2003, art. 23(2). Further, "[i]n determining the basic amount of the fine to be imposed, the Commission will take the value of the undertaking's sales of goods or services to which the infringement directly or indirectly . . . relates in the relevant geographic area within the EEA," and "will normally take the sales made by the undertaking during the last full business year of its participation in the infringement. . . . The basic amount of the fine will be related to a proportion of the value of sales, depending on the degree of gravity of the infringement, multiplied by the number of years of infringement," with "the proportion of the value of sales taken into account . . . set at a level of up to 30% of the value of sales." Guidelines on the method of setting fines imposed pursuant to Article 23(2)(a) of Regulation No 1/2003, 2006/C 210/02, arts. 13, 19, 21. According to a recent empirical study of cartel fines, however, "[t]he EC has over the last decade been setting the base amount at 16–17% (with outliers up to 18–19%)," but "[f]or common vertical agreements that infringe Article 101 TFEU . . . the EC sets the base amount at 7–8% of their relevant sales." Moreover, "[t]he fining methodology of other cases (e.g., pay-for-delay agreements and cases with an abuse component) is less consistent," though according to one of the study's authors some consistency is found in article 102 cases "with base amounts concentrated in the 10–11% range." Bruno Van den Bosch & Friso Bostoen, *Opening the Black Box: Uncovering the European Commission's Cartel Fining Formula Through Computational Analysis*, 3 Stan. J. Computational Antitrust 158, 191–92 (2023).

(which might then be followed either by the court itself determining the terms of a FRAND license, or by the parties settling the matter).[66] For violations of those bodies of law that regulate wrongful patent assertion through the lens of unfair competition law, the remedies would again include injunctive relief and damages. Damages can take the form of lost profits or other actual financial losses, as well as (where appropriate) damages for reputational harm;[67] and, primarily in common-law countries, under some circumstances punitive or enhanced damages.[68]

Remedies will be an important aspect of the discussion that follows, because a remedy that is too generous (or too miserly) can exacerbate (or dampen) the use of any of the above legal doctrines as a tool for regulating wrongful assertion. A common law-and-economics justification for enhanced or punitive damages, for example, as applied to remedies for patent infringement, is that these remedies sometimes may be necessary to achieve optimal deterrence;[69] but at the same time their overliberal application risks chilling would-be technology users from engaging in lawful conduct.[70] The same tension applies in the present context. According to U.S. antitrust scholars, absent the possibility of a treble damages award, some antitrust offenses may never be litigated (or even if litigated, will still be on net profitable to the defendant), and thus will be underdeterred; given the risk of error, however, the prospect of incurring treble damages liability may discourage some firms from engaging in vigorous, but lawful, competition.[71] Perhaps in the present context, such concerns are

[66] *See, e.g.*, Jorge L. Contreras et al., *The Effect of FRAND Commitments on Patent Remedies*, *in* PATENT REMEDIES AND COMPLEX PRODUCTS: TOWARD A GLOBAL CONSENSUS 160, 165–66 (Brad Biddle et al. eds. 2019) [hereinafter COMPLEX PRODUCTS]. Chapter 6 notes some of the recent developments in FRAND litigation.

[67] *See generally* Cotter, *supra* note 64 (discussing circumstances under which U.S. law of unfair competition permits awards of punitive or enhanced damages); *cf.* Colleen Chien et al., *Enhanced Damages, Litigation Cost Recovery, and Interest*, *in* COMPLEX PRODUCTS, *supra* note 66, at 94–96 (noting the general unavailability of punitive or enhanced damages in civil law countries).

[68] For discussion, *see infra* chapter 4.

[69] *See* Chien et al., *supra* note 67, at 97–100.

[70] *See id.* at 100–102.

[71] *See* Cotter, *supra* note 18, at 11, 13 n.110 (noting the existence of "concerns over the potential overdeterrent effect of treble damages in private antitrust litigation," while acknowledging that "[p]erhaps the best argument in favor of treble damages is that antitrust offenses often cause dispersed or social harm extending beyond the quantifiable harm suffered by the individual plaintiff, and that by enabling plaintiffs to capture some of the value of this dispersed harm the regime comes closer to achieving optimal deterrence") (citing Makan Delrahim, *The "New Madison" Approach to Antitrust and Intellectual Property Law*, Keynote Address at the University of Pennsylvania Law School (Philadelphia, Pa., Mar. 16, 2018), https://www.justice.gov/opa/speech/assistant-attorney-general-makan-delrahim-delivers-keynote-address-university; Makan Delrahim, *Take It to the Limit: Respecting Innovation Incentives in the Application of Antitrust Law*, Remarks at USC Gould School of Law—Application of Competition Policy to Technology and IP Licensing (Los Angeles, Cal., Nov. 10, 2017), https://www.justice.gov/opa/speech/file/1010746/download; and EINER ELHAUGE, UNITED STATES ANTITRUST LAW AND ECONOMICS 14–15 (2d ed. 2011)).

of lesser moment, given that claims for conduct such as fraudulent procurement require such stringent proof that they almost always fail. On the other hand, it's possible that concerns over the overdeterrent effect of treble damages may at times render U.S. courts too cautious in applying antitrust law, especially in patent-related disputes, as we shall see. At the same time, the civil law countries' reluctance to withhold injunctive relief for patent infringement has caused them to rely, perhaps too heavily, on antitrust and abuse of right doctrines as a necessary safety valve. (I return to these issues in chapter 6.)

The broader point is that the many different doctrines that address wrongful patent assertion do so primarily for different reasons—sometimes because the perceived misuse of a patent threatens to impede others from innovating, or to distort the market by enabling the patentee to expand its market power into related areas; and sometimes because an unwarranted threat of patent assertion will threaten the integrity of the marketplace or the judicial system, or simply reduce social welfare (perhaps for a combination of some or all of these reasons). Depending on which wrongful assertion claim or defense is at issue, defendants raising such a claim or defense may be entitled to very different remedies, and the liberality with which courts award these remedies in turn impacts the effectiveness of the doctrine—sometimes, perhaps, making it too effective, and other times not effective enough. The chapters that follow are intended to shed some light on these issues, though not before one additional preliminary consideration that the following chapter addresses: what should count as an "assertion" of patent rights, and should assertion be a requisite element at all?

3
Assertion

I stated in chapter 1 that this book would focus on doctrines relating to patent *assertion*, in the sense of either actual enforcement or, in some instances, threatened enforcement of patent rights. By "actual enforcement" I mean simply the initiation and maintenance of patent infringement litigation, which seems a pretty straightforward concept.[1] The meaning of "threatened enforcement," by contrast, is less clear, in particular as it relates to implicit, as opposed to express, threats to litigate. As noted in chapter 1, both offers to license and refusals to license can be understood as, in some sense, conveying the message that if the recipient of the communication doesn't accept or comply, the sender will sue.[2] Nevertheless, I've chosen not to address the legality of offers to license or of other agreements, or of refusals to deal, except insofar as they bear a close relationship to patent infringement litigation (primarily in relation to pay-for-delay agreements and the patent misuse doctrine, as discussed in chapters 5 and 6 respectively). That said, some legal doctrines, such as the U.K.'s law of unjustified threats, expressly address the threatened enforcement of IP rights; while others, including unfair competition claims targeting false communications, apply to false accusations of infringement which often, if not necessarily always, convey an express or implicit threat to litigate.[3] Consequently, I have chosen to include these bodies of law within the book's scope.

[1] *See, e.g.*, Agreement on Trade-Related Aspects of Intellectual Property Rights, Apr. 15, 1994, Marrakesh Agreement Establishing the World Trade Organization, Annex 1C, Legal Instruments-Results of the Uruguay Round vol. 31, 33 I.L.M. 1197 (1994) [hereinafter TRIPS], art. 4(1) ("Members shall ensure that enforcement procedures as specified in this Part are available under their law so as to permit effective action against any act of infringement of intellectual property rights covered by this Agreement, including expeditious remedies to prevent infringements and remedies which constitute a deterrent to further infringements."); Directive 2004/48/EC of the European Parliament and of the Council of 29 April 2004 on the Enforcement of Intellectual Property Rights, 2004 O.J. (L 195) 16, art. 1 ("This Directive concerns the measures, procedures and remedies necessary to ensure the enforcement of intellectual property rights.").

[2] *See supra* ch. 1 note 8 and accompanying text.

[3] Like other types of false statements, false accusations of infringement may injure the accused party's reputation; consumers may believe that the accused firm is unethical, or not much of an innovator, if it is merely copying someone else's innovation, and they may choose to shun the firm for these reasons. But false accusations of infringement also often communicate, at least implicitly, a threat of enforcement as well: regardless of how much (or how little) one may care about business ethics or about innovative firms, it may be rational to cease trading with an accused infringer if you think that the patent owner will soon take action to shut them (or you!) down.

Wrongful Patent Assertion. Thomas F. Cotter, Oxford University Press. © Oxford University Press 2026.
DOI: 10.1093/9780191994104.003.0003

Two principal sets of issues nevertheless remain. The first involves the question of whether, in a given context, enforcement (or threatened enforcement) should be considered a necessary element for liability to attach. To be sure, many claims, including not only abuse of process and sham litigation antitrust claims, but also claims by a prevailing party for its attorneys' fees or for compensation following the lifting of a wrongly-issued preliminary injunction, are themselves premised on the other party having used, or at least having threatened to use, the judicial system to enforce its alleged rights. In contrast, certain other types of claims have *no* necessary tie to the use of the court system, and for that reason are not covered in this book. (Product hopping, for example, involves gaming the regulatory system to impede competitors from being able to market their products; it doesn't necessarily involve patent owners suing or threatening to sue anyone.[4]) For yet other claims, however—including antitrust claims involving the fraudulent procurement of patents, which *is* one of the principal topics of this chapter—the relevant legal standards could go either way: they could condition liability on the defendant's having enforced or threatened to enforce its rights, or they could dilute or even dispense with that requirement altogether. One set of issues this chapter takes up, therefore, includes whether enforcement *should* be an element of such claims; if so, whether enforcement in this context should extend to threatened or only actual enforcement; and if not, whether liability nevertheless requires some additional misconduct on the part of the defendant, or only the mere acquisition or possession of a fraudulently acquired patent (coupled with whatever other elements would necessarily be required to prevail in, *e.g.*, an attempted monopolization or abuse of dominant position case). A second set of issues, to the extent relevant, centers on defining the scope of the term "threatened enforcement"—the dilemma being that if only express threats are actionable, patent owners may be able to evade liability by avoiding the use of expressly-threatening words, but if implicit threats count too, then courts sometimes will have to distinguish between (wrongful) implicit threats and other, possibly welfare-enhancing, communications.

I will argue that there are no uniformly correct answers to these questions, but that the differential treatment of various forms of assertion depends in part on the harms the legal system wishes to prevent and on the reasons for considering these harms to be unjustified. Put another way, the four elements of any wrongful assertion claim or defense—"assertion," "cognizable harm," "without justification," and "adverse consequences"—are interrelated

[4] *See supra* ch. 1 note 11.

and interdependent; and although in principle the same end result could be obtained by coupling a broad definition of assertion with narrower definitions of "without justification" or "adverse consequences" (or vice versa), in practice various contextual factors may render it preferable to adopt a relatively broad or narrow definition of one term or the other. A narrow definition of "assertion," for example, for purposes of fraudulent procurement claims, will screen out many claims at the outset, while a broader one may allow many more claims to proceed through litigation. The choice of which assertions count as potentially wrongful acts—or whether assertion should matter at all—therefore may depend, in part, on other features of the substantive or procedural law, including the existence of other options for challenging invalid patents; the availability of enhanced or treble damages for patentee misconduct; and the institutional competence of the relevant decisionmaker.

Before proceeding with the analysis, however, it's important to understand the lay of the land. The next two sections discuss the legal doctrines for which the above questions are most germane, namely fraudulent procurement and sham litigation antitrust claims, and unfair competition and other related claims premised on false accusations of infringement.[5] The third section returns to the above questions and provides a policy analysis.

Enforcement as Wrongful Assertion

The law of antitrust provides two of the most salient examples for which the actual enforcement of a patent can constitute a civil wrong, namely claims premised on the fraudulent procurement of patent rights and sham litigation claims. Taking these in order, the foundational U.S. decision addressing antitrust liability for fraudulent procurement is the 1965 case of *Walker Process Equipment, Inc. v. Food Machinery and Chemical Corp.*[6] The patent owner (Food Machinery and Chemical Corporation, or "FMC") had initiated matters

[5] These are relevant here, because fraudulent procurement antitrust claims present, as the text above indicates, a vehicle for considering whether assertion should be a necessary element for liability; and both fraudulent procurement and sham litigation antitrust claims pose the question whether threatened enforcement should be actionable to the same extent as actual enforcement. The legal standards pertaining to sham litigation and to the unfair competition claims discussed herein also present questions of how to reconcile litigants' rights of access to the courts with concerns over the abuse of those rights, although most of the analysis of that topic comes up in the following chapter. By contrast, the legal standards relating to fee awards, compensation for wrongly issued injunctions, and defenses which can limit the type of remedies available or render a patent in suit unenforceable, all necessarily involve actual litigation, and therefore are addressed in greater detail later in this book.

[6] 382 U.S. 172 (1965).

by filing an action against Walker Process, alleging infringement of a patent relating to sewage treatment.[7] In response, Walker Process filed a counterclaim alleging that FMC had obtained the patent by means of knowingly and intentionally misrepresenting to the United States Patent and Trademark Office (USPTO) the firm's prior use of the invention, and that FMC's subsequent enforcement of the patent constituted an act of monopolization in violation of § 2 of the Sherman Act.[8] The Supreme Court held that Walker Process had stated a claim for relief, though it cautioned that on remand the claimant would have to substantiate not only that FMC had "knowingly and willfully misrepresent[ed] facts to the Patent Office,"[9] but also that enforcement of the patent enabled FMC to monopolize a relevant market.[10] Put another way, enforcing a patent that one has knowingly and intentionally acquired by means of fraud on the Patent Office can constitute an act of monopolization or attempted monopolization, but only if the claimant can prove all of the elements of such a claim, in addition to the fraud.[11] Subsequent lower court decisions have held, moreover, that the claimant must prove the fraud by clear and convincing evidence.[12]

[7] *See id.* at 173.

[8] *See id.* at 174.

[9] *Id.* at 177.

[10] *See id.* at 174, 177–78 (stating, *inter alia*, "the enforcement of a patent procured by fraud on the Patent Office may be violative of s 2 of the Sherman Act provided the other elements necessary to a s 2 case are present"). The Court also stated that its "conclusion applies with equal force to an assignee who maintains and enforces the patent with knowledge of the patent's infirmity." *Id.* at 177 n.5. Some commentators have argued that the decision does not *require* proof of enforcement for a § 2 claim premised on fraudulent procurement, *see, e.g.*, B.D. Daniel, Walker Process *Proof: The Proper Prescription*, 41 Rutgers L.J. 105, 158 (2009) (stating that "[t]he references to enforcement . . . were only prefatory comments or descriptions of the particular circumstances of the case"), but the case law generally has interpreted the decision to require proof of enforcement or at least threatened enforcement. For discussion, see Herbert Hovenkamp et al., IP and Antitrust: An Analysis of Antitrust Principles Applied to Intellectual Property Law, § 11.02[E] (2023) (advocating, however, a broad interpretation of "enforcement").

[11] For a monopolization claim under U.S. law, this would mean that the claimant must show that the antitrust defendant has monopoly power in a well-defined market, and that the alleged fraud has enabled it to willfully acquire or maintain that monopoly. *See* United States v. Grinnell Corp., 384 U.S. 563, 570–71 (1966) (holding that a § 2 claim requires evidence of "the willful acquisition or maintenance of [monopoly] power as distinguished from growth or development as a consequence of a superior product, business acumen, or historic accident"). As Michael Carrier notes, "a market share of at least 70 percent 'generally establishes a prima facie case of monopoly power,' with some courts finding such power between 50 percent and 70 percent," and "the leading antitrust treatise suggest[ing] a presumption of monopoly power from a 'share of a well-defined market protected by sufficient entry barriers' that 'has exceeded 60 percent for the five years preceding the complaint.'" Michael A. Carrier, *The Antitrust Case Against Live Nation*, 15 Harv. J. Sports & Enter. L. 1, 11 (2024) (citations omitted). Mere ownership of a patent, moreover, does not create a presumption of market power, according to the Court's later decision in *Illinois Tool Works Inc. v. Independent Ink, Inc.*, 547 U.S. 28 (2006). For an attempted monopolization claim, the claimant would have to prove (1) a specific intent to monopolize, (2) predatory or anticompetitive conduct, and (3) a dangerous probability of success. *See* Spectrum Sports, Inc. v. McQuillan, 506 U.S. 447, 456 (1993).

[12] *See* C.R. Bard, Inc. v. M3 Sys., Inc., 157 F.3d 1340, 1364–65 (Fed. Cir. 1998) (citing Handgards, Inc. v. Ethicon, Inc., 601 F.2d 986, 996 (9th Cir. 1979)). For discussion of relevant cases, see Hovenkamp

A broader version of this type of claim can arise under E.U. law. The foundational decision, *AstraZeneca AB v. European Commission*,[13] arose when the European Commission initiated an investigation of two subsidiaries of AstraZeneca (AZ), a large pharmaceutical company. The Commission concluded that the firms had abused their dominant position in the market for omeprazole-based drugs in two ways, one involving the submission of misleading information to national patent offices and courts, the other involving the deregistration and withdrawal of existing products from certain markets in an effort to delay generic competition.[14] The General Court affirmed, subject to a few modifications,[15] and the CJEU affirmed the General Court. Focusing here on only the first of the alleged abuses, the CJEU cited the General Court's conclusions that (1) the submission of information that is liable to lead national authorities "into error and therefore to make possible the grant of an exclusive right" to which the defendants either were not entitled (or to which they were entitled for a shorter period of time), constituted an abuse of dominant position; and (2) "it followed from the objective nature of the concept of abuse that the misleading nature of representations made to public authorities had to be assessed on the basis of objective factors and that proof of the deliberate nature of the conduct and of the bad faith of the undertaking in a dominant position was not required, but could none the less constitute a relevant factor."[16] The CJEU also noted, however, the General Court's findings that "the Commission was right to find that AZ had deliberately tried to mislead the patent offices," and that "it was motivated by the intention of misleading the patent offices," and agreed that "AZ deliberately attempted to mislead the patent offices and judicial authorities in order to keep for as long as possible its monopoly," conduct that "fell outside the scope of competition on the merits."[17] Thus, while

ET AL., *supra* note 10, § 11.02[F] (noting, however, that because of the stringent standards of proof, "*Walker Process* claims are usually not successful").

[13] Case C-457/10 P, ECLI:EU:C:2012:770 (CJEU 2012).

[14] *Id.* ¶¶ 18–19. The misrepresentations consisted of statements made to authorities in several member states that AZ first obtained marketing authorization from the European Communities in March 1988, without notifying them that it had actually obtained "technical" authorization in France in 1987. Had the 1987 date been given, AZ would have been unable to obtain a supplemental protection certificate (SPC) in Denmark and in Germany, under rules applicable at that time. AZ defended its conduct on the ground that it was not authorized to begin selling products in France until the authorities there had published a price list, but in other contexts it used the date of technical authorization; and it understood that the patent offices and attorneys with which it communicated understood the relevant date to be the date of technical authorization, but never informed them of its alternative interpretation. *See id.* ¶¶ 77–97.

[15] *See* AstraZeneca AB v. Comm'n, ECLI:EU:T:2010:266, Case T-321/05 (Gen. Ct. 2010).

[16] *AstraZeneca AB*, ECLI:EU:C:2012:770, ¶¶ 62–63.

[17] *Id.* ¶¶ 66, 84, 93.

the CJEU did not embrace the defendants' arguments that "deliberate fraud or deceit should be a requirement for a finding of abuse in circumstances such as those of the present case,"[18] there was ample evidence that AZ intentionally misled the authorities; and the Court cited with approval the General Court's statement that dominant firms need not be infallible, but rather that "the assessment of whether representations made to public authorities for the purposes of improperly obtaining exclusive rights are misleading must be made *in concreto* and may vary according to the specific circumstances of each case."[19] That said, commentators have interpreted the *AstraZeneca* case as standing not only for the proposition that a dominant firm's "mere acquisition" of a patent by means of misleading representations has an anticompetitive effect, but also that evidence of intent is not a prerequisite (though it may be relevant "when looking to the abuse as a whole").[20]

A second type of wrongful assertion claim grounded in antitrust law arises from the pursuit of sham infringement litigation—assuming, once again, that

[18] *Id.* ¶ 71.

[19] *Id.* ¶ 99.

[20] World Intell. Prop. Org. Comm. on Dev. & Intell. Prop., *Study on the Anti-Competitive Enforcement of Intellectual Property (IP) Rights: Sham Litigation*, U.N. Doc. CDIP/9/INF/6 REV, annex 64 (July 30, 2012) [hereinafter CDIP Study]. The study relies in part on the analysis of Ola Rickardsson, "Patent Misuse and 'Sham'—Development of New Principles Under EU Competition Law" (2010) (Master Thesis, Lund University). Rickardsson argues that the E.U. and U.S. approaches differ in that "EU competition law is occupied with the regulation of the behavior of dominant firms rather than the actual effect of that behavior, while US antitrust law is more occupied with the exclusionary effects of the actual behavior." CDIP Study, *supra*, at annex 63 n.183 (quoting Rickardsson, *supra*, at 38).

One recent U.S. decision that at first blush might seem analogous to *AstraZeneca* is *Teva Branded Pharm. Prods. R&D, Inc. v. Amneal Pharms., LLC*, 124 F.4th 898 (Fed. Cir. 2024). As discussed in chapter 5, under U.S. law the owner of a patent that is properly listed on the FDA's Orange Book and that files suit within forty-five days of receiving a so-called Paragraph IV certification, indicating that the sender is planning to market a bioequivalent generic version of the owner's approved drug, obtains an automatic thirty-month stay of approval of the generic drug. The defendant can counterclaim, however, for an order that the owner's patents are incorrectly listed; such was the case here, where the patents did not claim the active ingredient of the approved drug. The only necessary consequence of an incorrect listing, however, would be that the owner is not entitled to the thirty-month stay. That said, the district court also denied Teva's motion to dismiss Amneal's antitrust counterclaims, which alleged that the improper listing enabled Teva to maintain monopoly power. *See* Teva Branded Pharm. Prods. R&D, Inc. v. Amneal Pharms., LLC, 736 F. Supp. 3d 227, 230–33 (D.N.J. 2024). The antitrust counterclaims were not before the Federal Circuit on interlocutory appeal, but the district court's denial of the motion to dismiss seems correct insofar as an incorrect listing can delay the entry of generic competition. To my knowledge, however, there was no allegation that the Teva patents were fraudulently procured, or that Teva's mere possession of those patents was anticompetitive. It is conceivable, though, that if the knowing possession of a fraudulently procured patent, without more, were to trigger some provision under U.S. law that automatically excluded competitors, then under those circumstances the knowing possession of such a patent could give rise to antitrust liability.

At present, there appear to be no decisions in China or Japan finding the assertion of a fraudulently procured patent to be an act in violation of competition law, *see* Takamitsu Shigetomi, Toshiya Furusho & Takashi Hirose, *Japan*, *in* 7 The Intellectual Property and Antitrust Review (Dieter Paemen ed. 2022); Nie Xin, *The Regulation Framework of Antitrust Law on Patent Malicious Litigation*, 21 J. Shanghai U. Fin. & Econ., no. 3, 2019, at 107, although Chinese law does recognize a more general claim for malicious litigation. *See infra* note 36 and accompanying text.

all of the other elements of such a claim (e.g., a dominant market share) are present, *and* subject to the plaintiff's success in overcoming protections intended to ensure litigants a right of access to the courts. The leading U.S. case addressing sham infringement litigation as a possible antitrust violation is *Professional Real Estate Investors, Inc. v. Columbia Pictures Industries, Inc.*[21] (hereinafter *PREI*). A group of movie studios filed an action for copyright infringement against a hotel operator, alleging that the hotel's rental of videos to guests for in-room viewing constituted a violation of the studios' exclusive right of public performance; in response, the hotel filed a counterclaim alleging that the infringement litigation was a sham intended to restrain trade, in violation of the Sherman Act.[22] Under U.S. law, however, the First Amendment guarantees, among other things, a constitutional right to petition the government.[23] As a result, beginning in the early 1960s the Supreme Court has decided a series of cases standing for the proposition that litigants are (in general) immune from antitrust liability where the alleged anticompetitive conduct is the act of petitioning the government.[24] This immunity from liability—referred to in the case law as *Noerr-Pennington* immunity—can be overcome when the petitioning is

[21] 508 U.S. 49 (1993). An earlier case, *California Motor Transport Co. v. Trucking Unltd.*, 404 U.S. 514 (1972), had held that *Noerr-Pennington* immunity did not shield a pattern of litigating "with or without probable cause, and regardless of merits." Although *PREI* did not purport to overrule *California Motor*, its holding that an antitrust plaintiff must demonstrate *inter alia* objective baselessness is in some tension with *California Motor*, in which the antitrust defendants had prevailed in about half of their cases against the antitrust plaintiffs. I discuss *California Motor* and the post-*PREI* case law addressing its continued vitality in chapter 4.

[22] *PREI*, 508 U.S. at 52.

[23] *See* U.S. Const. amend. I ("Congress shall make no law . . . abridging . . . the right of the people . . . to petition the Government for a redress of grievances.").

[24] *See* E.R.R. Presidents Conf. v. Noerr Motor Freight, Inc., 365 U.S. 127 (1961); United Mine Workers of Am. v. Pennington, 381 U.S. 657 (1965). Both cases are sometimes read as grounding the resulting immunity in *antitrust* law, not in the First Amendment, *see, e.g.*, Paul R. Gugliuzza, *Patent Trolls and Preemption*, 101 Va. L. Rev. 1579, 1639 (2015) (quoting *Noerr*, 365 U.S. at 137–38, for the proposition that the Court adopted "'a construction of the Sherman Act' . . . to avoid 'important . . . questions' about the right to petition, informed by the Sherman Act's purpose to regulate 'business activity,' not 'political activity'"), though the Court itself has sometimes characterized *Noerr-Pennington* immunity as a creature of First Amendment law. *See* Octane Fitness, LLC v. ICON Health & Fitness, Inc., 572 U.S. 545, 556 (2014) ("We crafted the *Noerr-Pennington* doctrine—and carved out only a narrow exception for 'sham' litigation—to avoid chilling the exercise of the First Amendment right to petition the government for the redress of grievances."); BE & K Constr. Co. v. NLRB, 536 U.S. 516, 524–28 (2002); *see also PREI*, 508 U.S. at 56 (quoting *Noerr*, 365 U.S. at 138, for the proposition that the Court did not "'impute to Congress an intent to invade' the First Amendment right to petition"); Hovenkamp et al., *supra* note 10, § 11.03[B][1], at 11–31 & n.122. On the other hand, as Minyu Zheng points out, Minyu Zheng, Legal Responses to Unjustified Threats of Patent Infringement – Intellectual Property Approach or Unfair Competition Approach? 98–99 (2024), in *Borough of Duryea v. Guarnieri*, 564 U.S. 379 (2011), both Justice Thomas (the author, eighteen years earlier, of the majority opinion in *PREI*) and the late Justice Scalia have expressed doubt that lawsuits qualify as "petitions" within the meaning of the First Amendment. *See Duryea*, 379 U.S. at 399 (Thomas, J., concurring in the judgment); *id.* at 401–04 (Scalia, J., concurring in the judgment in part and dissenting in part). Perhaps the Supreme Court will revisit the issue at some point in the future.

nothing more than a "sham," which has sometimes been described as the use of "governmental process—as opposed to the outcome of that process" as an anticompetitive weapon.[25] *PREI* was the first Supreme Court decision to expressly hold that an antitrust violation can be based on sham infringement litigation, albeit subject to two qualifications:

> First, the lawsuit must be objectively baseless in the sense that no reasonable litigant could realistically expect success on the merits. If an objective litigant could conclude that the suit is reasonably calculated to elicit a favorable outcome, the suit is immunized under *Noerr*, and an antitrust claim premised on the sham exception must fail.... Only if challenged litigation is objectively meritless may a court examine the litigant's subjective motivation. Under this second part of our definition of sham, the court should focus on whether the baseless lawsuit conceals "an attempt to interfere *directly* with the business relationships of a competitor," ... through the "use [of] the governmental *process*—as opposed to the *outcome* of that process—as an anticompetitive weapon" ....[26]

Lower court decisions have applied these standards to allegations of sham patent infringement litigation, sometimes referred to as *Handgards* claims after a pre-*PREI* decision that may have been the first example of the type.[27] As with *Walker Process* claims, moreover, the relevant burden of proof is clear

[25] City of Columbia v. Omni Outdoor Advert., Inc., 499 U.S. 365, 380 (1991).

[26] *PREI*, 508 U.S. at 60–61 (citations omitted). Commentators have pointed out that the Court's various articulations of what "objective baselessness" means can seem difficult to reconcile. In one portion of the opinion, after noting that the lower courts had concluded that the antitrust defendant had probable cause to allege copyright infringement, the Court stated:

> The existence of probable cause to institute legal proceedings precludes a finding that an antitrust defendant has engaged in sham litigation. The notion of probable cause, as understood and applied in the common-law tort of wrongful civil proceedings ... requires the plaintiff to prove that the defendant lacked probable cause to institute an unsuccessful civil lawsuit and that the defendant pressed the action for an improper, malicious purpose.... Probable cause to institute civil proceedings requires no more than a "reasonabl[e] belie[f] that there is a chance that [a] claim may be held valid upon adjudication."

[27] *Id.* at 62 (citations omitted).

(For discussion of the "common-law tort of wrongful civil proceedings," *see infra* note 34.) Another portion, however, noted that, even though Columbia Pictures' infringement claim "did not survive PRE's motion for summary judgment," it "was arguably 'warranted by existing law' or at the very least was based on an objectively 'good faith argument for the extension, modification, or reversal of existing law." *Id.* at 65 (quoting Fed. R. Civ. P. 11). Thus, "[e]ven in the absence of supporting authority, Columbia would have been entitled to press a novel copyright claim as long as a similarly situated reasonable litigant could have perceived some likelihood of success." *Id.* As Hovenkamp et al. note, "[t]his second test is analogous to—but even easier to meet than—the standard set forth in Rule 11," which requires that pleadings "be both objectively grounded ... *and* ... not 'presented for any improper purpose, such as to harass or to cause unnecessary delay or needless increase in the cost of litigation." Because "Rule 11 requires that a pleading be both objectively and subjectively nonfrivolous, while under *PREI* either an objective *or* a subjective basis will suffice to confer antitrust immunity," "it is

and convincing evidence, rather than the normal preponderance of evidence standard. Thus, only if the antitrust claimant demonstrates, by clear and convincing evidence, that the litigation was a sham does the case proceed to the substantive issue (subject to the normal preponderance standard) of whether the antitrust defendant's conduct enabled it to monopolize (or attempt to monopolize) a defined market.[28]

The foundational E.U. decision on sham litigation as an abuse of dominant position is *ITT Promedia NV v. Commission of the European Communities*[29] (which, however, like *PREI*, did not involve allegedly sham *patent* litigation).[30] The Commission adopted a standard, which the applicant Promedia did not oppose and the Court of First Instance applied, under which "in principle the bringing of an action, which is the expression of the fundamental right of access to a judge, cannot be characterised as an abuse" unless "an undertaking in a dominant position brings an action (i) which cannot reasonably be considered as an attempt to establish its rights and can therefore only serve to harass the opposite party, and (ii) which is conceived in the framework of a plan whose goal is to eliminate competition."[31] As others have noted, the second element "does not concern the subjective element that the US Supreme Court applied

reasonable to assume that some infringement lawsuits that are frivolous under Rule 11 will nonetheless receive antitrust immunity under *PREI*." Hovenkamp et al., *supra* note 10, § 11.03[B][4] at 11–37 & n.147. Probable cause, however, might appear to be an even stricter standard than Rule 11, which leads Hovenkamp et al. to suggest that the passages on probable cause and on Rule 11 can be reconciled by considering probable cause as "a 'safe harbor' for antitrust defendants," and that "[e]ven if infringement actions lack probable cause, the intellectual property owner may still be entitled to antitrust immunity under the objective prong if she can demonstrate that her claims, though incorrect, were nonfrivolous under the objective prong of Rule 11." *Id.* at 11–37 to -38.

See Handgards, Inc. v. Ethicon, Inc., 601 F.2d 986 (9th Cir. 1979). For discussion of relevant cases, see Hovenkamp et al., *supra* note 10, § 11.03[B][4].

[28] *See* C.R. Bard, Inc. v. M3 Sys., Inc., 157 F.3d 1340, 1364–65 (Fed. Cir. 1998) (citing Handgards, Inc. v. Ethicon, Inc., 601 F.2d 986, 996 (9th Cir. 1979)); FTC v. AbbVie Inc., 329 F. Supp. 3d 98, 120–21 (E.D. Pa. 2018), *aff'd in part, rev'd in part on other grounds*, 976 F.3d 327 (3d Cir. 2020); *see also* Golan v. Pingel Enter. Inc., 310 F.3d 1360, 1371 (Fed. Cir. 2002) (stating, in the context of unfair competition claims premised on allegedly false assertions of patent rights, that the claimant "must offer clear and convincing evidence that [the defendant] had no reasonable basis to believe that the [accused product] infringed [defendant's] patents or that [defendant] knew it was enforcing an expired, and therefore unenforceable, patent"). The Federal Circuit doesn't subject *Walker Process* claims to *Noerr-Pennington* analysis, however, *see* Nobelpharma AB v. Implant Innovations, Inc., 141 F.3d 1059, 1071 (Fed. Cir. 1998), although the Ninth Circuit, which occasionally hears such cases, does. *See* Hydranautics v. FilmTec Corp., 70 F.3d 533 (9th Cir. 1995). For discussion, *see* Hovenkamp et al., *supra* note 10, § 11.02[B].

[29] Case T-111/96, ECLI:EU:T:1998:183 (CJEU 1998).

[30] It was, in fact, premised on allegedly sham breach of contract litigation. For more detailed background on the case, *see* Ioannis Lianos & Pierre Régibeau, *"Sham" Litigation: When Can It Arise and How Can It Be Reduced?*, 62 Antitrust Bull. 643, 657–58 (2017).

[31] *ITT Promedia NV*, ECLI:EU:T:1998:183, ¶ 30; *see also id.* ¶ 55 (repeating these two cumulative criteria); *id.* ¶¶ 57–58 (noting that Promedia was not challenging the criteria, and that as a result there was "no need for [the court] to rule on the correctness of the criteria").

in *PREI*, perhaps because the EU notion of abuse is traditionally an objective one," but it does "resemble[] another US idea, namely the idea that the anticompetitive intent of a plaintiff can be derived from the existence of a pattern of baseless, repetitive lawsuits," and that "[a]s a whole . . . the EU approach does not differ a lot from the US one."[32] One subsequent CJEU decision has applied the *ITT Promedia* standard in relation to intellectual property litigation, stating that only in "quite exceptional circumstances" is it possible that asserting a claim for relief can be understood as an abuse of dominant position.[33]

Other bodies of law also sometimes target sham, baseless, or bad-faith patent litigation. Occasionally such claims may arise under generally applicable legal doctrines such as the common-law torts of wrongful use of civil proceedings[34] and abuse of process;[35] or, in civil law countries, abuse of rights or

[32] Mariateresa Maggiolino, Intellectual Property and Antitrust: A Comparative Economic Analysis of US and EU Law 198 (2011). *See also* CDIP Study, *supra* note 20, at annex 14 (quoting Rickardsson, *supra* note 20, at 46, for the proposition that the U.S. and E.U. tests "are very similar"); Simonetta Vezzoso, *Towards an EU Doctrine of Anticompetitive IP-Related Litigation*, 3 J. Eur. Comp. L. & Prac. 521, 533 (2012) (stating that "the subjective element of the *PREI* test is not absent from *ITT Promedia*, but it is to be inferred from the fact that the litigation is objectively baseless ('and can *therefore* only serve to harass the opposite party', emphasis added)"; but also suggesting that the CJEU's reference to "a *plan* whose goal is to eliminate competition" might suggest "a competition assessment more stringent than in other cases of abusive conduct," and that "the litigation patterns could still be anticompetitive even if by chance some aspect of it turns out not to have been 'unreasonable'")). I return to the issue of whether U.S. law requires, or should require, a claimant arguing that a pattern of filing suit constitutes anticompetitive sham petitioning to prove that each individual suit is objectively baseless, in chapter 4.

[33] Protégé Int'l Ltd. v. Commission européenne, Case T-119/09, ¶ 48 (CJEU 2012) (trademarks) (discussed in Lianos & Régibeau, *supra* note 30, at 659). *See also* Agria Polska sp. z o.o. v. European Commission, Case C-373/17 P, ECLI:EU:C:2018:756 (CJEU 2018) (dismissing an appeal in a case alleging wrongful claims of infringement of intellectual property rights, without reaching the merits); Merck Sharp Dohme S.A. v. Human Health Holdings, B.V., S/0026/19 (CNMC 2022) (Sp.) (awarding €38.9 million for abuse of dominant position by means of abusive litigation) (discussed in Marcos Araujo Boyd, *Patent Litigation as a Form of Abuse—The Spanish Decision Against MSD*, Kluwer Competition Law Blog, Nov. 2, 2022, https://competitionlawblog.kluwercompetitionlaw.com/2022/11/02/patent-litigation-as-a-form-of-abuse-the-spanish-decision-against-msd/).

[34] *See* Restatement (Third) of Torts: Liability for Economic Harm § 24 (Am. L. Inst. 2020) ("An actor is subject to liability . . . when (a) the actor initiates, procures, or continues a civil proceeding against another without probable cause; (b) the civil proceeding has a primary purpose other than securing the proper adjudication of the lawsuit; and (c) the lawsuit terminates in favor of the party against whom it is brought"). Parts (a) and (b) bear a close resemblance to the *Noerr-Pennington* standard articulated in *PREI*. *See PREI*, 508 U.S. at 62 (citing the earlier Restatement provision on wrongful civil proceedings, Restatement (Second) of Torts § 674 (Am. L. Inst. 1977), and noting that the "tort is frequently called 'malicious prosecution,' which (strictly speaking) governs the malicious pursuit of criminal proceedings without probable cause"); cf. *id.* at 66, 67 (Souter, J., concurring) (expressing his understanding that the Court did not intend to "transplant[] every substantive nuance and procedural quirk of the common-law tort of wrongful civil proceedings into federal antitrust law").

[35] *See* Restatement (Third) of Torts: Liability for Economic Harm § 26 (Am. L. Inst. 2020) ("An actor is subject to liability for the abuse of judicially issued process to achieve an objective that is outside the purpose for which the process is intended"); *see also id.* cmts. b, d (stating that "'process' generally means orders that are issued by courts at the behest of one of the parties, or that are otherwise backed by judicial authority"; that liability for abuse of process "typically arises . . . from the issuance of process *within* a case" and that it "requires a showing that the defendant's primary reason for invoking judicial process was outside the purpose for which the process was intended").

other related doctrines.[36] Independently of whether a patent applicant's conduct would constitute fraud for purposes of a *Walker Process* claim, moreover, if an infringement defendant proves that the applicant intentionally withheld material information from the patent office during the course of patent prosecution, the patent can be rendered unenforceable under the U.S. inequitable conduct defense, as discussed in chapter 6.[37]

Cf. High Concrete Structures, Inc. v. Nat'l Union Fire Ins. Co., No. 1264, 2004 WL 213235, at *2 (Pa. Ct. Com. Pl. Feb. 3, 2004) (stating that "a patent holder that had an improper motive in bringing a civil action for patent infringement may be charged with the state law tort of abuse of process by way of a counterclaim in the infringement action," but that "a patent holder that obtained a patent from the PTO by improper means may not be charged with abuse of process") (citations omitted).

[36] For discussion of abuse of rights, *see infra* ch. 6 notes 86–115 and accompanying text. For additional discussion of the (rare) circumstances in which filing a patent infringement lawsuit might constitute a tort, *see, e.g.*, Christof Karl, Björn Kalbfus, Hubertus Schacht & Michael Schneider, *Unjustified Allegations of Infringement of Intellectual Property Rights from a German Perspective*, 74 GRUR INT. 950, 953 (2025) (stating that, although the filing of a lawsuit is generally privileged, "[i]n the (very) exceptional case of abusive court proceedings, the procedural privilege does not" apply, though to the authors' knowledge there is "no decision in Germany finding that an IP right holder has abusively asserted his right in a court proceeding"); Monya Takatoshi, AIPPI Question Q292-SR-G-2024: Unjustified allegations of infringement of IP rights (Japan) (July 10, 2024) (stating that, because "the right of access to the courts is guaranteed by Article 32 of the Constitution of Japan, an allegation will be found unlawful (unjustified), in exceptional cases where the plaintiff was aware or a reasonable person could have easily been aware that the allegation lacked factual or legal grounds") (citing Judgment of Jan. 26, 1988, 1985 (o) 122 (S. Ct.) (Japan)). In China, courts have applied the "malicious litigation" doctrine to alleged abuses of patent rights. *See* Xiang Yu & Di Lu, *Mainland China*, *in* THE ENFORCEMENT OF PATENTS 89, 111–12 & nn. 92–93 (Kung-Chung Liu & Reto M. Hilty eds. 2012); Xin, *supra* note 20, at 117. Both of the preceding sources describe *Tongfa Pneumatic Valve Actuators Plant v. Yuan Li*, Ning Min San Chu Zi No. 188 (Nanjing Intermediate People's Ct. 2006), in which the owner obtained a patent knowing that the claimed invention was in the public domain, as the first case in which a Chinese court applied the malicious litigation tort to a patent infringement action. They also both note, however, that the law has not necessarily been consistently applied. More recent commentary suggests that the current approach would be to litigate cases like these under the abuse of right doctrine. *See* Yazhou Zhang, AIPPI Question Q292-SR-G-2024: Unjustified allegations of infringement of IP rights (China) (July 10, 2024).

[37] *See infra* ch. 6 notes 149–89 and accompanying text. Litigants sometimes raise other, more creative, theories as well. In the United States, for example, under some limited circumstances a private actor may be able to invoke the U.S. False Claims Act, 31 U.S.C. §§ 3729–33, against a firm that allegedly overcharged the United States government for drugs covered by fraudulently obtained patents. *See* Silbersher v. Valeant Pharms. Int'l, Inc., 89 F.4th 1154, 1159–60 (9th Cir.) (setting forth the conditions under which a claimant may proceed with such a claim, which if successful would entitle the claimant to up to 30% of the proceeds the government would be entitled to recover from the defendant; such claims are precluded if "substantially the same allegations or transactions as alleged in the action or claim were publicly disclosed—(i) in a Federal criminal, civil, or administrative hearing in which the Government or its agent is a party; (ii) in a congressional, Government Accountability Office, or other Federal Report, hearing, audit, or investigation; or (iii) from the news media, unless the action is brought by the Attorney General or the person bringing the action is an original source of the information"), *cert. denied*, 145 S. Ct.140 (2024). Another possibility, albeit rarely if ever successful, is to assert a civil claim under the Racketeering Influenced and Corrupt Organizations (RICO) Act—a statute that typically requires some showing of a pattern of fraudulent conduct. *See, e.g.*, Semiconductor Energy Lab'y Co. v. Samsung Elecs. Co., 204 F.3d 1368, 1380 (Fed. Cir. 2000), amended (Apr. 5, 2000) (stating that "inequitable conduct before the USPTO cannot qualify as an act of mail fraud or wire fraud for purposes of the predicate act requirement" of RICO because "to defraud" requires "wronging one in his property rights by dishonest methods or schemes" and "an application that has not yet matured into a patent cannot properly be deemed government property") (internal quotations and citations omitted).

Finally, even if the patent in suit was not obtained by fraud and the lawsuit itself is not baseless or in bad faith, the maintenance of the suit or the manner in which it is litigated can sometimes result in patent owner liability. First, if the defendant prevails on liability and/or validity, the defendant may qualify for reimbursement of at least some portion of the expenses it incurred in its defense—though as discussed in the following chapter, the specifics vary considerably from one country to another.[38] Second, as also discussed in chapter 4, defendants who were excluded from the market under the terms of a preliminary (or in some countries, even a permanent) injunction may be entitled to compensation, if the relevant claims of the patent in suit are subsequently held to be invalid.[39] Third, as discussed in chapter 6, even if the patent in suit is valid and infringed, legal doctrines including (in civil-law countries) abuse of dominant position or abuse of right, or (in common-law countries) equitable discretion and/or equitable defenses, may preclude the entry of injunctive relief or preclude enforceability altogether. Fourth, other generally applicable legal doctrines may penalize litigants or their attorneys for pursuing frivolous litigation or for engaging in misconduct during the course of litigation, as in any other type of case.[40] Some possible applications of these doctrines will come up, albeit briefly, in chapters 4 and 6.[41]

Another creative but unsuccessful theory arose in *Sec'y of State for Health v. Servier Labs. Ltd.* [2021] UKSC 24, in which the U.K. Supreme Court rejected a claim that the defendants, who allegedly caused the U.K.'s National Health Service to suffer economic harm by defrauding the EPO into issuing a patent that later was found to be invalid, could be liable under the common law doctrine of "unlawful means." The Court held that this type of claim, premised on a defendant's unlawful conduct toward a third party causing the plaintiff to suffer economic harm, does not arise unless the defendant's conduct affected the third party's freedom to deal with the plaintiff.

[38] *See infra* ch. 4 notes 5–14 and accompanying text.

[39] *See infra* ch. 4 notes 49–125 and accompanying text; *see also supra* ch. 2 note 52 and accompanying text.

[40] *See, e.g.*, Fed. R. Civ. P. 11(b)–(c) (stating that "[b]y presenting to the court a pleading, written motion, or other paper," an attorney "certifies that to the best of the person's knowledge, information, and belief, formed after an inquiry reasonable under the circumstances . . . it is not being presented for any improper purpose, such as to harass, cause unnecessary delay, or needlessly increase the cost of litigation," the "legal contentions are warranted by existing law or by a nonfrivolous argument for extending, modifying, or reversing existing law or for establishing new law," and that "the factual contentions have evidentiary support"; and providing that sanctions awarded for violations "must be limited to what suffices to deter repetition of the conduct or comparable conduct by others similarly situated," and "may include nonmonetary directives; an order to pay a penalty into court; or, if imposed on motion and warranted for effective deterrence, an order directing payment to the movant of part or all of the reasonable attorney's fees and other expenses directly resulting from the violation"); Goodyear Tire & Rubber Co. v. Haeger, 581 U.S. 101, 107–08 (2017) (holding that courts have inherent authority to award fees incurred in civil actions as a result of litigation misconduct); Chambers v. NASCO, Inc., 501 U.S. 32, 42–50 (1991) (discussing statutory and inherent authority to sanction litigation misconduct). The availability of such sanctions may vary substantially from country to country, however. For discussion, *see* Jacques Normand, *Final Report: The Two Approaches to the Abuse of Procedural Rights*, *in* Abuse of Procedural Rights: Comparative Standards of Procedural Fairness 237, 246–47 (Michele Tartuffo ed. 1998).

[41] *See infra* ch. 4 notes 252–53 and accompanying text; ch. 6 note 186.

Express or Implicit Threats of Enforcement as Wrongful Assertion

With the exception of *AstraZeneca*, all of the cases discussed in the preceding section involved the actual enforcement, that is, litigation, of patent rights. It seems reasonably clear, nonetheless, that under U.S. law an explicit *threat* to enforce a fraudulently procured patent, or to engage in sham infringement litigation, also can be sufficient to sustain antitrust liability under *Walker Process*[42] or *PREI*,[43] as the case may be—though whether an *implicit* threat of litigation can suffice has not always been so clear. In 2004, the Federal Circuit held in *Unitherm Food Systems, Inc. v. Swift-Eckrich, Inc.*[44] that "the standards . . . for determining jurisdiction in a Declaratory Judgment Action of patent invalidity also define the minimum level of 'enforcement' necessary to expose the patentee to a *Walker Process* claim for attempted monopolization."[45] Under the court's then-existing standard for obtaining declaratory relief, a putative infringer had to prove, *inter alia*, that the patent owner's conduct created a "reasonable apprehension of suit,"[46] the best evidence of which would be an explicit threat to file suit.[47] The corresponding standard for proving *Walker Process* "enforcement" similarly appeared generally to exclude conduct short of an explicit threat.[48] In 2007, however, the U.S. Supreme Court in *MedImmune, Inc. v. Genentech, Inc.*[49] overruled the rigid "reasonable apprehension of suit" standard for declaratory relief,[50] following which the Federal Circuit has held that a declaratory judgment action may proceed as long as the "patentee asserts rights under a patent based on certain identified ongoing or planned activity of

[42] *See* Hovenkamp et al., *supra* note 10, § 11.02[E]; Christopher R. Leslie, *Patents of Damocles*, 83 Ind. L.J. 133, 141 (2008) (citing Indium Corp. of Am. v. Semi-Alloys, Inc., 566 F. Supp. 1344, 1352–53 (N.D.N.Y. 1983)).

[43] *See, e.g.*, Miller Pipeline Corp. v. British Gas PLC, 69 F. Supp. 2d 1129, 1138–39 (S.D. Ind. 1999) (collecting cases); Hovenkamp et al., *supra* note 10, § 11.04[B][4][d] (noting with approval that the majority of circuits to have considered the issue have concluded that threatened litigation falls within the scope of *Noerr-Pennington* immunity, but that "there is far less justification for immunizing public communications regarding the litigation," notwithstanding dictum in *Zenith Elecs. Corp. v. Exzec, Inc.*, 183 F.3d 1340, 1353 (Fed. Cir. 1999), that would extend petitioning immunity to merely publicizing a patent in the marketplace).

[44] 375 F.3d 1341 (Fed. Cir. 2004), *rev'd on other grounds*, 546 U.S. 394 (2006).

[45] *Id.* at 1358.

[46] *See* Arrowhead Indus. Water, Inc. v. Ecolochem, Inc., 846 F.2d 731, 736–37 (Fed. Cir. 1988).

[47] *See, e.g.*, Vanguard Rsch., Inc. v. PEAT, Inc., 304 F.3d 1249, 1254–55 (Fed. Cir. 2002) ("Although the best evidence of a reasonable apprehension of suit comes in the form of an express threat of litigation, an express threat is not required. . . . To invoke the court's declaratory judgment jurisdiction, a plaintiff must show 'more than the nervous state of mind of a possible infringer,' but does not have to show that the patentee is 'poised on the courthouse steps.'") (citations omitted).

[48] *See* Leslie, *supra* note 42, at 144–61.

[49] 549 U.S. 118 (2007).

[50] *See id.* at 132 n.11 (2007).

another party, and . . . that party contends that it has the right to engage in the accused activity without license . . . ."[51] Subsequent cases have emphasized the totality-of-the-circumstances nature of the inquiry—such that, for example, correspondence from a nonpracticing entity identifying its patent, describing it as "relating to" the recipient's products, and requesting an opportunity to discuss it, can constitute an "implied assertion" sufficient to justify the recipient in seeking declaratory relief.[52] Assuming then that *Unitherm*'s equation of the standards for declaratory relief and for *Walker Process* "enforcement" remains good law, conduct falling short of an express threat to litigate may now satisfy the latter,[53] though the Federal Circuit itself has yet to expressly address this issue.

Sometimes an express or implicit threat to sue will suffice under other bodies of law as well. Since 1883, for example, the U.K. has recognized a statutory cause of action for making unjustified threats (sometimes referred to alternatively as "unlawful threats" or "groundless threats") against so-called "secondary" infringers, that is, entities who occupy a place in the distribution chain below the initial, "primary" infringer (typically, the manufacturer of the infringing subject matter).[54] Most recently amended in 2017, the current

[51] SanDisk Corp. v. STMicroelectronics, Inc., 480 F.3d 1372, 1381 & n.2 (Fed. Cir. 2007). The court went on to state that:

> In the context of conduct prior to the existence of a license, declaratory judgment jurisdiction generally will not arise merely on the basis that a party learns of the existence of a patent owned by another or even perceives such a patent to pose a risk of infringement, without some affirmative act by the patentee. But Article III jurisdiction may be met where the patentee takes a position that puts the declaratory judgment plaintiff in the position of either pursuing arguably illegal behavior or abandoning that which he claims a right to do. . . . We hold . . . that where a patentee asserts rights under a patent based on certain identified ongoing or planned activity of another party, and where that party contends that it has the right to engage in the accused activity without license, an Article III case or controversy will arise and the party need not risk a suit for infringement by engaging in the identified activity before seeking a declaration of its legal rights.

Id. at 1380–81.

[52] *See* Hewlett-Packard Co. v. Acceleron LLC, 587 F.3d 1358, 1361–64 (Fed. Cir. 2009).

[53] *See* Xitronix Corp. v. KLA-Tencor Corp., No. A-14-CA-1113, 2015 WL 5037387, at *3–7 (W.D. Tex. Aug. 24, 2015) (holding that merely advertising one's patent does not qualify as enforcement, but that an "overt act of enforcement" is also unnecessary to sustain a *Walker Process* claim); *see also* Hovenkamp et al., *supra* note 10, § 11.02[E], at 11–24 (stating that the elimination of the "reasonable apprehension of suit" test "may mean that the test no longer makes sense in the *Walker Process* context either," or that "the standard is correspondingly easier to meet," such that "a licensee in good standing might bring a *Walker Process* claim alleging that being coerced into signing the license was sufficient market effect from the enforcement of the patent").

[54] *See* Joshua Marshall, *Unjustified Threats as a Cause of Action*, 42 European Intell. Prop. Rev. 150, 150 (2020). Some other countries also have "unjustified" or "groundless" threat actions, and may even extend such actions to primary infringers. *See, e.g.*, Patents Act 1990 (Cth) §§ 128–32 (Austl.) ("Where a person, by means of circulars, advertisements or otherwise, threatens a person with infringement proceedings, or other similar proceedings, a person aggrieved may apply to a prescribed court . . . for" a declaration the threats were unjustifiable, an injunction against future threats, and damages sustained as a result of the threats); The Patents Act, 1970, § 106 (India) (stating it is unlawful

version of the law applies to unjustified threats of patent, design, and trademark infringement. Focusing specifically on the patent-related provision, a communication is defined as containing "a 'threat of infringement proceedings' if a reasonable person in the position of a recipient would understand from the communication that . . . (a) a patent exists, and (b) a person intends to bring proceedings (whether in a court in the United Kingdom or elsewhere) against another person for infringement of the patent by . . . (i) an act done in the United Kingdom, or (ii) an act which, if done, would be done in the United Kingdom."[55] The act states that "a threat of infringement proceedings made by any person is actionable by any person aggrieved by the threat,"[56] and thus is understood to confer standing on "any person whose commercial interests are, or are likely to be, adversely affected in a real, as opposed to a fanciful, way"—even if that person is not, itself, "the recipient of the threat."[57]

for "any person (whether entitled to or interested in a patent or an application for patent or not)" to threaten "any other person by circulars or advertisements or by communications" if the "threats are unjustifiable"); Canada regulates unjustified threats under a provision of its Trademark Law, in a manner that differs from both the U.K. model and the common law of product disparagement, as discussed *infra* at notes 71–80 and accompanying text.

[55] Patents Act 1977, c. 37, § 70(1) (U.K.). There are exemptions for threats directed against "making a product for disposal or importing a product for disposal" and against use of a patented process. *See id.* § 70A(2), (3), (4). The statute also exempts a threat "which is not an express threat . . . if it is contained in a permitted communication," *id.* § 70A(5), and defines a "permitted communication" as a "communication . . . made for a permitted purpose," where "all of the information that relates to the threat is information that . . . is necessary for that purpose . . . and . . . the person making the communication reasonably believes is true." *Id.* § 70B(1). A "permitted purpose" includes "(a) giving notice that a patent exists; (b) discovering whether, or by whom, a patent has been infringed by an act mentioned in section 70A(2)(a) or (b); and (c) giving notice that a person has a right in or under a patent, where another person's awareness of the right is relevant to any proceedings that may be brought in respect of the patent." *Id.* § 70B(2). In addition, a court may "treat any other purpose as a 'permitted purpose' if it considers that it is in the interests of justice to do so," *id.* § 70B(3), but a permitted purpose does not include "(a) requesting a person to cease doing, for commercial purposes, anything in relation to a product or process, (b) requesting a person to deliver up or destroy a product, or (c) requesting a person to give an undertaking relating to a product or process." *Id.* § 70B(4). Finally, "[i]f any of the following information is included in a communication made for a permitted purpose, it is information that is 'necessary for that purpose' . . . (a) a statement that a patent exists and is in force or that an application for a patent has been made; (b) details of the patent, or of a right in or under the patent, which—(i) are accurate in all material respects, and (ii) are not misleading in any material respect; and (c)information enabling the identification of the products or processes in respect of which it is alleged that acts infringing the patent have been carried out." *Id.* § 70B(5). In addition to all of the above, it is a defense if the party threatening the secondary infringer has been unable, after taking reasonable steps, to identify the primary infringer. *See id.* § 70C(4).

[56] *Id.* § 70A(1).

[57] Marshall, *supra* note 54, at 151 (citing Brain v. Ingledew Brown Bennison & Garrett (No. 3) [1997] F.S.R. 511 (Ch) (Eng.)). Despite its relatively narrow applicability, *Walker Process* is similarly generous in terms of conferring standing upon parties in addition to the immediate recipient of the threat. *See* Ritz Camera & Image, LLC v. SanDisk Corp., 700 F.3d 503 (Fed. Cir. 2012) (reversing dismissal of *Walker Process* claim asserted by a customer of the patent owner, which patent owner allegedly enforced its patent against other competing suppliers of flash memory products); Hydril Co. LP v. Grant Prideco LP, 474 F.3d 1344 (Fed. Cir. 2007) (reversing the dismissal of a *Walker Process* claim asserted by a competitor of the patent owner, which patent owner had allegedly threatened to sue the competitor's customers for patent infringement).

The statute may strike non-U.K. observers as unusual in several respects. First, the claim is available *only* for threats made against alleged secondary infringers,[58] on the theory that patent owners otherwise may use the threat of litigation "to isolate and intimidate the secondary and tertiary levels of the supply chain."[59] Second, a claim based on an otherwise actionable threat fails if the person making the threat "show[s] that the act in respect of which proceedings were threatened constitutes (or if done would constitute) an infringement of the patent."[60] Third, and following from the preceding point, the statute creates a form of strict liability, in that it renders unlawful a threat of litigation if *in fact* the patent at issue is invalid or not infringed, even if the accusation of infringement (though wrong) was reasonable.[61] Violations of the statute can result in a declaration, an injunction, and damages,[62] although the 2017 version of the statute protects attorneys and other professional advisers from personal liability if they are "acting on the instructions of another person" whom they identify when making the communication.[63]

Although the U.S. lacks an unlawful threats doctrine as such, express or implicit threats can sometimes give rise to liability under the anti-troll laws enacted by a majority of U.S. states over the past decade. Starting with Vermont in 2013, over thirty states have enacted such laws to date; most are incorporated into the state's existing Deceptive Trade Practices Act, Unfair Trade Practices

[58] *See* Patents Act 1977, c. 37, § 70A(2), (3), (4) (U.K.).

[59] James Fox et al., *UK Threats: Worldwide Consequences?*, 40 EUROPEAN INTELL. PROP. REV. 74, 75 (2018); *see also* Marshall, *supra* note 54, at 150 (stating that the original motivation for the statute was that "secondary infringers would often cease trading with the primary infringer, or cease selling the primary infringer's goods, rather than become embroiled in legal proceedings," such that "the primary infringer's business was strangled").

[60] Patents Act 1977, c. 37 § 70C(3) (U.K.).

[61] *See* Marshall, *supra* note 54, at 153. From 2004 to 2017, a patentee was exempt from liability if he could prove that, "at the time of the threat, 'he did not know, and had no reason to suspect, that the patent was invalid,'" but this provision was repealed. *See* U.K. LAW COMMISSION, PATENTS, TRADE MARKS, AND DESIGNS: UNJUSTIFIED THREATS, LAW COM NO 360, ¶¶ 6.135–6.141 (Oct. 12, 2015) (recommending the repeal, subsequently carried out, of this provision); ZHENG, *supra* note 24, at 31 (noting that "the good faith defence has been repealed," so that "threat-makers cannot now be immune from remedy for the person aggrieved by showing that they did not know and had no reason to suspect that the patent was invalid at the point of making the threat"). The rule appears to be the same in Australia. *See* Evgeny Guglyuvatyy, Natalai Stoianoff & Shanti Das, *Patents and Unjustified Threats—Legal Solutions in Australia*, 27 J. WORLD INTELL. PROP. L. 112, 115 (2023) (stating that "the provisions do not differentiate between threats made in good faith or bad faith"). The latter authors also discuss the possibility of liability for unjustified threats under other provisions of Australian law, including consumer protection law.

[62] Patents Act 1977, c. 37, § 70C(1) (U.K.). By way of comparison, the Australian statute expressly permits courts to award additional damages if they consider it "appropriate to do so having regard to: (a) the flagrancy of the threats; and (b) the need to deter similar threats; and (c) the conduct of the person who made the threats, being conduct that occurred after the person made the threats; and (d) any benefit shown to have accrued to the person who made the threats because of the threats; and (e) all other relevant matters." Patents Act 1990 (Cth) § 128(1A) (Austl.).

[63] *Id.* § 70D(3).

Act, Consumer Protection Act, or the like.[64] The Vermont statute, after which many of the others are patterned, states that "A person shall not make a bad faith assertion of patent infringement,"[65] and that a court may consider as evidence of bad faith factors such as (1) the transmission of a demand letter that (a) does not contain the patent number, the name and address of the patent owner, and specific factual allegations concerning the allegedly infringing activity; or (b) demands payment within an unreasonably short time; (2) offering to license the patent on unreasonable terms; and (3) sending a demand letter, where the sender knows or should know that the infringement claim is meritless.[66] The statute also states that a court may consider, as evidence that a person has not made a bad faith assertion, factors such as the sender's efforts to establish that the target has infringed, or has been successful in litigating the patent.[67] Although the statute does not define the term "assertion," it defines the term "demand letter" as "a letter, e-mail, or other communication asserting or claiming that the target has engaged in patent infringement,"[68] and states further that a "target" includes not only the recipient of such a letter, but also any person "against whom an assertion or allegation of patent infringement has been made; . . . who has been threatened with litigation or against whom

[64] Alternatively, on at least one occasion the Federal Trade Commission threatened to sue a patent assertion entity (PAE) for violating § 5 of the Federal Trade Commission Act by engaging in unfair or deceptive trade practices. The target was MPHJ Technology Investments, a PAE "whose 101 subsidiaries sent demands to thousands of small businesses threatening suit for the infringement of certain 'scan to email' patents, in some instances proposing a settlement amounting to $1,000 or $1,200 per employee." THOMAS F. COTTER, PATENT WARS: HOW PATENTS IMPACT OUR DAILY LIVES 214 (2018). In response MPHJ, which also had been facing investigations in New York and Minnesota for violating those states' unfair competition and consumer protection laws, "agreed to a consent order forbidding it from making misleading representations about the patent licenses it had granted to others, and from falsely representing its intent to file suit for infringement." *Id.* (citing Complaint, MPHJ Tech. Invs., LLC, 142 F.T.C. 3003 (Mar. 17, 2015) (No. C-4513), https://www.ftc.gov/system/files/documents/cases/150317mphjtechcmpt.pdf; Decision and Order, MPHJ Tech. Invs., LLC, 142 F.T.C. 3003 (Mar. 17, 2015) (No. C-4513), https://www.ftc.gov/system/files/documents/cases/150317mphjtechdo.pdf).

[65] *See, e.g.*, VT. STAT. ANN. tit. 9, § 4197(a) (2023). For discussion of similarities and differences among the state anti-troll laws, *see* Rebecca Schoff Curtin, *Slapping Patent Trolls: What Anti-Trolling Legislation Can Learn from the Anti-SLAPP Movement*, 18 STAN. TECH. L. REV. 39, 56–58 (2014); Gugliuzza, *supra* note 24, at 1591–99; Paul R. Gugliuzza, *Regulating Patent Assertions*, *in* PATENT ASSERTION ENTITIES AND COMPETITION POLICY 85, 88–90 (D. Daniel Sokol ed. 2017); Swathi Srinivasan et al., *Patent Trolling in the United States*, HARV. INST. OF POLS. 20–128 (Jan. 2019), https://iop.harvard.edu/sites/default/files/2023-02/IOP%20Tech%20Policy%20Full.pdf. Among the salient differences are that (1) some state laws target only non-practicing entities; (2) at least one requires the demand letter to disclose substantial additional information, *e.g.*, other litigation the patent owner has commenced; (3) some do not provide a private right of action, limiting enforcement to, *e.g.*, the state attorney-general, or limit recovery of punitive damages; and, somewhat analogous to the U.K.'s unlawful threats statute, some limit actions to bad faith assertions against end users only, and/or expressly permit actions to be based on threats that the patentee does not intend to carry out. *See* Curtin, *supra*, at 56–58; Gugliuzza, *supra* note 24, at 1593–96.

[66] *See* VT. STAT. ANN. tit. 9, § 4197(b) (2023).

[67] *See id.* § 4197(c).

[68] *Id.* § 4196(1).

a lawsuit has been filed alleging patent infringement; or . . . whose customers have received a demand letter asserting that the person's product, service, or technology has infringed a patent."[69] Anti-troll laws typically permit claims to be brought by the State Attorney General or by the recipient, and permit the recipient to recover enhanced damages and attorneys' fees.[70]

The law of unfair competition and business torts also sometimes plays a role in regulating false assertions (in the sense of communications) that the defendant or a third party is infringing a valid patent, although an express or implicit threat to sue (while often present) is typically not a necessary element. In the U.S., for example, a common-law commercial disparagement claim requires proof that the defendant intentionally made a false and disparaging statement, of and concerning the plaintiff's goods, services, or property, that caused the plaintiff to suffer "special harm" (for example, lost profits on specific diverted sales).[71] A claim therefore may arise from a false representation that a competitor's products infringe valid IP rights owned by the speaker.[72] Similar claims also sometimes may arise under the U.S. law of tortious interference with prospective business relations, if for example the false communication causes the plaintiff's customers to forgo doing business with the plaintiff.[73] The Federal Circuit has held, however, that these sorts of unfair competition and business tort claims are subject to the standards set out in the Supreme Court's *PREI* decision, meaning that they may proceed only if the communication falsely asserting infringement is both objectively baseless and subjectively motivated by the intent

[69] *Id.* § 4196(2).

[70] *See, e.g.*, *id.* § 4199 (authorizing remedies including "(1) equitable relief; (2) damages; (3) costs and fees, including reasonable attorney's fees; and (4) exemplary damages in an amount equal to $50,000.00 or three times the total of damages, costs, and fees, whichever is greater").

[71] *See, e.g.*, Paidar v. Hughes, 615 N.W.2d 276, 279–80 (Minn. 2000); Hurlbut v. Gulf Atl. Life Ins. Co., 749 S.W.2d 762, 766 (Tex. 1987). The tort goes by other names, including product disparagement, and in certain specific settings trade libel and "slander on title." A somewhat more expansive version, referred to as "injurious falsehood," dispenses with the requirement that the statement was "of and concerning the plaintiff's goods, services, or property." *See* Restatement (Second) of Torts § 623A (Am. L. Inst. 1977). Proof of an additional element, "actual malice," is required in some jurisdictions, while in others a rebuttable presumption of actual malice arises once the other elements are proven. For discussion, see Barton Beebe et al., Trademarks, Unfair Competition, and Business Torts 547–48 (2d ed. 2016). Disparaging statements made in the course of commercial advertising and promotion also sometimes can give rise to liability as a type of false advertising actionable under the Lanham Act. *See* Lexmark Int'l, Inc. v. Static Control Components, Inc., 572 U.S. 118 (2014).

[72] For citations to U.S. cases, see Beebe et al., *supra* note 71, at 568–73; Gugliuzza, *supra* note 24, at 1589–90, 1617–28. As noted in chapter 1, moreover, under U.S. law claims for false advertising or for false patent marking may arise in cases in which the patent owner materially misrepresents that *its own products* are patented, regardless of whether the representation involves an express threat of enforcement. *See supra* ch. 1 notes 9–10 and accompanying text.

[73] *See, e.g.*, SSI Techs., LLC v. Dongguan Zhengyang Elec. Mech. Ltd., 59 F.4th 1328 (Fed. Cir. 2023).

to injure the plaintiff.[74] These additional requirements depart from the common law—under which disparagement and tortious interference claims could be premised on false allegations of infringement, unless the party asserting infringement proved that it made the statement in subjective good faith[75]—and have, not surprisingly, made it much more difficult for them to succeed.[76] Following the Federal Circuit's example, some state courts considering claims under the anti-troll statutes have held that parties asserting claims under these laws also must satisfy the objective baselessness/subjective motivation standard that applies to sham litigation antitrust claims.[77] Critics such as Paul Gugliuzza nevertheless argue that the extension of the objective/subject standard to unfair competition and business torts claims is unwarranted, because the *Noerr-Pennington* doctrine on which *PREI* is based is grounded in antitrust law, not the First Amendment.[78] Even if this is a correct interpretation of the original decisions, however, as noted above some more recent Supreme Court cases appear to characterize *Noerr-Pennington* immunity as based on the First Amendment.[79] Be that as it may, as Gugliuzza points out, there would seem to be little justification for extending petitioning immunity to threatened litigation that the patent owner never intends to carry out, or to false statements relating to matters "peripheral" to infringement and validity (such as deceptive statements concerning what other parties have paid for a license).[80]

Outside the United States, unfair competition or other laws sometimes constrain IP owners from threatening purported infringers without adequate justification, though the specifics can vary. In the U.K., the elements of a claim for trade libel parallel the elements of a claim for commercial disparagement under U.S. law, but because such claims are generally harder to prove than are statutory claims for unjustified threats, the trade libel option is less commonly used.[81] Similarly in Canada, the common law claim is, as a practical matter,

[74] *See, e.g.*, Lite-Netics, LLC v. Nu Tsai Cap. LLC, 60 F.4th 1335, 1343–44 (Fed. Cir. 2023) (citing cases).

[75] *See* Gugliuzza, *supra* note 24, at 1617–20 (collecting cases).

[76] *See id.* at 1627; *see also* Curtin, *supra* note 65, at 62 (2014) (stating that the application of the *Noerr-Pennington* standard to the analogous "state anti-trolling laws will preempt most claims under them").

[77] *See* Paul R. Gugliuzza, *State Anti-Troll Statutes at the Federal Circuit. Or Not*, 51 AIPLA Q.J. 395, 403 n.49 (2023) (listing cases).

[78] Gugliuzza, *supra* note 24, at 1639.

[79] *See supra* note 24 and accompanying text.

[80] *See* Gugliuzza, *supra* note 24, at 1639–42.

[81] *See* Hans-Peter Brack, *Patent Infringement Warnings in a Common Law Versus a Civil Law Jurisdiction—An Actionable Threat?*, 37 Int'l Rev. Intell. Prop. & Competition L. 1, 5 (2006) (stating that "[t]here seems to be little to be gained" from pursuing the trade libel option, "unless it is not possible to bring an action" for unlawful threats, "because the burden of proof on a plaintiff is much higher," comprising evidence "that (1) the statement is false, (2) it was published with malice . . .,

superseded by § 7(a) of the Trademark Act, which states simply that "No person shall . . . make a false or misleading statement tending to discredit the business, goods or services of a competitor."[82] Canadian courts have interpreted this section as creating a strict-liability claim based on the communication of a threat to sue a firm's customers for the infringement of an invalid or noninfringed patent, where such threat causes the plaintiff to suffer losses.[83] Such claims therefore resemble claims under U.K. law for unlawful threats, albeit without the specific limitations on those claims under U.K. law as discussed above.[84]

The relevant standards also vary among the civil law countries. Under German law, for example, only explicit threats are actionable,[85] and only if the claimant proves the requisite degree of fault in making the false accusation of infringement—which, however, can vary depending on the identity of the accused (e.g., primary or secondary infringer) and the type of right at issue.[86]

and (3) that damage occurred to the plaintiff as a direct result of the publication"). Brack also notes the possibility, under some circumstances, of a claim for contempt of court (grounded in making "false statements that would have the effect of interfering with pending or imminent court proceedings, for example, by anticipating a verdict"), or for abuse of process (for example, where the claim is "intended to harass [a] competitor and its distributors" rather than being motivated by "genuine[] concern[] with asserting [one's] patent rights"). *Id.* at 6–7.

[82] Trademarks Act, R.S.C., 1985, c. T-13, § 7(a).

[83] For an excellent summary of the Canadian case law, see Norman V. Siebrasse, *Trademarks Act 7(a) Unjustified Threats Claim Fails on Second Branch*, Sufficient Description, Mar. 7, 2024, http://www.sufficientdescription.com/2024/03/trademarks-act-7a-unjustified-threats.html. Siebrasse argues that this strict liability standard—which departs from the common law's requirement of proof of actual malice—is sound because a threat directed at a customer that causes the customer to cease doing business with a supplier has the same effect as a preliminary injunction, and a patentee who obtains a preliminary injunction against the use of a patent later found to be invalid or not infringed should be (and, under Canadian law, is) strictly liable for the losses caused by the injunction's interim enforcement. He also argues, however, that liability should not hinge on whether the patentee communicates a threat or merely an "informative letter," where the latter has the same effect as an express threat. The discussion suggests a recurring problem in this area of law, to which I return at the end of the chapter, namely that the distinction between actionable threats and nonactionable non-threats is not always clear. Cf. Zheng, *supra* note 24, at 34–35 & n.7 (noting that, under German law, "authorisation enquiries (*Berechtigungsanfragen*) bear a formal resemblance to threats of infringement of exclusive rights," but "the crucial differences lie mainly in the form and intensity of the aimed influence"; that "authorisation enquiries are used to initiate an opportunity for both parties to exchange their views on legal situations, with the purpose of better protecting the exclusive rights," and are therefore "considered lawful in practice"; but that critics "point out that authorisation enquiries implicitly contain the same message sent in threats").

[84] *See supra* text accompanying note 63 (noting, *inter alia*, that since 2017 advisers such as attorneys are expressly exempt from liability).

[85] *See* Brack, *supra* note 81, at 16 (stating that "an actionable threat must be explicit in Germany," and that "a warning must (1) contain a clear demand for a specific person to stop a specific activity (*Unterlassungsverlangen*) and (2) warn the infringer that the right holder will file an action if the warning goes unheeded (*Androhung gerichtlicher Schritte*)"—though also that a warning will be considered unlawful "if a formal justification is missing, for example, if the warning is misleading or does not give complete and clear information") (citations omitted).

[86] *See id.* at 17:

> In general, a higher level of due care is required in warning parties further removed from the primary act of infringement, for example, resellers or customers. The breadth of the

Christopher Heath notes that French courts have indicated that "warning letters against primary infringers are not actionable,"[87] but that they "view the court action as the appropriate form and forum for making allegations of infringement against secondary infringers, while warning letters are considered improper regardless if the allegation of infringement is well-founded or not, although such action may be justified if done in an inoffensive and discrete manner."[88] As for Japan, Heath states that as of 2008 there were "no known cases where the sending of a warning letter to the manufacturer or importer was regarded as unlawful"[89]—but that Japanese courts considered the transmission of such letters to customers as per se illegal in cases in which there was, in fact, no infringement, until a 2002 Tokyo High Court decision, subsequently followed by other courts, that applied a more forgiving multifactor test.[90] Similarly in China, courts consider a variety of factors to determine whether

> warning is also important. Making a pronounced public warning that has significant effects requires significant due care. Higher levels of due care are also required when the warning is based on an unexamined right. For example, the courts have often indicated that great care is required when warning secondary infringers or customers about unexamined rights like utility models....

Liability may arise under article 823(1) of the Civil Code (*BGB*), as an aspect of the right to carry on an established and active business, or in some cases under unfair competition law. *See* ZHENG, *supra* note 24, ch. 3 (providing an overview of relevant case law and commentary); *see also* AMANDINE LÉONARD, ABUSE OF RIGHTS IN EUROPEAN PATENT LAW: RECONSIDERING THE PRINCIPLE OF THE PROHIBITION OF ABUSE OF RIGHTS AS AN INTERNAL CORRECTION MECHANISM AGAINST OVER-ENFORCEMENT PRACTICES BY RIGHT HOLDERS 96–98 (Apr. 30, 2019) (unpublished Ph.D. thesis submitted to KU Leuven, on file with author); Brack, *supra* note 81, at 18–20; Christopher Heath, *Wrongful Patent Enforcement: Threats and Post-Infringement Invalidity in Comparative Perspective*, 39 INT'L REV. INTELL. PROP. & COMPETITION L. 307, 312 (2008) (noting, in addition, the "financial incentive of lawyers to send out warning letters," because "the costs thereof can be recovered if the addressee undertakes to stop the allegedly infringing behaviour"); Karl et al., *supra* note 36, at 951–52.

[87] Heath, *supra* note 86, at 312 (citing Cour de cassation, Judgment of May 13, 1964, 1963 Annales 266 (Fr.)).

[88] *Id.* (citing Cour de cassation, Judgment of Mar. 2, 1965, 1996 Annales 1 (Fr.) (with comment by Mathély); Cour de cassation, Judgment of June 12, 2007 (Fr.), 39 INT'L REV. INTELL. PROP. & COMPETITION L. 354 (2008)—*False Ceiling* (Fr.); Tribunal de la Seine, Judgment of March 18, 1932, 1933 Annales 14 (Fr.)). Heath states, further, that "[n]ot only warning letters, but also information about a pending lawsuit against the manufacturer may give rise to an action for denigration." *Id.* (citing Cour de cassation, Judgment of May 12, 2004, Case 02-16623 (Fr.)). For further discussion, *see* Thomas Bouvet, AIPPI Question Q292-SR-G-2024: Unjustified allegations of infringement of IP rights (France) (July 10, 2024); Thomas F. Cotter, *Unfair Competition by Publicizing a Pending Infringement Action*, COMPARATIVE PATENT REMEDIES BLOG, May 17, 2025, https://comparativepatentremedies.blogspot.com/2025/05/unfair-competition-by-publicizing.html.

[89] *Id.* at 312–13.

[90] *Id.* at 313 (citing Judgment of Aug. 29, 2022, 2001 (ne) 5555 (Tokyo High Ct.) (Japan), 37 INT'L REV. INTELL. PROP. & COMPETITION L. 758 (2006)—*Warning Letter/Metallic Powder*). The factors include:

> the synthesis of the negotiation process with the competitor up to the warning, the timing and the distribution of the warning letter, the number and range of customers to whom the letter was distributed, the size and type of business concerned, the relationship and style of dealing with the competitor, the allegedly infringing products, the manner in which a patent infringement can be dealt with at the level of customers who are supplied with the allegedly

the transmission of warning letters constitutes a violation of unfair competition law, taking into account for example whether the recipient is a primary or secondary accused infringer, whether the patent owner has exercised due diligence to substantiate its claim of infringement, and whether the patentee has publicized the accusation of infringement.[91] On the other hand, Krista Rantasaari states that Dutch law makes "no formal distinction between primary and secondary infringers," but rather considers that a threat may be "unlawful where it is known, or ought reasonably to be known, that at the time of issuing the threat its patent was not valid and/or not infringed"—or, as in France, where the threat was "unnecessarily offensive or unnecessarily public."[92]

Enforcement or Threatened Enforcement as a Necessary Element

Having sketched out how various legal regimes address fraudulent procurement, sham litigation, and unjustified threats, I now turn to the questions with which this chapter opened: whether the law should dispense with proof of

> infringing goods, the reaction to the distribution of the warning letter, the conduct of the patentee and the customers after the distribution, and other circumstances.

Warning Letter/Metallic Powder, 37 IIC at 760. *Cf.* Christopher Heath, *Case No. 56, Threats—Warning Letter alleging Patent Infringement—Standard of Liability*, *in* Japanese Patent Law: Cases and Comments 601, 607 (Christopher Heath & Atsuhiro Furuta eds. 2019) (stating that "a different standard of liability is applied for (unexamined) utility models that can only be enforced based on a prior assessment report," under which negligence is presumed if the report is negative).

[91] The two leading cases to date are *Shenzhen Libang Precision Instr. Co. v. Shenzhen Mairui Biomed. Elecs. Co.*, Case No. (2015) Min Shen I No. 191 (Supreme People's Ct. 2015) (China), and *Shijiazhuang Shuanghuan Automobile Co. v. Honda Motor Co.*, Case No. (2014) Min San Zhong Zi No. 7 (Supreme People's Ct. 2015) (China), https://enipc.court.gov.cn/zh-cn/news/view-35.html. According to commentators, the court in *Libang* held that the sending of warning letters to the primary infringer's dealers and to the public did not constitute actionable commercial slander, where the patent owner exercised due care. In *Shuanghuan*, on the other hand, the court held that although Honda was not liable for warning letters sent to the alleged primary infringer, it had engaged in unfair competition by, *inter alia*, sending warning letters, lacking sufficient detail, to claimant Shuanghuan's distributors, warning them of the infringement of a patent that was later found to be noninfringed and causing Shuanghuan to suffer economic loss (though not an injury to its reputation). For discussion of these and other cases on commercial disparagement and defamation as they relate to false accusations of IP rights, *see* Zheng, *supra* note 24, ch. 4; Yu Du, *Unjustified Threats of Legal Proceedings in IP Actions in China*, HG.org, https://www.hg.org/legal-articles/unjustified-threats-of-legal-proceedings-in-ip-actions-in-china-48693 (last visited Jan. 10, 2024); Liang Kun, *Abuse of Patent Infringement Notices and Its Regulation*, China Pats. & Trademarks No. 2, 2023, at 47, 52–53.

[92] Krista Rantasaari, *Abuse of Patent Enforcement in Europe: How Can Start-ups and Growth Companies Fight Back?*, 11 J. Intell. Prop., Info. Tech. & E-Com. L. 358, 375 (2020) (citations omitted); *see also* Léonard, *supra* note 86, at 96–100 (discussing Belgian, French, and Dutch cases); Zheng, *supra* note 24, at 90, 104–05 (noting that, whereas China, Germany, and the U.K. differentiate among threats aimed at primary and at secondary infringers, the U.S. does not, except for a few of the state anti-troll laws).

actual or threatened enforcement where today it requires it, or alternatively whether it should require such proof where today it does not; and second, if the law does or should require proof of threatened enforcement, what sort of evidence should suffice to demonstrate the threat's existence?

The leading academic voice in favor of disposing with (or diluting) actual or threatened enforcement as a necessary element for antitrust liability is Christopher Leslie, in his two provocative articles, "The Anticompetitive Effects of Unenforced Invalid Patents"[93] and "Patents of Damocles."[94] The first of the two articles argues broadly that the mere possession of a patent the owner knows to be invalid and does not disavow can sometimes enable the owner to acquire or maintain monopoly power by frightening away would-be competitors, and that when this is so, such possession should be understood as an act of unlawful monopolization under § 2 of the Sherman Act.[95] Leslie further argues that U.S. antitrust law is well-suited to address the problems resulting from the knowing possession of invalid patents, because (1) such conduct distorts markets in favor of monopolists; and (2) the availability of treble damages helps to overcome the legal and practical obstacles that otherwise can discourage validity challenges under other bodies of law, and provides an effective deterrent.[96] The second article argues that even if the enforcement requirement is retained, courts should recognize a broader range of conduct as species of enforcement, including "publicly flaunting one's patent; stating a general intent to sue infringers; accusing competitors of infringement; threatening competitors' business partners; and licensing activities,"[97] as well as refusing to license one's invalid patent on royalty-free terms.[98] Leslie contends

[93] 91 Minn. L. Rev. 101 (2006).

[94] *See supra* note 42.

[95] *See* Leslie, *supra* note 93, at 155–70. Notice that, under this proposal, the patentee's knowledge that the patent is invalid would not necessarily depend upon the patent having been fraudulently procured, as it is for *Walker Process* claims as such. *See id.* at 103 n.2 ("This Article focuses on those invalid patents either that are procured by the applicant's fraud on the Patent and Trademark Office, or that the patent owner later discovers should not have been issued because the patent (or one of its claims) failed one of the patentability requirements.").

[96] *See id.* at 171–75. Among the legal obstacles to validity challenges, as of the date of the article's publication, were the United States' lack of an effective system of post-issuance review of issued patents, and the onerous standing requirement for initiating actions for declaratory relief. *See id.* at 139–52. The practical obstacle Leslie identifies is a collective action problem, *i.e.*, the fact that the party seeking to invalidate a patent bestows a benefit on itself and others, for which it otherwise may not be compensated. *See id.* at 171–72. As discussed below, however, since publication of the article, the U.S. has adopted a system for post-issuance review that is similar to that available in Europe and elsewhere, and has relaxed the standard for obtaining declaratory relief, *see infra* notes 132–35 and accompanying text—though Leslie argued that even if (as it happened) such reforms were adopted, his proposal "could easily be pursued in conjunction with" such reforms. Leslie, *supra* note 93, at 174.

[97] Leslie, *supra* note 42, at 143.

[98] *See id.* at 160.

that such "soft enforcement" on the part of a monopolist can distort the market by deterring or delaying potential competition, and that when it does so it violates § 2.[99] As in the first article, Leslie also argues that antitrust "can address the problem of fraudulently procured patents more effectively than can the patent system alone."[100]

On the other side of the ledger, Leslie also considers the social costs of a more expansive liability regime, applying the familiar decision-theoretic framework that counsels policymakers to craft antitrust rules and standards so as to minimize the aggregate costs of false positives, false negatives, and administrative/adjudicative costs.[101] A false positive occurs when the applicable rule or standard results in the actual or expected imposition of liability, despite the fact that permitting the conduct at issue would neither distort the market nor impair consumer welfare; put another way, although policy would counsel in favor of exonerating the conduct at issue, the governing rule or standard results either in liability or in a settlement, favorable to the claimant, premised on a substantial risk of liability. A false negative involves precisely the opposite, by exonerating conduct that threatens to distort the market and to reduce consumer welfare. Finally, adjudicative and administrative costs include not only the litigation and compliance costs borne by the parties, but also the costs (time, money, resources) incurred by policy- and decisionmakers. (In this regard, bright-line rules, such as per se legality or illegality, tend to reduce adjudicative costs, but if they result in fewer accurate outcomes—outcomes aligned with the underlying purpose of antitrust law—they may generate correspondingly more false positives or negatives.) Each one of these costs, in turn, is a function of both its frequency and its magnitude, though neither of these is often readily quantifiable.

Leslie recognizes that his proposals risk generating some false positives,[102] but he argues that these risks are minimal, for several reasons. First, he notes

[99] *See id.* at 143–61, 172.

[100] *Id.* at 171. *See also* Mordechay Sorek, Miriam Marcowitz-Bitton & Yotam Kaplan, *Patent Fraud by Design*, 38 CARDOZO ARTS & ENTER. L.J. 359, 378 (2020) (arguing that, in view of the difficulties of detection and the inadequacy of existing remedies, current law encourages applicants to defraud the patent office).

[101] *See, e.g.*, Alden F. Abbott & D. Bruce Hoffman, Ohio v. American Express *and the Continued Evolution of Economic Reasoning in Supreme Court Jurisprudence*, 33 ANTITRUST 37, 37 (2018) ("[T]he [U.S. Supreme] Court has adopted principled screening rules designed to minimize the sum of antitrust error costs (false positives plus false negatives) and administrative costs in antitrust enforcement.").

[102] *See* Leslie, *supra* note 42, at 174 (stating that "if patent enforcement is defined too broadly for the purposes of antitrust claims, inventors could be more reluctant to seek patents or to exercise their legitimate rights"; "[f]earing antitrust litigation and potential liability, patentees may be less willing or eager to engage in licensing activity or to flaunt the range and importance of their patents," which "could reduce the expected value of patents and make investments in innovation less attractive").

that while "false positives could result if a patentee is found liable for violating Section Two when the fact-finder incorrectly concludes that the monopolist's patent is invalid," "[t]his result seems unlikely given the difficulty of proving that a patent is invalid."[103] Second, "a false positive would result if the fact-finder . . . incorrectly concludes that the monopolist knew of the patent's invalidity"[104] or, in connection with the second proposal, incorrectly finds "that the monopolist committed fraud against the PTO to obtain the patent."[105] Leslie believes that these risks are relatively low, given that U.S. law requires both invalidity and fraud to be proven by clear and convincing evidence.[106] Third, Leslie notes that, in addition to proving invalidity or fraud, the claimant must prove both the existence of monopoly power[107] and a sufficient causal connection between that power and ownership of the invalid or fraudulently-procured patent,[108] and argues that the burden of proving these two elements also tends to "screen" or "filter" out false positives.[109] Fourth, Leslie concedes that an expansion of antitrust liability could generate nuisance litigation, which in turn can sometimes compel innocent defendants to settle, but argues that such risks exist under current law as well; that courts can police this risk through the imposition of litigation sanctions, such as those noted above;[110] and that evidentiary requirements of the sort already in place for *Walker Process* claims (which require compliance with a heightened pleading requirement[111] and, as above, proof of fraud by clear and convincing evidence[112]) further reduce the incidence of nuisance suits.

Overall, Leslie makes a powerful case for expanding the scope of U.S. antitrust liability; and while the arguments raised in the first article, under which a monopolist's mere knowledge that it possesses an invalid patent could amount

[103] Leslie, *supra* note 93, at 178; *see also* Leslie, *supra* note 42, at 175 (noting that the antitrust claimant "must establish by clear and convincing evidence that the monopolist's patent is invalid, an extremely demanding standard").

[104] Leslie, *supra* note 93, at 178 (noting, in addition, that in regard to knowing possession of invalid patents, firms "may disavow patents known to be invalid, thereby avoiding false positives," and that "the fact that non-monopolists, too, might have an incentive to disavow their invalid patents is not necessarily a bad outcome").

[105] Leslie, *supra* note 42, at 175.

[106] *See id.* (referring to proving fraud on the patent office, in particular, as "notoriously difficult").

[107] *See* Leslie, *supra* note 93, at 178; Leslie, *supra* note 42, at 174–75.

[108] *See* Leslie, *supra* note 42, at 175–76.

[109] *See id.* at 174.

[110] *See* Leslie, *supra* note 93, at 179–83; *see also supra* note 41 and accompanying text.

[111] *See* Baxalta Inc. v. Bayer Healthcare LLC, No. 17-1316-RGA, 2020 WL 5445375, at *3 (D. Del. July 13, 2020) (stating that "[t]he heightened pleading requirements of [Federal Rule of Civil Procedure] 9(b)," under which a claimant must "state with particularity the circumstances constituting fraud or mistake" apply to "causes of action for inequitable conduct, unclean hands, and *Walker Process* claims") (citations omitted).

[112] *See supra* notes 12, 106 and accompanying text.

to an antitrust violation, would expand liability farther than any nation (to my knowledge) has attempted thus far, the proposal advanced in the second article would move U.S. law in the direction of E.U. law as expressed in *AstraZeneca*.[113] It also would align with unfair competition torts such as product disparagement, under which liability depends upon, in the present context, a false representation that another's goods are infringing, whether or not accompanied by an express or implicit threat to sue.[114] Of course, there may be good reasons for also recognizing claims specifically targeting false accusations of infringement, such as the U.K.'s law of unjustified threats, if for example the doctrinal specifics of torts such as trade libel render them insufficient to remedy some of the harms resulting from false accusations.[115] But just as it may be desirable, nonetheless, to have available as a backstop a broadly applicable unfair competition tort that includes, but is not limited to, false accusations of infringement, perhaps it is desirable to have a broadly applicable antitrust claim directed against monopolization by means of fraudulently procured patents, regardless of whether the patent owner enforces or threatens to enforce them; or such, at least, is Leslie's view.

All that said, I remain skeptical that U.S. courts should remove actual or threatened enforcement as a condition to *Walker Process* liability—or define "threatened enforcement" so broadly as to include merely publicizing a patent, stating a general intent to sue infringers, etc.[116]—for the following reasons.

[113] Recall that in *AstraZeneca*, the defendant submitted misleading information to obtain SPCs that excluded generic competition in Denmark and Germany. *See supra* note 13. Even if U.S. and E.U. law aligned in this respect, however, there would remain other differences. "Dominance" under E.U. competition law, for example, does not require as substantial a market share as "monopolization" does under U.S. law. *See* Daniel J. Gifford & Robert T. Kudrle, The Atlantic Divide in Antitrust: An Examination of US and EU Competition Policy 10 (2015) ("'[D]ominant' firms ... in German national law may be ones with a market share as low at [sic] 30 percent, although the usual threshold at the EU level is generally 40 to 50 percent ...."). In addition, and as noted above, in *AstraZeneca* the CJEU expressly declined to require proof of fraudulent intent. *See supra* notes 13–20 and accompanying text.

[114] As discussed in chapter 2, materially false representations can harm both consumers and honest competitors by impairing the integrity of the market. In the present context, a false accusation of infringement may divert business from the accused if, for example, its customers come to believe that the accused is unethical—or not much of an innovator, if it is merely copying someone else's innovation. Or it may divert trade because the recipient of the communication perceives it, at least implicitly, to threaten enforcement either against the recipient or someone with whom it does business.

[115] *See supra* note 81 and accompanying text (noting the difficulty in proving trade libel under U.K. law).

[116] Note, however, that if the *Unitherm* court's equation of the standards for declaratory judgment jurisdiction and for the "minimum level of 'enforcement' necessary to expose the patentee to a *Walker Process* claim," *see supra* text accompanying note 45, remains good law, it would appear that after *MedImmune, Inc. v. Genentech, Inc.*, 549 U.S. 118 (2007), licensees now *can* assert *Walker Process* claims. *See* Hovenkamp et al., *supra* note 10, § 11.02[E] (stating that "after *MedImmune* it is possible that a licensee in good standing might bring a *Walker Process* claim alleging that being coerced into signing the license was sufficient market effect from the enforcement of the patent"); *see also supra* note 53 and accompanying text (suggesting that, in view of *MedImmune*, some "conduct falling short of an express threat to litigate may now" suffice, although the Federal Circuit "has yet to expressly address the issue").

First, I should note that I agree with Leslie[117]—and with the courts[118]—that *Walker Process* liability should extend not only to the actual enforcement of a fraudulently procured patent, but also to its threatened enforcement, because a sufficiently credible threat to litigate can have much the same exclusionary effect as actually litigating. And if express threats count, then it would seem logical for implicit threats, which convey the same message, to do so as well—though much may hinge on how the term "implicit" is defined, a point I return to below. (As noted above, however, the Federal Circuit has yet to address whether implicit threats count for purposes of *Walker Process* claims following the Supreme Court's decision in *MedImmune*;[119] and according to commentators, German law relating to the sending of warning letters restricts liability to express threats.[120]) But if this line of reasoning is correct, then it is fair to ask, as Leslie does, why conduct such as "publicly flaunting one's patent," "stating a general intent to sue infringers," and so on, which may have the "same exclusionary effects [of] deterring (or delaying) market entry . . . and raising rivals' costs of entry" should not count as well.[121] The answer, in my view, is that the extension of liability to non-threats would increase the risk of socially costly false positives, to some degree at least, without a correspondingly large reduction in the cost of false negatives—though I concede that neither nor I anyone else can be certain of the magnitude of either harm, and that reasonable minds may differ in their estimates.

As for the false positives, my principal concern is less that courts would wrongly condemn innocent patent holders, should the matter be litigated all the way through to judgment, than with the risk of claimants asserting weak claims of fraudulent procurement to extract unwarranted settlements from owners. As Frank Easterbrook observed several decades ago, U.S. antitrust law is susceptible to this type of abuse because the costs of antitrust litigation are asymmetric:

> The plaintiff's costs of litigation will be smaller than the defendant's. The plaintiff need only file the complaint and serve demands for discovery. If the plaintiff wins, the defendant will bear these legal costs. The defendant, on the other hand, faces treble damages and injunction, as well as its own (and even its rival's) costs of litigation. The principal burden of discovery falls on the

[117] *See* Leslie, *supra* note 42, at 142–43.
[118] *See supra* notes 49–53 and accompanying text.
[119] *See supra* notes 49–53 and accompanying text.
[120] *See supra* note 85 and accompanying text.
[121] Leslie, *supra* note 42, at 142.

defendant. The defendant is apt to be larger, with more files to search, and to have control of more pertinent documents than the plaintiff.[122]

To be sure, the Chicago School perspective on antitrust, of which Easterbrook's article is an exemplar, is often criticized today for exhibiting an undue fear of false positives, the result of which has been a decades-long underenforcement that has harmed U.S. consumers.[123] Moreover, while treble damages—a feature that appears to be unique to U.S. antitrust law, in comparison with competition law elsewhere—do present a risk of overdeterrence under some circumstances, as I have previously noted myself,[124] under other circumstances they may be necessary to attain the optimal deterrence of anticompetitive conduct that otherwise would remain undetected or profitable (as Leslie argues would be the case here).[125] Nevertheless, one might imagine situations in which a competitor of a dominant patent owner might be tempted to push the envelope, especially if as under Leslie's first proposal no conduct beyond knowing possession of an invalid patent were a necessary prerequisite to proceeding with the § 2 analysis. But even under Leslie's second proposal, which requires some conduct (flaunting, etc.) even if not threatened enforcement as such, a heightened risk of false positives could generate some social costs. A competitor whose request for a royalty-free license is rebuffed, for example, may well be tempted to try litigation as a cudgel to achieve what it wants; and even if such a claim ultimately would be found to lack merit, if litigated to conclusion, society would bear unnecessary administrative and adjudicative costs. There also may be some risk that, if conduct

[122] Frank H. Easterbook, *The Limits of Antitrust*, 63 TEX. L. REV. 1, 34 (1984) (stating further that "[b]ecause of the asymmetries of the costs, antitrust may be a cheaper (and more effective) means of imposing costs on one's rivals than is resort to the political and administrative process"). As for what the costs of litigation actually are, I have not been able to find any reliable estimates of the cost of prosecuting or defending a U.S. antitrust action. As noted in chapter 1, the median cost of litigating even a small-stakes (less than $1 million in dispute) patent infringement action, just through discovery and claim construction, is $300,000. *See supra* ch. 1 n.4. The cost of defending an antitrust claim premised on the knowing possession of an invalid patent would share some (though not all) of these same costs, plus others relating to issues such as market definition, barriers to entry, and causation.

[123] *See, e.g.*, JONATHAN B. BAKER, THE ANTITRUST PARADIGM: RESTORING A COMPETITIVE ECONOMY 73–74 (2019).

[124] *See* Thomas F. Cotter, *Antitrust, Intellectual Property, and Dynamic Efficiency: An Essay in Honor of Herbert Hovenkamp*, CONCURRENCES, no. 3-2020, at 13 (2020).

[125] *See* Leslie, *supra* note 42, at 171–72; *see also* Cotter, *supra* note 124, at 13 n.110 (stating that treble damages are "sometimes defended on the ground that some anticompetitive conduct is difficult to detect, thus necessitating a damages multiplier to achieve optimal deterrence," or because "antitrust offenses often cause dispersed or social harm extending beyond the quantifiable harm suffered by the individual plaintiff"); Sorek, Marcowitz-Bitton & Kaplan, *supra* note 100, at 377–88 (arguing that, even with treble damages and the possibility, recognized by some not all courts, of private actions by consumers, disgorgement would be the better option for ensuring that patent fraud doesn't pay). For discussion of fines under E.U. law, *see supra* ch. 2 note 65.

such as publicizing one's patent could provoke an antitrust suit, owners could be chilled from engaging in the lawful exercise of free speech—or perceive the need to quickly file suit against, rather than inform or negotiate with, a putative infringer. Finally, although competitors remain the most common class of plaintiffs to assert *Walker Process* claims—most often, however, as counterclaims after having been sued for infringement—in 2012 the Federal Circuit held that direct purchasers of products incorporating allegedly fraudulently-procured patents also have standing to assert such claims.[126] Perhaps because liability still depends upon the patent being enforced (or its enforcement being threatened) against someone, such as the manufacturer of the goods that consumers have bought, this development has not resulted in a flood of consumer *Walker Process* claims; but elimination of the enforcement element might risk doing so.[127]

On the other hand, such concerns could be overblown. A monopolization case is only credible, after all, if brought against a firm that, by some conceivable measure, has substantial market power, and such firms are unlikely to be pushovers when confronted with weak antitrust claims. Further, as Leslie notes, in addition to the usual deterrents against unfounded litigation such as Rule 11 sanctions, claimants would have to satisfy the heightened requirements for pleading fraud;[128] and to have a plausible chance even of settling on favorable terms, would have to convince the patent owner that they might be able to prove (by clear and convincing evidence) both fraud and invalidity, along with the usual § 2 requirements that the owner has monopoly power in some well-defined market and that the conduct at issue contributed to its acquisition or maintenance of that power (albeit these last two under only the normal preponderance of the evidence standard). That is a tall order, and even under a more plaintiff-friendly regime it may only rarely be met. But if that is

[126] *See* Ritz Camera & Image, LLC v. SanDisk Corp., 700 F.3d 503 (Fed. Cir. 2012).

[127] *See* Christopher Leslie, *The Role of Consumers in* Walker Process *Litigation*, 13 Sw. J. L. & Trade Am. 281, 300 (2007) (noting, *inter alia*, that "frivolous litigation is more likely to be brought in the form of a consumer class action than by excluded competitors"; that "increasing the pool of potential plaintiffs from 5 competitors to 5 million consumers should increase deterrence," but "also magnifies the risk of nuisance suits"; and that "the cost to targeted patentees could be substantial, especially if firms were repeatedly sued by different consumers each seeking a meager payment to go away"). Leslie suggests that, as "a filter against frivolous lawsuits against patentholders," the law could permit consumers to sue only if a competitor has already "successfully sued on a *Walker Process* claim," though he sees some downsides to this approach; or perhaps state governments could bring actions as *parens patriae*. *See id.* at 302–11. Sorek, Marcowitz-Bitton, and Kaplan propose instead that, because competitors are likely to have better information about potential fraud than consumers, but the incentive to commit fraud remains if consumers' injuries are not compensated, the law should confer upon competitors "*sui generis* standing to assert *Walker Process* claims in class actions" and allow them "to serve as representatives of consumer classes." Sorek, Marcowitz-Bitton & Kaplan, *supra* note 100, at 382–85.

[128] *See supra* notes 12, 106, 112 and accompanying text.

so, then the gains from adopting more plaintiff-friendly rules are also likely to be pretty limited.

As for false negatives, it is important to note that, since the publication of Leslie's two articles the United States has enacted legislation enabling anyone to petition for post-grant review of issued patents within nine months of grant, on any grounds,[129] and thereafter to petition for *inter partes* review (IPR) of issued patents for lack of novelty or nonobviousness, in light of other issued patents and printed publications.[130] Firms have not been shy to take advantage of these procedures, especially IPRs, and when they do so they succeed in invalidating one or more of the challenged claims roughly 30 to 40% of the time—about the same success rate as accused infringers have when they assert invalidation as a defense in infringement litigation.[131] In addition, the Supreme Court's decisions in *MedImmune, Inc. v. Genentech, Inc.*[132] (released in between Leslie's first and second articles), and in *Medtronic, Inc. v. Mirowski Family Ventures, LLC*[133] have not only made it easier for potential infringement defendants to assert claims for a declaratory judgment of invalidity or noninfringement,[134] but also (arguably) have expanded the potential availability of *Walker Process* claims to a parallel extent.[135]

[129] *See* 35 U.S.C. §§ 321–29.

[130] *See id.* §§ 311–19.

[131] In fiscal year 2024, 1,288 petitions for IPR were filed; the Patent Trial and Appeal Board instituted 740 IPRs; and the Patent Trial and Appeal Board issued final written decisions invalidating some or all of the challenged claims of 379 patents (32%). 32% of cases settled, and in 2% the patentee requested an adverse judgment. Historically, the invalidation rate is 41%. *See* U.S. Pat. & Trademark Off., PTAB Trial Statistics FY24 End of Year Outcome Roundup IPR, PGR (2024), https://www.uspto.gov/sites/default/files/documents/ptab_aia_fy2024__roundup.pdf. Brian Love also suggests that the lack of a standing requirement for IPRs "facilitates the sharing of the cost of patent challenges through entities such as Unified Patents" and others, which may reduce the collective action problems noted *supra* note 96. Brian J. Love, Personal Correspondence with Author, Aug. 15, 2024 (on file with author). Moreover, as Alan Shampine has observed, a patent strong enough to enable the acquisition or maintenance of monopoly power is hardly unlikely to go unnoticed by the patentee's competitors. *See* Allan Shampine, *A Primer on the Economics of Intellectual Property Antitrust Claims*, A.B.A.: Antitrust Mag. Online, June 2023.

One caveat to all of the above: as this book goes to press, the Trump-appointed Acting Director and, since September 2025, the permanent Director of the USPTO have exercised their statutorily granted discretion to dramatically decrease the rate at which IPRs are being instituted (i.e., being allowed to proceed to adjudication on the merits); and the agency also has proposed formal rules that would discourage challengers from filing petitions under a variety of circumstances. Where matters will end up remains, as of the beginning of 2026, uncertain, but if current trends persist, the force of my argument in the text above is, I concede, weakened.

[132] 549 U.S. 118 (2007).

[133] 571 U.S. 191 (2014).

[134] *See MedImmune*, 549 U.S. at 132 n.11, 137 (overturning the Federal Circuit's "reasonable apprehension of suit" standard for determining whether declaratory relief is appropriate, and holding that a patent licensee is "not required . . . to break or terminate its . . . license . . . before seeking a declaratory judgment . . . that the underlying patent is invalid, unenforceable, or not infringed"); *Medtronic*, 571 U.S. at 194 (holding that "when a licensee seeks a declaratory judgment against a patentee to establish that there is no infringement, the burden of proving infringement remains with the patentee").

[135] *See supra* notes 53, 119.

Further, as discussed earlier in this chapter, under some circumstances publicizing one's patent already can form the basis for actionable product disparagement or some other form of unfair competition;[136] and although, in the United States, unfair competition claims premised on false accusations of infringement can be difficult to prove under the objective baselessness/subjective motivation standard that the Federal Circuit applies in such cases,[137] in practice this standard may not be any more difficult to plead and prove than *Walker Process* cases, which as noted previously are subject to heightened pleading and proof standards.[138] Unfair competition claimants also do not need to define a market or prove monopoly power, which lightens their burden; and while unfair competition claims typically result in awards of actual damages,[139] and thus are not automatically trebled as U.S. antitrust damages are, for cases brought under the Lanham Act courts have discretion to award the defendant's profits[140]—and for cases brought under state law, to award punitive damages in appropriate cases.[141] Thus, while an antitrust claim premised on a monopolist's knowing possession of an invalid patent might provide greater protection against the market-distorting effects of such patents, the availability of these other options presumably reduces many of the social costs associated with *not* recognizing such a claim; and, when "deciding whether to apply or extend antitrust into gray areas," courts should and do "consider whether the risk of antitrust intervention is worthwhile, given the existence of other potential causes of action that can reduce the cost of false negatives."[142]

To be sure, these options are not perfect substitutes for antitrust liability. Throughout this chapter I have assumed that any patent that was procured by fraud is necessarily invalid or unenforceable;[143] but because IPRs are available

[136] *See infra* note 139 and accompanying text.

[137] *See supra* notes 74–77 and accompanying text.

[138] *See supra* notes 42–43, 107–109 and accompanying text.

[139] *See, e.g.*, Restatement (Third) of Unfair Competition § 36 (Am. L. Inst. 1995). On a policy basis, limiting awards to actual damages may reduce some of the risk of harm resulting from false positives that could flow from not requiring proof of actual or threatened enforcement (though as noted in the text above punitive damages may be available in egregious cases).

[140] *See* 15 U.S.C. § 1117(a).

[141] *See* Restatement (Third) of Unfair Competition § 36 cmt. n ("A successful plaintiff in an action for unfair competition may recover punitive damages under the rules generally applicable to awards of punitive damages in tort actions. . . . The purpose of punitive damages is to punish the wrongdoer for egregious conduct, and normally proof of malice or willful misconduct is required. Punitive damages are not available in actions under the Lanham Act.") (citation omitted); Rite Aid Corp. v. Lake Shore Invs., 471 A.2d 735, 742–43 (Md. 1984) ("[P]unitive damages may be recovered under 'appropriate circumstances' in both an action for interference with a contract and an action for injurious falsehood.").

[142] Thomas F. Cotter, *And Should I Then Presume?: A Response to Carrier and Tushnet's* An Antitrust Framework for False Advertising, 108 Iowa L. Rev. Online 22, 28 (2023) (citations omitted).

[143] Under U.S. law, it is possible to obtain a patent by concealing information that would have caused the patent examiner to reject a claim as drafted, but for the patent that subsequently issues to withstand

only for novelty and nonobviousness challenges, they cannot winnow out patents the claims of which are invalid because, for example, the specification describes make-believe experimentation substantiating the invention's operability.[144] Moreover, to the extent Leslie's proposals would render potentially actionable the possession, licensing, or refusal to license on royalty-free terms, of a fraudulently-procured patent, they would go beyond anything that standard unfair competition law would be able to address. And one can readily comprehend the injustice of a case in which, say, a patent owner acquires a patent by fraud; the risk of infringement liability deters those competitors from infringing the patent, even in the absence of any express or implicit threat to sue; and the fraud comes to light only several years after it occurred. In such a case, the patentee may wind up benefiting, perhaps quite substantially, from its deceit, even if the patent is eventually invalidated *and* the patentee is required to compensate a *Walker Process* plaintiff for treble the amount of the latter's injury.[145] (The facts leading up to the *Walker Process* litigation may have presented similar facts.[146]) I nevertheless remain concerned that a more expansive antitrust rule would offer only marginal procompetitive benefits, while running the risk of increasing the cost of false positives. I could be wrong, however; and even if I am correct in my assessment of U.S. law, the calculus may well be different for other jurisdictions such as the E.U. As I suggested at the beginning of this chapter, although in principle the same end result could be obtained by coupling a broad definition of assertion with narrow definitions of "without justification" or "adverse consequences" (or vice versa), in practice various contextual factors may render it preferable to adopt a relatively broad or narrow definition of one term or the other. In the U.S., with its high costs of litigation (including pretrial discovery) and the availability of treble

an invalidation challenge in infringement litigation, where claims are construed more narrowly, and the burden of proving invalidation is higher, than during prosecution. In such a case, as discussed in chapter 6, the patent might be unenforceable under the inequitable conduct doctrine, but valid. *See Therasense, Inc. v. Becton, Dickinson & Co.*, 649 F.3d 1276, 1291–92 (Fed. Cir. 2011) (en banc). If the fraud were sufficient to satisfy *Walker Process* liability, it almost certainly would suffice to render the patent unenforceable under the inequitable conduct doctrine. *See infra* ch. 6 note 187.

144 *See, e.g.*, Jorge L. Contreras, *Patent Reality Checks: Eliminating Patents on Fake, Impossible and Other Inoperative Inventions*, 102 J. PAT. & TRADEMARK OFF. SOC'Y 2, 16 (2021) (proposing that "the penalties for fraud on the USPTO should be expanded in the case of inoperative inventions (i.e., these procured through deception beyond the simple omission of prior art references)," such as the many patents procured by defunct company Theranos, "to include both criminal penalties and substantial fines"); *see also* Kyle Kroll, *Prosecuting Inequitable Conduct*, 109 MINN. L. REV. HEADNOTES 49 (2020) (discussing possible criminal penalties for fraudulently procured patents).

145 *See* Leslie, *supra* note 127, at 293 (cited in Sorek, Marcowitz-Bitton & Kaplan, *supra* note 100, at 378).

146 *See* Leslie, *supra* note 93, at 123.

damages for antitrust violations, these contextual factors may counsel in favor of screening out a larger number of claims at an early stage, even if we can be reasonably confident that courts would reach the right decisions most of the time in cases that proceeded all the way to trial.[147] By contrast, a more expansive rule of antitrust liability, such as that applied in *AstraZeneca*, may be sensible in jurisdictions in which treble damages are not available for antitrust violations, and fee-shifting rules make tenuous private antitrust claims more risky.

* * *

If we assume nonetheless that in some cases—whether as a matter of antitrust law, unfair competition law, the law of unjustified threats, or whatever else—liability hinges on whether something constitutes threatened enforcement, the question arises how courts should go about distinguishing actionable threats from nonactionable non-threats. Following from the above, if courts are too hasty to infer that a communication constitutes an implicit threat, they risk generating false positives. In addition, an expansive definition of implied threat also may encourage owners to "jump the gun," that is, to file suit without warning, or any effort to negotiate, or even to obtain a clear grasp of the facts.[148] Imagine, for example, a practicing patent owner sending a competitor a letter stating something along the lines of "We think you are infringing, but we want to talk about exactly how your device operates and how the claims should be construed before we sue."[149] The hypothetical letter contains what might be termed a "contingent threat" to sue, the outcome of which depends on what the patentee's proposed investigation reveals, but communications of this sort could wind up saving substantial time and effort, and

[147] The availability of jury trials in United States District Court, however, may suggest some reasons to doubt whether the district courts are necessarily more institutionally competent to make validity and other related decisions than, say, the PTAB, which adjudicates IPRs in bench trials at which three patent-specialist administrative law judges preside. On the other hand, IPRs and the other options noted in the text above do not eliminate all fraudulently procured patents (much less, all known-to-be-invalid ones, given the imperfections of the examination process); these options primarily serve other interests than the prevention of market distortion, which is antitrust's domain; and the remedies associated with them are generally, if not universally, more modest than the remedies available under U.S. law for an antitrust violation.

[148] *See* Guglyuvatyy, Stoianoff & Das, *supra* note 61, at 115 (stating that, in the context of the Australian law on unjustified threats, that "the most cautious approach is" sometimes "to proceed straight to court," rather than to work matters out; but also that "small players" are sometimes "hesitant to write letters of demand to 'goliaths', knowing that the latter would invoke the unjustified threats provisions," which apparently are not interpreted as being limited, as in the U.K., to threats made to secondary and tertiary infringers).

[149] The above is a quote from Norman V. Siebrasse, Personal Correspondence with Author, Aug. 1, 2024 (on file with author).

it would seem a mistake to discourage patent owners from making them. On the other hand, a rule that limits liability to explicit threats only, or to threats that are worded in a particular fashion, may be both underinclusive and easily circumvented. If so, then it may be necessary to confer discretion upon courts to determine whether a given communication constitutes a threat, under some sort of totality of the circumstances standard, but as with all such standards there are potential drawbacks in terms of predictability, consistency, and the risk of error.

There are nevertheless some rules that courts and legislatures could consider adopting, if they have not done so already, to mitigate these problems. First, as this chapter has shown, threats (however defined) against alleged secondary infringers can be more insidious than threats against primary infringers, if secondary infringers are more likely simply to give in and stop using or selling the primary infringer's goods;[150] in effect, communicating such threats to secondary parties can enable the patent owner to obtain the functional equivalent of a preliminary injunction without having to prove its case to a court and post security.[151] For this reason, it may make sense (1) to apply a broader definition of "implied threat" when the communication is made to a secondary infringer than to a primary infringer; or (2) to apply a stricter standard of liability (*e.g.*, one that gives relatively little weight to the sender's good faith belief that the patent was valid and infringed) where a threat, however defined, is made against a secondary infringer;[152] or (3) to create a specialized cause of action, as in the U.K. and some other common law countries, the effect of which is to nudge patent owners into threatening primary rather than secondary infringers whenever possible.[153] Second, subject to the preceding recommendations concerning secondary infringers, in considering whether to adopt a broad or narrow definition of threatened enforcement for a given body of law, courts and legislatures may conclude

[150] *See supra* notes 59, 83.

[151] *See supra* note 83 (discussing Siebrasse's argument to this effect).

[152] *See, e.g.*, Karl et al., *supra* note 36, at 951–52 (stating that, although German law "provides for damages, on the condition that the unjustified warning letter was culpably issued, i.e. with negligence or intent," the courts apply this standard more strictly in regard to customer versus manufacturer warnings); *see also* ZHENG, *supra* note 24, at 47.

[153] In carrying out this "nudging" function, the law of unlawful threats arguably is somewhat analogous to the legal prohibition of blackmail, which (as Richard Posner once put it) can be viewed as penalizing "a costly and apparently sterile redistributive activity" that plays only a "speculative . . . socially productive role as an auxiliary form of law enforcement." Richard A. Posner, *Blackmail, Privacy, and Freedom of Contract*, 141 U. PENN. L. REV. 1817, 1827 (1993). Threats against secondary infringers arguably are, in most instances, a similarly dubious "auxiliary form of law enforcement."

that expansive definitions of threatened infringement pair better with relatively forgiving standards of liability (that is, standards that focus attention on the patent owner's subjective good faith), and narrow definitions with less forgiving standards (that is, standards that put more weight on whether, ex post, the patent was invalid or not infringed, than on the patentee's ex ante state of mind). Minyu Zheng's suggestion, if I understand correctly, that German courts apply a relatively strict standard to explicit threats, even if made to a primary infringer,[154] would seem consistent with this logic. Third, the more detailed the communication, the more likely it would seem to be, all other things being equal, that the owner is investigating and negotiating in good faith, as in the hypothetical presented in the preceding paragraph. In this regard, some of the factors listed in the U.S. anti-troll laws as relevant to whether a demand letter is a "bad faith assertion"—*e.g.*, does it contain the patent number, the name and address of the patent owner, and specific factual allegations concerning the allegedly infringing activity[155]—arguably could be relevant as well in determining whether, in the first instance, to characterize the communication *as* an assertion. Alternatively, legislators could come up with specific exemptions for permitted communications, as under U.K.[156] and German law,[157] to ensure that merely informative or investigatory letters are not actionable. Fourth, and relatedly, perhaps contingent threats, of the type suggested by the hypothetical letter, should be presumptively nonactionable, even if made to a primary infringer. Finally, if remedies are limited to actual damages and/or fee shifting is routine practice

[154] *See id.* at 34, 103; *see also* Brack, *supra* note 81, at 16 (stating that actionable threats must be explicit). Again, though, for secondary infringers a strict standard of liability may be optimal even if the definition of threat is broad. Such a pairing would comport with the U.K. law, which couples a broad definition of "threatened enforcement"—asking whether "a reasonable person in the position of a recipient would understand" that "a person intends to bring proceedings," Patents Act 1977, c. 37, § 70(1) (Eng.)—with what is effectively a strict liability rule, *see supra* note 61 and accompanying text, subject to exemptions for certain permitted purposes, *see supra* note 55. For a recent case finding that a manufacturer's notification to Amazon, pursuant to Amazon's IPR Policy, that third parties were selling allegedly infringing goods on Amazon's platform constituted threats to sue "Amazon in the event that it did not delist" those products, see Noco Co. v. Shenzhen Carku Tech. Co. Ltd., [2023] EWCA Civ 1502, ¶¶ 40–41 (Eng.).

[155] *See supra* note 66 and accompanying text.

[156] *See* Patents Act 1977, c. 37, §§ 70B, 70(C)(4) (Eng.) (exempting from liability communications made for various "permitted purposes"), discussed *supra* note 55; *see also Patents Act 1990* (Cth) § 131 (Austl.) (stating that "[t]he mere notification of the existence of a patent, or an application for a patent, does not constitute a threat of proceedings for the purposes of section 128").

[157] *See* Zheng, *supra* note 24, at 34 & n.7 (distinguishing between potentially actionable warning letters and non-actionable authorization enquiries under German law, with the latter differing "in the form and intensity of the aimed influence" and intended "to initiate an opportunity for both parties to exchange their views on legal situations," despite arguably "implicitly contain[ing] the same message sent in threats"); Karl et al., *supra* note 36, at 952.

in a given jurisdiction, there would seem to be fewer incentives for the recipient of a communication to engage in opportunistic litigation. Under these conditions, policymakers may opt for a relatively broad definition of threatened enforcement without having to worry too much about generating false positives.[158]

[158] Two other considerations that, in my view, are not relevant to distinguishing threats from non-threats are the extent to which the sender publicizes the communication (which is, however, relevant in determining liability for certain unfair competition torts such as commercial disparagement, *see supra* note 71), and whether the sender is a nonpracticing entity. The fact that an entity, whether practicing or not, has a reputation for litigating may however have some bearing on whether a communication should be deemed threatening. *See* Hewlett-Packard Co. v. Acceleron LLC, 587 F.3d 1358, 1364 n.1 (Fed. Cir. 2009) (stating that "[a] history, or the lack thereof, of litigating in the industry can certainly be a factor to be considered" in determining whether there was an implicit threat of assertion sufficient to sustain jurisdiction for declaratory relief).

4

"Without Sufficient Justification," Case 1

Chapter 1 proposed a universal definition of wrongful patent assertion as "an assertion of patent rights that may (or should) result in the owner suffering adverse consequences, by reason of having harmed or threatened to harm a cognizable interest without sufficient justification." Previous chapters have focused on what it means (or could mean) to "assert" one's patent (and, relatedly, whether assertion should be a condition to liability at all), and on the various possible harms resulting from the assertion of patent rights that are (or could be) legally cognizable. In this and the following two chapters, I will address what it might mean to assert one's patent "without sufficient justification"—though as I have emphasized throughout, the constituent elements of a wrongful assertion claim or defense are interrelated: a harm needs no justification if it is not cognizable, or (for present purposes) it is not caused by something that can be characterized as an assertion, while the severity of the adverse consequences potentially impacts both the effectiveness of the relevant legal standard and the harm that could result from its erroneous application. Moreover, in principle one could achieve the same end result by combining narrow definitions of cognizable harm and assertion with a narrow range of offsetting justifications, as one could with broad definitions of all of the elements, or some combination of various intermediate positions—though within various real-world settings, some combinations may be more practicable than others; and the overall desirability of any given outcome will depend in part on how much weight to accord other potentially relevant considerations, including fundamental rights to speak, petition the government, compete, or engage in business.

Subject to these understandings, this chapter will begin the analysis of "without sufficient justification" by considering under what circumstances an assertion of patent rights is, or should be deemed, wrongful precisely *because* the asserted claim or claims are adjudicated invalid or not infringed. More precisely, should the mere fact that the claims in suit are adjudicated invalid or not infringed ever suffice to render an assertion (in some sense) wrongful—and if so, what consequences should follow to remedy the resulting harm?

Wrongful Patent Assertion. Thomas F. Cotter, Oxford University Press. © Oxford University Press 2026.
DOI: 10.1093/9780191994104.003.0004

Alternatively, under what circumstances should the assertion of invalid or noninfringed claims be considered wrongful, but only if coupled with other facts—and what should those other facts be, and what consequences should follow upon proof of their existence? What are the relevant interests at stake, and how should the law balance these interests when, as will inevitably be the case from time to time, they conflict?

Harms Resulting from the Assertion of Invalid or Noninfringed Patent Claims, Full Stop

Let's begin with a thought experiment, by imagining a world in which the assertion of patent claims that are ultimately found to be invalid or not infringed would result in the patent owner becoming legally obligated to compensate all persons who have suffered some negative effect as a result of the assertion. Who would those persons be, and what harm would they have suffered?

To state the obvious, the most direct victim of such an assertion would be the accused infringer, who at the very least would have incurred attorneys' fees and other expenses related to defending itself against the lawsuit—and potentially other losses as well, including opportunity costs (diverting time, money, and resources to the lawsuit instead of to more productive, potentially profitable activities) and pecuniary losses resulting from any (interim or final) enforcement that was ordered prior to the finding of invalidity or noninfringement. These pecuniary losses, in turn, could take the form of lost profits or increased expenditures resulting from an injunction that barred the defendant from the manufacture, use, or sale of the patented technology; relatedly, losses resulting from corrective measures, if any, such as recall, removal, or destruction; and any damages or other compensation the defendant was required to pay, even if only on an interim basis. There also could be reputational effects, to the extent the adjudication (even if only temporarily) succeeded in branding the defendant as an infringer; and, depending on how far we want to take this, other noneconomic harms such as mental distress—this last perhaps questionable if the accused infringer is a corporation or other artificial entity, though certainly a possibility for corporate managers and other employees, who also might suffer their own losses if they are let go in response to losses directly suffered by the accused infringer. In addition, there may be consumers and other prospective purchasers of the defendant's goods or services who suffer losses if those products are pulled from the market, and on and on, causal chains reaching, as they do, out into infinity.

Not surprisingly, no body of law aspires to such a comprehensive system of compensation. Familiar common-law tort law concepts, for example, duty (which limits the class of potential claimants to whom one is responsible),[1] proximate cause (which tends to limit recovery to victims whose injuries are direct and foreseeable),[2] and rules requiring claimants to quantify their injuries with some degree of certainty,[3] all work to minimize the number of persons to whom and the circumstances under which the wrongdoer will be liable. In this regard, the law of wrongful assertion is no different. Even if one wanted to adopt such a comprehensive system, identifying all of the victims and quantifying their losses in some rational manner would present insurmountable difficulties, and would impose enormous costs on the courts and parties—to say nothing of the potentially negative effect of such a broad rule on the patent incentive scheme, and on incommensurables such as plaintiffs' fundamental rights of access to the courts.[4]

[1] *See, e.g.*, Keith N. Hylton, *Duty in Tort Law: An Economic Approach*, 75 FORDHAM L. REV. 1501 (2006) (positing that a no-duty rule may be appropriate when the actor's conduct generates substantial external benefits compared to external costs).

[2] *See* Thomas F. Cotter, *Extraterritorial Damages in Patent Law*, 39 CARDOZO ARTS & ENTER. L.J. 1, 23 & n.14 (2020) (stating that doctrines such as proximate cause "are premised on the assumption that extending liability too far is unlikely to deter the type of wrongful act at issue, and may instead either over-deter actors from engaging in beneficial conduct or, alternatively, undermine the purposes the body of law is intended to carry out or other important public policies") (citations omitted).

[3] *See* Roger D. Blair & William H. Page, *Speculative Antitrust Damages*, 70 WASH. L. REV. 423, 427 (1995) (arguing that damages are unduly speculative if they "fail[] to account rationally for factors other than the defendant's illegal conduct that may have caused (or significantly contributed to) the asserted difference between" the actual state of the world and the counterfactual that would have obtained "but for the violation from a base experience unaffected by the violation").

[4] Malani and Masur have argued, however, that one could improve the working of the patent system by requiring the losing patentee to pay the prevailing defendant more than just the latter's attorneys' fees, to discourage patent owners from asserting "weak" claims (which, despite their weakness, impose a nonzero risk of liability on the defendant, and thus may compel an unwarranted settlement); and by entitling the prevailing patentee to recover additional damages or a patent term extension, for having been forced to assume a nonzero risk of collecting nothing. *See* Anup Malani & Jonathan S. Masur, *Raising the Stakes in Patent Cases*, 101 GEO. L.J. 637 (2013); *see also* David D. Friedman, *Beyond Fee Shifting: A Proposal for Tort Reform* (unpublished draft, on file with author) (similar). Malani and Masur argue that such a system would encourage owners of patents with a high social value to assert them, while discouraging the owners of patents with low social value from asserting theirs. Their proposal, however, requires someone to determine the error rate in a typical case (that is, the probability that a court will invalidate a valid patent, or validate an invalid one). *See* Malani & Masur, *supra*, at 665. Although they recommend that this task be delegated to an administrative agency or panel of outside experts, *see id.* at 682, I remain skeptical that such a system would be feasible in the real world.

For a somewhat different perspective, *see* Thomas J. Miceli & Michael P. Stone, *"Piggyback" Lawsuits and Deterrence: Can Frivolous Litigation Improve Welfare?*, 39 INT'L REV. L. & ECON. 49, 55 (2014) (arguing that "frivolous litigation is not necessarily detrimental to social welfare," because it can "correct for" some degree of underdeterrence, but also cautioning that "[t]he amount of the 'correction' . . . is not related in any systematic way to the amount of underdeterrence, so as a general matter it is not possible to say whether frivolous suits improve or worsen welfare"). Whatever the merits of this argument may be in other contexts—even if one believes that patent rights are being underenforced notwithstanding the existence of PAEs, litigation financing, and remedies such as injunctions (in most countries) or enhanced damages (in the United States)—I think it is highly unlikely that frivolous patent litigation would be a socially valuable corrective, given its manifest risk of abuse. That said, there

Indeed, in the absence of additional facts that might implicate doctrines sounding in antitrust or unfair competition law, in most countries the wrongful asserter will be responsible for, at most, the accused infringer's attorneys' fees and related costs—and even then, often only a portion of the actual costs incurred, and typically only if the patent is found to be invalid or not infringed in the litigation at hand, as opposed to some unrelated future proceeding.[5] IPRED article 14, for example, requires E.U. member states to "ensure that reasonable and proportionate legal costs and other expenses incurred by the successful party shall, as a general rule, be borne by the unsuccessful party, unless equity does not allow this,"[6] but in practice many member states provide only partial compensation to the prevailing party, sometimes based on the amount at stake[7]—though the CJEU has held that laws awarding flat rate

may be an argument to be made for tolerating some measure of nonfrivolous but ex ante weak claims that provide courts with an opportunity to modify an existing but suboptimal legal rule, as explained in an American Law Institute commentary on the U.S. tort of wrongful use of civil proceedings. *See* Restatement (Second) of Torts, § 675 cmt. f (Am. L. Inst. 1977) ("To hold that the person initiating civil proceedings is liable unless the claim proves to be valid, would throw an undesirable burden upon those who by advancing claims not heretofore recognized nevertheless aid in making the law consistent with changing conditions and changing opinions. There are many instances in which a line of authority has been modified or rejected. To subject those who challenge this authority to liability for wrongful use of civil proceedings might prove a deterrent to the overturn.")

[5] A note on terminology: outside the United States, courts and commentators often use the term "fee awards" and "cost awards" (or "awards of costs") interchangeably. In the U.S., by contrast, an award of costs usually refers to an award of the court costs alone (e.g., docket and witness fees), which are trivial compared to attorneys' fees. For discussion, see Thomas F. Cotter, Comparative Patent Remedies: A Legal and Economic Analysis 146–47 & n.283 (2013), and sources cited therein. In the text above, I will follow the majority practice and use "fee awards" and "awards of costs" interchangeably, unless otherwise noted.

[6] Directive 2004/48/EC of the European Parliament and of the Council of 29 April 2004 on the Enforcement of Intellectual Property Rights, 2004 O.J. (L 195) 16 [hereinafter IPRED], art. 14.

[7] For recent commentary, see Krista Rantasaari, *Patent Litigation in Europe: Intermediate Fee Shifting and the UPC*, 18 JIPLP 642 (2023) (noting, *inter alia*, that according to a survey conducted by the European Patent Litigators Association (EPLIT) of costs awarded in Austria, Finland, France, Germany, Hungary, Italy, the Netherlands, and the U.K., "total costs reimbursed from a losing party" range from lows of "up to 25 percent" in Italy to a high of "between 75 per cent and 100 per cent in Finland") (citing EPLIT, Survey on Costs of Patent Litigation Across Europe (2021) (on file with author)). For other estimates, *see, e.g.*, Giovanni Casucci, *Patent Enforcement in Italy*, *in* Patent Enforcement Worldwide: Writings in Honour of Dieter Stauder 205, 223 (Christopher Heath ed., 3d ed. 2015) [hereinafter Patent Enforcement Worldwide] (stating that "Italian courts never order the effective costs suffered by the winning party, usually awarding less than 40 per cent of the overall value"); Christian Osterrieth, *Patent Enforcement in Germany*, *in* Patent Enforcement Worldwide, *supra*, at 111, 142 (stating that "the party who loses the lawsuit bears the total costs including attorneys' and patent attorneys' fees of the prevailing party, but only the amount of the statutory minimum fees" which is based on the estimated value in dispute); Isabelle Romet et al., *Patent Enforcement in France*, *in* Patent Enforcement Worldwide, *supra*, at 145, 174 (stating that fee awards are discretionary, but "usually . . . represent one- to two-thirds of the actual costs"). Some EU member states apply a similar loser-pays rule to patent opposition or invalidation proceedings, *see, e.g.*, WIPO, International Case Management Guide for Judges § 5.7.7 (2023) (discussing the German system), but cost shifting is discretionary for opposition proceedings before the EPO. *See* EPC art. 104(1) ("Each party to the opposition proceedings shall bear the costs it has incurred, unless the

fees must compensate for "a significant and appropriate part of the reasonable costs" actually incurred (as well as fees for technical advisers whose work is "directly and closely linked to" the proceeding).[8] Fees in Commonwealth countries are often said to be undercompensatory as well.[9] In Japan and China, courts award fees to the prevailing party only in a minority of cases, and the amounts awarded tend to be undercompensatory.[10] By contrast, in U.S. patent cases the prevailing party is not even formally entitled to recover its fees and costs. Instead, courts award fees only in "exceptional" patent infringement cases,[11] employing a totality of the circumstances test;[12] as a result, the prevailing party obtains a fee award in only a small percentage of U.S. patent cases.[13] Thus, while conceding that the broad rule sketched above as a thought

Opposition Division, for reasons of equity, orders, in accordance with the Implementing Regulations, a different apportionment of costs"); EPC Implementing Regulations R.88.

[8] *See* United Video Properties, Inc. v. Telenet NV, Case C-57/15, ECLI:EU:C:2016:611 (CJEU 2016).

[9] *See* Cotter, *supra* note 5, at 209, and sources cited therein (discussing fee awards in the U.K., Canada, and Australia); Christopher Rennie-Smith, *Patent Enforcement in the United Kingdom*, *in* Patent Enforcement Worldwide, *supra*, at 81, 109 (stating that fee awards "rarely amount to the costs actually incurred," and noting that "costs in patent actions are increasingly assessed on an issue basis"); *see also* ABB Tech. AG v. Hyundai Heavy Indus. Co., 2013 FC 1050, ¶ 4 (Can.) (noting "the growing disparity between the Federal Court tariff [costs schedule] and the actual costs of patent litigation"), discussed in Norman V. Siebrasse, *Does Canada Really Follow the "English Rule" for Costs?*, Sufficient Description Blog, Nov. 6, 2013, http://www.sufficientdescription.com/2013/11/does-canada-really-follow-english-rule.html. As noted below, moreover, both the U.K.'s Intellectual Property Enterprise Court and the Unified Patent Court impose caps on the amount of recoverable fees. *See infra* notes 20, 31 and accompanying text.

[10] For discussion of fee-shifting in Japan, *see* Cotter, *supra* note 5, at 328, and sources cited therein; Christopher Heath, *Patent Enforcement in Japan*, *in* Patent Enforcement Worldwide, *supra* note 7, at 383, 415. Chinese courts generally do not award fees, though in some IP cases they award them to the prevailing plaintiff, albeit typically below the amount actually incurred. For discussion, *see, e.g.*, Guodong Du, *Attorney's Fees in China: Does the Losing Party Pay?*, China Justice Observer, Sept. 1, 2019 (stating that in patent disputes, the court may order the infringer to pay the patentee's attorney's fees, and may order fee awards for wrongful acts such as malicious litigation) (citations omitted); *see also* Cotter, *supra*, at 360, and sources cited therein; Thomas Pattloch, *Patent Enforcement in China*, *in* Patent Enforcement Worldwide, *supra*, at 316, 347.

[11] *See* 35 U.S.C. § 285.

[12] *See* Octane Fitness, LLC v. ICON Health & Fitness, Inc., 572 U.S. 545, 554 (2014) (defining an exceptional case as "simply one that stands out from others with respect to the substantive strength of a party's litigating position (considering both the governing law and the facts of the case) or the unreasonable manner in which the case was litigated," and stating that "courts may determine whether a case is 'exceptional' in the case-by-case exercise of their discretion, considering the totality of the circumstances"). A finding of willful infringement weighs in favor of a finding that a case is exceptional, but is not dispositive. *See* SiOnyx LLC v. Hamamatsu Photonics K.K., 981 F.3d 1339 (Fed. Cir. 2020) (affirming the denial of a fee award, and observing that "despite the jury's finding of willful infringement, the district court concluded that Hamamatsu's noninfringement and invalidity defenses were not so weak as to be exceptional").

[13] For discussion of fee awards in the U.S., *see, e.g.*, Geneva Clark, 2020 Lex Machina Patent Litigation Report 15 (Rachel Bailey & Jason Maples eds. 2021) (excluding consent and default judgments, as well as voluntary dismissals, reporting 132 decisions on the merits in all of 2020); John Skenyon et al., Patent Damages Law and Practice § 4.35 (2023) (noting, *inter alia*, that when U.S. courts award fees, the award typically is not for the entire litigation). One way for patent owners to avoid liability for fees under 35 U.S.C. § 285 is to voluntarily dismiss the action without prejudice. For discussion, *see* Skenyon et al., *supra*, § 4.34 (discussing Federal Circuit decisions standing for

experiment is neither feasible nor desirable, the question arises whether limiting the accused infringer's recovery in these respects, as many countries do, is optimal—or conversely, whether the recovery *even of* fees and costs should be disallowed, absent additional facts, as it normally is in the United States.[14]

To help in analyzing this question, we can begin by reviewing the economic literature on fee shifting. Most of the theoretical literature on this topic centers on comparing the effects of a pure English versus pure American Rule. As my coauthors and I have previously observed, this literature generally predicts that, all other things being equal, the English Rule will have two primary effects. The first is that fee shifting "will enhance the overall quality of the pool of lawsuits that are filed," because potential plaintiffs will be (1) less inclined to bring weak claims, that is, claims they are ex ante likely to lose and for which they would, as a result, have to pay not only their own but their opponent's fees; and (2) more inclined to bring likely winning claims, for which they will not bear the full cost.[15] The second effect is that "cost recovery can increase the duration and complexity of legal disputes," because (1) it "exaggerate[s] the gap between the parties' estimates of the expected value of their respective recovery or payout if the case is litigated," and "[t]he wider this gap, the less likely parties are to reach a mutually agreeable settlement"; and (2) it may encourage "well-resourced parties to devote more resources to litigation," on the assumption that doing so increases the chances of winning (and thus being reimbursed for the additional cost).[16] On the other hand, and somewhat at odds

the proposition that, although a voluntary dismissal with prejudice can qualify the defendant as a prevailing party for purposes of § 285, a voluntary dismissal without prejudice cannot); Lionel Lavenue et al., *Evolving Case Law Elucidates Atty Fees for Patent Litigants*, LAW360, July 17, 2020. This loophole is one of several features of U.S. practice that may enable intellectual property owners to profit from "Schedule A" litigation, discussed *infra* at note 160. In a case in which the patent owner prevails on some claims but the defendant succeeds in proving that other asserted claims are invalid, the case law appears to permit the court to deny fees altogether or to award partial fees to the party who on balance prevailed, the latter however still subject to the "exceptional cases" requirement. *See* SKENYON ET AL., *supra*, § 4.34.

[14] The TRIPS Agreement takes essentially a neutral stance on the issue. *See* Agreement on Trade-Related Aspects of Intellectual Property Rights, Apr. 15, 1994, Marrakesh Agreement Establishing the World Trade Organization, Annex 1C, Legal Instruments-Results of the Uruguay Round vol. 31, 33 I.L.M. 1197 (1994) [hereinafter TRIPS], art. 45(2) (stating that "the judicial authorities shall also have the authority to order the infringer to pay the right holder expenses, which may include appropriate attorney's fees"); DANIEL GERVAIS, THE TRIPS AGREEMENT: DRAFTING HISTORY AND ANALYSIS 583 (4th ed. 2012) (suggesting that the first sentence of article 45(2) requires only that courts have authority to award fees in cases in which the defendant knew or had reasonable grounds to know it was infringing, but that even if the provision requires that courts have authority to award fees against innocent infringers "the court could use its discretion and refuse the remedy in cases where its application would be inappropriate").

[15] Colleen V. Chien et al., *Enhanced Damages, Litigation Cost Recovery, and Interest*, *in* PATENT REMEDIES AND COMPLEX PRODUCTS: TOWARD A GLOBAL CONSENSUS 90, 108 (Brad Biddle et al. eds. 2019) [hereinafter COMPLEX PRODUCTS] (citations omitted).

[16] *Id.* (citations omitted).

with the second effect noted above, is the possibility that risk-averse litigants will be more likely to settle, or to avoid bringing some meritorious claims altogether, to avoid the risk of incurring the counterparty's fees—and this result is substantively unfair, particularly if the risk-averse party is financially disadvantaged compared to the counterparty.[17] An additional complicating factor is that if the prevailing party is entitled to recover its fees, courts either may have to devote time to "satellite" litigation to determine how much would be reasonable to award—and to whom, if each party prevailed on some issues but not others—or resort to the use of possibly arbitrary statutory rates.[18]

Empirical studies testing the above theoretical predictions have been somewhat inconclusive, though a few have reported (as expected) that fee shifting tends to screen out weaker cases and to reduce settlement rates.[19] Specifically in regard to IP cases, Helmers et al. conducted a study of the U.K.'s Intellectual Property Enterprise Court (IPEC), a tribunal that hears relatively small-stakes IP disputes—specifically, cases in which the value in suit is £500,000 or less—and which in 2010 introduced a cap on recoverable fees (£50,000, plus an additional £25,000 for proceedings relating to damages).[20] Helmers et al. first developed a model which predicts that (1) the effect of a costs cap is ambiguous (it could result in either more or less litigation overall); but (2) when a costs cap results in more litigation, plaintiffs' win rates will decline, settlements will increase, and plaintiffs on average will devote fewer resources to

[17] *See id.* at 108–09. These potential chilling effects on plaintiff behavior might be further exacerbated, if plaintiffs are obligated to post security for the defendant's costs. German courts typically require this when the plaintiff is based outside of Germany, subject to certain exceptions. *See* Thomas Kühnen, Handbuch der Patentverletzung 840–53 (16th ed. 2024). Article 69(4) of the Unified Patent Court Agreement confers discretion to award security for costs in cases before the UPC. *See* Agreement on a Unified Patent Court, 2013/C 175/01 [hereinafter UPCA], art. 69(4). For discussion, *see, e.g.*, Volkswagen AG v. Network Sys. Techs. LLC, UPC_CFI_514/2023, Application Nos. 11434/2024, 11453/2024, 11833/2024 (L.D. Munich Apr. 23, 2024) (denying a request for security for costs, absent evidence that the plaintiff would be unable to pay the defendant's costs or that enforcing the judgment would prove difficult); IP-Portal: European IP Law, *Article 69*, https://www.ippt.eu/legal-texts/upc-agreement/article-69 (summarizing the preceding and other UPC decisions on security for costs).

Note also that, aside from fairness considerations, under some circumstances there may be a public benefit arising from the filing of ex ante weak claims that provide courts with an opportunity to improve existing law. *See supra* note 4.

[18] *See* Chien et al., *supra* note 15, at 110.

[19] *See id.* at 109 (citing sources). *But see* Mark Schankerman & Florian Schuett, *Patent Screening, Innovation, and Welfare*, 89 Rev. Econ. Stud. 2101, 2142 (2021) (estimating, on the basis of simulations calibrated on U.S. data, that "a loser-pays rule would reduce overall social welfare in the United States, because increased litigation costs would outweigh avoided deadweight loss").

[20] These amounts were increased in 2021 to £60,000 and £30,000, respectively (but IPEC's jurisdiction over patent matters remains limited to those with a maximum value of £500,000, absent agreement of the parties). *See* U.K. Courts and Tribunals Judiciary, Intellectual Property Enterprise Court Guide (updated Oct. 2022).

litigation.[21] The authors then conducted an empirical study of the effects of the IPEC costs cap, and reported that (1) IPEC litigation did increase, even relative to an overall increase in U.K. patent litigation that began in 2011; and (2) smaller plaintiffs' win rates declined and they settled more often, and larger plaintiffs devoted fewer resources to litigating.[22]

In another study conducted by some of the same authors, Love et al. conclude that fee shifting is the "key reason" for the relative absence of PAE cases in the U.K. and Germany, compared to the United States, both because it deters PAEs from suing and because, when they do sue, it encourages defendants to litigate rather than agree to a quick settlement.[23] Whether one views this in a positive or a negative light, of course, depends on one's views of PAE litigation generally, though I have argued previously that PAE litigation in the United States has been, on balance, a negative.[24] There are several reasons for this conclusion, among them that PAEs behave opportunistically, meaning that they typically do not transfer technology to their licensees,[25] but rather seek out and assert claims against companies whose independently-invented products allegedly fall within the scope of the subject patent claims; and the evidence that PAE lawsuits against startups, in particular, can hinder innovation.[26] Moreover, in 2016 the United States Federal Trade Commission (FTC) published a study of PAEs that, among other things, distinguished between "Portfolio PAEs" and "Litigation PAEs."[27] Whereas the former generally

[21] *See* Christian Helmers et al., *The Effect of Fee Shifting on Litigation: Evidence from a Policy Innovation in Intermediate Cost Shifting*, 23 Am. L. & Econ. Rev. 56, 67–72 (2021).

[22] *See id.* at 88–95. The authors distinguish between small and medium-sized enterprises (SMEs), as defined by EU criteria, and large firms. *See id.* Online Appendix xviii; European Commission, SME Definition, https://single-market-economy.ec.europa.eu/smes/sme-definition_en.

[23] *See* Brian J. Love et al., *Patent Assertion Entities in Europe*, *in* Patent Assertion Entities and Competition Policy 104 (D. Daniel Sokol ed. 2017); Christian Helmers et al., *Is There a Patent Troll Problem in the U.K.?*, 24 Fordham Intell. Prop. Media & Ent. L.J. 509 (2014). In addition, shortly before this book went to press, Love, Helmers, and a third author posted a paper on ssrn reporting that, according to their empirical analysis of U.S. cases pre- and post-*Octane Fitness*, that decision "increased defendants' willingness to contest weak claims and prompted plaintiffs, especially PAEs, to file stronger ones." Tommaso Alba, Christian Helmers & Brian J. Love, *A Tale of Trolls and Fees: The Role of Fee-Shifting in Patent Litigation* (Nov. 24, 2025), https://ssrn.com/abstract=5796263.

[24] For discussion and citation to sources, *see* Thomas F. Cotter, Patent Wars: How Patents Impact Our Daily Lives 209–19 (2018).

[25] *See* Robin C. Feldman & Mark A. Lemley, *The Sound and the Fury of Patent Activity*, 103 Minn. L. Rev. 1793 (2019); *see also* Cotter, *supra* note 24, at 216; Mark A. Lemley & A. Douglas Melamed, *Missing the Forest for the Trolls*, 113 Colum. L. Rev. 2117, 2167 (2013).

[26] *See* Colleen V. Chien, *Startups and Patent Trolls*, 17 Stan. Tech. L. Rev. 461, 474–77 (2014); Lauren Cohen et al., *Patent Trolls: Evidence from Targeted Firms*, 65 Mgt. Sci. 5461 (2019); Stephen Kiebczak et al., *The Effect of Patent Litigation and Patent Assertion Entities on Entrepreneurial Activity*, 45 Res. Pol'y 218 (2015); Roger Smeets, *Does Patent Litigation Reduce Corporate R&D? An Analysis of US Public Firms* (Dec. 2015), https://papers.ssrn.com/sol3/papers.cfm?abstract_id=2443048.

[27] Fed. Trade Comm'n, Patent Assertion Entity Activity: An FTC Study 1 (Oct. 2016) [hereinafter "FTC Study"].

are highly capitalized and tend to license large portfolios of patents—think Intellectual Ventures—the latter typically are structured as Limited Liability Companies (LLCs) that own one or a small number of patents, and that tend to settle for sums far below what it would cost the defendant to litigate.[28] This evidence that Litigation PAEs settle most of their claims for the defendant's avoided litigation costs seems extremely difficult to square with any sort of coherent innovation policy.[29] That said, as others have observed, the better strategy for dealing with such abuses is not to eliminate PAEs altogether (assuming that were even possible), but rather to address the features of the patent system that enable the abuse.[30] In this regard, and consistent with Love et al.'s findings that the English Rule discourages PAE suits generally, adoption of the English Rule would have the salutary effect of substantially reducing the ability of Litigation PAEs to extract nuisance settlements—though to be sure, as discussed above mandatory fee shifting also could discourage some smaller, less solvent, and less sophisticated entities from bringing meritorious suits, and/or encourage them to settle on less favorable terms.

There are a few ways, admittedly none of them perfect, for trying to reconcile these tensions between, on the one hand, wanting to deter suits that lack merit, and on the other not wanting to deter the meritorious ones. First, a nation could adopt a partial-recovery rule, under which the prevailing party would be entitled to obtain only some portion of its actual expenses. As noted above, this is what many nations actually do, whether as a matter of judicial discretion or statutory command in the form of costs caps (as in Germany, the U.K.'s IPEC, and more recently the UPC[31]); and the practice is not irrational. It can be understood as a compromise among the competing interests—the prevailing party receives some compensation, while the risks of chilling parties from asserting valid claims and of encouraging better-off parties to overinvest in litigation effort are reduced, though not eliminated. On the downside, it achieves these goals at a cost of leaving all prevailing parties worse off than they would have been, had the counterparty's wrongful (as I have defined it) conduct never occurred; nor is there any guarantee that the portion awarded, whether set by judges on a case-by-case basis or by statutory fiat, will bear a reasonable relation to the effort actually needed to prosecute or defend a

[28] *Id.* at 2–4, 45.
[29] *See* Cotter, supra note 24, at 216.
[30] *See* Lemley & Melamed, *supra* note 25, at 2121 (arguing that, instead of "search[ing] for 'bad actors,'" we should "focus instead on aspects of the patent system itself that give rise to the problems and on specific, objectionable conduct in which both trolls and practicing entities sometimes engage").
[31] *See* Unified Patent Court Administrative Committee, Decision on scale of ceilings, D AC/10/24042023_E (Apr. 24, 2023).

case—and where the amount is not fixed by statute, there also is no guarantee that awards will be consistent from one action to another. Nonetheless, if the statutory rates are not *too* far below market value, on balance a partial-recovery regime may be a sensible solution, particularly if combined with other tweaks to minimize the negative effects of fee-shifting. In this regard, for example, Filipe Fischmann argues that the U.K.'s practice of awarding costs on an issue-by-issue basis reduces litigants' incentives to overlitigate, and thus "may help to speed litigation."[32] He also suggests that nations can avoid "over-rigid costs scales" by authorizing courts to depart upwards in cases in which the court disapproves of the losing party's conduct.[33]

Second, one could limit fee-shifting to only the worst cases—which is, effectively, what the United States does—but with the result that the vast majority of prevailing parties are not made whole. In practice, moreover, even when U.S. courts do award fees, as in Europe the fees tend to be only partial,[34] thus further diluting the potential benefits of fee-shifting.

A third possibility would be to adopt mandatory fee-shifting subject to exceptions. In 2013, the United States came close to adopting this sort of rule, when the House of Representatives approved a bill—which, however, died in the Senate—that would have imposed mandatory fee shifting in patent infringement actions "unless the court finds that the position and conduct of the nonprevailing party or parties were reasonably justified in law and fact or that special circumstances (such as severe economic hardship to a named inventor) make an award unjust."[35] The first exception, under which fee shifting would not apply if the losing party was "reasonably justified in law and fact," was inspired by another federal statute, the Equal Access to Justice Act,[36] which in certain cases brought against the United States government requires the

[32] Filipe Fischmann, *Patent litigation and cost-shifting in Europe: critical appraisal and proposal of alternative solutions*, 10 JIPLP 98, 106 (2015).

[33] As Fischmann notes, the Patents Court has the authority to resolve doubts in favor of the losing party where it disapproves of that party's conduct. *See id.* at 100.

[34] *See supra* n.13.

[35] *See* Innovation Act, H.R. 3309, § 3(b)(1) 113th Cong., 1st Sess. (referred to the Senate Committee on the Judiciary, Dec. 9, 2013), https://www.congress.gov/113/cprt/HPRT85655/CPRT-113HPRT85655.pdf. An earlier bill would have introduced mandatory fee shifting in the limited circumstances in which, as summarized by Lemley and Melamed, "a patent is found invalid or not infringed and the patent holder is (1) not the original inventor or the original assignee of the patent, (2) has not practiced the patent, and (3) is not a university or a technology transfer organization the primary purpose of which is to facilitate commercialization of university patents." Lemley and Melamed, *supra* note 25, at 2177 n.247 (quoting Saving High-Tech Innovators from Egregious Legal Disputes Act of 2013 (SHIELD Act), H.R. 845, 113th Cong., § 2 (2013)).

[36] *See* 5 U.S.C. § 504; 28 U.S.C. § 2412. The awards tend to be under $10,000 in amount, and are granted mostly in Social Security and veterans' benefits disputes. See Equal Access to Justice Act Reporting, https://eaja.acus.gov/.

government to pay the prevailing plaintiff's fees unless the government's position was "substantially justified."[37] Although this exception presumably would have resulted in more fee awards than under the current "exceptional case" rule, it hardly would have amounted to mandatory fee shifting; according to the legislative history accompanying the House bill, there would have been "no presumption that the nonprevailing party's position was not reasonably justified simply because it lost the case," and a plaintiff would have been "immune from a fee award so long as its position had a reasonable basis in law and fact."[38]

The second exception ("severe economic hardship to a named inventor"), on the other hand, went directly to the point of trying to alleviate the burdens on SMEs,[39] though much would have depended on how the exception was interpreted; the fact that it didn't mention defendants at all, and specifically referred only to hardship "to a named inventor" rather than "to the patent owner," suggests that it would have been quite narrow. More promisingly, perhaps, Krista Rantasaari argues that the UPC has authority to invoke "equity" as a rationale for reducing the burden of fee shifting on SMEs under UPCA article 69;[40] and costs caps that correlate with the value in dispute might be seen as an attempt to achieve a similar result, to the extent the amount at stake is a rough proxy for a party's status as an SME. Yet another variation on this theme might be to adopt "one-way" fee shifting, either in favor of SMEs or some other

[37] 5 U.S.C. § 504(a)(1); 28 U.S.C. § 2412(d)(1)(A). The original text of the Innovation Act mirrored this "substantially justified" standard, but the language subsequently was changed to "reasonably justified" specifically to "lower[] the standard of justification," that is, to make it marginally more difficult to obtain a fee award. *See* H. Rep. 113–279, 113th Cong., 1st Sess., at 108 n.55 (Dec. 2, 2013), https://www.congress.gov/113/crpt/hrpt279/CRPT-113hrpt279.pdf.

[38] H. Rep. 113–279, *supra* note 37, at 58–59 (further stating, with citations to cases interpreting the EAJA, that fees would not "be awarded if the nonprevailing party's case was justified to a degree that could satisfy a reasonable person . . . or there was at least a dispute over which reasonable minds could differ," and that "[w]hen a case turns on a legal question, courts have looked to the clarity of the governing law—that is, whether judicial decision on the issue left the status of the law unsettled, and whether the legal issue was novel or difficult. . . . On questions of statutory interpretation, for example, courts have asked whether the Federal courts were split on the matter . . . or whether the nonprevailing party interpreted a statute in a manner that is contrary to its plain language and unsupported by its legislative history") (citations omitted).

[39] *See id.* at 59 (stating that "courts have discretion in special circumstances to protect from a fee award, for example, the unsophisticated independent inventor who brought a lawsuit to protect what he may have understood to be his claimed invention but whose complaint was ultimately determined not to be reasonably justified").

[40] *See* Rantasaari, *supra* note 7, at 652–53. Article 69(1) states that "Reasonable and proportionate legal costs and other expenses incurred by the successful party shall, as a general rule, be borne by the unsuccessful party, unless equity requires otherwise, up to a ceiling set in accordance with the Rules of Procedure," and article 69(2) that "[w]here a party succeeds only in part or in exceptional circumstances, the Court may order that costs be apportioned equitably or that the parties bear their own costs." Rantasaari also notes, however, that although the UPCA allows SMEs to benefit from various cost reductions, *see id.* at 646, the Rules of Procedure do not clearly indicate that the prevailing party can recover its court fees, even though article 69 would appear generally to require this, *see id.* at 653.

favored parties,[41] or specifically in favor of patent challengers,[42] though either of these variations would leave prevailing patentees undercompensated, which might seem unfair;[43] and, depending on how SMEs are defined, might actually encourage litigation by undercapitalized PAEs.

Strictly speaking, it is impossible to say which rule (English or American), or which variation of these rules, is optimal, because the answer depends on how much weight one accords to the right of access to courts; on this issue, different countries and regions may simply have different cultural preferences, making it futile to try proving one side right or wrong. Nevertheless, a few matters are reasonably clear. *First*, as discussed above, some form of routine fee shifting probably would have an outsize negative impact on Litigation PAEs, which all other things being equal would seem to be a social good.[44] *Second*, the invalidation of invalid patents—patents that do not, in fact, satisfy the statutory criteria for patentability—is also a public good, because it prevents patent owners from benefiting from a statutorily unwarranted restriction of free competition.[45] As with other public goods, however, there is a risk of a collective action problem, insofar as the public benefit of invalidation exceeds the private benefit to the invalidator. The English Rule mitigates this problem to some degree, by increasing the payoff to the invalidator, at least in those cases in which invalidation can be, and is, raised as a counterclaim or defense. *Third*, by ensuring that the prevailing party is rendered no worse off than it otherwise would have been, but for the other party's conduct, the English Rule relieves some of the pressure for other, perhaps more error-prone, doctrines (e.g., enhanced damages) or bodies of law (e.g., antitrust) to discourage infringer or

[41] Some U.S. departures from the American Rule are in fact one-way. These include all claims that are subject to the Equal Access to Justice Act, as well as plaintiffs' claims for violations of the federal antitrust and civil rights laws. For discussion of one-way fee shifting, *see, e.g.*, Collen V. Chien, *Reforming Software Patents*, 50 HOUS. L. REV. 325, 375–78 (2012); Harold J. Krent, *Explaining One-Way Fee Shifting*, 79 VA. L REV. 2039 (1993).

[42] *See* Jay P. Kesan, *Carrots and Sticks to Create a Better Patent System*, 17 BERKELEY TECH. L.J. 763, 787 (2002) (proposing one-way fee shifting "when a patent is revoked or invalidated based on certain categories of prior art that are reasonably discoverable by a patentee's diligent prior art search").

[43] Cf. Fischmann, supra note 32, at 107–08 (arguing that a better solution would be a "'modulated two-way fee shifting system,' which would permit a limited amount of reimbursement of the patentee, if she prevailed in good-faith litigation, until she obtained a . . . certificate of contested validity," which would entitle the patentee to a higher fee award in any future litigation over the patent).

[44] *See supra* notes 28–30 and accompanying text.

[45] This assumes that the statutory criteria themselves are correctly calibrated, and that the final determination by the appropriate court or agency whether they are satisfied is error-free. It is doubtful that these assumptions are always accurate, but as I have previously argued in the related context of patent remedies, it would be unwise to authorize judges to second-guess those criteria on a case-by-case basis. *See* Thomas F. Cotter, *Patent Remedies and Practical Reason*, 88 TEX. L. REV. SEE ALSO 125, 130–31 (2010).

patentee misconduct.[46] *Fourth*, if one suspects that, for the preceding reasons, the pure English Rule is in general superior to the pure American Rule, then some type of a partial or modified English Rule—for example, one that awards partial but nontrivial costs, or that generally exempts SMEs, or that provides courts with discretion to award higher fees when the counterparty has acted unreasonably—would probably be superior to the pure American Rule as well, since the expected effect of a partial rule would be to mitigate the English Rule's drawbacks, to some degree. The current practices of some countries, however, to award no fees at all absent exceptional circumstances, or to routinely award less than half of the fees actually incurred, would seem difficult to justify. *Fifth*, a partial English Rule may be more politically feasible than a pure English Rule, given the revealed preferences of most jurisdictions for awarding only partial recoveries,[47] although it would be illuminating if some countries, at least for some classes of cases, began experimenting with a full-blown application of the English Rule, to provide data for further evaluation of its effects.

Aside from awarding fees, countries could provide additional compensation to the prevailing defendant, either to make up for other losses the defendant suffers, or to deter patent assertions that threaten third-party interests—and in fact some do so, in certain types of cases, though typically not just because the plaintiff lost its case.[48] As noted in chapter 2, however, German law permits an adjudicated infringer to recover back the damages paid prior to patent invalidation, as well as the costs of the first infringement action.[49] These practices arguably make sense in a bifurcated system like Germany's, where invalidation sometimes does not occur until long after a judgment of infringement has

[46] *See* Mark A. Lemley & Ragesh Tangri, *Ending Patent Law's Willfulness Game*, 18 BERKELEY TECH. L.J. 1085, 1123–24 (2003) (arguing that courts should award fees but not damages enhancements for willful infringement).

[47] Partial recoveries based on statutory flat rates also reduce the adjudicative cost of determining the amount of the fee to be awarded, though at potentially high risk of undercompensation. So does awarding fees based on some percentage (e.g., 10%) of the plaintiff's recovery, as Japanese courts reportedly do on some occasions when they do award fees, *see* COTTER, *supra* note 5, at 328; but the amount awarded can be entirely arbitrary, and this sort of rule does not seem readily transferrable to awards of fees to defendants.

[48] As noted in chapter 3, for example, to prevail on a common-law claim for wrongful use of civil proceedings, a plaintiff must establish that the defendant initiated, continued, or procured (ultimately unsuccessful) civil proceedings "without probable cause, and primarily for a purpose other than that of securing the proper adjudication of the claim in which the proceedings are based"—a standard that, if not identical with the very-difficult-to-satisfy *Noerr-Pennington* standard as articulated by the U.S. Supreme Court in *PREI*, bears more than a passing resemblance to it. *See supra* ch. 3 n.34. In the rare case in which such a claim succeeds, damages can include not only actual pecuniary losses but also, where appropriate, damages for harm to reputation and for emotional distress, and punitive damages. *See* RESTATEMENT (SECOND) OF TORTS § 681 & cmt. a (Am. L. Inst. 1977).

[49] *See supra* ch. 2 note 52 and accompanying text.

been rendered and executed;[50] but it also undermines the policies that generally favor the finality of judgments, specifically the reliance interests of the prevailing party (and, possibly, innocent third parties), which one would expect to increase over time.[51] To be sure, these policies are not so absolute that they necessarily preclude the reopening of a judgment obtained by fraud, or require compliance with an injunction forbidding the use of what later turns to have been an invalid patent.[52] But it is not surprising to see that, in countries in which an accused infringer is afforded the opportunity of asserting invalidity as a defense or counterclaim, the accused is not entitled to compensation for the effects of an adverse judgment simply because some other party, in some subsequent proceeding, succeeds where the first party failed.[53] (Similarly, although a licensee who has paid royalties for the use of what later turns out to be an invalid patent will in many countries no longer be obligated to continue paying them post-invalidation, it is generally not entitled to recover back the royalties already paid.[54] This rule makes sense not only because it protects reliance interests, but also because one would assume the negotiated royalty to have reflected the parties' perceptions of the risk of subsequent invalidity and noninfringement; and presumably, the parties could have agreed ex ante to the return of royalties in the event of invalidation, if they wished to depart from the default rule.[55]) Indeed, even in Japan and China, which like Germany have bifurcated systems, the adjudicated infringer is not entitled to recover back the damages it paid or to recover damages for its own losses (though in Japan and, at least under some circumstances in China, the defendant can raise invalidity as a defense, subject to the qualification that a finding of invalidity applies only *inter partes*).[56] Arguably the first-best solution would be to eliminate bifurcation and, therefore, either the perceived need for ex post reimbursement,

[50] *See id.* notes 50–51 and accompanying text (noting, however, that recent legislation is intended to reduce the "injunction gap"). It is also possible to obtain a stay of enforcement pending resolution of an invalidation proceeding, though traditionally German courts have been reluctant to grant such stays. *See* Cotter, *supra* note 5, at 225 n.45.

[51] *See, e.g.*, Restatement (Second) of Judgments, § 74 cmt. c (Am. L. Inst.1982).

[52] *See, e.g.*, Flexiteek Ams., Inc. v. PlasTEAK, Inc., No. 08-60996-CIV-COHN/SELTZER, 2012 WL 5364247, at *2 (S.D. Fla. Oct. 31, 2012).

[53] *See supra* ch. 2 notes 47–48 and accompanying text.

[54] *See id.* note 48.

[55] *See* Thomas F. Cotter, *Should Licensees Have a Right to Recover Royalties Paid on a Patent That Is Later Found to Be Invalid or Not Infringed?*, Comparative Patent Remedies Blog, Feb. 11, 2015, http://comparativepatentremedies.blogspot.com/2015/02/should-licensees-have-right-to-recover.html. The Coase Theorem, of course, tells us that the choice of default rule is irrelevant if transaction costs and other bargaining obstacles are zero. *See* Ronald H. Coase, *The Problem of Social Cost*, 3 J.L. & Econ. 1 (1960). Nonetheless, I suspect it would be more difficult to move away from a default rule under which the licensee is presumptively entitled to reimbursement, if doing so would reveal the patent owner's private beliefs about the probability of validity and infringement.

[56] *See supra* ch. 2 notes 39–41 and accompanying text.

or the risk of injustice to defendants who are unable to invalidate the patents they stand accused of infringing prior to the judgment of infringement being rendered and carried out. (Note too that, in bifurcated systems, this injustice extends not only to the adjudicated infringer, but also to third parties and to consumers who are negatively affected by the infringement judgment and any resulting remedies.)[57]

On the other hand, for cases in which courts enter provisional measures (preliminary injunctions) against the manufacture, use, or sale of patents that

[57] Consider, however, the following variation on the topic discussed in the paragraph above: the patent owner, in good faith, obtains a judgment of infringement in a court of first instance, and while the appeal is pending enforces its judgment by excluding the defendant/appellant from competing against it. The appellate court subsequently issues a final nonappealable judgment of noninfringement and/or invalidity. Should the excluded defendant—or even, as alluded to in the text above, third party insurers and consumers—be eligible to recover compensation, perhaps by way of analogy to the compensation some courts require patentees to pay when a preliminary injunction is vacated (for discussion of which, see infra notes 61–125 and accompanying text)? Should the law go even further, by requiring the patent owner to disgorge the profit it earned by enforcing the invalid or noninfringing patent while the appeal was pending?

To my knowledge, courts have not been receptive to the idea that, under such circumstances, a patentee must provide compensation, or disgorge its interim profits, to third parties. *See* Menzis Zorgversekeraar N.V. v. AstraZeneca B.V., Case No. 22/01071, ECLI:NL:HR:2023:1513 (S. Ct. 2023) (Neth.) (holding that plaintiff health insurer could not recover for losses suffered, absent culpable behavior by the patentee); Low v. Pfizer Canada, Inc., [2015] BCCA 506 (Can.) (holding that a class of consumers is not entitled to recover for unjust enrichment or tortious interference with economic relations, where a drug company allegedly retained a monopoly prior to the eventual invalidation of its patent); *see also* Apotex Inc. v. Eli Lilly & Co., [2015] ONCA 305 (Can.) (holding that, although the plaintiff generic drug company was entitled to recover compensatory damages under a special provision of Canadian law applicable to drug patent disputes (and discussed *infra* note 72), it is not entitled *in addition* to disgorgement of the patentee's monopoly profit "over and above what [the generic firm] would have earned from sales of the generic drug at lower prices," because the generic firm itself was not deprived of that additional profit); SmithKline Beecham plc v. Apotex Europe Ltd., [2006] EWCA Civ 658 (Eng.). In some countries, however, the defendant may be afforded some form of compensation if the injunction is reversed on appeal. For brief discussion of German practice, for example, *see* Stefan Richter, Tobias J. Hessel & Thomas Misgaiski, Clifford Chance, *Enforcement security before German courts and the Unified Patent Court in comparison*, JUVE Patent, May 2, 2025 (discussing the German courts' practice under article 709(1) of the German Code of Civil Procedure of requiring the prevailing the plaintiff to provide security pending appeal from a first-instance judgment, and the corresponding but more limited practice under the UPCA). Similarly, in Japan, judgments may be stayed pending appeal, but when judges permit provisional execution and the judgment is reversed, under article 260 of the Civil Procedure Act "the plaintiff must compensate the defendant for any damages suffered," and "[c]ourts and most scholars consider this compensation to be a strict liability." Email from Professor Masabumi Suzuki, Waseda University, to Thomas F. Cotter, June 6, 2024 (on file with author). Israeli courts may award restitution under an unjust enrichment theory. *See* Palimport Ltd. v. Ciba-Geigy Ltd., P.D. 29(1) 597 (1975) (discussed in, *inter alia*, *SmithKline Beecham*, *supra*, and Daniel Friedmann, *Restitution of Benefits Obtained Through the Appropriation of Property or the Commission of a Wrong*, 80 Colum. L. Rev. 504, 537–38 (1980) (arguing that the absence of a tort on the part of the patentee "does not justify allowing retention of gains made at the expense of the party that eventually won")). (My understanding of U.S. practice, in contrast, is that the defendant would not be entitled to compensation absent a bond, and that a bond securing a permanent injunction would be uncommon.) My own view is that compensation of some sort may be appropriate, though I would be inclined to counsel against conferring standing on third parties or consumers, or requiring the disgorgement of the patentee's entire interim profit (assuming, reasonably, that it exceeds the defendant's interim loss), both of which expansions might risk overdeterring the legitimate exercise of valid rights. I thank Christopher Heath for stimulating discussion of this issue.

subsequently are determined to be invalid or not infringed, most countries offer some measure of recovery for the interim losses the defendant suffers. The TRIPS Agreement addresses the topic in two articles. The first is article 48(1), which is included in the section on civil and administrative procedures and remedies. It states that

> The judicial authorities shall have the authority to order a party at whose request measures were taken and who has abused enforcement procedures to provide to a party wrongfully enjoined or restrained adequate compensation for the injury suffered because of such abuse. The judicial authorities shall also have the authority to order the applicant to pay the defendant expenses, which may include appropriate attorney's fees.[58]

Second, under the section heading "Provisional Measures," article 50(3) requires WTO members to confer authority upon courts to "order the applicant to provide a security or equivalent assurance sufficient to protect the defendant and to prevent abuse,"[59] and article 50(7) states that:

> Where the provisional measures are revoked or where they lapse due to any act or omission by the applicant, or where it is subsequently found that there has been no infringement or threat of infringement of an intellectual property right, the judicial authorities shall have the authority to order the applicant, upon request of the defendant, to provide the defendant appropriate compensation for any injury caused by these measures.[60]

Consistent with these provisions, WTO member states authorize some form of compensation for wrongly granted preliminary injunctions, although the specifics can vary considerably. In the U.K., for example, courts require a party seeking a preliminary injunction to execute a "cross-undertaking"—a legally enforceable promise that it will compensate the defendant for losses suffered

[58] TRIPS, *supra* note 14, art. 48(1). As noted previously, moreover, article 8(2) states that "[a]ppropriate measures, provided that they are consistent with the provisions of this Agreement, may be needed to prevent the abuse of intellectual property rights by right holders or the resort to practices which unreasonably restrain trade or adversely affect the international transfer of technology." *See also* Gervais, *supra* note 14, at 592 (stating that "abuse need not necessarily imply demonstrable bad faith, but a serious departure from reasonable use of legal proceedings"; and that "WTO Members may provide compensation in other cases," but that "this should not become a deterrent to use courts in bona fide disputes").

[59] TRIPS, *supra* note 14, art. 50(3).

[60] *Id.* art. 50(7); *see also* Gervais, *supra* note 14, at 608–09 (suggesting that the term "appropriate compensation," as distinct from "adequate compensation," may imply a case-by-case analysis).

as a result of a preliminary injunction that subsequently is discharged.[61] In an oft-cited opinion in *Hoffmann-La Roche & Co. AG v. Secretary of State*,[62] Lord Diplock observed that this practice had become standard by the late nineteenth century, and is intended to mitigate the risk facing a defendant who may turn out to have been wrongly enjoined on the basis of the incomplete information available at the beginning of the case.[63] Moreover, although "[t]he undertaking is not given to the defendant but to the court itself," and the court "retains a discretion not to enforce the undertaking if it considers that the conduct of the defendant in relation to the obtaining or continuing of the injunction or the enforcement of the undertaking makes it inequitable to do so," the standard assessment of compensation "is made upon the same basis as that upon which damages for breach of contract would be assessed if the undertaking had been a contract between the plaintiff and the defendant that the plaintiff would not prevent the defendant from doing that which he was restrained from doing by the terms of the injunction."[64] Subsequent decisions have clarified, however, that because "the jurisdiction to award compensation on a cross-undertaking is equitable and is not contractual . . . it requires a degree of flexibility to ensure that the inquiry claimant receives the amount, and only the amount, for which it 'should be compensated.' "[65] That said, the compensation that would be "just and equitable, or fair and reasonable, in all the circumstances" typically will be that which would have been foreseeable to the moving party "from circumstances known to him at the time."[66] In the context of patent litigation specifically, compensation typically will consist of lost profits on sales the defendant would have made had it not been temporarily excluded from the U.K. market,[67] but also may include "loss of business reputation or lost opportunity to extend into the market."[68] In addition, English courts may require the movant to undertake to compensate third parties who

[61] Civ. Proc. Rule 25.9(3)(a) (U.K.) (stating that, subject to an exception not relevant here, "unless the court orders otherwise, an order for an interim injunction must contain . . . an undertaking by the applicant to the court to pay any damages which the respondent sustains and which the court considers the applicant should pay"); Rennie-Smith, *supra* note 9, at 93. The court also may require the plaintiff to post a bond, to ensure that it will be able to pay the damages if needed.

[62] [1975] AC 295 (H.L.) (U.K.).

[63] *See id.* at 360–61.

[64] *Id.* at 361.

[65] Dr. Reddy's Labs. (UK) Ltd. v. Warner-Lambert Co. LLC, [2023] EWCA Civ. 73 [88] (Eng.) (citing Abbey Forwarding Ltd. v. Hone (No.3) [2014] EWCA Civ. 711, [2015] Ch. 309 (Eng.)).

[66] *Id.* [89]–[90] (citing *Abbey Forwarding* quoting *Air Express Ltd. v. Ansett Transport Indus. (Operations) Proprietary Ltd.* (1979) 146 CLR 249 (High Ct.) (Austl.)).

[67] *See, e.g.*, Astrazeneca AB v. KRKA, d.d. Novo Mesto, [2014] EWHC 84 (Pat.) (Eng.).

[68] Rennie-Smith, *supra* note 9, at 93.

could be negatively affected by the injunction—such as, in pharmaceutical cases, the National Health Service.[69] If a cross-undertaking for the benefit of third parties is not made, however, any resulting losses those third parties suffer are likely to remain uncompensated.[70]

The system works largely the same way in other common law countries, including Australia,[71] Canada,[72] and Ireland,[73] but not in the United States. In the U.S., the Federal Rules of Civil Procedure authorize courts to award preliminary relief only if the moving party provides "security in an amount that the court considers proper to pay the costs and damages sustained by any party found to have been wrongfully enjoined or restrained,"[74] but in practice

[69] Civ. Proc. Rule 25.9(5) (U.K.) (stating that, subject to an exception not relevant here, "when the court makes an order for an interim injunction, it must consider whether to require an undertaking by the applicant to pay any damages sustained by a person other than the respondent, including another party to the proceedings or any other person who may suffer loss as a consequence of the order"); 2025 Patent Courts Guide ¶ 10.1 (stating that "where a party seeks an interim injunction which would affect dealings in a pharmaceutical product or medical device purchased by the National Health Service ('NHS'), the Court will consider whether the applicant should give such an undertaking in favour of the NHS. The applicant must notify the Department of Health by email . . . of (i) the application when it is made and (ii) any order made following the application as soon as practicable").

[70] *See* Sec'y of State for Health v. Servier Labs. Ltd, [2021] UKSC 24 (rejecting application of the "unlawful means" tort to the NHS' claim that the defendants had caused the NHS to suffer economic harm by defrauding the EPO into issuing a patent that later was found to be invalid, on the ground that "liability for unlawful means does not arise unless the defendant's conduct affected the third party's freedom to deal with the plaintiff," and noting the risk that the tort otherwise would result in virtually unlimited liability to persons who suffer economic loss caused by the conduct targeting a third party).

[71] *See* Fed. Ct. Australia, Usual Undertaking as to Damages Practice Note (GPN-UNDR) (Oct. 25, 2016).

[72] *See* R. Civ. P. 40.03 (Can.) ("On a motion for an interlocutory injunction or mandatory order, the moving party shall, unless the court orders otherwise, undertake to abide by any order concerning damages that the court may make if it ultimately appears that the granting of the order has caused damage to the responding party for which the moving party ought to compensate the responding party"); United States v. Yemec, 2013 ONSC 50 [13]–[19] (Can.). In addition, under Canada's Regulations Respecting a Notice of Compliance Pertaining to Patented Medicines, SOR/93-133 (the "PM(NOC) Regulations"), once a firm that intends to market a generic version of a patented drug serves a Notice of Allegation (NOA) on the patent owner, alleging that the owner's patent is invalid or would not be infringed by the generic equivalent, the patent owner obtains an automatic stay against the marketing of the generic drug if the owner files suit within 45 days. If the defendant succeeds in proving that the patented drug is invalid or would not be infringed, the defendant is entitled to so-called section 8 damages to compensate it for the profit it would have earned during the period of exclusion. For an overview, *see* BLAKE'S GUIDE TO LITIGATION AND DISPUTES RESOLUTION IN CANADA, SECTION X: PM(NOC) PROCEEDINGS (July 2024). For discussion of the case law, including the section 8 case law, *see* BRUCE STRATTON, ANNOTATED PATENT ACT, App. J (Dec. 2024). By contrast, under the somewhat analogous U.S. Hatch-Waxman Act, which is discussed in the following chapter, the generic firm is not entitled to damages for the period of time the automatic stay is in place.

[73] Cf. Bristol Myers Squibb Holdings Ireland Unltd. v. Norton (Waterford) Ltd. t/a Teva Pharms. Ireland, [2024] IECA 49, [17]–[68], [106]–[111] (Ire.) (comparing Irish and English law on cross-undertakings, and concluding that on at least one point—the inclusion of third-party losses within the scope of the undertaking—Irish law takes a more conservative approach).

[74] Fed. R. Civ. P. 65(c). This subsection includes one exception, that "The United States, its officers, and its agencies are not required to give security." *Id.*

the amount of the bond is believed often to be undercompensatory, for a variety of reasons;[75] and, importantly, the damages payable to the wrongly enjoined defendant are almost always capped by the amount of the bond.[76] Moreover, although it is theoretically possible for a U.S. (or, for that matter, other common-law) court to order restitution of the plaintiff's benefit instead, this is rare, because doctrinally restitution is limited to restitution in kind or money had and received.[77] Thus, if the plaintiff's gains exceed the defendant's losses—as will normally be the case if the patent enables the exercise of monopoly power, and competition from the defendant would create a duopoly[78]—the plaintiff may be better off for having obtained the preliminary injunction, even if it later has to compensate the defendant for (some portion of) the latter's losses.

The civil law countries, for their part, are divided, with some holding the moving party liable to the defendant only if that party is at fault (e.g., if the

[75] *See* Ofer Grosskopf & Barak Medina, *Remedies for Wrongfully-Issued Preliminary Injunctions: The Case for Disgorgement of Profits*, 32 Seattle U. L. Rev. 903, 907–09 (2009) (noting that, under longstanding practice, U.S. courts "consider the equities of the case before imposing liability upon the bond," and thus "retain their discretionary power to deny full, or even any, recovery on the bond"; and that "[t]he court sets the bond at an early stage . . . when the defendant's possible costs and harms are often underestimated"). The defendant can request that the amount of the bond be increased, however, during the pendency of litigation. *See, e.g.*, Int'l Game Tech. v. WMS Gaming, Inc., 217 F.3d 850 (Fed. Cir. 1999); Nintendo of Am. Inc. v. Lewis Galoob Toys, Inc., 16 F.3d 1032 (9th Cir. 1994). Outright denial of recovery on the bond appears to be rare, and the majority of federal circuits apply a rebuttable presumption that the defendant is entitled to recover its provable damages up to the amount of the bond. *See* Nat'l Collegiate Athletic Ass'n v. Governor of New Jersey, 939 F.3d 597, 606–09 (3d Cir. 2019) (reviewing cases). Though not common, awards of damages in excess in the bond may be possible, where the plaintiff has engaged in bad faith or fraud. *See, e.g.*, AstraZeneca LP v. Breath Ltd., 542 Fed. Appx. 971, 984 (Fed. Cir. 2013), *as amended on reh'g* (Dec. 12, 2013); Nat'l Collegiate Athletic Ass'n v. Murphy, Civ. Action No. 14-06450 (FLW), 2020 WL 7074398, at *6 & n.11 (D.N.J. Dec. 3, 2020). Finally, there is relatively little case law guidance on how to set the amount of the bond; for a rare example, see Sanofi-Synthelabo v. Apotex, Inc., 470 F.3d 1368, 1384–85 (Fed. Cir. 2006).

[76] *See* Grosskopf & Medina, *supra* note 75, at 908–09 & n.25 (citing W.R. Grace & Co. v. Local Union 759, 461 U.S. 757, 770 n.14 (1983)).

[77] *See id.* at 909–14 (noting U.S., U.K., and Australian case law); *see also* Sandoz AG v. Bayer Intellectual Property GmbH, [2025] EWHC 2201 (Pat.) (Eng.) (rejecting the claimants' request for the disgorgement of the profits the patentee earned prior to the lifting of a preliminary injunction). An exception, according to Grosskopf and Medina, is Israel, which they describe as "allow[ing] an expansive use of the restitutionary remedy in this context." Grosskopf & Medina, *supra* note 75, at 911 (citing the *Palimport* decision noted *supra* note 57); *see also* Uri Y. Haconen, *Evergreening at Risk*, 33 Harv. J.L. & Tech. 479, 550–55 (2020) (advocating this approach).

[78] *See* Steven C. Salop, *Potential Competition and Antitrust Analysis: Monopoly Profits Exceed Duopoly Profits*, Org. Econ. Coop. & Dev. 15 (June 10, 2021), https://one.oecd.org/document/DAF/COMP/WD(2021)37/en/pdf (stating that "monopoly profits typically exceed the total market profits earned by the dominant firm and the entrant combined in the duopoly market that occurs if there is successful entry"); Marco Stieff & Anja Geller, *Ersatzansprüche bei ungerechtfertigen einstweiligen Verfügungen im Pharmabereich: Ansprüche des Antragsgegners under geschädigte Dritter*, 2023 GRUR 931 (noting that the patentee's profits often exceed the generic defendant's profits "by a wide margin"). Most patents do not enable the exercise of monopoly power, but some—particularly those in the pharmaceutical sector—do.

moving party acted in bad faith in seeking the injunction), and others holding the movant strictly liable for interim harm suffered by the defendant. In China, the Supreme People's Court recently adopted guidelines that effectively endorse a strict liability approach.[79] Somewhat similarly, in Japan when an order granting a preliminary injunction is reversed, the patentee "is presumed to have been negligent about the false allegation in her filing for the preliminary injunction,"[80] and therefore liable in tort under article 709 of the Civil Code.[81] Within the E.U., some member states traditionally have applied a strict liability approach, while others require a showing of fault.[82] IPRED article 9(7) simply mirrors TRIPS article 50(7), stating that where "provisional measures are revoked or where they lapse due to any act or omission by the applicant, or where it is subsequently found that there has been no infringement or threat of infringement of an intellectual property right, the judicial authorities shall have the authority to order the applicant, upon request of the defendant, to provide the defendant appropriate compensation for any

[79] *See* Provisions of The Supreme People's Court on Several Issues Concerning the Application of Laws in Adjudication of Action Preservation Cases Involving IP Disputes, art. 16 (Jan. 1, 2019) [hereinafter PI Provisions], *English language translation available at* https://www.lindapatent.com/en/law_patent/803.html (characterizing as "defective" under article 105 (now article 108) of the Civil Procedure Law applications with respect to which the applicant waits more than thirty days to file suit, the IP is invalid, or the IP is not infringed); China Civil Procedure Law art. 108, *English language translation available in* Yang Li, *China*, *in* PRELIMINARY INJUNCTIONS: WHAT APPROACH TO LIABILITY IS TAKEN ACROSS THE GLOBE? 13 (Bird & Bird LLP, Apr. 2024) [hereinafter PRELIMINARY INJUNCTIONS] (stating that, if the application "is erroneous, the applicant shall compensate the respondent for losses caused by the preservation measure"). For discussion, *see* Hui Zhang, *China: Comments on the New Rules on Preliminary Injunction and Representative Precedents*, KLUWER PATENT BLOG, Feb. 19, 2019, https://patentblog.kluweriplaw.com/2019/02/19/china-comments-on-the-new-rules-on-preliminary-injunction-and-representative-precedents/ (stating that "Article 16 indicates that . . . strict liability shall be applied in determining whether a PI is wrongly issued, regardless of whether the moving party has subjective fault or not"). To obtain a preliminary injunction, the applicant normally must post a bond. *See* PI Provisions, *supra*, art. 11 (stating further that the amount "shall be equivalent to the possible loss to be suffered by the respondent due to the act preservation measures, including the reasonable loss of sale proceeds and custody expenses of the products involved in order to stop the infringement," and that "where the possible loss to be suffered by the respondent may exceed the amount of the applicant's guarantee, the people's court may order the applicant to add a corresponding amount of guarantees and may decide to cancel or partially cancel the preservation measures provided that the applicant refuses to add to the guarantee").

[80] Masabumi Suzuki & Yoshiyuki Tamura, *Patent Enforcement in Japan*, 3 ZGE/IPJ 435, 469–70 (2011) (citing Judgment of Dec. 24, 1968, 22 Minshū 3428 (S. Ct.) (Japan)).

[81] *See, e.g., id.*; Makoto Hattori, *Case No. 48, Interim Procedures and Protective Orders*, *in* JAPANESE PATENT LAW: CASES AND COMMENTS 524–25 (Christopher Heath & Atsuhiro Furuta eds. 2019). I understand, however, that "in practice, there are many cases in which the plaintiff's negligence and liability were denied"; on the other hand, as noted above, when a judgment is provisionally executed pending appeal and then reversed, the plaintiff is strictly liable to the defendant for any damages suffered. *See* Suzuki, *supra* note 57. On the bonding requirement under Japanese law, *see* COTTER, *supra* note 5, at 304 n.73 (citing sources); Hattori, *supra*, at 521–22.

[82] Those opting for a strict liability approach include Denmark, Finland, France, Germany, and Sweden. Those applying a fault-based approach include Belgium and Italy. The Hungarian practice at issue in the CJEU decision noted in the text above has since been amended, *see infra* note 94.

injury caused by those measures."[83] The UPCA includes substantively identical language.[84]

Since 2019, the CJEU has issued two (arguably inconsistent) decisions interpreting IPRED article 9(7). Both cases involved generic drug manufacturers who launched at risk and, as a result, were preliminarily enjoined on the basis of rights later determined to be invalid. The first was *Bayer Pharma AG v. Richter Gedeon Vegyészeti Gyár Nyrt.*[85] In 2002, Bayer filed with the Hungarian National Intellectual Property Office an application for a patent relating to a contraceptive ingredient; the application was published shortly thereafter but not granted until 2010.[86] A few months before the patent issued, Richter began marketing a contraceptive product in Hungary, while another firm, Exeltis, entered the Hungarian market the same month the patent issued.[87] Shortly after issuance, Richter initiated an action for a declaratory judgment of noninfringement.[88] The following day, Bayer applied for a preliminary injunction against Richter and Exeltis, which however was denied for lack of a plausible claim of infringement.[89] Richter and Exeltis then commenced an invalidation action in the Hungarian Intellectual Property Office, during the pendency of which Bayer moved again for a preliminary injunction, which this time was successful.[90] Bayer then initiated infringement actions which, however, were stayed pending resolution of the invalidation action (Hungary, like Germany, having a bifurcated system).[91] An appellate court then vacated the

[83] IPRED, *supra* note 6, art. 9(7); *see also id.* art. 9(6) (stating that "judicial authorities may make . . . provisional measures . . . subject to the lodging by the applicant of adequate security or an equivalent assurance intended to ensure compensation for any prejudice suffered by the defendant as provided for in paragraph 7"); *id.* recital 22 (stating that "[i]t is . . . essential to provide for provisional measures for the immediate termination of infringements, without awaiting a decision on the substance of the case, while observing the rights of the defence, ensuring the proportionality of the provisional measures as appropriate to the characteristics of the case in question and providing the guarantees needed to cover the costs and the injury caused to the defendant by an unjustified request. Such measures are particularly justified where any delay would cause irreparable harm to the holder of an intellectual property right").

[84] *See* UPCA, *supra* note 17, art. 60(9) (stating that "Where the measures to preserve evidence are revoked, or where they lapse due to any act or omission by the applicant, or where it is subsequently found that there has been no infringement or threat of infringement of the patent, the Court may order the applicant, at the defendant's request, to provide the defendant with appropriate compensation for any damage suffered as a result of those measures"); *id.* art. 60(7) ("The measures to preserve evidence may be subject to the lodging by the applicant of adequate security or an equivalent assurance intended to ensure compensation for any prejudice suffered by the defendant as provided for in paragraph 9"); *id.* art. 62(5) (stating that "[a]rticle 60(5) to 60(9) shall apply by analogy to" preliminary injunctions).

[85] Case C-688/17, ECLI:EU:C:2019:722 (CJEU 2019).

[86] *See id.* at ¶¶ 15, 17.

[87] *See id.* at ¶ 16.

[88] *See id.* at ¶ 18.

[89] *See id.* at ¶ 19.

[90] *See id.* at ¶¶ 20–21.

[91] *See id.* at ¶ 22.

preliminary injunction on procedural grounds and remanded the matter back to the trial court, which denied Bayer's renewed motion for a preliminary injunction in view of "the advanced stage of the proceedings for a declaration for invalidity . . . and for revocation . . . ."[92] The patent in suit was thereafter declared invalid in its entirety and the infringement action dismissed, after which Richter and Exeltis requested compensation for their interim losses.[93] Bayer opposed these claims, arguing that Richter and Exeltis "themselves caused the losses they claim to have suffered by having intentionally and unlawfully placed the products in question on the market," such that under Hungary's Civil Code, "there is . . . no justification for their claim for compensation for these losses."[94] The trial court—apparently sensing that Bayer had the better of the argument as a matter of domestic Hungarian law[95]—then referred two questions to the CJEU, which the latter body summarized as whether IPRED article 9(7), "and in particular [its] concept of 'appropriate compensation' . . . must be interpreted as precluding national legislation which provides that a party shall not be compensated for losses which he has suffered due to his not having acted as may generally be expected in order to avoid or mitigate his loss and which, in circumstances such as those in the main proceedings, results in the court not making an order for provisional measures against the applicant obliging him to provide compensation for losses caused by those measures even though the patent on the basis of which these were requested and granted has subsequently been found to be invalid."[96]

The CJEU held that article 9(7) does not preclude national legislation that denies compensation under the stated conditions.[97] In reaching this

[92] *See id.* at ¶¶ 23–24.

[93] *See id.* at ¶¶ 25–30.

[94] *Id.* at ¶ 31. The Civil Code provision at issue stated that "[t]he injured party is under an obligation to act as would generally be expected in the circumstances in question in order to avoid or to mitigate the loss. A party shall not be compensated for loss resulting from the injured party's failure to comply with that obligation." *Id.* ¶ 14. It has since been superseded by Hungarian Civil Code article 6:525, which states that "[t]he injured party has a duty to prevent, repair and remedy damage" (machine translation). *See* Agnieszka Sztoldman, *Compensation for a Wrongful Enforcement of a Preliminary Injunction under the Enforcement Directive (2004/48/EC)*, 42 EIPR 721, 725–26 (2020). According to one source, moreover, subsequent to the *Bayer* decision Hungary amended its law to provide for strict liability in the event a preliminary injunction issues on what later turns out to be an invalid patent. *See* Bálint Halász, *Hungary, in* Preliminary Injunctions, *supra* note 79, at 6.

[95] *See id.* ¶ 57 ("It is apparent from the order for reference and the questions in it that were put to the Court of Justice that, in those circumstances, the national legislation at issue in the main proceedings would not allow a court to order the applicant to provide compensation for the losses caused to the defendant by those provisional measures which had been set aside.").

[96] *Id.* ¶ 34.

[97] *See id.* (operational portion), stating that article 9(7) must be interpreted as not precluding national legislation which provides that a party shall not be compensated for losses which he has suffered due to his not having acted as may generally be expected in order to avoid or mitigate his loss and which, in circumstances such as those in the main proceedings, results in the court not making an order for provisional measures against the applicant obliging him to provide compensation for losses caused by those measures even though the patent on the basis of which those had been requested and granted has

conclusion, the Court stated, first, that "the concept of 'appropriate compensation' must be regarded as an autonomous concept of EU law which must be given a uniform interpretation throughout the territory of the [E.U.],"[98] citing both the need for uniformity in the application of E.U. law, as well as the risk that permitting diverse interpretations of the concept might compromise IPRED's stated "objective of equivalence and homogeneity in the high level of protection of intellectual property . . . ."[99] Second, the Court stated that the fact that the conditions specified in article 9(7) are satisfied does not necessarily "mean that the competent national courts will automatically and in any event be obliged to order the applicant to provide compensation for any losses suffered by the defendant as a result of those measures."[100] Rather, "a finding that an application for provisional measures is unjustified presupposes, primarily, that there is no risk that irreparable harm may be caused to the holder of an intellectual property right in the event of delay in the adoption of the measures sought by him";[101] and the defendants' marketing of products despite the existence of a potentially "hindering" patent or patent application "may, prima facie, be regarded as objectively indicative of the existence of a risk, for the holder of that patent, of irreparable harm" such that the application for preliminary relief "cannot be regarded a priori as 'unjustified' for the purposes of [IPRED] Article 9(7) . . . read in the light of recital 22 of that directive."[102] The mere fact that the provisional measures have been repealed therefore "cannot be regarded in itself as a decisive factor in proving the unjustified nature of the application which gave rise to the provisional measures which have been set aside";[103] "[a] different conclusion could have the effect, in circumstances such as those of the main proceedings, of discouraging the holder of the patent in question from availing himself of" provisional measures "and would thus run counter to the directive's objective of ensuring a high level of protection of intellectual property."[104] Finally, the Court reasoned that article 9(7) also must

subsequently been found to be invalid, to the extent that that legislation permits the court to take due account of all the objective circumstances of the case, including the conduct of the parties, in order, inter alia, to determine that the applicant has not abused those measures.

[98] *Id.* ¶ 49.
[99] *See id.* ¶¶ 37–49.
[100] *Id.* ¶ 52.
[101] *Id.* at ¶¶ 62.
[102] *Id.* ¶ 63. As noted above, recital 22 refers to the need to provide "guarantees . . . to cover the costs and the injury caused to the defendant by an unjustified request," and states that provisional "measures are particularly justified where any delay would cause irreparable harm to the holder of an intellectual property right."
[103] *Id.* ¶ 64.
[104] *Id.* ¶ 65.

be read in light of article 3(2)'s requirement that courts provide "safeguards" against the abuse of IP remedies, and thus in deciding whether to award compensation "national courts must determine whether, in a given case, the applicant has not abused those measures and procedures," taking "due account of all the objective circumstances of the case, including the conduct of the parties."[105]

The *Bayer* decision elicited mixed reactions. Supporters expressed the view that the Court's interpretation of article 9(7) was consistent with the intent of the E.U. legislator to limit compensation to cases involving abusive—that is to say, ex ante unjustified—enforcement.[106] Supporters also have argued that the "high level of protection of intellectual property" referenced in the decision and in IPRED is, indeed, socially beneficial, and that patent owners who have acted reasonably (that is, in good faith) ex ante therefore need some assurance that they will not be held responsible for excluding potential competitors based upon an ex post determination of invalidity or noninfringement.[107] Detractors argued, in contrast, that the decision would encourage patent owners to misuse their rights and to impose upon defendants "an excessive preventive obligation" to "clear the way" before launching a possibly infringing product;[108] and described limiting compensation to cases of abuse as "puzzling," insofar as a successful abuse of rights claim under national law would authorize a compensatory remedy in any event.[109] Commentators on both sides of the issue, however, speculated that EU member states that had been applying a strict liability standard might have to amend their laws.

[105] *See id.* ¶¶ 66–70.

[106] *See* Tanguy de Haan, *The CJEU Sides with IP Right Holders: The* Bayer Pharma *Judgment (C-688/17) and the Consequences of the Europeanisation of Provisional and Precautionary Measures Relating to IP Rights*, 42 EIPR 767, 769 (2020); Miquel Montaña, *The CJEU Judgment of 11 January 2024 in* Gilead v. Mylan: *Will it Prompt an Exodus of Patent Owners to the UPC?*, Kluwer Patent Blog, Jan. 15, 2024, https://patentblog.kluweriplaw.com/2024/01/15/the-cjeu-judgment-of-11-january-2024-in-gilead-v-mylan-will-it-prompt-an-exodus-of-patent-owners-to-the-upc/. Montaña further argues that the intent of the EU legislator was for IPRED article 9(7) to implement TRIPS article 50(7), which in his view is subject to the more general article 48(1), which as noted above authorizes compensation for injuries suffered as a result of "abused enforcement procedures." On this reading, *Bayer* correctly limits compensation to cases of abuse, which also presumably would include only those in which the enforcement was unjustified ex ante. *See also* Grosskopf & Medina, *supra* note 75, at 922 n.86 (noting that, from a corrective justice perspective, one might argue that "the harms inflicted by a wrongfully-issued preliminary injunction . . . are the result of the inability of the legal system to quickly decide the case and provide an effective remedy for the protection of rights," and thus "when there is a bona fide controversy about the parties' rights . . . it is far from self-evident that it is the plaintiff who should be liable for the harms inflicted by" the injunction). A corrective justice perspective that rejects liability without fault would seem to be consistent with those portions of the *Bayer* decision that would appear to limit the patent owner's liability to cases in which the owner has abused its rights. Query, though, whether such an approach would be consistent with the utilitarian justifications for patent rights.

[107] *See* de Haan, *supra* note 106, at 770–71.

[108] Sztoldman, *supra* note 94, at 726.

[109] Léon Dijkman, *CJEU Rules that Repeal of Provisional Measure does not Automatically Create Liability for Wrongful Enforcement*, 14 JIPLP 917, 918 (2019).

Nevertheless, five years after *Bayer* the CJEU upheld member states' authority to hold owners strictly liable in *Mylan AB v. Gilead Sciences Finland Oy*.[110] In 2009 Gilead, the owner of a European Patent directed to certain compounds useful in the treatment of viral infections, obtained from the Finnish Patent and Registration Office a corresponding supplementary protection certificate (SPC) covering an antiretroviral medication for the treatment of persons with HIV.[111] Shortly before the patent expired in 2017, Mylan sought marketing authorization for a generic version of the medication, prompting Gilead to file suit for infringement of the SPC later that year.[112] Gilead obtained a preliminary injunction but, as in *Bayer*, the injunction was subsequently revoked and the IP right at issue (here, the SPC) invalidated.[113] Mylan then sought compensation under Finnish law, which typically holds the owner strictly liable under such circumstances.[114] The trial court referred to the CJEU the question of whether such strict liability is compatible with article 9(7).[115] In a decision that surprised many observers, the CJEU answered in the affirmative.[116]

Noting first that article 9(7) itself does not expressly require a showing of fault,[117] the Court then asserted, without reference to the "autonomous concept" language from *Bayer*, that article 9(7) is not intended "to harmonise the rules on compensation for defendants beyond what is required by" the TRIPS Agreement, and that member states have discretion as to the article's specific implementation.[118] For this reason, member states have "leeway to opt, as the case may be, for a strict liability regime or a fault-based liability regime."[119] In so holding, the Court adopted a narrow reading of *Bayer*, stating that that decision held only that "national legislation refusing compensation to a defendant subject to provisional measures where that defendant had not acted as would generally be expected of any person seeking to avoid or mitigate his

110 Case C-473/22, ECLI:EU:C:2024:8 (CJEU 2024).
111 *See id.* ¶ 13.
112 *See id.* ¶¶ 14–16.
113 *See id.* ¶¶ 17–19.
114 *See id.* ¶ 20. According to the referring court, however, the court has some discretion in setting the amount of the compensation based on fault. *See id.* ¶ 23. As discussed in the text above, this discretion may have been crucial to the outcome of the case.
115 *See id.* ¶ 26.
116 *See id.* (operative portion) (holding that article 9(7) "must be interpreted as not precluding national legislation which provides for a mechanism for compensation for any injury caused by a provisional measure . . . based on a system of strict liability of the applicant for those measures, in the context of which the court is entitled to adjust the amount of damages by taking into account the circumstances of the case, including whether the defendant played a part in the occurrence of the injury").
117 *See id.* ¶ 31.
118 *See id.* ¶ 35.
119 *Id.* ¶ 37.

or her loss" was compatible with article 9(7) "only if the court could take into account . . . all the circumstances of the case."[120] The Court further cautioned that, "irrespective of the liability regime adopted," a court must "take into account all the circumstances of the case before it, including the conduct of the parties . . . ."[121] Thus, "[i]n order to determine whether a system of strict liability complies with the requirements of [IPRED] [a]rticle 3 . . . it is necessary to place it in the context of the provisional measures provided for in Article 9 of that directive and to examine whether the system resulting from the combination thereof is equitable and proportionate and whether it does not create a barrier to legitimate trade while remaining dissuasive."[122] Applying this standard to the case before it, the Court noted that Finnish case law permits the court to reduce compensation where the defendant "enabled the injury to occur or failed to take reasonable measures to avoid or mitigate the injury," before concluding that "a strict liability mechanism such as that at issue in the main proceedings would not upset the balance" between rightsholders and defendants by deterring the latter from bringing legal proceedings.[123] The Finnish standard therefore was consistent with the requirement that compensation be equitable, proportional, and dissuasive, and that it not constitute a barrier to legitimate trade.[124]

Mylan therefore would seem to stand for the proposition that either a fault-based or strict liability standard is acceptable under EU law, as long as the standard permits the court to consider the totality of the circumstances, including the fault if any of either party, before either on the one hand denying relief, or on the other setting the "appropriate compensation." One might imagine, for example, that under this framework a court might award less than full compensation (but how much less?) in a case in which the patentee acted in good faith while the defendant launched at risk. Neither decision, however, addresses whether IPRED permits E.U. member state courts to order movants to compensate third parties. This issue was recently noted, but not resolved, in

[120] *Id.* ¶ 38; *see also id.* ¶ 39 (stating that *Bayer* does not stand for the proposition that article 9(7) permits compensation "only in the event of fault on the part of the applicant," but rather that "the Court merely intended to remind the judicial authority that it is for it to assess the particular circumstances of the case before it in order to decide whether the applicant should be ordered to pay the defendant 'appropriate' compensation, that is to say, compensation justified in the light of those circumstances").

[121] *Id.* ¶ 40.

[122] *Id.* ¶ 42.

[123] *Id.* ¶¶ 43, 46 (reiterating, in addition, that Finnish law "makes it possible . . . to adjust the amount of damages and thereby mitigate any deterrent effect for the holder of the intellectual property right"). Regarding the "balance," *see also id.* ¶ 48 (stating that "[t]he fact that the defendant does not have to demonstrate fault committed by the applicant is a counterweight to the fact that that applicant was able to obtain such measures without having to adduce definitive evidence of any infringement").

[124] *See id.* ¶¶ 44–50.

a decision from the Republic of Ireland which, like the U.K., typically requires the moving party to make a cross-undertaking for damages.[125]

To date, there has been relatively little policy analysis of these issues, one of the few exceptions being a 2009 article by Ofer Grosskopf and Barak Medina.[126] The authors start from the premise that, as a policy matter, the goal of the law of preliminary injunctions should be to minimize "the expected irreparable social costs that result from the delay in deciding the case on the merits";[127] and that irreparable harm includes not only the familiar private harms (harms that are difficult to value, such as loss of first-mover advantage or injury to reputation, or that may result from the other party becoming insolvent),[128] but also irreparable *social* harms. Relevant to patent law, when a

[125] *See* Bristol Myers Squibb Holdings Ireland Unltd. v. Norton (Waterford) Ltd. t/a Teva Pharms. Ireland, [2024] IECA 49, [81] (Ire.) (declining to address the question of whether such compensation would be consistent with IPRED article 9(7)). As noted above, however, the court expressed the view that, although Irish law may permit courts to include third parties within the scope of the undertaking, the point is not clearly established; and to the extent it is permissible, Irish law may take a more conservative approach to the practice than do English courts. *See id.* [106]–[111]. Further, although German law may permit a defendant to recover losses suffered by a related company, see Düsseldorf Regional Court, Judgment of Sept. 29, 2022, 2023 GRUR 957 (Ger.), there appears to be no basis for compensating unrelated third parties in France, Germany, or the Netherlands, absent an abuse of right. *See* Synteco SpA v. Laboratoires Negma SAS, Cour de cassation, Judgment of Feb. 10, 2015, PIBD No. 1025, III-260 (Fr.); Marco Stief & Anja Geller, *Ersatzansprüche bei ungerechtfertigten einstweiligen Verfügungen im Pharmabereich: Ansprüche des Antragsgegners und geschädigter Dritter*, 2023 GRUR 931.

[126] Grosskopf & Medina, *supra* note 75.

[127] *Id.* at 920. This is a common, though not universally held, assumption in the law-and-economics literature, often expressed as the Leubsdorf-Posner rule. *See* Am. Hosp. Supply Corp. v. Hosp. Prods., 780 F.2d 589, 593–94 (7th Cir. 1986) (Posner, J.) (stating that a court should "grant the preliminary injunction if but only if P x HP > (1 – P) x HD, or, in words, only if the harm to the plaintiff if the injunction is denied, multiplied by the probability that the denial would be an error (that the plaintiff, in other words, will win at trial), exceeds the harm to the defendant if the injunction is granted, multiplied by the probability that granting the injunction would be an error"); John Leubsdorf, *The Standard for Preliminary Injunctions*, 91 Harv. L. Rev. 525, 542 (1978). For other possibilities, *see, e.g.*, Douglas Lichtman, *Irreparable Benefits*, 116 Yale L.J. 1284, 1287 n.3 (2007) (suggesting that, in principle, the law of preliminary injunctions could serve other goals, such as to "maximally encourage settlement, or . . . clearly signal to the parties the most likely outcome on the merits"—or, citing Richard R.W. Brooks & Warren F. Schwartz, *Legal Uncertainty, Economic Efficiency, and the Preliminary Injunction Doctrine*, 58 Stan. L. Rev. 381 (2005), "to create incentives for defendants to engage in efficient conduct before and during litigation"). Rasmus and Peter Bogetoft also argue that the Leubsdorf-Posner and Brooks-Schwartz rules "focus only on the properties of the parties, i.e. their irreparable harm or their joint surplus," and not on social irreparable harms resulting from loss of innovation or unnecessary loss of consumer surplus, *see* Rasmus Arler Bogetoft & Peter Bogetoft, *Market entrance, patents, and preliminary injunctions: a model of pharmaceutical patent litigation*, 53 Eur. J. L. & Econ. 379, 408 (2022), but Grosskopf, Medina, and Lichtman do take these social harms into account in their applications of Leubsdorf-Posner. Bogetoft and Bogetoft also note that actual U.S. law is probably more restrictive than Leubsdorf-Posner, because the latter would permit some injunctions to issue with less than a 50% probability of success on the merits. *See* Bogetoft & Bogetoft, *supra*, at 406; *see also* Grosskopf & Medina, *supra* note 75, at 923 n.90, 917 n.70. The current U.S. standard phrases the requirements in the conjunctive. *See* Winter v. Natural Resources Defense Council, Inc., 555 U.S. 7, 20 (2008) (stating that "[a] plaintiff seeking a preliminary injunction must establish that he is likely to succeed on the merits, that he is likely to suffer irreparable harm in the absence of preliminary relief, that the balance of equities tips in his favor, and that an injunction is in the public interest").

[128] *See id.* at 916.

preliminary injunction is wrongly granted these irreparable social harms may include the deadweight loss resulting from the patentee's exercise of market power,[129] as well as any harms to third parties that under applicable law are not compensable.[130] When a preliminary injunction is wrongly denied, on the other hand, the irreparable social harm "includes the adverse effects of such a decision on the incentives to invest in research."[131] Their analysis suggests that, in general, the optimal sanction for a wrongly-issued preliminary injunction would be a restitutionary award, by which they mean awarding the defendant the amount the plaintiff gained at the defendant's expense, which they refer to as undeserved wealth transfers.[132] This rule would increase the probability of a correct decision, they claim—meaning, again, one that minimizes "the expected irreparable social costs that result from the delay in deciding the case on the merits"[133]—by eliminating the need to consider, when balancing hardships between the parties,[134] mere wealth transfers from defendant to plaintiff. All of the latter would now be *reparable* harms, leaving the court free to focus on the irreparable harms alone.[135] It also would ensure that defendants be compensated for the resulting undeserved wealth transfers to plaintiffs, though not for additional social harms such as deadweight loss or harms to third parties (unless the third parties are entitled to a restitutionary claim of their own, a matter the authors do not resolve).[136] The authors concede, however, that a rule limiting recovery to wealth transfers would be underdeterrent in cases in which plaintiffs' expected interim profits exceed defendants' interim losses;[137] and as noted above, this would seem to be a fairly common occurrence in patent cases.[138] Grosskopf and Medina therefore acknowledge that there might be other situations in which it would be optimal to require plaintiffs to disgorge their own benefit even if it exceeds the

[129] *See id.* at 920 (noting that "a deadweight-loss suffered by one party is *socially* irreparable even if this party's private loss can be cured by a remedy after trial"; even if the defendant were to be compensated for it, that compensation would "merely reallocate[] the damage but . . . not eliminate it").

[130] *See id.* at 927. They also might include, as with corrective measures such as destruction, irreparable environmental costs. *See* Charlotte J.S. Vrendenbarg, *Towards a Judicial Sustainability Test in Cases Concerning the Enforcement of Intellectual Property Rights*, 2023 GRUR Int. 1125 (2023).

[131] *See* Grosskopf & Medina, *supra* note 75, at 919 (citing Lichtman, *supra* note 127, at 1289).

[132] *See id.* at 925.

[133] *Id.* at 920.

[134] *See* Thomas F. Cotter, Principles of Intellectual Property Law: Remedies 75–85 (2026) (noting that courts generally consider the balance of hardships, among other factors, in deciding whether to grant preliminary injunctions).

[135] *See* Grosskopf & Medina, *supra* note 75, at 923. It is not clear how one would go about quantifying *literally* future irreparable harms, as in the authors' numerical illustrations, though the prevailing test does seem to require courts somehow to balance them.

[136] *See id.* at 927.

[137] *See id.* at 939.

[138] *See supra* note 78 and accompanying text.

defendant's loss, such as where the "errant gain creates a social loss because it might skew the plaintiff's incentives," noting Doug Lichtman's argument that awarding the patentee a mistaken benefit distorts the patent incentive.[139] On the other hand, they also worry that mitigating the risk of underdeterrence might increase the risk of overdeterrence, since courts have discretion to deny preliminary injunctions that strike them as "socially inefficient," but no way of monitoring whether plaintiffs *should* be granted preliminary injunctions they do not request.[140]

A somewhat different take can be found in an article by John Boyce and Aidan Hollis.[141] Boyce and Hollis present a game theoretic model involving two players, an innovator and prospective defendant, under which *both* parties benefit from having a preliminary injunction issue, and the innovator/patentee will be *more* likely to seek preliminary relief when it believes the odds of prevailing at trial are low.[142] The intuitions behind these counterintuitive results derive from the fact, noted above, that the patent owner/monopolist often has more to lose than a defendant/potential duopolist to gain from the defendant's entry. As a result, a patentee who obtains an interim monopoly as a result of a preliminary injunction is better off—even if, after losing at trial, it must compensate the defendant for the latter's forgone duopoly profit—than is a patentee who does not seek preliminary relief but loses at trial, and therefore enjoys only whatever duopoly profit it earned in competition with the defendant during the pretrial stage.[143] In addition, the defendant is better off if it is temporarily enjoined but fully compensated thereafter in the event the patentee loses, than if it competes during the pretrial stage but loses at trial (and therefore incurs liability for the losses it caused the patentee to suffer pretrial).[144] Consumers, however, are worse off if a court enters an unwarranted preliminary injunction, which leads the authors to advocate a rule under which the patentee would be obligated, if it loses at trial, to pay the defendant

[139] Grosskopf & Medina, *supra* note 75, at 927 (citing Lichtman, *supra* note 127, at 1289–90, 1297). Other possible reasons for awarding a higher restitutionary award might be if the defendant is expected to pass on these excess benefits to third parties at whose expense they were derived, or simply to deter weak claims. *See id.*

[140] *See id.* at 934.

[141] John R. Boyce & Aidan Hollis, *Preliminary Injunctions and Damage Rules in Patent Law*, 16 J. ECON. & MGT. STRATEGY 385 (2007).

[142] *See id.* at 391–400.

[143] *See id.* at 387 (stating that "preliminary injunctions create extra profits to be shared between the firms in the industry. The patentee gets monopoly profits less a (possible) payment to the imitator; and the imitator obtains its expected profits without the risk of having to pay damages to the incumbent. The injunction can thus be seen as a court-ordered collusive scheme to charge monopoly prices and share profits").

[144] *See id.* at 397–98.

damages for the defendant's interim losses *and* a fine (presumably payable to the state) equal to the amount of the lost consumer surplus.[145]

The Boyce and Hollis model nevertheless rests on some unrealistic assumptions—among them, that both parties know the likelihood of obtaining an injunction and the likelihood of success at trial,[146] and that all of the losses each party suffers are, in fact, reparable and fully compensable after trial.[147] Regarding this second assumption in particular, the conventional view has long been that some private harms are irreparable in the sense of being either incalculable or uncollectable;[148] and, as we have seen, it is unlikely that defendants are fully compensated for their interim losses in the United States or in countries that apply a fault-based standard. Legislators could address the latter problem by amending the compensation standard, but this would not address the former problem of some private losses remaining, in some meaningful sense, irreparable.[149] On the other hand, the authors' prediction that "preliminary injunctions may be sought to obtain market power ... on patents of questionable merit,"[150] seems consistent with the observation that many cases in which drug companies seek preliminary injunctions involve "secondary" patents that are intended to extend the effective scope of protection of a drug.[151] As noted in chapter 5, such patents make up a disproportionate number of those involved in pay-for-delay settlements, and at least in that context also are significantly more likely to be invalidated or found noninfringing than are primary patents.[152] Perhaps, then, as Boyce and Hollis suggest, the current state of the law invites too much abuse, even within the strict liability nations.

As the above discussion indicates, the optimal standard for rectifying the consequences of preliminary injunctions that prove, ex post, to have been

[145] *See id.* at 400–04. This may not be as difficult to achieve as it sounds, if in any event a court must estimate what the defendant's profit would have been, but for the preliminary injunction. Constructing this but-for market would entail estimating aggregate price and output with and without the injunction, from which one should be able readily to calculate the forgone consumer surplus.

[146] *See id.* at 390–91.

[147] *See id.* at 387, 391.

[148] *Cf.* Lichtman, *supra* note 127, at 1292 (stating that in practice "[m]ost irreparable harms ... are irreparable only in the sense that the harm at issue is difficult for a court to value").

[149] One possible implication of the Boyce & Hollis model, however, might be that if all private harm *is* in principle reparable, society might be better off if defendants' private harms went uncompensated, because this would reduce defendants' incentive in effect to "collude" with plaintiffs for preliminary injunctive relief. *See* Boyce & Hollis, *supra* note 141, at 399, 404 (suggesting that under current law "preliminary injunction hearings may lack the adversarial characteristic one might expect," and describing current law as enabling "a court-directed collusive arrangement"). On the other hand, if all private harm were reparable, it's not clear what the point would be of having any law of preliminary injunctions to begin with.

[150] *See* Boyce & Hollis, *supra* note 141, at 404.

[151] *See* Stief & Geller, *supra* note 125, at 934.

[152] *See infra* ch. 5 n.117.

undeserved is elusive. Even assuming, as above, that the overarching goal of the law of preliminary injunctions should be to minimize the irreparable harm resulting from delays in adjudication, the importance of this goal will depend on how long those delays typically last—a matter that varies from one country to another—and, more fundamentally, on how courts articulate and apply the standards for granting preliminary injunctions.[153] The relief, if any, granted in the event of an ex post wrongful injunction surely is a factor, but only one factor, that affects plaintiffs' decisions to seek such relief in the first place and potential defendants' decisions to launch at risk. Other factors besides these that may enter in to the mix may include how accurately courts establish the amount of the bond or undertaking, particularly if the matter is not likely to be revisited;[154] the extent to which preliminary relief induces the parties to settle[155] or the court to enter final judgment in conformity with its preliminary analysis;[156] the extent, if any, to which the parties are risk-averse;[157] the extent to which courts or agencies, including those that adjudicate validity, are error-prone; and the extent to which the substantive law accurately calibrates which inventions merit patent protection. In regard to these last points, if adjudication is error-prone or the calibration is not optimized, such that *too many* validity challenges are successful, a strict liability rule marginally exacerbates these errors by making patent assertion even more risky than it ought to be.[158]

[153] The rules vary a bit from one jurisdiction to another, *see* COTTER, *supra* note 134—and in theory could vary even more if for example courts took into account "irreparable benefits," *see* Lichtman, *supra* note 127, at 1294–1301, or the variance in the expected outcome, *see* Douglas Lichtman, *Uncertainty and the Standard for Preliminary Relief*, 70 U. CHI. L. REV. 197, 205–10 (2004), though for now these remain only theoretical possibilities.

[154] *See* Lichtman, *supra* note 127, at 211 (noting that "overstating" the bond causes plaintiffs to decline even a correctly offered injunction, and this changes "both the likelihood of an errant result and its expected magnitude"); *but see* Grosskopf & Medina, *supra* note 75, at 907–09 (stating that, in U.S. practice, bonds typically are believed to be undercompensatory).

[155] *See* Jean O. Lanjouw & Josh Lerner, *Tilting the Table? The Use of Preliminary Injunctions*, 44 J.L. & ECON. 573, 577 (2001).

[156] *See* Lichtman, *supra* note 127, at 1295 & n.19; Lichtman, *supra* note 153, at 203–04.

[157] *See* Lichtman, *supra* note 153, at 201 (noting that firms "are typically risk-neutral," but that corporate managers may not always be).

[158] One additional wrinkle is that in some jurisdictions *defendants* may be allowed to post security, or to make interim payments, to avoid being preliminarily enjoined. Courts in India, for example, have allowed defendants in FRAND cases to deposit interim royalties to avoid being prohibited from using the claimed patents pending trial. *See, e.g. Intex Techs. (India) Ltd. v. Telefonaktiebolaget LM Ericsson*, 2023:DHC:2243-DB (Delhi High Ct. Mar. 29, 2023) (India). IPRED requires E.U. member states to make this practice available, *see* IPRED, *supra* note 6, art. 9(1)(a) (stating that member states shall ensure that courts may condition the continuation of an infringement "subject to the lodging of guarantees intended to ensure the compensation of the rightholder"), and the UPCA also authorizes this practice, *see* UPCA, *supra* note 17, art. 62(1) (authorizing the court "to prohibit, on a provisional basis and subject, where appropriate, to a recurring penalty payment, the continuation of the alleged infringement or to make such continuation subject to the lodging of guarantees intended to ensure the compensation of the right holder"). Nevertheless, awarding interim damages in lieu of preliminary relief appear to be uncommon in Europe for now; and some other jurisdictions generally disapprove of it, albeit subject to some possible exceptions. (Article 12 of the Chinese PI Provisions noted above,

All that said, notwithstanding these many sources of uncertainty, it's hard to see how innovation policy is served by allowing patent owners to benefit from errors in granting preliminary relief, even if those errors appeared justified at the time. As Lichtman cogently puts it,

> If the patentee is mistakenly awarded preliminary relief, the patentee is admittedly privately better off. But it would be surprising were society to applaud that error. Patent law is intended to award the patentee a certain payoff. . . . Any deviation from that baseline distorts those incentives and undermines the desired distributional outcome.[159]

Moreover, while a strict liability standard obviously makes patent assertion riskier than it otherwise would be, essentially the same principle is reflected in

for example, states that preliminary injunctions granted by Chinese courts "are generally not cancelled because the respondent provides a guarantee, except with the applicant's consent"); and although there are some isolated examples of U.S. courts deploying the procedure, *see, e.g.*, Flo-Con Sys., Inc. v. Leco Corp., 845 F. Supp. 1576, 1583 (S.D. Ga. 1993) (cited in Michael Meurer, *Controlling Opportunistic and Anti-Competitive Intellectual Property Litigation*, 44 B.C. L. Rev. 509, 528 (2003)), there is no explicit authority for doing so under the Federal Rules of Civil Procedure, *see* Thomas F. Cotter, *Setting the Amount of an Injunction Bond (and a Brief Digression about the Wright Brothers)*, Comparative Patent Remedies Blog, Apr. 18, 2014, http://comparativepatentremedies.blogspot.com/2014/04/setting-amount-of-injunction-bond-and.html. The effect of conditioning interim use on the payment or posting of security would be to render some of the plaintiff's allegedly irreparable harm—such as the risk of the defendant's insolvency, or of a final damages judgment failing to properly account for the time value of money or other advantages accruing to the defendant from delay—reparable. More generally, such practices could allow a defendant who believes the court has erroneously balanced the relative hardships to "repair" some of the plaintiff's allegedly irreparable harm by compensating the plaintiff for harms that otherwise would be, at least as a practical matter, non-compensable under governing law, such as harm to reputation or moral prejudice—though one probably would expect such cases to be rare.

In addition, in some recent cases the Court of Appeals for England and Wales held that an implementer was entitled to a declaration that a willing licensor would enter into an interim global license of FRAND-committed SEPs, pending the Patent Court's determination of the terms of final license. *See* Lenovo Group Ltd. v. Telefonaktiebolaget LM Ericsson (Publ), [2025] EWCA Civ 182 (Eng.); Panasonic Holdings Corp. v. Xiaomi Tech. UK Ltd., [2024] EWCA Civ 1143 (Eng.). The declarations sought in these cases, however, which I return to in chapter 6, were not entered in lieu of preliminary injunctive relief.

[159] Lichtman, *supra* note 127, at 1297; *see also* Thomas F. Cotter, *Antitrust, Intellectual Property, and Dynamic Efficiency: An Essay in Honor of Herbert Hovenkamp*, Concurrences No. 3, 2020, at 8 (arguing, in response to the claim that "[r]equiring pharmaceutical companies to continue marketing superseded drugs so that generic competitors can take many of their customers reduces incentives for innovation," and that preventing drug companies "from operating in a profit-maximizing way may harm innovation and drug development throughout the pharmaceutical industry," that if "[t]aken to its logical conclusion, this reasoning would lead to the untenable conclusion that drug companies should be immune from liability—for anything—since any potential exposure reduces their ability to maximize profits"). Note also that, whatever the merits may be of the argument that the assertion of nonfrivolous but ex ante weak claims sometimes provides courts with an opportunity to modify suboptimal legal rules, *see supra* note 4, that argument is unpersuasive in the context of preliminary injunctions which, by definition, are provisional rulings, typically made on a limited factual record and under abbreviated deadlines.

mandatory fee shifting rules (albeit with the amount of compensation at stake probably being, on average, considerably lower in the latter than in the former context). And as with fee shifting, the strict liability standard as carried out in practice often may be less than fully compensatory, thus reducing some of the risk of overdeterrence. Indeed, as suggested above, perhaps even a strict liability standard does not go far enough, to the extent it leaves patentees with some incentive to seek unwarranted relief and imposes unnecessary losses on consumers and other third parties. That said, requiring patent owners to disgorge their entire profit, or imposing a fine based on lost consumer surplus, simply for having obtained an ex post unwarranted preliminary injunction would be a substantial departure from most courts' existing practice; and whether such far-reaching reforms would have merit, or would generate unforeseeable negative consequences, remains for now anyone's guess.[160] Those countries whose standards at present are undercompensatory, however, whether de jure (e.g.,

[160] That said, the time may be ripe for courts in the United States to consider more robust measures to guard against abuse in one particular type of intellectual property litigation, the so-called "Schedule A" cases. The majority of these involve allegations of trademark or design patent infringement, though some allege violations of copyrights or of utility patents. The typical case involves an owner who files a complaint and a motion for an ex parte temporary restraining order, often under seal, against multiple, often foreign, defendants, who are identified in an accompanying list, often referred to as "Schedule A." The papers allege that the defendants are offering allegedly infringing products for sale online. Over the past decade or so, several U.S. judges have granted these motions, notwithstanding the difficulties (especially in design and utility patent cases) of determining on the basis of ex parte, preliminary evidence that the accused products infringe. The orders are then forwarded to the online platforms on which the defendants are offering merchandise for sale, after which the platforms typically make the accused products, and sometimes all of a defendant's products, unavailable, sometimes for longer than the fourteen days that a temporary restraining order is supposed to last. Judges also have issued asset-freezing orders, sometimes in cases in which such orders are not permitted under U.S. law. *See* Zorro Productions, Inc. v. The Individuals, Corporations, Limited Liability Companies, Partnerships, and Unincorporated Associations Identified on Schedule A Hereto, Case No. 23-cv-5761, 2023 WL 8807254, at *4 (N.D. Ill. Dec. 20, 2023) (noting the unavailability of asset-freeing orders under U.S. law except where the plaintiff is seeking equitable monetary relief, such as the "disgorgement of ill-gotten gains"). Given the cost of litigation, the end result is often that defendants either settle or default. Plaintiffs may voluntarily dismiss their claims against those who do not settle or default, and those parties may be eligible for compensation in the amount of the injunction bond; but they are not automatically awarded their fees, and U.S. courts can be reluctant to award litigation sanctions. *See, e.g.*, Jiangsu Huari Webbing Leather Co., Ltd. v. Joes Identified in Schedule A, No. 1:23-cv-02605 (S.D.N.Y. Jan. 2, 2024) (denying an award of fees and sanctions sought by two defendants, in a case alleging utility patent infringement on the part of 163 defendants, despite (1) the apparent violation of the limitations on party joinder set forth in 35 U.S.C. § 299; (2) the lack of evidence that the two moving defendants' products infringed the patent in suit; and (3) the court's finding that the plaintiff (a) made no effort to contact the defendants in advance; (b) engaged in a strategy of freezing competitors' accounts and then voluntarily dismissing its claims against objecting parties; (c) informed other platforms, not listed in the restraining order, of the order's existence; and (d) falsely claimed that it had provided one of the moving defendants with documents it requested) (cited in Sarah Burstein, *Sanctions & Schedule A*, PATENTLY-O, Jan. 23, 2024, https://patentlyo.com/patent/2024/01/burstein-sanctions-schedule.html). For illuminating discussion of Schedule A cases—and suggestions for reform, including greater use of fee shifting and sanctions—*see* Burstein, *supra*; Sarah Fackrell, *The Counterfeit Sham*, 138 HARV. L. REV. 472, 493–500 (2024); Eric Goldman, *A SAD Scheme of Abusive Intellectual Property Litigation*, 123 COLUM. L. REV. FORUM 183 (2023) (stating, among many other points, that judges in Schedule A cases "routinely undervalue bonds").

Hungary prior to statutory amendment) or de facto (e.g., the United States), might do well to consider experimenting with some version of the British model, which at least promises something approaching full compensation to defendants and even to some third parties, even if it does not address *all* of the negative consequences that may flow from a wrongly granted injunction. Finally, as for those E.U. member states that traditionally have applied a strict liability standard, or that might be motivated to do so post-*Mylan*,[161] it is to be hoped that they do not apply the flexibilities that decision mentions in crafting appropriate compensation so liberally as to allow patentees to profit substantially from judicial error.

Liability Conditioned on Invalidity or Noninfringement Only If Coupled with Other Facts

Unlike costs awarded to the prevailing party in litigation, and claims for compensation for wrongly-issued preliminary injunctions—both of which, as we have seen, are available in some countries as a matter of right—the other claims discussed in chapter 3, including sham litigation antitrust claims,[162] unfair competition claims arising from false assertions of patent infringement, and claims arising under the U.K.'s law of unjustified threats, depend upon the patent claims in suit being not only invalid or not infringed, but also on additional elements. For these other types of claims, in other words, noninfringement or invalidity is a necessary but not sufficient condition for liability to attach.[163] In itself, the existence of these additional requirements is not surprising. Sham litigation antitrust claims, after all, are just a specific type of antitrust claim which, like other antitrust claims, require proof of harm to competition; similarly, unfair competition claims arising from false assertions of infringement may, like other unfair competition claims, require evidence of deceptive intent and special harm to the claimant. In addition, however—as discussed in chapter 3

[161] *See Mylan*, ECLI:EU:C:2024:8, ¶ 40 (stating that "irrespective of the liability regime adopted," a court must "take into account all the circumstances of the case before it, including the conduct of the parties").

[162] For purposes of this analysis, I do not focus on *Walker Process* claims, which I discussed at length in chapter 3.

[163] *Cf.* Herbert Hovenkamp et al., IP and Antitrust: An Analysis of Antitrust Principles Applied to Intellectual Property Law, ch. 11.02 (2023) (stating that "after *PREI* . . . a successful infringement lawsuit cannot, without more, be the basis for an anticompetitive litigation claim," but that "[t]he 'without more' is an important qualifier because even a successful infringement lawsuit could conceivably provide the basis for an anticompetitive litigation claim if the patentee prevailed in its prior infringement suit only because it successfully concealed its fraud against the PTO, which has since been exposed").

and again below—for sham litigation antitrust claims and unfair competition claims, courts also require evidence of the defendant's objective and/or subjective intent or purpose or motivation in filing the infringement action. As we have seen, the impetus behind this additional requirement is the perceived need to avoid both unduly interfering with owners' fundamental rights of access to the courts or petitioning the government for redress, as well as chilling the legitimate, presumably innovation-enhancing, exercise of IP rights.[164] As I have stressed throughout, the weight accorded to intangible considerations such as the right of access to courts may vary from one legal culture to another, and is not a matter on which universal consensus is likely to be attained; and although the question whether, on balance, a regime that is marginally more aggressive in responding to a given type of allegedly wrongful patent assertion advances or impedes innovation is in principle subject to empirical analysis, the difficulty of teasing out causal relationships in the midst of numerous confounding variables presents insuperable obstacles in drawing many firm conclusions.[165] Nonetheless, in this section I will argue that, subject to these limitations, some reforms would be desirable. In particular, I will argue that the current E.U. and (especially) U.S. standards for evaluating whether sham litigation antitrust claims may proceed probably screen out too much anticompetitive conduct; and, *a fortiori*, that unfair competition and other claims based on the owner's threats or other communications concerning allegedly infringing activity also should not require proof of objective baselessness. Consistent with this analysis, the U.K.'s strict liability standard for unjustified threats against secondary infringers makes sense, whereas the U.S. Federal Circuit's extension of the sham litigation standard to unfair competition-type claims does not, at least as a policy matter.

Turning first to antitrust claims, as noted in the preceding chapter, to succeed on a sham litigation antitrust claim a U.S. claimant must first overcome the defendant's *Noerr-Pennington* immunity by proving, by clear and convincing evidence (1) that the defendant's infringement suit was "objectively baseless in the sense that no reasonable litigant could realistically expect success on the merits" (meaning that it lacked probable cause or at least an "objectively 'good faith argument for the extension, modification, or reversal of existing law'");

[164] As the previous section showed, these concerns also sometimes lead countries to place limits on awards of attorneys' fees and on compensation for wrongly-issued injunctions—though typically as a matter of policy rather than of constitutional obligation, and often only by limiting the amount of compensation due or the conditions under which compensation will be awarded, rather than by rejecting liability altogether.

[165] Decisions may sometimes come down to policymakers' underlying values or "priors." For citations to some of the relevant literature making this point, *see* Cotter, *supra* note 159, at 11 n.92.

and (2) that the lawsuit also "conceals 'an attempt to interfere *directly* with the business relationships of a competitor,' . . . through the 'use [of] the governmental *process*—as opposed to the *outcome* of that process—as an anticompetitive weapon.' "[166] If the claimant succeeds in demonstrating these two elements, the defendant loses its immunity and the claimant can then seek to prove that the sham litigation caused or posed a dangerous probability of causing the defendant to acquire or maintain monopoly power.[167] Applying a standard that commentators have described as substantively similar, E.U. courts would find this type of claim actionable as an abuse of dominant position, subject to proof that a dominant undertaking brought an infringement action "which cannot reasonably be considered as an attempt to establish its rights and can therefore only serve to harass the opposite party, and . . . is conceived in the framework of a plan whose goal is to eliminate competition."[168] Not surprisingly, under these formulations successful sham litigation antitrust claims are extremely rare.[169] Perhaps that is how it should be, if sham litigation itself is rare; but if not, then it seems reasonable to conclude that much anticompetitive litigation simply goes unremedied, because of the difficulty of overcoming litigants' immunity from suit.

In theory, the law could be otherwise. If neither jurisdiction recognized a constitutional right to petition the government or fundamental right of access to the courts, the law could be structured such that the filing (or threatened filing) of an ultimately unsuccessful infringement suit that causes anticompetitive harm would be an actionable antitrust violation. The fact that no country (to my knowledge) has adopted such a rule nonetheless is testament to the fact that the right of access to the courts and to petition the government not only is recognized but is accorded substantial, albeit unquantifiable, weight just about everywhere.[170] Even putting those fundamental interests aside, however, a

[166] Professional Real Estate Investors, Inc. v. Columbia Pictures Industries, Inc., 508 U.S. 49, 60–62, 65 (1993) [hereinafter *PREI*].

[167] *See supra* ch. 3 notes 21–28 and accompanying text.

[168] ITT Promedia NV v. Commission of the European Communities, Case T-111/96, ECLI:EU:T:1998:183, ¶ 30 (CJEU 1998).

[169] For discussion of the U.S. case law, *see* HOVENKAMP ET AL., *supra* note 163, § 11.03[B][4]. For a rare example of a (partial) win for the antitrust plaintiff, *see* FTC v. AbbVie Inc., 976 F.3d 327 (3d Cir. 2020) (affirming a judgment that defendants engaged in sham litigation alleging that one generic firm's product infringed under the doctrine of equivalents, but reversing a judgment that they engaged in sham litigation alleging that another firm's product infringed under the doctrine of equivalents).

[170] For an expression of this point of view, *see PREI*, 508 U.S. 67, 69 (Stevens, J., concurring) ("Access to the courts is far too precious a right for us to infer wrongdoing from nothing more than using the judicial process to seek a competitive advantage in a doubtful case"). As noted above, moreover, various legal doctrines aside from the standard of liability (including duty, proximate cause, and limitations on the recovery of speculative damages) further narrow the scope of an actor's responsibility. *See supra* notes 1–3 and accompanying text.

standard that rendered unsuccessful litigants strictly liable for any anticompetitive harm resulting from the unsuccessful assertion of their rights would risk encouraging nuisance litigation ("sham-sham" suits[171])— particularly in the United States, where damages are automatically trebled and consumer class actions can impose additional penalties. Given that a substantial plurality or even majority of patent infringement actions are, in fact, unsuccessful,[172] a strict liability standard (assuming it were constitutionally permissible to implement) would almost surely result in either a dramatic increase in the number of sham litigation claims directed against unsuccessful patent owners, or a substantial reduction in the number of patent infringement actions filed, or both[173]—notwithstanding the difficulty claimants would face in ultimately proving an actionable antitrust violation, were the matter to be litigated all the way through to judgment.[174] In any event, given existing constitutional strictures, adoption of a strict liability standard for sham litigation antitrust actions is not a serious policy proposal; my point is simply that, even in the absence of such strictures, nations probably are right to be cautious about radically opening the doors to sham litigation antitrust suits.

That said, there are reasons to think that the current standards for adjudicating sham litigation are too strict. Among the legal analysts who have expressed concern over underestimating the anticompetitive effects of sham (or "predatory") litigation are two that one would not normally classify as antitrust hawks, Robert Bork and Richard Posner. As initially sketched by Bork in his 1978 book *The Antitrust Paradox*, and elaborated upon by others over the past forty-some years, predatory litigation can be quite a promising strategy for maintaining monopoly power, for several reasons.[175] The first is that, despite

[171] For a time, I thought I was the first to coin this phrase, but I wasn't. *See* Einer Elhauge, *Making Sense of Antitrust Petitioning Immunity*, 80 CAL. L. REV. 1177, 1234 (1992); Christopher C. Klein, *Strategic Sham Litigation: Economic Incentives in the Context of the Case Law*, 6 INT'L REV. L. & ECON. 241, 249 (1986).

[172] For statistics, *see supra* ch. 1 n.6.

[173] *See* Klein, *supra* note 171, at 249–50.

[174] See the parallel discussion of *Walker Process* claims in chapter 3. The effect would be less dramatic outside the United States, where treble damages are off the table and the applicable legal standard is already marginally more plaintiff-friendly, insofar as proof by clear and convincing evidence is not required and the owner's subjective motivation may be less relevant.

[175] *See* ROBERT H. BORK, THE ANTITRUST PARADOX: A POLICY AT WAR WITH ITSELF 347–48 (1978). I should note, however, that I am not aware of any evidence whether Bork approved or disapproved of the legal standard subsequently articulated in *Professional Real Estate Investors*. The antitrust *defendants* in that case cited *The Antitrust Paradox* in their Supreme Court brief. *See* Brief for the Respondents at 13, 20, 43 Professional Real Estate Investors, Inc. v. Columbia Pictures Industries, Inc., 508 U.S. 49 (1993), No. 91-1043, 1992 WL 541278 (quoting BORK, *supra*, at 358–59 for the propositions that "[r]egardless of intent, parties can be held liable only if they employ means of influencing governmental action that are themselves illegal or reprehensible," and that "unprotected sham activity" is "either making 'deliberate misrepresentations to . . . tribunals' or pressing 'baseless claims for the ulterior purpose of wreaking economic injury upon a competitor' "). On the other hand, at pages 353–55 of his

the fact that litigation (especially patent litigation, and especially in the United States) is notoriously expensive, investing in litigation against a potential rival can be a rational strategy for a monopolist—even if the lawsuit has relatively little chance of succeeding on the merits if litigated through to conclusion—as long as there is a positive expected return from scaring off, delaying, or otherwise disadvantaging the rival.[176] A drug company with a portfolio of patents relating to a blockbuster drug, for example, can earn hundreds of millions of dollars or more by delaying new entry for even a single year.[177] (Relatedly, predatory litigation may induce the target to cooperate—for example, to delay entry in return for a share of the monopolist's interim profits,[178] as can happen in the context of pay-for-delay settlements of pharmaceutical patent litigation, as discussed in the following chapter.) Second, and again notwithstanding the cost of litigation itself, predatory litigation can be a much *more* attractive strategy for a monopolist than are other forms of anticompetitive behavior. Unlike predatory pricing, for example, which requires the monopolist

book Bork himself cited with approval *California Motor Transport v. Trucking Unlimited*, 404 U.S. 508 (1972), a case in which the Supreme Court held that the complaint stated a claim under the Sherman Act even though more than half of the defendants' petitions were successful in obtaining the sought-after relief. *See infra* notes 230–34 and accompanying text. In any event, my citations to Bork herein are intended merely to convey his view that predatory litigation was, as he put it, "particularly insidious," BORK, *supra*, at 348, for the reasons discussed in the text above.

[176] An analogy might be made to PAEs, who lose a disproportionate share of the cases they file and do not settle, *see* Eric Rogers & Young Jeon, *Inhibiting Patent Trolling: A New Approach for Applying Rule 11*, 12 NW. J. TECH. & INTELL. PROP. 291, 308 n.87 (2014) (citing sources), but whose existence nevertheless suggests that even weak infringement claims can promise a positive return on investment. The reasons for the positive return are different, however. Since PAEs don't make or sell any products, they are unlikely to be monopolists themselves, and instead look to maximize licensing revenue rather than to exclude competitors. Moreover, the fact that PAEs don't make or sell products also means that they typically are not amenable to countersuits for patent infringement, whereas a practicing entity with monopoly power may well provoke such a countersuit if it initiates litigation, whether sham or not. Thus, in comparison with a PAE, a practicing monopolist who files an ex ante weak infringement claim may foresee a different type of benefit (exclusion) as well as a different type of cost (the cost of responding to a retaliatory lawsuit), and its conduct primarily implicates a different type of cognizable harm (market distortion). Those differences notwithstanding, the filing of substantively weak infringement claims can be a rational strategy for both PAEs and practicing entities.

[177] *See, e.g.*, FED. TRADE COMM'N, PAY-FOR-DELAY: HOW DRUG COMPANY PAY-OFFS COST CONSUMERS BILLIONS (Jan. 2010), at 8–10 (estimating that, as of 2009, the average pay-for-delay settlement of pharmaceutical patent litigation delayed generic entry by seventeen months over what it otherwise would have been, and enabled the patent owner to earn on average an additional $3.5 billion); FTC v. AbbVie Inc., 976 F.3d 327, 345, 357 (3d Cir. 2020) (stating that the antitrust defendant expected to protect "billions of dollars" of revenue "by deferring competition . . . for three years"). My purpose here is not to condemn or justify pay-for-delay settlements (that's chapter 5), but merely to point out that delay can be lucrative, especially in markets for pharmaceutical products.

[178] *See* Gary Myers, *Litigation as a Predatory Practice*, 80 KY. L.J. 565, 589 (1991) (citing James D. Hurwitz, *Abuse of Government Process, the First Amendment, and the Boundaries of* Noerr, 74 GEO. L.J. 65, 75 (1985)); Ioannis Lianos & Pierre Régibeau, *"Sham" Litigation: When Can It Arise and How Can It Be Reduced?*, 62 ANTITRUST BULL. 643, 668 (2017).

to incur substantial, typically asymmetric, ex ante losses to drive out or discipline competitors, in the hope of eventually recouping those losses ex post, predatory litigation generally does not impose materially higher costs on the predator than on the victim.[179] More generally, though, as Bork observed, this combination of factors indicates that sham litigation need not "require that the predator be able to impose larger costs on the victim, that the predator have greater reserves than the victim, or that the predator have better access to capital than the victim. No other technique of predation is able to escape all of these requirements, and that fact indicates both the danger and the probability of predation by misuse of governmental processes."[180] Moreover, "[t]his mode of predation is particularly insidious because of its relatively low antirust visibility,"[181] an observation the accuracy of which has only increased after *PREI*; and there are reasons to doubt whether fee awards, even if they were widely

[179] *See* Bork, *supra* note 175, at 347–48 (observing that "expenses in complex business litigation can be enormous, not merely in direct legal fees and costs but in the diversion of executive time and effort and in the disruption of the organization's regular activities," and that as a result the monopolist "can impose equal or greater costs upon the entrant and, if it has greater or even equal reserves, may be able to outlast the potential rival"; further, that sham litigation can be "a useful tactic against any size firm, regardless of relative reserves, for it may be worth the price of litigation to purchase a delay of a year or several years in a rival's entry into a lucrative market"); *see also* Michael W. Bien, *Litigation as an Antitrust Violation: Conflict Between the First Amendment and the Sherman Act*, 16 U.S.F.L. Rev. 41, 42 n.2 (1981) (stating that "[l]itigation . . . provides an attractive alternative to predatory pricing because instituting litigation is much less expensive to the dominant firm, but can still accomplish all of the 'desired' anticompetitive effects"); Elhauge, *supra* note 171, at 1229–30 (stating that "a threat to inflict proportionate costs on both sides can still deter competition if the threatener can make a credible commitment to inflict those costs regardless of the injury he himself suffers"; and that "strategic litigation is . . . a far more useful tool for driving competitors out of business than predatory pricing," because while the latter "costs a large producer *more* than a small producer," predatory litigation can "inflict greater per unit costs on small producers than the large producer suffers"); Myers, *supra* note 178, at 596–602 (stating that predatory litigation "may allow the dominant firm to impose asymmetrical costs on the entrant," in part due to economies of scale achieved by repeat litigators, while "the benefits of abusive litigation may be as great or greater than those of other techniques").

One might make a similar argument about *Walker Process* claims, assuming that the cost of fraudulently procuring a patent is not materially higher than what it normally costs to procure a patent. Moreover, if "soft" enforcement, such as publicizing one's patent—or for that matter, merely the knowing possession of an invalid patent—were sufficient potentially to trigger antitrust liability, the predator's costs would be even lower than with actual (or even, possibly, threatened) litigation. *See* Christopher Leslie, *Patents of Damocles*, 83 Ind. L.J. 133, 147–48 (2007) (stating that "[i]n some ways, the holder of a fraudulently procured patent can achieve more cost-effective market exclusion by just brandishing the patent and not undertaking the costs of actual litigation"). Nevertheless, I argued in chapter 3 that liability under U.S. antitrust law should not attach unless the patent owner has engaged in actual or threatened enforcement, and that too expansive a definition of threatened enforcement risks generating unintended negative consequences. In the present chapter, I assume that sham litigation claims will be viable only if there *is* litigation or at least threatened litigation, as opposed to soft enforcement or mere possession. The question then is whether the standard for proving sham litigation under U.S. law post-*PREI* is too stringent, and for the reasons to be developed in the text above I believe that the answer to that question is yes.

[180] Bork, *supra* note 175, at 348.

[181] *Id.*

available or more generous than they are at present, would suffice to deter much anticompetitive litigation.[182]

Much of the legal and economic literature critiquing the *PREI* standard also cites back to Judge Posner's analysis in a pre-*PREI* decision, *Grip-Pak, Inc. v. Illinois Tool Works, Inc.*[183] Among the questions presented in the case was whether plaintiff Grip-Pak, a potential competitor in the market for plastic holders for beverage six-packs, could proceed with an antitrust claim against defendant Tool Works, which allegedly controlled 90% of the relevant market, based in part on the latter's having pursued ultimately unsuccessful, but arguably non-malicious,[184] trade secret litigation against the former.[185] Framing the issue as whether "a lack of probable cause is essential to make a lawsuit

[182] *See* Meurer, *supra* note 158, at 537–38 (stating that "[t]he prospect of recovering attorney's fees after trial has no value to a defendant who goes bankrupt before trial, and perhaps little value to a defendant who suffers financial distress because of trial cost and delay," though it might "be more effective against litigation that attempts to discourage a defendant from making a certain product variety" and "encourage some marginal defendants to fight the predator and reduce the credibility of predatory litigation"); cf. Lianos & Régibeau, *supra* note 178, at 667, 681, 687 (stating that cost-shifting "is not particularly effective in targeting . . . sham litigation," albeit under a definition of sham litigation that would encompass even litigation that "has a relatively high chance of winning" but "would not have [been] started in the absence of any sham benefits").

[183] 694 F.2d 466 (7th Cir. 1982). Consistent with my caveat above about Bork's writing on predatory litigation, *see supra* note 175, I should note here that Posner in his book *Antitrust Law* states, in the context of discussing whether § 2 of the Sherman Act could be repealed, that "bringing a harassing lawsuit against a competitor . . . can be adequately punished" by "abuse of process," and that because "acontractual exclusionary practices" "invariably violate other laws with heavy penalties, their loss would not be significant." Richard A. Posner, Antitrust Law 259–60 (2d ed. 2001). Even assuming that *PREI* does not alter the common-law tort of abuse of process, however—*see, e.g., Nader v. Democratic Nat'l Ctee.*, 567 F.3d 692, 696–99 (D. C. Cir. 2009) (posing but not resolving the question)—the adequacy of abuse of process seems doubtful if that tort, as distinct from wrongful use of civil proceedings, applies only to the use of the court's process (issuance of subpoenas, etc.) and not to the initiation of litigation. Moreover, the adequacy of the tort of wrongful use of civil proceedings also is doubtful. That tort, like *PREI*, requires proof that an actor "initiate[d], procure[d], or continue[d] a civil proceeding against another without probable cause," and that "the civil proceeding has a primary purpose other than securing the proper adjudication of the lawsuit," *see supra* ch. 3 n.34; and the expected damages recovery is likely to be substantially less than the treble damages awarded under U.S. law for antitrust violations.

[184] The trial court hearing the trade secret claim had made a finding that Tool Works had not acted maliciously in asserting that claim, and therefore could not be liable under Illinois law for Grip-Pak's attorneys' fees. *See id.* at 468–69. The Seventh Circuit nonetheless found the record ambiguous on the question of whether the issue of malice was actually litigated by the parties and thus "determined in the sense relevant to collateral estoppel," but went on to consider "whether, if collateral estoppel were applied, the finding that the Illinois suit was not malicious would bar Grip-Pak from seeking to recover in this antitrust suit the expenses it incurred in defending the Illinois suit." *Id.* at 470.

[185] *See id.* at 468. There were additional suits and threats as well. *See id.* (stating that the plaintiff accused the defendant or "threatening groundless patent-infringement suits to deter would-be competitors" and "prosecuting three 'baseless and groundless lawsuits in bad faith," including the suit against Grip-Pak for trade secret misappropriation, along with unlawfully "acquiring every patent there is on plastic beverage holders" and "filing a fraudulent patent application"). Noting some commentary expressing "[c]oncern with the evidentiary problems" of "disentangling real from professed motives" as a reason why some courts at the time had held "that a single lawsuit cannot provide a basis for an antitrust claim," the court stated that it "need not face" that issue given that "three improper lawsuits are alleged, and it can make no difference that they were not all against Grip-Pak." *Id.* at 472.

actionable under the Sherman Act,"[186] the court concluded that the answer was no. In reaching this conclusion, the court noted first that "[i]f all nonmalicious litigation were immunized from government regulation by the First Amendment, the tort of abuse of process would be unconstitutional," differing as it does from the tort of malicious prosecution in not requiring proof "that the lawsuit was brought without probable cause."[187] Doubting that this was a fair reading of the *Noerr-Pennington* case law as of 1982, the court then went on to consider "whether, as a matter of antitrust principle, the Sherman Act should be interpreted to forbid using litigation to suppress competition."[188] Conceding that "[d]istinguishing a lawful from an unlawful anticompetitive purpose is harder than distinguishing lawful from unlawful purpose in abuse of process cases," Judge Posner nonetheless concluded that this difficulty is not "so acute that such litigation can never be considered an actionable restraint of trade, provided it has some, though perhaps only threadbare, basis in law."[189] Judge Posner's explanation of the preceding principle is worth quoting largely in full (as, in fact, it was in Justice Stevens' concurring opinion in *PREI*[190]):

> Many claims not wholly groundless would never be sued on for their own sake; the stakes, discounted by the probability of winning, would be too low to repay the investment in litigation. Suppose a monopolist brought a tort action against its single, tiny competitor; the action had a colorable basis in law; but in fact the monopolist would never have brought the suit—its chances of winning, or the damages it could hope to get if it did win, were too small compared to what it would have to spend on the litigation—except that it wanted to use pretrial discovery to discover its competitor's trade secrets; or hoped

[186] *Id.* at 470. More precisely, the court cited Grip-Pak's argument that the trial court's finding of a lack of malice, "unelaborated as it is, implied only that the Illinois suit could not be the basis of an action for malicious prosecution under Illinois tort law," which requires proof of "improper purpose . . . and lack of probable cause to believe that the lawsuit may have merit." *Id.* "One cannot tell from the state court's finding which element it thought was missing here—assuming, contrary to what we said earlier, that its finding was intended to determine an actually litigated issue. If the missing element was improper purpose, Grip-Pak's effort to characterize the state court action as anticompetitive would be devastated. A lawsuit could not be thought anticompetitive if it was no part of the plaintiff's purpose to suppress competition. But the judge may instead have thought although the state court action was ultimately determined not have to merit, it had had enough apparent merit when brought to satisfy probable cause . . . . We must consider therefore whether a lack of probable cause is essential to make a lawsuit actionable under the Sherman Act." *Id.* As noted in chapter 3, although the American Law Institute refers to this tort as "wrongful use of civil proceedings," it "is frequently called 'malicious prosecution,' which (strictly speaking) governs the malicious pursuit of criminal proceedings without probable cause"). *See supra* ch. 3 n.34 (quoting *PREI*, 508 U.S. at 62).

[187] *Grip-Pak*, 694 F.2d at 471.

[188] *Id.* at 472.

[189] *Id.*

[190] *See PREI*, 508 U.S. at 73–75 (Stevens, J., concurring).

> that the competitor would be required to make public disclosure of its potential liability in the suit and that this disclosure would increase the interest rate that the competitor had to pay for bank financing; or just wanted to impose heavy legal costs on the competitor in the hope of deterring entry by other firms. In these examples the plaintiff wants to hurt a competitor not by getting a judgment against him, which would be a proper objective, but just by the maintenance of the suit, regardless of its outcome. . . .
>
> . . . [W]e think it is premature to hold that litigation, unless malicious in the tort sense, can never be actionable under the antitrust laws. The existence of a tort of abuse of process shows that it has long been thought that litigation could be used for improper purposes even when there is probable cause for the litigation; and if the improper purpose is to use litigation as a tool for suppressing competition in its antitrust sense . . . it becomes a matter of antitrust concern. This is not to say that litigation is actionable under the antitrust laws merely because the plaintiff is trying to get a monopoly. He is entitled to pursue such a goal through lawful means, including litigation against competitors. The line is crossed when his purpose is not to win a favorable judgment against a competitor but to harass him, and deter others, by the process itself—regardless of outcome—of litigating. The difficulty of determining the true purpose is great but no more so than in many other areas of antitrust law.[191]

Under Judge Posner's analysis, in short, all that would be necessary to strip a defendant of immunity from suit would be evidence that the defendant filed suit not "to get damages" but rather "only in the hope that the expense and burden of defending [the suit] will make the defendant abandon its competitive behavior."[192] As we have seen, nonetheless, the Supreme Court majority charted a different path in *PREI*, effectively opting for the "malicious prosecution" model over the "abuse of process" model.[193]

Critics of *PREI* generally proceed from the central insight of Judge Posner's approach, namely that a litigant typically will not file a lawsuit supported by probable cause unless it expects a positive return on its investment in litigating. A litigant therefore would choose not to sue if, as Posner describes it, "the stakes, discounted by the probability of winning, would be too low to repay the investment"—*unless* its motive is to attain collateral benefits, such as the delay

[191] *Grip-Pak*, 694 F.2d at 472 (citations omitted).
[192] *PREI*, 508 U.S. at 73 (Stevens, J., concurring).
[193] *See id.* at 62 & n.7.

or exclusion of potential competition, which arise solely "from the institution of the suit [and] are not outcome dependent."[194] Building on prior work by Christopher Klein[195] and Gary Myers,[196] Nicholas Hakun in a recent article defines a "legitimate suit" as one in which the plaintiff expects a positive return on its investment, such that $xJ > C$, where x is the ex ante probability of success, J the monetary value of the judgment, and C the cost of litigation.[197] Absent collateral benefits, then, where $xJ < C$ the lawsuit would be "irrational."[198] Hakun then defines a "strategic" or "predatory" suit as one in which $xJ < C$ but $xJ + A > C$, where A is the "value conferred to the plaintiff merely for initiating the suit."[199] Thus, for example, if J = $1 million, x is 30%, and C is $500,000, initiating litigation is irrational absent expected collateral benefits A equal to or greater than $200,000.[200]

Given that some amount of strategic or predatory litigation surely exists in the real world, the question then is what, if anything, to do about it. Taking the *PREI* majority's articulation of the relevant standard at face value, a "baseless" lawsuit would be one in which the objective, ex ante value of x is 0.[201] This test has the virtues of being relatively simple to apply[202] and avoiding false positives; but it also surely underdeters some amount of anticompetitive litigation—i.e., any litigation in which x exceeds 0, no matter by how little, while $xJ < C$ and $xJ + A > C$. Judge Posner's analysis, by contrast, can be read to imply that, anytime $xJ < C$, the litigant would lose its *Noerr-Pennington* immunity and thus potentially be subject to antitrust liability[203]—though to succeed the antitrust claimant would still have to prove that the defendant's lawsuit caused, or posed a dangerous probability of causing, the defendant to acquire or maintain monopoly power. As Einer Elhauge notes, however, this test "seems somewhat biased toward finding an abusive intent"[204]—perhaps overly so. For one thing,

194 Nicholas E. Hakun, *Strategic Litigation and Antitrust Petitioning Immunity*, 12 UC Irvine L. Rev. 865, 900 (2022).
195 Klein, *supra* note 171.
196 Gary Myers, *Litigation as a Predatory Practice*, 80 Ky. L.J. 565 (1992).
197 *See* Hakun, *supra* note 194, at 885–86.
198 *See id.* at 886.
199 *Id.*
200 *See id.*
201 *See id.* at 890.
202 One possible complication, perhaps more theoretical than real, would be a case in which the initiation of litigation was objectively warranted ex ante but becomes objectively baseless as litigation progresses, in which its continuation probably could be actionable. *Cf.* Hovenkamp et al., *supra* note 163, § 11.03[B][2] (suggesting that "there may be rare circumstances in which an intellectual property owner's continued prosecution of a suit might itself be objectively baseless").
203 *See Grip-Pak*, 694 F.2d at 472 ("The line is crossed when his purpose is not to win a favorable judgment against a competitor but to harass him, and deter others, by the process itself—regardless of outcome—of litigating").
204 Elhauge, *supra* note 171, at 1233.

as Elhauge observes, "penalizing litigation whenever the chances of success are low would bar 'creative' legal arguments from legal discourse."[205] More importantly, arguably, litigants for whom $xJ < C$ (but for whom $xJ + A$, presumably, is greater than C) would lose their immunity even if the collateral benefit, standing alone, is less than the cost of litigating ($A < C$), or indeed even if $A < xJ$. Put another way, a litigant who expects to derive some benefit from the possibility of victory, albeit not enough by itself to justify litigating, as well some benefit from the collateral consequences of litigating, albeit not enough by itself to justify the lawsuit, would always lose its immunity from suit. Elhauge argues that this result could cause firms to "fear . . . bring[ing] even meritorious litigation.[206]

Elhauge therefore concludes that, unless we fall back on the *PREI* standard, "[s]ome weighing of the motives must be made."[207] In principle, this could entail determining the defendant's subjective motivation for suit and evaluating whether it "dominated the defendant's mind," but Elhauge (rightly, in my view) expresses concern such an approach would induce speculation and potentially introduce bias.[208] Alternatively, one could opt for "an objective test for determining intent," though again he cautions that some possible candidates for such an approach—asking whether the litigant acted "reasonably" or whether "the motive of securing judicial relief was a 'significant' factor behind the decision to sue"—would either chill "creative" legal arguments or "leave[] the judicial inquiry unstructured."[209] To resolve this contretemps, Elhauge proceeds from the premise that, contra Posner, there is "a greater need to encourage legitimate suits than to deter strategic suits," insofar as "[l]egitimate suits are already somewhat deterred by their costs,"[210] and also because of the risk of otherwise inducing "sham-sham" suits.[211] Elhauge therefore concludes that a "better test" would be one that strips the defendant of immunity "only if the direct injury was a necessary *and* sufficient objective motivation for the strategic litigation."[212] Put another way:

[205] *See id.* at 1232; *see also supra* notes 4, 17 (making this point in connection with both mandatory fee shifting and wrongful use of civil proceedings litigation).

[206] Elhauge, *supra* note 171, at 1231.

[207] *Id.* For this reason, Elhauge prefers the term "predatory litigation" to "sham litigation," since in his analysis a claimant may litigate to obtain both the legitimate benefits from winning and anticompetitive collateral benefits. *See id.* at 1227.

[208] *See id.* at 1232.

[209] *Id.*

[210] *Id.* at 1233.

[211] *See id.* at 1234.

[212] *Id.*

> ... the antitrust plaintiff alleging strategic litigation would (in addition to defendant market power) have to show: (1) that the antitrust defendant would not have brought the original suit but for the direct injury imposed on his competitor, and (2) that the defendant would have brought suit even without any prospect of winning in order to inflict the direct costs or delays on his competitor.[213]

Using Hakun's mathematical notation, condition (1) would require proof that $xJ < C$ (a necessary condition for suit), and condition (2) that $C < A$ (the sufficient condition). Requiring condition (2) reduces the risk of discouraging novel legal claims, and conforms better to the abuse of process tort's focus on the litigant's "primary" motivation—albeit at the cost of immunizing some suits for which A was a decisive factor (namely, those for which $xJ + A > C$ but $xJ < C$ and $A < C$).

Hakun's more recent contribution to the literature seeks to improve upon Elhauge's by structuring the analysis into a series of steps or "screens." As he describes it, "to plead a proper case of predatory litigation, the plaintiff must first pass the 'antitrust screen'" by "establishing '(1) evidence of market structure (i.e. market power and relevant markets . . .) and (2) 'exclusionary effect' (i.e., foreclosure of a competitor from a market . . .)," to "indicate that an antitrust violation is plausible."[214] Second, to overcome petitioning immunity, the claimant "would have to plausibly allege that 'the defendant would have brought suit even without any prospect of winning in order to inflict the direct [anticompetitive harm] on his competitor"—in other words, Elhauge's "sufficient condition" that $C < A$.[215] Third, the claimant would have to establish that the defendant's primary motive for suing "was to harm competition through the litigation process, not the outcome," by presenting "objective evidence that the conduct was irrational but for the collateral anticompetitive benefit, as well as any subjective evidence ... that could be useful to assist the finder of fact."[216] This last screen might seem to duplicate Elhauge's "necessary" condition ($xJ < C$); and since it has already been established at the second step that $C < A$, then xJ is also necessarily $< A$, meaning that the primary motive was anticompetitive.[217] Hakun's test would result in the same false negatives as Elhauge's, but

[213] *Id.*
[214] Hakun, *supra* note 194, at 905 (citations omitted).
[215] *Id.* (quoting Elhauge, *supra* note 171, at 1234).
[216] *Id.* at 906.
[217] *Cf. id.* (stating that whether deciding the primary motive "is done via a calculation of expected benefit versus the collateral anticompetitive benefit or is done qualitatively is not necessary to define now").

presumably would reduce adjudicative costs to some extent by eliminating the need to determine if $xJ < C$ if the claim failed to satisfy the second screen.

The issue, then, is whether the net effect of any of these departures from *PREI* would be to improve social welfare, by deterring anticompetitive litigation that currently receives a free pass, or to reduce social welfare by discouraging too many litigants with valid claims from coming forward. That question, of course, cannot be answered with confidence absent empirical evidence of how frequently patent owners engage in sham litigation under the current standards, the losses consumers suffer as a result, and any estimate of how much sham (and nonsham) litigation would be deterred under a more rigorous standard.[218] Moreover, even with such evidence, it would be difficult to estimate what the impact on innovation might be if some legitimate suits are deterred; and to the extent many observers would place some inherent, but unquantifiable, value on the right of access to the courts, independent of its value in preserving the patent incentive scheme, the question may defy empirical analysis altogether. All that said, the preceding analysis strongly suggests that *PREI* generates substantial false negatives by immunizing infringement litigation the primary purpose of which is to exclude competition "by means of the process itself . . . regardless of outcome."[219]

On the other side of the equation, of course, are the twin concerns over false positives and adjudication costs, neither of which can be predicted with confidence either—though, again, there are some plausible reasons why concerns over false positives, at least, should not trouble policymakers too much. First off, under an approach like the ones proposed by Elhauge and Hakun, the only claims that would proceed to trial would be those in which there is sufficient evidence for the trier of fact to conclude that the antitrust defendant possesses, or has a dangerous probability of possessing, monopoly power, and that the effect of the litigation was or would be to enable the acquisition or maintenance of that power. Lack of sufficient evidence of market power should screen out many claims, since under U.S. law monopolization claims generally require evidence of a 50% or greater market share, coupled with barriers to entry.[220]

[218] *See* Christopher C. Klein, *Anticompetitive Litigation and Antitrust Liability*, Dep't of Econ. & Fin. Working Paper Series (Aug. 2007), at 15–16, *available at* https://capone.mtsu.edu/berc/working/SHAM07WP.pdf; Lianos & Régibeau, *supra* note 178, at 672–73.

[219] *Grip-Pak*, 694 F.2d at 472.

[220] *See* Michael A. Carrier, *The Antitrust Case Against Live Nation*, 15 Harv. J. Sports & Enter. L. 1, 11 (2024) (citations omitted). Elsewhere, Carrier notes that courts "dispose of 97% of rule of reason cases on the grounds that the plaintiff cannot show an anticompetitive effect"). *See* Michael Carrier, *The Rule of Reason: An Empirical Update for the 21st Century*, 16 Geo. Mason L. Rev. 827, 837 (2009). His empirical analysis may pick up primarily Sherman Act § 1 rather than § 2 (monopolization and attempted monopolization) cases, but courts hearing § 2 claims also apply a type of Rule of Reason analysis. *See, e.g.*, LePage's, Inc. v. 3M, 277 F.3d 365, 396 n.5 (3d Cir. 2002) (noting that "the

In addition, if need be, courts or legislators could couple the proposed analytical framework with certain safe harbors. In this regard, Gary Myers has suggested that courts could implement a series a presumptions, specifically a conclusive presumption that successful litigation is nonpredatory; a rebuttable presumption that litigation that survived a motion for summary judgment is nonpredatory; and a rebuttable presumption that litigation filed or pursued in violation of Rule 11 is sham.[221] Nevertheless, if the case proceeded past these initial screens, courts would have to consider evidence relating to the motivation for the lawsuit. In the formal terms presented above, this would mean determining whether the collateral benefit of litigating, if any, was expected to exceed the cost of litigation, and if so whether the noncollateral benefit also was expected to exceed the cost of litigation (that is, whether the litigant foresaw "a reasonable likelihood of obtaining a sufficiently large recovery to merit litigation"[222]). This would not be easy, though perhaps not very different in kind from the type of evidence needed to prevail in a pay-for-delay case, as discussed in the next chapter. Aside from whatever other evidence might be available, legal experts might provide opinions of the defendant's ex ante likelihood of success on the merits of the infringement litigation, as circumstantial evidence of the defendant's actual subjective estimate;[223] and economic experts could quantify the benefit to the defendant of delay or deterrence. The case for adopting a more aggressive antitrust standard nevertheless would be marginally stronger if coupled with a loser-pays rule, to deter "sham-sham" claims, as Klein has noted elsewhere.[224]

legal frameworks for analyzing rule of reason violations of § 1 and monopolization claims under § 2 are similar" (citations omitted).

[221] Myers, *supra* note 178, at 626–28. Recall from chapter 3 that Rule 11 of the Federal Rules of Civil Procedure states that "[b]y presenting to the court a pleading, written motion, or other paper," an attorney "certifies that to the best of the person's knowledge, information, and belief, formed after an inquiry reasonable under the circumstances . . . it is not being presented for any improper purpose, such as to harass, cause unnecessary delay, or needlessly increase the cost of litigation," the "legal contentions are warranted by existing law or by a nonfrivolous argument for extending, modifying, or reversing existing law or for establishing new law," and that "the factual contentions have evidentiary support." Note, in addition, that in the absence of Myers' proposed safe harbors, under Elhauge's or Hakun's proposals sham litigation antitrust claims would no longer necessarily depend, as they do now, on the patent claims in suit being found invalid or not infringed. These antitrust claims would be more akin to those I discuss in chapter 6, for which invalidity or noninfringement is not a prerequisite to liability.

[222] Myers, *supra* note 178, at 619.

[223] *Cf. AbbVie*, 976 F.3d at 370 (stating, in the context of the current *PREI* standard, that "a reasonable litigant's subject motivation for filing an objectively baseless lawsuit must be something besides success on the merits," but also that "[i]t does not necessarily follow that the motivation was to thwart competition" if a company filed "an objectively baseless lawsuit because it subjectively (though unreasonably) expected the lawsuit to succeed").

[224] *See* Klein, *supra* note 171, at 16–17. Lianos and Régibeau propose, as an alternative to antitrust liability, a "mechanism design" approach under which the court would first determine if there is "sufficient evidence of sham payoffs," and if so a defendant could make a unilateral offer of settlement; if the

To be sure, any change to U.S. law that depended on the overruling of *PREI* would have to come from the Supreme Court (assuming, as seems correct, that *PREI* and other more recent Supreme Court decisions stand for the proposition that *Noerr-Pennington* immunity arises under the First Amendment). The above does suggest, however, that countries that have yet to confront these issues may wish to consider a more aggressive stance toward sham litigation. And even U.S. courts, arguably, could construe *PREI* narrowly, particularly as applied to serial petitioning and to the application of petitioning immunity to some unfair competition claims, as discussed below.

First, as for serial petitioning, prior to *PREI* the only Supreme Court decision expressly addressing sham litigation was a 1972 decision, *California Motor Transport Co. v. Trucking Unlimited.*[225] The plaintiff trucking companies alleged that the defendant trucking companies conspired to oppose, "with or without probable cause, and regardless of [the] merits," the plaintiffs' applications to the California Public Utility Commission and the Interstate Commerce Commission to operate within the State of California.[226] Although the antitrust defendants prevailed in twenty-one of the forty petitions they filed,[227] the Ninth Circuit held that the plaintiffs stated a claim for relief under the sham petitioning exception to *Noerr-Pennington.*[228] The Supreme Court affirmed, stating that "a pattern of baseless, repetitive claims may emerge which leads the factfinder to conclude that the administrative and judicial processes have been abused."[229]

Although the *PREI* Court did not purport to overrule *California Motor*,[230] the Court's requirement that litigation be objectively baseless—unsupported

litigant rejects the offer and loses at trial, it would then pay the defendant the offered amount. Lianos & Régibeau, *supra* note 178, at 682–84. This approach, they argue, would deter predatory but not legitimate litigation; it would require legislation, however, and in my view would not be an easy sell.

[225] 404 U.S. 508 (1972). In dictum, the Supreme Court had alluded to a sham exception in the original *Noerr* decision. *See Eastern R.R. Presidents Conference v. Noerr Motor Freight Inc.*, 365 U.S. 127, 144 (1961).

[226] Trucking Unltd. v. Cal. Motor Transp. Co., 432 F.2d 755, 762 (9th Cir. 1970), *aff'd*, 404 U.S. 508 (1972).

[227] *See* Elhauge, *supra* note 171, at 1184 (citing Trucking Unltd. v. Cal. Motor Transp. Co. 1967 Trade Cas. (CCH) ¶ 72,298, at 84,744 (N.D. Cal.), *rev'd on other grounds*, 432 F.2d 755 (9th Cir. 1970), *aff'd*, 404 U.S. 508 U.S. (1972).

[228] Trucking Unltd., 432 F.2d at 762–63 (stating, *inter alia*, that the fact that defendants' "joint activity took the form, in part, of solicitation of governmental action and that they made a genuine effort to support all protests as effectively as possible would not negate a primary purpose to restrain competition directly").

[229] 404 U.S. at 513.

[230] *See PREI*, 508 U.S. at 66–67 & n.4 (stating that, on the facts alleged in *California Motor*, the defendants were not entitled to immunity where they instituted proceedings "with or without probable cause," but that "[w]e left unresolved the question . . . whether litigation may be sham merely because a subjective expectation of success does not motivate the litigant," and that the case did "not transform the sham inquiry into a purely subjective investigation").

by probable cause, or even an "objectively 'good faith argument for the extension, modification, or reversal of existing law' "[231]—to qualify as a sham is difficult to square with the result in *California Motor*, where more than half of the defendant's objections prevailed on the merits.[232] For this reasons, some courts and commentators have concluded that *PREI* in effect overruled, or at least limited, *California Motor*, such that only those petitions within a series that lack probable cause or are otherwise objectively baseless can be shams.[233] Nevertheless, to date the majority of U.S. Courts of Appeals that have addressed the issue have held that *PREI* applies to cases involving a single petition or lawsuit, but that a pattern can constitute a sham, even if some of the individual petitions are supported by probable cause, as long as the defendant's motivation for engaging in the pattern was to disadvantage the defendant regardless of the outcome.[234] This interpretation accepts the ongoing precedential value of *California Motor* but, as above, can be difficult to reconcile with the holding in *PREI*. It also requires some line-drawing as to what constitutes a pattern, with courts generally requiring four or more petitions or lawsuits, while declining to draw any bright lines.[235]

[231] *Id.* at 62, 65.

[232] *See* Elhauge, *supra* note 171, at 1227 n.236 (rejecting the counterargument that the *California Motor* Court "sustained the complaint only as to those of the 40 legal proceedings that lacked probable cause," because "the complaint carefully refrained from charging that *any* of the 40 proceedings was in fact instituted without probable cause"; "[r]ather, the gravamen of the complaint was that the defendants were instituting proceedings automatically, without really considering the merits or whether or not probable cause existed").

[233] *See* U.S. Futures Exch., LLC v. Bd. Of Trade of City of Chicago, 953 F.3d 955, 964–66 (7th Cir. 2020); Hovenkamp et al., *supra* note 163, § 11.03[5][b] (proposing that each lawsuit in a series be tested for objective baselessness, and that for those (if any) that are objectively baseless, "an antitrust plaintiff might point to the pattern of suits as evidence of the intellectual property owner's subjective motivation in bringing the suits"). *Cf.* Puerto Rico Tel. Co. v. San Juan Cable LLC, 874 F.3d 767, 771–72 (1st Cir. 2017) (expressing skepticism over the antitrust plaintiff's argument, but limiting its holding to the facts).

[234] The leading case is *USS-POSCO Indus. v. Contra Costa County Bldg. & Constr. Trade Council*, 31 F.3d 800, 810–11 (9th Cir. 1994) (reading *PREI* as "provid[ing] a strict two-step analysis to assess whether a single action constitutes sham petitioning," under which "[i]f the suit turns out to have objective merit, the plaintiff can't proceed to inquire into subjective purposes, and the action is perforce not a sham," and *California Motor* as requiring an inquiry whether legal filings were "made, not out of a genuine interest in redressing grievances, but as part of a pattern or practice of successive filings undertaken essentially for purposes of harassment"; but holding, on the facts, "that more than half of all the actions as to which we know the results turn out to have merit cannot be reconciled with the charge that the unions were filing lawsuits and other actions willy-nilly without regard to success"). *See also* Hanover 3201 Realty, LLC v. Village Supermarkets, Inc., 806 F.3d 162, 180–81 (3d Cir. 2015); Waugh Chapel v. United Food & Comm'l Workers, 728 F.3d 354, 364–67 (4th Cir. 2013); Primetime 24 Joint Venture v. Nat'l Broadcasting Co., 219 F.3d 92, 100–02 (2d Cir. 2000).

[235] *See Hanover 3201 Realty*, 806 F.3d at 181; Hovenkamp et al., *supra* note 163, § 11.03[5][b] (citing cases).

A recent paper by James Cooper and Emily Kral nevertheless provides an interesting theoretical case for the majority view.[236] The gist of their argument rests on two key premises. The first is that the evidence before a court often is ambiguous, in the sense that it could be consistent with the defendant's motivation for filing suit being either a sham—meaning that "the defendant is using the process to harm competition"—or legitimate, meaning that "the defendant genuinely [is] attempting to vindicate First Amendment rights."[237] The second is that "as long as the probability of winning is positively correlated with the underlying quality of the case, which in turn is an objective proxy for motive, the win-rate provides an informative objective metric to assess the likelihood that a pattern of petitioning is a sham."[238] In regard to the latter, the authors present a formal analysis, consistent with the decision-theoretical approach that governs much of U.S. antitrust law,[239] under which "the optimal legal rule given two possible evidence-generating distributions ... is determined by the ratio of type-I [false positive] to type-II [false negative] error costs."[240] If the costs associated with either type of error are equal, the likelihood ratio would be one, but under *PREI* the costs associated with a false positive (wrongly condemning as sham a legitimate petition) are accorded more weight than the costs associated with a false negative (wrongly vindicating a sham as legitimate). (Cooper and Kral assume, for purposes of exposition, that the likelihood ratio is 2—i.e., that in view of the First Amendment right to petition the government, a false positive is twice as costly as a false negative in the present context.) Crucially, with a sufficiently large number of petitions filed by the same entity, the optimal evidentiary threshold for maintaining the desired (constant) likelihood ratio can be lowered, because a court will have more information from which to judge if the defendant's principal motive was legitimate or sham: in other words, "a larger sample means the court can ... reduce type-II errors ... with no increase

[236] James C. Cooper & Emily Kral, *Shambles: Making Sense of the Confused State of* Noerr*'s Sham Exception*, 76 Case Western Reserve L. Rev. (forthcoming), *manuscript available at* https://papers.ssrn.com/sol3/papers.cfm?abstract_id=4740979. *See also* Susan Creighton et al., *Cheap Exclusion*, 72 Antitrust L.J. 975, 992–93 & n.59 (2005) (arguing that "immunity should not be available to abusive repetitive litigation," because the cost asymmetries noted in the text above will be greater: "the incremental cost of filing an additional sham complaint is negligible, but the cost of defending against the complaint is high in comparison," and "may be particularly acute when the sham litigation is against a rival's customers").

[237] Cooper & Kral, *supra* note 236 (manuscript at 5). Since, as noted above, both motives may be present in some cases, I assume that under the authors' definitions "sham" means that the motive to harm competition predominates, and that "legitimate" means the reverse.

[238] *Id.* (manuscript at 6).

[239] *See supra* ch. 3 note 101 and accompanying text.

[240] Cooper & Kral, *supra* note 236 (manuscript at 28). For technical explication, *see id.* at 27–28.

in type-I errors."[241] Operationally, this means that if the court observes a series of petitions with a sufficiently low, but not necessarily zero, win rate, inferring a sham motivation for the series would reduce the aggregate cost of error—or, to put it another way, would be a Pareto-superior rule to *PREI* in the context of serial petitioning.[242]

To be sure, the analysis rests on the assumption that the right to petition the government is entitled to substantial weight, but not to *so* much weight that a few winning petitions within the sample necessarily immunize the defendant from liability. This would be consistent with the post-*PREI* case law that has continued to follow *California Motor*, but might be objectionable to observers who place an extremely high value on the right to petition. In addition, as the authors concede, one cannot expect courts or parties to perform the relevant calculations with precision.[243] Nevertheless, the analysis provides a principled theoretical basis for the majority view that a series of petitions having a sufficiently low win rate is consistent with the series as a whole—understood "holistically," as the Third Circuit expressed it in *Hanover 3201 Realty*[244]—having been a sham. In practical terms, moreover, a win rate of 20% or lower can, "under reasonable parameter values . . . provide objective evidence of a sham with as few as five cases,"[245] which would be generally consistent with the post-*PREI* case law.[246] And again, as I have noted throughout, even then not all such cases ultimately would result in liability, given the plaintiff's burden of proving the other elements (monopoly power, causation) of its antitrust case. Imposing unduly high hurdles for relief, on the other hand, would seem to guarantee that some, perhaps most, predatory litigation will go substantially unchecked.

A few final points remain. First, even if one were to conclude, contrary to the above, that the current U.S. and E.U. standards are optimal for antitrust claims premised on sham petitioning, it wouldn't necessarily follow that the exact same standard should apply to other claims premised on the assertion of patent rights that are invalid or not infringed. As discussed in chapter 3, for example, subject to some exceptions the U.K.'s law of unjustified threats

[241] *Id.* (manuscript at 35). More technically, "as sample sizes increase, a greater proportion of the draws will come from the central area near the mean, causing the distribution to take on its true form. In this manner, more observations collectively provide more information about the underlying conduct giving rise to the observed evidence." *Id.* (manuscript at 32).

[242] *See id.* (manuscript at 31–38).

[243] *See id.* (manuscript at 44–45).

[244] *Hanover 3201 Realty*, 806 F.3d at 180 (stating that "[i]n deciding whether there was such a policy of filing petitions with or without regard to merit, a court should perform a holistic review that may include looking at the defendant's filing success—i.e., win-loss percentage—as circumstantial evidence of the defendant's subjective motivations").

[245] Cooper & Kral, *supra* note 236 (manuscript at 45).

[246] *See supra* notes 234–35 and accompanying text.

renders the patent owner strictly liable for threats made against alleged secondary infringers, assuming that the patent at issue is invalid or noninfringed. This standard arguably makes sense, if the purpose of the law is to encourage owners to litigate against primary infringers when it is feasible to do so, and thus to protect (presumably more vulnerable) secondary parties and prevent owners from, in effect, obtaining do-it-yourself preliminary injunctions.[247] Absent such a legislative policy, however, applying a strict liability standard to unfair competition claims premised on threats potentially would interfere unduly with the right of access to the courts. Bad faith, in turn, may entail some mix of objective or subjective considerations, but in no country that I am aware of does the statutory or common law require proof of objective baselessness. Again, though, even if one believes that a showing of objective baselessness is necessary in the antitrust context to dispel the risk of socially costly false positives, it would not follow that a similar requirement would be optimal in the context of unfair competition claims. Because antitrust violations distort entire markets, damages or fines will be on average higher (especially in the U.S., where damages are automatically trebled) than the damages assessed for unfair competition torts, which typically compensate for specific lost sales.[248] Unfair competition claims also usually depend upon the initiative of private litigants, who may or may not be motivated to sue, whereas antitrust claims can be brought by public authorities, thus adding to their deterrent (though, if not well-managed, potentially overdeterrent) effect. (The exception here is for the U.S. anti-troll claims and related actions under consumer protection laws, which are sometimes enforced by public authorities.) For these reasons, the costs associated with false positives should be systematically lower for unfair competition-type claims than for antitrust claims, thus justifying a lower liability standard. That said, as a purely legal matter courts in the United States may be required to apply the *PREI* standard to non-antitrust claims, if as the Federal Circuit infers that standard is constitutionally obligatory for any type of claim premised on actual or threatened litigation.[249] Even if this reading is correct, however, one could argue that it shouldn't affect unfair competition or other claims premised merely on communications that fall short of express or implicit threats to sue, or which otherwise do not implicate petitioning the

[247] *See supra* ch. 3 notes 54–63, 153 and accompanying text.
[248] *See supra* ch. 2 note 71 and accompanying text; ch. 3 notes 71, 96, 124–25 and accompanying text. Put another way, there are distinct cognizable harms at issue, which might provide a principled rationale for applying a lesser standard of proof for unfair competition and anti-troll violations. Of course, if punitive or enhanced damages are a possibility, as may sometimes be the case, the risk of harm from false positives increases.
[249] *See supra* ch. 3 notes 78–79 and accompanying text.

government;[250] and false commercial speech, as such, enjoys no constitutional protection, even in the United States.[251]

The second point to note is that there may be other claims available for predatory litigation besides those discussed above, such as the U.S. anti-troll laws discussed in chapter 5 and the civil law abuse of right doctrine discussed in chapter 6. In addition, as noted previously, in U.S. civil litigation Rule 11 of the Federal Rules of Civil Procedure obligates attorneys to certify that any paper presented to a court is, "to the best of the person's knowledge, information, and belief, formed after an inquiry reasonable under the circumstances . . . not being presented for any improper purpose, such as to harass, cause unnecessary delay, or needlessly increase the cost of litigation"; that the "legal contentions are warranted by existing law or by a nonfrivolous argument for extending, modifying, or reversing existing law or for establishing new law"; and that "the factual contentions have evidentiary support."[252] As in other countries, however, U.S. courts are in general reluctant to sanction attorneys, absent exceptional circumstances.[253]

To be sure, in principle the existing laws could be amended. Eric Rogers and Young Jeon have argued that, for example, to reduce the costs of PAE activity, Rule 11 should be amended to require courts, *sua sponte*, to stay litigation when presented with "suspect-class factors indicative of bad-faith patent assertion," and to require the plaintiff to "frontload" proof that it has fulfilled its Rule 11 obligations, before the counterparty would be required to comply with discovery.[254] The proposal is not necessarily unreasonable, but would require action from the United States Judicial Conference, which promulgates

[250] *See supra* ch. 3 text accompanying note 80 (noting with approval Paul Gugliuzza's argument that the rationale for extending petitioning immunity to threated litigation the owner never intends to carry out, or to false statements relating to peripheral matters, is weak).

[251] *See* In re R.M.J., 455 U.S. 191, 203 (1982).

[252] Fed. R. Civ. P. 11(b)(1)–(3).

[253] *See supra* note 160 (discussing Schedule A cases); Jacques Normand, *Final Report: The Two Approaches to the Abuse of Procedural Rights*, *in* ABUSE OF PROCEDURAL RIGHTS: COMPARATIVE STANDARDS OF PROCEDURAL FAIRNESS 237, 246–47 (Michele Tartuffo ed. 1998).

[254] Rogers & Jeon, *supra* note 176. According to the proposal:

> [a] suspect class of patent infringement claimants can be defined by certain indicia of patent trolling. Some easily determinable characteristics indicative of a predisposition to patent trolling are: 1) the litigant was not in privity of employment with the named inventor, including through subsidiaries, affiliates, or its business predecessor or successor (leaving merely a relationship through contract originating from the transfer of intellectual property); 2) the litigant does not make available any commercial products or services in relation to the patent; and 3) the litigant's lines of business for the past three years share no commonality with the subject matter of the patent. If two or more of the mentioned characteristics apply, the entity's patent infringement complaint should be subject to increased scrutiny.

Id. at 327. The authors then specify steps for the court to conduct to determine if *sua sponte* scrutiny is warranted. *See id.* at 330–31.

the Rules of Civil Procedure, or from Congress—and probably would receive considerable blowback from PAEs (for singling them out as meriting such extra scrutiny) as well as from district court judges (for giving them extra work to do, on their own initiative). In addition, although a violation of Rule 11 can result in sanctions against the attorney, firm, or party responsible for the violation, the current version of the rule limits sanctions "to what suffices to deter repetition of the conduct or comparable conduct by others similarly situated"; and while the sanction may include "a penalty into court; or, if imposed on motion and warranted for effective deterrence, an order directing payment to the movant of part or all of the reasonable attorney's fees and other expenses directly resulting from the violation," under the current version represented parties, as opposed to their lawyers, are not financially responsible for making unwarranted legal contentions.[255] In any event, it seems unlikely that a Rule 11 amended along the lines proposed by Rogers and Jeon would eliminate the need for appropriate scrutiny under antitrust or unfair competition law of claims premised on false assertions of patent rights, since as noted the amendment would apply only to firms with possible PAE characteristics.

Perhaps more promisingly, Rebecca Schoff Curtin has proposed that the United States enact a federal anti-SLAPP law, under which

> A patent infringement claim that is objectively baseless, or brought in subjective bad faith, shall be subject to a special motion to strike, unless, in the case of a finding of subjective bad faith only, the plaintiff can demonstrate on the pleadings that the claim has a reasonable basis in fact and law, which would be defined as a heightened standard of particularity in the pleadings.[256]

[255] *See* Fed. R. Civ. P. 11(c)(4), (5).

[256] Rebecca Schoff Curtin, *SLAPPing Patent Trolls: What Anti-Trolling Legislation Can Learn from the Anti-SLAPP Movement*, 18 Stan. Tech. L. Rev. 39, 67 (2014). "SLAPP" is an acronym for "strategic lawsuits against public participation." Anti-SLAPP laws, as enacted for example in California, enable defendants to obtain expedited hearings on motions to strike claims that could have a chilling effect on free speech. *See, e.g.*, Cal. Civ. Proc. Code § 425.16 (stating, *inter alia*, a legislative finding that "there has been a disturbing increase in lawsuits brought primarily to chill the valid exercise of the constitutional rights of freedom of speech and petition for the redress of grievances," and providing that "[a] cause of action against a person arising from any act of that person in furtherance of the person's right of petition or free speech under the United States Constitution or the California Constitution in connection with a public issue shall be subject to a special motion to strike, unless the court determines that the plaintiff has established that there is a probability that the plaintiff will prevail on the claim"); *see also* Directive (EU) 2024/1069 of the European Parliament and of the Council of 11 April 2024 on protecting persons who engage in public participation from manifestly unfounded claims or abusive court proceedings ('Strategic lawsuits against public participation'), OJ L., 16.4.2024. Curtin's proposal is novel in extending anti-SLAPP protection to a type of claim that does not generally impact free speech concerns, but rather "concern about the cost of litigation abuse, not just to private parties, but to society at large." Curtin, *supra*, at 45.

Discovery would be stayed while the motion is pending, absent special circumstances.[257] Curtin proposes a range of factors that courts could employ to determine at this initial stage whether an infringement claim is objectively or subjectively baseless, patterned after factors identified in Federal Circuit case law and state anti-troll laws.[258] She also would include certain procedural safeguards, including a right to an immediate appeal; mandatory fee-shifting in the event the motion were granted; and discretionary fee-shifting, to deter frivolous motions to strike, if the motion were denied.[259] Overall, her proposal seems plausibly welfare-enhancing—though I also suspect that at present any new federal legislation that might be viewed as weakening U.S. patent rights, as this might be, would be a difficult sell.

Finally, although it is hard to know how much of an effect standards of proof ultimately have on litigation, perhaps it would be advisable to revisit the requirements that U.S. antitrust plaintiffs asserting *Walker Process* or sham litigation claims prove fraud or sham by clear and convincing evidence, rather than the normal preponderance of evidence standard—though to the extent requirements are viewed as constitutionally based, any such change would need to come from the Supreme Court, not Congress. One possible lesson to be drawn from this chapter, therefore, is that countries that have yet to address the issues discussed above should consider in advance the loss of flexibility that can result from over-constitutionalizing the standards governing antitrust and IP disputes. Safeguarding the right to petition is important, but elevating that goal above all others risks, in Cooper and Kral's colorful phrase, leaving competition in a shambles.

[257] *See id.* at 67, 74.

[258] *See id.* at 68–73. Curtin acknowledges, however, that it may be "the rare case in which a showing can be made that a claim is objectively baseless near the time of filing." *Id.* at 69.

[259] *See id.* at 73–77.

5

"Without Sufficient Justification," Case 2

The preceding chapter addressed various types of wrongful assertion claims, the success of which depends upon the patent having been asserted without justification, where the lack of justification depends, in whole or in part, upon an asserted patent claim being adjudicated invalid or not infringed. This chapter will consider the possibility of wrongful assertion claims, the success of which does not necessarily depend upon an adjudication of invalidity or noninfringement, but rather (in some sense) on the *ex ante probability* of validity and infringement. The principal example is a "pay-for-delay" or "reverse payment" antitrust claim arising from an allegedly anticompetitive settlement of pharmaceutical patent litigation.[1] To be sure, in this type of case it is the settlement of the litigation on possibly anticompetitive terms, rather than an

[1] Settlements of patent disputes can present antitrust issues in other contexts as well—though as Hovenkamp et al. have long noted, the majority of such cases can be resolved without considering whether the asserted patent claims were valid and infringed, because the settlement would be lawful (or unlawful, as the case may be) either way. For example, the settlement of a garden-variety patent infringement action that results in the defendant taking a nonexclusive license to the patented technology typically generates no antitrust scrutiny, absent other suspect facts, whereas a settlement under which the parties agree to a horizontal allocation of the market for some nonpatented good would likely be a per se violation regardless of the merits of the originating patent dispute. *See* Herbert Hovenkamp et al., IP and Antitrust: An Analysis of Antitrust Principles Applied to Intellectual Property Law, §§ 7.01, 7.02[A], [B] (2023). In the minority of cases in which this is not so, courts may need to inquire into validity and infringement. *See id.* § 7.03[B], at 7–21 (citing *Standard Oil Co. (Ind.) v. United States*, 283 U.S. 163, 180–81 (1931), in which "the Supreme Court approved the appointment of special master to determine whether the patents held by the various parties were sufficiently broad to warrant a conclusion that they interfered with one another," and *United States v. Singer Mfg. Co.*, 374 U.S. 174, 199 (1963), in which "the record suggested that the parties had reached a settlement in part in order to avoid drawing attention to prior art that might have resulted in the invalidation of several of their patents"). As a practical matter, such cases appear to be uncommon outside the pharmaceutical context. In any event, under the analytical framework employed in this book, to the extent such cases hinge on a finding of invalidity or noninfringement, they would fall into Case 1; to the extent they hinge on a finding of probable invalidity or noninfringement, they would fall into Case 2, and the analysis presented in this chapter concerning how courts might draw such probabilistic inferences would be applicable, as individual circumstances permit. *See also* Erik Hovenkamp, *Antitrust Law and Patent Settlement Design*, 32 Harv. J.L. & Tech. 418 (2019) (proposing that courts focus on settlement design, rather than inquiring into validity and infringement, in the broad range of antitrust disputes premised on allegedly anticompetitive settlements). I discuss Erik Hovenkamp's analysis as it applies to reverse payments *infra* notes 82–83 and accompanying text. For a more technical explication of the analysis underlying his paper, *see* Erik Hovenkamp & Jorge Lemus, *Antitrust Limits on Patent Settlements: A New Approach*, 70 J. Indus. Econ. 257 (2022).

Wrongful Patent Assertion. Thomas F. Cotter, Oxford University Press. © Oxford University Press 2026.
DOI: 10.1093/9780191994104.003.0005

initial act of actual or threatened patent assertion as such, that potentially gives rise to antitrust liability. Nevertheless, an initial act of actual or threatened assertion typically is a proximate cause of the subsequent settlement;[2] and I will argue below that liability should hinge on whether the patentee and the accused infringer agreed to delay generic entry for a longer period of time than was warranted by the ex ante probability of success on the merits of the infringement suit.

A second example would be a claim under one of the U.S. anti-troll laws, albeit subject to the caveat that the issue is unlikely to arise unless the Federal Circuit modifies its ostensible view that *Noerr-Pennington* applies to unfair competition and business tort claims premised on accusations of patent infringement.[3] That said, the situation I have in mind is the following. Suppose that a state attorney general alleges that a demand letter the patentee has sent to various recipients constitutes a bad faith assertion under the relevant anti-troll law, but that the patent itself has not been adjudicated invalid or not infringed.[4] The plaintiff concedes, however, that as of the date the demand letter was sent, the ex ante probability of validity and infringement was greater than zero, so the ground for alleging bad faith assertion cannot be that the sender "knew, or should have known, that the claim or assertion is meritless"[5]—at least, not in any literal sense of the word "meritless." Rather, the argument is that the ex ante probability of validity and infringement was too low to justify filing suit other than for the collateral purpose

[2] More precisely, the regulatory regime in the United States encourages patent owners to file suit shortly before generic entry otherwise would occur; upon doing so, generic approval is automatically stayed for thirty months, and the settlements to be discussed in this chapter often are reached during this period. *See infra* notes 99–101 and accompanying text. Under the E.U.'s regulatory regime, settlements sometimes occur after the patent owner commences legal proceedings, and/or the generic firm initiates a patent invalidation action, but in other instances the generic firm settles under threat of infringement proceedings or to avoid such proceedings. *See* Servier v. European Commission, Case C-201/19 P, ECLI:EU:C:2024:552, ¶¶ 12–20 (CJEU 2024); H. Lundbeck A/S v. European Commission, Case C-591/16 P, ECLI:EU:C:2021:243, ¶¶ 26, 35, 42, 47 (CJEU 2021); Generics (UK) Ltd. v. Competition and Markets Authority, Case C-307/18, ECLI:EU:C:2020:52, ¶ 13, 14, 144, 158.

[3] *See supra* ch. 3 notes 74–76 and accompanying text (noting Federal Circuit case law requiring proof that an assertion of patent rights was, *inter alia*, objectively baseless—which would seem to render irrelevant evidence that the patent owner had a low but nonzero ex ante probability of success).

[4] *See* Paul R. Gugliuzza, *Patent Trolls and Preemption*, 101 VA. L. REV. 1579, 1582 (2015) (stating that "[w]hen MPHJ finally did file suit, it did so only after numerous state attorneys general had begun investigating the company's enforcement tactics").

[5] *See* VT. STAT. ANN., tit. 9, § 4197(b)(6) (stating that "[a] court may consider . . . as evidence that a person has made a bad faith assertion of patent infringement," that the "[t]he claim or assertion of patent infringement is meritless, and the person knew, or should have known, that the claim or assertion is meritless").

of extracting nuisance payments.[6] Should the court entertain such probabilistic evidence?[7]

Pay-for-delay and Probability

This section addresses antitrust claims arising from the settlement of pharmaceutical patent litigation, in which the patent owner transfers cash or other consideration to the defendant (a generic drug company) in return for the latter's agreement not to market a generic version of a patented drug for a period of time. These "pay for delay" (otherwise known as "reverse payment" or "exclusion payment") settlements first came to the attention of antitrust regulators over twenty-five years ago, and have generated a considerable body of case law and commentary ever since. The following paragraphs provide a brief overview of why the pharmaceutical industry has proven to be fertile ground for these settlements, before proceeding to a discussion of how courts and agencies in the United States and the European Union have come to evaluate

[6] *See id.* § 4197(b)(5), (9) (stating that "[a] court may consider . . . as evidence that a person has made a bad faith assertion of patent infringement," that the offer to license is "for an amount that is not based on a reasonable estimate of the value of the license"; and "[a]ny other factor that the court finds relevant").

[7] In principle, the question of whether courts should entertain evidence of the ex ante probability of validity and infringement also could arise in cases, unlike the hypothetical presented in the text above, in which liability normally depends on an adjudication of noninfringement or invalidity: for example, unfair competition claims premised on false accusations of infringement, in which the patent owner's good faith would be an exonerating or mitigating factor. In these cases, which would fall into Case 1 in terms of this book's taxonomy, evidence of the ex ante probability of validity and infringement would seem relevant to the patentees' good faith or lack thereof—in which case the issue I will be addressing later in this chapter in connection with anti-troll laws could come up in this context as well. To the extent the resolution of the issue depends on expert testimony, however, it may be unlikely to arise outside of common-law countries in which extensive use of expert testimony is permitted—and even then, for reasons discussed later in this chapter, it may be rare for the stakes of the litigation to justify the expense.

Another type of case in which evidence of the ex ante probability of success on the merits could in principle be useful would be a sham litigation antitrust claim, if as discussed in the preceding chapter the law was modified to permit such claims to proceed if, *inter alia*, (1) the expected collateral benefit of litigating exceeded the expected cost of litigation, and (2) the expected noncollateral benefit of litigating appears to be less than the expected cost of litigation. *See supra* ch. 4 text accompanying notes 215–16; *see also infra* text accompanying note 95. Even with such a modification to existing law, however, I think it is extremely unlikely that courts would find an antitrust violation in a case in which the asserted patent was adjudicated to be infringed and not invalid, even if the preceding conditions were met (which is why I classify sham litigation antitrust claims under Case 1). The one possible exception might be a sham litigation antitrust claim premised on a series of lawsuits having a sufficiently low win-rate over time. *See supra* ch. 4 notes 225–46 and accompanying text (discussing how a win-rate of 20% or less over a series of five or more cases may support a probabilistic inference of sham litigation).

Yet another type of case that, in principle, could come within Case 2 would be one in which the patent owner has allegedly abused its dominant position by gaming the use of divisional or continuation applications—a matter that was the subject of a recent European Commission investigation, *see infra* note 130.

them.[8] The key policy questions, to be discussed later in this chapter, are whether it is appropriate to adjudge these settlements to be anticompetitive on the basis of probabilistic evidence, and if so what sort of probabilistic evidence decisionmakers should rely upon in making such estimates.

At the outset, it's useful to have some understanding of the monetary stakes involved. Although estimates vary, by most accounts drug companies incur, on average, hundreds of millions of dollars—perhaps more—to bring a new drug to market, from the initial applied research through the clinical studies needed to obtain marketing approval.[9] Typically drug companies will obtain at least one patent on the active pharmaceutical ingredient (API) or ingredients comprising a prescription drug; often they follow up with a series of secondary patents on new uses, methods of delivery, or variations on the original API. The patent term for each of these patents begins on the date the patent issues and, assuming that periodic maintenance fees are paid, expires twenty years from the date the application was filed. (Pendency periods vary from one year to another, but on average patent applications remain pending for about two years in the United States, about three years in the European Patent Office.[10]) To market the drug to the public, however, the drug company must obtain marketing authorization from the Food and Drug Administration (FDA) in the United States; the European Medicines Agency (EMA), or regulatory authorities in individual member states, in the E.U.;[11] and/or counterpart agencies in

[8] As will be discussed in the text, courts in the U.S. and E.U. have now adjudicated several pay-for-delay antitrust actions. Reverse payments also have been the subject of one short decision of China's Supreme People's Court, *AstraZeneca AB v. Jiangsu Aisaikang Pharm. Co.*, (2021) SPX Zhi Civil Final No. 388, and also are briefly addressed in the recently published *Interpretation of the Supreme People's Court on Several Issues Concerning the Application of Law in the Trial of Civil Disputes over Monopoly* (June 2024). I discuss the competing approaches of the U.S., the E.U., and China *infra* notes 53–75 and accompanying text.

[9] I review the various economic studies as of 2017 in chapter 6 of my book PATENT WARS: HOW PATENTS IMPACT OF OUR DAILY LIVES (2018). For the small-molecule compounds that comprise the active pharmaceutical ingredient (API) of most new drugs, these estimates ranged from a low of $43 million (in 2000 dollars) to a high of $2.6 billion (in 2013 dollars) for drugs comprising self-originated new chemical entities (NCEs). ($2.6 billion in 2013 would be worth about $3.5 billion in 2025.) In my view, the most credible estimates fall within the middle-to-high range in between these extremes. The highest estimates properly take into account opportunity costs (most new drug candidates fail somewhere along the way, and the money spent pursuing them could have been profitably invested somewhere else), but they do not account for the drug companies' ability to claim tax deductions for R&D (which would effectively lower the cost incurred). Moreover, in the U.S. the bulk of applications submitted to the FDA for regulatory approval are not for NCEs (or for new biologic entities (NBEs), which probably require even greater expenditures) but for "new uses of, or variations on, existing drugs, for which development costs are likely to be much lower." *Id.* at 147.

[10] *See* IP5 STATISTICS REPORT 2021 66–67, 97–98, https://link.epo.org/ip5/IP5%20Statistics%20Report%202021_1.pdf; USPTO, PATENTS PENDENCY DATA JULY 2024, https://www.uspto.gov/dashboard/patents/pendency.html.

[11] The EMA is an E.U. agency that evaluates applications for marketing authorization throughout the E.U. and the European Economic Area (EEA) (which includes all E.U. member states plus Iceland, Liechtenstein, and Norway). *See* European Medicines Agency, *What we do*, https://www.ema.europa.eu/en/about-us/what-we-do#evaluate-applications-for-marketing-authorisation-12355. Applicants have

other countries. Marketing approval almost always takes a much longer time than it takes to obtain a patent. In the United States, the median times from submission of an Investigational New Drug (IND) application to marketing approval is, according to one study, a little over eight years;[12] and it is probably at least that long or longer in the E.U.[13] Since the patent owner cannot lawfully market the drug until it obtains marketing authorization, the effective term of a patent on a new drug therefore is usually much shorter than the nominal patent term. One way for authorities to make up for some of this lost time is to offer patent term extensions, or functional approximations thereof. In the United States, for example, drug patents can receive up to five additional years of patent protection to compensate for regulatory delay,[14] whereas in the E.U., member states can grant a *sui generis* form of protection known as the supplemental protection certificate (SPC). SPCs, which can last for up to five years following expiration of the relevant domestic or European patent, prevent others from marketing specific EMA-approved medicinal or plant protection products.[15] Nations also may offer additional periods of marketing exclusivity for a variety of reasons, including the development of "orphan" drugs for rare diseases, or undertaking studies of the safety and effectiveness of drugs to treat

the option, however, of bypassing the EMA and applying for marketing authorization from national authorities within individual member states of the EEA. *See* European Medicines Agency, *National competent authorities (human)*, https://www.ema.europa.eu/en/partners-networks/eu-partners/eu-member-states/national-competent-authorities-human#list-of-national-competent-authorities-in-the-eea-11541. For a brief overview of the E.U. regulatory process, see Margherita Colangelo, *Reverse Payment Patent Settlements in the Pharmaceutical Sector Under EU and US Competition Laws: A Comparative Analysis*, 40 World Competition: Law & Econ. Rev. 471, 478–79 (2017).

[12] *See* Dean G. Brown et al., *Clinical development times for innovative drugs*, 21 Nat'l Rev. Drug Discovery 793 (2022) (reporting median of 8.2 years from submission of IND to marketing authorization). The overall time from drug discovery to marketing authorization, including preclinical testing conducted prior to submission of the IND, is sometimes said to take an average of 10–15 years. *See* Benjamin Zycher et al., *Private Sector Contributions to Pharmaceutical Science: Thirty-Five Summary Case Histories*, 17 Am. J. Therapeutics 101, 105 (2010).

[13] The European Federation of Pharmaceutical Industries and Associations asserts that "[m]edicine development takes an average of 12 years until approval for use in patients," presumably including preclinical testing. *See* EFPIA, *Clinical Trials*, https://www.efpia.eu/about-medicines/development-of-medicines/regulations-safety-supply/clinical-trials/.

[14] *See* 35 U.S.C. § 156(g)(6). The period of extension is reduced if the drug otherwise would be subject to patent protection for more than fourteen years following FDA approval. *See id.* § 156(c)(3).

[15] See Regulation (EC) No. 469/2009 of the European Parliament and of the Council of 6 May 2009 concerning the supplementary protection certificate for medicinal products, L 152/1; Regulation (EC) No 1610/96 of the European Parliament and of the Council of 23 July 1996 concerning the creation of a supplementary protection certificate for plant protection products, L 198/30. For discussion, *see, e.g.*, European SPCs Unravelled: A Practitioner's Guide to Supplementary Protection Certificates in Europe (Oswin Ridderbusch & Alexa von Uexküll 2d ed. 2021); Georgia A. Roussou, Supplementary Protection Certificates for Medicinal Products (2023); Supplementary Protection Certificates (SPC): A Handbook (Marco Stieff ed., 2d ed. 2021).

children.[16] Finally, nations may offer drug patent owners periods of *data* exclusivity, meaning that prospective generic competitors may not rely upon the clinical studies used to demonstrate the safety and effectiveness of the original ("reference") drug until after a specified period of time has passed.

The existence of this last form of exclusivity reflects a certain ambiguity inherent to the regulation of pharmaceutical products. On the one hand, in view of the high cost of pharmaceutical R&D and the (comparatively) low cost of developing generic bioequivalents to the small-molecule compounds that make up most prescription drugs,[17] economists generally agree that patent protection is necessary to encourage the development and commercialization of new drugs from which the public derives enormous benefits. At the same time, however, because public health depends not only upon development and commercialization, but also upon access to these drugs, and because access is affected by price, nations also engage in various forms of price regulation, often through the purchasing power of national health services. (In this regard, the United States remains an outlier among developed countries, with comparatively limited government regulation of drug prices to date.) Another way to keep the price of prescription drugs in check, which most countries including the United States also have adopted, is through legislation intended to promote competition from generic drug manufacturers; and this is where data exclusivities fit in. Generic firms are permitted, albeit only after a specified period of time following the approval of a brand-name drug, to apply for marketing approval for a bioequivalent version of an approved drug, and to rely upon the clinical studies submitted by the owner of the approved drug to prove that the drug is safe and effective. Since the patent rights covering the reference drug may still be in force, however, once the generic drug is approved or its approval is imminent, the brand owner may re-enter the picture and sue for the

[16] *See, e.g.*, Regulation (EC) No 141/2000 of the European Parliament and of the Council of 16 December 1999 on orphan medicinal products, L 18/1, art. 8 (ten years of marketing exclusivity for orphan drugs); Regulation (EC) No 1901/2006 of the European Parliament and of the Council of 12 December 2006 on medicinal products for paediatric use and amending Regulation (EEC) No 1768/92, Directive 2001/20/EC, Directive 2001/83/EC and Regulation (EC) No 726/2004, L 378/1, art. 36 (six-month extension of the patent or SPC term for conducting pediatric studies). (Some modifications to the exclusivities mentioned here and *infra* note 26 and accompanying text may take effect in 2026, following an agreement, shortly before this book went to press, among the EU institutions concerning pharmaceutical legislation reform.) For discussion of the various exclusivities under U.S. law, *see* Robin Feldman, *Regulatory Property: The New IP*, 40 COLUM. J. L. & ARTS 53 (2016).

[17] Biologics, on the other hand, are more complex molecules and therefore have proven both more costly to develop, and more difficult and expensive to reverse-engineer. For discussion, see W. Nicholson Price II & Arti Rai, *Manufacturing Barriers to Biologics Competition and Innovation*, 101 IOWA L. REV. 1023 (2016). The text above focuses on drugs, which have been the subject of most of the pay-for-delay case law.

infringement of any such patents that a generic substitute might infringe. The incentive to sue will be greatest where the brand-name drug confers substantial market power; moreover, in the limiting case in which the brand-name drug previously enjoyed monopoly power, and the brand and generic firms thereafter would compete as duopolists, the duopoly profits earned by the brand and the generic will be lower than the brand's monopoly profit prior to generic entry.[18] Real-world complications, including the possibility of entry by other generic firms, may further complicate the picture, but the fact remains that the brand often has a substantial incentive to delay generic entry as much as possible—and that incentive can be exacerbated by other features of the drug approval process, particularly in the United States.

To see why requires a slightly more detailed description of the drug approval process in the U.S. and the E.U. The U.S. approach is unusually complex, in part because of a piece of legislation enacted in 1984 and known as the Hatch-Waxman Act, which was intended to speed up the entry of generic drugs to the marketplace (but in doing so, also created some unintended incentives for potentially anticompetitive conduct). In the U.S., once the FDA approves the brand's new drug application (NDA), the brand will cause the drug, along with any "related patent and exclusivity information," to be listed in the FDA's publicly accessible "Orange Book."[19] A competitor who wants to market a bioequivalent version of the original ("reference") drug, and to rely upon the clinical studies referenced in support of the NDA, may file an "Abbreviated New Drug Application" (ANDA)[20]—though it must wait until five years following approval of the NDA, reduced to four if it intends to challenge patent validity or infringement.[21] It also must certify that its proposed generic drug will not infringe any Orange Book listed patent in force, so if there are any potentially relevant Orange Book listed patents, the generic will make a "Paragraph IV" certification asserting that its proposed generic drug will not infringe and/or that the patents at issue are invalid or unenforceable.[22] The first generic to file an ANDA, moreover, will obtain 180 days of exclusivity

[18] *See* ch. 4 note 78 and sources cited therein.

[19] *See Approved Drug Products with Therapeutic Equivalence Evaluations (Orange Book)*, U.S. Food & Drug Admin., http://www.fda.gov/Drugs/InformationOnDrugs/ucm129662.htm.

[20] See 21 U.S.C. § 355(j)(2).

[21] *See id.* § 355(j)(5)(F)(ii). By way of information, there is an analogous (albeit even more complicated) pathway for the marketing of generic version of biologics, known as "biosimilars." Because of the greater complexity of biologics, though, the brand is entitled to twelve years of exclusivity before an applicant may request authorization to market a biosimilar. *See* 42 U.S.C. § 262(k)(7)(A). For a brief overview, see FDA, *Review and Approval*, https://www.fda.gov/drugs/biosimilars/review-and-approval.

[22] *See id.* § 355(j)(2)(A)(vii)(IV).

from competition from later-filing generic firms.[23] Upon receiving notification of the filing of the paragraph IV certification, however, the brand has forty-five days to file an action for infringement against the generic, the submission of the ANDA being considered an act of so-called "technical" infringement; if it does so, it obtains a thirty-month stay of approval of the ANDA.[24] The thirty-month stay is the functional equivalent of an automatic preliminary injunction—and if it pertains to the first-filing generic, it blocks not only that firm from marketing the generic drug but also any subsequent generic firms, since the first-filer has yet to use its 180-day exclusivity.[25]

The EMA process involves fewer legal complexities, though arguably just as many factual complications. Generics must wait a bit longer than in the United States—eight years before they can seek approval to market a generic drug (or a biosimilar), and another two before they can place the generic drug on the market.[26] There is no automatic stay of authorization, however; nor is there any counterpart to the FDA's Orange Book, in which drug patent owners list the patents they claim are relevant to their approved drugs. To keep the generic off the market, then, the brand must affirmatively request a preliminary injunction; and the brand would need to do so in each member state of interest, individually.[27] It also may need to file actions against multiple generics, given the absence of any right of exclusivity for the first generic to file.

It should be apparent from the above that the U.S. system in particular enhances whatever incentive may already exist for the brand and the first-filing generic to settle on terms that keep the generic off-market in exchange for

[23] More precisely, other generic manufacturers will be prohibited from marketing a generic version of the drug until 180 days after the first ANDA applicant does so, or a court enters judgment finding the patent in suit to be invalid or noninfringed. *See id.* § 355(j)(5)(B)(iv). More than one company may file an ANDA on the first day it is possible to do so, but there can be only one 180-day period of exclusivity per drug product; it begins to run upon the "first commercial marketing of the drug . . . by the first applicant." *Id.* § 355(j)(5)(B)(iv)(I). Thus, "whether multiple first applicants enjoy the full 180-day exclusivity period depends on when those ANDAs are approved in relation to when the 180-day exclusivity period is triggered." U.S. Dep't of Health & Human Servs. et al., Guidance of Industry: 180-Day Exclusivity: Questions and Answers 9–11 (Jan. 2017 draft). The 180-day exclusivity period can be forfeited if it is not used within a statutorily-specified time frame. *See id.* at 15–19.

[24] More precisely, it obtains a stay of approval of the ANDA until the earliest of (1) the date the patent expires, (2) the entry of a final judgment of invalidity or noninfringement, or (3) thirty months. *See id.* § 355(j)(5)(B)(iii).

[25] *See supra* note 23.

[26] *See* Regulation (EC) No. 726/2004 of the European Parliament and of the Council of 31 March 2004 laying down Community procedures for the authorisation and supervision of medicinal products for human and veterinary use and establishing a European Medicines Agency, L 136/1, article 14(11) (providing, in addition, for an additional year of market exclusivity in cases in which the original drug has a new indication with significant clinical benefit).

[27] For some cases arising on or after June 1, 2023, the Unified Patent Court might be an option, at least for those E.U. member states that have ratified the Unified Patent Court Agreement.

some portion of the additional profit the brand expects to earn in the absence of generic competition. First, upon receiving notice of the generic's Paragraph IV certification, the brand will almost always sue for infringement because, as noted above, the automatic stay provides the brand with the functional equivalent of a (virtually costless) thirty-month preliminary injunction. Second, whether the parties settle on terms that allow the generic to enter the market only upon patent expiration, or some period of time prior to expiration, the brand is largely assured of earning (at the limit, monopoly) profits for that period of time, because the first-filing generic likely will still be entitled to its 180-days of generic exclusivity, once it finally enters the market.[28] Third, because the monopolist's profit prior to generic entry likely will exceed its own and the generic's duopoly profits following generic entry, a brand that enjoys monopoly power can share some portion of its monopoly profit with the first-filing generic and still be better off than it would be competing with the generic. All of this suggests that settling on terms that keep the generic out of the market in exchange for cash or other valuable consideration—which is the form that pay-for-delay settlements take—would be a tempting response, albeit one that might appear at first blush to be a per se illegal market allocation scheme. As Jeremy Bulow puts it, "you don't get to pay your competitor to stay out of the market."[29]

Similar considerations might work to encourage anticompetitive settlements in the E.U., although the different regulatory environment could either enhance or dampen the incentives to collude, depending on the circumstances. Since there is no automatic stay, the brand will need to quickly file (and prevail on) a preliminary injunction to keep the generic off the market entirely—though even if it does so, as discussed in the preceding chapter it may be obligated to compensate the generic later on, if the injunction is lifted. On the other hand, the fact that numerous generics may be poised to compete with the brand can make collusion much more expensive, too. Instead of paying off just one competitor, the brand may have to pay off several, thus increasing transaction costs, reducing the benefits of collusion,[30] and perhaps signaling its own

[28] As noted above, there are scenarios under which the 180-day period can be forfeited, but—for reasons more technical than need be presented here—these are unlikely to arise in many cases. For discussion, see U.S. Dep't of Health & Human Servs. et al., Guidance of Industry: 180-Day Exclusivity: Questions and Answers 15–19 (Jan. 2017 draft).

[29] Jeremy Bulow, *The Gaming of Pharmaceutical Patents, in* 4 Innovation Policy and the Economy 145, 166 (Adam B. Jaffe et al. eds. 2004).

[30] *See* Hovenkamp, *supra* note 1, at 460–62 (showing that, in the U.S., the 180-day exclusivity period provides the settling generic with an incentive to accept a longer period of delay). *Cf.* FTC v. Actavis Inc., 570 U.S. 136, 154–55 (2013) (posing the question whether "a high reverse payment [would] signal to other potential challengers that the patentee lacks confidence in its patent, thereby provoking

perceptions concerning the weakness of its patent[31]—although, depending on the circumstances, a given generic may operate in only certain parts of the E.U., rather than the entire region.

There are, however, other considerations to keep in mind—foremost among them, that the generic might actually be infringing a valid patent, and if so that valid patent entitles the brand to exclude the generic from the market until patent expiration. In addition, although the fact that in pay-for-delay cases consideration flows from plaintiff to defendant may seem odd—intuition suggests that, most of the time, it's the defendant who pays to settle litigation, in the hope of avoiding potentially greater liability if the case were to proceed to trial—in this context, settlements with consideration flowing from plaintiff to defendant can be consistent with a high probability of the plaintiff's prevailing on the merits, particularly where the defendant has yet to earn much or any revenue from sales of infringing products.

Some illustrations, initially premised on the U.S. system, may help to clarify why this is so.[32] Suppose that the defendant begins its alleged infringement at time t_0; that the parties consider settlement at time t_1; and that trial is expected to take place at time t_2. As of t_1, the patent owner has incurred lost profits of $30 million. The present value of its estimated future lost profits if the alleged infringement does not cease is $100 million, consisting of an additional $10 million in lost profits from t_1 to t_2 and $90 million thereafter. The present value of the defendant's estimate of its own loss if it stops marketing the accused product at t_1 is $50 million, consisting of $5 million in lost profits from t_1 to t_2 (call this $G_{\Delta,t2}$) and $45 million thereafter. As of t_1, the expected benefit to the plaintiff (Π) from going to trial can be expressed as

$$E[B]_{\Pi,T} = P_{\Pi}[I_{\Pi} + \delta_{\Pi}(D_{\Pi,t1} + D_{\Pi,t2})] - C_{\Pi,T}, \tag{1}$$

additional challenges, perhaps too many for the patentee to 'buy off,'" but concluding that under U.S. law the 180-day exclusivity afforded to the first generic to file an ANDA, along with the 30-month stay, means that "a reverse payment settlement with the first filer (or, as in this case, all of the initial filers) 'removes from consideration the most motivated challenger, and the one closest to introducing competition'") (quoting C. Scott Hemphill, *Paying for Delay: Pharmaceutical Patent Settlement as a Regulatory Design Problem*, 81 N.Y.U. L. Rev. 1553, 1586 (2006)).

[31] *Cf. FTC v. Actavis*, 570 U.S. at 175 (Roberts, C.J., dissenting) (stating that "a patent holder who gives away notably large sums of money because it is . . . concerned about the strength of its patent, would be putting blood in water where sharks are always near").

[32] The illustrations that follow are adapted from my article *Refining the "Presumptive Illegality" Approach to Settlements of Patent Disputes Involving Reverse Payments: A Commentary on Hovenkamp, Janis & Lemley*, 87 Minn. L. Rev. 1789 (2003).

where P_{Π} is the plaintiff's estimate of the probability of success on the merits; I_{Π} is the plaintiff's estimate of the present value to it of obtaining an injunction at t_2; $D_{\Pi,t1}$ is the plaintiff's estimate of its damages at t_1; $D_{\Pi,t2}$ is the plaintiff's estimate of the additional damages it will incur from t_1 to t_2; δ_{Π} is the portion of its damages that the plaintiff expects to be able to collect from the defendant, where $0 \leq \delta \leq 1$; and $C_{\Pi,T}$ is the plaintiff's estimate of the present value of its future litigation costs. (Assume for now that each party bears its own costs, as is usually the case in the U.S.) The expected liability of the defendant (Δ) if the matter goes to trial can be expressed as

$$E[L]_{\Delta,T} = P_{\Delta}[I_{\Delta} + \delta_{\Delta}(D_{\Delta,t1} + D_{\Delta,t2})] + C_{\Delta,T}, \quad (2)$$

where P_{Δ} is the defendant's estimate of the plaintiff's probability of success on the merits; I_{Δ} is the defendant's estimate of the present value of its loss if an injunction issues at t_2; $\delta_{\Delta}(D_{\Delta,t1} + D_{\Delta,t2})$ is the defendant's estimate of the amount of damages it will pay if it is found liable; and $C_{\Delta,T}$ is the defendant's estimate of the present value of its future litigation costs. For simplicity, assume symmetric information, *i.e.*, $P_{\Pi} = P_{\Delta}$; that the defendant will not be judgment-proof, *i.e.*, $\delta = 1$; and that $P = .75$, *i.e.*, the plaintiff has a 75% chance of prevailing at trial. On these facts, the plaintiff's expected benefit from proceeding with litigation is $.75(90 + 30 + 10) - C_{\Pi,T} = \$97.5$ million $- C_{\Pi,T}$; the defendant's expected loss is $.75(45 + 30 + 10) + C_{\Delta,T} = \$63.75$ million $+ C_{\Delta,T}$. A settlement under which the defendant immediately ceases its infringement, and neither party pays any money to the other, brings the plaintiff \$100 million in immediate benefits $(I_{\Pi} + D_{\Pi,t2})$ and brings the defendant \$50 million in immediate losses/forgone gains $(I_{\Delta} + G_{\Delta,t2})$. A rational defendant therefore would be willing to settle the case by agreeing to cease infringement and pay the plaintiff up to \$13.75 million $+ C_{\Delta,T}$.[33] A rational plaintiff would be willing to accept the promise to cease infringement and to accept "payment" of at least $-\$2.5$ million $- C_{\Pi,T}$. In other words, the plaintiff would be willing to *pay* the defendant as much as \$2.5 million $+ C_{\Pi,T}$ to settle the case. Put another way, the range of possible payments stretches from a reverse payment of \$2.5 million, to a payment from defendant to plaintiff of \$13.75 million, aside from litigation costs. Thus, even when the

[33] More realistically, one might not expect the defendant to continue marketing during t_2 if its expected loss from doing so (here \$7.5 million) exceeded its expected gain (here \$5 million), although strategic considerations or other factors may weigh in the defendant's calculation.

plaintiff's chances of prevailing at trial are quite good, it is conceivable that the parties might agree to a settlement under which the plaintiff would pay the defendant.

Generally, one would expect the parties to settle when the expected benefit of settlement exceeds the expected benefit of litigation. The monetary aspect of the settlement agreement will satisfy the following condition:

$$E[B]_{\Pi,T} - E[B]_{\Pi,S} \leq SP \leq E[L]_{\Delta,T} - E[L]_{\Delta,S}, \tag{3}$$

where $E[B]_{\Pi,S}$ is the expected benefit to the plaintiff of settling; $E[L]_{\Delta,S}$ is the expected loss to the defendant of settling; and SP is the settlement payment. Substituting terms shows that

$$\begin{aligned} P_{\Pi}[I_{\Pi} + \delta_{\Pi}(D_{\Pi,t1} + D_{\Pi,t2})] - C_{\Pi,T} - (I_{\Pi} + D_{\Pi,t2}) &\leq SP \\ \leq P_{\Delta}[I_{\Delta} + \delta_{\Delta}(D_{\Delta,t1} + D_{\Delta,t2})] + C_{\Delta,T} - (I_{\Delta} + G_{\Delta,t2}) & \end{aligned} \tag{4}$$

Now consider the parties' incentives under the U.S. regulatory regime as described above. Once the plaintiff files suit, it obtains an automatic thirty-month stay, so the defendant may not market any infringing product as of t_1. D_{t1} therefore equals 0. D_{t2} and $G_{\Delta,t2}$ may be greater than or equal to zero, but they will tend toward zero if trial is expected to occur within thirty months of t_0 because the automatic stay will preclude the defendant's product from being on the market prior to t_2, at the earliest. (δ also could be less than 1, if the generic manufacturer has few assets or sources of income other than the drug at issue.) In any event, as $D_{\Pi,t2}$ and $G_{\Delta,t2}$ approach zero, inequality (4) simplifies to

$$-(1 - P_{\Pi})I_{\Pi} - C_{\Pi,T} \leq SP \leq (1 - P_{\Delta})I_{\Delta} + C_{\Delta,T}, \tag{5}$$

or, to phrase it in terms of how much money (positively) the plaintiff would be willing to pay, instead of how much (negatively) it would accept,

$$(1 - P_{\Pi})I_{\Pi} + C_{\Pi,T} \geq SP \geq (1 - P_{\Delta})I_{\Delta} - C_{\Delta,T}. \tag{6}$$

Table 5.1 Assume that $P_{\Pi} = P_{\Delta} = P$; $I_{\Pi} = 90$ million; and $I_{\Delta} = 45$ million.

P	Amount plaintiff will pay defendant
0	$90m + C_{\Pi,T} \geq SP \geq 45m - C_{\Delta,T}$
.25	$67.5m + C_{\Pi,T} \geq SP \geq 33.75m - C_{\Delta,T}$
.50	$45m + C_{\Pi,T} \geq SP \geq 22.5m - C_{\Delta,T}$
.75	$22.5m + C_{\Pi,T} \geq SP \geq 11.25m - C_{\Delta,T}$
1	$C_{\Pi,T} \geq SP \geq - C_{\Delta,T}$

Two observations follow from this inequality. The first is that the amount the plaintiff will agree to pay ranges from a maximum of $C_{\Pi,T}$ when $P_{\Pi} = 1$ (i.e., the plaintiff is 100% certain of victory at trial) to a maximum of $C_{\Pi,T} + I_{\Pi}$ when $P_{\Pi} = 0$ (*i.e.*, the plaintiff is 100% certain of losing at trial). At any probability in between, the plaintiff will agree to pay the defendant up to $C_{\Pi,T}$ plus some portion of I_{Π}, as set forth in Table 5.1. Significantly, the plaintiff will always be willing to pay the defendant something to settle. Second, when the defendant is 100% certain that its product would infringe ($P_{\Delta} = 1$), the defendant will be willing to pay up to $C_{\Delta,T}$ to settle. When the defendant is sure that its product would not infringe ($P_{\Delta} = 0$), the minimum the defendant would be willing to accept is $I_{\Delta} - C_{\Delta,T}$. At some intermediate probability, the defendant would be willing to accept some portion of I_{Δ}, minus the litigation expenses it will avoid by settling. Table 5.1 illustrates the range of likely settlement values for different probabilities of success.

The E.U. system can be illustrated in a similar fashion, subject to a few tweaks to reflect (1) the prevailing party's entitlement to recover a portion of its litigation costs, and (2) the lack of an automatic stay, in consequence of which the brand must decide whether to move for a preliminary injunction, knowing that if it succeeds in obtaining one it may be obligated to compensate the generic for its interim losses if the brand loses at trial. As shown in the appendix to this chapter, the same general results nevertheless obtain, in that if the brand believes it has a 100% chance of winning, it will pay only up to the sum of (1) the portion of its expected litigation costs it expects will be uncompensable, minus (2) whatever damages it expects to collect from the generic for products sold during the initial, pre-settlement period. More generally, as in the U.S., a higher payment correlates with a lower probability of infringement and validity, though a payment in excess of avoided litigation costs can be consistent with a greater than 50% ex ante probability of validity and infringement.

The above illustration assumes that the parties settle on terms that keep the generic off the market until the date the patent expires, but in fact real-world settlements often allow for earlier generic entry (sometimes coupled with a reverse payment, sometimes not). To illustrate, suppose that the patent at issue has five years until expiration, and that for each year the brand retains its monopoly it earns $100 million in profits.[34] If instead the generic enters and the two firms compete as duopolists, assume that the brand will earn $60 million and the generic $30 million per year, until patent expiration.[35] Retention of its monopoly therefore is worth $40 million per year to the brand, or $200 million over the five-year period. Suppose further that $P_\Pi = P_\Delta = .8$. The brand's expected payoff from litigating at t_0 is $160 million – $C_{\Pi,T}$, and the generic's is $30 million – $C_{\Delta,T}$. If antitrust liability is not a concern, one would expect the parties to settle on terms that keep the generic off market until the end of the fifth year, with the brand paying some amount between $40 million + $C_{\Pi,T}$ and $30 million – $C_{\Delta,T}$. The parties' aggregate profit would be $500 million, and in an expectations sense each would be at least as well off, or better off, than if the matter proceeded to litigation.

Alternatively, in the above scenario the parties could agree to a lower payment coupled with earlier generic entry. Because P = .8, the generic's anticipated date of entry (in an expectations sense) as of t_0 would be the beginning of the final year. If the generic were to enter at that date, the brand would expect to earn $460 million ($100 million during Years 1–4 and $60 million in Year 5), and the generic $30 million (in Year 5). The most the brand would be willing to pay to achieve this settlement would be its avoided litigation costs, $C_{\Pi,T}$. Absent the risk of antitrust liability, however, such a settlement seems unlikely, since the parties' aggregate profit would now be $490 million, or $10 million less than it could be with the reverse payment. (Consumer surplus correspondingly would be $10 million greater.) Other possibilities, though again unlikely absent a risk of antitrust liability, would be to permit entry somewhere in between the beginning and end of Year 5, with a maximum reverse payment greater than $C_{\Pi,T}$ but less than $40 million + $C_{\Pi,T}$ (the maximum the brand would pay to ensure exclusivity until the end of Year 5).[36]

[34] This example is modified from Thomas F. Cotter, *Antitrust Implications of Patent Settlements Involving Reverse Payments: Defending a Rebuttable Presumption of Illegality in Light of Some Recent Scholarship*, 71 ANTITRUST L.J.1069, 1085–86 (2004).

[35] It has long been the case that, after generic entry, the brand often raises the price of the branded drug, which it sells to consumers who prefer the brand-name to the generic equivalent. For recent evidence, *see* Mohammed Jamjoom et al., *Generic entry and effect of market competition on outpatient pharmacy drug prices*, 20 J. GENERIC MEDICINES 69 (2024) (reporting that, in the U.S. from 2013 to 2018, "[t]he median brand-name drug NADAC price increased by 1.0% per month before generic entry, remained stable during the generic entry period, and increased by 0.4% per month afterwards"). The brand's overall profit nevertheless is expected to decline as a result of competition from the generic, which will sell to consumers for whom the brand-name and generic drugs are acceptable substitutes.

[36] As several commentators have noted, the fact that something is a feasible settlement does not mean that it is an equilibrium or Pareto optimal settlement. Absent some risk of antitrust liability, one would

Based on the above, it would seem that banning reverse payment settlements in excess of $C_{\Pi,T}$ would be certain to increase consumer surplus, in comparison with allowing such settlements to occur. Some economists have posited, however, that under certain conditions a ban on reverse payment settlements could make consumers worse off.[37] The leading example involves a risk-averse brand coupled with the parties' asymmetric expectations concerning the likely outcome of litigation.[38]

To illustrate, suppose that the brand accurately foresees an 80% probability of success at trial ($P_{\Pi} = .8$), but the generic estimates the brand's probability of success at only 60% (and its own, correspondingly, at 40%). Suppose further that the brand is risk averse, such that its expected payoff from litigating, net of litigation expenses, is only $125 million (instead of $160 million – $C_{\Pi,T}$, as above). The generic is risk-neutral and expects to incur only $3 million in fees if the case proceeds to trial. On these facts, the brand would be indifferent between litigating and allowing generic entry at Year 3.125, since the expected payoff from either would be $125 million. (Put another way, the brand is indifferent between litigating and competing as a duopolist for 1.875 years.) The generic is indifferent between litigating (expected payoff of $57 million) or settling on terms that permit it to enter at Year 3.1. (Put another way, the generic is indifferent between litigating and competing as a duopolist for 1.9 years.) The parties are close, but absent a reverse payment there will be no settlement; and the expected date of generic entry would be at the beginning of Year 4 (reflecting an objective 80% probability the brand will prevail at trial). If reverse payments are permitted, on the other hand, the brand could pay the generic (say) $15 million on condition that the generic enters at Year 3.55. The generic's expected payoff then would be $58.5 million, and the brand's $127 million.

expect the parties to agree to the generic's delaying entry until patent expiration. *See, e.g.*, Aaron Edlin et al., Actavis *and Error Costs: A Reply to Critics*, ANTITRUST SOURCE, Oct. 2014, at 5; Hovenkamp, *supra* note 1, at 456–57, 474.

[37] *See* Barry C. Harris et al., *Activating* Actavis*: A More Complete Story*, ANTITRUST, Spring 2013, at 83; Marc G. Schildkraut, *Patent Splitting Settlements and the Reverse Payment Fallacy*, 71 ANTITRUST L.J. 1033 (2004); Robert D. Willig & John P. Bigelow, *Antitrust Policy Towards Agreements that Settle Patent Litigation*, 49 ANTITRUST BULL. 655 (2004); Barry C. Harris et al., *Activating* Actavis*: A More Complete Story*, ANTITRUST, Spring 2013, at 83.

[38] A risk-averse person, "when faced with a choice between two gambles with the same expected value, will usually choose the one with a smaller variability of return," WALTER NICHOLSON, MICROECONOMIC THEORY: BASIC PRINCIPLES AND EXTENSIONS 538 (9th ed. 2004). In the present context, a risk-averse brand would be willing to pay a risk premium *R* to "ensure an immediate payoff (or payout) below the actuarial value of litigating to judgment." Cotter, *supra* note 34, at 1073. Proponents of the analysis discussed in the text above also have posited that there may be other cases in which a reverse payment is needed to facilitate a settlement, such as when the generic is a risk preferrer, or the incumbent is aware of possible entry by a third party. *See* Cotter, *supra* note 34, at 1089 n.60 (citing sources).

Both parties are better off than they would expect to be from litigating, and consumers would benefit from earlier generic entry than would be expected under litigation. As in the preceding illustration, however, the parties could do even better if reverse payments are lawful no matter the amount. In that case, brand should be willing to pay up to $75 million, and generic should be willing to accept as little as $57 million, to settle on condition that generic delay entry until the patent term ends in five years.[39]

Obviously, the numbers in the above example have been chosen to illustrate a situation in which a reverse payment would be necessary to induce a desirable settlement (and even then, it's not clear that the amount of the payment must be more than the brand's avoided litigation costs, which were left unspecified). How often such situations would arise in the real world is debatable—as is the question of how readily a court could determine whether the brand was risk averse, and that the parties' litigation expectations diverged.[40] I will return to this issues below, in the context of discussing how courts should evaluate the legality of reverse payment settlements of the type under consideration in this chapter.

The Case Law on Reverse Payments

The first few cases addressing whether reverse payment settlements violate antitrust law arose in the United States. Although a few early decisions applied a rule of per se liability,[41] the majority of U.S. courts prior to 2013 adopted the "scope of the patent" test, under which a settlement would be lawful, absent sham litigation or fraud in the procurement, as long as the terms of the settlement fell within the *potential* exclusionary scope of the patent.[42] In 2012, however, the Third Circuit departed from this trend by adopting the so-called "quick-look" or presumptive illegality approach, under which "the finder of fact must treat any payment from a patent holder to a generic patent challenger who agrees to delay entry into the market as *prima facie* evidence of an unreasonable restraint of trade, which could be rebutted by showing that the payment (1) was for a purpose other than delayed entry or (2) offers

[39] *See* Edlin et al., *supra* note 36, at 7.
[40] *See id.*
[41] *See* In re Cardizem Antitrust Litig., 332 F.3d 896 (6th Cir. 2003).
[42] *See* FTC v. Watson Pharms., Inc., 677 F.3d 1298, 1312 (11th Cir. 2012), *rev'd and remanded*, 570 U.S. 136 (2013).

some procompetitive benefit."[43] The Supreme Court granted certiorari to resolve the conflict, and issued its resulting decision in *FTC v Actavis, Inc.* in 2013.[44]

Writing for a 5–3 majority, Justice Breyer rejected the scope of the patent test, reasoning that "it would be incongruous to determine antitrust legality by measuring the settlement's anticompetitive effects solely against patent law policy, rather than by measuring them against procompetitive antitrust policies as well."[45] Thus, rather than focusing on whether the parties agreed to terms falling within the potential exclusionary scope of the patent, courts should instead consider whether the "payment in effect amounts to a purchase by the patentee of the exclusive right to sell its product, a right it . . . would lose if the . . . patent were held invalid or not infringed by the generic product."[46] Put another way, the relevant question is whether "a patentee is using its monopoly profits to *avoid the risk* of patent invalidation or a finding of noninfringement."[47] Further emphasizing this avoidance-of-risk point, the Court continued:

> The reverse payment . . . may amount to no more than a rough approximation of the litigation expenses saved through the settlement. That payment may reflect compensation for other services that the generic has promised to perform—such as distributing the patented item or helping to develop a market for that item. There may be other justifications. Where a reverse payment reflects traditional settlement considerations, such as avoided litigation costs or fair value for services, there is not the same concern that a patentee is using its monopoly profits to *avoid the risk* of patent invalidation or a finding of noninfringement. In such cases, the parties may have provided for a reverse payment without having sought or brought about the anticompetitive consequences we mentioned above.[48]

That said, the Court cautioned that it should "normally not [be] necessary to litigate patent validity to answer the antitrust question (unless, perhaps, to determine whether the patent litigation is a sham)".[49] Rather:

[43] *See* In re K-Dur Antitrust Litig., 686 F.3d 197, 218 (3d Cir. 2012), *vacated and remanded*, 570 U.S. 913 (2013).
[44] 570 U.S. 136 (2013).
[45] *Id.* at 146.
[46] *Id.* at 153–54.
[47] *Id.* at 156 (emphasis added).
[48] *Id.* (emphasis added).
[49] *Id.* at 157.

> An unexplained large reverse payment itself would normally suggest that the patentee has serious doubts about the patent's survival. And that fact, in turn, suggests that the payment's objective is to maintain supracompetitive prices to be shared among the patentee and the challenger rather than face what might have been a competitive market—the very anticompetitive consequence that underlies the claim of antitrust unlawfulness. The owner of a particularly valuable patent might contend, of course, that even a small risk of invalidity justifies a large payment. But, be that as it may, the payment (if otherwise unexplained) likely seeks to *prevent the risk of competition*. And, as we have said, that consequence constitutes the relevant anticompetitive harm. In a word, the size of the unexplained reverse payment can provide a workable surrogate for a patent's weakness, all without forcing a court to conduct a detailed exploration of the validity of the patent itself.[50]

The Court nevertheless also rejected the Third Circuit's quick-look approach, in favor of the Rule of Reason,[51] although the difference between the two approaches in the present context seems scant. A fair reading of the Court's approach would require the antitrust plaintiff to show a large, apparently unjustified payment—as opposed to *any* payment, under the Third Circuit's approach—but would then shift the burden of production to the defendants to demonstrate that the payment was, in fact, justified or otherwise procompetitive.[52]

Several U.S. trial and appellate court decisions have addressed reverse payment settlements in the years following the *Actavis* decision.[53] Courts generally have followed *Actavis* in concluding that a large and ostensibly unjustified payment permits an inference of anticompetitive harm.[54] Most have agreed,

[50] *Id.* at 157–58 (emphasis added).

[51] *See id.* at 158–59.

[52] *See* Thomas F. Cotter, FTC v. Actavis, Inc.: *When Is the Rule of Reason Not the Rule of Reason?*, 15 MINN. J.L. SCI. & TECH. 41, 43 (2014) (asserting that "the Court appears to have all but in name adopted the presumptive illegality approach it purported to reject"); Edlin et al., *supra* note 36, at 3–4 (suggesting that the Rule of Reason envisioned in *Actavis* differs from the quick-look approach in that "the plaintiff bear[s] the burden of production as to avoided litigation expense and the burden of persuasion overall," and in "permitting the defendant to offer a wider range of responses" such as a lack of market power).

[53] Over thirty, actually. For a recent overview of the case law interpreting *Actavis*, *see* Kristen O'Shaughnessy et al., *A Decade of FTC v. Actavis: The Reverse Payment Framework Is Older, But Are the Courts Wiser in Applying It?*, 86 ANTITRUST L.J. 473 (2024).

[54] *See, e.g.*, Impax Labs., Inc. v. FTC, 994 F.3d 464, 495 (5th Cir. 2021) (rejecting the argument that the FTC needed to "assess the likely outcome of the patent case in order to find anticompetitive effects," and reading *Actavis* to stand for the proposition that "[t]he fact that generic competition was possible, and that Endo was willing to pay a large amount to prevent that risk, is enough to infer anticompetitive effect"); HOVENKAMP ET AL., *supra* note 1, § 16.01[D][i], at 16–31 to -32 nn. 119 & 120 (citing additional cases).

in addition, that "payments" are not limited to cash transfers, but can include any other transfer of valuable consideration from brand to generic, including an agreement on the part of the brand not to market or license an authorized generic that would compete with the alleged infringer's product.[55] (Such cases present obvious practical difficulties, of course, to the extent courts must determine the cash value to attribute to such noncash transfers.) At least one court also has allowed defendants to present evidence that a reverse payment was justified by reason of the brand's aversion to risk,[56] though this appears to be a minority view in light of the *Actavis* majority's characterization, as noted above, of payments intended to avoid the risk of competition as anticompetitive.[57] On the other hand, some decisions have taken a narrower approach to reverse payment antitrust suits brought by private parties, as opposed to the FTC, in holding that private parties cannot rely on the *Actavis* inference alone to establish an antitrust violation, but rather must also prove that, absent the settlement, the generic would have entered the market earlier because it would have prevailed in the infringement litigation or entered at risk, or because the parties would have negotiated a settlement permitting earlier entry.[58] As other courts and commentators have noted, however, nothing in *Actavis* itself hints at a heightened standard for private plaintiffs merely to demonstrate an antitrust violation.[59] That said, to *quantify* the amount of its damages, a private plaintiff may have to provide evidence from which the trier of fact can estimate

[55] *See* In re Loestrin 24 Fe Antitrust Litigation, 814 F.3d 538 (1st Cir. 2016); King Drug Co. v. SmithKline Beecham, 791 F.3d 388 (3d Cir. 2015). Other cases may involve the settlement of other litigation on terms that favor the generic, or that purport to compensate the generic for products or services the generic agrees to provide to the brand. For discussion, see HOVENKAMP ET AL., *supra* note 1, § 16.01[D](ii); *cf.* Michael A. Carrier & Edward Bank, *The Missing Caselaw of Reverse-Payment Settlements*, 97 ST. JOHN'S L. REV. 959, 995–96 (2025) (noting that such "side deals" may include "co-promotion deals, backup manufacturing, the provision of active ingredients, and joint-development agreements," but that empirical evidence suggests that such arrangements between brands and generics are rare outside the settlement context).

[56] *See* In re Wellbutrin XL Antitrust Litig. Indirect Purchaser Class, 868 F.3d 132, 168–69 (3d Cir. 2017).

[57] *See supra* notes 47–50 and accompanying text.

[58] *See, e.g.*, In re Wellbutrin XL Antitrust Litig., 133 F. Supp. 3d 734, 764–67 (E.D. Pa. 2015) (acknowledging that *Actavis* "explained that it is 'normally not necessary to litigate patent validity to answer the antitrust question' because '[a]n unexplained large reverse payment itself would normally suggest that the patentee has serious doubts about the patent's survival,'" but concluding that in a case litigated under the Clayton Act, rather than (like *Actavis*) under the FTC Act, "the causation requirement cannot be satisfied by using the size of the payment as a proxy for patent strength and the success of the underlying patent litigation"), *aff'd*, 868 F.3d 132, 169 (3d Cir. 2017); *see also* In re Nexium (Esomeprazole) Antitrust Litig., 842 F.3d 34, 60–64 (1st Cir. 2016); Apotex, Inc. v. Cephalon, Inc., 255 F. Supp. 3d 604, 612 (E.D. Pa. 2017).

[59] *See, e.g.*, United Food & Com. Workers Loc. 1776 & Participating Emps. Health & Welfare Fund v. Teikoku Pharma USA, 296 F. Supp. 3d 1142, 1152–54 (N.D. Cal. 2017); HOVENKAMP ET AL., *supra* note 1, § 16.01[J], at 16-66.61–.62 (citing additional cases); Kevin B. Soter, Note, *Causation in Reverse Payment Antitrust Claims*, 70 STAN. L. REV. 1295, 1310 (2018).

the date on which the generic would have entered the market, absent the reverse payment, and this inquiry may indeed entail investigation into the ex ante probability of validity and infringement.[60] For this reason, in private antitrust actions courts applying the *Actavis* inference and those requiring proof of actual delay of generic entry have both permitted expert testimony concerning the ex ante probability that the brand would have prevailed had the infringement lawsuit proceeded to judgment.[61]

For its part, the CJEU has issued decisions in several reverse payments cases, beginning in 2020 with *Generics (UK)*,[62] continuing in 2021 with a series of related decisions involving the Swedish firm Lundbeck,[63] and culminating in 2024 with a series of related decisions involving the French company Servier.[64] Without going into the particulars of these enormously complex cases, suffice to say that the standard the CJEU employs requires courts to consider, on a case-by-case basis, whether there were "real and concrete possibilities" for the generic firms to compete, absent the settlement agreements.[65] In this regard, the fact that the brand paid the generic an amount greater than or equal to the profit the generic would have earned from competing may be relevant in determining whether a settlement is an unlawful restriction "by object"[66] (the practical effect of which is that any procompetitive justification in defense of the restriction is very unlikely to succeed), but the amount need not be this high to raise suspicion.[67] Rather, the issue is whether the amount corresponded to

[60] *See* Hovenkamp, *supra* note 1, at 423; Soter, *supra* note 59, at 1312–13 n.76.

[61] See In re Wellbutrin XL Antitrust Litig., 133 F. Supp. 3d 734, 764–67 (E.D. Pa. 2015), *aff'd*, 868 F.3d 132, 169 (3d Cir. 2017); *see also* In re Zetia (Ezetimibe) Antitrust Litig., MDL No. 2:18-md-2836, 2022 WL 3344191, at *8–20 (E.D. Va. Aug. 3, 2022); In re Intuniv Antitrust Litig., Civil Action Nos. 1:16-cv-12653-ADB, 1:16-cv-12396-ADB, 2020 WL 5995326, at *12–14 (D. Mass. Oct. 10, 2020); In re Loestrin 24 Fe Antitrust Litig., 433 F. Supp. 3d 274, 306 (D.R.I. 2019); In re Namenda Direct-Purchaser Antitrust Litig., 331 F. Supp. 3d 152, 188 (S.D.N.Y. 2018); In re Solodyn (Minocycline Hydrochloride) Antitrust Litig., No. CV 14-MD-02503, 2018 WL 563144, at *16–19 (D. Mass. Jan. 25, 2018); United Food & Com. Workers Loc. 1776 & Participating Emps. Health & Welfare Fund v. Teikoku Pharma USA, 296 F. Supp. 3d 1142, 1184 (N.D. Cal. 2017); cf. Fresenius Kabi USA, LLC v. Par Sterile Prods., LLC, Case No. 16-4544 (SDW) (LDW), 2020 WL 901967, at *6 (D.N.J. Feb. 25, 2020), *vacated and remanded on other grounds*, 841 Fed. Appx. 399 (3d Cir. 2021).

[62] Generics (UK) Ltd. v. Competition and Markets Authority, Case C-307/18, ECLI:EU:C:2020:52 (CJEU 2020).

[63] The leading case is *H. Lundbeck A/S v. European Commission*, Case C-591/16 P, ECLI:EU:C:2021:243 (CJEU 2021).

[64] The leading case is *Servier v. European Commission*, Case C-201/19 P, ECLI:EU:C:2024:552 (CJEU 2024). Shortly before this book went to press, the CJEU dismissed an appeal brought by the defendants in yet another reverse-payments decision. *See* Case C-2/24 P, Teva Pharm. Indus. Ltd. v. Eur. Comm'n, ECLI:EU:C:2025:825 (CJEU 2025). The decision applies the principles set forth in the aforementioned decisions and does not appear to break new legal ground.

[65] *See id.* ¶¶ 100–02; *Generics (UK)*, Case C-307/18 P, ECLI:EU:C:2020:52, ¶¶ 36, 50; *Lundbeck*, Case C-591/16 P, ECLI:EU:C:2021:243, ¶¶ 54–55.

[66] *See Lundbeck*, Case C-591/16 P, ECLI:EU:C:2021:243, ¶¶ 63, 65, 66.

[67] *See id.* ¶ 115:

arm's-length compensation to the generic for services rendered, or made up to the generic for "the costs of or disruption caused by the litigation between them."[68] (Note that, unlike the *Actavis* inference, this phrasing does not explicitly inquire into whether the payment exceeded the brand's avoided litigation costs.[69]) Moreover, the Court has emphasized that "it is not for the competition authority concerned to carry out a review of the strength of the patent at issue

> For the purpose of that examination, it is appropriate to assess on a case-by-case basis whether the net gain of the transfers of value from the manufacturer of originator medicines to the manufacturer of generic medicines was sufficiently significant actually to act as an incentive to the manufacturer of generic medicines to refrain from entering the market concerned and, consequently, not to compete on the merits with the manufacturer of originator medicines; however, there is no requirement that the net gain should necessarily be greater than the profits which that manufacturer of generic medicines would have made if it had been successful in the patent proceedings (see, to that effect, judgment of 30 January 2020, *Generics (UK) and Others*, C-307/18, EU:C:2020:52, paragraphs 93 and 94).

See also Servier, Case C-201/19 P, ECLI:EU:C:2024:552, ¶ 333; Lupin Ltd. v. European Commission, Case C-144/19 P, ECLI:EU:C:2024:545, ¶ 128 (CJEU 2024).

[68] *See Generics (UK)*, Case C-307/18, ECLI:EU:C:2020:52, ¶¶ 85–87:

> The fact that such an agreement involves transfers of value, either pecuniary or non-pecuniary, made by the manufacturer of the originator medicine to the manufacturer of generic medicines is not sufficient ground to classify it as a "restriction by object," since those transfers of value may prove to be justified, that is, appropriate and strictly necessary having regard to the legitimate objectives of the parties to the agreement.
>
> That may, in particular, be the case where the manufacturer of generic medicines receives from the manufacturer of the originator medicine sums that correspond in fact to compensation for the costs of or disruption caused by the litigation between them, or that correspond to remuneration for the actual supply, immediate or subsequent, of goods or services to the manufacturer of the originator medicines. That may also be the case when the manufacturer of the generic medicines discharges undertakings, particularly financial, given by the patent holder to him, such as a cross-undertaking in damages.
>
> However, such a characterisation as a "restriction by object" must be adopted when it is plain from the analysis of the settlement agreement concerned that the transfers of value provided for by it cannot have any explanation other than the commercial interest of both the holder of the patent and the party allegedly infringing the patent not to engage in competition on the merits.

See also Servier, Case C-201/19 P, ECLI:EU:C:2024:552, ¶ 160, stating that, according to the General Court (Court of First Instance):

> it is necessary to examine whether that reverse payment is aimed at compensating costs inherent in the settlement that are borne by the manufacturer of generic medicines. The General Court stated that those costs include, in particular, expenses incurred in the context of the disputes which are the subject of the settlement agreement, provided that those expenses have been established by the parties to that agreement and that they are not disproportionate to the amount of the expenses that are objectively indispensable to the litigation. By contrast, according to the judgment under appeal, those costs do not include either the value of the stock of infringing medicinal products or the research and development costs incurred in developing those medicinal products. Those costs also exclude, as a general rule, sums payable as compensation under contracts concluded by the manufacturer of generic medicines with third parties, including for termination.

[69] In *Generics*, one of the questions posed was whether there is a restriction by object when "the patent holder agrees to make a transfer of value to the generic company in an amount substantially greater than the avoided litigation costs," *see Generics*, *supra*, ¶¶ 21, 61, 65, but the Court did not squarely address it.

or of the probability of a dispute between the patent holder and a manufacturer of generic medicines being brought to an end with a finding that the patent is valid and has been infringed."[70] As under the U.S. *Actavis* decision, "the fact that it is not possible to determine with certainty whether [the generic] would have actually entered those markets has no bearing on the fact that, although it wished to enter those markets and had the means to do so, it agreed with [the brand] to forego such a possibility, on terms mutually beneficial to those two undertakings."[71]

Finally, in 2021 China's Supreme People's Court issued a decision in a case in which there appears to have been a reverse payment settlement between Bristol-Myers Squibb (BMS) and an affiliate of a Chinese firm, referred to as VCare.[72] Because the patent in suit had expired by the date of the decision, the Court did not, ultimately, conclude whether it violated China's Anti-Monopoly Law. It did suggest, however, that in reverse payment cases it sometimes may be necessary to predict what the outcome would have been had the case proceeded to trial.[73] Subsequent to this decision, the Court released its

[70] *Lundbeck*, Case C-591/16 P, ECLI:EU:C:2021:243, ¶ 60.

[71] *Servier*, Case C 176/19 P, ECLI:EU:C:2024:552, ¶ 485; *see also id.* ¶¶ 339, 355, stating that "the counterfactual method" of "compar[ing] the competitive situation resulting from that agreement and the situation that would exist in its absence"—

> is not intended to predict what a party's conduct would have been if it had not concluded an agreement with its competitor or competitors, but to highlight a causal relationship between that agreement and a deterioration in the competitive situation on the market, on the basis of a counterfactual scenario which, although hypothetical, must nevertheless be realistic and credible. In that regard, the Court has already had occasion to state, in the context of a patent dispute settlement agreement in return for reverse payment, that the sole purpose of the counterfactual scenario is to establish the realistic possibilities with respect to the conduct of the manufacturer of generic medicines in the absence of that agreement. While that counterfactual scenario cannot be unaffected by the chances of success of that manufacturer in the patent proceedings or again in relation to the probability of conclusion of a less restrictive agreement, those factors constitute, however, only one of the factors among many to be taken into consideration. Consequently, it is not for the entity bearing the burden of proving the existence of appreciable potential or real effects on competition, when it establishes the counterfactual scenario, to make a definitive finding in relation to the chances of success of the manufacturer of generic medicines in the patent dispute or to the probability of the conclusion of a less restrictive agreement.

[72] *See* AstraZeneca AB v. Jiangsu Aisaikang Pharm. Co., (2021) SPX Zhi Civil Final No. 388 (China).

[73] *See id.* at 10 (machine translation):

> . . . it is generally possible to analyze whether and to what extent the agreement has caused competition harm in the relevant market by comparing the actual situation of signing and fulfilling the agreement with the hypothetical situation of not signing and fulfilling the agreement, and by focusing on the possibility of the patent right of the drug concerned being invalidated as a result of the request for declaration of invalidity in the event that the generic applicant has not withdrawn the request for declaration of invalidity, and then analyzing whether or not the agreement has caused competition harm to the relevant market on that basis. . . . In principle, if the patent right holder gives high benefit compensation to the generic applicant to make the generic applicant withdraw its request for declaration of invalidity without justifiable reasons, it can be considered as one of the important factors to determine that the patent right is more likely to be invalidated due to the request for declaration of

Interpretation of the Supreme People's Court on Several Issues Concerning the Application of Law in the Trial of Civil Disputes over Monopoly (June 2024), article 20 of which states:

> Where the plaintiff has evidence to prove that the agreement reached and implemented by the generic drug applicant and the patent right holder of the generic drug meets the following conditions at the same time, and claims that the agreement constitutes a monopoly agreement as provided for in Article 17 of the Anti-Monopoly Law, the People's Court may support the claim:
>
> (1) The generic drug patent right holder gives or promises to give the generic drug applicant obviously unreasonable monetary or other forms of compensation;
>
> (2) The generic drug applicant undertakes not to question the validity of the patent rights of the generic drug or delay entering the relevant market of the generic drug.
>
> If the defendant has evidence to prove that the compensation referred to in the preceding paragraph is only to make up for the costs of resolving disputes related to the patents of the generic drugs or has other legitimate reasons, or that the agreement complies with Article 20 of the Anti-Monopoly Law and claims that it does not constitute a monopoly agreement as stipulated in Article 17 of the Anti-Monopoly Law, the people's court shall support it.[74]

The *Interpretation* arguably departs from the dictum in the 2021 decision suggesting that courts would need to predict what the outcome of the underlying

invalidity filed by the generic applicant, and at the same time, it is also generally necessary to make a prediction on the relevant examination results in the case of the assumption that the generic applicant has not withdrawn its request for declaration of invalidity. The competitive harm of the agreement should generally be examined in terms of whether it materially prolongs the patentee's monopoly of the market, and whether it materially delays or precludes the entry of actual or potential generic applicants into the market. If the possibility of the patent right being invalidated due to the invalidation request is small, then the conclusion and performance of the relevant agreement will generally have no substantive impact on the market monopoly of the patentee and the market entry of the generic applicant in the relevant market, and it can be preliminarily concluded that the possibility of its having an exclusionary or restrictive effect on competition in the relevant market is small, and it will generally not constitute a monopoly agreement subject to the Antimonopoly Law.

[74] Interpretation of the Supreme People's Court on Several Issues Concerning the Application of Law in the Trial of Civil Disputes over Monopoly (June 2024), *translated and quoted in* Aaron Wininger, *China's Supreme People's Court: Drug Patent Reverse Payment Agreements May Violate the Anti-Monopoly Law*, China IP Law Update, June 24, 2024, https://www.chinaiplawupdate.com/2024/06/chinas-supreme-peoples-court-drug-patent-reverse-payment-agreements-may-violate-the-anti-monopoly-law/.

lawsuit would have been, in favor of an approach similar to the CJEU's under which payments exceeding the expected cost of resolving the dispute and not otherwise justified would be facially unlawful.[75]

Evaluating the Standards as a Matter of Policy

Broadly speaking, there are four possible standards by which courts could evaluate the lawfulness of reverse payment settlements. First, one could adopt a rule under which a settlement is lawful if its terms fall within the potential exclusionary scope of the patent (the "scope of the patent" test). Second, one could adopt a rule under which the settlement is lawful if the ex ante probability the patentee would have prevailed in litigation had the case not settled is sufficiently high. The leads to the question, however, of what a sufficiently high probability is (50%? higher?), and how a court would be able to determine this. Third, one could define an anticompetitive settlement not as one in which the ex ante probability of success is low in comparison with some benchmark, but rather one that unnecessarily delays generic entry past the point at which, in a probabilistic sense, it would have occurred with litigation. Under this test, settlements in excess of the brand's avoided litigation costs would be unnecessarily restrictive, even though some of these settlements might be consistent with an ex ante high (> 50%) probability of success. Fourth, one could adopt a rule of per se illegality or restriction by object, under which pay-for-delay settlements are unlawful on their face, and it would be unlikely that any further inquiry into possible procompetitive justifications would be availing. I will argue that the third test is optimal, but that (with some slight modification) the E.U.'s "restriction by object" standard is not very different.

The "scope of the patent" test

The first approach to consider is one that would render reverse payment settlements lawful as long as the terms of the settlement fall within the potential exclusionary scope of the patent. As noted above, this was the test applied by

[75] *See* Yi Yang, Yong Bai & Ling Ho, *Antitrust Review of Reverse Payment Agreements to Settle Patent Disputes—The Emerging Legal Landscape in Mainland China*, ANTITRUST INTELL. PROP. HEALTHCARE & LIFE SCIENCES, Nov. 27, 2023, https://www.cliffordchance.com/insights/resources/blogs/talking-tech/en/articles/2023/11/antitrust-review-of-reverse-payment-agreements-to-settle-patent-disputes.html.

some courts in the United States prior to *Actavis*, and advocated by Chief Justice Roberts in his dissenting opinion in that case.[76] One argument in favor of this approach, more jurisprudential than economic in nature, is that as long as the parties have agreed to terms that fall within the scope of the (presumptively valid) patent—i.e., requiring the generic to refrain from practicing the patented technology during the remainder of the patent term—they are doing precisely what patent law permits them to do, and therefore (absent sham litigation or fraud in the procurement) should not be deemed guilty of violating the antitrust laws.[77] So stated, however, this position merely states its own conclusion, namely that patent law necessarily immunizes the patent owner from antitrust liability as long as its conduct falls within the patent's potential scope. If the position is to be persuasive, it needs some rationale beyond mere intuition.[78]

One possible rationale is that there's nothing about reverse payment settlements of patent litigation that demands intensive antitrust scrutiny, because *all* settlements involve plaintiffs transferring *something* to defendants to induce agreement; even in the (presumably) more typical case in which the defendant pays money to the plaintiff to settle the case, the plaintiff is forgoing *something*, if only a chance of recovering higher damages or a longer period of exclusion, in return for certainty.[79] Moreover, as the discussion in footnote 1 above suggests, it's even possible for reverse payments, in the literal sense of cash going from plaintiff to defendant, to occur outside the context of pharmaceutical patent litigation.[80] On this logic, reverse payment settlements do not deserve any special antitrust scrutiny, as long as the terms fall within the potential

[76] *See Actavis*, 570 U.S. at 160 (Roberts, C.J., dissenting).

[77] *See id.* at 163 (Roberts, C.J., dissenting) (stating that "a patent holder acting within the scope of its patent has an obvious defense to any antitrust suit: that its patent allows it to engage in conduct that would otherwise violate the antitrust laws. But again, that's the whole point of a patent: to confer a limited monopoly").

[78] *Cf. id.* (stating that the *Actavis* majority's position, that "the legality of the settlement should be 'measur[ed]' by 'procompetitive antitrust policies,' rather than 'patent law policy,'" "simply states [its] conclusion"). To be fair, the dissent also argues that the scope of the patent test is more consistent with then-existing U.S. case law, *see id.* at 165–68, and goes on to present other reasons in support of its more limited reading of antitrust law, as discussed in text above. Note also that the scope of the patent test is not entirely toothless, since it would condemn settlements in which the parties agreed to some restraint outside the scope of the patent, such as the generic's agreement not to market some other product or to compete in some other territory. But it would absolve almost all other reverse payment settlements, for which reason it is sometimes viewed as almost a rule of per se legality.

[79] *See* Asahi Glass Co. v. Pentech Pharms., Inc., 289 F. Supp. 2d 986, 994 (N.D. Ill. 2003) (Posner, J.) (stating that "*any* settlement agreement can be characterized as involving 'compensation' to the defendant, who would not settle unless he had something to show for the settlement"); *see also Actavis*, 570 U.S. at 169 (Roberts, C.J., dissenting) (stating that "[w]hile the alleged infringer may not be suing for the patent holder's money, it is suing for the right to use and market the (intellectual) property, which is worth money"). More accurately, the infringer is not necessarily *suing* for anything, unless (as in some of the E.U. cases) it files its own invalidation action, though in the U.S. it typically will assert by way of an affirmative defense that the claims in suit are invalid.

[80] *See supra* note 1 and accompanying text.

exclusionary scope of the patent—or if they do, then logically we should subject all settlements to intensive antitrust scrutiny, a conclusion that virtually everyone would reject out of hand as being impractical.

These arguments are unpersuasive, however. True, all settlements involve some sort of consideration flowing from plaintiffs to defendants; but not all settlements *are* legal, for good reason.[81] From the standpoint of social welfare, the question should be whether a particular type of settlement threatens to restrict competition unnecessarily; if it does, there is no categorical reason why antitrust law should defer to the settling parties, even if the terms fall within the patent's exclusionary scope. And as explained above, there *are* good reasons to think that reverse payment settlements are such a type, given the very real risk that many of these settlements may amount to little more than brands paying off generics to forestall legitimate competition. More generally, as Erik Hovenkamp demonstrates, one would expect most settlements, in most areas of private law, to "emulate the parties' expectations about how litigation would play out."[82] IP settlements between competitors are, in this sense, different, because the parties cannot lawfully contract around a judgment of noninfringement or invalidity; such a judgment gives the defendant "an inalienable right to compete."[83] To forestall a judgment that would permit the defendant to compete freely with the plaintiff, therefore, the parties may settle—but on terms that provide for a longer period of exclusion than would be warranted in view of the ex ante probability of validity and infringement, since the plaintiff can share some of the gains from a longer exclusion period with the defendant in such a way as to make both parties better off (but consumers worse off, in comparison with the state of the world in which the settlement is consistent with the ex ante probability of success).[84] This is precisely

[81] *See supra* note 1.

[82] Hovenkamp, *supra* note 1, at 427. Hovenkamp goes on to explain that, in most areas of private law, "an ex ante settlement will delimit rights in the same way they are expected to end up ex post," "because the parties simply cannot mutually agree on anything else." *Id.* at 427–28. To illustrate, he uses a simple example of two parties, P and D, one of whom (D) uses a noisy machine the abandonment of which would benefit P in the amount of $10,000 but would cost D $6,000. Joint welfare is maximized, in the amount of $4,000, if D abandons use. If P sues D for nuisance, and the court orders D to abandon use, that judgment would maximize the parties' joint welfare; if P loses, the parties would bargain around the outcome, with P paying between $6,000 and $10,000 to induce D to abandon, again maximizing joint welfare. Alternatively, the parties could settle before trial—but regardless of what they perceive to be the ex ante probability of P's prevailing at trial, one would expect them to bargain toward the joint welfare maximizing outcome. *See id.* at 428. However they divide up the gains between themselves, the increase in joint welfare will be the same amount, D will abandon use of the machine, and the settlement will "emulate the parties' expectations about how litigation," include post-litigation settlement, "would play out."

[83] *Id.* at 429.

[84] To illustrate, Hovenkamp presents an example in which P's expected monopoly profit is $100 million, and the parties jointly would expect a total of $60 million if competing as duopolists. If P's ex ante probability of prevailing at trial is 50%, P's expected profit from litigation is $80 million. P would accept

the reason why some patent settlements, and especially reverse payment settlements, deserve greater scrutiny than settlements generally.

A better argument in support of the scope of the patent test is that, as discussed below, the leading alternatives to it (other than per se illegality) all rest, expressly or implicitly, on a probabilistic assessment of either the likely outcome of the infringement suit[85] or the probabilistic date of generic entry. These alternatives, especially the former, at first blush may seem either administratively cumbersome or susceptible to error (or both). Moreover, if one believes, as Chief Justice Roberts states in his dissenting opinion, that a more aggressive antitrust standard will discourage some risk-averse plaintiffs from settling,[86] it's theoretically *possible*, for reasons discussed above,[87] that departing from the scope of the patent test could discourage some settlements that actually would make consumers better off. The question then is whether these problems are sufficiently difficult, troubling, or realistic, that antitrust liability should never result from settlements that fall within the potential exclusionary scope of the patent, despite the false negative risks. To answer this question, let's move on to the next two candidates for an antitrust standard, the "ex ante probability" test and the "less restrictive alternatives" test.

Ex-ante probability test

Suppose instead then that antitrust liability hinges on a determination that the brand's ex ante probability of success was low—say, below 50%. In theory, this would leave the parties free to settle using reverse payments that are consistent with the brand having a greater than 50% ex ante probability of success on the

a settlement on terms—say, a certain period of exclusion—that would leave it with at least an $80 million in expected profit. But, as Hovenkamp says, "Why stop there? They would maximize their joint wellbeing . . . by further restraining competition to the monopoly or cartel level," leaving P and D with an additional $20 million to divide up. In short, "the firms' settlement must restrain competition to *some* degree in order to be mutually acceptable; and yet . . . the firms always prefer to restrain competition all the way to monopoly." *Id.* at 427.

85 *See Actavis*, 570 U.S. at 171 (Roberts, C.J., dissenting) (stating that "I therefore don't see how the majority can conclude that it won't normally be 'necessary to litigate patent validity to answer the antitrust question,' unless it means to suggest that the defendant (patent holder) cannot raise his patent as a defense in an antitrust suit. But depriving him of such a defense—if that's what the majority means to do—defeats the point of the patent, which is to confer a lawful monopoly on its holder"; and that the proposition that "even if the patent is valid, a patent holder violates the antitrust laws merely because the settlement took away some chance that his patent would be declared invalid by a court" is unsound).

86 *See id.* at 172 (stating that "[a] patent holder may be 95% sure about the validity of its patent, but particularly risk averse or litigation averse, and willing to pay a good deal of money to rid itself of the 5% chance of a finding of invalidity").

87 *See supra* notes 37–40 and accompanying text.

merits. Assuming, for the moment, that this would be a desirable rule—that is, that the antitrust plaintiff should bear the burden of proving that the brand would have lost the underlying infringement action—the question then is how to go about determining the ex ante probability of success.

The first possibility is that the antitrust court could hold a patent infringement trial within the antitrust trial. It should come as no surprise, however, that nobody wants to do this; antitrust trials are complicated enough without the added burden of injecting a complicated patent infringement trial into them. Requiring such a procedure also would put the generic in the odd position of having to defend the settlement to which it agreed by arguing that it was destined to lose. Perhaps more likely, a trial-within-a-trial requirement simply would deter such settlements altogether—but if that is the optimal outcome, a rule of per se liability would do just as well. (I don't think that would be the optimal outcome, though, for reasons discussed below.) Wisely, both the U.S. Supreme Court and the CJEU have declined to go down this road, as discussed above.[88]

Second, the antitrust court could entertain evidence in the form of expert testimony concerning the brand's ex ante probability of success. As noted above, several U.S. courts have permitted such testimony in private antitrust actions challenging reverse payment settlements,[89] but this procedure has its drawbacks. In a case between two more or less equally-matched parties, one would expect both to retain well-credentialed experts to offer competing opinions on the brand's likelihood of prevailing. Each would have to satisfy the admissibility standards under the relevant evidentiary rules,[90] but assuming each does so to the court's satisfaction there may be no clear criterion for finding one expert more credible than the other. This is, of course, a recurring, and well-recognized, problem with the extensive use of expert testimony generally,

[88] That said, there are other areas of law, such as legal malpractice actions, in which it sometimes may be necessary to try a case within a case. For discussion, specific to the United States, *see* David Winnett, *Legal Malpractice: Proving the Case-Within-a-Case*, PLAINTIFF, Nov. 2015, at 1.

[89] *See supra* note 61 and accompanying text.

[90] In the United States, this would mean compliance with, *inter alia*, Federal Rule of Evidence 702. In its recently amended form, this rule states:

> A witness who is qualified as an expert by knowledge, skill, experience, training, or education may testify in the form of an opinion or otherwise if the proponent demonstrates to the court that it is more likely than not that:
>
> > the expert's scientific, technical, or other specialized knowledge will help the trier of fact to understand the evidence or to determine a fact in issue;
> >
> > the testimony is based on sufficient facts or data;
> >
> > the testimony is the product of reliable principles and methods; and
> >
> > the expert's opinion reflects a reliable application of the principles and methods to the facts of the case.

particularly in the United States;[91] and while there may be some procedures judges can use to reduce abuses, such as "hot tubbing"[92] or the use of court-selected, neutral experts,[93] neither is commonly used in the U.S. For these reasons, among others, civil law systems such as the E.U.'s generally make much less use of party experts.[94] Personally, I remain skeptical that expert testimony on this issue would prove very useful for reaching an accurate result, though it may be a necessary evil if some sort of probabilistic estimate is needed to determine damages.[95] To permit it in all cases, however—including government-initiated actions in which causation and damages are not at issue—simply to establish (or refute) liability, seems dubious.

If not experts, though, then what other evidence could be used to establish liability, *if* an ex ante probability of invalidity or noninfringement is a necessary element of the plaintiff's case? In some of my early work on this topic, I suggested that the size of the payment could be a useful indicium—as, in fact, it is, if it can be established that the size is greater than the generic's expected profits from sales of the generic drug, over the relevant period of time.[96] But while some reverse payments have in fact exceeded the generic's expected profit, others have not, and in these latter cases there may be no way to accurately translate the amount into an ex ante probability of success. Recognizing this problem, and building on suggestions by Dan Crane and others, I also

[91] *See, e.g.*, Jeffrey L. Harrison, *Reconceptualizing the Expert Witness: Social Costs, Current Controls, and Proposed Responses*, 18 YALE J. REG. 253 (2001).

[92] *See, e.g.*, Lisa Wood, *Hot Tub Redux*, ANTITRUST (Spring 2018), at 31 (discussing the use of "hot tubbing"—a procedure used in Australia, Canada, and the U.K., but only sparingly in the U.S., in which "experts present their testimony concurrently to the court, without lawyers acting as intermediaries," and the court may "directly question the experts in real time about areas of agreement and disagreement"). For recent discussion, see Samuel Kim, *Post-*Daubert*: Expert Hot-Tubbing as a Workable Tool for Trial Judges*, 34 FED. CIR. B.J. 121 (2025).

[93] *See, e.g.*, Stephanie Domitrovich, *Fulfilling Daubert's Gatekeeping Mandate Through Court-Appointed Experts*, 106 J. CRIM. L. & CRIMINOLOGY 35 (2016) (advocating greater use of court-appointed neutral experts, in both civil and criminal proceedings).

[94] *See id.* at 42.

[95] To be sure, there are other areas of law in which the trier of fact or a government agency may have to make probabilistic estimates of what the outcome of litigation would have been, including legal malpractice actions, *see supra* note 88, and offers to compromise tax liability, *see Tucker v. Comm'r*, 676 F.3d 1129, 1134 (D.C. Cir. 2012); and in cases involving damages awarded under the "loss of chance" doctrine, to compensate a plaintiff for the probabilistic loss of some profitable venture, *see* THOMAS F. COTTER, PRINCIPLES OF INTELLECTUAL PROPERTY LAW—REMEDIES 166–68 (2026). Moreover, if courts were to adopt the sham litigation standard recommended in the preceding chapter—under which a crucial fact would be whether the expected noncollateral benefit of litigating exceeded the expected cost of litigation, *see supra* note 7—this would seem necessarily to require expert testimony concerning the patentee's ex ante probability of success. Thus, despites its drawbacks, there may be no substitute for probabilistic expert testimony in situations such as these.

[96] *See* Cotter, *supra* note 52, at 42 (stating that "where the amount of consideration flowing from patent owner to generic manufacture exceeds the generic firm's expected profit from the sale of the generic drug in question, the inference that the patent owner is simply paying a potential competitor to exit the market is much stronger, and the presumption of illegality should be very difficult to rebut").

suggested that the presence of a reverse payment should give rise to a rebuttable presumption of illegality, and that courts could determine whether the defendants rebutted that presumption in view of a range of additional factors:

> Where that amount is less than the amount of the patent owner's expected litigation costs, this fact alone may be sufficient to rebut the presumption, and thus shift to the antitrust plaintiff the burden of proving that the anti-competitive harm outweighs the procompetitive benefit of the settlement.... Other relevant evidence may include the presence of other agreements between the settling parties (for example, authorizing the defendant to market an authorized generic drug, or licensing the defendant other intellectual property rights), which should be taken into account for the limited purpose of accurately estimating the value of the consideration flowing from plaintiff to defendant; whether the generic is "cash-strapped," and therefore willing to accept a later entry date to remain in business; whether the patent owner sought, and succeeded in obtaining, a preliminary injunction against the generic manufacturer; whether the generic manufacturer agrees to waive its 180-day exclusivity, thus removing the risk of a bottleneck potentially blocking other ANDA applicants; and whether the patent in suit has withstood other validity challenges arising after the filing of the settled action.[97]

Of the above considerations, one might think that the brand's success in obtaining a preliminary injunction would be a relatively strong indicium of likely success, since the court issuing the injunction must have concluded that there *was* a likelihood of success on the merits.[98] On the other hand, in the types of cases of interest here parties do not always seek preliminary injunctions—especially in the United States, where the brand typically obtains an automatic thirty-month stay of generic entry—and outside the U.S., courts sometimes have been known to give "likelihood of success on the merits" short shrift.[99] Some commentators have suggested, in addition, that courts

[97] *Id.*

[98] *See* Daniel A. Crane, *Exit Payments in Settlement of Patent Infringement Lawsuits: Antitrust Rules and Economic Implications*, 54 FLA. L. REV. 747, 783–85 (2002) (adding, however, that "the preliminary injunction must have been genuinely contested").

[99] *See* COTTER, *supra* note 95, at 80–82 (noting that, in Commonwealth jurisdictions, courts sometimes require the moving party only to show that "the claim is not frivolous or vexatious, in other words, that there is a serious question to be tried," and if so the court should proceed to consider the balance of conveniences, in accordance with Lord Diplock's opinion in *American Cyanamid Co. v. Ethicon Ltd.* [1975] A.C. 396 (H.L.) (U.K.); but that "Commonwealth courts do not always take the *Cyanamid* standard quite so literally... particularly where there is a substantial risk that a decision favorable to the movant will, as a practical matter, end the litigation").

could employ some form of truncated procedure similar to a preliminary injunction hearing,[100] or that courts could seek advice from specialized agencies (really just a variation on the court-appointed experts suggestion noted above), to ascertain the brand's ex ante likelihood of success.[101] How feasible such recommendations would be, or how much they would reduce the administrative burden of having a full-blown trial-within-a-trial, nevertheless seems questionable.

Finally, to return to an issue alluded to above, a court applying the ex ante probability rule also would need to decide how much, if any, weight to accord to the parties' claims that the settlement was motivated in part by the brand's risk aversion, and that the presence of risk aversion can reconcile a high reverse payment with an objectively high ex ante probability of success. (For that matter, if taken to its logical conclusion, the risk-aversion argument could lead us all the way back to the scope of the patent test, as suggested by Chief Justice Roberts.[102]) The argument that courts should be permitted to consider risk aversion as a defense nevertheless has been pretty convincingly demolished, both doctrinally[103] and as a matter of policy. With regard to the latter, as many others have noted it is a standard assumption of economic analysis that

[100] *See* Cotter, *supra* note 34, at 1811–12 (reviewing various proposals).

[101] *See* Colangelo, *supra* note 11, at 21 (suggesting that courts "should conduct a case-by-case analysis which cannot disregard a summary inquiry of patent strength," and that "an option would be to imagine a range of regulatory actors involved in these issues . . . such as the PTO and FDA in the US, the EPO, EMA and national regulators in Europe . . . providing information more directly relevant to the antitrust analysis than the direction of the settlement payment") (citing Daniel A. Crane, Actavis, *the Reverse Payment Fallacy, and the Continuing Need for Regulatory Solutions*, 15 Minn. J.L. Sci. & Tech. 51, 59 (2014)); *see also* Crane, *supra* note 98, at 786 (suggesting that U.S. courts could appoint temporary officials known as "special masters" to aid in this process). It also has been suggested that the parties' own documents could shed light on their expectations of success, though one would expect most such documents to be privileged under U.S. law. *See* Hovenkamp et al., *supra* note 1, § 7.03[C], at 7-22 to -23 (stating that "[i]deally, the antitrust court would have access to the honest internal assessments the settling parties made of the case at the time," but that "[m]uch of that information is likely to be privileged . . . as—to a lesser extent—are the settlement negotiations themselves"; and suggesting that "courts might wish to consider whether a party that wishes to defend an antitrust claim by arguing that it would have won the case it settled ought to be required to waive privilege and disclose the actual advice it received before settling").

[102] *See supra* note 86.

[103] Doctrinally, recall that the *Actavis* majority frames the antitrust inquiry into whether the settling parties agreed to delay generic entry "to prevent the risk of competition." *Actavis*, 570 U.S. at 157. The CJEU decisions point in a similar direction. *See Lundbeck*, Case C-591/16, ECLI:EU:C:2021:243, ¶¶ 114, 126 (stating that "agreements whereby competitors deliberately substitute practical cooperation between them for the risks of competition can clearly be characterised as 'restrictions by object'"; and that "to the extent the agreements at issue reflect the fact . . . that the damages to which manufacturers of originator medicines may be entitled in the event of the unlawful entry of generic medicines on the market are often substantially lower than the damage suffered by the former, it should be recalled that it is for public authorities and not private undertakings to ensure compliance with statutory requirements") (citing *Generics (UK)*, Case C-307/18, ECLI:EU:C:2020:52, ¶¶ 83, 87–88).

profit-maximizing corporations are risk neutral.[104] A second problem is that if risk aversion is a cognizable justification for a reverse payment that otherwise seems difficult to defend, it is difficult to imagine how antitrust plaintiffs can effectively refute the assertion that risk aversion was, in fact, the brand's motivation for agreeing to the deal; and if brands have no incentive not to proffer the argument, whether true or not, brands and generics would have every reason to settle on the most restrictive terms possible.[105] Third, unless the numbers are just right, it's unlikely that risk aversion actually would derail settlement altogether; in many, probably most, cases, a risk averse plaintiff could still manage to settle on terms with earlier entry, which increases consumer surplus.[106] Finally, even if risk aversion were to derail *some* settlements if reverse payments are unavailable, it is doubtful that the avoidance of that risk outweighs the above negative consequences of recognizing risk aversion as a cognizable defense.[107] For similar reasons, one may doubt the rationale that the *generic's* supposed risk aversion, or its willingness to delay generic entry in return for an immediate infusion of cash necessary to remain in business, are good reasons for tolerating reverse payment settlements that otherwise seem suspect.[108]

Even if risk aversion is not a cognizable justification, however, the ex ante probability test would seem to entail substantial, perhaps enormous, complexity in operation. The costs of carrying out the necessary inquiries, including the costs of error in doing so, therefore would need to be balanced against the expected benefit of discouraging settlements that delay generic entry despite the likelihood that the brand would have lost the infringement suit. Perhaps there is a better way.

[104] *See* Bulow, *supra* note 29, at 167, 184 n.37 (noting, in addition, that firms can hedge risk in other ways that do not involve settlements below fair market value); Einer Elhauge & Alex Krueger, *Solving the Patent Settlement Puzzle*, 91 TEX. L. REV. 283, 311–12 (2012); Hovenkamp, *supra* note 1, at 473.

[105] *See* Edlin et al., *supra* note 36, at 5; Hovenkamp, *supra* note 1, at 476.

[106] *See* Edlin et al., *supra* note 36, at 7 ("carefully constructed"); Hovenkamp, *supra* note 1, at 475–76; *see also* In re Cipro Cases I & II, 348 P.3d 835, 869 (Cal. 2015) (stating that "[a]ttempts to quantitatively estimate the frequency with which risk aversion would produce an efficient settlement despite payment in excess of litigation costs suggest such occurrences would be exceedingly rare") (citing, *inter alia*, Keith Leffler & Cristofer Leffler, *The Probabilistic Nature of Patent Rights*, ANTITRUST, Summer 2003, at 77, 79–80).

[107] *See* Hovenkamp, *supra* note 1, at 476.

[108] *See* Elhauge & Krueger, *supra* note 104, at 311–12 (noting, *inter alia*, that entrants are typically public corporations with a market capitalization that exceeds the potential patent damages from the case at hand," such that their "managers and shareholders have incentives to behave in a risk-neutral manner that maximizes expected profits"); Hovenkamp, *supra* note 1, at 475 (noting, in respect of the "cash-strapped generic" rationale, that "[i]f the rival is too poor to survive until the proportional entry date, then, in light of the high cost of patent litigation it is unlikely that it would have a credible litigation threat, in which case there would not be any settlement in the first place").

Less restrictive alternative test

A third possibility, advocated by (among others) Edlin et al. and by Erik Hovenkamp, is that a settlement should be deemed anticompetitive if it unnecessarily delays generic entry past the point at which, in a probabilistic sense, it would have occurred *with* litigation.[109] Although this may sound much like the ex ante probability test, it is different in the following sense: under this test, a settlement is "anticompetitive if consumers are worse off under the settlement than they would be under one of two benchmarks: (1) the outcome of litigation, in expectation; or (2) an alternative settlement that did not include a large payment."[110] Doctrinally, this means that, under this standard, reverse payment settlements are anticompetitive when there is a less restrictive alternative—a settlement with no reverse payment and earlier entry—that the parties would have agreed to, absent the reverse payment.[111] Practically, it means that reverse payments in excess of avoided litigation costs should be presumptively illegal.[112]

This standard is attractive for several reasons. First, as Hovenkamp argues, it puts reverse payment settlements on par with the mill run of other settlements in private litigation, where the settlement outcome is expected to mirror the outcome of litigation.[113] Condemning settlements that extend beyond the generic's ex ante expected date of entry absent the settlement therefore would be consistent with what Hovenkamp refers to as a "proportional-effects rule," under which "antitrust's goal is for settlements to be proportional: to restrain competition to an extent commensurate with the expected result of patent litigation."[114] Secondly, although the standard rests upon the premise that reverse payment settlements in excess of avoided litigation costs are anticompetitive because they delay generic entry past the expected date of entry under litigation, it obviates the need for a court to actually calculate that date (or, what amounts to the same thing, to estimate the ex ante probability of validity and infringement, albeit subject to the caveat that such an inquiry ultimately may be unavoidable if it becomes necessary to calculate damages). Put another way, the standard condemns reverse payments where the parties could have settled

[109] *See supra* text accompanying note 36.
[110] Edlin et al., *supra* note 36, at 4.
[111] *See* Aaron Edlin et al., *The* Actavis *Inference: Theory and Practice*, 67 Rutgers Univ. L. Rev. 585, 609 (2015); Hovenkamp, *supra* note 1, at 467–68.
[112] The rationale being that, even if the brand were certain to win, and thus to exclude the generic for the entire remaining patent term, it would be willing to pay its avoided litigation costs to settle. *See supra* Table 5.1; Edlin et al., *supra* note 111, at 591–92, 625.
[113] *See* Hovenkamp, *supra* note 1, at 427–29.
[114] *Id.* at 420.

on terms with earlier entry, *whatever* the ex ante probability of success may have been. Third, as Edlin et al. have formally demonstrated, in every case in which the parties settle with a reverse payment, they could have settled on mutually agreeable terms without a reverse payment, subject to earlier generic entry.[115] For this reason, the risk of false positives is nonexistent.[116] Relatedly, the standard does not undermine the patent incentive, insofar as it permits brands to enforce their patents up through the generic's expected date of entry, though not beyond.[117] Finally, the standard is consistent with the *Actavis* inference in that the transfer of cash or other consideration "to prevent the risk of competition" constitutes anticompetitive harm.[118]

Of the three choices so far, the least restrictive alternative test appears to be the best of the available options. Operationally, it would permit reverse payment settlements in which the brand pays up to its avoided litigation costs, but not beyond. Adjudication costs would be lower than under the ex ante probability test (though hardly zero given the possible need, *inter alia*, to quantify the brand's avoided litigation costs, as well as the value of noncash consideration provided to induce settlement). The cost of false positives should be low, as above, and consumer welfare should be higher than under the two preceding standards.

Per se illegality/restriction by object

As discussed in chapter 2, agreements or practices that appear to have no cognizable offsetting procompetitive justification are considered unlawful on their face—referred to as per se illegal in the United States, or restrictions by object

[115] *See* Edlin et al., *supra* note 111, at 624–25. There may be some situations in which risk aversion confounds this result, but for reasons discussed above these can be safely ignored. *See supra* notes 103–08 and accompanying text.

[116] *See* Edlin et al., *supra* note 111, at 634.

[117] Arguments that any restriction on patent owners' conduct risks harming dynamic efficiency by reducing the value of patents—*see, e.g.*, Joanna Shepherd, *Deterring Innovation:* New York v. Actavis *and the Duty to Subsidize Competitors' Market Entry*, 17 MINN. J. L. SCI. & TECH. 663, 703–04 (2016) (stating that preventing drug companies "from operating in a profit-maximizing way may harm innovation and drug development throughout the pharmaceutical industry")—prove too much, in that they provide no meaningful limitation on patent rights whatsoever. In the present context, moreover, empirical evidence indicates that reverse payment settlements of patent infringement litigation disproportionately involve secondary patents, covering some variation over the initial, active ingredient patent; and that patent owners are, in general, significantly less likely to win nonsettled lawsuits involving secondary patents. *See* C. Scott Hemphill & Bhaven N. Sampat, *Drug Patents at the Supreme Court*, 339 SCI. 1386, 1387 (2013); C. Scott Hemphill & Bhaven N. Sampat, *When Do Generics Challenge Drug Patents?*, 8 J. EMPIRICAL LEGAL STUD. 613, 643 (2011).

[118] *Actavis*, 570 U.S. at 157; *see also Lundbeck*, Case C-591/16, ECLI:EU:C:2021:243, ¶ 114.

in the E.U. And as discussed earlier in this chapter, a few early U.S. decisions appeared to embrace a rule of per se illegality for reverse payment settlements, before other courts adopted a more lenient approach, and the U.S. Supreme Court in *Actavis* rejected all of the previous approaches in favor of the Rule of Reason. U.S. commentary, however, generally supports the Supreme Court's rejection of per se illegality, on the ground that, if taken to its logical conclusion, per se illegality would be overinclusive in rendering any cash or noncash payment from brand to generic unlawful on its face, even if the payment is less than the brand's avoided litigation costs, or compensates the generic for other legitimate goods or services.[119] On the other hand, as noted above the CJEU has confirmed that reverse payment settlements can be considered restrictions by object under E.U. law,[120] thus creating an apparent disparity between the two jurisdictions, and requiring further inquiry into which approach makes more sense.

One needs to be careful with terminology, however. As noted above, the *Actavis* decision can (and should) be read not as requiring courts to conduct some amorphous, open-ended version of the Rule of Reason, but rather something functionally closer to a rule of presumptive illegality with respect to reverse payment settlements.[121] Similarly, the E.U. approach does not mean that all reverse payment settlements are unlawful. The Court has been careful to state that "[t]he fact that . . . an agreement involves transfers of value" from brand to generic "is not sufficient ground to classify it as a 'restriction by object,' since those transfers of value may prove justified, that is, appropriate and strictly necessary having regard to the legitimate objectives of the parties to the agreement."[122] The question instead is whether the generic receives "sums that correspond in fact to the compensation for the costs of or disruption caused by the litigation between them, or that correspond to remuneration for the actual supply . . . of goods or services . . . ."[123] Thus, in the E.U. as in the U.S., there are cognizable justifications for reverse payments; moreover, as in the U.S.,

[119] *See, e.g.*, Elhauge & Krueger, *supra* note 104, at 289.
[120] *See supra* notes 103, 122, and accompanying text.
[121] *See supra* note 52 and accompanying text.
[122] *Generics (UK)*, Case C-307/18, ECLI:EU:C:2020:52, ¶ 85.
[123] *Id.* ¶ 86. So understood, in some respects the CJEU's approach to reverse payment settlements calls to mind the U.S. Supreme Court's discussion in *Broadcast Music, Inc. v. Columbia Broadcasting Systems, Inc.*, 441 U.S. 1 (1979), of whether the blanket licenses offered by collective rights organizations such as ASCAP and BMI, permitting the public performance of musical works, constituted per se illegal price fixing. As the Court stated, "'price fixing' is a shorthand way of describing certain categories of business behavior to which the per se rule has been held applicable"; to determine whether it applies "it is necessary to characterize the challenged conduct as falling within or without that category of behavior to which we apply the label 'per se price fixing,'" which is "often, but not always . . . a simple matter." *Id.* at 8–9.

the antitrust plaintiff must prove that, but for the settlement, the brand and generic would have been, in some meaningful sense, potential competitors.[124] Once those justifications are ruled out, however, the CJEU would classify the agreement as a restriction by object, and no further defense to liability would likely be of much avail. This may go beyond how some U.S. courts interpret *Actavis*, but the differences between the two approaches are not great. Both characterize the elimination of a risk of competition as anticompetitive conduct, absent a cognizable justification,[125] and both reject any need to construct the ex ante probability of success as a prerequisite to liability.[126]

That said, the CJEU's phrasing of the test as whether the generic had "real and concrete possibilities" to compete can seem vague; and, as quoted in the preceding paragraph, although the Court asks whether the payment compensated the generic for "the costs of or disruption caused by the litigation," it does not expressly inquire into whether the payment exceeded the *brand*'s avoided litigation costs.[127] Given that payments in the latter amount can rightly be characterized as anticompetitive,[128] in the sense of deferring generic entry past the ex ante expected date of entry, the Court's failure to make this amount the touchstone seems surprising—as it its apparent interest in whether the payment compensates the generic for the *latter*'s litigation costs, since the only reason the brand would pay some or all of the generic's costs would be to avoid the risk of an adverse judgment.[129] Perhaps in future cases the Court will clarify its position on this matter; doing so would both align the CJEU's standard with *Actavis* and, more importantly, better articulate an economically defensible heuristic for distinguishing pro- from anticompetitive settlements.[130]

[124] *See Generics (UK)*, Case C-307/18, ECLI:EU:C:2020:52, ¶¶ 30–58.

[125] *See Actavis*, 570 U.S at 157 (characterizing elimination of "the risk of competition" as "the relevant anticompetitive harm"); *Lundbeck*, Case C-591/16 P, ECLI:EU:C:2021:243, ¶ 114 (stating that "agreements whereby competitors deliberately substitute practical cooperation between them for the risks of competition can clearly be characterised as 'restrictions by object'"). Moreover, for reasons discussed above, a straightforward reading of *Actavis* would seem to exclude some possible procompetitive justifications, including likelihood of success on the merits and risk aversion. *See supra* notes 30, 103, and accompanying text.

[126] *See Generics (UK)*, Case C-307/18, ECLI:EU:C:2020:52, ¶¶ 50, 122; *see also Servier*, Case C-176/19 P, ECLI:EU:C:2024:552, ¶¶ 102, 353; *Lundbeck*, Case C-591/16 P, ECLI:EU:C:2021:243, ¶ 60.

[127] *See supra* notes 62–70 and accompanying text.

[128] More precisely, given that in Europe the prevailing party is entitled to a portion of its costs, any payment by the brand in excess of its expected-to-be-uncompensable litigation costs, minus whatever damages it would expect to collect from the generic were the matter to proceed to litigation, is equivalent to a payment to avoid the risk of litigation. *See* Appendix, *infra*. Strictly speaking, then, the acceptable amount of a reverse payment in the E.U. should be smaller, all other things being equal, than in the United States.

[129] More specifically, unless the settlement is intended to avoid the risk of a judgment adverse to the patent owner, the *generic* should be willing to pay its own anticipated cost of litigating to judgment, plus the portion of the brand's fees *it* would expect to pay. *See id.*

[130] Before closing out this section, I should note as well the European Commission's recent proceeding in Case AT.40588—*Teva Copaxone* (though in view of the likelihood of an appeal pending

Anti-troll Laws

As discussed in chapter 3, since 2013 a majority of states within the United States have enacted anti-patent troll laws forbidding the "bad faith assertion" of patent rights. Most of these statutes list various factors that a court may consider as evidence of bad faith. The Vermont statute, for example, states that the following factors may be relevant:

(1) The demand letter does not contain the following information:
  (A) the patent number;
  (B) the name and address of the patent owner or owners and assignee or assignees, if any; and
  (C) factual allegations concerning the specific areas in which the target's products, services, and technology infringe the patent or are covered by the claims in the patent.
(2) Prior to sending the demand letter, the person fails to conduct an analysis comparing the claims in the patent to the target's products, services,

publication of this book, I will not dwell too long on the matter). In this case, the E.C. concluded that Teva abused its dominant position in the market for glatiramer acetate (GA)—the active ingredient in Copaxone, an immunomodulator drug—through a combination of two strategies: the misuse of divisional applications and the disparagement of a rival generic drug. Focusing here on the alleged divisional abuse, the divisional applications at issue were derived from two families of secondary patents: one derived from a parent patent claiming a production process for GA, from which Teva later split off two divisionals, and one derived from a parent "dosage" patent, relating to a 40 mg formulation of the drug, from which it split off four divisionals. *See id.* ¶¶ 102–03 & tables 13–14. According to the Commission, Teva staggered its divisional filings, sought preliminary injunctions on the basis of patents which the EPO had granted, and then (sometimes) "strategically withdrew the challenged patents before the adoption of a reasoned decision of those challenged patents by the" EPO Technical Board of Appeals, because "a reasoned revocation would have had a strong precedent effect on the remaining divisional patents of the same patent family." *Id.* ¶¶ 1019–20. In this manner, the Commission found, "Teva managed to obstruct effective legal review of its patents and to prolong legal uncertainty surrounding their validity, thereby hindering" prospective entrant Synthon from entering the relevant markets. *Id.* ¶ 140. In concluding that this conduct contributed to an abuse of dominant position, the E.C. reaffirms that an abuse of dominant position may "consist of behaviour which is otherwise lawful under branches of law other than competition law," *id.* ¶ 1061 (citing *AstraZeneca AB v. Comm'n*, Case C-457/10 P, ECLI:EU:C:2012:770 (CJEU 2012)); and repeatedly notes that the divisional patents at issue were weak, were likely to be invalidated despite having been initially granted and, in some instances, having survived an initial opposition, and that Teva personnel were aware of these infirmities. *See id.* ¶¶ 1136, 1141, 1160, 1178, 1181, 1182–1213, 1255, 1258, 1290, 1294, 1296, 1315, 1357. What remains unclear to me is whether the decision hinges on the likely invalidity of the divisionals at issue, which would justify classifying *Teva* as a "Category 2" decision, or whether it is independent of that determination, which would justify classifying the case as "Category 3." Might it be enough, in other words, for a dominant firm to employ the strategy of strategic filing and withdrawal, just to avoid the possibility of a reasoned decision on invalidity that could, potentially, topple all of the dominoes? For a variety of reasons, I am inclined to think that the probable-albeit-not-certain invalidity of the divisionals was a crucial, and seemingly well-substantiated, aspect of the Commission's case, *see* Thomas F. Cotter, *Some Thoughts on Teva Copaxone (Anticompetitive Misuse of Divisionals)*, Comparative Patent Remedies Blog, Apr. 21, 2025, but will withhold definitive judgment pending further evaluation by the General Court.

and technology, or such an analysis was done but does not identify specific areas in which the products, services, and technology are covered by the claims in the patent.

(3) The demand letter lacks the information described in subdivision (1) of this subsection, the target requests the information, and the person fails to provide the information within a reasonable period of time.

(4) The demand letter demands payment of a license fee or response within an unreasonably short period of time.

(5) The person offers to license the patent for an amount that is not based on a reasonable estimate of the value of the license.

(6) The claim or assertion of patent infringement is meritless, and the person knew, or should have known, that the claim or assertion is meritless.

(7) The claim or assertion of patent infringement is deceptive.

(8) The person or its subsidiaries or affiliates have previously filed or threatened to file one or more lawsuits based on the same or similar claim of patent infringement, and:

  (A) those threats or lawsuits lacked the information described in subdivision (1) of this subsection; or

  (B) the person attempted to enforce the claim of patent infringement in litigation, and a court found the claim to be meritless.

(9) Any other factor the court finds relevant.[131]

[131] VT. STAT. ANN. tit. 9, § 4197(b) (2023). The statute goes on to state that

> A court may consider the following factors as evidence that a person has not made a bad faith assertion of patent infringement:
>
> (1) The demand letter contains the information described in subdivision (b)(1) of this section.
> (2) Where the demand letter lacks the information described in subdivision (b)(1) of this section and the target requests the information, the person provides the information within a reasonable period of time.
> (3) The person engages in a good faith effort to establish that the target has infringed the patent and to negotiate an appropriate remedy.
> (4) The person makes a substantial investment in the use of the patent or in the production or sale of a product or item covered by the patent.
> (5) The person is:
>   (A) the inventor or joint inventor of the patent or, in the case of a patent filed by and awarded to an assignee of the original inventor or joint inventor, is the original assignee; or
>   (B) an institution of higher education or a technology transfer organization owned or affiliated with an institution of higher education.
> (6) The person has:
>   (A) demonstrated good faith business practices in previous efforts to enforce the patent, or a substantially similar patent; or
>   (B) successfully enforced the patent, or a substantially similar patent, through litigation.
> (7) Any other factor the court finds relevant.

Id. § 4197(c).

The enactment of these laws coincided with increased public awareness of the practices of patent assertion entities (PAEs)—particularly those, referred to as "Litigation PAEs"[132] by the FTC and as "bottom feeders" by Mark Lemley and Doug Melamed[133]—whose business model depends on suing or threatening to sue multiple defendants, and settling for a sum less than each defendant's avoided litigation costs. As noted in chapter 3, for example, a firm called MPHJ Technology Investments, LLC, was alleged to have sent, through 101 subsidiaries, demand letters to thousands of small businesses alleging the latter's infringement of certain "scan to email" patents, and in some instances proposing settlements in the amount of $1,000 or $1,200 per employee. The attorneys general of New York and Minnesota, and later the FTC, succeeded in obtaining settlements from MPHJ under existing consumer protection and unfair competition laws, with MPJH eventually agreeing to cease making misleading representations about the licenses it had granted to others, and from falsely representing that it intended to initiate infringement litigation.[134]

The anti-troll laws enacted in response to this and other cases nevertheless have resulted in few, if any, final judgments, partly due to serious questions (still largely unresolved) over whether state or only federal courts may adjudicate these types of cases under the Supreme Court's 2013 decision in *Gunn v. Minton*,[135] and also whether (as discussed in chapter 4) the *Noerr-Pennington* doctrine requires the plaintiff asserting a bad faith assertion claim to prove that the assertion is both objectively and subjectively baseless.[136]

[132] Fed. Trade Comm'n, Patent Assertion Entity Activity: An FTC Study 4 (Oct. 2016) (describing "Litigation PAEs" as PAES that "typically sued potential licensees and settled shortly afterward by entering into license agreements with defendants covering small portfolios," and finding that these firms tended to settle for less than the avoided cost to the licensee of litigation).

[133] *See* Mark A. Lemley & A. Douglas Melamed, *Missing the Forest for the Trolls*, 113 Colum. L. Rev. 2117, 2126, 2163 (2013) (describing as "bottom feeders" PAEs "interested in quick, low-value settlements for a variety of patents," and "the point of the bottom-feeder business model" as "to collect avoided litigation costs").

[134] *See* Gugliuzza, *supra* note 4, at 1580–81, 1599–600. For the FTC complaint and consent order, *see* Complaint, In the Matter of MPHJ Tech. Investments, LLC, Docket No. C-4513 (Fed. Trade Comm'n Mar. 13, 2015), https://www.ftc.gov/system/files/documents/cases/150317mphjtechcmpt.pdf; Decision and Order, In the Matter of MPHJ Tech. Investments, LLC, Docket No. C-4513 (Fed. Trade Comm'n Mar. 13, 2015), https://www.ftc.gov/system/files/documents/cases/150317mphjtechdo.pdf. In 2015, the PTAB invalidated the primary patent at issue. *See* MPHJ Tech. Investments, LLC v. Ricoh Ams. Corp., 847 F.3d 1363 (Fed. Cir. 2017) (affirming the PTAB decision).

[135] 568 U.S. 251, 258 (2013) (holding that "federal jurisdiction over a state law claim will lie if a federal issue is: (1) necessarily raised, (2) actually disputed, (3) substantial, and (4) capable of resolution in federal court without disrupting the federal-state balance approved by Congress"). On the facts of the case, the Court held that a state court had jurisdiction over legal malpractice action arising from an attorney's failure to raise an "experimental use" argument that allegedly would have prevented the invalidation of an inventor's patent).

[136] *See supra* ch. 3 notes 77–80 and accompanying text.

If the answer to this last question is yes, then by way of analogy to sham litigation antitrust suits the anti-troll plaintiff probably would have to prove that the assertion was both objectively baseless and subjectively motivated by the intent to injure the recipient; and a necessary but not sufficient condition for objective baselessness would be proof that the asserted patent was invalid, not infringed, or unenforceable.[137]

If, on the other hand, U.S. courts eventually come around to the view that *Noerr-Pennington* doesn't apply to these types of claims, then (at least in principle) claimants might be able to use probabilistic evidence in certain cases. Returning to the hypothetical presented at the beginning of this chapter, suppose that a patent owner sends demand letters to numerous recipients, but doesn't actually sue any of them for infringement (or at least hasn't done so yet);[138] a state attorney-general (AG) files suit against the owner for bad faith assertion, in violation of an anti-troll law; but the AG concedes that, as of the date the owner sent the letters, the ex ante probability of validity and infringement was greater than zero, thus (it would seem) eliminating as a possible ground for alleging bad faith assertion that the sender "knew, or should have known, that the claim or assertion is meritless."[139] Instead, the AG intends to show, among other things, that the ex ante probability of validity and infringement was too low to justify filing suit other than for the collateral purpose of

[137] You might think that, even if *Noerr-Pennington* immunizes the patentee from liability for asserting objectively justifiable patent claims, it would not preclude the state from imposing liability, for example, for the patentee's failure to include statutorily required information, or its inclusion of deceptive information, in a demand letter. Gugliuzza worries, however, that if the First Amendment is understood to "require[] that patent holders receive broad, *Noerr*-like immunity for all communications related to patent enforcement, then governments—both state and federal—are largely powerless to engage the problem that has captured the attention of policymakers and the public: demand letters that contain plausible allegations of infringement but that also contain statements that are deceptive or false." Gugliuzza, *supra* note 4, at 1616–17; *see also id.* 1629–32.

[138] Alternatively, perhaps by the time the bad faith assertion case goes to trial, the patent in suit has been found invalid, or has expired.

[139] *See* VT. STAT. ANN., tit. 9, § 4197(b)(6) (stating that "[a] court may consider . . . as evidence that a person has made a bad faith assertion of patent infringement," that the "[t]he claim or assertion of patent infringement is meritless, and the person knew, or should have known, that the claim or assertion is meritless"). In an appropriate case, however, the plaintiff might be able to prove meritlessness, if for example the claim language clearly precluded the claim construction that the patentee relied upon in support of validity and infringement, or if that construction was "so unreasonable that no reasonable litigant could believe it would succeed," *see* Rebecca Schoff Curtin, *SLAPPing Patent Trolls: What Anti-Trolling Legislation Can Learn from the Anti-SLAPP Movement*, 18 STAN. TECH. L. REV. 39, 68 (2014) (proposing that courts consider factors such as these, in the context of her model anti-SLAPP statute); or if there was clear evidence that by the time the demand letters were sent the patent in suit had expired, or that it was owned by someone else, or that the recipients' use was permitted under the exhaustion doctrine. For what may be other examples, *see* Gugliuzza, *supra* note 4, at 1619 & n.245 (citing cases in which, for example, the patent owner failed to produce any evidence at trial in support of its claim for infringement, or voluntarily dismissed every case it commenced).

extracting nuisance payments.[140] On these facts, should the court permit the AG to introduce evidence that the patentee has (or had) a *low but nonzero* ex ante probability of success on the merits of its infringement assertions—coupled, perhaps, with evidence that that probability, whatever it is, would not have justified the royalties the patentee demanded?

In principle, it seems that the answer to the above question should be yes—though again, it bears emphasizing that the issue would come up, if at all, only if the courts eventually conclude that anti-troll claimants are not obligated to prove objective baselessness. If that were to happen, however, then under the standards that applied prior to the Federal Circuit's embrace of the *Noerr-Pennington* standard, courts might consider as proof of bad faith "both subjective considerations (such as the patent holder's lack of intent to file a threatened infringement suit) and objective considerations (such as the weakness of the infringement claim on the merits)."[141] Evidence suggesting that the owner had a low but nonzero ex ante probability of success therefore would seem relevant in the present context, though it's an open question exactly what such evidence would consist of; there may be no useful heuristic, comparable to an "unexplained large reverse payment" in the pay-for-delay context, for drawing critical probabilistic inferences. Evidence that the owner typically demanded royalties in an amount below the recipients' avoided litigation costs, for example, might be consistent with bad faith behavior, but it isn't dispositive if the value of the invention itself is low.[142] Similarly, evidence that while the case was pending the patent in suit was invalidated in parallel infringement litigation or in a PTAB proceeding might be suggestive, but would not necessarily exclude the possibility that the patentee had an ex ante nonzero chance of prevailing. In addition, party admissions, as revealed in discovery, might shed light on the patentee's ex ante expectations, but cannot be counted upon to exist.

Perhaps, then, a more precise estimate of the ex ante probability of success would be called for. Any such estimate, however, would need to take into account not only potential validity problems, but also whether (at least a sample of) the recipients' products plausibly fall within the patent's claims, and the

[140] *See id.* §§ 4197(b)(5), (9) (stating that "[a] court may consider . . . as evidence that a person has made a bad faith assertion of patent infringement," that the offer to license is "for an amount that is not based on a reasonable estimate of the value of the license"; and "[a]ny other factor that the court finds relevant").

[141] Gugliuzza, *supra* note 4, at 1642.

[142] Evidence of comparable licenses might be useful as well, though it may be quite difficult to uncover other licenses, especially licenses involving nonparties, that are sufficiently technologically and economically comparable to the license offered by the patent owner.

damages the patent owner might have expected from infringement litigation. In this regard, courts might permit the use of probabilistic expert testimony, which as noted above may be necessary in some pay-for-delay cases, and would be necessary under a sham litigation standard reformulated in accordance with the analysis presented in chapter 4.[143] Nevertheless, it may be the rare case in which an anti-troll litigant would consider the expense of producing such probabilistic evidence to be a wise use of resources, given what would (in my view, typically) be the substantially lower stakes of such cases in comparison with major antitrust litigation. Nonetheless, to the extent such cases could arise, there seems to be no reason why plaintiffs shouldn't be allowed to introduce probabilistic evidence, insofar as it may be relevant to bad faith, to the same extent they would be permitted to do so in antitrust litigation[144]—though again, all of this may be academic, as long as the objective baselessness standard remains in place.

Appendix to Chapter 5

The E.U. system requires some tweaks to the model presented in the text, to reflect the fact that the prevailing party is usually entitled to recover a portion $(1-\gamma)$ of its litigation costs, and the lack of an automatic stay. In consequence of the latter difference, the brand must decide whether to move for a preliminary injunction, but if it obtains one it may be obligated to compensate the generic for its interim losses $(G_{\Delta,t2})$ if the brand loses at trial.[145] Thus, we have two equations illustrating the expected benefit to the brand, (7) on the assumption that a preliminary injunction issues, and (8) on the assumption it does not (either because the brand does not seek one, or its request is denied):

$$E[B]_{\Pi,T} = P_{\Pi}(I_{\Pi} + \delta_{\Pi} D_{\Pi,t1}) - (1-P_{\Pi})G_{\Delta,t2} \\ -[P_{\Pi}\gamma C_{\Pi,T} + (1-P_{\Pi})(C_{\Pi,T} + (1-\gamma)C_{\Delta,T})], \tag{7}$$

[143] *See supra* note 7.

[144] For a possible example, *see* Katana Silicon Techs. v. Micron Techs., Inc., 671 F. Supp. 3d 1138 (D. Idaho 2023) (in a case in which the patent owner filed suit for the infringement of three patents, and the defendant responded with a claim under the Idaho anti-troll law, imposing an $8 million bond reflecting approximately treble the cost of defending against the infringement suit).

[145] As discussed in chapter 4, the amount the plaintiff may be obligated to pay if the preliminary injunction turns out, ex post, to be unwarranted may be less than the full amount of the defendant's loss. Including that complication above would make the math even messier, however, without materially altering the results.

$$E[B]_{\Pi,T} = P_\Pi\left[I_\Pi + \delta_\Pi(D_{\Pi,t1} + D_{\Pi,t2})\right] \\ -\left[P_\Pi \gamma C_{\Pi,T} + (1-P_\Pi)(C_{\Pi,T} + (1-\gamma)C_{\Delta,T})\right] \tag{8}$$

Similarly, the generic's expected loss with (10) and without (11) a preliminary injunction can be expressed as:

$$E[L]_{\Delta,T} = P_\Delta\left[I_\Delta + \delta_\Delta D_{\Delta,t1} + G_{\Delta,t2}\right] \\ +\left[P_\Delta((1-\gamma)C_{\Pi,T} + C_{\Delta,T}) + (1-P_\Delta)(\gamma C_{\Delta,T})\right], \tag{10}$$

$$E[L]_{\Delta,T} = P_\Delta\left[I_\Delta + \delta_\Delta(D_{\Delta,t1} + D_{\Delta,t2})\right] \\ +\left[P_\Delta((1-\gamma)C_{\Pi,T} + C_{\Delta,T}) + (1-P_\Delta)(\gamma C_{\Delta,T})\right] \tag{11}$$

A settlement at t_1, expressed in terms of payment from brand to generic, will be rational as long as SP falls within the following ranges:

$$(1-P_\Pi)(I_\Pi + G_{\Delta,t2} + C_{\Pi,T} + (1-\gamma)C_{\Delta,T}) + P_\Pi(\gamma C_{\Pi,T} - \delta_\Pi D_{\Pi,t1}) \geq SP \\ \geq (1-P_\Delta)(I_\Delta + G_{\Delta,t2} - \gamma C_{\Delta,T}) - P_\Delta[\delta_\Delta D_{\Delta,t1} + (1-\gamma)C_{\Pi,T} + C_{\Delta,T}] \tag{12}$$

$$(1-P_\Pi)(I_\Pi + C_{\Pi,T} + (1-\gamma)C_{\Delta,T}) + (1-\ P_\Pi\delta_\Pi)D_{\Pi,t2} \\ + P_\Pi(\gamma C_{\Pi,T} - \delta_\Pi D_{\Pi,t1}) \geq\ SP\ \geq (1-P_\Delta)(I_\Delta - \gamma C_{\Delta,T}) \\ -P_\Delta[\delta_\Delta(D_{\Delta,t1} + D_{\Delta,t2}) + (1-\gamma)C_{\Pi,T} + C_{\Delta,T}] + G_{\Delta,t2} \tag{13}$$

The math is messier, but under both scenarios, if the brand believes it has a 100% chance of winning, it will pay only up to the sum of its avoided expected-to-be-uncompensable litigation costs minus whatever damages it expects to collect from the generic for products sold during the initial, pre-settlement period. If it believes it has a zero chance, it seems unlikely that it would pursue preliminary injunctive relief, but it would be willing to pay up to $(I_\Pi + C_{\Pi,T} + (1-\gamma)C_{\Delta,T} + D_{\Pi,t2})$ to settle at t_1. Table 5.2 illustrates the outcomes with the same numbers used before, on the simplifying assumptions that $\delta = 1$; $D_{t1} = 0$; the parties have symmetric information and are risk-neutral; and that a preliminary injunction would not issue unless $P \geq .50$.

Table 5.2 Assume that $I_{\Pi} = 90$ million; $D_{\Pi,t2} = 10$ million; $G_{\Delta,t2} = 5$ million; $I_{\Delta} = 45$ million.

P	Amount plaintiff will pay defendant
0	$100m + C_{\Pi,T} + (1-\gamma)C_{\Delta,T} \geq SP \geq 50m - \gamma C_{\Delta,T}$
.25	$75m + .75(1-\gamma)C_{\Delta,T} + (C_{\Pi,T})(.75 + .25\gamma) \geq SP \geq 36.25m - (.25 + .75\gamma)C_{\Delta,T} - .25(1-\gamma)C_{\Pi,T}$
.50	$47.5m + .5(1+\gamma)C_{\Pi,T} + 5(1-\gamma)C_{\Delta,T} \geq SP \geq 25m - .5(1+\gamma)C_{\Delta,T} - .5(1-\gamma) C_{\Pi,T}$
.75	$23.75m + C_{\Pi,T}(.25 + .75\gamma) + .25(1-\gamma)C_{\Delta,T} \geq SP \geq 12.5m - (.75 + .25\gamma)C_{\Delta,T} - .75(1-\gamma)C_{\Pi,T}$
1	$\gamma C_{\Pi,T} \geq SP \geq -[(1-\gamma)C_{\Pi,T} + C_{\Delta,T}]$

6

"Without Sufficient Justification," Case 3

We come now to the final substantive chapter of the book, which will address claims, defenses, and remedies that constrain the exercise of patent rights even though the patent at issue may be both valid and infringed. These include the "abuse" doctrines (abuse of dominant position, abuse of right, and abuse of economic dependence); equitable defenses including patent misuse, equitable estoppel, inequitable conduct, and unclean hands; and discretionary denials of injunctive relief, whether as a matter of equity, proportionality, or one of the above-mentioned doctrines. Tied into this last subtopic of injunctive relief is the question of whether courts should be authorized to grant antisuit (or anti-antisuit) injunctions against a litigant's prosecution or enforcement of patent rights in another jurisdiction. The common question raised by all of these bodies of legal doctrine is under what circumstances legislators or courts should restrain what would otherwise be the lawful and legitimate exercise of patent rights.

One way to approach this question is by way of noting, as in the previous chapter, that some patent licenses (often entered into in settlement of patent litigation) violate antitrust law, because even if the patent at issue were valid and infringed, it could not possibly justify the agreed-upon terms. The example cited there, adapted from one originally propounded by Hovenkamp, Janis, and Lemley, would be for two auto manufacturers to settle litigation involving a windshield wiper patent by agreeing to a license under which each manufacturer may use the patented technology, *and* to a naked market allocation whereby one will sell pickup trucks only east of the Mississippi River and the other only west.[1] In other instances, however, antitrust law condemns

[1] Herbert Hovenkamp, Mark A. Lemley & Mark D. Janis, *Anticompetitive Settlement of Intellectual Property Disputes*, 87 MINN. L. REV. 1719, 1726 (2003). The example is presented again in the authors' treatise, which also notes that, conversely, many other licenses—e.g., vertical licenses in which neither licensor nor licensee has market power—would attract little if any antitrust scrutiny, again without inquiry into whether the licensed rights are valid and otherwise would be infringed. *See* HERBERT HOVENKAMP ET AL., IP AND ANTITRUST: AN ANALYSIS OF ANTITRUST PRINCIPLES APPLIED TO INTELLECTUAL PROPERTY LAW, §§ 7.01, 7.02[A], [B] (2023). Another example of when courts can condemn a license without considering validity and infringement is when owners of blocking patents agree to cross-license one another *and* to fix the prices of their competing end products. *See, e.g.*, In re

Wrongful Patent Assertion. Thomas F. Cotter, Oxford University Press. © Oxford University Press 2026.
DOI: 10.1093/9780191994104.003.0006

licenses or conduct involving valid and infringed patents that *may* be, but are not as in the preceding example *necessarily*, harmful in the sense of unnecessarily distorting the market, harming consumers, and/or impeding innovation. These include, for example, tying arrangements, grantbacks, reach-through licenses, and refusals to deal, whether litigated as stand-alone claims or where applicable as aspects of an abuse of dominant position. When antitrust plaintiffs assert these types of claims, their success will depend, in large part, on whether legislative or judicial decisions have previously concluded that permitting the type of conduct at issue would enable the patent owner to reap anticompetitive benefits that extend beyond the legitimate scope of the patent.[2] Given this book's focus, however, on claims and defenses related to the actual or threatened assertion of patent rights, beyond whatever implicit threat may back up an offer to license or a refusal to deal, and that it does not aspire to provide a comprehensive overview of patent-related antitrust claims, I will not spend much time addressing how the world's competition authorities define the concept of "beyond the scope" other than to note the following two points.

The first is that, in the United States, facts that might give rise to a patent-related antitrust claim also will sometimes give rise to a patent misuse defense to a claim for patent infringement—though as we shall see, patent misuse also extends to some conduct that does not violate the antitrust laws, while for conduct that simultaneously violates antitrust *and* constitutes misuse, the obvious question is whether two doctrines are needed, or if one alone would suffice.

The second is that application of the concept of *proportionality* sometimes may justify characterizing conduct as extending beyond the legitimate scope of the patent, regardless of the patent's infringement and validity. In the preceding chapter, for example, I concurred with Erik Hovenkamp's recommendation that antitrust standards should ensure that settlements of actual or threatened patent litigation are proportional, in the sense of restraining competition only "to an extent commensurate with the expected result of patent litigation."[3]

Summit Tech., Inc., No. 9286, Decision and Order (FTC Feb. 23, 1999), https://www.ftc.gov/sites/default/files/documents/cases/1999/03/ftc.gov-d09286visx.do_.htm.

[2] See, e.g., FTC v. Actavis, Inc., 570 U.S. 136, 167 (2013) (Roberts, C.J., dissenting) (stating that "any agreements relating to patents . . . are subject to antitrust scrutiny if they confer benefits beyond the scope of the patent," albeit while rejecting the majority's view that the defendants' agreement in that case went beyond what I refer to above as the *legitimate* scope of the patent).

[3] Erik Hovenkamp, *Antitrust Law and Patent Settlement Design*, 32 Harv. J.L. & Tech. 418, 420 (2019) (proposing a "proportional-effects rule," under which "antitrust's goal is for settlements to be *proportional*: to restrain competition to an extent commensurate with the expected result of patent litigation").

On this view, settlements that would delay generic entry past the ex ante expected date of entry are disproportional to the (desirable) normative goal of aligning the ex ante and ex post dates of generic entry—and, if you will, can be viewed as extending the *legitimate* scope of the patent. And while that chapter applied this principle only to reverse-payment settlements, one might view the same principle as being at play in at least some of the other cases in which antitrust or other law condemns patent-related conduct. In the hypothetical involving the windshield wiper patent litigation, for example, even if the patent owner were sure to win had the case proceeded to trial instead of settling, no court would have entered a judgment dividing up the geographic market for pickup trucks between the owner and the defendant. At most, it would have enjoined the defendant's use of the patented blade, but this too hardly would have resulted in the *de facto* exclusion of the rival from any substantial portion, much less half, of the U.S. market for pickup trucks; presumably, there would be plenty of imperfect but noninfringing alternatives available to the rival, and no matter how inventive the patented blades might be it seems unlikely that their absence would be a dealbreaker for many consumers. Other cases, however, are not quite so simple; by way of example, whether the (legitimate) threat of an injunction against the infringement of a valid patent should be understood as justifying a settlement or license permitting the use of the patented technology subject to condition *X* may depend on whether the consequences resulting from imposition of condition *X* would enable the owner to obtain some benefit or inflict some harm that is disproportionate in view of an appropriate normative baseline—which might be commensurability with the expected outcome of litigation, or something else.[4] This chapter therefore will begin with a short riff on proportionality and its various possible meanings. I then turn to a discussion of antitrust and the sometimes related abuse doctrines, before turning to what is probably the common law's closest analogue to the abuse of rights principle, equity.

[4] Put another way, the question is whether the patentee is justified in demanding compliance with condition *X* in exchange for permission to use the patented technology. Condition *X* might be an agreement to pay a royalty in some amount *Y*, or to engage in some conduct *Z*, such as agreeing to purchase another product or to license another patent from the owner. If the benefit to the patentee and/or the harm to the counterparty or to third parties resulting from the counterparty's agreeing to pay amount *Y* or engage in conduct *Z* exceeds what is understood to be the appropriate baseline, the question then becomes whether this disproportionality by itself should be sufficient to condemn the condition, or whether proof of additional factors, or some specific quantitative departure from proportionality such as "gross" disproportionality, should be necessary.

Proportionality

As I discuss in an essay to be published in a forthcoming edited volume,[5] one way of thinking about the topic of wrongful patent assertion is through the lens of proportionality: in other words, to characterize a patent assertion as "wrongful" is to say that, in some meaningful sense, the assertion would confer some benefit upon the patentee, or inflict some cognizable harm upon the accused, third parties, or the general public, that is "disproportionate." Of course, to state that an assertion is "disproportionate" is not, without more, any more helpful than characterizing the assertion as "wrongful"; what is needed are criteria by which to distinguish wrongful (or disproportionate) assertions from legitimate (proportional) ones. The proportionality concept nevertheless sometimes can be helpful in this regard, from both a legal and a policy perspective.

In terms of legal analysis, proportionality is an important concept in several legal systems,[6] but is perhaps most closely associated with the European Union, for which proportionality is a foundational legal principle. Article 5(1) of the Treaty on European Union (TEU) states that "[t]he limits of Union competences are governed by the principle of conferral," and that "[t]he use of Union competences is governed by the principles of subsidiarity and proportionality."[7] Article 5(4) further elaborates:

> Under the principle of proportionality, the content and form of Union action shall not exceed what is necessary to achieve the objectives of the Treaties. The institutions of the Union shall apply the principle of proportionality as laid down in the Protocol on the application of the principles of subsidiarity and proportionality.[8]

[5] *See* Thomas F. Cotter, *Wrongfulness as Disproportionality: Toward a Law-and-Economics Approach to Wrongful Patent Assertion, in* Intellectual Property and the Principle of Proportionality (Christopher Heath & Anselm Kamperman Sanders eds., forthcoming 2026).

[6] *See, e.g.*, Minyu Zheng, Legal Responses to Unjustified Threats of Patent Infringement – Intellectual Property Approach or Unfair Competition Approach? 131–44 (2024) (providing a brief overview of proportionality in international (WTO), E.U., and domestic law). The concept is also referenced, and applied, by the European Court of Human Rights. *See, e.g.*, Jonathan Griffiths, *Enforcement of Intellectual Property Rights and the Right to a Fair Trial, in* Research Handbook on Human Rights and Intellectual Property 438, 453 (Christophe Geiger ed. 2015) (citing cases).

[7] Consolidated Version of the Treaty on European Union art. 5(1), Oct. 26, 2012, 2012 O.J. (C 326) 18.

[8] *Id.* art. 5(4). *See also id.* Protocol (No. 2) on the Application of the Principles of Subsidiarity and Proportionality (detailing the procedures to be followed in reviewing legislation for compliance with the principles of subsidiarity and proportionality).

Further breaking down the concept, the E.U.'s official website explains that "[u]nder this principle, EU measures . . . must be suitable to achieve the desired end; must be necessary to achieve the desired end; and must not impose a burden on the individual that is excessive in relation to the objective sought to be achieved (proportionality in the narrow sense)."[9] These three conditions—of suitability (appropriateness), necessity (i.e., is the measure the least restrictive option to achieve the desired end?), and proportionality *stricto sensu* (requiring some sort of balancing of benefits and costs)—are relevant both for determining whether E.U. legislation is consistent with the TEU and, at least where courts are understood to have authority to determine whether a specific application of domestic or E.U. law would be lawful, in cases involving private law rights.[10] In regard to intellectual property rights in particular, moreover, article 3(2) of the Intellectual Property Rights Enforcement Directive (IPRED) states that "remedies shall . . . be effective, proportionate and dissuasive and shall be applied in such a manner as to avoid the creation of barriers to legitimate trade and to provide for safeguards against their abuse."[11] On this basis, some scholars have argued that the laws of E.U. member states need to be more accommodating than many traditionally have been toward denying, or at least staying, injunctive relief in some patent infringement actions,[12] though others contend that proportionality is already "built in" to existing systems that generally award injunctions as a matter of right.[13] I will have more to say about

[9] European Union, Principle of Proportionality, https://eur-lex.europa.eu/EN/legal-content/glossary/principle-of-proportionality.html.

[10] For discussion of CJEU case law and of commentary regarding the applicability of the proportionality concept to intellectual property rights, *see, e.g.*, Léon Dijkman, The Proportionality Test in European Patent Law: Patent Injunctions Before EU Courts and the UPC 147–48, 153–57 (2023) (discussing cases); Zheng, *supra* note 6, at 135–38; Peter Teunissen, *Intellectual Property, Injunctions, and Proportionality: Towards a Uniform Approach*, 74 GRUR Int. 805, 808–09 (2025).

[11] Directive 2004/48/EC of the European Parliament and of the Council of 29 April 2004 on the Enforcement of Intellectual Property Rights [hereinafter IPRED], art. 3(2). The Directive expressly references proportionality in several other parts as well. *See id.* art. 8(1) (the right of information); art. 10 (corrective measures); art. 14 (legal costs); recitals 22, 25.

[12] *See, e.g.*, Dijkman, *supra* note 10, at 149–61; Ansgar Ohly, *Three Principles of European IP Enforcement Law: Effectiveness, Proportionality, Dissuasiveness*, *in* Technology and Competition: Contributions in Honour of Hanns Ullrich 257, 265–67 (Josef Drexl ed. 2009); Teunissen, *supra* note 10, at 810–16. *See also* HTC Corp. v. Nokia Corp., [2013] EWHC 3778 [32] (Pat.) (Eng.) (pre-Brexit decision, concluding IPRED article 3(2) "requires the court to refuse to grant an injunction where it would be disproportionate to grant one even having regard to the requirements of efficacy and dissuasiveness," and suggesting that "the practical effect of this approach is little different" from pre-IPRED English case law that would deny injunctive relief if such relief would be "grossly disproportionate").

[13] See, e.g., Lea Tochtermann, *Injunctions in European Patent Law*, 11 ZGE/IPJ 257, 265, 269–70 (2019) (arguing, *inter alia*, that "[a] guarantee for proportionality may . . . be derived from the functioning of the patent system as a whole"; and noting that, in Germany, "injunctions are only declared provisionally enforceable against security" pending appellate review, and defendants may request a temporary stay of enforcement if "enforcement would entail a disadvantage that it is impossible to

these positions, and about the specific proposals referenced above, later in this chapter.

Proportionality also can be a useful concept for evaluating the various wrongful assertion doctrines, whether formulated by legislatures, courts, or other actors, as a matter of policy. In this regard, the rule ostensibly adopted by the U.S. Supreme Court in *FTC v. Actavis, Inc.*,[14] that a patent owner's agreement to settle patent litigation by transferring consideration in excess of its avoided litigation costs to the accused infringer can be prima facie evidence of an antitrust violation, is correct if the underlying principle is that competition law should condemn settlements that enable patent owners to obtain effective terms of exclusivity that are disproportionate, in the sense of exceeding the patent's ex ante probabilistic term of protection.[15] More generally, as noted above, one might argue that the broader principle encompassing the *Actavis* inference is that antitrust should condemn any settlement or license that restrains competition to an extent disproportionate to the expected result of patent litigation.[16] In some situations, the application of this principle would be simple and uncontroversial—*of course* antitrust law would condemn the hypothetical settlement involving the windshield wiper patent, because the economic value the patentee would derive from the settlement would be so clearly disproportionate (incommensurate) with the scope of the comparatively trivial patent. Of course, in this example the terms of the settlement also would exceed the patent's *potential* exclusionary scope, because there's nothing about a windshield wiper patent that would authorize two rivals to divide up the geographic market for pickup trucks. In this example, therefore, whichever normative principle one invokes—"terms should be commensurate with the expected result of patent litigation," or "terms should be commensurate with the patent's potential exclusionary scope"[17]—it's clear that the settlement should be condemned, because it's simply a disguise for a per se unlawful market allocation. But in other cases, whether antitrust or other bodies of law should condemn a given settlement, license, or conduct by a patent owner will depend in large part on the policymaker's initial choice of an appropriate normative principle. With regard to reverse payments, if "terms should be commensurate with the

compensate or remedy"); DIJKMAN, *supra* note 10, at 149–50 (noting this view among other German and Dutch commentators).

[14] *See* FTC v. Actavis, Inc., 570 U.S. 136, 158 (2013).
[15] *See supra* ch. 5 notes 109–18 and accompanying text.
[16] *See supra* text accompanying note 4.
[17] The latter is, in a sense, a subset of the former, since anything outside the potential exclusionary scope might appear necessarily to be disproportionate to the expected result of litigation.

expected result of patent litigation" is the appropriate normative principle, then payments exceeding the patentee's avoided litigation costs are highly suspect, because for reasons discussed in chapter 5 the term of exclusivity agreed upon in the settlement will be disproportionate to the ex ante probabilistic term. If instead the appropriate normative principle is "terms should be commensurate with the potential exclusionary scope," then most such settlements will be lawful because the agreed-upon term of exclusivity usually will be less than or equal, and therefore proportional, to that potential scope. The point is that, in this and other examples to be discussed later in this chapter, much of the heavy lifting comes in choosing the appropriate normative principle, after which determining whether the settlement, license, or other conduct would generate benefits or harms that are disproportionate in view of that principle may be comparatively easy.

Does that mean, then, that proportionality ultimately is something of an empty concept? I don't think so, for a couple of reasons. The first is that characterizing wrongful assertion doctrine as a response to disproportionate exercises of patent rights requires one to ask, "Disproportionate to what?", and thus goads one into thinking more precisely about exactly what the appropriate normative principle *is*. In the context of reverse payment settlements, for example, as discussed in chapter 5 I believe the case is strong that application of the principle "terms should be commensurate with the expected result of patent litigation" would increase consumer welfare and decrease market distortion in comparison with the principle "terms should be commensurate with the potential exclusionary scope," and also that the former principle can be implemented at relatively low administrative cost. In other settings, such as those cases, alluded to above and discussed in greater detail toward the end of this chapter, in which the patent misuse defense may arise under U.S. law, one could similarly ask whether the licensing of a patent on condition *X* enables the patentee to extract value that would exceed the incremental value (ex ante or ex post) of the patent absent the condition; if so, whether policymakers should view this extraction as a problem; and if not, whether policymakers should view the extraction as a problem for other reasons, such as a normative commitment against price discrimination. Similarly, in regard to whether courts should have discretion to stay or deny injunctive relief for patent infringement, it seems reasonably clear that in the absence of such discretion patent owners sometimes can extract value from potential licensees ex post that is disproportionate to the value they could have extracted ex ante. This ability may or may not be dispositive in the crafting of legislative rules, but recognizing that the extraction of such "holdup" value is one of the possible effects of automatic injunctive relief should be an indispensable aspect of legislative rulemaking.

Further, in cases involving assertions the wrongfulness of which depends, in whole or in part, on the patent being invalid or not infringed, such assertions clearly are disproportionate if the appropriate normative principle in such cases is that "patentees should not extract benefits or inflict harms incommensurate with ex post incremental value"; but whether any such extraction *should* be considered wrongful is the difficult normative question. In regard to awards of attorneys' fees, some legislatures or courts apparently have concluded that "patentees should not extract benefits and inflict harms incommensurate with ex post incremental value," *is* the appropriate normative principle *vel non*. Others may agree only that it is a necessary, but not sufficient, condition for liability; and for other situations, such as compensation for wrongly issued preliminary (or permanent) injunctions, reasonable minds may differ whether "commensurate with ex post incremental value" is an appropriate baseline at all, in comparison with, say, "commensurate with ex ante incremental value," or even "commensurate with an amount not grossly in excess of the ex ante incremental value," this last perhaps being consistent with some sort of bad faith standard. Presenting the issues in these terms, however, might at least compel decisionmakers to think more carefully about whether an assertion that would be disproportionate in view of ex post but not ex ante incremental value (or vice versa) should subject the owner to liability, and if not why not: is it because of the potential effects on the patent incentive scheme, or the risk of chilling legitimate exercises of rights, or something else?

The other reason that proportionality can be useful goes back to its legal meaning. As noted above, courts, particularly in the E.U., have developed specific criteria that inform the proportionality test; and even if those criteria do not always lead to one single conclusion, it still can be useful to try and reason through whether a doctrine, or its application in a particular case, would generate results that would be suitable to a legitimate purpose, necessary to effectively carry out that purpose, and justifiable in view of the net social benefits to be obtained from carrying out the purpose. As suggested by Minyu Zheng, proportionality in this sense can be viewed not only as "a method of rational thinking . . . but also a comprehensive and concise expression of purposive rationality."[18]

[18] ZHENG, *supra* note 6, at 139 (citing AHARON BARAK, PROPORTIONALITY: CONSTITUTIONAL RIGHTS AND THEIR LIMITATIONS 175 (2012), and MAX WEBER, ECONOMY AND SOCIETY: AN OUTLINE OF INTERPRETIVE SOCIOLOGY 26 (Guenther Roth & Claus Wittich trs., 1978)).

The Abuse Doctrines: Abuse of Dominant Position

Abuse of dominant position is an antitrust claim common to many countries and regions, though notably not the United States. In the E.U., for example, the claim is set forth in article 102 of the Treaty on the Functioning of the European Union (formerly article 82 of the Treaty Establishing the European Community), which states:

> Any abuse by one or more undertakings of a dominant position within the internal market or in a substantial part of it shall be prohibited as incompatible with the internal market in so far as it may affect trade between Member States.
>
> Such abuse may, in particular, consist in:
>
> (a) directly or indirectly imposing unfair purchase or selling prices or other unfair trading conditions;
>
> (b) limiting production, markets or technical development to the prejudice of consumers;
>
> (c) applying dissimilar conditions to equivalent transactions with other trading parties, thereby placing them at a competitive disadvantage;
>
> (d) making the conclusion of contracts subject to acceptance by the other parties of supplementary obligations which, by their nature or according to commercial usage, have no connection with the subject of such contracts.[19]

Similar provisions can be found in China's Anti-Monopoly Law[20] and India's Competition Act,[21] while the closest analogy in Japan is the Monopoly Law's

[19] Treaty on the Functioning of the European Union (TFEU), art. 102.

[20] *See* Anti-Monopoly Law (China) art. 22 (2022 rev.), *English language translation available at* https://www.chinalawtranslate.com/en/anti-monopoly-law-2022/. *See also id.* arts. 23, 24 (setting forth factors for determining if an undertaking holds a dominant position); State Administration for Market Regulation (SAMR), State Council Anti-Monopoly Committee Ant-Monopoly Guidelines in the Field of Intellectual Property Rights, arts. 14–19 (Aug. 6, 2020); SAMR, Provisions Prohibiting Abuse of Dominant Market Positions, arts. 14–20 (Apr. 15, 2023); SAMR, Provisions Prohibiting Abuse of Intellectual Property Rights to Exclude and Restrict Competition, arts. 8–14 (Aug. 1, 2023). Some provisions of these documents address patent pools and standard-essential patents, discussed *infra* at notes 76–78 and accompanying text.

[21] *See* Competition Act, 2002, art. 4(2) (India):

> There shall be an abuse of dominant position [under subsection (1), if an enterprise or a group].—
>
> (a) directly or indirectly, imposes unfair or discriminatory—(i) condition in purchase or sale of goods or service; or (ii) price in purchase or sale (including predatory price) of goods or service; . . . or
>
> (b) limits or restricts—(i) production of goods or provision of services or market therefor; or (ii) technical or scientific development relating to goods or services to the prejudice of consumers; or

prohibition of "unfair competition," which is defined to include a variety of practices by which an undertaking takes unfair advantage of its superior bargaining power (and thus would appear to embrace both abuse of dominant position and, as discussed below, abuse of economic dependence).[22] In all of these jurisdictions, a dominant undertaking's conduct with regard to its intellectual property can, under some circumstances, constitute an abuse of dominant position.

Most of the reported decisions addressing the circumstances under which enforcement or threatened enforcement constitutes an abuse nevertheless come from the E.U. or its member states.[23] As discussed in chapter 3, for example, the Court of First Instance in *ITT Promedia* held that it can be an abuse for a dominant firm to file an action "(i) which cannot reasonably be considered as an attempt to establish its rights and can therefore only serve to harass the opposite party, and (ii) which is conceived in the framework of a plan whose goal is to eliminate competition."[24] Although *ITT Promedia* did not involve IP rights, subsequent case law and commentary provides support for the proposition that, in exceptional cases, sham litigation of IP rights can violate article 102.[25] Similarly, in *AstraZeneca AB*

(c) indulges in practice or practices resulting in denial of market access [in any manner]; or
(d) makes conclusion of contracts subject to acceptance by other parties of supplementary obligations which, by their nature or according to commercial usage, have no connection with the subject of such contracts; or
(e) uses its dominant position in one relevant market to enter into, or protect, other relevant market.

[22] *See* Act on Prohibition of Private Monopolization and Maintenance of Fair Trade art. 2(9) (Japan) [hereinafter Japan Anti-Monopoly Act] (defining "unfair trade practices" as including, *inter alia*: "engaging in any act specified in one of the following by making use of one's superior bargaining position over the counterparty unjustly, in light of normal business practices: (a) causing the counterparty in continuous transactions (including a party with whom one newly intends to engage in continuous transactions; the same applies in (b) below) to purchase goods or services other than those to which the relevant transactions pertain[;] (b) causing the counterparty in continuous transactions to provide money, services or other economic benefits[; and] (c) refusing to receive goods in transactions with the counterparty, causing the counterparty to take back such goods after receiving them from the counterparty, delaying payment to the counterparty or reducing the amount of payment, or otherwise establishing or changing trade terms or executing transactions in a way disadvantageous to the counterparty.") *See also* Japan Fair Trade Commission, Guidelines Concerning Abuse of Superior Bargaining Position under the Antimonopoly Act (Nov. 30, 2010); Michael Underdown, *Abuse of Dominant Position and the Public Interest in Japanese Competition Law*, 4 MACARTHUR L. REV. 173 (2000) (contrasting the Japanese approach to that of other countries or regions, including the E.U.).

[23] In addition, some of the E.U. case law addressing whether a refusal to license one's IP can constitute an abuse of dominant position will be relevant to the related "abuse of economic dependence" doctrine, discussed *infra* notes 116–42 and accompanying text.

[24] ITT Promedia NV v. Comm'n of Eur. Cmtys., Case T-111/96, ECLI:EU:T:1998:183, ¶ 30 (CJEU 1998).

[25] *See supra* ch. 3 note 33 and accompanying text.

v. European Commission[26] the Court held that the submission of misleading information, liable to lead national authorities "into error and therefore to make possible the grant of an exclusive right" to which the defendants were not entitled, could constitute an abuse of dominant position, though (unlike in the United States) this sort of claim does not necessarily depend on the enforcement or threatened enforcement of the wrongly-procured rights.[27] Further, as discussed in chapter 5 there is an evolving body of CJEU case law considering the circumstances under which the settlement of actual or threatened patent litigation by means of reverse payments constitutes an abuse;[28] and more recently, the European Commission fined Teva €462.6 million for allegedly artificially extending the latter's exclusivity in the market for glatiramer acetate medicines by, *inter alia*, obtaining a series of divisional patents covering methods of manufacture, threatening to enforce these patents by means of preliminary injunctions, and then timely withdrawing its requests for preliminary injunctions to avoid judgments of invalidity.[29]

Most of the recent European case law addressing enforcement as a possible abuse of dominant position, however, involves standard-essential patents (SEPs), the leading decision being the CJEU's 2015 judgment in *Huawei Technologies Co. Ltd. v. ZTE Corp.*[30] As noted in chapter 3, standard-setting organizations (SSOs) (sometimes referred to in the alternative as standards development organizations, or SDOs) such as the European Telecommunications Standards Institute (ETSI) or the Institute of Electrical and Electronics Engineers (IEEE), promulgate standards that enable devices to interoperate. To constrain the market power that otherwise might follow from owning a patent, or portfolio of patents, the practice of which would be essential to standard compliance, SSOs often require members to declare any patents or pending patent applications that may be essential to the practice of a standard under consideration, and to commit to licensing their SEPs on (undefined) fair, reasonable, and nondiscriminatory (FRAND) terms.[31] In this context, the Court summarized the questions presented in the *Huawei* case as "in what circumstances the bringing of an action for infringement, by an undertaking in

[26] AstraZeneca AB v. Eur. Comm'n, Case C-457/10 P, CLI:EU:C:2012:770 (CJEU 2012).
[27] *See supra* ch. 3 notes 13–20 and accompanying text.
[28] *See supra* ch. 5 note 130.
[29] *See id.* note 130.
[30] Case C-170/13, ECLI:EU:C:2015:477 (CJEU 2015).
[31] *See, e.g.*, ETSI Rules of Procedure, Annex 6 Rules 4.1, 6.1, 6bis (Nov. 29–30, 2022), https://www.etsi.org/images/files/IPR/etsi-ipr-policy.pdf.

a dominant position and holding an SEP, which has given an undertaking to the standardisation body to grant licences to third parties on FRAND terms, seeking an injunction prohibiting the infringement of that SEP or seeking the recall of products for the manufacture of which the SEP has been used, is to be regarded as constituting an abuse contrary to Article 102 TFEU."[32] Citing the indispensability of the technology to the implementer, the possible difficulty the implementer faces in identifying all relevant SEPs in advance, and the irrevocable nature of the SEP owner's commitment to license on FRAND terms,[33] the Court set forth a series of steps—sometimes referred to in subsequent commentary as the "FRAND dance"—to aid in determining whether a request for injunctive relief is abusive.[34] First, the SEP owner must "alert the alleged infringer of the infringement complained about by designating that SEP and specifying the way in which it has been infringed."[35] Second, "after the alleged infringer has expressed its willingness to conclude a licensing agreement on FRAND terms, it is for the proprietor of the SEP to present to that alleged infringer a specific, written offer for a licence on FRAND terms, in accordance with the undertaking given to the standardisation body, specifying, in particular, the amount of the royalty and the way in which that royalty is to be calculated."[36] (As the case law has subsequently developed, the implementer's expression of its willingness to license, and the owner's submission of a written offer, are considered separate steps 2 and 3, respectively.) Next, the implementer should "diligently to respond to that offer, in accordance with recognised commercial practices in the field and in good faith, a point which must be established on the basis of objective factors and which implies, in particular, that there are no delaying tactics.... Should the alleged infringer not accept the offer made to it, it may rely on the abusive nature of an action for a prohibitory injunction or for the recall of products only if it has submitted to the proprietor of the SEP in question, promptly and in writing, a specific counter-offer that corresponds to FRAND terms."[37] Further, "where the alleged infringer is using the teachings of the SEP before a licensing agreement has been concluded, it is for that alleged infringer, from the point at which its counter-offer is rejected, to provide appropriate security, in accordance with recognised commercial

[32] *Huawei*, ECLI:EU:C:2015:477, at ¶ 44.
[33] *See id.* ¶¶ 49, 51, 62.
[34] Whether the steps are mandatory (and if so, should necessarily be followed in strict sequence)—or, as the U.K. Supreme Court viewed them, more in the nature of a safe harbor, *see Unwired Planet Int'l Ltd. v. Huawei Techs. (UK) Co. Ltd.* [2020] UKSC 37 [153]—remains a matter of debate.
[35] *Huawei*, ECLI:EU:C:2015:477, at ¶ 61.
[36] *Id.* ¶ 63.
[37] *Id.* ¶¶ 65–66.

practices in the field, for example by providing a bank guarantee or by placing the amounts necessary on deposit"; and where the parties fail to reach agreement, they "may, by common agreement, request that the amount of the royalty be determined by an independent third party, by decision without delay."[38] At all times, however, the implementer may retain the right to challenge the validity and essentiality of the SEP claims at issue.[39]

Since 2015, much (probably most) of the national case law interpreting the *Huawei v. ZTE* competition-law defense has come from Germany—though courts in the Netherlands, France, the U.K., and elsewhere also have contributed, and more recently the Unified Patent Court (UPC) has begun to weigh in as well. By and large, the German courts have interpreted the decision to mean that the implementer's expression of willingness to license (step 2, following the initial notification by the SEP owner) is not merely a formal requirement, but must be manifested throughout the course of negotiations,[40] and that the owner's initial offer need only avoid being "evidently non-FRAND."[41] As a consequence, perhaps, relatively few German decisions post-*Huawei v. ZTE* have found the SEP owner's conduct to be an abuse of dominant position resulting in the loss of the right to injunctive relief. Whether this will remain the case nevertheless remains to be seen. In 2024, the European Commission (EC) took the unusual step of filing an amicus brief in a pending German SEP appeal, arguing *inter alia* that *Huawei v. ZTE* obligates domestic courts to follow the steps of the FRAND dance sequentially, rather than to consider the implementer's overall course of conduct to determine if the implementer has adequately expressed its willingness to license.[42] In March 2025, however, the Munich Higher Regional Court rejected this approach, while holding that a willing prospective licensee could avoid an injunction if it posted security in the amount of the SEP owner's last offer.[43] Two late 2024 decisions from the Mannheim and Munich Local Divisions of the Unified Patent Court also

[38] *Id.* ¶¶ 67–68.

[39] *See id.* ¶ 69.

[40] *See, e.g.*, Erik Habich, *Willingness to License on FRAND Terms*, *in* FRAND: German Case Law and Global Perspectives 2, 4–11 (Peter Georg Picht, Thomas F. Cotter & Erik Habich eds. 2024) (discussing the German Federal Supreme Court's decisions to this effect in the Judgment of May 5, 2020, KZR 36/17–*FRAND-Einwand I* (Ger.), and the Judgment of Nov. 24, 2020, KZR 35/17– *FRAND-Einwand II* (Ger.)).

[41] See Erik Habich, Peter Georg Picht & Thomas F. Cotter, *FRAND Offer*, *in* FRAND: German Case Law and Global Perspectives, *supra* note 40, at 62, 65–98 (discussing cases).

[42] *See* Brief of the European Commission as Amicus Curiae, Munich Higher Regional Court, 6 U 3824/22, *HMD Global Oy v. VoiceAge EVS GmbH & Co KG* (filed Apr. 15, 2024), *available at* https://competition-policy.ec.europa.eu/document/download/66e0bd63-36da-4b27-9eef-70602a8c7be2_en?filename=2024_Amicus_Curiae_6U3824_22Kart_de.pdf.

[43] *See* OLG Munich, Case 6 U 3824/22 Kart (Mar. 20, 2025) (Ger.). As of December 2025, an appeal was pending before Germany's Federal Supreme Court.

rejected the EC's view that the implementer needs only to formally express its willingness to license before the court moves on the next step of evaluating the SEP owner's offer.[44] So far, none of these post-amicus brief cases have resulted in a referral to the CJEU.

As discussed later in this chapter, the German approach to SEP cases contrasts sharply with that of the United States and the United Kingdom, where (among other differences) equity plays the dominant role in determining whether SEP owners may obtain injunctive relief. Another difference, specific to the United States, is the outright absence from the latter of an abuse of dominant position doctrine. Doctrinally, U.S. courts interpret § 2 of the Sherman Act, which condemns monopolization,[45] as prohibiting the willful acquisition or maintenance of monopoly power,[46] but not its mere possession or exercise, much less the broader concept of abuse of dominant position. In a recent paper, however, Herb Hovenkamp argues that U.S. antitrust law would benefit from the addition of an abuse of dominant position doctrine that would constrain a dominant firm's use of its power in one market to gain a competitive (but not necessarily monopolistic) advantage in a complementary market.[47] To curtail potential abuses of the abuse doctrine, however, in Hovenkamp's formulation the doctrine would apply only in situations in which the dominant firm's conduct poses a substantial risk of "higher prices, lower market output, or reduced innovation in the secondary market"[48]; one possible example might be a digital platform's self-preferencing of its own products or services.[49] More relevant here would be how the doctrine might constrain some forms of "harmful extraction rather than exclusion," such as the conduct alleged in *Rambus Inc. v. FTC*.[50] In that case, the Federal Trade Commission alleged that Rambus had violated Sherman Act § 2 by deceiving JEDEC, an SSO to which it belonged, into believing that it had no existing or pending patents relevant to

[44] *See* LG Munich, Judgment of Sept. 19, 2024, 7 O 14174/23 (Ger.); Huawei Techs. Co. Ltd. v. Netgear Deutschland GmbH, UPC_CFI_9/2023 (Munich Local Division Dec. 18, 2024); Panasonic Holdings Corp. v. Guangdong OPPO Mobile Telecommunications Corp. Ltd., UPC_CFI_ 210/2023, (Mannheim Local Division, Nov. 22, 2024).

[45] *See* 15 U.S.C. § 2 (subjecting to penalties "[e]very person who shall monopolize, or attempt to monopolize, or combine or conspire with any other person or persons, to monopolize any part of the trade or commerce among the several States, or with foreign nations").

[46] *See* United States v. Grinnell Corp., 384 U.S. 563, 570–71 (1966).

[47] *See* Herbert Hovenkamp, *Monopolizing Digital Commerce*, 64 Wm. & Mary L. Rev. 1677 (2023).

[48] *Id.* at 1722.

[49] *See id.* at 1716–18 (discussing, *inter alia*, "Apple's practice of requiring makers of games or other apps to sell exclusively through its own store and requiring payment of a high commission," which was unlikely to result in Apple's acquisition of monopoly power in the market for electronic games, but which "very likely resulted in higher prices").

[50] 522 F.3d 456 (D.C. Cir. 2008).

standards that JEDEC was developing; and then, after withdrawing from the SSO, demanding allegedly above-FRAND royalties for the use of technologies that it had, in fact, been developing.[51] The D.C. Circuit held, however, that absent evidence that the SSO would have chosen a non-proprietary standard had it been aware of Rambus' pending applications, the FTC had not proven that Rambus willfully acquired or maintained monopoly power.[52] As Hovenkamp suggests, an "'abuse' standard would have seen the issue differently—not whether the conduct threatened additional monopoly but rather whether it threatened competitive harm at all," which "it clearly did"[53]—as evidenced by the parallel investigation brought by the European Commission, which fined Rambus for an abuse of dominant position.[54]

In other work, however, Hovenkamp (and others) have cautioned against extending U.S. antitrust law to address other conduct that might be perceived as an abuse in the E.U. or elsewhere, such as a lawful monopolist's mere extraction of high prices for the goods or services over which it has market power,[55] or other than in extraordinary circumstances unilateral refusals to

[51] *See id.* at 459. On appeal, the D.C. Circuit expressed doubt that Rambus actually had violated JEDEC's disclosure policy, insofar as it failed to disclose pending applications that were (following Rambus' departure from JEDEC) amended to read on the standards at issue, *see id.* at 467–68; but as noted in the text above, the principal holding is that even if Rambus did violate that policy, there was no § 2 violation.

[52] *See id.* at 461–67. In reaching this conclusion, the court cited *NYNEX Corp. v. Discon, Inc.*, 525 U.S. 128 (1998)—a case in which the Supreme Court rejected the proposition that a concerted vertical refusal to deal that enabled a regulated industry to evade price regulation was per se illegal—for the proposition that deceptive conduct that enables a monopolist to avoid price constraints does not "present a harm to competition in the monopolized market." *Rambus*, 522 F.3d at 466. Cf. *Broadcom Corp. v. Qualcomm Inc.*, 501 F.3d 297, 314 (3d Cir. 2007) (holding that "that (1) in a consensus-oriented private standard-setting environment, (2) a patent holder's intentionally false promise to license essential proprietary technology on FRAND terms, (3) coupled with an SDO's reliance on that promise when including the technology in a standard, and (4) the patent holder's subsequent breach of that promise, is actionable anticompetitive conduct").

[53] Hovenkamp, *supra* note 47, at 1722. In other work, I have suggested that the case could have come out differently under § 2 if the court had distinguished between monopoly status (which any owner of a SEP might have) and monopoly power (which SEP owners who abide by FRAND commitments do not have). If the facts were as alleged, Rambus did not necessarily acquire the former by means of deceptive conduct, but it did so acquire the latter. *See* Thomas F. Cotter, *Patent Holdup, Patent Remedies, and Antitrust Responses*, 34 J. Corp. L. 1151, 1194 (2009). I also suggested that the analogy to *NYNEX* was flawed for a variety of reasons, among them the risk that finding a vertical refusal to deal per se illegal would have opened the floodgates for disappointed suppliers to assert nuisance claims. *See id.* at 1196–1200.

[54] *See* European Commission, *Press Release, Antitrust: Commission accepts commitments from Rambus lowering memory chip royalty rates - frequently asked questions* (Dec. 9, 2009), https://ec.europa.eu/commission/presscorner/detail/en/memo_09_544.

[55] *See, e.g.*, Herbert Hovenkamp, *The Monopolization Offense*, 61 Ohio St. L.J. 1035, 1044 (2010) (asserting that, "as a matter of principle, public utility style price regulation is not the antitrust solution to a failure of competition"). Even in the E.U., claims asserting that a firm has abused its dominant position by charging unfairly high prices are infrequent, though not an empty set. For discussion of the principal cases over past forty years, *see* Miroslava Marinova, *Unmasking Excessive Pricing: Evolution of EU Law on Excessive Pricing from* United Brands *to* Aspen, 20 Eur. Comp. J. 315 (2024).

deal (including unilateral refusals to license one's IP)[56]—though on the latter issue, the U.S. case law has not always been a model of clarity. Some U.S. cases, for example, have recognized an "essential facilities" doctrine, under which a monopolist may be obligated to permit access to some asset others need to compete, subject to proof of "(1) control of the essential facility by a monopolist; (2) a competitor's inability practically or reasonably to duplicate the essential facility; (3) the denial of the use of the facility to a competitor; and (4) the feasibility of providing the facility."[57] The U.S. Supreme Court has never expressly recognized the doctrine, however,[58] and its two most prominent decisions, over the past forty years, on monopolists' duties to deal—*Aspen Skiing Co. v. Aspen Highlands Skiing Corp.*[59] and *Verizon Commc'ns Inc. v. Law Offices of Curtis V. Trinko, LLP*[60]—are often viewed as pointing in opposite directions. Briefly, in *Aspen Skiing*, the Court held that an alleged monopolist may be liable under Sherman Act § 2 if it lacks a legitimate business justification for terminating a profitable venture with a competitor,[61] whereas in *Trinko* the Court rejected a claim that Verizon's failure to provide competing local exchange carriers (LECs), as required under the Telecommunications Act of 1996, also violated § 2.[62] In the latter decision, the Court noted that the facts of *Aspen Skiing* differed from *Trinko* in that the defendant in *Aspen* terminated a preexisting course of dealing between the parties, despite its short-term profitability; and in any event characterized *Aspen* as standing "at or near the outer boundary of § 2 liability."[63] The Court also cited, as prudential reasons for not imposing a duty to share, the concern that doing so would reduce potential monopolists' ex ante incentives to innovate, would require courts to undertake the difficult task of regulating price and output, might encourage collusion between monopolists and potential competitors, and could generate substantial

[56] *See* HOVENKAMP ET AL., *supra* note 1, § 13.02[D].

[57] MCI Commc'ns Corp. v. Am. Tel. & Tel. Co., 708 F.2d 1081, 1132–33 (7th Cir. 1983). The precise meaning of each of the court's elements (*e.g.*, what it means for a facility to be "essential"), as well as what sorts of business justifications for denying access might provide a viable defense, may be open for debate. Moreover, according to some authorities, the plaintiff must prove that the monopolist uses the facility to control another, vertically related, market, and that the plaintiff is a potential competitor in one of the two markets. For discussion, *see* Thomas F. Cotter, *Essential Facilities*, *in* ANTITRUST LAW AND ECONOMICS 157, 162 (Keith N. Hylton ed. 2010).

[58] *See* Cotter, *supra* note 57, at 158–61 (discussing the principal Supreme Court decisions—*United States v. Terminal R.R. Ass'n of St. Louis*, 224 U.S. 383 (1912), *Associated Press v. United States*, 326 U.S. 1 (1945), and *Otter Tail Power Co. v. United States*, 410 U.S. 366 (1973)—that are sometimes cited as authority for the doctrine, albeit without explicitly endorsing it).

[59] 472 U.S. 585 (1985).

[60] 540 U.S. 398 (2004).

[61] *See Aspen Skiing*, 472 U.S. at 608–11.

[62] *See Trinko*, 540 U.S. at 402, 415–16.

[63] *See id.* at 409–10.

(and, given the regulatory oversight imposed by the Telecommunications Act in the case at hand, unnecessary) error and administrative costs.[64]

In view of these cases, U.S. courts, including the Federal Circuit, have been even more loath to interpret antitrust law as imposing a duty to license intellectual property, absent some *other* violation of Sherman Act §§ 1 or 2.[65] By way of comparison, aside from the *Huawei v. ZTE* decision noted above, the leading cases from within the E.U appear collectively to stand for the proposition that, although such cases are "exceptional," a dominant undertaking's refusal to license IP can be abusive where the IP is "indispensable for carrying on a particular business," and three cumulative conditions are satisfied, specifically, that the refusal is preventing the emergence of a new product or service for which there is a potential consumer demand, or a new technical development; that it is unjustified; and that the refusal excludes competition in a secondary market.[66] And perhaps U.S. law should be slightly more receptive than it currently is, under some circumstances. In this regard, Hovenkamp interprets *Aspen Skiing* as offering a viable, and needed, exception to the no-duty-to-license rule when, *inter alia*, a dominant firm reneges on a commitment to license (at all, or on FRAND terms) and thus is able, ex post, to extract higher rents or exclude competition.[67] In Hovenkamp's view, *Rambus* itself might

[64] *See id.* at 407–08, 411–15. *See also* Pac. Bell Tel. Co. v. linkLine Commc'ns, Inc., 555 U.S. 438 (2009) (holding that a vertically integrated firm that engages in a price "squeeze"—using its monopoly power to raise prices in the market for inputs, while cutting prices in the associated market for outputs, to the disadvantage of competitors in the output market—does not violate § 2, where the firm labors under no antitrust duty to sell the input to those competitors in the first place).

[65] *See* In re Indep. Serv. Orgs. Antitrust Litig., 203 F.3d 1322, 1325–28 (Fed. Cir. 2000) (holding that unilateral refusal to license does not violate § 2, absent evidence of fraud in the procurement, sham petitioning, or an attempt to extend its patent beyond the scope of the grant); Intergraph Corp. v. Intel Corp., 195 F.3d 1346, 1356–62 (Fed. Cir. 1999) (holding that Intel's refusal to share proprietary information with Intergraph did not violate § 2). A few other circuits have, on occasion, been slightly more receptive to such claims, at least in the copyright context. *See* Data Gen. Corp. v. Grumman Sys. Support Corp., 36 F.3d 1147, 1187 & n.64 (1st Cir. 1994) (holding that a unilateral refusal to license a copyright might violate § 2, in the "rare" case in which the plaintiff can rebut a presumption that the defendant was motivated by a valid business justification); Image Tech. Servs., Inc. v. Eastman Kodak Co., 125 F.3d 1195, 1218–20 (9th Cir. 1997) (affirming a jury verdict that defendant lacked a legitimate business justification for its refusal to license, and therefore was liable under § 2). As Jorge Contreras notes, however, U.S. courts sometimes have required patentees to license their patents on "fair" or "reasonable" terms as a remedy for a stand-alone violation of antitrust law. *See* Jorge Contreras, *A Brief History of FRAND: Analyzing Current Debates in Standard Setting and Antitrust Through a Historical Lens*, 80 ANTITRUST L.J. 39 (2015).

[66] *See* IMS Health GmbH & Co. OHG v. NDC Health GmbH & Co. KG, Case C-418/01, ECLI:EU:C:2004:257, ¶ 52 (CJEU 2004); Radio Telefis Eireann (RTE) v. Comm'n of Eur. Cmtys. (Magill II), Case C-241/91, ECLI:EU:C:1995:98, ¶¶ 53–57 (CJEU 1995); Microsoft Corp. v. Comm'n of Eur. Cmtys., Case T-201/04, ECLI:EU:T:2007:289, ¶¶ 331–33, 647 (Court of First Instance, Grand Chamber, 2007).

[67] *See* Herbert Hovenkamp, *FRAND and Antitrust*, 105 CORNELL L. REV. 1683, 1710 (2020) (proposing that a necessary condition for liability should be the existence of an "original cooperative dealing [that] led to significant, asset-specific investment from which extraction or significant modification

be such a case, as might also be the FTC's (ultimately unsuccessful) case addressing Qualcomm's refusal to license rival chipmakers.[68]

Even so, whether the integration of such a principle into U.S. antitrust law would (or should) provide an alternative tool for precluding SEP owners from seeking injunctive relief against willing licensees, as under *Huawei v. ZTE*, is in my view much less clear,[69] for reasons similar to those I cited in chapter 3 in cautioning against extending liability under U.S. antitrust law to a monopolist's mere possession of a fraudulently-acquired patent. These include the automatic trebling of damages in private antitrust actions, as well as the prevalence of such private actions (including class action lawsuits and claims brought under parallel but sometimes more plaintiff-friendly state antitrust laws), both of which pose some risk of overdeterrence; and the availability of other options for responding to SEP owner misconduct, including (as discussed later in this chapter) actions for breach of contract and the denial of injunctive relief as a matter of equitable discretion.[70] On the other hand, where these features of U.S. antitrust law are not present or are of lesser import (namely, pretty much everywhere else in the world), and where the alternative options for constraining opportunistic conduct by SEP owners are limited (as in E.U. member states such as Germany), antitrust may be a necessary fallback.[71] That said, one possible drawback of the exclusive or near-exclusive reliance on antitrust law to regulate SEP owners' requests for injunctions is that, unless courts are willing to establish the terms of a FRAND license themselves—something that,

would be costly"). Hovenkamp is doubtful that the facts of the *Aspen* case satisfy the necessary conditions, however. *See id.* at 1713–14.

[68] *See id.* at 1722 (discussing *FTC v. Qualcomm Inc.*, 411 F. Supp. 3d 658, 669–80 (N.D. Cal. 2019), *rev'd*, 969 F.3d 974 (9th Cir. 2020)); *see also id.* at 1724–25 (stating that "evading a FRAND requirement by licensing selectively only to noncompetitors threatens to undermine the entire competitive purpose of the [SSO] joint venture," because "[t]he purpose of standard setting is to design a standard so that goods can be produced competitively within a shared technology"). In brief, the FTC claimed, among other things, that Qualcomm's breach of its commitment to license rival chipmakers, and its refusal to sell chips to OEMs that declined to license Qualcomm's SEPs, enabled Qualcomm to maintain its monopoly in the markets for CDMA and LTE modem chips. The district court agreed, but the Ninth Circuit concluded that, as a matter of law, Qualcomm's conduct did not violate § 2. *See* F.T.C. v. Qualcomm, 969 F.3d at 993–1003.

[69] To be clear, Hovenkamp doesn't appear to advocate that either, other than in cases involving sham petitioning. *See* Hovenkamp, *supra* note 67, at 1741–43.

[70] In a similar vein, *see* Carl Shapiro & Mark A. Lemley, *The Role of Antitrust in Preventing Patent Holdup*, 168 U. PENN. L. REV. 2019, 2056–59 (2020) (arguing that "[i]f courts effectively enforce FRAND commitments, most of the holdup problem can be solved without resort to antitrust," while cautioning that "antitrust still has an important role to play" in cases such as *Qualcomm*, "when contract law and anti-fraud laws fail to fully address the patent holdup problem"). As will be discussed later in this chapter, in adjudicating SEP cases U.K. courts also primarily focus on equitable discretion, rather than on antitrust.

[71] *See* Thomas F. Cotter, *Comparative Law and Economics of Standard-Essential Patents and FRAND Royalties*, 22 TEX. INTELL. PROP. L.J. 311, 353–56 (2014).

for example, the German courts to date have never done—they also may be hesitant to find a violation of antitrust law (which, absent settlement, might require them to do precisely that). As I have suggested elsewhere, this reluctance, if that is what it is, may reflect "the German courts' preference that the parties work matters out for themselves."[72] To be sure, such a preference may be justified, if courts lack the institutional capacity to establish the terms of FRAND licenses for themselves; indeed, the concern about courts' lack of insight, in comparison with the parties, of how to accurately value technology is the leading theoretical reason for protecting patent rights by means of a "property" rule, the effect of which is to compel prospective licensors and licensees to engage in private bargaining.[73] On the other hand, when implementers are compelled to bargain under threat of injunctive relief, they may wind up paying substantially more than the technology's economic value—the holdup phenomenon alluded to earlier in this chapter, and discussed at greater length below—particularly where, as in many SEP cases, they have few if any alternatives to using the patented technology. The U.S. and U.K. approach, which as discussed below considers the availability of injunctive relief primarily from the standpoint of equitable discretion and relegates antitrust to a subsidiary role, arguably is more sensitive to this latter risk. Indeed, from the perspective of these courts, whether the SEP owner's proposed terms are in fact FRAND is the key issue, and compliance with the *Huawei v. ZTE* FRAND dance can seem like a sideshow at best, a set of formalities divorced from substance at worst.[74]

For their part, courts and agencies in China and India have adopted an approach to SEP owners' requests for injunctions that merges aspects of both the E.U. and U.S./U.K. approaches. As in the E.U., antitrust law sometimes has played an important role. Guangliang Zhang notes, for example, that China's Anti-Monopoly Law may be applicable where SEP owners engage in "abuse of market dominance such as excessive pricing and 'patent holdup,'" citing as examples the 2013 decision in *Huawei Tech. Ltd. v. InterDigital Tech. Corp.*[75] and a

[72] Thomas F. Cotter, *US and German Approaches to FRAND Disputes: Like Ships That Pass in the Night*, *in* FRAND: GERMAN CASE LAW AND GLOBAL PERSPECTIVES, *supra* note 40, at 212, 213.

[73] *See* Thomas F. Cotter, *On the Economics of Injunctions in Patent Cases*, 11 ZGE 293, 294–95 (2019).

[74] For a succinct statement of this perspective, *see Webinar: German FRAND Cases: the EC's Amicus Brief and Other Developments* (Nov. 14, 2024) (comments of Arnold, L.J., beginning at 46:20) (stating that "[t]he reality, as everybody surely knows, is that any SEP holder is a willing licensor if the price is high, and any implementer is a willing licensee if the price is low. So, we take the view that all of this discussion of whether people are willing licensors or willing licensees is actually a distraction from what matters. There is only one thing that matters, and that is, what is the right price? In other words, what terms are actually FRAND? That is why the increasing tendency of the UK courts, since *Unwired Planet*, has been to try and focus upon that question"), https://www.youtube.com/watch?v=joNiD2UeWOo.

[75] Yue Gao Fa Min San Zhong Zi No. 306 (Guangdong High Ct. 2013) (China). For discussion, *see, e.g.*, Guangliang Zhang, *Determination of the Global Royalty Rate of Standard Essential Patents: Judicial*

2015 investigation by China's National Development and Reform Commission that fined Qualcomm RMB 6.088 billion—though he states that an antimonopoly lawsuit "itself cannot resolve the issue of royalty rate determinations,"[76] which may however be resolved in patent infringement actions or in stand-alone actions to determine FRAND royalty rates.[77] Chinese courts and agencies in recent years also have advocated a fault-based framework similar to *Huawei v. ZTE*, albeit one that is not necessarily grounded in competition law and does not require a finding of abuse of dominant position. According to guidelines issued by courts in Beijing in 2017 and in Guangdong in 2018, for example, courts should deny injunctive relief if the SEP owner breached its FRAND commitment and the implementer acted in good faith, if neither party was at fault and the implementer deposits with the court the royalty it has offered, or if both parties are at fault but the SEP owner's fault is greater.[78] In general and in principle, the Chinese approach sounds reasonable—though

Jurisdiction and Determination Method from Chinese Law Perspective, *in* FRAND: GERMAN CASE LAW AND GLOBAL PERSPECTIVES, *supra* note 40, at 234, 245–46.

[76] *See* Zhang, *supra* note 75, at 237–38. Also of relevance, from an antitrust standpoint, is a 2023 publication of the State Administration for Market Regulation (SAMR), *Prohibiting Abuse of Intellectual Property Rights to Exclude and Restrict Competition* (Aug. 1, 2023). Article 19, as translated and quoted in Aaron Wininger, *China's State Administration for Market Regulation Releases "Provisions Prohibiting Abuse of Intellectual Property Rights to Exclude and Restrict Competition"*, CHINA IP LAW UPDATE, June 29, 2023, https://www.chinaiplawupdate.com/2023/06/chinas-state-administration-for-market-regulation-releases-provisions-prohibiting-abuse-of-intellectual-property-rights-to-exclude-and-restrict-competition/, requires operators with a dominant market position to abide by principles of "fairness, reasonableness and non-discrimination," among other matters. *See also* MA Butian & Pyeng Liu, *China Seps and FRAND—Litigation, Policy and Latest Developments*, IAM, Oct. 27, 2023, https://www.iam-media.com/hub/sepfrand-hub/2023/article/china-seps-and-frand-litigation-policy-and-latest-developments (discussing the above Provisions and other relevant Guidelines issued by Chinese agencies or courts).

[77] For an example of the former, see the Supreme People's Court decision in *Advanced Codec Techs. v. OPPO*, 2022 Zuigaofa ZhiMinZhong, Nos. 907, 910, 911, 916, 917, and 918 (Dec. 12, 2023), discussed in MA Butian, *Second-instance Judgment in ACT v Oppo Sheds Light on Comparable Agreements and how to Find Fault in SEP Licensing Negotiations*, GLOBAL COMP. REV., Feb. 1, 2024, https://globalcompetitionreview.com/hub/sepfrand-hub/2023/article/second-instance-judgment-in-act-v-oppo-sheds-light-comparable-agreements-and-how-find-fault-in-sep-licensing-negotiations. For an example of the latter, see *Nokia Techs. v. OPPO*, Case No. (2021) Yu Min Chu 1232 (Chongqing Intermed. People's Ct. Dec. 13, 2023), as discussed in Enrico Bonadio & Dyuti Pandya, *Global FRAND Rates in China*, KLUWER PATENT BLOG, Dec. 21, 2023, https://patentblog.kluweriplaw.com/2023/12/21/global-frand-rates-in-china/.

[78] For discussion, *see, e.g.*, Butian & Liu, *supra* note 76; Yabing Cui, *Across the Fault Lines: Chinese Judicial Approaches to Injunctions and SEP's*, CHINA IPR BLOG, June 5, 2018, https://chinaipr.com/2018/06/05/across-the-fault-lines-chinese-judicial-approaches-to-injunctions-and-seps/; Jie Gao, *Development of the FRAND Jurisprudence in China*, 21 COLUM. SCI. & TECH. L. REV. 446 (2020). *See also* SAMR, Anti-Monopoly Guidelines in the Field of SEPs, art. 8 (Nov. 8, 2024), translated and quoted in Aaron Wininger, *China's State Administration for Market Regulation Releases Anti-monopoly Guidelines in the Field of Standard Essential Patents*, CHINA IP LAW UPDATE, Nov. 11, 2024, https://www.chinaiplawupdate.com/2024/11/chinas-state-administration-for-market-regulation-releases-anti-monopoly-guidelines-in-the-field-of-standard-essential-patents/ (also largely mirroring the *Huawei v. ZTE* framework).

critics charge, among other things, that the royalties awarded by Chinese courts are too low,[79] and the courts' willingness to set global rates without both parties' consent (a practice pioneered, however, by the Patents Court of England and Wales in 2017,[80] as discussed below) and to award lower rates for the Chinese market (again, a practice that sometimes has been observed elsewhere),[81] also rankles some outside observers.

Courts in India also have cited *Huawei v. ZTE* with approval, as in for example the Delhi High Court's 2023 *Intex v. Ericsson* decision.[82] Indian practice as reflected in *Intex* is (so far) unique, however, in that Indian courts hearing FRAND cases often require defendants to deposit interim royalties pending trial, in lieu of an interim prohibition on use[83] (though unlike the situation in China, critics might argue that the amounts Indian courts award on an interim basis risk being potentially too high, as reflected by the Delhi High Court's interim award of 100% of Ericsson's asking price). Moreover, although India's Competition Commission has intervened in some SEP disputes—sometimes siding with implementers over patent owners, at least on a preliminary basis, on matters such as the appropriate royalty base[84]—a 2023 decision of the Delhi High Court takes the contrary position that the resolution of these

[79] *See, e.g.*, Mark Cohen, *Oppo v. Nokia in Context*, China IPR, Dec. 18, 2023, https://chinaipr.com/2023/12/18/oppo-v-nokia-in-context/; Aaron Wininger, *China's Supreme People's Court Sets Low FRAND Rate in Another OPPO Case*, China IP Law Update, Jan. 15, 2024, https://www.chinaiplawupdate.com/2024/01/chinas-supreme-peoples-court-sets-low-frand-rate-in-another-oppo-case/; Aaron Wininger, *Chongqing No. 1 Intermediate People's Court Sets Global FRAND Rate for 5G SPEs at $0.707 in Nokia/OPPO Case*, China IP Law Update, Dec. 16, 2023, https://www.chinaiplawupdate.com/2023/12/chongqing-no-1-intermediate-peoples-court-sets-global-frand-rate-for-5g-seps-at-0-707-unit-in-nokia-oppo-case/.

[80] *See* Unwired Planet Int'l Ltd. v. Huawei Techs. Co. Ltd., [2017] EWHC (Pat) 711 (Eng.), *aff'd*, [2020] UKSC 37 (appeal taken from Eng.).

[81] *See Unwired Planet*, [2017] EWHC (Pat) 711 (Eng.) (different rates for "Major Markets" and for "China and Other Markets"); TCL Commc'n Tech. Holdings, Ltd. v. Telefonaktiebolaget LM Ericsson, No. SACV 14-341, 2018 WL 4488286 (C.D. Cal. Sept. 14, 2018), *vacated in part, rev'd in part, and remanded on other grounds*, 943 F.3d 1360 (Fed Cir. 2019) (different rates for the U.S., Europe, and the rest of the world).

[82] Intex Techs. (India) Ltd. v. Telefonaktiebolaget LM Ericsson, 2023:DHC:2243-DB (Delhi High Ct. Mar. 29, 2023).

[83] In addition to *Intex*, see cases cited in J. Gregory Sidak, *FRAND in India*, in The Cambridge Handbook of Technical Standardization Law: Competition, Antitrust, and Patents 336 (Jorge L. Contreras ed. 2018); *see also* Pravin Anand, Tusha Malhotra & Udita M Patro, *India*, *in* International Patent Litigation: Developing an Effective Strategy 201, 212–13 (Gwilym Roberts ed. 2018). One reason for the development of this practice in India may be that, traditionally, it has sometimes taken a very long time to litigate a case all the way through to judgment. Payment of interim royalties in lieu of preliminary injunctive relief is available in principle in other jurisdictions, including the UPC, as is the posting of security following the rejection of a counteroffer under *Huawei v. ZTE*, Case C-170/13, ¶ 67, but to date these practices are uncommon—though as discussed toward the end of this chapter, in some recent decisions the Court of Appeal for England and Wales has concluded that, on the specific facts before it, a willing licensor and licensee in a FRAND dispute would agree to an interim license, pending the court's adjudication of the terms of a permanent FRAND license. *See infra* notes 345–47 and accompanying text.

[84] *See* Sidak, *supra* note 83, at 346–50 (discussing interim decisions of the CCI).

cases is a matter to be governed exclusively by patent law.[85] In September 2025, the Indian Supreme Court dismissed the appeal against the Delhi court's judgment.

In summary, courts and regulators in all of the principal jurisdictions for FRAND litigation appear to recognize that the FRAND commitment can limit the SEP owner's right to seek injunctive relief, and that antitrust law sometimes provides an effective means for enforcing that limitation. Moreover, in countries such as Germany, antitrust's abuse of dominant position doctrine may be the exclusive or near-exclusive means for constraining SEP owners' right to enjoin implementers. Whether it is optimal to rely so heavily on antitrust nevertheless is questionable, particularly if the practical effect is to discourage courts from closely examining whether SEP owners' offers are FRAND-compliant. On the other hand, where courts have greater flexibility to deny injunctive relief, whether under antitrust or other bodies of law, the question arises whether courts have the institutional capacity fairly and accurately to establish the terms of FRAND licenses on their own. I return to this issue below in the context of the abuse of right doctrine and, later, equitable discretion.

The Abuse Doctrines: Abuse of Right

As noted in chapter 2, within the civil law tradition courts, and sometimes legislatures, impose a generally applicable duty that persons not "abuse" their rights.[86] The resulting "abuse of rights" (*abus de droit*) doctrine is therefore

[85] Telefonaktiebolaget Ericsson AG (Publ) v. Competition Comm'n of India, LPA 247/2016 (Delhi High Court July 13, 2023). For a critical take, *see* Ambika Aggarwal & Anindya Sircar, *Jurisdictional Changes in Indian Patent Enforcement—Comment on the* Ericsson v. CCI *Decision*, 55 IIC 954 (2024).

[86] Commentators view the abuse of right doctrine as a general principle of E.U. law, as expressed in decisions such as *Kofoed v. Statteministeriet*, Case C-321/05, ECLI:EU:C:2007:408, ¶ 38 (CJEU 2007) (referring to "the general Community law principle that abuse of rights is prohibited"). For discussion of relevant case law and commentary, including commentary that posits a distinction among fraud, abuse of right, and/or abuse of law (circumvention), see AMANDINE LÉONARD, ABUSE OF RIGHTS IN EUROPEAN PATENT LAW: RECONSIDERING THE PRINCIPLE OF THE PROHIBITION OF ABUSE OF RIGHTS AS AN INTERNAL CORRECTION MECHANISM AGAINST OVER-ENFORCEMENT PRACTICES BY RIGHT HOLDERS 43–51 (Apr. 30, 2019) (unpublished Ph.D. thesis submitted to KU Leuven, on file with author) (concluding that the distinction is neither straightforward nor of much practical significance); *see also id.* at 192 (noting that "[s]olely relying on the word 'abuse' leads to a very narrow understanding of misconducts by right holders," by excluding over-enforcement practices "such as an exercise of rights which may be considered to violate the principle of good faith in Germany, the principle of reasonableness and farness in the Netherlands, or the role of equitable considerations in the UK"); *id.* at 195–96 (noting the courts' frequent aggregation of abuse of rights and unfair competition claims in France and Belgium). International and regional instruments also recognize the need to constrain the abusive enforcement of IP rights, albeit without specifically invoking an abuse of rights doctrine as such. *See, e.g.*, Paris Convention for the Protection of Industrial Property, Sept. 28, 1979, 828 U.N.T.S. 305,

sometimes described as constraining the "unreasonable" assertion of a person's legal rights, affording courts the flexibility to "reject[] a rigid adherence to the letter of the law"[87] under circumstances where, for example, such rigidity might undermine the purpose of the law or cause disproportionate harm to the defendant, third parties, or the general public. (As we shall see, however, in regard to the exercise of IP rights courts also sometimes invoke the doctrine to provide an additional sanction, where the right at issue is not infringed or is found to be invalid. The applications of greatest interest to this chapter, nonetheless, are those that constrain what would otherwise be a legitimate exercise of patent rights.) Courts and commentators also recognize, however, as they do with the abuse of dominant position doctrine in competition law, the countervailing need to avoid an interpretation of the doctrine that is too open-ended and unpredictable. To achieve some semblance of balance between flexibility

art. 5(2) (stating that member states "shall have the right to take legislative measures providing for the grant of compulsory licenses to prevent the abuses which might result from the exercise of the exclusive rights conferred by the patent, for example, failure to work"); Agreement on Trade-Related Aspects of Intellectual Property Rights, Apr. 15, 1994, Marrakesh Agreement Establishing the World Trade Organization, Annex 1C, Legal Instruments-Results of the Uruguay Round vol. 31, 33 I.L.M. 1197, arts. 8(2), 41(1), 48, 50(3) (1994) [hereinafter TRIPS] (stating, *inter alia*, that "[a]ppropriate measures, provided that they are consistent with the provisions of this Agreement, may be needed to prevent the abuse of intellectual property rights by right holders," and that enforcement "procedures shall be applied in such a manner as to avoid the creation of barriers to legitimate trade and to provide for safeguards against their abuse"); Directive 2004/48/EC of the European Parliament and of the Council of 29 April 2004 on the Enforcement of Intellectual Property Rights, 2004 O.J. (L 195) 16, art. 3(2) [hereinafter IPRED] (stating that "remedies shall . . . be effective, proportionate and dissuasive and shall be applied in such a manner as to avoid the creation of barriers to legitimate trade and to provide for safeguards against their abuse").

[87] Amandine Léonard, *"Abuse of Rights" in Belgian and French Patent Law – A Case Law Analysis*, 7 JIPITEC 30, 32 2016) (suggesting further that, while the doctrine is flexible, courts in Belgium and France generally look for proof of fault, harm, and causation); *see also* Peter Georg Picht & Anna-Lena Karczewski, *Germany*, *in* INJUNCTIONS IN PATENT LAW: TRANS-ATLANTIC DIALOGUES ON FLEXIBILITY AND TAILORING 142, 155 (stating that "[i]n general German civil law, the abuse of right is usually interpreted as one form of violating the duty to 'perform according to the requirements of good faith, taking customary practice into consideration'"); Krista Rantasaari, *Abuse of Patent Enforcement in Europe: How Can Start-ups and Growth Companies Fight Back?*, 11 JIPITEC 358, 366 (2020) (stating that the doctrine often "is associated with situations where there is no visible infringement of a formal legal requirement," but cautioning that "it seems rather impractical that a court would apply such general provisions in the case of an abusive exertion of an IP right"); Norman V. Siebrasse et al., *Injunctive Relief*, *in* PATENT REMEDIES AND COMPLEX PRODUCTS: TOWARD A GLOBAL CONSENSUS 115, 141–42 (Brad Biddle et al. eds. 2019) (describing the abuse of rights doctrine "as a corrective mechanism" that limits the otherwise lawful exercise of rights, based on "such standards of behavior by the rightsholders as morality, good faith, fairness, and proportionality as well as reasonableness and social functions of rights"); Richard Steppe & Amandine Léonard, *Catching Patent Trolls in the Net of Abuse of Rights: Applying the General Principle of Union Law in the Context of the Unitary Patent Package*, 39 E.I.P.R. 163, 167 (2017) (analogizing the doctrine to a "safety valve") (citing Stefan Vogenauer, *The Prohibition of Abuse in Law: An Emerging General Principle of EU Law*, *in* PROHIBITION OF ABUSE OF LAW: A NEW GENERAL PRINCIPLE OF EU LAW? 521, 570 (Rita de la Feria & Stefan Vogenauer eds. 2011)). Although most of the above citations discuss E.U. law, versions of an abuse of rights doctrine also are recognized in legislation and/or case law outside the E.U., including in Japan, South Korea, and China, as noted below.

and predictability, therefore, courts in civil law countries have come to recognize certain categories of conduct as potentially triggering application of the doctrine, while at the same time leaving open the possibility that over time new categories might emerge. In this regard, the abuse of right doctrine bears something of a family resemblance to the common law's various equitable remedies and defenses, discussed later in this chapter, though its roots and the specifics of its application remain distinct.

Following from the above, and focusing for present purposes on applications of the abuse of rights doctrine to patent assertion in particular, it may be useful to consider the specific categories of conduct that courts in various nations have considered to possible abuses of right, or to violate other related doctrines, as well as the sanctions meted out for such abuses. In this regard, Amandine Léonard's detailed examination of court decisions from Belgium, France, Germany, the Netherlands, and the U.K. applying what she refers to as "abuse *sensu lato*" provides a good start by breaking down the judicial application of the doctrine into six general categories, as below.

(1) The illegal exercise of patent rights

The cases Léonard surveyed that fall into this category consist primarily of those in which the patent owner has knowingly asserted rights in an expired, exhausted, or clearly invalid or noninfringed patent, or in which an assignee has filed an infringement action before registering its assignment (as required under the laws of some countries, such as France).[88] In such cases, courts applying the doctrine would not be constraining the otherwise legitimate exercise of substantive rights, and the sanction might be nothing more than dismissal of the action and costs—though in principle, application of the doctrine also could result in an award of compensatory or nominal damages.[89] Probably the closest analogue in common-law countries would be actions for wrongful civil proceedings (malicious prosecution),[90] abuse of

[88] *See* LÉONARD, *supra* note 86, at 108–22, 202–03 (citing cases).

[89] *See id.* at 169–71, 183–84, 372 & n.1665, 390–91. For a recent case, *see* San-Ei Gen FFI v. Nexira SASU, PIBD 179-III-1 (Cour de cassation 2022) (Fr.) (holding that a patent owner abused its right by filing an infringement action with knowledge that its claim, which was the subject of a pending nullity action, was likely to be invalid).

[90] *See* RESTATEMENT (SECOND) OF TORTS § 674 (Am. L. Inst. 1977) (stating that "[o]ne who takes an active part in the initiation, continuation or procurement of civil proceedings against another is subject to liability to the other for wrongful civil proceedings if (a) he acts without probable cause, and primarily for a purpose other than that of securing the proper adjudication of the claim in which the proceedings are based, and (b) except when they are ex parte, the proceedings have terminated in favor of the person against whom they are brought").

process,[91] or (depending on the circumstances) a claim for wrongful threats in the U.K. and some other common-law countries (which Léonard discusses at some length). In Japan and South Korea, moreover, where infringement and validity determinations are bifurcated, courts hearing infringement actions have invoked the abuse of rights doctrine to render unenforceable, albeit only *inter partes*, patent claims that the infringement defendant proves to be invalid.[92] In China, some applications of the malicious litigation tort might correspond to this category as well, as discussed in chapter 3,[93] though since 2021 article 132 of China's Civil Code also has recognized a more general abuse of rights doctrine, the precise contours of which remain to be determined.[94]

(2) Conduct that undermines "the general principle of proportionality interpreted in light of considerations of fairness and equity"[95]

Among the cases that might fall within this category of Léonard's taxonomy are those in which the patent owner sues for disproportionate damages,[96] or requests injunctive relief under circumstances in which the harm to the defendant, third parties, or the general public would be grossly disproportionate.[97] (Léonard also suggests, however, that the abuse of rights doctrine could target some cases involving requests for injunctive relief for reasons

[91] *See id.* § 682 (stating that "[o]ne who uses a legal process, whether criminal or civil, against another primarily to accomplish a purpose for which it is not designed, is subject to liability to the other for harm caused by the abuse of process").

[92] *See* Siebrasse et al., *supra* note 87, at 142 n.155 (citing *Texas Instruments v. Fujitsu*, Case No. Hei 10(O) 364 (S. Ct. Apr. 11, 2000) (Japan), and *LG Elecs., Inc. v. Daewoo Elecs., Inc.*, 2010da95390 (S. Ct. Jan. 19, 2012) (S. Kor.), for the proposition that "it can constitute an abuse of right to seek injunctive relief against infringement of a patent that will clearly be invalidated in a separate invalidation proceeding"); Thomas F. Cotter, Comparative Patent Remedies: A Legal and Economic Analysis 295–96 (2013).

[93] *See* ch. 3 n.40 (discussing a case premised on the fraudulent acquisition of a patent with knowledge that the claimed invention was in the public domain).

[94] For discussion, *see* Jialin Dong, *The Interpretation and function orientation of the principle of prohibiting abuse of rights*, 14 J. Educ., Humanities & Soc. Sci. 602 (2023) (discussing various possible interpretations of article 132, and proposing adoption of a formulation of the doctrine advocated by the French jurist Louis Josserand). Article 132 reads, in Dong's translation, as "Civil subjects shall not abuse civil rights to harm the interests of the state, the social public interests or the legitimate rights and interests of others." *See also* Supreme People's Court, Interpretation of Several Issues Concerning the Application of the General Provisions of the Civil Code of the PRC, art. 3 (Feb. 22, 2022), *English language translation available at* https://www.chinalawtranslate.com/en/%E5%85%B3%E4%BA%8E%E9%80%82%E7%94%A8%E3%80%8A%E4%B8%AD%E5%8D%8E%E4%BA%BA%E6%B0%91%E5%85%B1%E5%92%8C%E5%9B%BD%E6%B0%91%E6%B3%95%E5%85%B8%E3%80%8B%-E6%80%BB%E5%88%99%E7%BC%96%E8%8B%A5%E5%B9%B2%E9%97%AE/.

[95] Léonard, *supra* note 86, at 202.

[96] *See id.* at 153, 233–38.

[97] *See id.* at 218–32.

other than, or in addition to, disproportionately, including those in which the patentee's intention is to harm the defendant[98] (abuse *stricto sensu*, discussed below) or in which granting an injunction would undermine the purpose of patent protection,[99] also discussed below.) Thus far, however, few infringement defendants appear to have invoked the abuse of rights defense in these types of cases. An excessive damages claim nevertheless did succeed in one Belgian case Léonard discusses[100]; and in a case involving the question of whether IPRED article 13(1)(b) precluded a provision of Polish copyright law authorizing awards "corresponding to twice . . . the amount of the appropriate fee which would have been due at the time it was sought if the rightholder had given permission for the work to be used," the CJEU noted—albeit in dictum, in the course of answering the question before it in the negative—the possibility "that, in exceptional cases, payment for a loss calculated on the basis of twice the amount of the hypothetical royalty will exceed the loss actually suffered so clearly and substantially that a claim to that effect could constitute an abuse of rights, prohibited by Article 3(2) of Directive 2004/48."[101] Courts in the Netherlands,[102] Japan,[103] and South Korea also have held that the owner of a FRAND-committed SEP may abuse its rights by seeking injunctive relief

[98] *See id.* at 229–30.

[99] *See id.* at 230–31.

[100] *See id.* at 153 (citing *X v. SPRL Green & Co.*, 2012/RG/1003 (Mons Ct. App. Dec. 2, 2013) (Belg.), and noting among other additional factors that the plaintiff initially intended to license the defendant, that the parties had collaborated in presenting the patented product at trade shows, and that the defendant had invested in preparing to commercialize the product, before the parties had a falling out).

[101] *See* Stowarzyszenie 'Oławska Telewizja Kablowa' v. Stowarzyszenie Filmowców Polskich, Case C-367/15, ECLI:EU:C:2017:36, ¶¶ 25, 31 (CJEU 2017), noted in Léonard, *supra* note 86, at 234.

[102] *See* Samsung Elecs. Co. v. Apple Inc., Rb.'s-Gravenhage, HA ZA 11-2215, HA ZA 11-2213 (June 20, 2012), and HA ZA 11-2212, HA ZA 11-2213, and HA ZA 11-2215 (Mar. 14, 2012), discussed in Léonard, *supra* note 86, at 136; Cotter, *supra* note 92, at 324; and Gertjan Kuipers, Douwe Groenevelt & Oscar Lamme, *A Further Perspective On Apple v Samsung: How To Successfully Enforce Standard Essential Patents (SEPs) In The Netherlands*, Mondaq, Sept. 11, 2012, https://www.mondaq.com/patent/196082/a-further-perspective-on-apple-v-samsung-how-to-successfully-enforce-standard-essential-patents-seps-in-the-netherlands. To be clear, the court did not hold that it was abusive per se for a SEP owner to seek injunctive relief, but that on the facts presented Samsung had not negotiated in good faith and Apple was a willing licensee.

[103] *See* Samsung Elecs. Co., Ltd. v. Apple Japan Godo Kaisha, Judgment of May 16, 2014, 2013 (Ne) 10043 (IP High Court, Grand Panel) (Japan), *translated at* http://www.ip.courts.go.jp/eng/vcms_lf/25ne10043full.pdf. In a subsequent decision, *Imation Corp. Japan v. One-Blue LLC*, Tokyo Dist. Ct., Feb. 18, 2015, Case No. 2013 (Wa) 21383, the court held that the defendant (the manager/operator of a patent pool that included some SEPs) had engaged in unfair competition by sending a warning letter to three retailers threatening injunctive relief, because under the *Samsung v. Apple* decision, the act of seeking an injunction for the infringement of a FRAND-committed SEP against a willing licensee is an abuse of right. The decision therefore appears to read *Samsung v. Apple* as holding that it is an abuse of right per se to seek injunctive relief against a willing licensee for the infringement of a FRAND-committed SEP. Cf. Yuzuki Nagakoshi & Katsuya Tama, *Japan Without FRANDS? Recent Developments on Injunctions and FRAND-Encumbered Patents in Japan*, 44 AIPLA Q.J. 243 (2016) (critiquing *Samsung v. Apple* for arguably creating such a per se rule and for ignoring, as part of the abuse of rights calculus, the rightsholder's subjective intent; and proposing that Japanese courts hearing FRAND cases instead consider whether the rightsholder has satisfied its statutory duty to negotiate in good faith).

against a willing licensee (though in the South Korean case, no such abuse was found on the facts of the case).[104] As noted at the beginning of this chapter, however, several commentators view disproportionality as a separate, stand-alone ground for staying or denying injunctive relief, and I will return to the topic of proportionality and injunctive relief later in this chapter, in connection with the discussion of equitable discretion.[105] What I will note here is that the above three FRAND cases arguably do point to the need, at least in principle, for a tool in addition to competition law to address situations in which the owner of a FRAND-committed SEP seeks to enjoin a willing licensee, but the conditions for invoking competition law are not present (perhaps because there are competing standards, such that the SEP at issue does not confer sufficient market power to qualify as "dominance"). The Japanese case, in which Apple successfully raised the abuse of right argument against Samsung, nevertheless also points to the need, suggested earlier in this chapter, to ensure that courts compensate for denials of injunctive relief with adequate monetary relief. On the facts presented, it's possible that the relief the Japanese IP High Court awarded to Samsung actually may have been below-FRAND.[106]

(3) Contradictory behavior

A third category in Léonard's taxonomy consists of cases in which patent owners engage in some form of contradictory behavior, for example by

[104] *See* Seoul District Court [Dist. Ct.], 2011Kahap39552, Aug. 24, 2012 (S. Kor.)), discussed in Siebrasse et al., *supra* note 87, at 142 n.156.

[105] *See infra* notes 280–85 and accompanying text.

[106] *See* Norman V. Siebrasse & Thomas F. Cotter, *Judicially Determined FRAND Royalties*, *in* 1 Cambridge Handbook of Technical Standardization Law 365, 384–85 (Jorge L. Contreras ed. 2017) (noting that the court calculated a FRAND royalty based upon the assumption that aggregate royalties for the standard at issue would not exceed 5% of the value the standard contributed to the end devices, rather than, as the evidence suggested, 5% of the product price); *see also* Nagakoshi & Tamai, *supra* note 103, at 269 (noting that the damages awarded in *Samsung v. Apple* amounted to ¥9,955,854, equal to about $83,400 as of May 2015, "which would most likely not even cover the attorneys' fees"). Other examples in which Léonard argues courts might consider enforcement to be an abusive, on proportionality or other grounds, might include requests for unnecessarily broad discovery *see* Léonard, *supra* note 86, at 126, and cases in which the rights holder intentionally delays negotiating a license or filing suit to maximize the damages to be awarded or the royalties ultimately to be negotiated under threat of injunctive relief, in view of the defendant's having in the interim invested substantial sunk costs on the assumption it was not infringing, *see id.* at 236–37. In common-law countries, intentional, prejudicial delay certainly would be a factor weighing against the entry of an injunction. *See infra* notes 298–309 and accompanying text (discussing the doctrines of laches, prosecution laches, and equitable estoppel). Also of interest is the Paris Court of Appeals' decision in *Laboratoires Negma SAS v. Biogaran SAS*, Cour d'appel de Paris, Jan. 27, 2014, in which the court awarded damages to compensate for losses incurred by reason of a preliminary injunction against forbidding use of a patent that was subsequently invalidated, *and* additional damages for abuse of right in connection with the exclusive licensee's overall campaign against the generic drug company. *See* Léonard, *supra* note 86, at 139–40.

proposing a claim construction that contradicts positions the owner previously took as recorded in the prosecution history, or by misleading an accused infringer into believing that the owner would not sue.[107] Defenses premised on this type of behavior are not often successful, however, within the jurisdictions Léonard studied. In common-law countries, courts may apply equitable doctrines such as estoppel or laches to preclude patent owners from litigating or from obtaining injunctive relief in some cases of this type, as discussed below.[108]

(4) Conduct that undermines the function of patent rights

The principle that rightsholders should not exercise their rights in a manner that would undermine the function of those rights is common to the jurisdictions Léonard studies. An alleged violation of this "rights-function" principle therefore may inform a court's decision whether the challenged exercise is an abuse of right, though one or more of the other criteria, and one or more other bodies of law, also may be relevant in such cases: for example, when a patent owner engages in litigation for a collateral purpose, or attempts to obtain a competitive advantage by falsely asserting that a competitor or its customers is engaging in infringement.[109] Another possible example, more pertinent to this chapter (though potentially dovetailing with the disproportionality category above), would be when a SEP owner or patent assertion entity (PAE) uses the threat of injunctive relief to obtain a royalty that is based in part on the holdup value of the patent.[110] I will return to this topic later in this chapter, in connection with the discussion of equitable discretion and proportionality.[111]

(5) Abuse *stricto sensu*

The paradigm case falling into this category (and potentially overlapping with some cases falling within Léonard's first category as well) occurs when the owner asserts a patent in subjective bad faith, with the intention of harming the defendant for a collateral purpose, not tied to the benefits of exercising patent

[107] *See* Léonard, *supra* note 86, at 111–12, 122–26.
[108] *See infra* notes 143–48 and accompanying text.
[109] *See* Léonard, *supra* note 86, at 93–104.
[110] *See id.* at 321–26, 390–96.
[111] *See infra* notes 279–86 and accompanying text.

rights as such.[112] As previously noted in chapters 3 and 4, a common-law analogue to this category might be the abuse of process and malicious prosecution doctrines. The extent to which these claims remain viable in the United States, however, when the allegedly abusive assertion of rights is subjectively motivated by the desire to harm another but not objectively baseless, is unclear after *Professional Real Estate Investors, Inc. v. Columbia Pictures Industries, Inc.*[113]—though for reasons discussed in chapter 4, there is a reasonable policy argument for continuing to recognize them.

(6) Fraudulent acts

The paradigm example here is when the owner submits misleading information to the Patent Office to obtain its patent.[114] If the patent would not have issued absent the fraudulent information, this is yet another example of what this book classifies as a "Category 1" case. Where the fraud infects one or more claims of an issued patent, those claims should be subject to invalidation; and when the fraud enables the patent owner to obtain monopoly power or a dominant position, it may be actionable under competition law, as discussed in chapter 3. The abuse of right doctrine nevertheless might fill the gap where the requisite elements for an antitrust claim are lacking, or provide some additional punch if it results in the imposition of a sanction—whether of a monetary nature, or the rendering invalid or unenforceable of the other claims for which the fraud was not material—beyond merely invalidating the infected claims. As discussed later in this chapter, unenforceability of the patent in its entirety is the standard penalty for such fraud under the U.S. doctrine of inequitable conduct.[115]

As the above discussion shows, the categories of greatest interest for purposes of the chapter are numbers two and four, for which the abuse of right doctrine may constrain the enforcement of patent rights that would be disproportionate or that would undermine the function of patent rights. Indeed, the two categories might seem to converge, in cases in which the alleged abuse is the use of a patent to extract revenue that (substantially?) exceeds the value of the patented technology in comparison with alternatives. Because either equity

[112] *See id.* at 203–04.
[113] 508 U.S. 49 (1993).
[114] *See* LÉONARD, *supra* note 86, at 159–65, 202–03.
[115] *See infra* notes 149–74 and accompanying text.

or a stand-alone proportionality doctrine might serve much the same purpose, I defer discussion of these possible applications of the abuse of right doctrine to later in this chapter. Relatedly, some applications of the doctrine might cover much the same ground as the U.S. patent misuse or inequitable conduct doctrines, as we shall see. Whichever doctrinal tool might apply, however, the key question is how best to balance the needed flexibility against the potential for uncertainty. Dividing potential applications of the abuse of right doctrine into the above six categories is a good start, though both the disproportionality and rights-function categories may need some further refinement to ensure that judicial discretion is not unlimited.

The Abuse Doctrines: Abuse of Economic Dependence

Before moving on to equitable doctrines and proportionality, however, it is appropriate to consider one more abuse doctrine, the potential applicability of which to patent assertion came up in a recent Belgian decision. This is the "abuse of economic dependence" (or "abuse of superior bargaining power") doctrine, found in some European and Asian civil codes, which generally forbids a firm with relative strength in comparison with another from abusing that strength. Conduct falling within the proscription may include, as deemed appropriate, refusals to deal, discriminatory trading conditions, and tie-ins.[116] Some of these laws may be, or as originally conceived may have been, intended specifically to protect small and medium-sized enterprises.[117]

[116] *See, e.g.*, Japan Anti-Monopoly Act, *supra* note 22; Monopoly Regulation and Fair Trade Act, art. 45(1)(6) (Feb. 6, 2024) (S. Korea) (defining as an "unfair trade practice" "[m]aking transactions with the other party to the transaction by unfairly taking advantage of the bargaining position of the business entity itself"). In Europe, see Code of Economic Law, art. IV.2/1 (Bel.) (in force 2020) (forbidding abuse of economic dependence, and listing various considerations that may be considered abusive, including refusals to deal, unfair pricing, and inflicting unequal conditions on economic partners); Code de Commerce (Fr.), art. L420-2, para. 2; Competition Act (Ger.), art. 20 (as amended, 2020). For discussion of abuse of economic dependence and analogous doctrines elsewhere, *see generally* Abusive Practices in Competition Law (Fabiana Di Porto & Rupprecht Podszun eds. 2018), and especially chapter 8 therein, Mor Bakhoum, *Abuse without Dominance in Competition Law: Abuse of Economic Dependence and its Interface with Abuse of Dominance* (pp. 157–84). For short overviews, highlighting some recent applications to digital markets, *see* Marion Baumann et al., *The Enforcement of Abuse of Economic Dependence in the EU*, K&L Gates European Antitrust, Competition, and Trade Regulation Alert (Jan. 28, 2021), https://www.klgates.com/The-Enforcement-of-Abuse-of-Economic-Dependence-in-the-EU-1-28-2021; Vassili Moussis & Atsushi Yamada, *Abuse of Economic Dependence*, Concurrences, https://www.concurrences.com/en/dictionary/abuse-of-economic-dependence.

[117] *See* Tunstall Grp. Holdings Ltd. v. Victrix Socsan, Trib. Entr. Bruxelles, July 26, 2022, ICIP 2022, 637, ¶ 92 (citing D. Philippe & G. Sorreaux, *L'abus de la concurrence*, *in* G. Sorreaux, L'abus de dépendence économique, les clauses abusive et les pratiques du marché déloyales: premières regards

The recent case considering the doctrine within the context of a patent infringement action is *Tunstall Integrated Health & Care Limited v. Victrix Socsan SL*,[118] the facts of which were as follows. The plaintiffs (collectively, "Tunstall"), were active in the home health care monitoring sector. To this end, the firm sold devices, called "reception units," that were installed in individual homes; marketed and licensed software implementing a platform and protocols for use with these devices; and owned a European Patent, validated in Belgium, related to these protocols.[119] Télé-Secours, which marketed televigilance services for elderly and vulnerable people, had been a customer/licensee of Tunstall for several years but was unhappy with Tunstall's delay in providing an updated platform, and planned to hire another firm (Victrix) as a replacement. Tunstall asserted that Victrix's activity would infringe Tunstall's patent, and rebuffed Victrix's request to negotiate a license.[120] Tunstall then sued Télé-Secours and Victrix, arguing that Victrix had infringed by offering to supply its platform to Télé-Secours, and that that certain "test calls" between Télé-Secours and Tunstall constituted infringing uses.[121] The defendants in turn counterclaimed for abuse of dominant position and for abuse of economic dependence. The trial court rejected the competition-law claim on the ground that Tunstall was not dominant throughout the entire E.U.[122] It nevertheless found that Tunstall had abused both defendants' economic dependence, and ordered the plaintiffs to conclude a license in line with market value[123]—which in turn appears to have rendered moot the claim for patent

sur la loi du 4 avril 2019, DAOR 2019, no. 131, p.27), for the proposition that "the legislator's objective is . . . to protect small and medium-sized enterprises, not competition"), *aff'd in part, rev'd in part*, Tunstall Integrated Health & Care Ltd. v. Victrix Socsan SL, Cour d'appel de Bruxelles, June 8, 2023, ICIP 2023, 507, *rev'd*, Cour de cassation d Belgique, Feb. 20, 2025. The German statute cited in the preceding footnote also was originally expressly limited to the protection of SMEs, but this limitation was deleted by a 2020 amendment. *See* Baumann et al., *supra* note 116. A focus on the protection of small and medium-sized enterprises also is often associated with the neo-Brandeisian movement in U.S. antitrust law, as noted in chapter 2.

118 Tunstall Grp. Holdings Ltd. v. Victrix Socsan, Trib. Entr. Bruxelles, July 26, 2022, ICIP 2022, 637, *aff'd in part, rev'd in part*, Cour d'appel de Bruxelles, June 8, 2023, ICIP 2023, 507, *rev'd*, Cour de cassation de Belgique, Feb. 20, 2025. The decision of Cour d'appel provides a more comprehensive recitation of the facts than does the decision of the Cour de cassation, and is therefore the primary source for my discussion of the facts in the text above.

119 *See* Tunstall Grp. Holdings Ltd. v. Victrix Socsan, Cour d'appel de Bruxelles, June 8, 2023, ICIP 2023, 507, ¶¶ 1–2.

120 *See id.* ¶ 3.

121 *See id.* ¶ 18.

122 *See Tunstall Grp. Holdings*, ICIP 2022, 637, ¶¶ 6–53. Whether dominance throughout the entire E.U. is a requisite element of an abuse of dominant position claim under E.U. law turned out not to matter on appeal, as discussed in the text above.

123 *See id.* ¶¶ 54–97.

infringement, though earlier in the decision the court characterized the patent infringement claim as a "pretext."[124]

On appeal, the Brussels Court of Appeal agreed that there was no infringement, and also (albeit for a different reason) no abuse of dominant position. On the latter issue, the appellate court concluded that, under governing CJEU case law, Tunstall's refusal to license Victrix would not constitute an abuse of dominant position, absent evidence that (1) Tunstall's refusal to license precluded the development of a new product or new technology for which there exists potential consumer demand, (2) Tunstall lacked an objective justification for the refusal, and (3) the refusal would tend to exclude all competition in a derivative market.[125] The court concluded that the evidentiary basis for such a claim was lacking, noting also that if the above conditions are too readily found, there would be less of an incentive to invest in creating the asset at issue.[126]

As for abuse of economic dependence, the Court of Appeal agreed with the trial court that the doctrine entails three cumulative conditions: a situation of economic dependence, an abuse, and damage to competition, with the first of these elements being defined as "a position of subjection of one enterprise toward another or many other enterprises, characterized by the absence of an alternative reasonably equivalent and available without delay, on reasonable conditions and at reasonable cost, enabling the enterprise or each of them to extract benefits or conditions which could not be obtained under normal market conditions."[127] The appellate court's interpretation of this element nevertheless sharply differed from that of the trial court. The trial court had reasoned that Télé-Secours was dependent on Tunstall, because its only alternative to dealing directly with Tunstall would have been to deal with one of Tunstall's Belgian licensees.[128] From the appellate court's perspective, however, those licensees were reasonable alternatives; the facts that none of them offered precisely the advantages Télé-Secours expected from the use of Victrix's equipment, and that the price would have been a few thousand euros more than Victrix would have charged over a five-year period, were irrelevant.[129] The appellate court therefore did not need to consider the second element, whether Tunstall had

[124] *Compare id.* ¶ 98 (stating that because Tunstall was, "by the present judgment, ordered to grant the defendants a license for its patent, it cannot pursue its action for patent infringement against the same parties"), *with id.* ¶ 89 (characterizing Tunstall's refusal to license as being "on the basis of a false pretext of patent infringement").

[125] For citations to the relevant CJEU cases, *see supra* note 66.

[126] *See Tunstall Grp. Holdings*, ICIP 2023, 507, ¶¶ 32–37.

[127] *Id.*, ¶ 22.

[128] *See Tunstall Grp. Holdings*, ICIP 2022, 637, ¶ 70.

[129] *Tunstall Grp. Holdings*, ICIP 2023, 507, ¶¶ 25–28.

demanded benefits or imposed conditions upon Télé-Secours that would have been "abnormal."[130] Turning then to Victrix's abuse of economic dependence claim, the appellate court concluded, contrary to the court of first instance, that the claim does not extend to precontractual negotiations, but rather can be brought only by a party that is already in a business relation with the alleged abuser. Since Victrix had no such relationship with Tunstall, Victrix's abuse of economic dependence claim also was unsustainable.[131]

Both sides then filed further appeals with the Cour de cassation. Tunstall argued that Victrix's offer had in fact constituted an act of infringement under Belgian law, and for reasons not altogether relevant to the present discussion, the Cour de cassation agreed.[132] More important here, Victrix and Télé-Secours argued that, under Belgian law, an abuse of economic dependence claim does not hinge on the presence of an existing contractual relationship. The Court agreed and therefore quashed the appellate decision, albeit without addressing other aspects of the appellate decision's reasoning regarding abuse of economic dependence, or explaining its own reasoning.[133] Presumably, though, the Court was persuaded by Advocate-General Inghels' opinion in favor of reversal, which argued that the Belgian legislator had intended a broad understanding of abuse of economic dependence, with "economic dependence" not being limited to contractual dependence but rather to be evaluated under the totality of the circumstances.[134]

In my view, the appellate court's narrower interpretation of the doctrine is more sensible than that of the Cour de cassation. To be sure, Tunstall's conduct, as described by the court of first instance, may seem unfair, even spiteful

[130] *See id.* ¶ 28. The lower court thought that was the case because Victrix offered to pay the "market price" for a license, *see Tunstall Grp. Holdings*, ICIP 2022, 637, ¶ 75; *see also id.* ¶ 89 (referring to Tunstall's "unjustified and discriminatory refusal" to license Victrix, when it licensed others, and characterizing Tunstall's refusal to license as being "on the basis of a false pretext of patent infringement" and therefore abusive). Elsewhere, however, the court suggested that Tunstall's actual justification was simply to reserve business for itself, *see id.* ¶ 86 (referring to Tunstall's "corporate strategy" as being "to develop an *end-to-end* solution for" Télé-Secours).

[131] *See Tunstall Grp. Holdings*, ICIP 2023, 507, ¶ 30.

[132] *See* Victrix Socsan S.L. v. Tunstall Group Holdings Ltd., Cour de cassation d Belgique, Feb. 20, 2025, at 5–6.

[133] *See id.* at 6–7.

[134] *See* Opinion of Advocate General Inghels, C.23.0375.F-C.24.0002.F, ¶¶ 13–19. Advocate-General Inghels indicated that a nonexhaustive list of criteria for evaluating economic dependence would include the relative market power of the defendant; the share of the plaintiff's business that depends on the defendant; the defendant's technology or know-how; the reputation of the brand, the rarity or perishable nature of it product, or the loyalty of consumers; the defendant's access to essential resources or infrastructures; "fear of serious economic disadvantage, retaliation or termination of the contractual relationship"; the defendant's regular granting of special conditions, such as discounts, which are not granted in similar cases; and whether the plaintiff is constrained to placing itself into a situation of economic dependence. *See id.* ¶ 16 (citations omitted).

(though Tunstall's motivation was at least in part to retain business for itself), given that Tunstall wouldn't license Victrix but would license other providers.[135] But the administrative costs of a more accommodating standard could be high, with courts in a greater number of cases now having to determine how close an alternative provider comes to satisfying the claimant's preferences; having to consider numerous factors relevant to economic dependence, as set forth in the Advocate General's opinion cited above; and, in some cases, having to establish the terms for what would amount to a compulsory license. (In the *Tunstall* case itself, Tunstall may have charged the same or substantially the price to all of its licensees, which would have reduced the administrative burden of determining a court-ordered royalty. From a purely economic perspective, however, it's not clear that a patentee's interest in price discrimination is something that necessarily should be condemned,[136] although the statutes recognizing an abuse of economic dependence doctrine, like the U.S. Robinson-Patman Act,[137] appear to take issue with price discrimination on normative grounds.) In addition, as the Court of Appeals suggested, sounding a bit like the U.S. Supreme Court in *Trinko*, forced sharing may reduce the incentive to produce a better product—here, either by Victrix designing around the patent or by the licensees developing a more user-friendly

[135] Difficulties in determining actors' subjective motivations, as well as the very real possibility that spite between business rivals may be difficult to disentangle from economic self-interest, have resulted in what some perceive to be a movement away from the recognition of spite-based torts in U.S. law. *See* Restatement (Third) of Unfair Competition, § 1 cmt. c & Reporter's Note (Am. L. Inst. 1995) (stating that, although "[s]everal cases recite, mostly in dicta, that one who engages in competition solely or primarily for the purpose of causing harm to another is subject to liability to the other, apparently without regard to the nature of the actor's business methods," "the rule has had little practical effect," and recommending that liability be "determined by an analysis of the business methods employed by the actor and not by the actor's motivation"); Roger D. Blair & Thomas F. Cotter, *An Economic Analysis of Seller and User Liability in Intellectual Property Law*, 68 U. Cincinnati L. Rev. 1, 44 n.164 (1999) (stating that, at least as of 1999, a few U.S. states continued to "recognize a cause of action for 'prima facie tort,' defined as intentionally causing harm to another without justification," but that such an approach "may be problematic . . . insofar as it leaves the courts with vast discretion to determine exactly what actions are harmful, and what reasons qualify as sufficient justification for the harm") (citations omitted).

[136] For discussion, *see* Thomas F. Cotter, *The Procompetitive Interest in Intellectual Property Law*, 48 Wm. & Mary L. Rev. 483, 547–49 (2006) (discussing the pros and cons of price discrimination, among them (1) that "first-degree price discrimination, in which a seller with market power offers each individual buyer the maximum price she is willing to pay above marginal cost, is economically efficient in comparison with offering a single price above marginal cost," though "almost impossible to implement" in the real world; and (2) that the welfare effects of "second-degree discrimination, in which different versions of a product were offered to consumers at different prices," or third-degree price discrimination, which exists when "a supplier offers a product to different groups at different prices, based on a prediction of different groups' willingness to pay," are ambiguous—though in some, perhaps many, such cases price discrimination makes the product at issue available to buyers who would not otherwise pay the going rate, and thus also increases output). Even in such cases, however, people may disapprove of price discrimination for reasons of perceived fairness or equality.

[137] *See infra* note 142.

platform—though as the court also recognized, there may be exceptional cases in which the CJEU's competition case law would require licensing, in order to prevent the IP owner from altogether blocking the development of a new product.[138] The reading adopted by the Cour de cassation, by contrast, may threaten to provide every disappointed business suitor with a potential cause of action.[139]

On the other hand, where there *is* a contractual relationship, the abuse of economic dependence doctrine arguably could fill a gap by discouraging "holdup" in the sense originally developed by Oliver Williamson and others—as a form of opportunism on the part of the dominant party in a contractual relationship, the ex ante possibility of which could discourage some non-dominant undertakings from proceeding with otherwise beneficial transactions, or induce parties to incur inefficient ex ante costs to prevent such opportunism.[140] (Hovenkamp's proposed rationale for and application of the rule in *Aspen Skiing* might be seen in a similar light.)[141] Still and all, much depends on the courts' ability to apply the doctrine sensibly; and some risk would remain that courts would become entangled in everyday business disputes for which they have no special expertise, or wind up applying the doctrine in ways that harm more than help consumers[142]—in which case the question is whether the benefits provided by the rule, whether grounded in economic analysis (holdup prevention) or substantive fairness (views of which may vary from one culture to another) are worth that risk.

Equitable Defenses, Remedies, and Discretion

In common-law countries, courts of equity developed in parallel with courts of law, with the former crafting over time various types of claims, defenses, and

[138] *See supra* note 66.

[139] *Compare supra* note 52 (suggesting this as a rationale for the holding in *NYNEX Corp. v. Discon, Inc.*, 525 U.S. 128 (1998)).

[140] *See infra* notes 248–52 and accompanying text.

[141] *See supra* notes 55–68 and accompanying text.

[142] Similar reasoning has resulted in the near obsolescence of claims for secondary-line price discrimination under the U.S. Robinson-Patman Act, 15 U.S.C. §§ 13a–13c, 21a, legislation enacted in the 1930s specifically to protect small businesses by curtailing the nascent power of chain stores to negotiate volume discounts. *See, e.g.*, Antitrust Modernization Commission, Report and Recommendations 311–32 (Apr. 2007), available at https://govinfo.library.unt.edu/amc/report_recommendation/amc_final_report.pdf (recommending the repeal of Robinson-Patman). More recently, the Neo-Brandeisian school of antitrust has advocated a revival of Robinson-Patman Act enforcement, notwithstanding the potential negative impact on consumer welfare. For recent discussion, *see, e.g.*, Congressional Research Service, *FTC Revives Enforcement of the Robinson-Patman Act*, Jan. 6, 2025, https://crsreports.congress.gov/product/pdf/LSB/LSB11257.

remedies that were intended to provide a degree of flexibility in response to, or to fill certain perceived gaps in, the rigorous application of the law by the law courts. Whereas the law courts would award monetary damages, for example, the courts of equity (chancery) had discretion to enter injunctions against ongoing or future wrongs that might threaten a rightsholder with irreparable harm. Eventually, the two systems merged, so that today, for example, the Patents Court of England and Wales, technically part of the Chancery Division of the High Court of Justice, can award where appropriate compensatory damages, the infringer's profits, and injunctive relief in one single action. The United States District Courts similarly have subject matter jurisdiction over civil actions, including patent infringement actions, and can award both damages and injunctions. Both courts also have authority to apply various defenses that trace their origin to the courts of equity and thus are classified as equitable; these include, as relevant here, various forms of estoppel and laches, as well as (in the United States) inequitable conduct and patent misuse. Overall, one of the hallmarks of equitable remedies and equitable defenses remains that courts have a degree of discretion in applying them—though, as the quotation from Chief Justice Roberts noted earlier in this chapter indicates, "discretion is not whim," but rather is guided by existing precedent even as it may be applied to new circumstances.

It is fair to state, nevertheless, that today courts in England and some other common-law countries have more discretion than their counterparts in the United States to modify traditional equitable remedies and defenses—as witness, for example, the United States Supreme Court's decision in *Grupo Mexicano de Desarrollo S.A. v. Alliance Bond Fund, Inc.*,[143] holding that U.S. district courts, unlike their British counterparts, lack jurisdiction to enter orders freezing a defendant's assets pending trial to ensure the eventual payment of compensatory damages, because such orders were not available in courts of equity in 1789.[144] In a similar vein, the U.S. Supreme Court interprets the Seventh

[143] 527 U.S. 308 (1999).

[144] *See id.* at 318–19 (stating that, under the Judiciary Act of 1789, which confers upon the federal courts jurisdiction over "all suits . . . in equity," these courts have "authority to administer in equity suits the principles of the system of judicial remedies which had been devised and was being administered by the English Court of Chancery at the time of the separation of the two countries," and that in 1789 the analogous type of relief, known as a "creditor's bill," normally "could be brought only by a creditor who had already obtained a judgment establishing the debt"). Asset preservation orders may be available, however, where the plaintiff is seeking *equitable* monetary relief, such as the "disgorgement of ill-gotten gains," *see* Zorro Prods., Inc. v. Individuals, Corps., Ltd. Liab. Cos., P'ships, & Unincorporated Ass'ns Identified on Schedule A Hereto, Case No. 23-cv-5761, 2023 WL 8807254, at *4 (N.D. Ill. Dec. 20, 2023), but this is not relevant to U.S. utility patent infringement cases, for which the disgorgement remedy has been unavailable since 1946. By contrast, the Court of Appeal for England and Wales, approved the issuance of this type of order in *Mareva Compania Naviera SA v. Int'l Carriers SA (The Mareva)* [1980] 1 All E.R. 213 (Ct. App. 1975), for which reason these orders often are referred to as

Amendment to the United States Constitution, which "preserve[s]" the right to trial by jury in suits at common law, as requiring inquiry into whether the type of claim or remedy sought is one that would have been litigated or available in a court of law or a court of equity in 1789.[145] For this reason, and in contrast to practice everywhere else in the world, the majority of U.S. patent infringement actions today are tried before juries. There also is an ongoing debate whether U.S. courts are statutorily bound to recognize equitable defenses such as estoppel and laches only under circumstances in which those defenses would have been available as of the enactment of the 1952 Patent Act[146]; and whether awards of ongoing royalties in lieu of injunctive relief, which the Federal Circuit has authorized in a series of decisions since *eBay Inc. v. MercExchange, L.L.C.*,[147] would have been an available option in 1789.[148]

The subsections below group the equitable doctrines relevant to this book into three categories. The first centers on the "unclean hands" and "inequitable conduct" doctrines, the latter being available in few countries other than the United States. These defenses can render patents unenforceable by reason of the patent owner or other associated persons having engaged in fraudulent or deceptive conduct that bears some relevance to the infringement action (though it may have arisen independently of it), and in this regard may overlap with *Walker Process* antitrust claims under some circumstances. The second subsection addresses the U.S. patent misuse doctrine, which as noted

Mareva orders. IPRED article 6(2) also authorizes courts in E.U. member states to enter *Mareva*-type orders.

More generally, the U.K. Supreme Court has recently reaffirmed that U.K. courts are not constrained to applying the law of equity as it existed at same point in the past. *See* Wolverhampton City Council v. London Gypsies and Travellers [2023] UKSC 47, [19]–[22], [145]–[153] (observing, *inter alia*, that "the principles and practice governing the exercise of the power to grant injunctions need to and do evolve over time as circumstances change"; that "practice has not stood still and is unrecognisable from the practice which existed before the 1873 [Supreme Court of Judicature] Act"; and that in view of "the continuing flexibility of equitable powers . . . injunctions may be issued in new circumstances when the principles underlying the existing law so require").

145 *See, e.g.*, Markman v. Westview Instruments, Inc., 517 U.S. 370, 376–78 (1996).

146 *See* Christa Laser, *Equitable Defenses in Patent Law*, 75 U. Miami L. Rev. 1, 27–75 (2020) (discussing whether 35 U.S.C. § 282, which states that "unenforceability" shall be a defense in actions for patent infringement, codifies "the decisional law of unenforceability that existed at the time of enactment" in the sense of freezing equitable defenses as they existed in 1952).

147 547 U.S. 388, 391 (2006). The above text notwithstanding, the *eBay* decision itself is often viewed as a departure from the tradition it itself invokes. *See infra* notes 271–73 and accompanying text.

148 *Compare* H. Tomás Gómez-Arostegui, *Prospective Compensation in Lieu of a Final Injunction in Patent and Copyright Cases*, 78 Fordham L. Rev. 1661, 1707 (2010) (arguing that such awards are equitable in nature, and that they conflict with *Grupo Mexicano* because courts of equity would not have made such awards in 1789), *with* Mark A. Lemley, *Ongoing Confusion over Ongoing Royalties*, 76 Mo. L. Rev. 695, 699 (2011) (stating that, although "the question is not free from doubt, there are reasonable arguments for treating ongoing royalties as within either the law or the equity power of the courts," and that "[c]ourts seem to agree that at least some authority exists for such an award").

previously also overlaps to some degree with antitrust law and, in some respects, resembles the civil law's abuse of right doctrine. One thing common to all three of unclean hands, inequitable conduct, and patent misuse is that these defenses render wrongful (in the nonjudgmental sense I adopted in chapter 1) the assertion of what otherwise may be valid and infringed patents, by reason of conduct that typically pre-dates, and (as above) may be independent of, the infringement litigation. The third subsection groups together the equitable defenses of estoppel and laches with discretionary denials of the equitable remedies of injunctions and accountings of the infringer's profits. From an economic perspective, the matters falling within this last grouping often can be understood as tools for restraining the exercise of patent holdup, as defined below; what renders the request for relief wrongful, in the sense used in this book, is the attempt to extract holdup value. A follow-up subsection will then compare the common law courts' discretion to deny equitable relief with the civil law's options of abuse of dominant position, abuse of right, and proportionality. This section, and chapter, will then conclude with some observations on the current debate over the use of the antisuit, and anti-antisuit, injunctions in FRAND cases.

Equitable Defenses: Unclean Hands and Inequitable Conduct

[149] Among the many equitable maxims the Anglo-American courts have articulated over the centuries is that equity will not aid a claimant who comes before the court with "unclean hands," albeit subject to the caveats that "[t]he grime on the hands must . . . be sufficiently closely connected with the equitable remedy that is sought"—that is, it must relate to the particular act or transaction at issue in the lawsuit—and that "whether there is or is not a sufficiently close connection must depend on the facts of each case."[150] The most

[149] Portions of this section are adapted from my article *An Economic Analysis of Patent Law's Inequitable Conduct Doctrine*, 53 Ariz. L. Rev. 735 (2011).

[150] Grobelaar v. Newsgroup Newspapers Ltd., [2002] UKHL 40, [90] (opinion of Lord Scott). *Cf.* Perma Life Mufflers, Inc. v. Int'l Parts Corp., 392 U.S. 134, 148, 151 (1968) (Marshall, J., concurring in the result) (stating that "[t]he principle that a wrongdoer shall not be permitted to profit through his own wrongdoing is fundamental in our jurisprudence," though agreeing with the majority that "because of the strong public interest in eliminating restraints on competition . . . many of the refinements of moral worth demanded of plaintiffs by such traditional legal and equitable doctrines as *volenti non fit injuria*, unclean hands, and many of the variations of *in pari delicto* should not be applicable in the antitrust field"). As Sean Seymore notes, under current U.S. law the unclean hands defense differs from inequitable conduct and patent misuse in that unclean hands results only in the dismissal of the lawsuit (what he refers to as "relational unenforceability"), whereas misuse and inequitable conduct result in the permanent (for inequitable conduct) or potentially only temporary (for misuse) unenforceability of the patent against the world. He argues, however, that as a normative matter the penalty for unclean

prominent recent decision applying the unclean hands doctrine in an action for patent infringement is *Gilead Sciences, Inc. v. Merck & Co., Inc.*[151] A jury had awarded Merck $200 million in damages for the infringement of two patents relating to treatments for Hepatitis C. Post-trial, however, the district judge concluded that the patents were unenforceable against Gilead by reason of "both pre-litigation business misconduct and litigation misconduct attributable to Merck";[152] and the Federal Circuit, relying on the judge's findings of fact, affirmed. In particular, the trial court found that Pharmasset, a company Gilead later acquired, had discovered a compound (PSI-6130) that was later modified to arrive at sofosbuvir, the active ingredient in Gilead's Hepatitis C treatment; that Pharmasset disclosed to Merck, in confidence, the structure of the compound during a conference call, on the understanding that Merck employees working on Merck's Hepatitis C project would not participate; that in fact a Merck chemist who was working, and continued to work, on the patent applications that later issued as the Merck patents in suit did participate; that the chemist falsely testified about his participation and its potential significance to the work he was doing, at his pretrial deposition and at trial; and that the misconduct infected the entire proceeding, in view of Gilead's defense that the Merck patents were derived from Pharmasset.[153] Significantly, the court affirmed the judgment that the misconduct precluded both injunctive relief and damages, a result that Christa Laser finds to be an extension of the pre-1952 case law.[154] Laser also notes that in some recent cases defendants have raised the defense in other contexts, albeit not necessarily successfully, such as in one case involving the alleged filing of "excessive numbers of patents 'intended to create a "legal thicket." ' "[155]

hands sometimes should be permanent unenforceability. *See* Sean B. Seymore, *Unclean Patents*, 102 B.U. L. Rev. 1491, 1510–11, 1515–17 (2021).

[151] 888 F.3d 1231 (Fed. Cir. 2018).

[152] *Id.* at 1233.

[153] *See id.* at 1236–48.

[154] *See* Laser, *supra* note 146, at 46 (stating that pre-1952, the doctrine was used to bar legal relief (damages) in cases involving "fraud in obtaining the judgment of relief or fraud in obtaining the patent," and that it would not have barred legal relief where, as in *Gilead*, the defense was premised in part "on prosecution misconduct that does not rise to the level of inequitable conduct or fraud in obtaining the patent").

[155] *Id.* at 46 (citing Nomadix, Inc. v. Hosp. Core Servs. LLC, No. CV 14-08256, 2015 WL 3948804, at *11 (C.D. Cal. June 29, 2015)); cf. *id.* (citing Intamin, Ltd. v. Magnetar Techs. Corp., 623 F. Supp. 2d 1055, 1073, 1078 (C.D. Cal. 2009), as "finding unclean hands barred all relief where patentee was 'threatening its competitors with intellectual property rights it did not own,' but also forged assignment documents and failed to disclose the forgery in discovery"). For a South African case invoking the unclean hands doctrine, *see Villa Crop Prot. (Pty) Ltd v. Bayer Intell. Prop. GmbH*, 2022 (4) BCLR 461 (CC) (S. Afr.). The defendant alleged that Bayer made statements to the South African Patent Office concerning the novelty of its claimed plant protection product, which contradicted its seeking of an SPC from the EPO concerning the same product. South Africa's Constitutional Court allowed the defendant to

The inequitable conduct defense is probably best viewed as an offshoot of unclean hands, originating as it did in three mid-twentieth century U.S. Supreme Court decisions—*Precision Instrument Manufacturing. Co. v. Automotive Maintenance Machinery Co.*,[156] *Hazel-Atlas Glass Co. v. Hartford-Empire Co.*,[157] and *Keystone Driller Co. v. General Excavator Co.*[158]—that invoked either unclean hands or general equitable principles to render unenforceable patents the prosecution and/or litigation of which had been pursued by means of serious misconduct such as fraud, bribery, or perjury. As Sean Seymore notes, however, the inequitable conduct doctrine, as subsequently developed by the lower courts, "addresses a breach of candor owed to the Patent Office," whereas "unclean hands encompasses a broader range of misconduct."[159] The duty of candor, in turn, is separately incorporated into Patent Rule 56, which the USPTO adopted in 1977 and which obligated patent applicants and persons associated with them affirmatively to disclose "information they are aware of which is material to the examination of the application."[160] An amended version of Rule 56 went into effect in 1992, and similarly imposes on "[e]ach individual associated with the filing and prosecution of a patent application . . . a duty to disclose to the Office all information known to that individual to be material to patentability," while providing a more detailed definition of materiality.[161]

proceed with two related defenses that seem analogous to the U.S. inequitable conduct doctrine: one based on § 61(1)(g) of South Africa's Patents Act, which states that "a false statement or representation which is material and which the patentee knew to be false at the time when the declaration was made" can be a ground for invalidating an issued patent; and second, the "common-law defence of unclean hands." The decision also cautions, however, that it may be rare for unclean hands to amount to an abuse of process resulting in unenforceability.

[156] 324 U.S. 806 (1945) (holding that, where the patent owner had every reason to believe that the purported inventor had submitted false testimony during the course of an interference proceeding relating to his dates of invention and conception, the resulting patent was rendered unenforceable).

[157] 322 U.S. 238 (1944) (setting aside a judgment of patent infringement, where the patent owner had caused the publication of a trade journal article authored by its patent attorney but attributed to a "disinterested expert" that falsely touted the subject invention's advances over the prior art, and had used that article to deceive both the Patent Office and the district court on the issue of patentability).

[158] 290 U.S. 245 (1933) (affirming the dismissal of a complaint for patent infringement, where the patent owner had corrupted a witness and suppressed evidence of another's prior use in order to defend against patent invalidity in a prior infringement action involving related patents).

[159] Seymore, *supra* note 150, at 1510.

[160] *See* 37 C.F.R. § 1.56 (1977) (further defining information as material if "there is a substantial likelihood that a reasonable examiner would consider it important in deciding whether to allow the application to issue as a patent").

[161] 37 C.F.R. § 1.56(a) (2009). This version of Rule 56 defines information as material if "it is not cumulative to information already of record or being made of record in the application," and it either "establishes, by itself or in combination with other information, a prima facie case of unpatentability of a claim," or "refutes, or is inconsistent with, a position the applicant takes in . . . [o]pposing an argument of unpatentability relied on by the Office, or . . . [a]sserting an argument of patentability." *Id.* § 1.56(b) (further defining a "prima facie case of unpatentability" as being "established when the information compels a conclusion that a claim is unpatentable under the preponderance of evidence, burden-of-proof

Tying these various strands together, the Federal Circuit has articulated the inequitable conduct defense as requiring proof, by clear and convincing evidence, that "(1) an individual associated with the filing and prosecution of a patent application made an affirmative misrepresentation of a material fact, failed to disclose material information, or submitted false material information; and (2) the individual did so with a specific intent to deceive the [US] PTO."[162] Over time, however, the court's confusing, sometimes contradictory, and often expansive interpretations of "materiality" and "intent"[163] provoked a backlash, as many observers—including even some Federal Circuit judges,

standard, giving each term in the claim its broadest reasonable construction consistent with the specification, and before any consideration is given to evidence which may be submitted in an attempt to establish a contrary conclusion of patentability"). In addition, "no patent will be granted on an application in connection with which fraud on the Office was practiced or attempted or the duty of disclosure was violated through bad faith or intentional misconduct." *Id.* § 1.56(a).

In a recent proceeding involving allegations of misconduct during the course of an *inter partes* review (IPR), the Director of the UPSTO concluded that Rule 56 does not apply to IPRs, but that several other provisions of the Code of Federal Regulations do impose a duty of candor and good faith in such proceedings. Based upon her determination that the "Patent Owner engaged in sanctionable misconduct by orchestrating a deliberate scheme to hide relevant factual evidence from the Board and thereby mislead the Board," involving "intentionally withholding and concealing relevant factual evidence in violation of 37 C.F.R. §§ 42.11(a) and 42.51(b)(1)(iii); intentionally relying on known falsely elicited expert testimony in violation of 37 C.F.R. §§ 42.11(a), 42.11(c), and 11.18(b)(2); and intentionally making a false statement of fact in violation of 37 C.F.R. § 42.11(c) and 11.18(b)(2)," she affirmed the PTAB's decision that an appropriate penalty was the cancellation of all 183 challenged claims. *See* Spectrum Solutions, LLC v. Longhorn Vaccines & Diagnostics, LLC, IPR2021-00847 (Patent 8,084,443 B2), IPR2021-00850 (Patent 8,293,467 B2), IPR2021-00854 (Patent 8,669,240 B2), IPR2021-00857 (Patent 9,212,399 B2), IPR2021-00860 (Patent 9,683,256 B2), 2024 WL3561972 (July 11, 2024). Just under one year later, on *sua sponte* reconsideration, the (new) Acting Director of the USPTO vacated this sanction, stating that "cancelling all challenged claims is not an appropriate sanction here"; "[e]ntry of compensatory expenses, including attorney fees . . . would have been appropriate," but for the fact that the petitioner had withdrawn from participation and agreed to a settlement under which each side would bear its own costs; and "[i]n the absence of other sanctions, Patent Owner is strongly admonished for its conduct and cautioned that any future misconduct before the Office will be met with additional sanctions." Order Modifying Entered Sanctions on Unopposed Remand and *Sua Sponte* Reconsideration, Spectrum Solutions, IILC v. Longhorn Vaccines & Diagnostics, LLC, IPR2021-00847 (Patent 8,084,443 B2), IPR2021-00850 (Patent 8,293,467 B2), IPR2021-00854 (Patent 8,669,240 B2), IPR2021-00857 (Patent 9,212,399 B2), IPR2021-00860 (Patent 9,683,256 B2) (June 5, 2025). The order "does not preclude the USPTO's Office of Enrollment and Discipline from exploring potential sanctions or discipline for violations of [37 C.F.R.] Part 11 based on the conduct in these proceedings." The author leaves it to the reader to judge whether a "strong[] admoni[tion]" is a proportionate sanction for the type of misconduct determined by the former Director, which the new order does not refute.

[162] Exergen Corp. v. Wal-Mart Stores, Inc., 575 F.3d 1312, 1327 n.3 (Fed. Cir. 2009) (citations omitted).

[163] Among the perceived problems were the existence of arguably conflicting lines of cases defining "intent to deceive"; multiple possible definitions of the term "material," including one that mirrored the 1977 Rule 56 focus on whether a "reasonable examiner" would have considered the information "important," as well as cases accepting as "material" deception conduct that had no bearing on patentability, such as an applicant's misrepresentation of its status as a small entity entitled to a fee reduction; the use of a "sliding scale," under which a greater showing of intent could compensate for a lesser showing of materiality, as long as both elements satisfied a minimum threshold; and the extension of the penalty of unenforceability, in some cases, to related applications. For discussion, see Cotter, *supra* note 136, at 744, 746–49 & n.55.

who called out what they perceived as an "absolute plague" of "charging inequitable conduct in almost every major patent case"[164]—concluded that the doctrine encouraged both patent owners to overdisclose relatively unimportant information, and accused infringers to overlitigate.[165] Mindful of these critiques, the court thereafter tightened the requirements for successfully invoking the defense in its 2011 *en banc* decision in *Therasense, Inc. v. Becton, Dickinson & Co.*[166] While retaining the two elements noted above, of (1) an affirmative misrepresentation of a material fact, a failure to disclose material information, or the submission of false material information, and (2) specific intent to deceive, the court narrowed the definition of materiality and clarified the meaning of specific intent. In particular, to prove materiality the defendant must show that the applicant misrepresented or failed to disclose "but-for" material evidence—for example, a prior art reference of which it was aware and that would have caused the examiner to reject a claim or claims. Alternatively, the materiality element may satisfied by proof of "affirmative egregious misconduct" such as "the filing of an unmistakably false affidavit."[167] In addition, the court clarified that the element of "specific intent to deceive" would not be satisfied by merely negligent or grossly negligent behavior.[168] The court also cautioned, moreover, that even if the defendant succeeds in meeting this burden, the district judge "must weigh the equities to determine whether the applicant's conduct before the [US]PTO warrants rendering the entire patent unenforceable,"[169] though the mandatory penalty for violations of the

[164] *See* Larson Mfg. Co. of S.D., Inc. v. Aluminart Prods. Ltd., 559 F.3d 1317, 1342 (Fed. Cir. 2009) (Linn, J., concurring) (quoting Kingsdown Med. Consultants, Ltd. v. Hollister Inc., 863 F.2d 867, 876 n.15 (Fed. Cir. 1988) (en banc)). The assertion that the doctrine was raised in "almost every major patent case" probably was something of an overstatement, however. Christian E. Mammen, *Controlling the "Plague": Reforming the Doctrine of Inequitable Conduct*, 24 BERKELEY TECH. L.J. 1329, 1358 tbl. 2 (2009) (presenting an empirical study concluding that the defense was raised in about 40% of all patent cases filed); Benjamin Brown, Comment, *Inequitable Conduct: A Standard in Motion*, 19 FORDHAM INTELL. PROP. MEDIA & ENT. L.J. 593, 605–15, 626 (2009) (reporting, *inter alia*, that from 2000–07 "courts addressed, on average, inequitable conduct in less than 20% of all reported patent cases," but that "it is almost impossible to ascertain the number of times inequitable conduct was pled"). *See also* Lee Petherbridge, Jason Rantanen & Polk Wagner, *Unenforceability*, 70 WASH. & LEE L. REV. 1751 (2013) (reporting findings, based on review of, *inter alia*, "every decision involving inequitable conduct made by the Federal Circuit, beginning with the creation of the court and ending May 27, 2010," that "patents held unenforceable have clear hallmarks of risky prosecution behavior, such as longer pendency and fewer disclosures of prior art, as compared to all other types we studied," thus suggesting that "the doctrine is likely operating better than conventional wisdom would suggest").

[165] Specifically, it was often alleged that the doctrine encouraged patent applicants to submit to the USPTO unnecessarily voluminous Information Disclosure Statements, the effect of which was to bury any truly material information in a sea of paper. The complex standards for proving inequitable conduct, as well as the perceived need on the part of defendants to review all of the forgoing information, also raised the cost of patent litigation. *See* Cotter, *supra* note 136, at 750.

[166] 649 F.3d 1276 (Fed. Cir. 2011) (en banc).

[167] *Id.* at 1292–93.

[168] *See id.* at 1287, 1290–92.

[169] *Id.* at 1288.

inequitable conduct doctrine remains the unenforceability of all of the patent's claims.[170] As a result of *Therasense*, the defense has become much more difficult to sustain. Not surprisingly, the "number of appeals related to this issue has dropped dramatically since" *Therasense*,[171] though it is not a dead letter; on occasion, defendants invoking the doctrine still succeed in having the patent they are accused of infringing declared unenforceable in its entirety.[172]

From an economic perspective, the key question is whether the doctrine, on net, makes a useful contribution to the proper functioning of the patent system. The answer, I think, comes in two parts. First, I would take it as a given that there is a compelling social interest in deterring patent applicants from affirmatively making "material" misrepresentations to the Patent Office, meaning misrepresentations that result in obtaining patent rights that otherwise would not have been granted, or that would have been narrower in scope. For this purpose, though, an inequitable conduct doctrine that is distinct from unclean hands may be unnecessary, if the latter would cover this situation anyway along with other forms of misconduct. (The principal issue with unclean hands, of course, is that courts need to be careful not to use the doctrine simply to penalize those it perceives as bad actors; but as noted above, the traditional contours of the doctrine are intended to guard against that possibility by requiring a nexus between the behavior and the exercise of the right.[173]) In the case of affirmative fraud, then, the only real distinction between inequitable conduct and unclean hands is that the traditional penalty for the latter is merely dismissal of the lawsuit; and in this regard, Seymore makes a good case for courts to have the discretion to impose the harsher penalty of unenforceability *erga omnes* for truly egregious behavior.[174]

Second, however, the question remains whether applicants also should be required, as they are in the United States and some other countries,[175]

[170] *See id.* at 1288–89 (reaffirming that a finding of inequitable conduct renders a patent unenforceable in its entirety, cannot be cured, and may result in related patents being held unenforceable); cf. *id.* at 1296, 1299 (O'Malley, J., concurring in part and dissenting in part) (arguing that district courts should have discretion to "choose to render fewer than all claims unenforceable, . . . simply dismiss the action before it, or . . . fashion some other reasonable remedy, so long as the remedy imposed by the court is 'commensurate with the violation'").

[171] *See* Dennis Crouch, *Discussions of Inequitable Conduct in CAFC Decisions*, PATENTLY-O, Jan. 29, 2025, https://patentlyo.com/patent/2025/01/discussions-inequitable-decisions.html (reporting a decline from a high of over forty such appeals in 2008 to fewer than ten in recent years).

[172] *See, e.g.*, GS Cleantech Corp. v. Adkins Energy LLC, 951 F.3d 1310, 1328–32 (Fed. Cir. 2020) (affirming judgment of inequitable conduct, where patent owner was aware of invalidating prior art and deliberately chose to conceal it).

[173] *See supra* note 150 and accompanying text.

[174] *See* Seymore, *supra* note 150, at 1515–17.

[175] *See* Andrea Schüßler et al., *AIPPI-Q289: Asking for Harmonization of Disclosure Requirements – Analysis and Opinion from a German and European Perspective*, 74 GRUR-INT. 103, 113–14 (2025) (stating that "a majority of countries in the world have only a very limited duty for applicants to disclose

to disclose prior art or other material information of which they aware; *and* if so whether the intentional violation of this norm should result in the unenforceability of the resulting patent.[176] From an economic perspective, the question then becomes whether the U.S. approach as embodied in the inequitable conduct doctrine works to achieve the optimal disclosure of information material to patentability.[177] In this regard, the argument would be that applicants who are aware of material information should be required to disclose it, because it is less costly for them to do so than for examiners to find it; indeed, without the applicant's assistance the examiner could miss something crucial, particularly given the time constraints under which examiners work. And if that is so, then arguably there should be some penalty in addition to merely invalidating the affected claim or claims ex post—given that invalidation probably (though not inevitably[178]) would be the result anyway, if the patent were

prior art," and yet "the patent systems work well"); Ari Laakkonen et al., *Summary Report: AIPPI Q289-SR-Patents-2024: Harmonisation of disclosure requirements and consequences of non-compliance* (July 10, 2024). According to the individual country reports filed by forty AIPPI member groups in response to AIPPI Q289-SR-Patents-2024, some countries impose no duty to disclose, while others impose an obligation to disclose the state of the prior art and/or to make disclosures in response to examiner requests. Sanctions for noncompliance may include rejection of the application, or in some countries revocation of an issued patent, but it is not clear how frequently these obligations are enforced. The U.S. and Israel appear to be unusual in having a broad disclosure obligation backed, potentially, by stringent sanctions, as discussed above and in the following footnote.

[176] There appear to be very few countries with anything analogous to the U.S. inequitable conduct doctrine. For discussion, *see* Thomas F. Cotter, Comparative Patent Remedies: A Legal and Economic Analysis 174 n.47 (2013) (noting Canadian case law rejecting the doctrine); R. Kehl Sink, Note, *Inequitable Outcomes from the Inequitable Conduct Defense: A Proposal for Revising an Employee-Inventor's Duty to Disclose*, 60 Santa Clara L. Rev. 185, 197–203 (2020) (asserting the absence of any close counterpart to the doctrine, at least as of 2020, in Australia, Canada, China, the EU, India, Japan, Mexico, or South Korea). Israel offers the closest counterpart of which I am aware. *See* Ran Vogel, Liam Whatstein & Ephraim Heilizaczer, *AIPPI Q289-SR-Patents-2024: Israel: Harmonisation of disclosure requirements and consequences of non-compliance*, at 5 (July 10, 2024) (stating that, if the examiner requests information from the applicant under Patents Act §§ 18(b), 18A (Isr.), and the applicant provides misleading information or fails to notify the office of any changes of which the applicant becomes aware, the court may cancel the patent, order it to be licensed, or shorten its term, or fine the applicant; and noting that in *Unipharm Ltd. v. Sanofi*, Case Nos. DNA 5679/21, DNA 5886/21 (S. Ct. Dec. 26, 2023) (Isr.), discussed *infra* note 184, the Israeli Supreme Court held that intentionally misleading the patent office can result in the applicant being liable for unjust enrichment).

[177] *See* Cotter, *supra* note 136, at 740 & n.12 (citing sources).

[178] There may be some cases in which information that would have been material to the examiner would not result in ex post invalidation (in litigation or a post-grant validity challenge), given the different burden of proof and claim construction standards that apply in prosecution and litigation under U.S. law (though I suspect that the number of such cases is small). *See Therasense*, 649 F.3d at 1291–92:

> When an applicant fails to disclose prior art to the PTO, that prior art is but-for material if the PTO would not have allowed a claim had it been aware of the undisclosed prior art. Hence, in assessing the materiality of a withheld reference, the court must determine whether the PTO would have allowed the claim if it had been aware of the undisclosed reference. In making this patentability determination, the court should apply the preponderance of the evidence standard and give claims their broadest reasonable construction . . . . Often the patentability of a claim will be congruent with the validity determination—if a claim is properly invalidated in district court based on the deliberately withheld reference, then that

subsequently litigated or its validity challenged and the missing information brought to light; otherwise the applicant's duty to disclose may be nothing more than a toothless honor system. Put another way, by rendering all claims of the patent unenforceable, the inequitable conduct doctrine increases the expected cost to the applicant of failing to disclose material information that the examiner otherwise might not be aware of, and thus encourages applicants to disclose in order to avoid that cost; and simultaneously reduces the likelihood of examiner error that otherwise may lead to the issuance, and potentially the interim enforcement, of invalid patents. And, as with some of the other topics discussed in this book (for example, wrongly issued preliminary injunctions, or PAEs using weak patents to extract nuisance value settlements), that interim enforcement can be socially costly.

All that said, most countries apparently don't think that the cost-benefit ratio weighs in favor of adopting a U.S.-style inequitable conduct doctrine—and they may be right. On the cost side, imposing an enforceable duty to disclose material information of which one is aware increases the cost faced by all applicants; and while this might seem to be a cost that society has good reason to impose, given the applicant's information advantage over the examiner, commentators outside the United States sometimes express concern over its impact, especially on small and medium-sized enterprises.[179] There also might be related concerns over possible uncertainties in defining what it means to be "aware" of material information—*e.g.*, does it include information of which the applicant *should* be aware—and, as in the U.S. prior to *Therasense*, over what "material" information is, although both of these problems could be reduced, though perhaps not eliminated, by carefully defining the scope of the duty. Second, introducing an inequitable conduct doctrine would increase overall adjudication costs by providing defendants with another possible defense to raise—though again, under a *Therasense*-style rule, it may be the unusual case in which the defendant finds it worthwhile to assert the defense at all, and the comparatively lean pretrial discovery available outside the United States might mean that relatively few defendants would have the necessary information even to make an informed decision. On the benefits side, moreover, there also is reason to doubt that the penalty of rendering all claims of an issued patent

reference is necessarily material because a finding of invalidity in a district court requires clear and convincing evidence, a higher evidentiary burden than that used in prosecution at the PTO. However, even if a district court does not invalidate a claim based on a deliberately withheld reference, the reference may be material if it would have blocked patent issuance under the PTO's different evidentiary standards.

179 *See* Schüßler et al., *supra* note 175, at 113, 117.

unenforceable contributes much to the goal of achieving optimal ex ante disclosure. For one thing, only a relatively small portion of all issued patents are ever litigated or have their validity challenged; knowing this in advance, an applicant may figure it's worth the gamble to refrain from disclosing, obtain its patent, and hope that the matter never comes to light.[180] (Of course, if a sufficiently large number of applicants feel this way, the aforementioned concerns about overburdening patent applicants may be exaggerated.) In addition, if, as critics argued prior to *Therasense*, the inequitable conduct encourages applicants to swamp the Patent Office with mostly useless Information Disclosure Statements that examiners largely ignore, the benefits of greater disclosure are achieved if at all only when the accused infringer accesses this information and finds some golden nugget that it otherwise would have overlooked; but again, that may be the rare case.

More significantly, as T.-J. Chiang has discussed, one might expect the unenforceability penalty to have little or no impact on an unscrupulous applicant's decision to disclose material information, if the disclosure of that information would mean that all or most of the claims as drafted would likely be invalid, because the marginal deterrent of having other, potentially less valuable claims rendered unenforceable in the event of litigation may be minimal.[181] For this reason, the benefits of adopting the doctrine may be meager indeed, unless courts are also free to increase the penalty. To this end, Chiang argues that, ideally, courts would impose a punitive fine, consisting of the value of whatever interim benefits the applicant derived from its failure to disclose—for example, the interim profits earned from enforcing a subsequently invalidated patent—multiplied by the inverse probability of detection.[182] Many countries, however, balk at the notion that civil courts should assess "punitive" sanctions,[183] so outside the few that do not the sanction could, at most, consist of disgorgement—and in fact, the Supreme Court of Israel, one of the few countries besides the United States with something functionally similar to an

[180] Even if it does not foresee litigation or a validity challenge, the applicant may hope to derive benefits from licensing its patent, or from whatever else motivates applicants to obtain patents despite the fact that, ex ante, they often can seem like a bad investment. *See* Mark A. Lemley, *The Surprising Resilience of the Patent System*, 95 TEX. L. REV. 1 (2016) (noting other theories of "why people obtain patents and then do nothing with them," including vanity, rewarding employee creativity, and social norms).

[181] *See* Tun-Jen Chiang, *The Upside-Down Inequitable Conduct Defense*, 107 NW. U. L. REV. 1243, 1253–54, 1261 (2013).

[182] *See id.* at 1286–91; *see also* Mordechay Soreka, Miriam Marcowitz-Bitton & Yotam Kaplan, *Patent Fraud by Design*, 38 CARDOZO ARTS & ENTER. L.J. 359 (2020) (proposing that courts authorize competitors to file *Walker Process* actions as representatives of a class of consumers, and that consumers be eligible to receive the profits earned as a result of the fraudulent procurement).

[183] *See, e.g.*, Schüßler et al., *supra* note 175, at 115–16.

inequitable conduct doctrine in place, recently approved that very sanction in a case in which the nondisclosing patentee may have earned substantial profits from the interim enforcement of an invalid patent.[184]

On the other hand, requiring courts to estimate the profit attributable to the ex ante failure to disclose is hardly costless or likely to be error-free.[185] More generally, the question remains whether the benefits produced by the doctrine, even if modified along the lines suggested by Chiang, would justify the cost. A full accounting would have to take into account the deterrent effect of other sanctions a patent lawyer or agent might personally incur for violating Patent Rule 56 or its counterpart in other countries, which in theory might obviate the need for other sanctions,[186] plus the possibility that conduct constituting inequitable conduct could also give rise to antitrust liability (though this may be a remote possibility in most cases, given among other things the other requirements needed to prove an abuse of dominant position or, in the U.S., a *Walker Process* monopolization suit[187]).

[184] *See* Unipharm Ltd. v. Sanofi, Case Nos. DNA 5679/21, DNA 5886/21 (S. Ct. Dec. 26, 2023) (Isr.) (original and machine translation on file with author). The facts of the case, as found by the lower court, were that Sanofi intentionally filed a patent application containing a misleading example concerning the production of a clopidogrel bisulfate crystal referred to as "Form 2"; intentionally omitted to disclose that Form 2 was originally discovered accidentally (which might have been relevant to inventive step); and benefited from this conduct, even though it eventually abandoned the patent application, because the application's pendency delayed generic competitors from entering the market. All five of the justices concluded, nonetheless, that Sanofi did not violate § 18C of Israel's Patent Act; but two (Justices Solberg and Amit) concluded that Sanofi violated § 29A(a) of the Competition Act, prohibiting abuse of dominant position, while the other three (Justices Baron, Hayut, and Fogelman) concluded that Sanofi violated a more general duty of good faith owed to the Patent Office. Justices Solberg, Baron, Amit, and Fogelman agreed, however, that the appropriate penalty for Sanofi's misconduct was restitution of profits attributable to the resulting delay in the approval of marketing applications filed by generic drug companies. Justice Amit would have limited the plaintiff Unipharm to compensatory damages.

[185] *See* Chiang, *supra* note 181, at 1288 (acknowledging that "assessing the difference between the actual monopoly profits gained under the improperly enlarged patent vis-à-vis the hypothetical monopoly profits that would have been earned under a properly issued patent may be difficult as a practical matter").

[186] *See* Cotter, *supra* note 136, at 720 & n.120; *but see* Chiang, *supra* note 181, at 1295–97 (arguing that this won't work, in part because the USPTO "has shown absolutely no interest in performing this policing function"); Jacques Normand, *Final Report: The Two Approaches to the Abuse of Procedural Rights*, *in* ABUSE OF PROCEDURAL RIGHTS: COMPARATIVE STANDARDS OF PROCEDURAL FAIRNESS 237, 246–47 (Michele Tartuffo ed. 1998) (discussing the general reluctance on the part of courts to sanction lawyers).

[187] The Federal Circuit also has held, pre-*Therasense*, that the conduct that would sustain a finding of inequitable conduct need not to rise to the level that would sustain a *Walker Process* claim, *see* Dippin' Dots, Inc. v. Mosey, 476 F.3d 1337, 1346–48 (Fed. Cir. 2007), though more recent case law has suggested that the conduct element may be "nearly identical." *See* Anne Brody & Elisabeth Ponce, *Courts Are Aligning Patent Fraud, Inequitable Conduct Claims*, LAW360 (May 18, 2021), https://www.law360.com/articles/1384168/courts-are-aligning-patent-fraud-inequitable-conduct-claims (citing cases); cf. *see also* HOVENKAMP ET AL., *supra* note 1, § 11.02[B], at 11–16.1 (stating that the "substantive changes to the inequitable conduct defense," which have made it "significantly harder to prove," "have undermined the court's reasoning in *Dippin' Dots*"). Further, as Chiang notes, *Walker Process* liability can be evaded by assigning the patent to an innocent party, whereas under similar circumstances a finding of inequitable conduct would still render the patent unenforceable. *See* Chiang, *supra* note 181, at 1293–94, 1297–99.

On balance, the extent to which the inequitable conduct doctrine, either in its existing or some modified form, produces net benefits by inducing optimal disclosure is unclear—which may go a long way toward explaining why few countries have adopted it. In this regard, readers may recall Fritz Machlup's famous dictum that "[i]f we did not have a patent system, it would be irresponsible, on the basis of our present knowledge of its economic consequences, to recommend instituting one. But since we have had a patent system for a long time, it would be irresponsible, on the basis of our present knowledge, to recommend abolishing it."[188] Much the same, I suspect, could be said of the inequitable conduct doctrine. Due to inertia, if nothing else, it probably will continue to play a role, albeit after *Therasense* a relatively small one, in the U.S., and will continue to be ignored (almost) everywhere else. By contrast, the general principle underlying the unclean hands doctrine—that wrongdoers should not benefit from their affirmative misconduct—appears to have reasonably broad support even in civil law countries,[189] and thus in appropriate circumstances might provide a basis for relief from a judgment obtained by intentional fraud, bribery, or other forms of corruption. As noted above, moreover, the submission of misleading information to procure patent rights can form the basis for an abuse of dominant position claim under competition law, though only if all of the other elements of such an offense are made out.

Equitable Doctrines: Patent Misuse

Also related to, but distinct from, unclean hands is the U.S. patent misuse doctrine.[190] Although there are some earlier cases that are sometimes viewed as having contributed to the development of this defense, the Supreme Court's

[188] Fritz Machlup, *An Economic Review of the Patent System*, Study of the Subcommittee on Patents, Trademarks, and Copyrights, of the Committee on the Judiciary of the United States Senate (1958), at 79–80.

[189] *See, e.g.*, Richard Kreindler, *Corruption in International Investment Arbitration: Jurisdiction and the Unclean Hands Doctrine*, *in* Between East and West: Essays in Honour of Ulf Franke 309, 317–18 (2010). The doctrine's status in investor-state arbitration, however, or international law more generally, is disputed. *See, e.g.*, Yueming Yan, *Corruption and the (Un)Clean Hands Doctrine in Investor-State Arbitration: Definitional and Reciprocity Challenges*, 38 ICSID Rev. – Foreign Investment L.J. 1 (2024).

[190] Portions of this discussion are adapted from my articles *Four Questionable Rationales for the Patent Misuse Doctrine*, 12 Minn. J.L. Sci. & Tech. 457 (2011) [hereinafter Cotter, *Four Questionable Rationales*]; *IP Misuse and Innovation Harm*, Iowa L. Rev. Bull. 52 (2011); and *Misuse*, 44 Hous. L. Rev. 901 (2007) [hereinafter Cotter, *Misuse*]. For a much more comprehensive discussion of the patent misuse doctrine than this chapter aspires to, *see* Daryl Lim, Patent Misuse and Antitrust Law: Empirical, Doctrinal, and Policy Perspectives (2013).

1942 decision in *Morton Salt Co. v. G.S. Suppiger Co.*[191] is usually considered to be foundational. The patentee Suppiger had filed an infringement action against Morton relating to Suppiger's patent on a machine for depositing salt tablets. In its defense, Morton cited Suppiger's practice of leasing machines incorporating the invention on condition that the machines be used only in conjunction with nonpatented salt tablets manufactured by a Suppiger subsidiary—a tying arrangement.[192] Without passing judgment on whether the tie violated federal antitrust law, the Supreme Court instead cited the unclean hands principle that courts "may appropriately withhold their aid where the plaintiff is using the right asserted contrary to the public interest," before concluding that the use of a patent "to suppress competition in the sale of an unpatented article may deprive the patentee of the aid of a court of equity to restrain an alleged infringement by one who is a competitor."[193] Suppiger therefore was foreclosed from obtaining relief, "at least until it is made to appear that the improper practice has been abandoned and that the consequences of the misuse . . . have been dissipated."[194] Subsequent Supreme Court decisions applied this "misuse" doctrine to the setting of royalty rates on the basis of the licensee's sales of unpatented products[195]; tying a patent license to the sale of a "nonstaple" product (one having no substantial use other than in connection with the patented article);[196] and contracts obligating a licensee to continue paying royalties post-patent expiration.[197]

These cases are curious in several ways. First, although the Court in *Morton* referred to the equitable doctrine of unclean hands, as noted above that doctrine would apply only if the plaintiff's misconduct related to the particular act or transaction at issue in the lawsuit—whereas in *Morton*, the defendant was not a party (willing or otherwise) to the offending leases.[198] Nor would it

[191] 314 U.S. 488 (1942); *see also* B.B. Chem. Co. v. Ellis, 314 U.S. 495 (1942) (companion case to *Morton*, reaching the same conclusion concerning the unenforceability of a tie-in).

[192] *See Morton Salt*, 314 U.S. at 489–91.

[193] *Id.* at 492.

[194] *Id.* at 494.

[195] *See* Zenith Radio Corp. v. Hazeltine Rsch., Inc., 395 U.S. 100, 135 (1969) (stating, however, that if the licensee is not coerced into taking unwanted patents, but rather the package is for the convenience of the parties, the arrangement is not misuse); cf. Automatic Radio Mfg. Co. v. Hazeltine Rsch., Inc., 339 U.S. 827 (1950) (finding no misuse in connection with a portfolio license).

[196] *See* Mercoid Corp. v. Mid-Continent Inv. Co., 320 U.S. 661 (1944); Mercoid Corp. v. Minneapolis-Honeywell Regul. Co., 320 U.S. 680 (1944). (The *B.B. Chemical* decision noted above also appears to have condemned the sale of material specially made for use with a patented method, *see* 314 U.S. at 496–98.) These cases have been legislatively overruled. *See infra* note 210 and accompanying text.

[197] *See* Brulotte v. Thys Co., 379 U.S. 29 (1964). The Federal Circuit reads the case as standing for the proposition that such a contract constitutes misuse per se. *See* Va. Panel Corp. v. MAC Panel Co., 133 F.3d 860, 869 (Fed. Cir. 1997). The Supreme Court reaffirmed *Brulotte* on stare decisis grounds in *Kimble v. Marvel Ent., LLC*, 576 U.S. 446 (2015).

[198] *See Morton*, 314 U.S. at 492–93.

matter, according to the Court, whether the defendant competed in the market for the tied product (though in fact Morton did compete against Suppiger's subsidiary in the market for salt tablets).[199] As a consequence, there is no "standing" requirement for asserting the defense of patent misuse. Second, despite misuse's status as an equitable doctrine, the standard penalty for misuse is unenforceability of the patent in suit, until the misuse is "purged,"[200] rather than merely finding an offending license provision (if such be the provenance of the misuse) null and void, or some other penalty to be determined within the court's discretion.[201] Third, the patentee's conduct may constitute misuse without necessarily violating antitrust law. In the *Morton* case itself, although the Court expressed concern over the use of patents "to suppress competition in the sale of an unpatented article" as a reason for withholding relief against "one who is a competitor,"[202] it did not reach the antitrust issue[203] (though a subsequent decision, *International Salt Co., Inc. v. United States*,[204] did hold that a similar arrangement violated the Clayton Act).

The principle that patent misuse reaches some conduct that does not violate competition law, as such, remains good law,[205] though it raises the obvious question of what the standard should be for adjudging a practice sufficiently anticompetitive (or contrary to public policy) to merit condemnation as patent misuse, if antitrust standards do not govern; is misuse some ill-defined "antitrust lite"? For that matter, it's doubtful that the practice at issue in *Morton* was itself anticompetitive in any meaningful sense. Even assuming, for the sake of argument, that the patent owner in *Morton* had monopoly power in the market

199 *See id.* at 491, 493–94.

200 *See id.* at 493 (stating that the patentee is precluded from obtaining relief, "at least until it is made to appear that the improper practice has been abandoned and that the consequences of the misuse . . . have been dissipated"); *see also* B.B. Chem. Co. v. Ellis, 314 U.S. 495, 498 (1942) (same). Laser argues, however, that a court applying the traditional, pre-1952 understanding of misuse as derived from the doctrine of unclean hands, "would likely not use patent misuse to bar a claim for damages at law." Laser, *supra* note 146, at 66.

201 There may be exceptions, however. *See* LIM, *supra* note 190, at 4 (noting that "[w]hat amounts to a successful dissipation [of the effects of misuse] depends on the nature and extent of the misuse," and that in some cases "[c]ancellation of an offending licensing clause may be sufficient"); *see also* Zila, Inc. v. Tinnell, 502 F.3d 1014, 1023 (9th Cir. 2007) (reading *Brulotte* not as "render[ing] an entire contract void and unenforceable merely because it includes an invalid licensing agreement," but rather as "render[ing] unenforceable only that portion of a license agreement that demands royalty payments beyond the expiration of the patent for which the royalties are paid").

202 *Id.* at 491.

203 *See id.* at 494.

204 332 U.S. 392 (1947).

205 *See, e.g.,* Monsanto Co. v. Scruggs, 459 F.3d 1328, 1339 (Fed. Cir. 2006) (stating that "[p]atent misuse may be found even where there is no antitrust violation, because '[p]atent misuse is . . . a broader wrong than [an] antitrust violation'") (quoting C.R. Bard, Inc. v. M3 Sys., Inc., 157 F.3d 1340, 1372 (Fed. Cir. 1998)); *see also* Zenith Radio Corp. v. Hazeltine Research, Inc., 395 U.S. 100, 140 (1969) (stating that, when there is patent misuse, "it does not necessarily follow that the misuse embodies the ingredients of a violation of either § 1 or § 2 of the Sherman Act").

for canning machines (a question the Court did not address),[206] it seems extremely unlikely that the owner had any reasonable prospect of leveraging that monopoly into a second monopoly in the market for the tied good (unpatented salt tablets)[207]—though, to be sure, some observers might argue that tying arrangements should be condemned because they limit consumer choice, or for other normative reasons such as an aversion to price discrimination, which tying can facilitate.[208] But in 1952, Congress itself effectively overruled the misuse cases that had condemned tying licenses to the sale of nonstaple products—the effect of which had been to call into doubt patent owners' ability to enforce their rights against contributory infringers[209]—when it included within the 1952 Patent Act a provision, § 271(d), expressly stating that it is not misuse for a patent owner to "derive[] revenue from acts which if performed by another without his consent would constitute contributory infringement of the patent," to "license[] or authorize[] another to perform acts which if performed without his consent would constitute contributory infringement of the patent," or to "enforce his patent rights against infringement or contributory infringement."[210] Congress also limited the scope of cases such as *Morton* in 1988, when it amended § 271(d) to state that refusing to license a patent is

[206] Under contemporary patent misuse and antitrust law, there is no longer a presumption that ownership of a patent confers monopoly power. *See* 35 U.S.C. § 271(d); Ill. Tool Works, Inc. v. Indep. Ink, Inc., 547 U.S. 28, 45–46 (2006).

[207] The Single Monopoly Profit Theory, as developed by the Chicago School beginning in the 1950s, posits that a monopolist can extract its full monopoly profit in the market for the monopolized good, or by means of a tying arrangement extract some portion of it in the market for the tying good and some portion in the market for the tied good, but cannot leverage the monopoly in the market for the tying good into a second monopoly in the market for the tied good. *See, e.g.*, Robert H. Bork, The Antitrust Paradox: A Policy at War with Itself 365–81 (1978) Ward S. Bowman, Jr., *Tying Arrangements and the Leverage Problem*, 67 Yale L.J. 19, 35 (1957). Among the conditions necessary for the Single Monopoly Profit Theory to hold, however, are that the market for the tied product is competitive and that the tied product is complementary to the tying product and purchased in fixed quantities. In the *Morton* case, purchasers would not have bought the unpatented salt tablets in fixed quantities. Nevertheless, it is unlikely that Suppiger or anyone else would have had the capacity to monopolize the market for salt tablets; a better explanation for the tie was that it was a means for engaging in imperfect price discrimination, by (in effect) charging a higher price, over the lifetime of the machine, to high-intensity users of the machine-plus-salt tablets bundle. *See, e.g.*, Herbert Hovenkamp & Fiona Scott Morton, *Framing the Chicago School of Antitrust Analysis*, 168 U. Penn. L. Rev. 1843, 1865–66 (2020) (stating that the Single Monopoly Profit result "can easily be broken if the setting is made more realistic," but that the use of tying to effect second degree price discrimination is "extremely common" and that such ties "produce uncertain but likely positive welfare effects, particularly since its effect would generally be to increase output"). For discussion of scenarios in which tying might facilitate leveraging or deter entry into an imperfectly competitive market for the tied good, *see, e.g.*, Dennis W. Carlton & Michael Waldman, *The Strategic Use of Tying to Preserve and Create Market Power in Evolving Industries*, 33 Rand J. Econ. 194 (2002); Einer Elhauge, *Tying, Bundled Discounts, and the Death of the Single Monopoly Profit Theory*, 123 Harv. L. Rev. 397 (2009).

[208] *See, e.g.*, Lim, *supra* note 190, at 99.

[209] *See* Cotter, *Misuse*, *supra* note 190, at 910 n.37.

[210] 35 U.S.C. § 271(d)(1)-(3); *see also* Dawson Chem. Co. v. Rohm & Haas Co., 448 U.S. 176 (1980) (interpreting § 271(d) as having overruled the *Mercoid* cases).

not misuse, and neither is conditioning "the license of any rights to the patent or the sale of the patented product on the acquisition of a license to rights in another patent or purchase of a separate product, unless, in view of the circumstances, the patent owner has market power in the relevant market for the patent or patented product on which the license or sale is conditioned."[211] The *Brulotte* rule as well has been generally condemned by law-and-economics commentators, who observe that an agreement to pay royalties post-expiration would be anticompetitive only under unusual circumstances (insofar as the contract does not restrain anyone other than the obligee from making free use of the technology claimed in the expired patent), and in most cases is more likely simply a means for spreading out financing over a longer period of time, like an installment contract.[212] Even the Supreme Court has come to recognize the formalism of the *Brulotte* rule, albeit in the course of retaining it on stare decisis grounds (and recommending that savvy parties simply draft around it, by making explicit that post-expiration royalties are for pre-expiration use, or for the use of other IP rights still in force).[213] To be sure, nobody's perfect; but this brief history of how the Supreme Court has defined misuse over the past eighty years hardly inspires confidence.

The Federal Circuit has tried to bring some order to the chaos by defining misuse as "impermissibly broaden[ing] the 'physical or temporal scope' of the patent grant with anticompetitive effect,"[214] and it has developed a three-step framework for evaluating assertions of misuse. The first step is to determine whether the challenged conduct is either per se misuse or per se lawful,[215] with per se misuse including obligating a licensee to pay post-expiration royalties and some tying arrangements,[216] and per se lawful conduct including anything that Congress has chosen to define as "not misuse" in § 271(d). Second, if the patentee's conduct is per se neither legal nor illegal, the court is to

> determine if that practice is "reasonably within the patent grant, i.e., that it relates to subject matter within the scope of the patent claims." If so, the practice does not have the effect of broadening the scope of the patent claims and thus cannot constitute patent misuse. If, on the other hand, the practice has

[211] *See* 35 U.S.C. § 271(d)(4)-(5).

[212] *See, e.g.*, Christina Bohannan & Herbert Hovenkamp, Creation Without Restraint: Promoting Liberty and Rivalry in Innovation 283 (2012).

[213] *See* Kimble v. Marvel Ent., LLC, 576 U.S. 446, 453–54 (2015).

[214] Windsurfing Int'l, Inc. v. AMF, Inc., 782 F.2d 995, 1001 (Fed. Cir. 1986) (quoting Blonder-Tongue Labs., Inc. v. Univ. of Ill. Found., 402 U.S. 313, 343 (1971)).

[215] *See* Va. Panel Corp. v. MAC Panel Co., 133 F.3d 860, 869 (Fed. Cir. 1997).

[216] *See id.*

the effect of extending the patentee's statutory rights and does so with an anticompetitive effect, that practice must then be analyzed in accordance with the "rule of reason." Under the rule of reason, "the finder of fact must decide whether the questioned practice imposes an unreasonable restraint on competition, taking into account a variety of factors, including specific information about the relevant business, its condition before and after the restraint was imposed, and the restraint's history, nature, and effect.[217]

Although this approach is more structured than anything found in *Morton* or other Supreme Court cases on misuse, it still begs the question of what "beyond the scope" and "anticompetitive" mean in this context—though in general, the court has applied the doctrine pretty narrowly. Consider, for example, two related cases from the early 2000s, *U.S. Philips Corp. v. ITC*[218] and *Princo Corp. v. ITC*.[219] *Philips* involved a challenge to the owner's practices of (1) licensing, as a package, its self-designated essential and non-essential patents on compact-disc related technology, in exchange for royalties based on the number of CDs produced rather than the number of patents used, and (2) declining to license any of the patents individually.[220] The alleged infringers argued that conditioning the license of the essential patents on the licensees' agreement to license nonessential patents constituted misuse.[221] Applying the three-step test, the court concluded first that, despite Philips' market power in the market for the essential patents, its practices were not misuse per se. In this regard, the court distinguished two (somewhat old) Supreme Court decisions addressing the circumstances under which the block booking of motion pictures was found to be a per se violation of the Sherman Act, on the grounds that Philips' licensees were not required to *use* the nonessential patents and that no portion of the royalty charged for the package could be attributed to those patents alone.[222] In addition, the court concluded that there was no proof of an anticompetitive foreclosure of commerce in the market for the tied patents, which the court viewed as another essential aspect of a per se misuse defense, and that there were potential procompetitive benefits arising from a reduction

[217] *Id.*
[218] 424 F.3d 1179 (Fed. Cir. 2005).
[219] 616 F.3d 1318 (Fed. Cir. 2010) (en banc).
[220] *See Philips*, 424 F.3d at 1182, 1184.
[221] *See id.* at 1183.
[222] *See id.* at 1188–91 (distinguishing *United States v. Paramount Pictures, Inc.*, 334 U.S. 131 (1948), and *United States v. Loew's, Inc.*, 371 U.S. 38 (1962)). Cf. Cotter, *Misuse*, *supra* note 190, at 921–23 (suggesting that, whatever the policy merits of the court's decision, its reading of the two preceding cases was somewhat disingenuous).

in transaction costs.[223] In *Princo*, the alleged infringers challenged an arrangement, also involving compact discs, under which Philips and Sony agreed to include within a patent pool two Philips patents ("Raaymakers") that claimed an analog method essential to the production of standard-compliant CDs, and a Sony patent ("Lagadec") that claimed a digital method but was not widely used (and in fact could not be used to produce standard-compliant CDs). The infringement defendants argued that this arrangement constituted misuse, because the parties had agreed to include Lagadec in the pool only to suppress it from becoming a viable future alternative to Raaymakers; there also was no option to license any of the pooled patents separately.[224] The en banc majority nevertheless rejected the misuse defense, reasoning that (1) misuse arises only when a patent owner leverages a patent to impose anticompetitive conditions outside the scope of the patent grant, and not from "collateral" agreements such as the alleged agreement between Philips and Sony to suppress the use of Lagadec; (2) Philips did not leverage the Raaymakers patent, and therefore did not misuse it; and (3) in any event, there was insufficient evidence of anticompetitive effect, because the infringement defendants did not prove there was a reasonable probability that Lagadec would have matured into a viable alternative to Raaymakers.[225]

Given its rather checkered past and current narrowness, the question arises whether there is any value in retaining the patent misuse doctrine. One possible rationale is that misuse might work to deter antitrust violations that otherwise would go undetected or unremedied.[226] Using the facts of the *Princo* case as an example, suppose that Philips and Sony really did agree to suppress the Lagadec technology, despite its possible being a better technology in the long run, so that they could share the monopoly profits generated from the licensing of Raaymakers. (To avoid such possibilities, patent pools generally are advised not to include substitute technologies.[227]) Such an agreement, if proven, might be unlawful as a matter of antitrust law, but also might escape detection on the part of, or simply not interest, the antitrust enforcement agencies. (On the other hand, on the facts of *Princo* the patentees might have had a credible argument that the pool was a type of joint venture between Philips and Sony, and that a restraint inhibiting either contributor from competing against the

[223] *See Philips*, 424 F.3d at 1192–95.

[224] *See Princo*, 616 F.3d at 1303, 1305–06, 1310, 1313.

[225] *See id.* at 1328–38.

[226] *See id.* at 460–68 (discussing the "optimal deterrence of substantive antitrust violations" rationale).

[227] *See, e.g.*, U.S. Dep't of Justice & Fed. Trade Comm'n, Antitrust Guidelines for the Licensing of Intellectual Property § 5.5 (2017).

venture by promoting an alternative technology would be reasonably ancillary to the venture's purpose, and therefore lawful.[228]) Perhaps some private party would have standing to assert an antitrust claim, but that's not entirely clear either, and in any event the difficulty of quantifying their damages would present a disincentive to filing suit.[229] On this view, the misuse defense might make up for antitrust's inability to remedy some forms of anticompetitive conduct, but the question is whether this additional deterrence would be cost-justified, in light of the corresponding additional risk of false positives and administrative costs. Moreover, the better response, if antitrust enforcement is deficient, might be to amend substantive antitrust law or bolster antitrust enforcement, rather to rely on the haphazard deterrent of relying on licensees to stop paying royalties, wait to be sued, and then raise the misuse defense.

Another argument, advanced initially by Christina Bohannan,[230] is that a misuse doctrine that goes beyond antitrust might remedy "innovation harm," a concept I noted earlier in chapter 2.[231] In a sense, this may be seen as a variation on the preceding rationale, insofar as standard antitrust enforcement may not adequately respond to conduct that threatens dynamic, as opposed to static, efficiency—though in Bohannan's formulation, misuse would be more like other doctrines internal to patent law, which balance social costs and benefits by, for example, limiting the scope and duration of patent rights and establishing the appropriate conditions for the granting of patent rights. To illustrate, suppose that the alleged misuse consists of the patentee's insistence upon some Condition X in return for its agreement to license the patent in suit; and that Condition X poses *some* risk to long-term innovation, though not quite enough or not quite so clearly as to merit scrutiny under existing antitrust law. In theory, it might make sense for patent law to penalize the patent owner for insisting upon Condition X, if the risk of harm to long-term innovation, though perhaps remote, is of sufficient gravity that its prohibition justifies what may be a relatively small diminution of the value of the patent (and thus of the patent incentive). In the context of *Philips* and *Princo*, for example,

[228] *See Princo*, 616 F.3d at 1336. For analysis, *see* Christopher A. Suarez, *Look Before You "Lock": Standards, Tipping, and the Future of Patent Misuse After* Princo, 13 COLUM. SCI. & TECH. L. REV. 371, 379–81 (2012).

[229] *See* Cotter, *Four Questionable Rationales*, supra note 190, at 466–67 & nn. 37, 38.

[230] *See* Christina Bohannan, *IP Misuse as Foreclosure*, 96 IOWA L. REV. 475, 505–25 (2011); *see also* BOHANNAN & HOVENKAMP, *supra* note 212, at 288 (summarizing the authors' view that misuse be available "when an IP holder's practice threatens unreasonable foreclosure of competition, innovation, or access to the public domain," with the last of these being more relevant to the doctrine of copyright misuse); LIM, *supra* note 190, at 27 (suggesting that patent policy can take some more speculative consequences into consideration than can antitrust policy).

[231] *See* ch. 2 notes 4–20 and accompanying text.

if the misuse defense rendered the conduct challenged in those cases unlawful, this might have had little if any negative impact on the patent incentive scheme or on static efficiency, while at the same time it might—albeit somewhat speculatively—have provided a greater incentive for implementers to develop better technological alternatives to the nonessential licensed patents (in *Philips*), or uses for an existing, but nascent, alternative (*Princo*).[232] That said, it remains to be seen how courts could be sufficiently confident that the conditions under which application of the misuse defense would increase long-term innovation, or more generally improve long-term social welfare, were in place.[233] As noted above, the block booking at issue in *Philips* and the alleged agreement at issue in *Princo* both might have increased both short- and long-term welfare, by in the first case decreasing the transaction costs of licensing, and in the second by precluding a joint venturer from undermining the purpose of the venture by licensing a potentially rival technology. Chalk that uncertainty up against the uncertain future harm resulting from the inclusion of nonessential patents in a package, or from the alleged suppression of what might (or might not) have been a viable future technology, and there would seem to be a substantial margin of error in the application of the doctrine.

To be sure, nothing in the preceding analysis rules out the possibility that it might be desirable for courts to be able to make use of the misuse doctrine in some, perhaps unforeseeable, cases in which it *is* possible to be reasonably confident that the risk of the challenged condition harming competition and/or future innovation outweighs any short-term benefits or any negative impacts on the patent incentive. More generally, having a safety valve available for rare cases may not be a bad idea—and in this sense, at least, misuse might be likened to the civil law's abuse of right doctrine.[234] Using Lèonard's framework, for example, one might imagine the misuse doctrine operating to preclude enforcement in cases in which the owner's exercise of its rights would undermine the underlying purpose of those rights: perhaps, by way of some hypothetical possibilities, in cases in which the owner uses its patent to prevent a third party from accessing a patented invention to assess its quality, or

[232] *See* Bohannan, *supra* note 230, at 510–15.

[233] Bohannan suggests what would appear to be a balancing approach, *see id.* at 511 (stating, with regard to arrangements like that in *Princo*, that courts may need to "weigh any evidence of foreclosure against the offsetting benefits to innovation of allowing the package license"), but I'm not sure exactly how courts would do this—or, alternatively, if they could, why the anticipated harm to dynamic innovation doesn't count as antitrust harm, but rather requires a separate misuse doctrine.

[234] *But see* Reto M. Hilty, *Legal Remedies Against Abuse, Misuse, and Other Forms of Inappropriate Conduct of IP Right Holders*, *in* Compulsory Licensing: Practical Experiences and Ways Forward 377, 380 (Reto M. Hilty & Kung-Chung Liu eds. 2015) (suggesting that "abuse" "has a stronger negative connotation" than "misuse").

sues to remedy the breach of a post-sale restraint on use or resale that otherwise would be permitted under the exhaustion doctrine. (Whether there are any such cases within the abuse of right case law, I do not know.) Absent other facts, however, it's doubtful that the misuse defense as currently applied would prevent the patent owner from enforcing its patent against an unlicensed party in the first example, given that prohibiting the unauthorized use of the invention falls squarely within the scope of the grant. Conceivably, if the patentee included a no-quality-assessment provision in a *license*, that provision might constitute misuse that would render the patent unenforceable against both licensee and third parties—but this would require finding that control over a licensee's ability to engage in quality assessment falls outside the scope of the patent grant *and* oversteps the rule of reason, and seems unlikely to succeed under current law.[235] If prohibiting a restraint like this is desirable, then, perhaps what the U.S. needs is not a misuse doctrine but something more akin to an abuse of right doctrine (or to copyright law's fair use doctrine, as others have suggested[236])—or perhaps better yet, legislation expressly exempting certain unauthorized uses that Congress deems to be social welfare-enhancing. (Many countries, for example, provide a broad exemption for experimental uses, but in the U.S. such uses, other than when "reasonably related to the development and submission of information" to the Food and Drug Administration,[237] are almost always unlawful.[238] It is often argued that the U.S. rule is suboptimal.[239]) As for the second example, now that the U.S. Supreme Court has ruled that the exhaustion doctrine precludes patent infringement claims premised upon breach of post-sale restraints on use or resale, but at the same time does not preclude liability under contract law,[240] a successful misuse defense would have to show that the restraint not only somehow extends the patent's scope but also violates misuse doctrine's ill-defined rule of reason—no small order if, as will usually be the case, there is no plausible antitrust claim against the restraint.[241] Conversely, if exhaustion doctrine did *not* preclude litigating

[235] For discussion, *see* Brenda M. Simon, *Patent Cover-Up*, 47 Hous. L. Rev. 1299 (2011).

[236] *See* Maureen A. O'Rourke, *Toward a Doctrine of Fair Use in Patent Law*, 100 Colum. L. Rev. 1177 (2000).

[237] 35 U.S.C. § 271(e)(1).

[238] See Madey v. Duke Univ., 307 F.3d 1351, 1362 (Fed. Cir. 2002) (stating that "so long as the act is in furtherance of the alleged infringer's legitimate business and is not solely for amusement, to satisfy idle curiosity, or for strictly philosophical inquiry, the act does not qualify for the very narrow and strictly limited experimental use defense").

[239] See, e.g., Katherine J. Strandburg, *What Does the Public Get? Experimental Use and the Patent Bargain*, 2004 Wis. L. Rev. 81.

[240] *See* Impression Prods., Inc. v. Lexmark Int'l, Inc., 581 U.S. 360, 373–74 (2017).

[241] *Cf.* Herbert J. Hovenkamp, *Post-Sale Restraints and Competitive Harm*, 67 N.Y.U. Ann. Surv. Am. L. 487, 521 (2011) (stating that "[i]f post-sale restraints serve potentially valuable functions and the

violations of post-sale restraints as acts of patent infringement—as the Federal Circuit understood the law to be prior to 2017[242]—the enforcement of the patent in such a situation might seem even more likely to fall within the scope of the grant, such that misuse would have little role to play in this situation either, under the three-step formula.[243]

In any event, if misuse is to play any useful role going forward, there are at least two reforms that might help to make its application more rational. The first would be for legislative guidance on the circumstances under which the misuse doctrine should apply. If deterring innovation harm that is not cognizable under antitrust law is to be the rationale, for example, it might be helpful for the legislature to spell that out and to provide criteria for determining how courts should evaluate proffered evidence of such harm. (Oddly enough, the only provision of the U.S. Patent Act that expressly references misuse—§ 271(d)—only defines what it is not.[244]) Second, it may be worth considering if unenforceability should always, or even usually, be the appropriate penalty for engaging in misuse. In previous work, I have suggested that unenforceability of the contractual provision giving rise to the finding of misuse would, in general, be a more proportionate sanction than unenforceability of the patent,[245]

only objection . . . is that they can take subsequent users or purchasers by surprise, a notice requirement seems much more suitable to the problem than the more draconian route of forbidding such restraints altogether").

242 *See* Mallinckrodt, Inc. v. Medipart, Inc., 976 F.2d 700, 709 (Fed. Cir. 1992). The court in *Mallinckrodt* nevertheless remanded for determination whether a restriction on post-sale use was "reasonably within the scope of the grant," *see id.* at 703, after which (I believe) the case settled.

243 Another possible example of patent misuse, according to Bohannan and Hovenkamp, might arise in connection with "reach-through" royalty agreements, under which "royalties are based not on the use of the patented technology directly but on products that result from the technology," though the authors concede that "it is not clear that many reach-through royalty agreements are, on balance, bad for innovation given their potential procompetitive consequences). BOHANNAN & HOVENKAMP, *supra* note 212, at 283, 285. *See also* Marshall Leaffer, *Patent Misuse and Innovation*, 10 J. HIGH TECH. L. 142, 161–62 (2010) (suggesting that exclusive grantbacks can be a form of misuse, because of their potential to undermine subsequent innovation). One other possible use of the misuse doctrine might be as an affirmative defense against vexatious litigation, insofar as *Noerr-Pennington* immunity does not apply to affirmative defenses as it would to antitrust claims premised on sham litigation. For discussion, *see* LIM, *supra* note 190, at 137 (citing *Int'l Motor Contest Ass'n v. Staley*, 434 F. Supp. 2d 650, 663 (N.D. Iowa 2006)).

244 *See* 35 U.S.C. § 271(d), previously cited in notes 206, 210–11 and accompanying text.

245 *See* Cotter, *Misuse*, *supra* note 190, at 960–61; *see also* BOHANNAN & HOVENKAMP, *supra* note 212, at 279, 282 (suggesting that, in the context of package licensing, "when there is no justification for packaging and a likelihood of foreclosure, the court should simply enjoin the package and require nondiscriminatory separate licensing," because "complete nonenforcement of the IP right . . . is too draconian," and similarly for the type of conduct at issue in *Princo*); LIM, *supra* note 190, at 199 (finding a "strong consensus that patent misuse needs to be better calibrated"); Bohannan, *supra* note 230, at 515 (suggesting that, where "a patent holder cannot justify the challenged license restriction but the court is unsure whether it would harm innovation, a court should find misuse but not hold the patent unenforceable").

though (for better or worse) the latter carries greater deterrent value.[246] At the very least, I would argue, courts should have greater discretion than they currently do to consider the lesser penalty.

Estoppel, Laches, Double Patenting, and Discretionary Stays or Denials of Equitable Relief

My approach to the topics addressed in this subsection—the equitable defenses of estoppel and laches; the (sometimes described, perhaps more colloquially than technically, as equitable) doctrine of obviousness-type double patenting; and discretionary stays or denials of equitable relief—is to present them primarily[247] as tools for restraining plaintiffs from exercising "holdup." Although holdup is a concept I have touched upon in other portions of this book and this chapter, its centrality to this subsection requires that I now define the term more clearly.

As discussed in a 2019 paper I published with Erik Hovenkamp and Norman Siebrasse,[248] the economic concept of holdup can be traced to work published beginning in the 1970s, by Nobel laureate Oliver Williamson and others, addressing the topic of opportunism in the context of long-term bilateral contracts.[249] As Williamson observed, "[t]ransactions that are supported by investments in durable, transaction-specific assets experience 'lock-in' effects" (or "asset specificity"), which in turn makes such investments "risky, in that specialized assets cannot be redeployed without sacrifice of productive value if contracts should be interrupted or prematurely terminated."[250] Further,

[246] *Cf.* Sean B. Seymore, *Patent Forfeiture*, 72 Duke L.J. 1019 (2023) (proposing that the various equitable defenses be bundled into one, and that upon proof of a violation the patent would, as under current misuse law, be rendered unenforceable but subject to reinstatement in the event of discontinuation and dissipation of effects).

[247] Primarily, but not exclusively. Courts in common-law countries sometimes may invoke the public interest as a reason for staying or denying injunctive relief, for example in cases involving life-saving drugs or medical devices. That rationale, which depending on the circumstances also might justify, where available, resort to compulsory licensing, is distinct from the holdup rationale discussed above.

[248] *Demystifying Patent Holdup*, 76 Wash. & Lee L. Rev. 1501 (2019), from which portions of the above are adapted. For a more comprehensive, and technical, discussion, the reader is advised to consult that paper and the sources cited therein.

[249] *See, e.g.*, Oliver E. Williamson, The Economic Institutions of Capitalism: Firms, Markets, Relational Contracting ch. 2 (1985); Victor P. Goldberg, *Regulation and Administered Contracts*, 7 Bell J. Econ. 426, 439–41 (1976); Benjamin Klein et al., *Vertical Integration, Appropriable Rents, and the Competitive Contracting Process*, 21 J.L. & Econ. 297 (1978); Oliver Hart, *Incomplete Contracts*, in 2 The New Palgrave: A Dictionary of Economics 752 (John Eatwell, Murray Milgate & Peter Newman eds. 1987); Benjamin Klein, *Why Hold-Ups Occur: The Self-Enforcing Range of Contractual Relationships*, 34 Econ. Inquiry 444 (1996); Oliver Williamson, *The Vertical Integration of Production: Market Failure Considerations*, 61 Am. Econ. Rev. 112 (1971).

[250] Williamson, *supra* note 249, at 52–54.

because it is costly, indeed impossible, to draft contracts addressing all possible future contingencies, each party to a long-term contract, despite having "a long-term interest in effecting adaptations of a joint profit-maximizing kind . . . also has an interest in appropriating as much of the gain as he can on each occasion to adapt"[251]—in other words, "holding up" the other for whatever short-term gains it can extract, e.g., by means of contractual renegotiations during the course of a long-term relationship. The risk of being held up, in turn, can cause parties to dissipate some of the gains from trade through haggling, monitoring, and demanding risk premiums to compensate for the future risk of being held up; or even deter some otherwise mutually beneficial transactions from going forward at all. An ongoing challenge, therefore, for the parties (and potentially for lawmakers), is to develop institutional responses that can minimize the risk of socially inefficient opportunism.[252]

The extension of the holdup concept to patent policy came some years later, with the most important contribution being Carl Shapiro's 2001 paper *Navigating the Patent Thicket: Cross Licenses, Patent Pools, and Standard Setting*.[253] Shapiro illustrated the concept of "patent holdup" with an example of a manufacturer who "could, with ease, invent around a given patent, if that manufacturer were aware of the patent and afforded sufficient lead time," in which "case the patented technology contributes little if anything to the final product, and any reasonable royalty would be modest at best."[254] (The assertion that, in such a case, the patented technology contributed little to the final product and that a royalty would be "modest" is consistent with the mainstream view among economists that the value of a technology to a prospective user is the incremental benefit the user expects to derive from the technology in comparison with the next-best alternative; that a royalty negotiated ex ante would reflect some portion of this value; and that, at least as a first approximation, royalties awarded in litigation also should reflect the user's expected incremental benefit.[255]) Problems may arise ex post, however, if the unaware manufacturer "has already designed its product and placed it into large scale production before the patent issues," because the patent owner now "can credibly seek far greater royalties, very likely backed up with the threat of shutting down the manufacturer if the Court indeed finds the patent valid and infringed and grants injunctive relief."[256] Shapiro's analysis identified three distinct

251 *Id.* at 63.
252 *See* Cotter, Hovenkamp & Siebrasse, *supra* note 248, at 1515–17.
253 1 INNOVATION POLICY AND THE ECONOMY 119 (Adam B. Jaffe et al. eds. 2001).
254 *Id.* at 125.
255 *See* Cotter, Hovenkamp & Siebrasse, *supra* note 248, at 1519 & n.70.
256 Shapiro, *supra* note 253, at 125.

sources that would contribute to these higher royalties, the first being the past (sunk) cost that the manufacturer has incurred to "design[] its product and place[] it into large scale production" prior to being made aware of the existence of the patent. As my coauthors and I have observed, "[t]o the extent these past or 'sunk' costs cannot be redeployed to produce a noninfringing product, they are, to use Williamson's terminology, 'asset-specific' and therefore capable of generating lock-in effects."[257] More precisely, "if the patent holder can credibly demand to enjoin the use of the infringing technology ex post, the manufacturer often would be better off agreeing to pay a royalty that exceeds the technology's ex ante value, rather than to write off those asset-specific sunk costs," which can thought of as a type of investment, as a loss.[258] The second potential source of patent holdup that Shapiro identified, the cost of redesigning a noninfringing product, is in our understanding the ex post *cost* of switching to an alternative technology at a higher price than would have been incurred ex ante.[259] Ex post, the manufacturer would pay some amount x to avoid incurring this higher incremental cost. The third source, which Shapiro referred to as "compatibility problems," we (following other analysts) identify as the loss of ex post *benefits*, potentially including network benefits, the manufacturer would have earned from using the patented technology in comparison with the next-best alternative.[260] Ex post, the manufacturer would pay some amount y to avoid forgoing these incrementally higher benefits. In the case of SEPs in particular, y may be enormous, if (as may well be the case) the benefits to be earned from using an alternative to the standardized technology are nil.

To state the matter in formal terms, my coauthors and I presented a model under which an implementer is considering two technologies (1 and 2), the first of which is patented but also superior to the alternative, in that the ex ante expected profit from its use is greater than the ex ante expected profit from the alternative.[261] If the implementer and patentee bargained ex ante, the maximal fee the patentee could charge would be

$$F^A = \pi_1 - k_1 - [\pi_2 - k_2],$$

[257] Cotter, Hovenkamp & Siebrasse, *supra* note 248, at 1520.

[258] *Id.* at 1521.

[259] *See id.* at 1524. If the ex post cost of switching to the alternative is the same as it would have been ex ante, however, that cost does not contribute to holdup, "since the user would have faced the very same calculus had the parties negotiated ex ante." *Id.*

[260] *See id.* at 1524–26 (citing, *inter alia*, Joseph Farrell et al., *Standard Setting, Patents, and Hold-up*, 74 ANTITRUST L.J. 603, 616 (2007)).

[261] For a more detailed exposition, *see* Cotter, Hovenkamp & Siebrasse, *supra* note 248, at 1529–33, 1562–65.

where π_1 and k_1 and the expected revenue and cost, respectively, of implementing technology 1, and π_2 and k_2 the expected revenue and cost of implementing technology 2. If the implementer has chosen technology 1 ex ante, however, the maximal fee the patentee could obtain through ex post negotiations is

$$F^P = \pi_1 - [\pi_{2|1} - k_{2|1}],$$

where $\pi_{2|1}$ is the ex post revenue expected to be earned from technology 2, given that the implementer has previously chosen technology 1, and $k_{2|1}$ is the ex post cost of implementing technology 2 given that the implementer has previously chosen technology 1. The maximum holdup rent the patentee can extract ex post therefore is the difference between $\mathcal{F}^A$ and $\mathcal{F}^P$, that is, the increase in the implementer's willingness to pay for a license when licensing terms are not negotiated until ex post:

$$\mathrm{H} = k_1 + \Delta\pi_2 + \Delta k_2,$$

where $\Delta\pi_2 \equiv \pi_2 - \pi_{2|1}$ *and* $\Delta k_2 \equiv k_{2|1} - k_2$. Translating this into English, the first term k_1 is the nonredeployable sunk cost of having invested, ex ante, in technology 1, while the second and third terms "reflect potential opportunity costs of adopting technology 2 ex post rather than ex ante."[262] More specifically, $\Delta\pi_2$ is the ex post higher incremental cost, and Δk_2 is the ex post lower incremental benefit, of adopting technology 2. Summarizing, the maximum holdup rent the patentee can extract ex post is the sum of the nonredeployable sunk costs invested in technology 1; the difference if any between the ex post and ex ante cost of implementing technology 2; and the difference if any between ex ante and ex post benefit of implementing technology 2. Crucially, given the assumption that the maximum royalty for the use of technology 1 should be no greater than F^A, holdup is socially inefficient for two reasons: "because the risk of being held up ex post may induce implementers to forgo otherwise productive investments, and because the holdup portion of the royalty exceeds the value of the patent over the state of the art."[263]

262 *Id.* at 1532.

263 Cotter, *supra* note 73, at 299 & n.26 (citing Norman V. Siebrasse & Thomas F. Cotter, *The Value of the Standard*, 101 MINN. L. REV. 1159, 1183–90 (2017), and suggesting further that "the extraction of unwarranted rents may be exacerbated in systems such as Germany's, where infringement and validity proceedings are bifurcated, and the latter take longer to resolve").

In theory, then, there is an argument for limiting injunctive relief—and other potentially supracompensatory remedies, such as excessive compensatory damages or the disgorgement of the infringer's profits—in cases in which there is a risk of holdup.[264] (Returning to a theme from earlier in this chapter, one could say that, in such cases, the royalty extracted by the patentee is disproportionate to the appropriate baseline.) Of course, just because there is a theoretical case for the proposition that patent owners sometimes may be able to extract ex post holdup rents does not prove (1) that patent owners invariably do so,[265] or (2) that courts can accurately perceive if or when the risk of, and consequences resulting from, holdup are substantial enough to outweigh the advantages of injunctions,[266] or (3) that implementers can never avoid being held up by negotiating in advance,[267] or (4) that staying or denying injunctive relief in preference to awarding court-determined royalties would avoid

For an illustrative example of holdup attributable to sunk costs, consider the facts of *Riles v. Shell Expl. & Prod. Co.*, 298 F.3d 1302 (Fed. Cir. 2002), in which Shell was found to have infringed Riles' patent on a method for installing the foundation for an oil drilling platform. Shell's evidence suggested that the ex ante value of the invention over alternative nonpatented methods was about $350,000, but Shell had subsequently built a platform on top of the foundation at a cost of $84 million. Had the court enjoined Shell from using the platform—or awarded a royalty reflecting what Shell would have been willing to pay if it had been enjoined, which is what Riles was requesting—the royalty Shell would have had to pay would have vastly exceeded the ex ante value of the invention. *See* Cotter, Hovenkamp & Siebrasse, *supra* note 248, at 1533–35.

[264] In common-law countries such as the U.K. and Canada, an award of the infringer's profits is in fact considered an equitable remedy, and is therefore discretionary rather than as of right. *See, e.g.*, Nova Chems. Corp. v. Dow Chem. Co., [2022] SCC 43, ¶109 (Can.); Hollister Inc. v. Medik Ostomy Supplies Ltd., [2012] EWCA Civ 1419, [55] (Eng.) (trademark case). In the U.S., Congress eliminated the disgorgement remedy for utility patents in 1946, though it continues to be available for design patent infringement—and does not appear to be discretionary, even though it may still qualify as an equitable remedy. *See* J.R. Simplot Co. v. McCain Foods USA, Inc., Case No. 1:16-cv-00449, 2024 WL 3796737, at *1–2 (D. Idaho Aug. 13, 2024) (recognizing a split of authority among the courts on whether, under U.S. law, an award of the infringer's profits for design patent infringement is an equitable remedy, for which there would be no constitutional right to trial by jury).

[265] Even without expecting owners to act altruistically, it may be the case that some are constrained by the reputational consequences that might follow from overreaching, especially if they are repeat players and/or are themselves both licensors and licensees. *See, e.g.*, Cotter, Hovenkamp & Siebrasse, *supra* note 248, at 1515.

[266] In general, protecting entitlements by means of so-called "property" rules (injunctive relief) promises two principal advantages: they encourage private bargaining, which may reduce the cost of adjudication; and the parties may have better information than would a court or other third party as to the value of the right at issue. In contrast, protecting entitlements by means of "liability" rules (damages) requires courts to determine value, and because they are at an information disadvantage in comparison with the parties they may err. On the other hand, liability rules may be preferable when there is reason to believe that private bargaining will fail, due to the presence of transaction costs or other impediments, or will fail to reflect important third-party interests. For discussion, see, e.g., Cotter, *supra* note 73, at 293–97 (relying primarily on the foundational analysis in Guido Calabresi & A. Douglas Melamed, *Property Rules, Liability Rules, and Inalienability: One View of the Cathedral*, 85 Harv. L. Rev. 1089, 1092 (1972)).

[267] Particularly in cases in involving complex products, which may incorporate hundreds of patented features, timely clearance in advance of product launch may be unattainable. For discussion, see, e.g., William F. Lee & A. Douglas Melamed, *Breaking the Vicious Cycle of Patent Damages*, 101 Cornell L. Rev. 385, 404–09 (2016).

generating worse problems, including opportunistic conduct on the part of implementers (referred to as "holdout"),[268] or a reduction in innovation incentives if courts routinely award undercompensatory damages.[269] Unfortunately, there is no decisive empirical evidence substantiating or refuting any of these propositions,[270] and reasonable minds therefore may differ on the issue of whether courts should have discretion to stay or deny injunctive relief, specifically to avoid holdup—though there is an accumulating body of evidence that, at least in the United States, the Supreme Court's decision in *eBay Inc. v. MercExchange, L.L.C.*,[271] which authorized courts to deny injunctive relief in

[268] Implementers may strategically delay negotiating, for example, if they believe that court-awarded damages—including prejudgment interest, which may be set below the owner's internal rate of return on capital, or (in some countries) may be discretionary or not subject to compounding—would not fully compensate the patentee for the time value of money; or if the owner needs ready access to capital to satisfy shareholders or creditors; or if, as suggested in *Optis Cellular Tech. LLC v Apple Retail UK Ltd.*, [2021] EWHC 2564, [236]–[244] (Pat.) (Eng.), delay induces owners to "discount the royalties/damages for past acts" or encourage other implementers to hold out. The difficulty, of course, lies in distinguishing such strategic behavior from the good faith refusal to accede to unreasonable terms, in view of the patent's likely validity and value.

[269] *See* Cotter, *supra* note 73, at 295–96, 300 (stating that "[o]n one view, if courts are vested with responsibility for valuing patents but are incapable of doing so with any degree of accuracy, the patent incentive scheme will be distorted," though "if judicial errors are random and, in the aggregate, cancel out, there may be no particular reason to worry about the effect of such errors distorting the patent incentive by either over- or under-stimulating the invention of new technologies;" that "[t]he possibility that damages are systematically undercompensatory might arise, however, if the damages methodologies courts use are unsound, or if the rules of procedure do not provide an effective means for determining the extent of the infringer's use of the invention"; and that the social harm resulting from valuation error may be greater in industries for which the patent incentive is a significant driver of innovation than for industries for which it is not).

[270] *See* Cotter, Hovenkamp & Siebrasse, *supra* note 248, at 1546–53. Studies that might be interpreted as showing that holdup is rampant in disputes over FRAND-committed SEPs, because in cases in which courts have awarded FRAND royalties they often have been substantially lower than SEP owner demands, *see, e.g.*, Jorge L. Contreras, *Much Ado About Hold-Up*, 2019 U. ILL. L. REV. 875, 888–92 (2019), or conversely that holdout is rampant because (predominantly German) courts often find implementers to be unwilling licensees, *see* Kirti Gupta & Urŝka Petrovčič, *Evidence of Systematic "Patent Holdout"*, 38 BERKELEY TECH. L.J. 575 (2023), are interesting but not dispositive, since (aside from leading to contradictory results) they depend on the courts' decisions in the relevant cases being accurate, which itself cannot be proven. Indeed, as Lemley and Shapiro have noted, the only way one could empirically determine the extent to which real-world licenses reflect holdup value would be to compare actual licenses (which are often not publicly available) with the ex ante value of the licensed technology (which is a non-observable counterfactual). *See* Mark A. Lemley & Carl Shapiro, *The Role of Antitrust in Preventing Patent Holdup*, 168 U. PENN. L. REV. 2019, 2030–31, 2039–40 (2020). Lemley and Shapiro argue, however, that the fact that companies in the high-technology sector "have overwhelmingly turned to SSOs in an effort to obtain global commitments to an ex ante royalty, which appear in the form of FRAND commitments" provides "strong evidence that companies view holdup as a problem they must build institutions to avoid." *See id.* at 2042. The argument that holdup cannot be "systemic" or "pervasive" in the telecommunications industry because otherwise that industry would not have made the astonishing progress it has achieved over the past generation is similarly interesting, but even if true hardly proves that holdup is never a problem, *see* Cotter, Hovenkamp & Siebrasse, *supra* note 248, at 1547, or that progress would not have been even faster absent holdup, *see* Lemley & Shapiro, *supra*, at 2040–41—and could just as easily be taken as evidence that the U.S. (and, I would add, U.K.) courts' disinclination to grant injunctive relief in SEP cases has prevented holdup from becoming systematic or pervasive, *see* Lemley & Shapiro, *supra*, at 2045–46.

[271] 547 U.S. 388 (2006).

a larger proportion of cases than previously, has on net promoted, rather than retarded, innovation.[272] That said, there may be no universally optimal practice, given the very different legal environments in which patent disputes are litigated. In countries with comparatively little discovery or tolerance for using damages experts, and aside from fee awards few if any tools, such as enhanced damages, for penalizing bad-faith infringers,[273] it is at least understandable that courts would be reluctant to deviate from the near-mandatory issuance of permanent injunctions—whereas in common-law countries such as the United States and the United Kingdom, courts are less hesitant to stay or deny injunctions, and to award ongoing royalties in lieu.

That said, the standards common law courts consider in deciding whether to exercise their discretion to stay or deny injunctive relief align only imperfectly with the factors that would be indicative of holdup. In the U.K., the courts are advised to stay or deny injunctive relief if granting the injunction would cause the defendant to suffer "grossly disproportionate" harm,[274] whereas in the U.S. the *eBay* decision states that to warrant an injunction the patentee "must demonstrate: (1) that it has suffered an irreparable injury; (2) that remedies available at law, such as monetary damages, are inadequate to compensate for that injury; (3) that, considering the balance of hardships between the plaintiff and defendant, a remedy in equity is warranted; and (4) that the public interest would not be disserved by a permanent injunction."[275] Although both standards rightly permit a court to award injunctive relief in favor of a practicing entity whose interest lies in exclusivity (in the U.S., because such an entity would be faced with irreparable harm if the defendant were permitted to continue using the patented technology, and an ongoing royalty likely would be inadequate to compensate for the loss of exclusivity), neither standard on its

[272] *See* Samuel Antill et al., *The Efficiency of Patent Litigation*, Jan. 21, 2025, https://papers.ssrn.com/sol3/papers.cfm?abstract_id= 4842424 (estimating the impact of "defendant-friendly reforms" such as limitations on injunctive relief as "improving welfare by up to 3.29%"); Filippo Mezzanotti, *Roadblock to Innovation: The Role of Patent Litigation in Corporate R&D*, 67 Mgmt. Sci. 7362 (2021) (concluding that *eBay* has had a positive impact on R&D spending by established firms). *See also* Fred Bereskin, Po-Hsuan Hsu & Huijun Wang, *Growth of Firms under Injunction Risk*, July 31, 2023, https://papers.ssrn.com/sol3/papers.cfm?abstract_id=4281493; Christian Helmers & Brian J. Love, *Patent Law Reform and Innovation: An Empirical Assessment of the Last 20 Years*, Oct. 19, 2023, https://ssrn.com/abstract=4580645; Filippo Mezzanotti & Timothy Simcoe, *Patent Policy and American Innovation After eBay: An Empirical Examination*, 48 Rsch. Pol'y 1271 (2019) (finding no reduction in innovation attributable to *eBay*).

[273] Although in cases in which the infringer's profit exceeds the plaintiff's own lost profits or lost royalties, one might think that the prospect of an award of that profit would have much the same deterrent effect as a possible award of enhanced damages.

[274] For discussion of the relevant case law, *see, e.g.*, Lionel Bently & Sir Richard Arnold, *United Kingdom*, *in* Injunctions in Patent Law: Trans-Atlantic Dialogues on Flexibility and Tailoring 261, 271–75 (Jorge L. Contreras & Martin Husovec eds. 2022).

[275] *eBay*, 547 U.S. at 391.

face provides guidance for determining whether the risk of holdup is substantial enough to warrant a stay or denial of injunctive relief in cases in which the patentee is willing—and perhaps, as in the case of some nonpracticing entities, *only*—able to license others to use the technology.

One way in which the law might improve would be for courts to expressly take into account factors that would be suggestive of the risk of holdup, in deciding whether to grant or deny injunctive relief. These might include the infringer's ex ante knowledge, or lack thereof, of the patent in suit; the presence of market forces necessitating a speedy product launch; the approximate number of patented features incorporated into the infringer's product; and any other evidence suggesting that the ex post royalty the parties would negotiate to avoid an injunction substantially exceeds the ex ante value.[276] Elsewhere, I also have suggested that courts could develop manageable heuristics for deciding when the social costs of injunctive relief would outweigh the social benefits, and have specifically proposed that—aside from cases involving compulsory licensing in the public interest—courts should (1) grant injunctions when the probability of holdup is low;[277] (2) deny injunctions when the probability of holdup is high, and the expected cost of valuation errors, based upon empirical evidence of the importance of the patent incentive in the industry sector at issue, is likely low to moderate;[278] and (3) when the matter is indeterminate, grant injunctions subject to stays.[279] At the practical level, this approach would counsel in favor of

[276] *See, e.g.*, Cotter, Hovenkamp & Siebrasse, supra note 248, at 1523 (also noting, however, that "if courts routinely deny injunctions based on the risk of sunk costs holdup, the incentive on the part of implementers to come up with ways of discovering and clearing the necessary rights in advance may be reduced—particularly if the damages courts award in lieu of injunctions are below the ex ante amount, due to error costs, or are otherwise undercompensatory"); Mark A. Lemley & Carl Shapiro, *Patent Holdup and Royalty Stacking*, 85 TEX. L. REV. 1991, 1992 (2007).

[277] *See* Cotter, *supra* note 73, at 303–05 (suggesting that "if the accused product embodies relatively few potentially patented features," or the defendant refused "to bargain in good faith prior to product launch," the court should probably find "that the probability of holdup was low"; but that "if transaction costs *were* high, the further finding that the defendant incurred substantial nonsalvageable sunk costs (or higher ex post switching costs, or lower ex post network benefits) would indicate both a high probability of, and substantial harm resulting from, holdup").

[278] *See id.* at 302–03, 305–06 (noting, *inter alia*, that "[s]urvey evidence . . . indicates that the patent incentive is most important in industries such as pharmaceuticals, medical devices and chemicals, and that in other fields patents play a lesser role in enabling firms to appropriate a return on research and development") (indirectly citing, *inter alia*, Wesley M. Cohen et al., *Protecting Their Intellectual Assets: Appropriability Conditions and Why U.S. Manufacturing Firms Patent (or Not)* (Nat'l Bureau Econ. Res., Working Paper No. 7552, 2000), http://www.nber.org/papers/w7552, and Bronwyn H. Hall & Dietmar Harhoff, *Recent Research on the Economics of Patents* 12–15 (Nat'l Bureau Econ. Res., Working Paper No. 1773, 2012), http://www.nber.org/papers/w17773).

[279] *See id.* at 306–07. By contrast, Lee and Melamed propose that, in view of the difficulty manufacturers often face of clearing all rights in advance of product launch, especially in cases involving complex products, courts should grant injunctions only in cases in which the patentee is an unwilling licensor (because its business model depends upon exclusivity); that in the subset of such cases in which the infringer is "innocent," meaning that it could not "cost-effectively have avoided infringement by negotiating a license ex ante," injunctive relief should be conditional on the patentee's obligation to

denying or at least staying injunctive relief in a fairly broad range of cases, including those involving SEPs (and complex products generally), albeit subject to consideration of whether the defendant has attempted to extract some benefit from strategic delay. Whether any courts will be willing to depart so far from more traditional, formal legal analysis, however, remains to be seen.

In any event, many other commentators, particularly in Europe's civil law jurisdictions, remain unpersuaded of the wisdom of according judges greater discretion to award ongoing monetary relief in lieu of injunctions, either for practical reasons (including skepticism that judges can accurately determine the appropriate royalties[280]), or legal reasons, including disagreement over the significance and/or proper application of the proportionality concept as articulated in the Intellectual Property Rights Enforcement Directive. Although some have argued in favor of an interpretation of proportionality that would confer upon judges limited discretion to dispense with injunctive relief, along the British model,[281] as noted above others have argued that domestic law adequately takes proportionality into account, without the need for independent

pay the infringer's design-around costs; and that in the subset of cases involving willing licensors and "guilty" infringers, courts should award enhanced damages, rather than injunctive relief, to penalize the infringer's failure to negotiate. *See* Lee & Melamed, *supra* note 267, at 404–11, 441–64. One problem with this approach, however—aside from the fact that, as with my proposed approach as well, it might require courts to undertake complex inquiries into the cost-effectiveness of preclearance search, as the authors acknowledge—is that it would eliminate the property-rule-associated social benefit of economizing on information costs, *see supra* note 267, even in cases in which holdup is not a serious ex ante risk. (It also might require some change to the law of enhanced damages, as it currently exists in the United States, to ensure that such damages would be available as a fallback.) Expanding on this theme, Siebrasse et al. argue that a bright-line rule precluding willing licensors from injunctive relief would cut too broadly:

> Even patentees who might be characterized as "willing licensors" can suffer noncompensable harm. For one, even if a patentee is an indiscriminate licensor whose typical or desired licensing arrangement is in the nature of a bare lump-sum payment or running royalty, equity has commonly recognized that uncertainty about the proper value of damages (such as a reasonable royalty) and courts' common lack of aptitude in price setting mean that monetary awards are an inadequate replacement for the capacity to license on privately agreed terms or not to license at all. In addition, patent licenses are often structured in ways that channel licensee behavior, whether by explicitly limiting what a licensee may do or by providing incentives for licensees to meet certain goals. Monetary awards for past infringement necessarily fail to replicate such structure, and ongoing royalties generally lack them as well. Further, an attempt to replicate such more complicated arrangements between unwilling partners and through a court order might be problematic for all sides and could upset a more targeted licensing program Finally, at least where the relevant patentees are business entities, patents are fundamentally held only to make money and, consequently, a so-called willing licensor is not so distinct from a supposedly "unwilling licensor" or competitor in terms of its ability to be satisfied with a large enough money payment.

Siebrasse et al., *supra* note 87, at 151–52.

280 *See, e.g.*, Peter Meier-Beck, *Should the Unified Patent Court Set FRAND Terms?*, 74 GRUR INT. 342, 348–49 (2025) (making this argument in the context of FRAND royalties in particular).

281 *See, e.g.*, Ansgar Ohly, *Injunctions in the UPC and the principle of proportionality*, STOCKHOLM INTELL. PROP. L. REV. 58 (2022). The British model is more favorable to patent owners than the U.S. *eBay* standard, in that injunctive relief remains the default remedy, subject to (as noted above) the defendant proving that an injunction would cause "grossly disproportionate" harm.

application.[282] German courts in particular have not shown much sympathy for arguments in favor of proportionality as a meaningful limitation on injunctive relief, even after a 2019 amendment to Germany's patent law explicitly permits them to do so in cases in which enforcement would cause disproportionate hardship to the defendant or third parties.[283]

Other European commentators envisage a meaningful role for proportionality as a check upon injunctive relief, albeit in a much more limited manner than in the United States. Léon Dijkman, for example, argues that courts are not well-positioned to engage in balancing the benefits and costs of injunctive relief in patent cases—and that E.U. legislators did not expect them to do so, either,[284] even though they did intend for proportionality to be a free-standing limitation on injunctive relief, distinct from whatever limitations are imposed by the abuse of dominant position and abuse of right doctrines.[285] Dijkman's principal concern therefore is that limitations on injunctive relief should be meaningful, but also susceptible to objective analysis and not so far-reaching that they deprive the patentee of an "effective sphere of exclusivity" that is "commensurate with the patent's contribution to the state of the art."[286] The this end, he argues that courts should prevent patentees from engaging in "overreach" by recognizing a rebuttable presumption in favor of staying injunctive relief for a reasonable period of time, but only if the infringer proves that the invention "is not indispensable for the core functionality of the products falling

[282] *See supra* note 13.

[283] *See* 2d Patent Law Modernization Act (Patentrechtmodernisierungsgesetz, 2.PatMoG), art. 36 (amending German Patent Act § 139). The amendment codifies the holding of the Federal Supreme Court in Judgment of 10 May 2016, X ZR 114/13—*Wärmetauscher*, which while denying the requested stay of injunctive relief recognized that stays were in principle permissible in cases of disproportionate harm. Thus far, however, the German courts have not seen fit to exercise such authority. (On the other hand, in one recent decision the Unified Patent Court's Court of Appeal did approve a limited carve-out of certain medical devices from the scope of injunctive relief. *See* Meril Italy Srl et al. v. Edwards Lifesciences Corp., UPC__CoA__A464/2024 et al. (Nov. 25, 2025)).

[284] *See* DIJKMAN, *supra* note 10, at 37, 39, 50, 157 (asserting, *inter alia*, that courts are incapable of knowing whether the grant or denial of an injunction will promote innovation and the diffusion of technological knowledge, and that "if patent courts would balance 'ad hoc' the interest of the patentee against those of the infringer, they would be substituting their own view on where that balance should lie for the EU legislator's").

[285] *See id.* at 150–53, 168 (stating, *inter alia*, that if the "safeguards against abuse" referenced in IPRED article 3(2) "were to refer only to Article 102 TFEU and abuse of rights doctrines, its inclusion in Article 3(2) . . . would be superfluous").

[286] *Id.* at 46. This "effective sphere" may extend beyond the metes and bounds of the claims, however, insofar as "[c]easing use of the invention may . . . necessarily require ceasing use of other technology not falling within the scope of the invention . . . . [O]verreach checks that the patent does not afford a measure of exclusivity that in practice reaches *far* beyond the patented invention." *Id.* at 190–91 (emphasis added); *see also id.* at 47 (arguing that "denial of an injunction any time its effect would extend beyond simple removal of the infringing component is untenable" and "would render the patent practically worthless in many cases"); *id.* at 192 ("a patented invention's sphere of exclusivity may reasonably extend to subordinate features in a device it enables").

within the effective scope of the injunction, and has "no notable commercial or technical advantages over alternative technologies."[287] (As examples of such "core functionality," Dijkman suggests, among others, the active ingredient of a pharmaceutical product or the time-tracking function of a clock.[288]) He would also authorize courts to deny injunctions to penalize patentees for "egregious" behavior,[289] and to stay injunctions when necessary to safeguard the interests of third parties.[290]

Echoing some of the same concerns, but more sanguine than Dijkman about the courts' ability to engage in principled balancing and to evaluate economic evidence, Peter Teunissen proposes that courts considering whether to stay injunctive relief should, absent a breach of good faith by either party, (1) examine the interests of the rightsholder, the defendant, and third parties; and (2) evaluate whether the effects of an injunction would be justified, in view of "the severity of the infringement" and the injunction's potential to cause "excessive harm on the interests of the infringer or third parties."[291] In patent cases in particular, Teunissen envisions that courts should be more cognizant than they currently are to the problems posed by "multi-component products such as cars or smartphones," where "it is sometimes impossible to remove or replace the infringing element directly at an acceptable cost."[292] Teunissen therefore proposes that in such cases courts should take into account "the disparity in market value between the protected subject matter and the harm caused by the injunction," which "[i]n the context of complex products" would entail

[287] *See id.* at 45–47, 192–201. Dijkman argues that "[a] focus on the technological significance of the invention in relation to the invention's effective scope" should be more attractive to courts that have technical, rather than economic, expertise, *id.* at 190–91—though he also concedes that some degree of subjectivity may be unavoidable. *See id.* at 190 ("To be sure, evaluating the significance of the patented technology for the infringing device is difficult and turns on an ultimately subjective assessment in that reasonable minds may differ over the correct outcome, but at least it is easier to formulate objective guidance for a technologically oriented evaluation than for a value-oriented evaluation," analogous to how the "problem solution approach boosts the objectivity and predictability of the inherently subjective assessment of inventive step").

[288] *See id.* at 192–93.

[289] Egregious behavior might include "patent ambush" (as was alleged in the *Rambus* investigation), divisional abuse (as was alleged in the *Teva* investigation), and strategic delay in either initiating litigation or prosecuting an application (topics I take up below under the rubrics of estoppel and laches). *See id.* at 201–02.

[290] *See id.* at 203–13 (defining "nonparties" to include entities that are "financially dependent on the infringement," such as suppliers, customers, resellers, distributors, and employees, and "third parties" as those who "depend on the infringing technology," such as patients and consumers; and discussing various scenarios in which these interests might outweigh the patentee's interest in exclusivity). Note that in these cases, some form of balancing cannot be avoided, *see id.* at 203–04, though Dijkman suggests some limiting principles to minimize the need for balancing, such as (among others) whether the patent owner is willing to license; whether reasonable alternatives exist; and whether an injunction would impede third parties from accessing noninfringing products.

[291] Teunissen, *supra* note 10, at 812.

[292] *Id.*

comparing "the value of the protected element" in relation to the "value of the overall product"—something that "may not always produce precise results," but for which a "rough estimate" may be good enough.[293] All that said, like Dijkman Teunissen believes that only in exceptional cases should courts exercise their authority to stay or deny injunctive relief.[294]

While both of these forgoing interpretations of proportionality may be closer in spirit both to what IPRED intends and to what courts within the E.U. are willing and able to carry out, their common emphasis on the exceptional nature of withholding injunctive relief potentially would enable patent owners to extract some measure of holdup value, under threat of injunctive relief—though whether, or what extent, patent owners would do so is of course an empirical question. Léonard, in contrast, in her discussion of how courts might apply the abuse of right doctrine *sensu lato* to rein in assertions that threaten disproportionate harm or that undermine the function of patent rights arguably envisages a somewhat more robust exercise of discretion to limit injunctive relief in the context of PAE litigation. In this regard, she suggests that, under the right-function category, courts consider "the purpose or objective of an injunction, i.e. to protect the business activities of a right holder against acts of infringement," as well as the "the purpose or objective of substantive patent law," and thus whether PAE plaintiffs who do not "help initial right holders in recouping their investment in R&D" or transfer technology to licensees "serve the purpose of stimulating innovation" might not merit injunctive relief.[295] She also argues that courts could invoke the proportionality criterion, whether as an aspect of an abuse of rights analysis or in applying IPRED article 3(2), by considering "whether 'the loss that the infringer is likely to suffer as a consequence of immediately terminating the use of the invention would grossly outweigh the licence fee on which reasonable parties would have agreed upon [or] whether the infringer has developed the infringing technology independently or whether it has copied it.' "[296] In addition, both Léonard, in her discussion of abuse of right, and Dijkman, in his discussion of article 3(2), make the important point that relying exclusively upon external bodies of law such as competition law to prevent the disproportionate harm from injunctive relief

[293] *Id.* at 812–13.
[294] *See id.* at 807, 810, 815.
[295] Léonard, *supra* note 86, at 394–95 (stating further that courts should take into account "NPE status . . . in determining whether a permanent injunction should be granted," and in particular whether "the use of its patents by an NPE is limited to obtain licensing fees from third parties, or alternatively that the NPE is not otherwise exercising its patent rights").
[296] *Id.* at 395 (quoting Ohly, *supra* note 12, at 264).

is likely to be an underinclusive response.[297] Moreover, whether one finds any of the three preceding proposals entirely persuasive in all their details, all three are rightly conscious of the need for courts to develop reasonably predictable, manageable criteria for assessing whether injunctive relief is appropriate in a given case, rather than relying upon "unlimited discretion."[298] Again, though, it remains to be seen whether courts within the E.U. see fit to depart from near-automatic injunctive relief, even under the limited circumstances envisioned by some of these authors.

The prevention of holdup also can be viewed as a rationale for applying, in patent infringement actions, the equitable defenses of estoppel and laches, as well as for rules precluding patent applicants from engaging in double patenting. Considering these in order, in the U.S. the Federal Circuit has held that a defendant asserting equitable estoppel must prove that (1) "[t]he patentee, through misleading conduct, leads the alleged infringer to reasonably infer that the patentee does not intend to enforce its patent against the alleged infringer," (2) "[t]he alleged infringer relies on that conduct," and (3) "[d]ue to its reliance, the alleged infringer will be materially prejudiced if the patentee is allowed to proceed with its claim."[299] (Although there is some case law

[297] *See* DIJKMAN, supra note 10, at 168 & n.99 (stating that "the unusually strong suite of remedies offered by the Enforcement Directive" can invite "gamesmanship," such as when "patentees giv[e] different interpretations of a claim before the EPO and the UPC," and that such gamesmanship need not "rise to the level of sanctionable abuse to be potentially problematic") (citations omitted); LÉONARD, *supra* note 86, at 395 (stating that "[t]he different categories of abuse *sensu lato* would alleviate the issues generated by a narrow interpretation of abuse which relies extensively on subjective considerations," and that "national courts would have a flexible tool at their disposal to assess the conduct of right holders without necessarily having to resort to an external, and highly demanding mechanism, such as competition law").

[298] Teunissen, *supra* note 10, at 806.

[299] A.C. Aukerman Co. v. R.L. Chaides Constr. Co., 960 F.2d 1020, 1028 (Fed. Cir. 1992) (en banc), *abrogated in part on other grounds by* SCA Hygiene Prods. Aktiebolag v. First Quality Baby Prods., LLC, 580 U.S. 328 (2017). The general contours appear to be largely the same in the U.K. and other common-law countries, though there can be nuances in regard to nomenclature or subcategories of estoppel—the common theme, however, being that the defendant has relied to its detriment on statements, conduct, or (where there was a duty to speak) silence on the part of the plaintiff. For discussion, *see, e.g.*, ELIZABETH COOKE, THE MODERN LAW OF ESTOPPEL (2000). For a discussion of analogous doctrines in some other countries, see, e.g., LÉONARD, *supra* note 86, at 122–26; *see also* DIJKMAN, *supra* note 10, at 201–02 (suggesting that practices such as patent ambush, divisional abuse, or strategic delay in enforcing one's rights may cause disproportionate harm justifying the withholding of injunctive relief).

U.S. law also recognizes prosecution history estoppel, under which a patentee who narrows its claims in response to an examiner's rejection is estopped from "later arguing that the subject matter covered by the original, broader claim was nothing more than an equivalent," so that "[c]ompetitors may rely on the estoppel to ensure that their own devices will not be found to infringe by equivalence," *Festo Corp. v. Skoketsu Kinzoku Kogyo Kabushiki Co., Ltd.*, 535 U.S. 722, 727 (2002), and the disclosure dedication rule, which precludes an application of the doctrine of equivalents that would render infringing unclaimed but disclosed subject matter, if a person of ordinary skill could "understand the unclaimed disclosed teaching upon reading the written description," *PSC Comput. Prods., Inc. v. Foxconn Int'l, Inc.*, 355 F.3d 1353, 1360 (Fed. Cir. 2004) ("[I]f one of ordinary skill in the art can understand the

suggesting that, for equitable estoppel to apply, the defendant must be aware of the existence of the patent in suit, in the absence of such proof it is likely that the closely related implied waiver or implied license defense would apply instead.[300]) Thus, where a patent owner has induced the defendant to believe that the owner has no relevant patents, or would not enforce its patents against the defendant, the owner may be precluded from subsequently reneging where the defendant reasonably relied on the owner's conduct or assertion to its detriment. One application of the doctrine would be in cases involving patent ambush, though of course only if the facts as proven by the defendant establish the elements of the defense.[301] Where the defense applies, it may preclude both injunctive relief and damages,[302] though the U.K. courts in particular emphasize the judge's discretion to craft an appropriate remedy.

The equitable doctrine of laches—defined as the "unreasonable, prejudicial delay in commencing suit"[303]—similarly may preclude a patent owner from obtaining injunctive relief, though in the U.S. it does not prevent the patentee from recovering any damages incurred within the relevant statute of limitations.[304] Again, one way of thinking about the doctrine is that, when applicable, it prevents a patentee from extracting a future royalty based on holdup value, where the defendant has been lulled into believing that the owner would not enforce. A variation on the conventional laches defense recognized

unclaimed disclosed teaching upon reading the written description, the alternative matter disclosed has been dedicated to the public."). Analogues to prosecution history estoppel also may be found in other countries, at least to the extent that owners are bound by their prior representations to the patent office. *See* Léonard, *supra* note 86, at 111–12 (providing examples); cf. Dijkman, *supra* note 10, at 168 (suggesting that such "gamesmanship" may be abusive under IPRED article 3(2)).

300 In *Aukerman*, the Federal Circuit stated that for equitable estoppel to apply, "the alleged infringer cannot be unaware . . . of the patentee and/or its patent." *Aukerman*, 960 F.2d at 1028. Whether or not this is an accurate statement of U.S. law, it appears that implied waiver theory could apply in such a case. *See* Qualcomm Inc. v. Broadcom Corp., 548 F.3d 1004, 1019–24 (Fed. Cir. 2008) (affirming a judgment that Qualcomm had implicitly waived its right to enforce patents, where it failed to disclose them in conformity with its obligation to an SSO, and remanding for determination whether it also was equitably estopped from enforcing those patents). *See also* Hynix Semiconductor Inc. v. Rambus Inc., 645 F.3d 1336, 1347–48 (Fed. Cir. 2011); Wang Lab'ys, Inc. v. Mitsubishi Elecs. Am., Inc., 103 F.3d 1571, 1581–82 (Fed. Cir. 1997); Cotter, *supra* note 190, at 130 n.140. For a recent (very thorough) English decision rejecting Apple's argument that Ericsson had breached its disclosure obligation to ETSI, and therefore was subject to an estoppel, *see* Optis Cellular Tech. LLC v. Apple Retail UK Ltd (Trial B), [2021] EWHC 1739 (Pat.) (Eng.).

301 *See Qualcomm*, 548 F.3d at 1019–24.

302 *See* Laser, *supra* note 146, at 35–36.

303 SCA Hygiene Prods. Aktiebolag v. First Quality Baby Prods., LLC, 580 U.S. 328, 333 (2017) (quoting Petrella v. Metro-Goldwyn-Mayer, Inc., 572 U.S. 663, 667 (2014)).

304 *See SCA Hygiene*, 580 U.S. at 334–34, 346. There is at least one Canadian decision expressing the same principle. *See* Uponor AB v. Heatlink Group Inc., [2016] FC 320, ¶ 290 (Can.). Under English law, by contrast, it appears to that laches can bar a claim brought within the statute of limitations. *See* P&O Nedlloyd B.V. v. Arab Metals Co, Stena Trading A.B., [2006] EWCA Civ 1717, [61] (Eng.).

in the United States is the defense of "prosecution laches," under which a patent may be rendered unenforceable if the owner engaged in unreasonable, unexplained, prejudicial delay in patent prosecution.[305] The doctrine had greater scope for application in regard to U.S. patent applications filed prior to June 1, 1995, insofar as those applications received a term of seventeen years measured from the date of grant—a feature that encouraged some applicants to keep their applications pending for several years, using the identical description but periodically amending their claims so that, upon grant, those claims would read on independently invented products that had come on the market in the interim.[306] The use of the doctrine to combat these so-called "submarine" patents is understandable, though a more recent application of the doctrine proved controversial. In *Sonos, Inc. v. Google LLC*,[307] the district judge overturned a jury verdict finding the claims of two continuation patents, filed in 2019 but claiming priority from a 2006 provisional and a 2007 nonprovisional application, infringed and not invalid, based on his conclusion that Sonos had strategically delayed the prosecution of the continuation patents so that it could later assert claims against companies like Google that, during the interim, had begun marketing services incorporating the claimed subject matter. Although the court held, in addition, that the claims in suit were invalid (because they were supported only by new matter incorporated after Google's service had come to qualify as prior art, and not by any of Sonos' earlier applications),[308] the gist of the court's decision was that prosecution laches barred the assertion of the claim even if it otherwise was valid and infringed:

> Sonos emphasizes that it complied with the statutory requirements and PTO regulations. Yet a patent applicant must "not only comply with the statutory requirements and PTO regulations but must also prosecute its application in an equitable way that avoids unreasonable, unexplained delay that prejudices others." . . .
>
> It was wrong that our patent system was used in this way. With its constitutional underpinnings, this system is intended to promote and protect

[305] *See, e.g.*, Cancer Rsch. Tech. Ltd. v. Barr Lab'ys, Inc., 625 F.3d 724, 728–32 (Fed Cir. 2010).

[306] *See, e.g.*, Symbol Techs., Inc. v. Lemelson Med., Educ. & Rsch. Found., 422 F.3d 1378 (Fed. Cir. 2005) (involving prosecutions pending for eighteen to thirty-nine years prior to issuance); *see also* Hyatt v. Hirshfeld, 998 F.3d 1347 (Fed. Cir. 2021) (holding that prosecution laches is a cognizable defense in an action filed against the USPTO under 35 U.S.C. § 145 to obtain a patent).

[307] No. C 20-06754, No. C 21-07559, 2023 WL 6542320 (N.D. Cal. Oct. 6, 2023), *aff'd in part, rev'd in part*, No. 2024-1097, 2025 WL 2473258, at *6–7 (Fed. Cir. Aug. 27, 2025).

[308] *See id.* at *20–30.

> innovation. Here, by contrast, it was used to punish an innovator and to enrich a pretender by delay and sleight of hand.[309]

The Federal Circuit nevertheless overturned the lower court's finding of prosecution laches, concluding that the evidence did not, in fact, support Google's claim that it had begun investing in developing its accused products as early as 2015; that Sonos' 2007 application, which was granted and issued in 2013, disclosed sufficient subject matter to support the claims of the 2019 continuation applications (which therefore were valid); and that Google therefore was not prejudiced by Sonos' delay in prosecuting those continuations.[310] The doctrine nevertheless remains a viable, albeit limited, safety valve for constraining opportunism, under appropriate circumstances.[311]

Finally, and in a similar vein, are the restrictions jurisdictions impose against double patenting—although the term "double patenting" can mean two distinct things. First, nations generally do not permit an applicant to obtain two patents claiming identical subject matter.[312] Second, the United States and Canada also restrict so-called "obviousness type" double patenting, which can be illustrated as follows. Suppose that a patent applicant files a first application claiming invention ABC; that while that application is pending, the applicant files a second application claiming ABC′; and that, from the perspective of a person of ordinary skill in the art, ABC′ is an obvious variation over ABC. In both countries, the courts have held that, despite the absence of any clear statutory basis for rejecting the second application, the Patent Office or the courts will invalidate the second application[313]—subject, however, to

[309] *Id.* at *17 (quoting *Hyatt*, 998 F.3d at 1360), *30.

[310] *See* Google LLC v. Sonos, Inc., No. 2024-1097, 2025 WL 2473258, at *6–7 (Fed. Cir. Aug. 27, 2025).

[311] In this regard, it arguably plays a role analogous to misuse or abuse or rights.

[312] In the United States, courts cite 35 U.S.C. § 101 ("Whoever invents or discovers any new and useful process, machine, manufacture, or composition of matter, or any new and useful improvement thereof, may obtain *a* patent therefor, subject to the conditions and requirements of this title" (emphasis added)), as the statutory basis for this restriction. *See, e.g.*, Application of Vogel, 422 F.2d 438, 440 (C.C.P.A. 1970). With respect to the EPO, the leading decision is that of the Enlarged Board of Appeal in G 0004/19 (Double patenting) 22-06-2021, ECLI:EP:BA:2021:G000419.20210622 (Société des Produits Nestlé S.A.), holding that "[a] European patent application can be refused under Articles 97(2) and 125 EPC if it claims the same subject-matter as a European patent which has been granted to the same applicant and does not form part of the state of the art pursuant to Article 54(2) and (3) EPC," and that "[t]he application can be refused on that legal basis, irrespective of whether it a) was filed on the same date as, or b) is an earlier application or a divisional application (Article 76(1) EPC) in respect of, or c) claims the same priority (Article 88 EPC) as the European patent application leading to the European patent already granted." *See also* Patent Act § 36(1) (Can.); Patent Act arts. 9, 22 (China); Patent Act art. 39 (Japan).

[313] *See* Whirlpool Corp. v. Camco Inc., 2000 SCC 67, ¶¶ 66–67 (Can.); In re Berg, 140 F.3d 1428, 1431–32 (Fed. Cir. 1998); *see also* Immunex Corp. v. Sandoz, Inc., 964 F.3d 1049, 1059 (Fed. Cir. 2020) (referring to obviousness-type double patenting as an equitable doctrine). As with prosecution

an exception available in the United States but not in Canada, namely that the inventor *can* obtain the patent on ABC′ if it files a "terminal disclaimer" forfeiting any portion of the patent term that would extend beyond the term for the original application claiming ABC.[314] The rationale for permitting the terminal disclaimer to avoid invalidation of the second patent is that, if the inventor could have included the claims of the second patent in the first application, the fact that the two patents expire on the same date renders the public no worse off than if the inventor had chosen to do so.[315]

By preventing the patent owner from effectively extending the patent term for identical or (in the U.S. and Canada) obvious variations over the originally-claimed subject matter, the rules against double patenting, like the other doctrines discussed in the preceding pages, can be understood as efforts to preclude patentees from extracting rents that are disproportionate in view of the technology's contribution to the art.[316] Arguably, though, the U.S. restrictions on obviousness-type double patenting do not go far enough; as Lemley and Ouellette have documented, even with terminal disclaimers as a countermeasure, there are reasons to believe that the proliferation of obvious secondary patents imposes substantial social costs.[317] A recent decision by the Federal Circuit interpreting the Patent Act as forbidding owners from obtaining patent term adjustments (for examiner-caused delay in prosecution) for such obvious secondary patents may help to alleviate some of these

history estoppel, the rule against obviousness-type double patenting elicits complaints from textualists. *See, e.g.*, Sherry Knowles & Anthony Prosser, *Let's Do Something About the Unauthorized Doctrine of Non-Statutory Judicially Created Obviousness-Type Double Patenting*, IP Watchdog, Sept. 6, 2022, https://ipwatchdog.com/2022/09/06/lets-something-unauthorized-doctrine-non-statutory-judicially-created-obviousness-type-double-patenting/id=151271/

[314] *See, e.g.*, 37 C.F.R. § 1.321(c) (stating, *inter alia*, that "[a] terminal disclaimer, when filed to obviate judicially created double patenting in a patent application or in a reexamination proceeding except as provided for in paragraph (d) of this section, must . . . [i]nclude a provision that any patent granted on that application or any patent subject to the reexamination proceeding shall be enforceable only for and during such period that said patent is commonly owned with the application or patent which formed the basis for the judicially created double patenting"). This last bit, requiring that the patents be "commonly owned," is intended to prevent harassment on the part of multiple patentees. *See, e.g.*, MyPort, Inc. v. Samsung Elecs. Co. Ltd., No. 2:22-CV-00114, 2023 WL 5612445, at *1 (E.D. Tex. Aug. 30, 2023).

[315] *See, e.g.*, Application of Braithwaite, 379 F.2d 594, 601 (C.C.P.A. 1967).

[316] Assuming that the first type of double patenting is illegal, you might think that after the expiration of the original patent other firms could compete using the invention claimed in that patent, whatever the status may be of the secondary patents. For a variety of reasons, however, that will not necessarily be the case. *See* Mark A. Lemley & Lisa Larrimore Ouellette, *Fixing Double Patenting*, 74 Am. U. L. Rev. 1013, 1030–32 (2025) (noting that, even with terminal disclaimers, "having too many patents in a field can create social costs," including "placing an increasing burden on the USPTO" and "impos[ing] costs on other innovators" by increasing the cost of challenging or defending against those patents; increasing the risk that "otherwise noninfringing design-arounds" will infringe; skewing the calculation of royalties for SEPs; and making it more difficult for generic drug manufacturers to clear the field).

[317] *See supra* note 316.

problems,[318] though there appears to be little prospect of going the Canadian route and eliminating the applicant's ability to obtain obvious secondary patents altogether.[319]

Antisuit Injunctions and FRAND Disputes[320]

The final topic in this lengthy chapter is the use of antisuit injunctions (ASIs), anti-enforcement injunctions (AEIs), anti-antisuit injunctions (AASIs), and the like, which have experienced a renaissance of sorts in recent years primarily in connection with disputes involving FRAND-committed SEPs. The typical fact pattern involving an ASI goes something like this: P sues, or threatens to sue, D for patent infringement in Country X; and D responds by asking the court in Country Y to enjoin P, assuming that the court in Country Y has jurisdiction over P's person, from litigating in Country X. An AEI is similar, except that it enjoins P from enforcing a judgment obtained or expected to be obtained in Country X, and may be coupled with or separate from an ASI. (For convenience, in the following paragraphs I will use the acronym ASI to include both antisuit and anti-enforcement injunctions, unless otherwise noted.) In response to, or in expectation of, finding itself on the receiving end of an ASI, P may ask the court in Country X to issue an AASI enjoining D from requesting or enforcing an ASI. In principle, the game may continue on with D requesting an anti-anti-antisuit injunction (AAASI), P requesting an anti-anti-anti-antisuit injunction (AAAASI), ad infinitum.

Courts in common-law countries have long understood themselves to have the power to enter ASIs under certain circumstances. Writing some thirty-five years ago, George Bermann distilled three types of situations in which courts might grant ASIs, namely "when the enjoining jurisdiction considers the out-of-state action to be (1) highly inconvenient, vexatious or oppressive (generally

[318] *See* In re Cellect, LLC, 81 F.4th 1216 (Fed. Cir. 2023); cf. Allergan USA, Inc. v. MSN Lab'ys Priv. Ltd., 111 F.4th 1358, 1368–71 (Fed. Cir. 2024) (holding that, if the first-filed patent benefits from a PTA, it is not rendered invalid on the basis of a second-filed application having a common priority date and a shorter term).

[319] In 2023, the USPTO proposed a rule that would have rendered any such obvious secondary patents automatically invalid, if any claims of the original patent were invalidated. The USPTO withdrew the rule in the wake of objections from the patent bar. For discussion, see Lemley & Ouellette, *supra* note 316, at 1039–45.

[320] Portions of this section are adapted from my article *Is Global FRAND Litigation Spinning Out of Control*, 2021 PATENTLY-O L.J. 1, https://patentlyo.com/media/2021/01/Cotter-Global-FRAND-Litigation-2021.pdf, and from my December 18, 2024 testimony before the United States House of Representatives Subcommittee on Courts, Intellectual Property, and the Internet of the Committee on the Judiciary: "IP and Strategic Competition with China: Part IV—Patents, Standards, and Lawfare."

to a local party), (2) in violation of a prior and independent obligation not to sue, or (3) a threat to the enjoining court's own jurisdiction or otherwise contrary to local public policy."[321] In the United States, the federal courts of appeal have developed slightly different approaches—sometimes classified as "liberal," "middle," and "conservative," with the liberal circuits being the most, and the conservative the least, accommodating—for determining whether an ASI is appropriate. Under the liberal approach, as applied in the Ninth Circuit, a court will first

> determine "whether or not the parties and the issues are the same" in both the domestic and foreign actions, "and whether or not the first action is dispositive of the action to be enjoined." Second, we determine whether at least one of the so-called "*Unterweser* factors" applies. Finally, we assess whether the injunction's "impact on comity is tolerable."[322]

Like the liberal approach, the conservative and middle approaches require identity of parties and issues. The former cautions, however, that courts should issue ASIs only if the foreign litigation would frustrate a policy of the forum or threaten its jurisdiction, while the latter applies a rebuttable presumption against issuance, which can be overcome if the aforementioned *Unterweser* factors outweigh the negative effect on comity.[323]

Since ASIs are not directed against the foreign court itself, but rather operate *in personam* against a party over whom the issuing court has jurisdiction, common-law courts do not consider them to be inherently an affront to

[321] George Bermann, *The Use of Anti-Suit Injunctions in International Litigation*, 28 COLUM. J. TRANSNAT'L L. 589, 595 (1990) (quoted in Christopher R. Drahozal, *Some Observations on the Economics of Comity*, *in* ECONOMIC ANALYSIS OF INTERNATIONAL LAW: CONTRIBUTIONS TO THE 13TH TRAVEMUNDE SYMPOSIUM ON THE ECONOMIC ANALYSIS OF LAW (Mar. 29–31, 2012) 147, 156 (Thomas Eger, Stefan Oeter & Stefan Voigt eds. 2014), https://papers.ssrn.com/sol3/papers.cfm?abstract_id=2101400); *see also* THOMAS RAPHAEL, THE ANTI-SUIT INJUNCTION 3 (2d ed. 2019) (stating that in England courts grant ASIs "predominantly . . . in two main situations: first, 'contractual' injunctions, where foreign proceedings are in breach of a contractual forum clause; and second, 'alternative forum' cases, where foreign proceedings overlap with matters that are being or can be litigated in England, and should be injuncted, in particular where they are considered vexatious or oppressive").

[322] Microsoft Corp. v. Motorola, Inc., 696 F.3d 872, 881 (9th Cir. 2012) (citations omitted). The *Unterweser* factors include "[whether the] foreign litigation . . . would (1) frustrate a policy of the forum issuing the injunction; (2) be vexatious or oppressive; (3) threaten the issuing court's in rem or quasi in rem jurisdiction; or (4) where the proceedings prejudice other equitable considerations." *Id.* (citations omitted); *see also See* Jorge L. Contreras & Michael A. Eixenberger, *The Anti-Suit Injunction—A Transnational Remedy for Multi-Jurisdictional SEP Litigation*, *in* THE CAMBRIDGE HANDBOOK OF TECHNICAL STANDARDIZATION LAW 451, 454 (Jorge L. Contreras ed. 2018) (expressing a fifth factor, namely "whether adjudication of the same issues in separate actions would result in delay, inconvenience, expense, inconsistency, or a race to judgment" (quoting VED P. NANDA ET AL., LITIGATION OF INTERNATIONAL DISPUTES IN U.S. COURTS § 16:15 (2017))).

[323] *See* Contreras & Eixenberger, *supra* note 322, at 454.

comity (though, as noted above, the impact on comity is a factor to be taken into account). Comity itself is a somewhat vague concept, but in general in understood to mean the due respect accorded to the institutions of other states: "the recognition which one nation allows within its territory to the legislative, executive or judicial acts of another nation, having due regard both to international duty and convenience, and to the rights of its own citizens, or of other persons who are under the protection of its laws."[324] Courts in civil law countries, by contrast, traditionally have viewed the *in personam* characterization of ASIs as something of a smokescreen for what is, in substance, an interference with the judiciary of another state, and (until recently, in any event) have eschewed granting them—a view embodied in, for example, the Brussels Regulation (Recast),[325] which is generally understood as forbidding courts of E.U. member states from enjoining litigation in another E.U. member.[326]

An interesting paper by Christopher Drahozal analyzes ASIs through the lens of game theory. Drahozal's thesis is that "[c]omity often serves a cooperative function: courts rely on comity as the basis for doctrines that enhanced cooperation with other States."[327] Drahozal then presents a state's decision whether to recognize a foreign judgment, or (more relevant here) to deny an ASI, as an example of an assurance game ("stag hunt") for which there are two possible equilibria: cooperate/cooperate or defect/defect.[328] In such a case, "the problem becomes one of coordination" to ensure that both actors choose to cooperate, and that comity might be "'cheap talk' that enables States to coordinate."[329] As an initial matter, therefore, one might expect that, if State X generally prefers that State Y not enjoin litigants from proceeding in State X,

[324] Hilton v. Guyot, 159 U.S. 113, 163–64 (1895); *see also, e.g.*, Raphael, *supra* note 321, at 8 (stating that comity "refers to several different concepts that bear a family relationship," and that "[t]he linking idea is the underlying notion that different nations, and in particular their courts and legal systems, owe each other mutual and reciprocal respect, sympathy, and deference, where appropriate"); Drahozal, *supra* note 321, at 149–50 (noting various formulations). William Dodge classifies comity into three types: "prescriptive," "adjudicatory," and "sovereign party," and divides each classification into two "principles," "principles of recognition" and "principles of restraint." *See* William Dodge, *International Comity in American Law*, 115 Colum. L. Rev. 2071 (2015). Most relevant here is adjudicatory comity, for which the relevant principle of restraint is the reluctance of courts to enter ASIs.

[325] Regulation (EU) No 1215/2012 of the European Parliament and of the Council of 12 December 2012 on jurisdiction and the recognition and enforcement of judgments in civil and commercial matters (recast), L 351/1.

[326] *See* Raphael, *supra* note 321, at 260–68; *see also* Drahozal, *supra* note 321, at 149–50 (describing the Brussels Regulation approach as embodying an "absolute" approach of "mutual trust" going "beyond comity").

[327] Drahozal, *supra* note 321, at 147.

[328] *See id.* at 154–55 (noting that "[a]n assurance game differs from a prisoners' dilemma game because it is no longer the case that each State individually has the incentive to defect," but rather that the game has dual equilibria).

[329] *Id.* at 155.

and vice versa, each state will signal the cooperative norm of denying ASIs as a matter of comity. Drahozal then asks, however, what might happen if one state or the other defects from the cooperative norm by opportunistically privileging its own citizens over those of other states. In such a case, he argues, the state whose citizens are negatively affected may punish, or at least not reward, the other state's defection by refusing to cooperate.[330] Proceeding then to the three types of situations in which common-law courts have been willing to grant ASIs,[331] Drahozal suggests that a court that issues an ASI to preserve its own jurisdiction can be viewed as punishing the other court for "acting opportunistically (defecting)."[332] Similarly, a court that enters an ASI to "vindicate[e] a prior and independent obligation not to sue," such as a forum selection clause, also can be understood as responding to a foreign court's having ignored that obligation.[333] The issuance of an ASI in response to "highly inconvenient or vexatious litigation," however, "is the most difficult to evaluate," because it

> seems to focus on the behavior of the parties rather than on the behavior of the foreign court . . . . On the other hand, if the foreign court is facilitating the vexatious litigation, that fact would provide evidence of opportunistic behavior such that comity would not preclude issuing an anti-suit injunction. But what if the party is merely taking advantage of a structural characteristic of the foreign court system that makes the litigation vexatious (such as lengthy delays in resolving cases, so that even if the foreign court sought to restrain the allegedly vexatious litigation it would take years before it could do so)? In such a case, my tentative view is that the failure or inability to provide sufficient procedural protections for foreign litigants could be viewed as

330 *See id.* at 155–56.

331 *See supra* text accompanying note 321.

332 Drahozal, *supra* note 321, at 156. Drahozal does not clarify what these types of cases would be, though many of Bermann's examples involve a foreign forum the application of whose substantive law would undermine some substantive policy of the issuing state (such as, in older cases, laws regulating gambling or divorce). *See* Bermann, *supra* note 321, at 597–98. Some of Bermann's examples, however, are more relevant here, particularly in the FRAND context as discussed in the text above. *See id.* at 613 (noting that, in cases of parallel litigation, the court that is the first seised of the action "may be tempted to issue an anti-suit injunction to protect its own jurisdiction," and to emphasize "the public and private interests in avoiding delay, inconvenience, a race to judgment and the risk of inconsistent rulings," but that "the inconvenience inherent in parallel proceedings is unlikely to be the only inconvenience factor of interest," along with "the advantage of having [the case] heard in the decidedly more convenient of two competing fora if in fact there is one").

333 *See* Drahozal, *supra* note 321, at 158–61 (distinguishing forum selection clauses, however, from arbitration clauses, which may be less clear about which forum is the appropriate one for matters relevant to the arbitration).

> defection by the foreign State such that comity would not preclude the grant of an anti-suit injunction.[334]

Although Drahozal doesn't take up the issue of AASIs, his analysis can be extended to cover such cases: if the granting of an ASI in a particular case is or would be a defection from comity, then an AASI is an appropriate response, rather than itself a defection. On the other hand, if the ASI is or would be an appropriate response to a defection on the part of the foreign court, then the foreign court's issuance of the AASI would be yet another defection.

Drahozal's analysis is insightful, though it also shows the inherent ambiguity of evaluating the policy merits of ASIs and AASIs; whether a given ASI is an appropriate response to a defection, or is itself a defection, can be determined only on a case-by-case basis, and even then there is likely to be considerable room for debate. In *Microsoft Corp. v. Motorola, Inc.*,[335] for example, Microsoft filed an action in U.S. district court, alleging that it was a third-party beneficiary of FRAND commitments Motorola had made to the IEEE and the ITU, and that Motorola had breached those commitments by demanding above-FRAND royalties. While that suit was pending, Motorola—taking advantage of the fact that infringement actions in Germany's bifurcated system are resolved quickly, and when successful almost always result in injunctive relief—sought and obtained an injunction in Germany for Microsoft's infringement of the German SEPs.[336] As a practical matter, the enforcement of the judgment in Germany probably would have forced Microsoft to capitulate, rather than to tolerate being excluded from the German market. The U.S. court therefore granted Microsoft's motion for an ASI, reasoning that (1) the U.S. contract action would be dispositive of the German patent dispute; (2) because "the German action raised 'concerns against inconsistent judgments,'" and of "forum shopping and duplicative and vexatious litigation," it potentially frustrated the court's "ability to adjudicate issues properly before it"; and (3) "the injunction's 'impact on comity would be tolerable'" because the U.S. action

[334] *Id.* at 156 (footnote omitted); *see also* Bermann, *supra* note 321, at 595–96 (stating that "what one party considers resort to legitimate litigation advantages of an out-of-state forum may strike the other as an exercise in inconvenience, vexatiousness and oppression," and that "while courts have developed some useful rules for deciding when recourse to a sister-state court is or is not abusive, none has devised a test that would neatly distinguish the two situations in all cases"; "[m]any courts, particularly in the older cases, appear to be on the lookout for evidence of fraud or collusion in resort to the chosen forum . . . or for an actual intent to cause undue hardship to the defendant . . . but the subjectivity of these conditions makes the inquiry difficult").

[335] Microsoft Corp. v. Motorola, Inc., 871 F. Supp. 2d 1089 (W.D. Wash. 2012), *aff'd*, 696 F.3d 872 (9th Cir. 2012).

[336] *See* Microsoft Corp. v. Motorola, Inc., 696 F.3d 872, 878–79.

was filed first, the injunction was limited in scope, and the court had a "strong interest" in adjudicating claims between two U.S. corporations.[337] For these reasons, the district court's issuance of an ASI can seem an appropriate response: the U.S. court, despite being first seised of the action, otherwise would have lost jurisdiction over the case, and Motorola clearly intended to exploit differences between the two forums' substantive and procedural law to effect that result. From the German courts' perspective, however, there was no "defection." To the contrary, "from the perspective of a German court," the paramount consideration (and thus the driving force behind countermeasures such as AASIs) is "the need to protect the patent holder's fundamental rights" that "guarantee access to the courts (right to justice) enshrined in" the E.U. Charter of Fundamental Rights, the German Constitution, and the Convention on Human Rights.[338] On this view, it was the U.S. court that was the defector.

Nevertheless, there is something to be said for restraining conduct like that of Motorola, which seems to go beyond the usual sort of forum shopping that is both widely tolerated and virtually inevitable in the context of FRAND disputes, given the very different legal norms that countries apply (including the availability, or not, of injunctive relief). But that hardly means that ASIs should be a commonplace remedy, as it appeared they were becoming when in 2020 courts in China granted ASIs in at least five separate FRAND cases[339]—this despite that, in one of them (*Oppo v. Sharp*) the Chinese court was not the first seised; that in some of them the order was initially entered *ex parte*; that some of them, unlike their counterparts elsewhere, prohibited the respondents from asserting claims relating to the subject SEPs anywhere else in the world, not just the specific jurisdiction in which parallel litigation was pending; and that China is a civil-law, not a common-law, country.[340]

[337] *Id.* at 880–81 (quoting *Microsoft*, 871 F. Supp. 2d at 1100–01). The Court of Appeals affirmed. *See id.* at 889.

[338] Mattias Zigann & Hubertus Schacht, *Anti-Antisuit Injunctions*, *in* FRAND: German Case Law and Global Perspectives, *supra* note 40, at 308, 311.

[339] Huawei v. Conversant, (2019) Zui Gao Fa Zhi Min Zhong 732, 733 & 734 No. 1 (SPC Aug. 20, 2020) (China); Xiaomi Commc'n Tech. Co., Ltd. v. InterDigital, Inc., E 01 Zhi Min Chu No. 169 (Wuhan Intermediate People's Ct. Sept. 23, 2020) (China); ZTE Corp. v. Conversant Wireless Licensing Co., (2018) Yue 03 Min Chu No. 335-1 (Shenzhen Intermediate People's Ct. Sept. 28, 2020) (China); Guangdong OPPO Mobile Telecomm. Corp., Ltd. v. Sharp Corp., Yue 03 Min Chu No. 689 (Shenzhen Intermediate People's Ct. Oct. 16, 2020) (China); Samsung Elecs. Co., Ltd. v. Telefonaktiebolaget LM Ericsson (Wuhan Intermediate People's Ct. Dec. 25, 2020) (China).

[340] For discussion, *see, e.g.*, Richard Arnold, *Arbitration of FRAND Disputes*, *in* FRAND: German Case Law and Global Perspectives, *supra* note 40, at 332, 341; Alexandr Svetlicinii & Fali Xie, *The anti-suit injunctions in patent litigation in China: what role for judicial restraint?*, 19 J. Intell. Prop. L. & Prac. 734 (2024); Yang Yu & Jorge L. Contreras, *Will China's New Anti-Suit Injunctions Shift the Balance of Global FRAND Litigation?*, Patently-O Blog, Oct. 22, 2020, https://patentlyo.com/patent/2020/10/contreras-injunctions-litigation.html.

As it turned out, however, courts in Germany, India, and the United States entered AASIs relating to three of the Chinese cases,[341] and in 2022 the E.U. initiated proceedings in the WTO arguing that Chinese courts' issuance of ASIs violates articles 1, 41, and 63 of the TRIPS Agreement.[342] Some German courts also have taken the position that defendants who apply for ASIs are unwilling prospective licensees,[343] which would mean they cannot rely on the *Huawei v. ZTE* defense against injunctive relief, and thus are likely to be subject to injunctive relief. In the aggregate, these developments may have contributed to implementers becoming more hesitant to seek ASIs over the last few years.

That said, ASIs are hardly dead and buried; the Federal Circuit reaffirmed their potential availability under U.S. law, for example, in a 2024 decision involving Ericsson and Lenovo.[344] Moreover, in October 2024 the Court of Appeal for England and Wales in *Panasonic Holdings Corp. v. Xiaomi Tech. UK Ltd.*, held that, in a case in which both parties had agreed to abide by the terms of a global FRAND license to be determined by the U.K. courts, and the SEP owner Panasonic thereafter appeared to undermine that agreement by proceeding with litigation in Germany, a willing licensor in the position of Panasonic "would agree to enter into, and would enter into, an interim licence of" Panasonic's portfolio of 3G and 4G SEPs, "pending the determination by the Patents Court of what terms for a final licence" are FRAND.[345] Although the court did not think it necessary to consider whether an ASI would have been appropriate, and the principal opinion took pains to distinguish its declaration from an ASI, the effect of such an order would be similar to an ASI where it induces the discontinuance of litigation in another forum. (The actual case settled shortly thereafter.) Whether such declarations should be available

[341] *See* Arnold, *supra* note 340, at 341 n.30 (citing InterDigital, Inc. v. Xiaomi Commc'n Tech. Co., Ltd., Delhi High Court, IA 8772/2020, (Delhi High Ct. Oct. 9, 2020) (India), and Ericsson Inc. v. Samsung Elecs. Co., Ltd., No. 2:20-CV-00380, 2021 WL 89980 (E.D. Tex. Jan. 11, 2021)); Svetlicinii & Xie, *supra* note 340, at 738–39 (also referring to German AASIs, and suggesting that "[d]espite the broad scope of Chinese ASIs in SEP disputes, the practice also reveals a relatively low level of compliance by the parties concerned").

[342] *See* WT/DS611—China—Enforcement of Intellectual Property Rights, https://policy.trade.ec.europa.eu/enforcement-and-protection/dispute-settlement/wto-dispute-settlement/wto-disputes-cases-involving-eu/wtds611-china-enforcement-intellectual-property-rights_en. The Panel Report, made public in April 2025, rejected the EU's claim that China's ASI policy violated TRIPS. The arbitration panel appointed to hear the appeal in the case, however, subsequently concluded that China's policy did in fact violate TRIPS articles 28(1) and 28(2), read in light of article 1.1 first sentence.

[343] *See* Peter Georg Picht, *Anti-Antisuit Injunctions*, *in* FRAND: German Case Law and Global Perspectives, *supra* note 40, at 200, 206–10 (citing decisions of the Munich and Düsseldorf courts).

[344] *See* Telefonaktiebolaget LM Ericsson v. Lenovo (U.S.), Inc., 120 F.4th 864 (Fed. Cir. 2024). In April 2025, the parties entered into a global settlement, thus mooting any further proceedings.

[345] *See* Panasonic Holdings Corp. v. Xiaomi Tech. UK Ltd., [2024] EWCA Civ 1143 (Eng.).

in cases presenting less extreme facts—for example, in cases in which the SEP owner has not consented to the U.K. court's determination of global FRAND terms—is surely debatable, though in early 2025 the Court of Appeal held that a similar declaration should issue in a case in which SEP owner Ericsson had not consented to the English court's establishment of a global royalty, much less reneged on such a commitment.[346]

In my view, the appropriate solution is not to eliminate ASIs (or interim licenses) altogether, but rather to confine their use to the most egregious cases—*e.g.*, in the context of SEP cases, to those in which, as in both *Microsoft* and *Panasonic*, a party has agreed to Court X making a global FRAND determination, and then reneges on that commitment by pursuing potentially dispositive relief elsewhere. The granting ASIs or interim licenses in a broader range of cases, by contrast, risks letting one country or a small number of countries effectively call the shots for the entire world. Of course, the underlying issue is how to deal with SEP cases, which present more clearly than perhaps any other type of patent case the clash between the traditional territorial understanding of patents and the global nature of commerce. In an ideal world, the best solution might be to take these matters out of the hands of domestic courts altogether, by instituting some sort of global tribunal for FRAND disputes, or alternatively by convincing SSOs to require mandatory arbitration. Proposals along these lines have been made by from to time,[347]

[346] *See* Lenovo Group Ltd. v. Telefonaktiebolaget LM Ericsson (Publ), [2025] EWCA Civ 182 (Eng.). As noted above, the parties thereafter reached a global settlement. In a subsequent decision in a case between Samsung and ZTE, however, a majority of the Court of Appeal held that an interim license was not appropriate where, among other things, the parties were involved in parallel litigation over a global FRAND rate in China. *See* Samsung Elecs. Co. v. ZTE Corp., [2025] EWCA Civ 1383 (Eng.). Nevertheless, by late 2025 tensions were flaring between the English courts, on the one hand, which (as discussed below) continue to entertain the prospect of determining global FRAND royalties and, at least under some circumstances, of issuing declarations concerning interim licenses, and on the other, the UPC and the Munich Regional Court, which have recently entered anti-interim license injunctions. The English court in one such case responded with an anti-anti-interim license injunction, while the UPC's Mannheim Division has intimated that it might not recognize English judgments concerning global FRAND royalties. For overviews of where matters stood as of the end of 2025, *see* Amazon.com, Inc. v. InterDigital VC Holdings, Inc., [2025] EWHC 3334 [27]–[33] (Pat.) (Eng.); Acer Inc. v. Nokia Techs. Oy, [2025] EWHC 3331 [392]–[404], [433]–[41] (Pat.) (Eng.); Florian Mueller, *UPC Threatens Amazon with Initial €50M ($59M) Fine, "Severe Consequences", Declares All UK Interim Licenses Unenforceable, Suggests EU WTO Action Against UK*, IP FRAY, Dec. 25, 2025. Observers will be keeping a close watch in 2026 on how this volatile situation plays out.

[347] *See* Arnold, *supra* note 340 (proposing mandatory arbitration); *see also* Jorge L. Contreras, *Global Rate-Setting: A Solution for Standards-Essential Patents?*, 94 WASH. L. REV. 701 (2019); Roya Ghafele, *Global FRAND Licensing in Light of* Unwired Planet v. Huawei, 24 UCLA J. L. & TECH. (2020). *But see* Eli Greenbaum, *No Forum to Rule Them All: Comity and Conflict in Transnational FRAND Disputes*, 94 WASH. L. REV. 1085, 1089, 1120 (2019) (arguing that "courts should resist the temptation to streamline worldwide FRAND litigation through consolidation of the dispute in one jurisdiction," in part because "territorial adjudication would allow jurisdictions to set independent FRAND policies appropriate to their specific social, economic, and political circumstances").

though at present there appears to be little enthusiasm for adopting them; and a 2023 proposal by the European Commission that would have required, among other things, the EUIPO to oversee the mandatory but nonbinding determination of global FRAND royalties as a precondition to the initiation of SEP litigation in the E.U. was withdrawn, following substantial criticism, in early 2025.

The situation therefore remains chaotic. One possibility would be to adhere to the territorial view, such that courts in Country X could establish the terms of FRAND licenses only with respect to Country X patents, absent consent of both parties for the court to set a global rate. This is, essentially, the position of the United States courts thus far,[348] but it risks forcing parties to litigate on a country-by-country basis, which seems highly inefficient. That said, it may be the rare case in which either party has the resources (and stamina) to litigate to judgment in more than two or three countries before settling; or, if even one court in a major market awards injunctive relief against the implementer, the implementer may feel compelled to enter into a global settlement to avoid the costs of remaining outside that market.

The downside of the latter result is that the settlement may reflect substantial holdup value, and while an implementer can in theory avoid that fate simply by being a "willing" licensee, the risk of being enjoined, whether deserved or not, shifts considerable bargaining power to the SEP owner. The other alternative is for courts to establish the terms of global FRAND licenses, even absent the consent of both parties, a practice the English courts pioneered beginning with the *Unwired Planet* decision in 2017.[349] The logic of this approach is, first, that if a freely negotiated FRAND license would be global in scope, then a willing licensee would agree to a global FRAND license; second, once it is established that the defendant has infringed one or more of the plaintiff's valid (domestic) SEPs, the court may enjoin the defendant from practicing the patented technology, if the defendant is an unwilling licensee; and third, on the basis of the forgoing principles, the court may offer the infringer the choice of either

[348] *See* Microsoft Corp. v. Motorola, Inc., 795 F.3d 1024 (9th Cir. 2015); TCL Commc'n Tech. Holdings, Ltd. v. Telefonaktiebolaget LM Ericsson, No. SACV 14-341, 2018 WL 4488286 (C.D. Cal. Sept. 14, 2018), *vacated in part, rev'd in part, and remanded on other grounds*, 943 F.3d 1360 (Fed Cir. 2019).

[349] *See* Unwired Planet Int'l Ltd. v. Huawei Techs. Co. Ltd. [2017] EWHC (Pat.) 711 (Eng.), *aff'd*, [2020] UKSC 37 (appeal taken from Eng.). Since then, courts in the U.K. have established the terms of FRAND licenses in two other cases, *InterDigital Tech. Corp. v. Lenovo Group Ltd.*, [2023] EWHC 539 (Pat.) (Eng.), *modified*, [2024] EWCA Civ. 743, and *Optis Cellular Tech. LLC v. Apple Retail UK Ltd.*, [2025] EWCA Civ 552 (Eng.). An appeal in the latter case is, as this book goes to press, pending before the U.K. Supreme Court.

agreeing to the court's determination of the terms of a global FRAND license (one that a willing licensee would accept), or (as an unwilling licensee) being enjoined from the domestic market.[350] This practice has its efficiency benefits, no doubt, and may work reasonably well if the English courts' FRAND determinations are reasonably accurate. One drawback, however, is that the practice encourages races to the courthouse, as litigants who think they can obtain a better deal in, say, Country X than in Country Y will hasten to file suit before their counterparties take the initiative in Country Y. Depending on the circumstances, Country X could be Germany or the UPC, where injunctive relief in FRAND cases remains common—or the U.S. International Trade Commission, which, unlike U.S. courts, is not bound by the *eBay* decision and therefore may be more likely to exclude infringing imports—or alternatively, a jurisdiction such as China which following *Unwired Planet* announced its willingness to establish global FRAND terms, albeit officially only when China is the country with the closer connection to the dispute.[351] In accordance with this policy, as noted previously a Chinese court established global FRAND terms for the first time in the 2023 decision in *Nokia Techs. v. OPPO*.[352] In response to that development, the European Union initiated a second matter under the auspices of the WTO, asserting that China's practice violates Paris Convention article 4bis, as incorporated under TRIPS article 2.1, as well as TRIPS articles 1(1), 28(1), and 28(2).[353] (Presumably the same argument, whatever its merits may be, could be made against former E.U. member the U.K. as well.) More generally, nations that object to nonconsensual global FRAND determinations perceive a loss of sovereignty, especially if the courts making those determinations feel the need to protect their jurisdiction to do so by issuing ASIs or interim licenses.

Where matters will end up remains for now anyone's guess. Perhaps the E.U.'s second WTO dispute against China will bring some clarity, though this assumes the continuing relevance of the WTO in the face of global trends toward

[350] *See Unwired Planet*, [2020] UKSC 37, [20], [27]–[29], [60], [165].
[351] *See supra* notes 339–42 and accompanying text.
[352] *See supra* note 79 and accompanying text.
[353] *See* WT/DS632-1—China—Measures Concerning Patent Licensing Terms: Request for Consultations by the European Union, Jan. 22, 2025, https://docs.wto.org/dol2fe/Pages/SS/directdoc.aspx?filename=q:/WT/DS/632-1.pdf&Open=True. Meanwhile, in February 2025, the CJEU ruled in *BSH Haugeräte GmbH v. Electrolux AB*, Case C-339/22, that where a patent owner sues a defendant in the E.U. member state in which the latter is domiciled, the court of that state may adjudicate the defendant's alleged infringement of corresponding foreign patents—and that, if the corresponding country is a non-E.U. member, may even adjudicate patent validity, albeit only on an *inter partes*, not an *erga omnes*, basis. We are living in interesting times.

protectionism and unilateralism. Meanwhile, one can expect SEP owners, implementers, and for that matter individual states[354] to continue jockeying for advantage, and ASIs, AASIs, and now interim licenses to remain potentially part of their arsenal—the concepts of "coordination" and "defection" tending to reside, like beauty, in the eye of the beholder.

[354] *See* Drahozal, *supra* note 321, at 161 (noting that "States' preferences for whether to cooperate or defect" "may be the result of rent-seeking behavior by businesses, lawyers, and others within the State," and that judges' interests too may "diverge from the preferences of the State itself"); *see also* Meier-Beck, *supra* note 280, at 347 n.38, 350 (stating that if courts determine global FRAND terms, it is possible that those "decisions may also be determined by aspects other than the fair, reasonable and non-discriminatory terms or the worldwide use of standard-essential patents," and that "in the global context in which conflicts of interest in question can be played out, it cannot be assumed that every state or judicial price fixing for licences to standard-essential patents worldwide is exclusively committed to the goal of finding a price that is analogous to competition").

7
Conclusion

This book has covered a lot of ground, in terms of both legal doctrine and global practice. In this final chapter, I provide a brief summary of its conclusions, and end with some thoughts on how policymakers might work to improve other features of the patent, regulatory, and litigation systems that sometimes enable wrongful patent assertion.

To recap, I defined the term "wrongful patent assertion" early on as "an *assertion* of patent rights that may (or should) result in the owner suffering *adverse consequences*, by reason of having harmed or threatened to harm a *cognizable interest* without *sufficient justification*." I also tried to make it clear that, as used throughout this book, the term "wrongful" would not necessarily connote any moral judgment, but rather would serve as a shorthand for conduct that, because of its potential for producing negative social welfare effects, subjects (or should subject) the patent owner to adverse consequences of one sort or another. I also emphasized that the term "wrongful patent assertion" would encompass not only the wrongful initiation or prosecution of litigation, but also situations in which something else—the relief sought, or some conduct occurring independently of the litigation, or conduct for which enforcement or threatened enforcement is an antecedent—results (or should result) in the patent owner suffering adverse consequences during the course of, or subsequent to, infringement litigation. The discussion nevertheless would be limited to doctrines that were in some way tethered to actual or threatened litigation; and it would center on how the various doctrines that regulate wrongful patent assertion operate, or could better operate, in the principal jurisdictions for patent litigation.

Chapter 2 then elaborated on the interests those doctrines, collectively, are intended to protect—including the promotion of innovation, competition, the integrity of the marketplace, and the integrity of the judicial system—while chapter 3 centered on "assertion," which I defined as the actual or threatened enforcement of patent rights. In this regard, I argued that it probably makes sense for U.S. law to limit antitrust liability for the fraudulent procurement of patent rights to cases involving the actual or threatened enforcement of those

Wrongful Patent Assertion. Thomas F. Cotter, Oxford University Press. © Oxford University Press 2026.
DOI: 10.1093/9780191994104.003.0007

rights, and not to define the term "threatened enforcement" so broadly as to encourage owners to "sue first, ask questions later" or implementers to engage in frivolous litigation. In other regions, by contrast, where the absence of treble damages and the presence of fee-shifting[1] reduce the risk of frivolous litigation, there is a stronger case for courts and regulators to view the fraudulent procurement of intellectual property rights as potentially an abuse of dominant position, even in the absence of threatened enforcement. Some unfair competition claims premised on a false accusation of infringement similarly do not depend upon proof that the accusation constitutes threatened enforcement, although others—including the U.K.'s law of unjustified threats—clearly do. For these latter claims, the task of the courts is to distinguish actionable threats from nonactionable non-threats, in order to effect the statutory policy of encouraging patent owners, when possible, to deal with primary rather than secondary infringers, while at the same time not discouraging good-faith negotiations between owners and users.

Chapters 4, 5, and 6 then addressed various possible ways of structuring the "wrongfulness" (or "without sufficient justification") element. Chapter 4 addressed claims that depend in whole or in part on the patent claims in suit being adjudicated invalid, not infringed, or otherwise unenforceable against the implementer. The first example presented under this heading was fee shifting. In theory, mandatory fee shifting ensures that the prevailing party (whether plaintiff or defendant) is fully compensated, either for the effects of the infringement or for having been the target of an unsuccessful infringement claim, as the case may be; empirically, fee shifting also appears to be associated with a lower incidence of infringement actions brought by patent assertion entities (PAEs). Among the downsides is the risk that fee shifting may increase litigation costs by encouraging parties with strong cases to divert more effort to litigation, while at the same time discouraging some small and medium-sized enterprises (SMEs) from vindicating their rights. Given these potential consequences, it is not surprising that there is substantial variation among countries. In some, including all of the member states of the European Union and the U.K., the general rule is that the prevailing party is presumptively entitled to recover its fees and costs—though in practice, the fees awarded typically are lower, sometimes substantially so, than the amounts actually incurred. In other places, including the United States and China, fee awards are relatively

[1] Some fees and costs can even be assessed against the European Commission. *See, e.g.*, United Parcel Service v. Commission, Case T-194/13, EU:T: 2017:144 (Gen. Ct. 2020) (awarding €270,250, pursuant to article 140(b) of the General Court's Rules of Procedure).

uncommon in patent infringement litigation. Although these variations may be attributable in part to the differing weight that different legal systems place upon the values of full compensation versus access to justice, I proposed that nations should consider adopting a "partial English Rule" that would presumptively entitle the winning party to full compensation, subject to judicial assessment and some exceptions, for example for SMEs. Similarly, I argued in favor of a general default principle that a defendant who is preliminarily enjoined on the basis of a patent that is subsequently adjudicated invalid or not infringed is entitled to full compensation for its temporary exclusion from the market, subject to some discretion for courts to depart from this rule where equitable considerations may so warrant. Many countries, including the U.K. and other members of the Commonwealth of Nations, follow this rule, and in 2024 the CJEU authorized E.U. members to follow suit. U.S. courts, on the other hand, rarely if ever award damages in excess of the injunction bond; and although courts can modify the amount of the bond as the litigation progresses, the risk remains that U.S. law undercompensates enjoined defendants and underdeters patent owners from wrongful assertion. For a third type of claim covered in chapter 3, however, sham litigation antitrust claims, legal systems generally place considerably more weight on the owner's interest in access to courts than on the victim's interest in compensation; in the U.S., for example, the Supreme Court has restricted sham litigation claims to cases in which the accusation of infringement is both objectively baseless and subjectively motivated by bad faith.[2] Following Elhauge, Hakun, and others, I argued that a better rule would be one that penalizes infringement litigation that would not have been undertaken but for its expected anticompetitive consequences. Under some circumstances, moreover, courts should continue to penalize serial litigation with a sufficiently low but nonzero success rate, as some U.S. courts have continued to do even after *Professional Real Estate Investors*.

Chapter 5 focused on claims the success of which may depend upon some sort of probabilistic assessment of infringement and validity. The principal example is a pay-for-delay antitrust claim, for which U.S. law as articulated in *FTC v. Actavis, Inc.*[3] holds that a payment in excess of the patent owner's avoided litigation costs is prima facie anticompetitive. As discussed in chapter 5, the effect of this standard is to condemn settlements that prolong patent exclusivity beyond the generic competitor's expected entry date, which itself is a function of the ex ante probability that the competitor's product infringes a valid

[2] *See* Professional Real Estate Inventors, Inc. v. Columbia Pictures Industries, Inc., 508 U.S. 49 (1993).
[3] 570 U.S. 136 (2013).

patent. Courts applying this standard in antitrust suits brought by the government nevertheless can avoid explicitly estimating that probability, though (for better or worse) the use of probabilistic expert testimony may be necessary to calculate damages in private actions. Chapter 5 also considers whether courts might entertain probabilistic evidence to assess claims of bad faith assertion in violation of anti-troll laws, but concludes that under current U.S. case law this is unlikely to happen, for both legal and practical reasons.

Finally, chapter 6 discussed claims, defenses, and remedies that limit the exercise of patent rights even when the patent claims at issue may be both valid and infringed. Here, much of the discussion centered on how courts in civil law countries may apply the abuse of dominant position, abuse of right, and proportionality concepts, and in common law countries equitable discretion, to stay or preclude prevailing patent owners from obtaining injunctive relief. I argued that, ideally, courts would apply these doctrines primarily to minimize the risk of patent holdup. To date, however, the civil law doctrines only rarely have resulted in stays or denials of injunctive relief, and thus may be ineffective in preventing holdup in many cases—though defenders of the status quo argue that, by relieving courts from having to calculate ongoing royalties, the current system reduces adjudication costs and better preserves the patent incentive. In common law countries, by contrast, the exercise of equitable discretion results in the delay or denial of injunctive relief in a broader range of cases—especially so in the United States, following the Supreme Court's 2006 in decision in *eBay Inc. v. MercExchange, LLC.*[4] Common law courts also apply a variety of equitable defenses, including estoppel and unclean hands, to limit the exercise of valid patent rights—though the U.S., once again, goes further than most by recognizing the equitable defenses of inequitable conduct and patent misuse, the contribution of which to optimal patent policy is probably at best marginal. But not all of the innovative legal responses to patent assertion have come from the United States. Chapter 6 also discusses, for example, a recent decision of the Belgian Cour de cassation authorizing broader use of the abuse of economic dependence doctrine to constrain patent rights (a development concerning which I expressed some skepticism). Meanwhile, the increasing use of antisuit injunctions (ASIs) and interim licenses in standard-essential patent (SEP) litigation presents a double-edged sword, in some cases arguably preventing patent owners from forum-shopping their way to the extraction of excessive royalties, while in others potentially contributing to forum shopping on the part of implementers. With regard to ASIs and related

[4] 547 U.S. 388, 391 (2006).

practices, I suggested that if judicial restraint cannot be guaranteed, the optimal solution might for standard-setting organizations to require mandatory arbitration, or for nations to agree on establishing a global forum for SEP disputes. There seems to be little chance of either solution being adopted in the near term, however; and where matters will eventually come to rest in this exceptionally important subcategory of patent infringement disputes remains highly uncertain.

I concede that there are several other topics related to the abuse of patent rights that the book did not address. As I noted in chapter 1, this volume would not center on abuses such as product hopping, that are not necessarily tied to patent litigation; nor would it, for the most part, address alleged abuses by implementers, which might however form a useful companion volume at some point in the future. Moreover, though perhaps it should go without saying, the law is simply not capable of addressing every conceivable opportunistic behavior in which patent owners (or implementers) may engage. Chapter 6 addressed how ASIs and related practices can either enable or inhibit some forms of forum shopping, for example; but in general, forum shopping is often endemic to patent infringement and other forms of litigation.[5] To be sure, neutral laws concerning matters such as venue and jurisdiction can alleviate the risk of forum shopping to some degree—as witness, for example, the U.S. Supreme Court's decision in *TC Heartland LLC v. Kraft Foods Group Brands LLC*,[6] which restricted patent infringement actions to districts in which the defendant either is incorporated or has committed allegedly infringing acts and has a regular and established place of business. But different jurisdictions will always be prone to enacting different laws, or following different practices, even when operating within frameworks such as TRIPS or the various E.U. Directives that are intended to achieve some degree of harmonization; and this is not necessarily a bad thing, to the extent such laws and practices reflect the preferences of local communities, and enable experimentation among different approaches to similar questions. Nevertheless, these differences provide opportunities for litigants to forum-shop, and absent specific, universally-applicable, uniform rules there may be little that anyone can do to eliminate it.

Similarly, as more than one person suggested to me during the course of my writing this book, one might view the selective enforcement of patent rights as a species of wrongful conduct. To cite one possible example, suppose that

[5] For discussion, *see* Thomas F. Cotter, *Is Global FRAND Litigation Spinning Out of Control?*, 2021 Patently-O L.J. 1 (providing a brief overview of forum shopping and of the related practice of forum *selling*, in which specific courts or even countries may vie for a particular type of litigation).

[6] 581 U.S. 258 (2017).

an owner offers nonexclusive licenses to one or more patents to one group of firms (x) for some nonzero royalty r, but offers royalty-free licenses to another group (y) (or simply tolerates the latter's use); or alternatively, licenses y and refuses to license x. This practice clearly disadvantages members of x; and on the right set of facts, it might even be an antitrust violation, if for example the owner perceives some mutual benefit in colluding with y to disadvantage x, or in withholding licenses from x because the owner competes in certain markets with members of x but not y.[7] But even that might be a longshot, given the courts' general reluctance, for good reason, to recognize an antitrust duty to license one's patents; and in the absence of facts suggesting such an anticompetitive motive on the owner's part, it's not clear there would be actionable harm under any body of law.[8] (Indeed, the owner's practice might even seem procompetitive, to the extent some implementers are being accorded the royalty-free use of the portfolio.) And perhaps that is just as well, given the risks of error and unintended consequences that might flow from courts imposing a duty to offer all takers identical terms (which courts themselves might then have to determine). Depending on one's perspective, however, the absence of any effective legal response might seem to leave a gap for owners, in some circumstances, to exploit.

Finally, there are numerous features of the patent system that enable owners to engage in the practices that the doctrines considered in this book sometimes, though only sometimes, succeed in constraining. Although certain reforms to those doctrines may improve social welfare, altering the underlying features that enable the abuse might be even more effective in constraining rent-seeking behavior. There are many such alterations that may be worth considering; and although an in-depth discussion of them would go far beyond this book's limited scope, I will mention three in brief.

Investments in Improving Patent Quality

Commentators have devoted considerable attention over the past thirty years to ways in which nations might improve patent quality—and thus reduce some

[7] I thank Erik Hovenkamp for illuminating discussion on this topic.

[8] There may be some exceptions, however. If the patents are FRAND-committed SEPs, for example, perhaps the practice described in the text above would be considered a breach of contract, depending on how the obligation to license SEPs on nondiscriminatory terms is interpreted. Or perhaps some regions or countries might consider such price discrimination to violate competition or unfair competition law, or to constitute an actionable abuse of economic dependence, even if there is no substantial market distortion.

of the opportunities for patent owners to exploit weak patents for private gain. Some of that commentary clearly has borne fruit, for example in the United States' adoption of post-grant and *inter partes* reviews in 2011. Some recent analyses suggest, moreover, that the current U.S. patent examination system actually performs surprisingly well in screening out invalid claims, and that the high invalidation rates observed in IPRs and in U.S. infringement litigation may be attributable to selection effects (that is, that only close cases proceed to judgment).[9] There may be some truth to this, although the evidence in support of this claim is not dispositive. The two econometric studies cited in the note below, for example, though highly sophisticated in their analyses, do not account for nonpatent prior art in estimating how many issued patents may be invalid;[10] do not rule out other possible reasons for the difference between

[9] *See* Ani Harutyunyan et al., *Patent Quality in the United States: Findings and Suggestions for Policymakers*, Sunwater Institute Policy Report (2024). The report cites three principal sources. The first is a paper by William Matcham and Mark Schankerman titled *Screening Property Rights for Innovation*, the current version of which can be found at https://papers.ssrn.com/sol3/papers.cfm?abstract_id=4519999. This paper presents a game theoretic model of the U.S. patent examination process, and uses natural language processing to estimate the "distance" between the claim of a given patent or application and previously granted claims. It estimates that only about 8% of U.S. patents contain claims that would be invalid in view of such prior art, whereas "over 35% of abandonments contain at least one valid claim," and therefore concludes that the current system for patent screening "is relatively effective, *given* the judicial standards of patentability the Patent Office is mandated to enforce." *Id.* at 3, 34. The second consists of the USPTO's Office of Patent Quality Assurance's annual reviews for 2017–23 of sampled office actions, which reports a noncompliance rate of about 7–8% for allowances and a higher rate for rejections. A summary of the review for fiscal year 2024 can be accessed at https://www.uspto.gov/sites/default/files/documents/mrf-data-fy24.xlsx. The third is Gaétan de Rassenfosse et al., *Low-Quality Patents in the Eye of the Beholder: Evidence from Multiple Examiners*, 37 J.L. Econ. & Org. 607 (2021), which compared patents with corresponding applications in at least two of five patent offices (the EPO, the U.S., China, Japan, and Korea) for the years 2000–06, and estimates comparative error rates (grants or rejections that differ among offices, and which are best explained as departures from the office's own internal standards). For the U.S., the estimated error rate is about 11%. On the basis of these studies, Harutyunyan et al. argue that the 40% or more invalidation rate observed in patent infringement litigation and in proceedings before the Patent Trial and Appeal Board (PTAB) is attributable to selection effects: "[s]ince only the most uncertain disputes go all the way to a judgment in litigation, the outcomes in trial become just as uncertain as coin tosses." Harutyunyan et al., *supra*, at 23 (citing George L. Priest & Benjamin Klein, *The Selection of Disputes for Litigation*, 13 J. Legal Stud. 1 (1984)).

[10] *See* de Rassenfosse et al., *supra* note 9, at 615–16 (positing the four sources of heterogeneity among office decisions on validity as "systematic office differences"; "systematic invention differences"; "application-patent office procedural differences," consisting of whether the applicant is local or foreign, whether the application is a priority filing, whether it is a Patent Cooperation Treaty filing, and the number of claims; and "examination idiosyncrasies"); Matcham & Schankerman, *supra* note 9, at 19 ("[t]o reflect the distance to the *prior* art, we compute the distance from each claim to every previously granted claim"). Examiners also focus most of their attention on patent prior art, *see* Christopher A. Cotropia, Mark A. Lemley & Bhaven Sampat, *Do Applicant Patent Citations Matter?*, 42 Res. Pol'y 844, 846–47, 852 n.26 (2013), but nonpatent prior art can play a substantial role in judicial and PTAB validity determinations. *See, e.g.*, Colleen V. Chien, *Rigorous Policy Pilots the USPTO Could Try*, 104 Iowa L. Rev. Online 1, 12–15 (2019) (making this point, and proposing, *inter alia*, that a pilot program to evaluate formally dividing search from examination, as in the EPO, would lead to more robust validity determinations); Stephen Yelderman, *Prior Art in the District Court*, 95 Notre Dame L. Rev. 837, 860–62 (2019).

predicted invalidity rates and invalidity rates in adversarial litigation;[11] and take the current standards for patentability as a given.[12] On this last point in particular, the coauthor of one of the two studies suggests elsewhere that a more rigorous inventive step requirement—one that excluded more inventions from patentability—would increase social welfare.[13]

That said, there are limits on how much any nation is or should be willing to invest in ex ante patent examination, given that most patents turn out to be of little or no commercial value expost (as Mark Lemley observed many years ago[14]). Still, there is reason to believe that more should be done to screen out patents that contribute little to the state of the art. For example, an April 2025 report of the United States Government Accountability Office—which reports, among other matters, a pervasive sentiment among examiners that they must prioritize quantity over quality—makes several recommendations (albeit at a somewhat high level of generality) for improving both real and perceived patent quality, most of which center on improving perceived deficiencies in the transparency and rigor with which the USPTO implements, monitors, and communicates its quality assurance programs.[15] In a more specific vein, Schankerman and Schuett suggest that substantially raising examination fees, coupled with the use of the additional revenue for hiring more examiners, would substantially increase social welfare.[16] Adopting measures such as these, however, would require political willpower in the face of powerful vested interests; and sometimes governments may exert pressure in precisely the opposite direction—for example, by rewarding the issuance of more and more patents,

[11] *See* de Rassenfosse et al., *supra* note 9, at 628–29 (suggesting that, in addition to selection effects, the difference in invalidity rates could be attributable to courts applying a stricter standard, or doing a more thorough review); *see also* Mark A. Lemley, *The Surprising Resilience of the Patent System*, 95 TEX L. REV. 1, 25, 27–28 (2016) (citing evidence the U.S. patentee win rates hover around 25–26%, and questioning the applicability of the strong form of the Priest-Klein hypothesis to patent litigation); Jason Rantanen, *Why Priest-Klein Cannot Apply to Individual Issues in Patent Cases* (Mar. 25, 2013), https://papers.ssrn.com/sol3/papers.cfm?abstract_id=2132810.

[12] *See* de Rassenfosse et al., *supra* note 9, at 612–16; Matcham & Schankerman, *supra* note 9, at 43.

[13] Mark Schankerman & Florian Schuett, *Patent Screening, Innovation, and Welfare*, 89 REV. ECON. STUD. 2101, 2133 (2021) (stating, on the basis of the authors' econometric model, that "the patent-quality problem is real," in that "almost half of all [U.S.] patents are issued on low-type inventions where patent rights are not needed to elicit their development, and thus impose unnecessary social costs").

[14] *See* Mark A. Lemley, *Rational Ignorance at the Patent Office*, 95 NW. U. L. REV. 1495 (2001); *see also* de Rassenfosse et al., *supra* note 9, at 629–30.

[15] *See* U.S. GOVERNMENT ACCOUNTABILITY OFFICE, INTELLECTUAL PROPERTY: PATENT OFFICE SHOULD STRENGTHEN ITS EFFORTS TO ADDRESS PERSISTENT EXAMINATION AND QUALITY CHALLENGES (April 30, 2025). The GAO summarizes these as including "take steps to evaluate ongoing initiatives related to patent examination challenges; formalize and document its approach for managing pilot programs; update guidance to address limitations in its supervisory quality reviews; establish and communicate an overall patent quality compliance goal; and assess and adopt alternative measures of the economic or scientific value of patents."

[16] *See* Schankerman & Schuett, *supra* note 13, at 2136–37.

of whatever quality, as is often alleged to be the case in China,[17] or by dramatically expanding the grounds for discretionary denials of *inter partes* review in parallel with infringement litigation, as the USPTO's interim director announced in March 2025.[18]

Eliminating Structural Features that can Induce Accused Infringers into Premature Settlement

In certain areas of patent law, the key to reducing abuse may be less a matter of improving patent quality, important though that may be, or of modifying antitrust or other substantive bodies of law, than of reforming the rules that enable owners to obtain engage in abuse in the first place. In the pharmaceutical field, for example, secondary patents, including continuations and divisionals, make up a disproportionate number of the patents that are the subject matter of double patenting[19] and reverse payment settlements,[20] and that contribute to the sort of abuses flagged in the European Commission's recent investigation of Teva.[21] Some of these problems might be ameliorated simply by limiting the ability of owners to obtain or assert multiple patents covering comparatively minor variations over the original patented subject matter. As was noted briefly in chapter 3, for example, under some circumstances the listing of drug patents on the FDA's Orange Book might violate antitrust law to the extent the listings are false and are intended to delay generic entry; but merely listing, or filing suit for the infringement of, multiple patents would not appear to constitute an antitrust offense absent evidence of sham litigation or an unlawful

[17] *See, e.g.*, Fen Lin, Waverly Ding & Shi Chen, *The Patent Gold Rush? An Empirical Study of Patent Bubbles in Chinese Universities (1990–2019)*, https://papers.ssrn.com/sol3/papers.cfm?abstract_id=4447754.

[18] *See* USPTO, *USPTO Rescinds Memorandum Addressing Discretionary Denial Procedures*, Feb. 28, 2025, https://www.uspto.gov/about-us/news-updates/uspto-rescinds-memorandum-addressing-discretionary-denial-procedures. As noted in chapter 3, the permanent director has continued, indeed expanded, the use of discretionary denials since assuming office in September 2025.

[19] Mark A. Lemley & Lisa Larrimore Ouellette, *Fixing Double Patenting*, 74 Am. U. L. Rev. 1013, 1027–28, 1032 (2025) (reporting that, in recent years, over 60% of patents listed in the FDA's Orange Book have terminal disclaimers; and stating that "life science companies often file a flurry of double patents once their FDA-granted period of data exclusivity ends, hoping to extend their period of control") (citing S. Sean Tu, Rachel Goode & William B. Feldman, *Biologic Patent Thickets and Terminal Disclaimers*, 331 J. Am. Med. Ass'n 355, 356–57 (2024)).

[20] *See supra* ch. 5 note 117 (citing C. Scott Hemphill & Bhaven N. Sampat, *Drug Patents at the Supreme Court*, 339 Sci. 1386, 1387 (2013), and C. Scott Hemphill & Bhaven N. Sampat, *When Do Generics Challenge Drug Patents?*, 8 J. Empirical Legal Stud. 613, 643 (2011)).

[21] *See supra* ch. 5 note 130; *see also* Katarina Foss-Solbrekk, *The Divisional Game: Using Procedural Rights to Impede Generic/Biosimilar Market Entry*, 53 Int'l Rev. Intell. Prop. & Comp. L. 1007 (2022).

reverse payment.[22] The maintenance of such "patent thickets" nevertheless can impede generic entry, simply by increasing the cost faced by would-be generic competitors to enter the market. A possible legislative response would be to limit the number of such patents relating to any given drug that can be listed or asserted, as legislation recently introduced in the United States would do in relation to biologic drugs[23]—though I suspect there would be a constitutional challenge, whether successful or not, to any such effort to broadly limit patent owners' ability to assert their patents. Other possible reforms would be to limit double patenting, either by abolishing the practice altogether (even when coupled with a terminal disclaimer), or by limiting the conditions under which it is permitted.[24] In a similar vein, Katarina Foss-Solbrekk has proposed ways in which the abuse of divisional practice within the EPO could be reduced, among them reducing the period during which applications remain pending (since divisionals can be filed only while the parent application is pending, which includes any time during which an appeal could be filed), introducing stricter conditions for the filing of divisionals (such as requiring applicants to describe how the claims differ from the parent), and tightening up the EPO's somewhat porous prohibition against double patenting.[25]

This book also has noted features of U.S. litigation that contribute to patent trolling, among them the presumption against fee-shifting; the high costs of litigation, given U.S. practice concerning matters such as discovery, jury trials, and the use of expert witnesses; and the difficulty of enforcing the anti-troll laws enacted by the states. These features—some of which, such as the constitutional right to trial by jury, are ineradicable—are less pronounced elsewhere.

[22] *See* Mayor & City Council of Baltimore v. AbbVie Inc., 42 F.4th 709 (7th Cir. 2022) (affirming a decision that AbbVie's assertion of 132 biologic drug patents did not violate the Sherman Act, as alleged by plaintiff third-party payors, absent evidence of actionable sham litigation or a reverse payment).

[23] For brief discussion, *see* Andrew Karpan, *New Bills Target 'Patent Thickets' and 'Product Hopping'*, LAW360 (Mar. 17, 2025), https://www.law360.com/articles/2311687/new-bills-target-patent-thickets-and-product-hopping-. The statutory framework for the marketing of biosimilars under the Biologics Price Competition and Innovation Act is somewhat similar to, but even more complex than, the Hatch-Waxman Act (although there is no automatic stay). It involves, among other things, two stages of litigation between the owner of a patented biologic drug and a firm that is planning to market a biosimilar. For an overview of the process, *see* Sandoz, Inc. v. Amgen, Inc., 582 U.S. 1 (2017).

[24] *See* Lemley & Ouellette, *supra* note 19, at 1046–48. Lemley and Oullette raise several other possibilities, including that patent owners be permitted "to replace one patent with another that covers an obvious variation of the first"; forbidding double patenting "for applications stemming from the same application or from applications filed on the same day by the same or overlapping inventors"; allowing "new claims to be added to an existing patent"; permitting "IPR challenges to include claims from related patent family members"; and raising fees substantially for continuations. *See id.* at 1050–56 (citing, *inter alia*, S. Sean Tu & Mark A. Lemley, *What Litigators Can Teach the Patent Office About Pharmaceutical Patents*, 99 WASH. U.L. REV. 1673, 1713–15 (2022)). On the other hand, a proposed USPTO rule that would have limited the number of continuations that an applicant could file was struck down in 2008, after which the agency voluntarily rescinded it.

[25] *See* Foss-Solbrekk, *supra* note 21, at 1031–34.

Other practices found outside the United States, however, including the near-automatic issuance of injunctive relief to prevailing patentees in civil law countries, may enable owners to extract holdup royalties and seem almost as difficult to modify. One reform that might be attainable, however, would be for countries such as Germany, Austria, and Hungary that bifurcate infringement and validity determinations to work toward eliminating it, or at least ameliorating its results by speeding up invalidation proceedings, as has been attempted in Germany;[26] routinely staying infringement litigation pending those proceedings; or permitting invalidity to be raised as an *inter partes* defense to infringement, as in Japan and (at least in some cases) China.[27] (To the extent the UPC comes to supplant more and more domestic European patent litigation in the years to come, moreover, bifurcation may become less of an issue over time, although the UPC can bifurcate under some circumstances.[28]) In the U.S., one reform that may not involve a huge investment of political capital would be to constrain the assertion of patent rights against customers of infringing manufacturers and against noncommercial users of patented inventions (such as consumers). The outright elimination of consumer liability would align U.S. law with the laws of many other countries, where only the commercial manufacture, use, or sale of a patented product can infringe.[29] Legislation that would codify the practice of staying litigation against customers of allegedly infringing manufacturers pending a declaratory judgment action filed by the manufacturers also would preserve the ability of the latter to avoid an unfavorable venue, and might reduce the incentive to harass users with demand letters.[30]

Implementing Rational Responses to Litigation Finance

The past decade has witnessed a substantial increase in the use of third-party litigation financing (TPLF), including third-party financing of patent infringement actions, in the United States and elsewhere. The third-party financing of

[26] *See supra* ch. 2 n.51.
[27] *See supra* ch. 2 notes 39–41 and accompanying text.
[28] *See* Agreement on a Unified Patent Court, 2013/C 175/01, art. 33(b)(3).
[29] *See, e.g., id.* art. 27(a) (stating that "[t]he rights conferred by a patent shall not extend to . . . acts done privately and for non-commercial purposes").
[30] *See* Thomas F. Cotter, Patent Wars: How Patents Impact Our Daily Lives 224–25 (2018); Colleen V. Chien & Edward Reines, *Why Technology Customers Are Being Sued En Masse for Patent Infringement and What Can Be Done*, 49 Wake Forest L. Rev. 235 (2014); Brian J. Love & James C. Yoon, *Expanding Patent Law's Customer Suit Exception*, 93 B.U. L. Rev. 1605 (2013).

patent actions raises two issues relevant to the topics discussed in this book, one narrow and one broad.

The narrow issue is whether courts or legislatures should require greater disclosure than the rules of practice currently mandate of the persons or entities involved in financing patent infringement actions. Calls for greater disclosure date back at least to the early 2010s, when alleged abuses by PAEs began to emerge as a major topic of concern. Some of these PAEs were believed to own hundreds of subsidiary shell companies,[31] some of which in turn owned one single patent. Concerns over the risk that such disaggregation of patent portfolios could result in inflated royalty awards, and/or enable PAE shareholders to better shield their assets against awards of attorneys' fees,[32] prompted both the USPTO[33] and the U.S. Congress[34] to consider enacting rules that would have obligated patent applicants and parties asserting infringement actions, respectively, to disclose their ultimate parent entities. As it happened, none of these proposals were signed into law, and as a consequence the disclosure that is mandated by the Federal Rules of Civil Procedure remains somewhat limited.[35] In recent years, however, some U.S. district and appellate courts

[31] MPHJ, for example, the company that was the subject of the FTC investigation noted in chapters 3 and 5, was the ultimate parent company of 101 subsidiaries.

[32] *See* Mark A. Lemley & A. Douglas Melamed, *Missing the Forest for the Trolls*, 113 Colum. L. Rev. 2117, 2159–60 (2013) (arguing that PAEs facilitate "double dipping" because (1) an accused who might negotiate a portfolio license with a single owner cannot readily do so when ownership is divided among many, perhaps unknown, owners; and (2) due to flaws in patent damages law, the damages awarded for the infringement of even a single patent may sometimes include some of the value of other components, such that multiple infringement actions relating to the same product expose the defendant to more risk than would a single action involving multiple patents). *See also* Taurus IP v. DaimlerChrysler, 726 F.3d 1306 (Fed. Cir. 2013) (affirming an award of attorneys' fees against a losing PAE, where the evidence showed, among other things, that in a previous action an affiliated company had misled the defendant into believing that it was settling all claims relating to certain products).

[33] *See* U.S. Dep't of Commerce, U.S. Pat. & Trademark Off., Proposed Rules: Changes to Require Identification of Attributable Owner, 79 Fed. Reg. 4105 (Jan. 24, 2014) (proposing a rule that would have required every patent applicant to identify the assignee, any "entity necessary to be joined in a lawsuit in order to have standing to enforce the patent," the "ultimate parent entity" of either of the preceding entities, and any entity that used any arrangement to temporarily divest itself or prevent the vesting of attributable ownership—along with updates during prosecution, upon payment of maintenance fees, and in connection with any postgrant USPTO proceedings).

[34] *See* H.R. 9, 114th Cong. § 4 (as reported by H. Comm. on the Judiciary, July 29, 2015), https://www.congress.gov/bill/114th-congress/house-bill/9/text#toc-H7E6F9EAE8263402492511BD54A562B0B; Another bill would have required any entity submitting more than twenty demand letters involving the same patent within a single year to disclose its ultimate parent entity to the USPTO. *See* H.R. 1896, 114th Cong. § 2 (as reported by H. Comm. on the Judiciary, Apr. 20, 2015), https://www.congress.gov/bill/114th-congress/house-bill/1896/text. None of these, however, was ever signed into law.

[35] *See* Fed. R. Civ. P. 7.1(a) (as relevant to patent infringement actions, requiring nongovernmental corporate parties to identify "any parent corporation and any publicly held corporation owning 10% or more of its stock); Fed. R. Civ. P. 26(a)(1)(A)(iv) (requiring the disclosure of insurance policies that may be "any insurance agreement under which an insurance business may be liable to satisfy all or part of a possible judgment in the action or to indemnify or reimburse for payments made to satisfy the judgment").

have adopted local rules requiring parties to disclose additional information concerning entities that may have a financial interest in the outcome of the litigation, principally to assist courts in avoiding judicial conflicts of interest and in case management.[36] One federal judge in particular, Colm Connolly of the District of Delaware, has gained prominence—and the wrath of some TPLFs—for imposing two standing orders requiring parties to provide information concerning litigation financing arrangements, including the identity of any person or persons who have authority to make decisions regarding litigation or settlement.[37] As David McGowan argues, these orders help to ensure that anyone whom an attorney would need to "call to clear an important decision . . . can be brought to the table if needed"—which in turn can help reduce the risk that the client's interest in settling may be compromised by the funder's interest in going to trial—and also, as suggested above, that "shot callers" are not immune from the risk of fee awards.[38] McGowan also recommends that Congress consider enacting legislation that would allow shot callers to submit to the court's jurisdiction, as a condition of allowing the case to proceed.[39]

The broader question is whether third-party litigation financing of patent infringement actions should be permitted at all. To be sure, recent decisions in the U.S. and elsewhere have set aside traditional common-law limits on champerty (the funding of litigation in return for a portion of the proceeds) and maintenance (a third party's improper interference with litigation) that would pose obstacles to litigation funding. These decisions have noted, among other things, that contrary to a strict understanding of the common-law prohibition of champerty, it has long been permitted, at least in the United States, for lawyers to take cases on a contingency basis; and more generally, that litigation finance might serve the public interest by enabling clients of limited means to vindicate their rights.[40] Whatever the merits might be of such arguments in

[36] *See* David McGowan, *Who's Suing You?*, 25 Minn. J. L. Sci. & Tech. 73, 77–78 & nn. 20–22 (2023).
[37] *See* Chief Judge Colm F. Connolly, United States District Court for the District of Delaware, Standing Order Regarding Disclosure Statements Required by Federal Rule of Civil Procedure 7.1 (Apr. 18, 2022), https://www.ded.uscourts.gov/sites/ded/files/Standing%20Order%20Regarding%20Disclosure%20Statements.pdf (requiring, "where a party is a nongovernmental joint venture, limited liability corporation, partnership, or limited liability corporation," the disclosure of "the name of every owner, member, and partner of the party, proceeding up the chain of ownership until the name of every individual and corporation with a direct or indirect interest in the party has been identified"); Chief Judge Colm F. Connolly, United States District Court for the District of Delaware, Standing Order Regarding Third-Party Litigation Funding Arrangements (Apr. 18, 2022), https://www.ded.uscourts.gov/sites/ded/files/Standing%20Order%20Regarding%20Third-Party%20Litigation%20Funding.pdf (requiring, "where a party has made arrangements to receive" third-party litigation funding, to disclose the funder, whether the funder's approval is necessary for litigation of settlement decisions, and the nature of the funder's financial interest).
[38] *See* McGowan, *supra* note 36 at 78, 90, 102.
[39] *See id.* at 111.
[40] *See, e.g.*, Maslowski v. Prospect Funding Partners LLC, 944 N.W.2d 235 (Minn. 2020).

favor of third-party financing of consumer or perhaps even some commercial claims, however, it is open to question whether third-party financing of patent actions improves social welfare. Analogous arguments from the early 2010s, to the effect that PAEs contributed to innovation by ensuring that individual inventors and SMEs who assigned their patents to such entities would have a chance of receiving compensation for their inventive efforts, were called into doubt by studies indicating that assignors typically receive relatively little in exchange for their patents.[41] But even if one assumes, for the sake of argument, that today's TPLFs offer the prospect of greater rewards for the originators of patented inventions than did the PAE model of ten or more years ago, the question remains whether the social benefits resulting from a putative increase in the incentive to innovate, itself resulting from an increase in enforceability, would outweigh the corresponding increases in adjudication costs and, potentially, deadweight loss from settlements or damages awards. I make no claim here that one necessarily outweighs the other, but I admit to being skeptical of the public benefits of TPLFs, and would welcome efforts by econometricians and others to model, simulate, and predict these effects.

More generally, I close with a simple recommendation: that in deciding the types of issues discussed in this book, policymakers should rely more on evidence and logic than on rhetoric and unexamined assumptions. What we don't need, in other words, is advice like that presented in the above-cited Sunwater Report, that "viewing the patent system as an economic utility-maximizing institution alone risks abandoning the notions of justice and natural rights on which the United States was founded and has thrived."[42] What we don't need are more statements defining the protection of intellectual property as a human right.[43] What we don't need are more politicians and business leaders asserting, without citation to evidence, that stronger patent rights are always better—or, conversely, that stronger antitrust, or consumer protection, or whatever laws are always better—even though it may well be the case that, within a specific context, evidence and logic suggest that patent rights or antitrust laws or other bodies of laws *do* in fact need to be strengthened. What we don't need, in other words, is what Lemley has referred to, disparagingly,

[41] *See* James E. Bessen & Michael J. Meurer, *The Direct Costs from NPE Disputes*, 99 Cornell L. Rev. 388, 410–11 (2014) (estimating that at most 20% of defendants' payments to NPEs went to patentees); Michael Risch, *Patent Troll Myths*, 42 Seton Hall L. Rev. 457, 461 (2012) (stating that "the evidence does not support a theory that NPEs incentivize investment by providing a market for patents," although they do "provide a better way for individual inventors to enforce their patents than bringing lawsuits themselves").

[42] Harutyunyan et al., *supra* note 9, at 27.

[43] *See* Charter of Fundamental Rights of the European Union, OJ C 364/1, Dec. 18, 2000, art. 17(2).

as “faith-based” intellectual property policy.[44] What would be helpful, instead, is a dose of honesty and humility, coupled with a willingness to experiment, to learn from experience, and to be open to new ideas on common problems. And one more thing, perhaps, beyond this: a (rebuttable) assumption that patent owners, implementers, business leaders, politicians, and others—for that matter, I would argue, most people most of the time—tend to act in their perceived self-interest. Armed with this assumption, courts and other decisionmakers, though potentially subject to some degree of self-interested bias themselves, might see their task as working to channel that self-interest so that private behavior better aligns with the public interest. Not a romantic vision of policymaking, to be sure, but one that may be more realistic—and more effective in promoting innovation, competition, and the integrity of the marketplace.

[44] *See* Mark A. Lemley, *Faith-Based Intellectual Property*, 62 UCLA L. Rev. 1328 (2015).

Bibliography

Articles, Books, Recordings

Abbott, Alden F., & D. Bruce Hoffman, Ohio v. American Express *and the Continued Evolution of Economic Reasoning in Supreme Court Jurisprudence*, 33 Antitrust 37 (2018).

Abusive Practices in Competition Law (Fabiana Di Porto & Rupprecht Podszun eds., Edward Elgar Publishing, Cheltenham, UK, 2018).

Agé, Sabine, & Lonni Bas, *France*, *in* Global Patent Litigation: How and Where to Win (Michael C. Elmer & C. Gregory Gramenopolous eds., Bloomberg Law, Arlington, VA, 2021) (ebook).

Agé, Sabine, & Marta Mendes Moreira, *Reginald Wehrkamp-Richter v Louis Paul Guitay, LPG Systems*, Intell. Prop. Magazine, May 2012.

Aggarwal, Ambika, & Anindya Sircar, *Jurisdictional Changes in Indian Patent Enforcement—Comment on the* Ericsson v. CCI *Decision*, 55 IIC 954 (2024).

Alba, Tommaso, Christian Helmers & Brian J. Love, *A Tale of Trolls and Fees: The Role of Fee-Shifting in Patent Litigation*, Nov. 24, 2025, https://ssrn.com/abstract=5796263.

Allison, John R. et al., *Our Divided Patent System*, 82 U. Chi. L. Rev. 1073 (2015).

Allison, John R. et al., *Understanding the Realities of Modern Patent Litigation*, 97 Tex. L. Rev. 1769 (2014).

Altmeyer, Stephan, & Christopher Weber, *Rückzahlung von Lizenzgebühren bei rückwirkender Vernichtung eines SEP?*, GRUR 1182 (2017).

Am. Intell. Prop. L. Ass'n, 2025 Report of the Economic Survey (2025).

Anand, Pravin, Tusha Malhotra & Udita M. Patro, *India*, *in* International Patent Litigation: Developing an Effective Strategy 201 (Gwilym Roberts ed., Globe Law and Business, London, 2018).

Antill, Samuel, et al., *The Efficiency of Patent Litigation*, Jan. 21, 2025, https://papers.ssrn.com/sol3/papers.cfm?abstract_id=4842424.

Arnold, Richard, *Arbitration of FRAND Disputes*, *in* FRAND: German Case Law and Global Perspectives 332 (Peter Georg Picht, Thomas F. Cotter & Erik Habich eds., Edward Elgar Publishing, Cheltenham, UK, 2024).

Bacher, Klaus, *Vernichtung des Patents nach rechtskräftigem Abschluss des Verletzungsprozesses*, GRUR 216 (2009).

Baker, Jonathan B., The Antitrust Paradigm: Restoring a Competitive Economy (Harvard University Press, Cambridge, MA, 2019).

Bakhoum, Mor, *Abuse Without Dominance in Competition Law: Abuse of Economic Dependence and its Interface with Abuse of Dominance*, *in* Abusive Practices in Competition Law 157–84 (Fabiana Di Porto & Rupprecht Podszun eds., Edward Elgar Publishing, Cheltenham, UK, 2018).

Barak, Aharon, Proportionality: Constitutional Rights and Their Limitations 175 (Cambridge University Press, Cambridge, UK, 2012).

Baumann, Marion, et al., *The Enforcement of Abuse of Economic Dependence in the EU*, K&L Gates European Antitrust, Competition, and Trade Regulation Alert (Jan. 28, 2021), https://www.klgates.com/The-Enforcement-of-Abuse-of-Economic-Dependence-in-the-EU-1-28-2021.

Beebe, Barton, et al., Trademarks, Unfair Competition, and Business Torts (2d ed., Wolters Kluwer Law & Business, New York, 2016).

Bently, Lionel, & Sir Richard Arnold, *United Kingdom*, *in* Injunctions in Patent Law: Trans-Atlantic Dialogues on Flexibility and Tailoring 261 (Jorge L. Contreras & Martin Husovec eds., Cambridge University Press, Cambridge, UK, 2022).

Bereskin, Fred, Po-Hsuan Hsu & Huijun Wang, *Growth of Firms under Injunction Risk*, July 31, 2023, https://papers.ssrn.com/sol3/papers.cfm?abstract_id=4281493.

Bermann, George, *The Use of Anti-Suit Injunctions in International Litigation*, 28 Colum. J. Transnat'l L. 589 (1990).

Bessen, James E., & Michael J. Meurer, *The Direct Costs from NPE Disputes*, 99 Cornell L. Rev. 388 (2014).

Bien, Michael W., *Litigation as an Antitrust Violation: Conflict Between the First Amendment and the Sherman Act*, 16 U.S.F.L. Rev. 41 (1981).

Bing, Guan, & Wang Ziqian, *Unknowns of 'No-Challenge Clause' in IP Licence Contracts*, China Bus. L.J., May 25, 2022, https://law.asia/ip-licence-no-challenge-clause-unknowns/.

Binns, Richard, & Nicola Walles, *Royalties for Unpatented Technology*, LII les Nouvelles 28, Mar. 2017.

Blair, Roger D., & Thomas F. Cotter, *An Economic Analysis of Seller and User Liability in Intellectual Property Law*, 68 U. Cincinnati L. Rev. 1 (1999).

Blair, Roger D., & William H. Page, *Speculative Antitrust Damages*, 70 Wash. L. Rev. 423 (1995).

Blake's Guide to Litigation and Disputes Resolution in Canada, Section X: PM(NOC) Proceedings (July 2024).

Bogetoft, Rasmus Arler, & Peter Bogetoft, *Market Entrance, Patents, and Preliminary Injunctions: A Model of Pharmaceutical Patent Litigation*, 53 Eur. J. L. & Econ. 379 (2022).

Bohannan, Christina, *IP Misuse as Foreclosure*, 96 Iowa L. Rev. 475 (2011).

Bohannan, Christina, & Herbert Hovenkamp, Creation Without Restraint: Promoting Liberty and Rivalry in Innovation (Oxford University Press, New York, 2012).

Bonadio, Enrico, & Dyuti Pandya, *Global FRAND rates in China*, Kluwer Patent Blog, Dec. 21, 2023, https://patentblog.kluweriplaw.com/2023/12/21/global-frand-rates-in-china/.

Bork, Robert H., The Antitrust Paradox: A Policy at War with Itself (Basic Books, Inc., New York, 1978).

Bouvet, Thomas, AIPPI Question Q292-SR-G-2024: Unjustified Allegations of Infringement of IP Rights (France) (July 10, 2024).

Bowman, Jr., Ward S., *Tying Arrangements and the Leverage Problem*, 67 Yale L.J. 19 (1957).

Boyce, John R., & Aidan Hollis, *Preliminary Injunctions and Damage Rules in Patent Law*, 16 J. Econ. & Mgt. Strategy 385 (2007).

Boyd, Marcos Araujo, *Patent Litigation as a Form of Abuse – The Spanish Decision Against MSD*, Kluwer Competition Law Blog, Nov. 2, 2022, https://competitionlawblog.kluwercompetitionlaw.com/2022/11/02/patent-litigation-as-a-form-of-abuse-the-spanish-decision-against-msd/.

Brack, Hans-Peter, *Patent Infringement Warnings in a Common Law Versus a Civil Law Jurisdiction—An Actionable Threat?*, 37 Int'l Rev. Intell. Prop. & Competition L. 1 (2006).

Brody, Anne, & Elisabeth Ponce, *Courts Are Aligning Patent Fraud, Inequitable Conduct Claims*, Law360 (May 18, 2021), https://www.law360.com/articles/1384168/courts-are-aligning-patent-fraud-inequitable-conduct-claims.

Brooks, Richard R.W., & Warren F. Schwartz, *Legal Uncertainty, Economic Efficiency, and the Preliminary Injunction Doctrine*, 58 Stan. L. Rev. 381 (2005).

Brown, Benjamin, Comment, *Inequitable Conduct: A Standard in Motion*, 19 Fordham Intell. Prop. Media & Ent. L.J. 593 (2009).

Brown, Dean G., et al., *Clinical development times for innovative drugs*, 21 Nat'l Rev. Drug Discovery 793 (2022).

Bulow, Jeremy, *The Gaming of Pharmaceutical Patents*, *in* 4 Innovation Policy and the Economy 145 (Adam B. Jaffe et al. eds., MIT Press, Cambridge, MA, 2004).

Burk, Dan L., & Mark A. Lemley, The Patent Crisis and How Courts Can Solve It (University of Chicago Press, Chicago, 2009).

Burstein, Sarah, *Sanctions & Schedule A*, Patently-O, Jan. 23, 2024, https://patentlyo.com/patent/2024/01/burstein-sanctions-schedule.html.

Butian, MA, *Second-Instance Judgment in ACT v Oppo Sheds Light on Comparable Agreements and How to Find Fault in SEP Licensing Negotiations*, Global Comp. Rev., Feb. 1, 2024, https://globalcompetitionreview.com/hub/sepfrand-hub/2023/article/second-instance-judgment-in-act-v-oppo-sheds-light-comparable-agreements-and-how-find-fault-in-sep-licensing-negotiations.

Butian, MA, & Pyeng Liu, *China Seps and FRAND—Litigation, Policy and Latest Developments*, IAM, Oct. 27, 2023, https://www.iam-media.com/hub/sepfrand-hub/2023/article/china-seps-and-frand-litigation-policy-and-latest-developments.

Calabresi, Guido, & A. Douglas Melamed, *Property Rules, Liability Rules, and Inalienability: One View of the Cathedral*, 85 Harv. L. Rev. 1089 (1972).

Carlton, Dennis W., & Michael Waldman, *The Strategic Use of Tying to Preserve and Create Market Power in Evolving Industries*, 33 RAND J. Econ. 194 (2002).

Carrier, Michael A., *The Antitrust Case Against Live Nation*, 15 Harv. J. Sports & Enter. L. 1 (2024).

Carrier, Michael A., *The Rule of Reason: An Empirical Update for the 21st Century*, 16 Geo. Mason L. Rev. 827 (2009).

Carrier, Michael A., & Edward Bank, *The Missing Caselaw of Reverse-Payment Settlements*, 97 St. John's L. Rev. 959 (2025).

Carrier, Michael, & Rebecca Tushnet, *An Antitrust Framework for False Advertising*, 106 Iowa L. Rev. 1841 (2021).

Casucci, Giovanni, *Patent Enforcement in Italy*, *in* Patent Enforcement Worldwide: Writings in Honour of Dieter Stauder 205 (Christopher Heath ed. 3d ed., Hart Publishing, Oxford, 2015).

Chen, Jian & Yunfeng Geng, *China*, *in* Global Patent Litigation: How and Where to Win (Michael C. Elmer & C. Gregory Gramenopolous eds., Bloomberg Law, Arlington, VA, 2021) (ebook).

Chiang, Tun-Jen, *The Upside-Down Inequitable Conduct Defense*, 107 Nw. U. L. Rev. 1243 (2013).

Chien, Colleen V., *Reforming Software Patents*, 50 Hous. L. Rev. 325 (2012).

Chien, Colleen V., *Rigorous Policy Pilots the USPTO Could Try*, 104 Iowa L. Rev. Online 1 (2019).

Chien, Colleen V., *Startups and Patent Trolls*, 17 Stan. Tech. L. Rev. 461 (2014).

Chien, Colleen V., et al., *Enhanced Damages, Litigation Cost Recovery, and Interest*, *in* Patent Remedies and Complex Products: Toward a Global Consensus (Brad Biddle et al. eds., Cambridge University Press, Cambridge, UK, 2019).

Chien, Colleen V., & Edward Reines, *Why Technology Customers Are Being Sued En Masse for Patent Infringement and What Can Be Done*, 49 Wake Forest L. Rev. 235 (2014).
Clark, Geneva, 2020 Lex Machina Patent Litigation Report 15 (Rachel Bailey & Jason Maples eds., 2021).
Coase, Ronald H., *The Problem of Social Cost*, 3 J.L. & Econ. 1 (1960).
Cohen, Lauren, et al., *Patent Trolls: Evidence from Targeted Firms*, 65 Mgt. Sci. 5461 (2019).
Cohen, Mark, *Oppo v. Nokia in Context*, China IPR, Dec. 18, 2023, https://chinaipr.com/2023/12/18/oppo-v-nokia-in-context/.
Cohen, Wesley M., et al., *Protecting Their Intellectual Assets: Appropriability Conditions and Why U.S. Manufacturing Firms Patent (or Not)* (Nat'l Bureau Econ. Res., Working Paper No. 7552, 2000), http://www.nber.org/papers/w7552.
Colangelo, Margherita, *Reverse Payment Patent Settlements in the Pharmaceutical Sector Under EU and US Competition Laws: A Comparative Analysis*, 40 World Competition: Law & Econ. Rev. 471 (2017).
Contreras, Jorge L., *A Brief History of FRAND: Analyzing Current Debates in Standard Setting and Antitrust Through a Historical Lens*, 80 Antitrust L.J. 39 (2015).
Contreras, Jorge L., *Global Rate-Setting: A Solution for Standards-Essential Patents?*, 94 Wash. L. Rev. 701 (2019).
Contreras, Jorge L., *Much Ado About Hold-Up*, 2019 U. Ill. L. Rev. 875 (2019).
Contreras, Jorge L., *Patent Reality Checks: Eliminating Patents on Fake, Impossible and Other Inoperative Inventions*, 102 J. Pat. & Trademark Off. Soc'y 2 (2021).
Contreras, Jorge L., et al., *The Effect of FRAND Commitments on Patent Remedies*, *in* Patent Remedies and Complex Products: Toward a Global Consensus (Brad Biddle et al. eds., Cambridge University Press, Cambridge, UK, 2019).
Contreras, Jorge L., & Michael A. Eixenberger, *The Anti-Suit Injunction—A Transnational Remedy for Multi-Jurisdictional SEP Litigation*, *in* The Cambridge Handbook of Technical Standardization Law 451 (Jorge L. Contreras ed., Cambridge University Press, Cambridge, UK, 2018).
Cooke, Elizabeth, The Modern Law of Estoppel (Oxford University Press, Oxford, NY, 2000).
Cooper, James C., & Emily Kral, *Shambles: Making Sense of the Confused State of* Noerr's *Sham Exception*, 76 Case Western Reserve L. Rev. (forthcoming), *manuscript available at* https://papers.ssrn.com/sol3/papers.cfm?abstract_id=4740979.
Cotropia, Christopher A., & Mark A. Lemley, *Copying in Patent Law*, 87 N.C. L. Rev. 1421 (2008).
Cotropia, Christopher A., Mark A. Lemley & Bhaven Sampat, *Do Applicant Patent Citations Matter?*, 42 Res. Pol'y 844 (2013).
Cotter, Thomas F., *An Economic Analysis of Patent Law's Inequitable Conduct Doctrine*, 53 Ariz. L. Rev. 735 (2011).
Cotter, Thomas F., *And Should I Then Presume?: A Response to Carrier and Tushnet's* An Antitrust Framework for False Advertising, 108 Iowa L. Rev. Online 22 (2023).
Cotter, Thomas F., *Antitrust, Intellectual Property, and Dynamic Efficiency: An Essay in Honor of Herbert Hovenkamp*, Concurrences No. 3, 2020.
Cotter, Thomas F., *Antitrust Implications of Patent Settlements Involving Reverse Payments: Defending a Rebuttable Presumption of Illegality in Light of Some Recent Scholarship*, 71 Antitrust L.J. 1069 (2004).
Cotter, Thomas F., *Comparative Law and Economics of Standard-Essential Patents and FRAND Royalties*, 22 Tex. Intell. Prop. L.J. 311 (2014).

Cotter, Thomas F., Comparative Patent Remedies: A Legal and Economic Analysis (Oxford University Press, Oxford, NY, 2013).

Cotter, Thomas F., *Damages for Noneconomic Harm in Intellectual Property Law*, 72 Hastings L.J. 1055 (2021).

Cotter, Thomas F., December 18, 2024 Testimony Before the United States House of Representatives Subcommittee on Courts, Intellectual Property, and the Internet of the Committee on the Judiciary: "IP and Strategic Competition with China: Part IV — Patents, Standards, and Lawfare."

Cotter, Thomas F., *Essential Facilities, in* Antitrust Law and Economics 157 (Keith N. Hylton ed., Edward Elgar Publishing, Cheltenham, UK, 2010).

Cotter, Thomas F., *Extraterritorial Damages in Patent Law*, 39 Cardozo Arts & Enter. L.J. 1 (2020).

Cotter, Thomas F., *Four Questionable Rationales for the Patent Misuse Doctrine*, 12 Minn. J.L. Sci. & Tech. 457 (2011).

Cotter, Thomas F., FTC v. Actavis, Inc.: *When Is the Rule of Reason Not the Rule of Reason?*, 15 Minn. J.L. Sci. & Tech. 41 (2014).

Cotter, Thomas F., *IP Misuse and Innovation Harm*, Iowa L. Rev. Bull. 52 (2011).

Cotter, Thomas F., *Is Global FRAND Litigation Spinning Out of Control?*, Patently-O L.J. 1 (2021).

Cotter, Thomas F., *Make No Little Plans: Response to Ted Sichelman*, Purging Patent Law of Private Law Remedies, 92 Tex. L. Rev. See Also 25 (2014).

Cotter, Thomas F., *Misuse*, 44 Hous. L. Rev. 901 (2007).

Cotter, Thomas F., *On the Economics of Injunctions in Patent Cases*, ZGE/IPJ 293 (2019).

Cotter, Thomas F., *Optimal Fines for False Patent Marking*, 17 Mich. Telecomms. & Tech. L. Rev. 181 (2010).

Cotter, Thomas F., *Patent Holdup, Patent Remedies, and Antitrust Responses*, 34 J. Corp. L. 1151 (2009).

Cotter, Thomas F., *Patent Remedies and Practical Reason*, 88 Tex. L. Rev. See Also 125 (2010).

Cotter, Thomas F., Patent Wars: How Patents Impact Our Everyday Lives (Oxford University Press, New York, 2018).

Cotter, Thomas F., *The Procompetitive Interest in Intellectual Property Law*, 48 Wm. & Mary L. Rev. 483 (2006).

Cotter, Thomas F., *Refining the "Presumptive Illegality" Approach to Settlements of Patent Disputes Involving Reverse Payments: A Commentary on Hovenkamp, Janis & Lemley*, 87 Minn. L. Rev. 1789 (2003).

Cotter, Thomas F., Remedies in Intellectual Property Law (Edward Elgar Publishing, Cheltenham, UK, 2026).

Cotter, Thomas F., *Setting the Amount of an Injunction Bond (and a Brief Digression about the Wright Brothers)*, Comparative Patent Remedies Blog, Apr. 18, 2014, http://comparativepatentremedies.blogspot.com/2014/04/setting-amount-of-injunction-bond-and.html.

Cotter, Thomas F., *Should Licensees Have a Right to Recover Royalties Paid on a Patent That Is Later Found to Be Invalid or Not Infringed?*, Comparative Patent Remedies Blog, Feb. 11, 2015, http://comparativepatentremedies.blogspot.com/2015/02/should-licensees-have-right-to-recover.html.

Cotter, Thomas F., *Some Thoughts on Teva Copaxone (Anticompetitive Misuse of Divisionals)*, Comparative Patent Remedies Blog, Apr. 21, 2025, https://comparativepatentremedies.blogspot.com/2025/04/some-thoughts-on-teva-copaxone.html.

Cotter, Thomas F., *Unfair Competition by Publicizing a Pending Infringement Action*, Comparative Patent Remedies Blog, May 17, 2025, https://comparativepatentremedies.blogspot.com/2025/05/unfair-competition-by-publicizing.html.

Cotter, Thomas F., *US and German Approaches to FRAND Disputes: Like Ships That Pass in the Night*, *in* FRAND: German Case Law and Global Perspectives 212 (Peter Georg Picht, Thomas F. Cotter & Erik Habich eds., Edward Elgar Publishing, Cheltenham, UK, 2024).

Cotter, Thomas F., *Wrongfulness as Disproportionality: Toward a Law-and-Economics Approach to Wrongful Patent Assertion*, *in* Intellectual Property and the Principle of Proportionality (Christopher Heath & Anselm Kamperman Sanders eds., Kluwer Law International, forthcoming 2026).

Cotter, Thomas F., Erik Hovenkamp & Norman Siebrasse, *Demystifying Patent Holdup*, 76 Wash. & Lee L. Rev. 1501 (2019).

Crane, Daniel A., Actavis, *the Reverse Payment Fallacy, and the Continuing Need for Regulatory Solutions*, 15 Minn. J.L. Sci. & Tech. 51 (2014).

Crane, Daniel A., *Exit Payments in Settlement of Patent Infringement Lawsuits: Antitrust Rules and Economic Implications*, 54 Fla. L. Rev. 747 (2002).

Creighton, Susan, et al., *Cheap Exclusion*, 72 Antitrust L.J. 975 (2005).

Crouch, Dennis, *Discussions of Inequitable Conduct in CAFC Decisions*, Patently-O, Jan. 29, 2025, https://patentlyo.com/patent/2025/01/discussions-inequitable-decisions.html.

Cui, Yabing, *Across the Fault Lines: Chinese Judicial Approaches to Injunctions and SEP's*, China IPR Blog, June 5, 2018, https://chinaipr.com/2018/06/05/across-the-fault-lines-chinese-judicial-approaches-to-injunctions-and-seps/.

Curtin, Rebecca Schoff, *Slapping Patent Trolls: What Anti-Trolling Legislation Can Learn from the Anti-SLAPP Movement*, 18 Stan. Tech. L. Rev. 39 (2014).

Daniel, B.D., *Walker Process Proof: The Proper Prescription*, 41 Rutgers L.J. 105 (2009).

de Haan, Tanguy, *The CJEU Sides With IP Right Holders: The* Bayer Pharma *Judgment (C-688/17) and the Consequences of the Europeanisation of Provisional and Precautionary Measures Relating to IP Rights*, 42 EIPR 767 (2020).

de Rassenfosse, Gaétan, et al., *Low-Quality Patents in the Eye of the Beholder: Evidence from Multiple Examiners*, 37 J.L. Econ. & Org. 607 (2021).

Delrahim, Makan, *The "New Madison" Approach to Antitrust and Intellectual Property Law*, Keynote Address at the University of Pennsylvania Law School (Philadelphia, PA, Mar. 16, 2018), https://www.justice.gov/opa/speech/assistant-attorney-general-makan-delrahim-delivers-keynote-address-university.

Delrahim, Makan, *Take It to the Limit: Respecting Innovation Incentives in the Application of Antitrust Law*, Remarks at USC Gould School of Law—Application of Competition Policy to Technology and IP Licensing (Los Angeles, Cal., Nov. 10, 2017), https://www.justice.gov/opa/speech/file/1010746/download.

Devlin, Alan, *Antitrust Limits on Targeted Patent Aggregation*, 67 Fla. L. Rev. 775 (2016).

Dijkman, Léon, *CJEU Rules that Repeal of Provisional Measure Does Not Automatically Create Liability for Wrongful Enforcement*, 14 JIPLP 917 (2019).

Dijkman, Léon, The Proportionality Test in European Patent Law: Patent Injunctions Before EU Courts and the UPC (Hart Publishing/Bloomsbury Publishing, London, 2023).

Dodge, William, *International Comity in American Law*, 115 Colum. L. Rev. 2071 (2015).

Domitrovich, Stephanie, *Fulfilling* Daubert*'s Gatekeeping Mandate Through Court-Appointed Experts*, 106 J. Crim. L. & Criminology 35 (2016).

Dong, Jialin, *The Interpretation and function orientation of the principle of prohibiting abuse of rights*, 14 J. Educ., Humanities & Soc. Sci. 602 (2023).

Drahozal, Christopher R., *Some Observations on the Economics of Comity*, *in* Economic Analysis of International Law: Contributions to the 13th Travemunde Symposium on the Economic Analysis of Law (Mar. 29–31, 2012) 147 (Thomas Eger, Stefan Oeter & Stefan Voigt eds., Mohr Siebeck, Tübingen, 2014), https://papers.ssrn.com/sol3/papers.cfm?abstract_id=2101400).

Du, Guodong, *Attorney's Fees in China: Does the Losing Party Pay?*, China Justice Observer, Sept. 1, 2019.

Du, Yu, *Unjustified Threats of Legal Proceedings in IP Actions in China*, HG.org, https://www.hg.org/legal-articles/unjustified-threats-of-legal-proceedings-in-ip-actions-in-china-48693.

Easterbook, Frank H., *The Limits of Antitrust*, 63 Tex. L. Rev. 1 (1984).

Edlin, Aaron, et al., Actavis *and Error Costs: A Reply to Critics*, Antitrust Source, Oct. 2014.

Edlin, Aaron, et al., *The* Actavis *Inference: Theory and Practice*, 67 Rutgers Univ. L. Rev. 585 (2015).

EFPIA, *Clinical Trials*, https://www.efpia.eu/about-medicines/development-of-medicines/regulations-safety-supply/clinical-trials/.

Elhauge, Einer, *Making Sense of Antitrust Petitioning Immunity*, 80 Cal. L. Rev. 1177 (1992).

Elhauge, Einer, *Tying, Bundled Discounts, and the Death of the Single Monopoly Profit Theory*, 123 Harv. L. Rev. 397 (2009).

Elhauge, Einer, United States Antitrust Law and Economics (2d ed., Thomson Reuters/Foundation Press, New York, 2011).

Elhauge, Einer, & Alex Krueger, *Solving the Patent Settlement Puzzle*, 91 Tex. L. Rev. 283 (2012).

EPLIT, Survey on Costs of Patent Litigation Across Europe (2021).

European SPCs Unravelled: A Practitioner's Guide to Supplementary Protection Certificates in Europe (Oswin Ridderbusch & Alexa von Uexküll 2d ed., Kluwer Law International, Alphen aan den Rijn, 2021).

Fackrell, Sarah, *The Counterfeit Sham*, 138 Harv. L. Rev. 472 (2024).

Farrell, Joseph, et al., *Standard Setting, Patents, and Hold-up*, 74 Antitrust L.J. 603 (2007).

Feldman, Robin C., *Regulatory Property: The New IP*, 40 Colum. J. L. & Arts 53 (2016).

Feldman, Robin C., & Mark A. Lemley, *The Sound and the Fury of Patent Activity*, 103 Minn. L. Rev. 1793 (2019).

Fischmann, Filipe, *Patent Litigation and Cost-Shifting in Europe: Critical Appraisal and Proposal of Alternative Solutions*, 10 JIPLP 98 (2015).

Foss-Solbrekk, Katarina, *The Divisional Game: Using Procedural Rights to Impede Generic/Biosimilar Market Entry*, 53 Int'l Rev. Intell. Prop. & Comp. L. 1007 (2022).

Fox, James, et al., *UK Threats: Worldwide Consequences?*, 40 European Intell. Prop. Rev. 74 (2018).

Friedman, David D., *Beyond Fee Shifting: A Proposal for Tort Reform* (unpublished draft, on file with author).

Friedmann, Daniel, *Restitution of Benefits Obtained Through the Appropriation of Property or the Commission of a Wrong*, 80 Colum. L. Rev. 504 (1980).

Gao, Jie, *Development of the FRAND Jurisprudence in China*, 21 Colum. Sci. & Tech. L. Rev. 446 (2020).

Gebru, Anan K., *Biopiracy as an Abuse of the Patent System*, *in* Intellectual Property Excesses: Exploring the Boundaries of IP Protection 111 (Enrico Bonadio & Aislinn O'Connell eds., Hart Publishing/Bloomsbury Publishing, Oxford, 2022).

Gervais, Daniel, The TRIPS Agreement: Drafting History and Analysis (4th ed., Sweet & Maxwell/Thomson Reuters, London, 2012).

Ghafele, Roya, *Global FRAND Licensing in Light of* Unwired Planet v. Huawei, 24 UCLA J. L. & Tech. (2020).

Gifford, Daniel J., & Robert T. Kudrle, The Atlantic Divide in Antitrust: An Examination of US and EU Competition Policy 10 (University of Chicago Press, Chicago, 2015).

Goldberg, Victor P., *Regulation and Administered Contracts*, 7 Bell J. Econ. 426 (1976).

Goldman, Eric, *A SAD Scheme of Abusive Intellectual Property Litigation*, 123 Colum. L. Rev. Forum 183 (2023).

Gómez-Arostegui, H. Tomás, *Prospective Compensation in Lieu of a Final Injunction in Patent and Copyright Cases*, 78 Fordham L. Rev. 1661 (2010).

Goold, Patrick, *Unbundling the "Tort" of Copyright Infringement*, 102 Va. L. Rev. 1833 (2016).

Greenbaum, Eli, *No Forum to Rule Them All: Comity and Conflict in Transnational FRAND Disputes*, 94 Wash. L. Rev. 1085 (2019).

Griffiths, Jonathan, *Enforcement of Intellectual Property Rights and the Right to a Fair Trial*, *in* Research Handbook on Human Rights and Intellectual Property 438 (Christophe Geiger ed., Edward Elgar Publishing, Cheltenham, UK, 2015).

Grosskopf, Ofer, & Barak Medina, *Remedies for Wrongfully-Issued Preliminary Injunctions: The Case for Disgorgement of Profits*, 32 Seattle U. L. Rev. 903 (2009).

Gugliuzza, Paul R., *Patent Trolls and Preemption*, 101 Va. L. Rev. 1579 (2015).

Gugliuzza, Paul R., *Regulating Patent Assertions*, *in* Patent Assertion Entities and Competition Policy 85 (D. Daniel Sokol ed., Cambridge University Press, Cambridge, NY, 2017).

Gugliuzza, Paul R., *State Anti-Troll Statutes at the Federal Circuit. Or Not*, 51 AIPLA Q.J. 395 (2023).

Guglyuvatyy, Evgeny, Natalai Stoianoff & Shanti Das, *Patents and Unjustified Threats—Legal Solutions in Australia*, 27 J. World Intell. Prop. L. 112 (2023).

Gupta, Kirti, & Urŝka Petrovčič, *Evidence of Systematic "Patent Holdout"*, 38 Berkeley Tech. L.J. 575 (2023).

Habich, Erik, *Willingness to License on FRAND Terms*, *in* FRAND: German Case Law and Global Perspectives 2 (Peter Georg Picht, Thomas F. Cotter & Erik Habich eds., Edward Elgar Publishing, Cheltenham, UK, 2024).

Haconen, Uri S., *Evergreening at Risk*, 33 Harv. J.L. & Tech. 479 (2020).

Hakun, Nicholas E., *Strategic Litigation and Antitrust Petitioning Immunity*, 12 UC Irvine L. Rev. 865 (2022).

Halász, Bálint, *Hungary*, *in* Preliminary Injunctions: What Approach to Liability is Taken Across the Globe? 13 (Bird & Bird LLP, Apr. 2024).

Hall, Bronwyn H., & Dietmar Harhoff, *Recent Research on the Economics of Patents* 12–15 (Nat'l Bureau Econ. Res., Working Paper No. 1773, 2012), http://www.nber.org/papers/w17773.

Harris, Barry C., et al., *Activating* Actavis*: A More Complete Story*, Antitrust, Spring 2013.

Harrison, Jeffrey L., *Reconceptualizing the Expert Witness: Social Costs, Current Controls, and Proposed Responses*, 18 Yale J. Reg. 253 (2001).

Hart, Oliver, *Incomplete Contracts*, in 2 The New Palgrave: A Dictionary of Economics 752 (John Eatwell, Murray Milgate & Peter Newman eds., W.W. Norton & Company, Inc., New York, 1987).

Harutyunyan, Ani, et al., *Patent Quality in the United States: Findings and Suggestions for Policymakers*, Sunwater Institute Policy Report (2024).

Hashiguchi, Mizuki, *Unraveling the Conundrums of Running Royalties in Cross-Border Patent License Agreements*, les Nouvelles, Mar. 2017.

Hattori, Makoto, *Case No. 48, Interim Procedures and Protective Orders, in* Japanese Patent Law: Cases and Comments 524 (Christopher Heath & Atsuhiro Furuta eds., Kluwer Law International, Alphen aan den Rijn, 2019).

Heath, Christopher, *Case No. 56, Threats—Warning Letter Alleging Patent Infringement—Standard of Liability, in* Japanese Patent Law: Cases and Comments 601 (Christopher Heath & Atsuhiro Furuta eds., Kluwer Law International, Alphen aan den Rijn, 2019).

Heath, Christopher, *Patent Enforcement in Japan, in* Patent Enforcement Worldwide: Writings in Honour of Dieter Stauder 383 (Christopher Heath ed. 3d ed., Hart Publishing, Oxford, 2015).

Heath, Christopher, *Wrongful Patent Enforcement—Threats and Post-Infringement invalidity in Comparative Perspective*, 39 IIC 307 (2008).

Helmers, Christian, & Brian J. Love, *Patent Law Reform and Innovation: An Empirical Assessment of the Last 20 Years*, Oct. 19, 2023, https://ssrn.com/abstract=4580645.

Helmers, Christian, et al., *Is There a Patent Troll Problem in the U.K.?*, 24 Fordham Intell. Prop. Media & Ent. L.J. 509 (2014).

Helmers, Christian, et al., *The Effect of Fee Shifting on Litigation: Evidence from a Policy Innovation in Intermediate Cost Shifting*, 23 Am. L. & Econ. Rev. 56 (2021).

Hemphill, C. Scott, *Paying for Delay: Pharmaceutical Patent Settlement as a Regulatory Design Problem*, 81 N.Y.U. L. Rev. 1553 (2006).

Hemphill, C. Scott, & Bhaven N. Sampat, *Drug Patents at the Supreme Court*, 339 Sci. 1386 (2013).

Hemphill, C. Scott, & Bhaven N. Sampat, *When Do Generics Challenge Drug Patents?*, 8 J. Empirical Legal Stud. 613 (2011).

Hemphill, C. Scott, & Tim Wu, *Nascent Competitors*, 168 U. Penn. L. Rev. 1879 (2020).

Hilty, Reto M., *Legal Remedies Against Abuse, Misuse, and Other Forms of Inappropriate Conduct of IP Right Holders, in* Compulsory Licensing: Practical Experiences and Ways Forward 377 (Reto M. Hilty & Kung-Chung Liu eds., Springer, Heidelberg, 2015).

Hovenkamp, Erik, *Antitrust Law and Patent Settlement Design*, 32 Harv. J.L. & Tech. 418 (2019).

Hovenkamp, Erik, & Jorge Lemus, *Antitrust Limits on Patent Settlements: A New Approach*, 70 J. Indu. Econ. 257 (2022).

Hovenkamp, Herbert, *Antitrust and the Patent System: A Reexamination*, 76 Ohio St. L.J. 467 (2015).

Hovenkamp, Herbert, *FRAND and Antitrust*, 105 Cornell L. Rev. 1683 (2020).

Hovenkamp, Herbert, *Monopolizing Digital Commerce*, 64 Wm. & Mary L. Rev. 1677 (2023).

Hovenkamp, Herbert, *Post-Sale Restraints and Competitive Harm*, 67 N.Y.U. Ann. Surv. Am. L. 487 (2011).

Hovenkamp, Herbert, *The Monopolization Offense*, 61 Ohio St. L.J. 1035, 1044 (2010).

Hovenkamp, Herbert, Mark A. Lemley & Mark D. Janis, *Anticompetitive Settlement of Intellectual Property Disputes*, 87 Minn. L. Rev. 1719 (2003).

Hovenkamp, Herbert, et al., IP and Antitrust: An Analysis of Antitrust Principles Applied to Intellectual Property Law (Wolters Kluwer Legal & Regulatory U.S., New York, 2023).

Hovenkamp, Herbert, & Fiona Scott Morton, *Framing the Chicago School of Antitrust Analysis*, 168 U. Penn. L. Rev. 1843 (2020).

Hurwitz, James D., *Abuse of Government Process, the First Amendment, and the Boundaries of* Noerr, 74 Geo. L.J. 65 (1985).

Hylton, Keith N., *Duty in Tort Law: An Economic Approach*, 75 Fordham L. Rev. 1501 (2006).

IP-Portal: European IP Law, *Article 69*, https://www.ippt.eu/legal-texts/upc-agreement/article-69.

Jamjoom, Mohammed, et al., *Generic Entry and Effect of Market Competition on Outpatient Pharmacy Drug Prices*, 20 J. Generic Medicines 69 (2024).

Karl, Christof, Björn Kalbfus, Hubertus Schacht & Michael Schneider, *Unjustified Allegations of Infringement of Intellectual Property Rights from a German Perspective*, 74 GRUR Int. 950 (2025).

Karpan, Andrew, *New Bills Target "Patent Thickets" and "Product Hopping"*, Law360 (Mar. 17, 2025), https://www.law360.com/articles/2311687/new-bills-target-patent-thickets-and-product-hopping-.

Kesan, Jay P., *Carrots and Sticks to Create a Better Patent System*, 17 Berkeley Tech. L.J. 763 (2002).

Khan, Lina, *The New Brandeis Movement: America's Antimonopoly Debate*, 9 J. Eur. Comp. L. & Prac. 131 (2018).

Kiebczak, Stephan, et al., *The Effect of Patent Litigation and Patent Assertion Entities on Entrepreneurial Activity*, 45 Res. Pol'y 218 (2015).

Kim, Samuel, *Post-*Daubert: *Expert Hot-Tubbing as a Workable Tool for Trial Judges*, 34 Fed. Cir. B.J. 121 (2025).

Klein, Benjamin, *Why Hold-Ups Occur: The Self-Enforcing Range of Contractual Relationships*, 34 Econ. Inquiry 444 (1996).

Klein, Benjamin, et al., *Vertical Integration, Appropriable Rents, and the Competitive Contracting Process*, 21 J.L. & Econ. 297 (1978).

Klein, Christopher C., *Anticompetitive Litigation and Antitrust Liability*, Dep't of Econ. & Fin. Working Paper Series (Aug. 2007), *available at* https://capone.mtsu.edu/berc/working/SHAM07WP.pdf.

Klein, Christopher C., *Strategic Sham Litigation: Economic Incentives in the Context of the Case Law*, 6 Int'l Rev. L. & Econ. 241 (1986).

Knowles, Sherry, & Anthony Prosser, *Let's Do Something About the Unauthorized Doctrine of Non-Statutory Judicially Created Obviousness-Type Double Patenting*, IP Watchdog, Sept. 6, 2022, https://ipwatchdog.com/2022/09/06/lets-something-unauthorized-doctrine-non-statutory-judicially-created-obviousness-type-double-patenting/id=151271/.

Kreindler, Richard, *Corruption in International Investment Arbitration: Jurisdiction and the Unclean Hands Doctrine*, *in* Between East and West: Essays in Honour of Ulf Franke 309 (JurisNet, LLC, Huntington, NY, 2010).

Krent, Harold J., *Explaining One-Way Fee Shifting*, 79 Va. L. Rev. 2039 (1993).

Kroll, Kyle, *Prosecuting Inequitable Conduct*, 109 Minn. L. Rev. Headnotes 49 (2020).

Kühnen, Thomas, Handbuch der Patentverletzung (16th ed., Heymanns, Hürth, 2024).

Kuipers, Gertjan, Douwe Groenevelt & Oscar Lamme, *A Further Perspective On Apple v Samsung: How to Successfully Enforce Standard Essential Patents (SEPs) In The Netherlands*, Mondaq, Sept. 11, 2012, https://www.mondaq.com/patent/196082/a-further-perspective-on-apple-v-samsung-how-to-successfully-enforce-standard-essential-patents-seps-in-the-netherlands.

Kun, Liang, *Abuse of Patent Infringement Notices and Its Regulation*, 2 China Pats. & Trademarks 47 (2023).

Küppers, Roland, & Nora Wessendorf, *Germany*, *in* Global Patent Litigation: How and Where to Win (Michael C. Elmer & C. Gregory Gramenopolous eds., Bloomberg Law, Arlington, VA, 2021) (ebook).

Laakkonen, Ari, et al., *Summary Report: AIPPI Q289-SR-Patents-2024: Harmonisation of Disclosure Requirements and Consequences of Non-compliance* (July 10, 2024).

Lanjouw, Jean O., & Josh Lerner, *Tilting the Table? The Use of Preliminary Injunctions*, 44 J.L. & Econ. 573 (2001).

Laser, Christa, *Equitable Defenses in Patent Law*, 75 U. Miami L. Rev. 1 (2020).

Lavenue, Lionel, et al., *Evolving Case Law Elucidates Atty Fees for Patent Litigants*, Law360, July 17, 2020.

Leaffer, Marshall, *Patent Misuse and Innovation*, 10 J. High Tech. L. 142 (2010).

Lee, William F., & A. Douglas Melamed, *Breaking the Vicious Cycle of Patent Damages*, 101 Cornell L. Rev. 385 (2016).

Leffler, Keith, & Cristofer Leffler, *The Probabilistic Nature of Patent Rights*, Antitrust, Summer 2003, at 77.

Lemley, Mark A., *Faith-Based Intellectual Property*, 62 UCLA L. Rev. 1328 (2015).

Lemley, Mark A., *Ongoing Confusion over Ongoing Royalties*, 76 Mo. L. Rev. 695 (2011).

Lemley, Mark A., *Rational Ignorance at the Patent Office*, 95 Nw. U. L. Rev. 1495 (2001).

Lemley, Mark A., *The Surprising Resilience of the Patent System*, 95 Tex L. Rev. 1 (2016).

Lemley, Mark A., & Lisa Larrimore Ouellette, *Fixing Double Patenting*, 74 Am. U. L. Rev. 1013 (2025).

Lemley, Mark A., & Christopher R. Leslie, *Categorical Analysis in Antitrust Jurisprudence*, 93 Iowa L. Rev. 1207 (2008).

Lemley, Mark A., & A. Douglas Melamed, *Missing the Forest for the Trolls*, 113 Colum. L. Rev. 2117 (2013).

Lemley, Mark A., & Carl Shapiro, *Patent Holdup and Royalty Stacking*, 85 Tex. L. Rev. 1991 (2007).

Lemley, Mark A., & Carl Shapiro, *The Role of Antitrust in Preventing Patent Holdup*, 168 U. Penn. L. Rev. 2019 (2020).

Lemley, Mark A., & Ragesh Tangri, *Ending Patent Law's Willfulness Game*, 18 Berkeley Tech. L.J. 1085 (2003).

Léonard, Amandine, *"Abuse of Rights" in Belgian and French Patent Law – A Case Law Analysis*, 7 JIPITEC 30 (2016).

Léonard, Amandine, Abuse of Rights in European Patent Law: Reconsidering the Principle of the Prohibition of Abuse of Rights as an Internal Correction Mechanism Against Over-Enforcement Practices by Right Holders (Apr. 30, 2019) (unpublished Ph.D. thesis submitted to KU Leuven, on file with author).

Leslie, Christopher R., *Patents of Damocles*, 83 Ind. L.J. 133 (2008).

Leslie, Christopher R., *The Anticompetitive Effects of Unenforced Invalid Patents*, 91 Minn. L. Rev. 101 (2006).

Leslie, Christopher R., *The Role of Consumers in* Walker Process *Litigation*, 13 Sw. J. L. & Trade Am. 281 (2007).

Leubsdorf, John, *The Standard for Preliminary Injunctions*, 91 Harv. L. Rev. 525 (1978).

Lianos, Ioannis, & Pierre Régibeau, *"Sham" Litigation: When Can It Arise and How Can It Be Reduced?*, 62 Antitrust Bull. 643 (2017).

Lichtman, Douglas, *Irreparable Benefits*, 116 Yale L.J. 1284 (2007).

Lichtman, Douglas, *Uncertainty and the Standard for Preliminary Relief*, 70 U. Chi. L. Rev. 197 (2004).

Lim, Daryl, Patent Misuse and Antitrust Law: Empirical, Doctrinal, and Policy Perspectives (Edward Elgar Publishing, Cheltenham, UK, 2013).

Lin, Fen, Waverly Ding & Shi Chen, *The Patent Gold Rush? An Empirical Study of Patent Bubbles in Chinese Universities (1990-2019)*, https://papers.ssrn.com/sol3/papers.cfm?abstract_id=4447754.

Love, Brian J., et al., *Patent Assertion Entities in Europe*, *in* Patent Assertion Entities and Competition Policy 104 (D. Daniel Sokol ed., Cambridge University Press, Cambridge, NY, 2017).

Love, Brian J., & James C. Yoon, *Expanding Patent Law's Customer Suit Exception*, 93 B.U. L. Rev. 1605 (2013).

Machlup, Fritz, *An Economic Review of the Patent System*, Study of the Subcommittee on Patents, Trademarks, and Copyrights, of the Committee on the Judiciary of the United States Senate (1958).

Maggiolino, Mariateresa, Intellectual Property and Antitrust: A Comparative Economic Analysis of US and EU Law (Edward Elgar Publishing, Cheltenham, UK, 2011).

Malani, Anup, & Jonathan S. Masur, *Raising the Stakes in Patent Cases*, 101 Geo. L.J. 637 (2013).

Mammen, Christian E., *Controlling the "Plague": Reforming the Doctrine of Inequitable Conduct*, 24 Berkeley Tech. L.J. 1329 (2009).

Marinova, Miroslava, *Unmasking Excessive Pricing: Evolution of EU Law on Excessive Pricing from* United Brands *to* Aspen, 20 Eur. Comp. J. 315 (2024).

Marshall, Joshua, *Unjustified Threats as a Cause of Action*, 42 European Intell. Prop. Rev. 150 (2020).

Matcham, William, & Mark Schankerman, *Screening Property Rights for Innovation*, https://papers.ssrn.com/sol3/papers.cfm?abstract_id=4519999.

McGowan, David, *Who's Suing You?*, 25 Minn. J. L. Sci. & Tech. 73 (2023).

Meier-Beck, Peter, *Should the Unified Patent Court Set FRAND Terms?*, 74 GRUR Int. 342 (2025).

Melamed, A. Douglas, *Mergers Involving Nascent Competition*, *in* Judging Big Tech: Insights on Applying U.S. Antitrust Laws to Digital Markets 38 (Erika M. Douglas et al. eds. 2022).

Meurer, Michael, *Controlling Opportunistic and Anti-Competitive Intellectual Property Litigation*, 44 B.C. L. Rev. 509 (2003).

Mezzanotti, Filippo, *Roadblock to Innovation: The Role of Patent Litigation in Corporate R&D*, 67 Mgmt. Sci. 7362 (2021).

Mezzanotti, Filippo, & Timothy Simcoe, *Patent Policy and American Innovation After* eBay*: An Empirical Examination*, 48 Rsch. Pol'y 1271 (2019).

Miceli, Thomas J., & Michael P. Stone, *"Piggyback" Lawsuits and Deterrence: Can Frivolous Litigation Improve Welfare?*, 39 Int'l Rev. L. & Econ. 49 (2014).

Montaña, Miquel, *The CJEU Judgment of 11 January 2024 in* Gilead v. Mylan*: Will it Prompt an Exodus of Patent Owners to the UPC?*, Kluwer Patent Blog, Jan. 15, 2024, https://patentblog.kluweriplaw.com/2024/01/15/the-cjeu-judgment-of-11-january-2024-in-gilead-v-mylan-will-it-prompt-an-exodus-of-patent-owners-to-the-upc/.

Mōri, Mineko, & Christopher Heath, *Comment on Decision of the Supreme Court, April 11, 2000—Case No. Hei 10 (O) 364, Texas Instruments v. Fujitsu* ("*Kilby III*"), 35 IIC 91 (2004).

Moussis, Vassili, & Atsushi Yamada, *Abuse of Economic Dependence*, Concurrences, https://www.concurrences.com/en/dictionary/abuse-of-economic-dependence.

Mueller, Florian, *UPC Threatens Amazon with Initial €50M ($59M) Fine, "Severe Consequences", Declares All UK Interim Licenses Unenforceable, Suggests EU WTO Action Against UK*, IP FRAY (Dec. 25, 2025). https://ipfray.com/upc-threatens-amazon-with-initial-e50m-59m-fine-severe-consequences-declares-all-uk-interim-licenses-unenforceable-suggests-eu-wto-action-against-uk/

Murata, Shinichi, *Japan*, *in* Global Patent Litigation: How and Where to Win (Michael C. Elmer & C. Gregory Gramenopolous eds., Bloomberg Law, Arlington, VA, 2021) (ebook).

Myers, Gary, *Litigation as a Predatory Practice*, 80 Ky. L.J. 565 (1991).

Nagakoshi, Yuzuki, & Katsuya Tama, *Japan Without FRANDS? Recent Developments on Injunctions and FRAND-Encumbered Patents in Japan*, 44 AIPLA Q.J. 243 (2016).

Nanda, Ved P., et al., Litigation of International Disputes in U.S. Courts (Thomson Reuters WEST, Eagan, MN, 2017).

Ncube, Caroline, *Limiting Access to Life-Saving Medications: Three South African Case Studies, in* Intellectual Property Excesses: Exploring the Boundaries of IP Protection 111 (Enrico Bonadio & Aislinn O'Connell eds., Hart Publishing/Bloomsbury Publishing, Oxford, NY, 2022).

Nicholson, Walter, Microeconomic Theory: Basic Principles and Extensions (9th ed., South-Western College Publishing, Cincinnati, OH, 2004).

Normand, Jacques, *Final Report: The Two Approaches to the Abuse of Procedural Rights, in* Abuse of Procedural Rights: Comparative Standards of Procedural Fairness 237 (Michele Tartuffo ed., Kluwer Law International, The Hague, 1998).

O'Rourke, Maureen A., *Toward a Doctrine of Fair Use in Patent Law,* 100 Colum. L. Rev. 1177 (2000).

O'Shaughnessy, Kristen, et al., *A Decade of FTC v. Actavis: The Reverse Payment Framework Is Older, But Are the Courts Wiser in Applying It?,* 86 Antitrust L.J. 473 (2024).

Ohly, Ansgar, *Injunctions in the UPC and the Principle of Proportionality,* Stockholm Intell. Prop. L. Rev. 58 (2022).

Ohly, Ansgar, *Three Principles of European IP Enforcement Law: Effectiveness, Proportionality, Dissuasiveness, in* Technology and Competition: Contributions in Honour of Hanns Ullrich 257 (Josef Drexl ed., Larcier, Brussels, 2009).

Ohly, Ansgar, & Martin Stierle, *Unverhältnismäßigkeit, Injunction Gap and Geheimnisschutz im Prozess: Das Zweite Patentrechtsmodernisierungsgesetz im Überblick,* GRUR 1229 (2021).

Osterrieth, Christian, *Patent Enforcement in Germany, in* Patent Enforcement Worldwide: Writings in Honour of Dieter Stauder 111 (Christopher Heath ed. 3d ed., Hart Publishing, Oxford, 2015).

Pattloch, Thomas, *Patent Enforcement in China, in* Patent Enforcement Worldwide: Writings in Honour of Dieter Stauder 316 (Christopher Heath ed. 3d ed., Hart Publishing, Oxford, 2015).

Petherbridge, Lee, Jason Rantanen & Polk Wagner, *Unenforceability,* 70 Wash. & Lee L. Rev. 1751 (2013).

Philippe, D., & G. Sorreaux, *L'abus de la concurrence, in* G. Sorreaux, L'abus de dépendence économique, les clauses abusives et les pratiques du marché déloyales: premières regards sur la loi du 4 avril 2019, 131 DAOR (2019).

Picht, Peter Georg, *Anti-Antisuit Injunctions, in* FRAND: German Case Law and Global Perspectives 200 (Peter Georg Picht, Thomas F. Cotter & Erik Habich eds., Edward Elgar Publishing, Cheltenham, 2024).

Picht, Peter Georg, & Anna-Lena Karczewski, *Germany, in* Injunctions in Patent Law: Trans-Atlantic Dialogues on Flexibility and Tailoring 142 (Jorge L. Contreras & Martin Husovec eds., Cambridge University Press, Cambridge, UK, 2022).

Posner, Richard A., Antitrust Law (2d ed., University of Chicago Press, Chicago, 2001).

Posner, Richard A., *Blackmail, Privacy, and Freedom of Contract,* 141 U. Penn. L. Rev. 1817 (1993).

Price II, W. Nicholson, & Arti Rai, *Manufacturing Barriers to Biologics Competition and Innovation,* 101 Iowa L. Rev. 1023 (2016).

Priest, George L., & Benjamin Klein, *The Selection of Disputes for Litigation,* 13 J. Legal Stud. 1 (1984).

Rantanen, Jason, *Why Priest-Klein Cannot Apply to Individual Issues in Patent Cases* (Mar. 25, 2013), https://papers.ssrn.com/sol3/papers.cfm?abstract_id=2132810.

Rantasaari, Krista, *Abuse of Patent Enforcement in Europe: How Can Start-ups and Growth Companies Fight Back?*, 11 J. Intell. Prop., Info. Tech. & E-Com. L. 358 (2020).

Rantasaari, Krista, *Patent Litigation in Europe: Intermediate Fee Shifting and the UPC*, 18 JIPLP 642 (2023).

Raphael, Thomas, The Anti-Suit Injunction (2d ed., Oxford University Press, Oxford, 2019).

Raynard, Jacques, *Anéantissement du brevet et sort des redevances de license: efficacité de la clause prévoyant la non-restitution des redevances acquitées*, Propriété Industrielle, July-Aug. 2017.

Raynard, Jacques, & Privat Vigand, *Incidence d'une decision d'annulation d'un brevet sur une decision irrevocable de condemnation pour contrefaçon rendue antérieurement*, Propriété Industrielle, April 2012.

Reilly, Greg, *Misleading Patent Signals*, 38 Harv. J. L. & Tech. 107 (2024).

Reilly, Greg, *The Justiciability of Cancelled Patents*, 79 Wash. & Lee L. Rev. 253 (2022).

Rennie-Smith, Christopher, *Patent Enforcement in the United Kingdom*, *in* Patent Enforcement Worldwide: Writings in Honour of Dieter Stauder 81 (Christopher Heath ed. 3d ed., Hart Publishing, Oxford, 2015).

Restatement (Second) of Judgments (Am. L. Inst.1982).

Restatement (Second) of Torts (Am. L. Inst. 1977).

Restatement (Third) of Torts: Liability for Economic Harm (Am. L. Inst. 2020).

Restatement (Third) of Unfair Competition (Am. L. Inst. 1995).

Richter, Stefan, Tobias J. Hessel & Thomas Misgaiski, *Enforcement Security Before German Courts and the Unified Patent Court in Comparison*, JUVE Patent, May 2, 2025.

Rickardsson, Ola, Patent Misuse and 'Sham'—Development of New Principles Under EU Competition Law (2010) (Master's Thesis, Lund University).

Risch, Michael, *Patent Troll Myths*, 42 Seton Hall L. Rev. 457 (2012).

Rogers, Eric, & Young Jeon, *Inhibiting Patent Trolling: A New Approach for Applying Rule 11*, 12 Nw. J. Tech. & Intell. Prop. 291 (2014).

Romet, Isabelle, et al., *Patent Enforcement in France*, *in* Patent Enforcement Worldwide: Writings in Honour of Dieter Stauder 145 (Christopher Heath ed. 3d ed., Hart Publishing, Oxford, 2015).

Roussou, Georgia A., Supplementary Protection Certificates for Medicinal Products (Edward Elgar Publishing, Cheltenham, UK, 2023).

Salop, Steven C., *Potential Competition and Antitrust Analysis: Monopoly Profits Exceed Duopoly Profits*, Org. Econ. Coop. & Dev. 15 (June 10, 2021), https://one.oecd.org/document/DAF/COMP/WD(2021)37/en/pdf.

Schankerman, Mark, & Florian Schuett, *Patent Screening, Innovation, and Welfare*, 89 Rev. Econ. Stud. 2101 (2021).

Schildkraut, Marc G., *Patent Splitting Settlements and the Reverse Payment Fallacy*, 71 Antitrust L.J. 1033 (2004).

Schüßler, Andrea, et al., *AIPPI-Q289: Asking for Harmonization of Disclosure Requirements – Analysis and Opinion from a German and European Perspective*, 74 GRUR Int. 103 (2025).

Seymore, Sean B., *Patent Forfeiture*, 72 Duke L.J. 1019 (2023).

Seymore, Sean B., *Unclean Patents*, 102 B.U. L. Rev. 1491 (2021).

Shampine, Allan, *A Primer on the Economics of Intellectual Property Antitrust Claims*, A.B.A.: Antitrust Mag. Online, June 2023.

Shapiro, Carl, *Navigating the Patent Thicket: Cross Licenses, Patent Pools, and Standard Setting*, *in* 1 Innovation Policy and the Economy 119 (Adam B. Jaffe et al. eds., MIT Press, Cambridge, MA, 2001).

Shapiro, Carl, & Mark A. Lemley, *The Role of Antitrust in Preventing Patent Holdup*, 168 U. Penn. L. Rev. 2019 (2020).

Shepherd, Joanna, *Deterring Innovation:* New York v. Actavis *and the Duty to Subsidize Competitors' Market Entry*, 17 Minn. J. L. Sci. & Tech. 663 (2016).

Shigetomi, Takamitsu, Toshiya Furusho & Takashi Hirose, *Japan*, *in* 7 The Intellectual Property and Antitrust Review (Dieter Paemen ed. 2022).

Sidak, J. Gregory, *FRAND in India*, in The Cambridge Handbook of Technical Standardization Law: Competition, Antitrust, and Patents 336 (Jorge L. Contreras ed., Cambridge University Press, Cambridge, UK, 2018).

Siebrasse, Norman V., *Does Canada Really Follow the "English Rule" for Costs?*, Sufficient Description Blog, Nov. 6, 2013, http://www.sufficientdescription.com/2013/11/does-canada-really-follow-english-rule.html.

Siebrasse, Norman V., Lear v. Adkins *Should Not Be Followed*, Sufficient Description Blog, Jan. 6, 2021, http://www.sufficientdescription.com/2021/01/lear-v-adkins-should-not-be-followed.html.

Siebrasse, Norman V., *No-Challenge Clause in Settlement Is Enforceable*, Sufficient Description Blog, Jan. 4, 2021, http://www.sufficientdescription.com/2021/01/no-challenge-clause-in-settlement-is.html.

Siebrasse, Norman V., *There Is No Such Thing as Licensee Estoppel*, Sufficient Description Blog, Jan. 5, 2021, http://www.sufficientdescription.com/2021/01/there-is-no-such-thing-as-licensee.html.

Siebrasse, Norman V., *Trademarks Act 7(a) Unjustified Threats Claim Fails on Second Branch*, Sufficient Description Blog, Mar. 7, 2024, http://www.sufficientdescription.com/2024/03/trademarks-act-7a-unjustified-threats.html.

Siebrasse, Norman V., et al., *Injunctive Relief*, *in* Patent Remedies and Complex Products: Toward a Global Consensus 115 (Brad Biddle et al. eds., Cambridge University Press, Cambridge, UK, 2019).

Siebrasse, Norman V., & Thomas F. Cotter, *Judicially Determined FRAND Royalties*, *in* 1 Cambridge Handbook of Technical Standardization Law 365 (Jorge L. Contreras ed., Cambridge University Press, Cambridge, UK, 2017).

Siebrasse, Norman V., & Thomas F. Cotter, *The Value of the Standard*, 101 Minn. L. Rev. 1159 (2017).

Simon, Brenda M., *Patent Cover-Up*, 47 Hous. L. Rev. 1299 (2011).

Sink, R. Kehl, Note, *Inequitable Outcomes from the Inequitable Conduct Defense: A Proposal for Revising an Employee-Inventor's Duty to Disclose*, 60 Santa Clara L. Rev. 185 (2020).

Skenyon, John, et al., Patent Damages Law and Practice (Thomson Reuters, Eagan, MN, 2023).

Smeets, Roger, *Does Patent Litigation Reduce Corporate R&D? An Analysis of US Public Firms* (Dec. 2015), https://papers.ssrn.com/sol3/papers.cfm?abstract_id=2443048.

Sorek, Mordechay, Miriam Marcowitz-Bitton & Yotam Kaplan, *Patent Fraud by Design*, 38 Cardozo Arts & Enter. L.J. 359 (2020).

Soter, Kevin B., Note, *Causation in Reverse Payment Antitrust Claims*, 70 Stan. L. Rev. 1295 (2018).

Srinivasan, Swathi, et al., *Patent Trolling in the United States*, Harv. Inst. of Pols. 20–128 (Jan. 2019), https://iop.harvard.edu/sites/default/files/2023-02/IOP%20Tech%20Policy%20Full.pdf.

Steppe, Richard, & Amandine Léonard, *Catching Patent Trolls in the Net of Abuse of Rights: Applying the General Principle of Union Law in the Context of the Unitary Patent Package*, 39 E.I.P.R. 163 (2017).

Stieff, Marco, & Anja Geller, *Ersatzansprüche bei ungerechtfertigten einstweiligen Verfügungen im Pharmabereich: Ansprüche des Antragsgegners und geschädigter Dritter*, GRUR 931 (2023).

Strandburg, Katherine J., *What Does the Public Get? Experimental Use and the Patent Bargain*, Wis. L. Rev. 81 (2004).

Stratton, Bruce, Annotated Patent Act (Dec., Carswell, Canada, 2024).

Supplementary Protection Certificates (SPC): A Handbook (Marco Stieff ed. 2d ed., Edward Elgar Publishing, Cheltenham, UK, 2021).

Svetlicinii, Alexandr, & Fali Xie, *The Anti-suit Injunctions in Patent Litigation in China: What Role for Judicial Restraint?*, 19 J. Intell. Prop. L. & Prac. 734 (2024).

Suarez, Christopher A., *Look Before You "Lock": Standards, Tipping, and the Future of Patent Misuse After* Princo, 13 Colum. Sci. & Tech. L. Rev. 371 (2012).

Suzuki, Masabumi, & Yoshiyuki Tamura, *Patent Enforcement in Japan*, 3 ZGE/IPJ 435 (2011).

Sztoldman, Agnieszka, *Compensation for a Wrongful Enforcement of a Preliminary Injunction under the Enforcement Directive (2004/48/EC)*, 42 EIPR 721 (2020).

Takatoshi, Monya, AIPPI Question Q292-SR-G-2024: Unjustified allegations of infringement of IP rights (Japan) (July 10, 2024).

Thornham, Christopher & Paul England, *England and Wales*, *in* Global Patent Litigation: How and Where to Win (Michael C. Elmer & C. Gregory Gramenopolous eds., Bloomberg Law, Arlington, VA, 2021) (ebook).

Tochtermann, Lea, *Injunctions in European Patent Law*, 11 ZGE/IPJ 257 (2019).

Trimble, Marketa, *The Extraterritorial Enforcement of Patent Rights*, *in* Patent Enforcement Worldwide: Writings in Honour of Dieter Stauder 569 (Christopher Heath ed. 3d ed., Hart Publishing, Oxford, 2015).

Tu, S. Sean, & Mark A. Lemley, *What Litigators Can Teach the Patent Office About Pharmaceutical Patents*, 99 Wash. U.L. Rev. 1673 (2022).

Tu, S. Sean, Rachel Goode & William B. Feldman, *Biologic Patent Thickets and Terminal Disclaimers*, 331 J. Am. Med. Ass'n 355 (2024).

Underdown, Michael, *Abuse of Dominant Position and the Public Interest in Japanese Competition Law*, 4 Macarthur L. Rev. 173 (2000).

Van den Bosch, Bruno, & Friso Bostoen, *Opening the Black Box: Uncovering the European Commission's Cartel Fining Formula Through Computational Analysis*, 3 Stan. J. Computational Antitrust 158 (2023).

Vande Walle, Simon, & Tadashi Shiraishi, *Competition Law in Japan*, *in* Comparative Competition Law 415 (John Duns, Arlen Duke & Brendan Sweeney eds. 2015).

Vogel, Ran, Liam Whatstein & Ephraim Heilizaczer, AIPPI Question Q289-SR-Patents-2024: Israel: Harmonisation of disclosure requirements and consequences of non-compliance (July 10, 2024).

Vogenauer, Stefan, *The Prohibition of Abuse in Law: An Emerging General Principle of EU Law*, *in* Prohibition of Abuse of Law: A New General Principle of EU Law? 521 (Rita de la Feria & Stefan Vogenauer eds., Hart Publishing, Oxford, 2011).

Vezzoso, Simonetta, *Towards an EU Doctrine of Anticompetitive IP-Related Litigation*, 3 J. Eur. Comp. L. & Prac. 521 (2012).

Vrendenbarg, Charlotte J. S., *Towards a Judicial Sustainability Test in Cases Concerning the Enforcement of Intellectual Property Rights*, 2023 GRUR Int. 1125 (2023).

Weatherall, Kimberlee & Elizabeth Webster, *Patent Enforcement: A Review of the Literature* (2013), https://papers.ssrn.com/sol3/papers.cfm?abstract_id=2284519.

Weber, Max, Economy and Society: An Outline of Interpretive Sociology (Guenther Roth & Claus Wittich trs., University of California Press, Berkeley, 1978).

Webinar: German FRAND Cases: the EC's Amicus Brief and Other Developments (Nov. 14, 2024), https://www.youtube.com/watch?v=joNiD2UeWOo.

Weck, Thomas, & Masako Wakui, Comparative Competition Law (World Scientific, Singapore, 2024).

Williamson, Oliver E., The Economic Institutions of Capitalism: Firms, Markets, Relational Contracting (The Free Press (Macmillan), New York, 1985).

Williamson, Oliver E., *The Vertical Integration of Production: Market Failure Considerations*, 61 Am. Econ. Rev. 112 (1971).

Willig, Robert D., & John P. Bigelow, *Antitrust Policy Towards Agreements that Settle Patent Litigation*, 49 Antitrust Bull. 655 (2004).

Wininger, Aaron, *China's State Administration for Market Regulation Releases "Provisions Prohibiting Abuse of Intellectual Property Rights to Exclude and Restrict Competition"*, China IP Law Update, June 29, 2023, https://www.chinaiplawupdate.com/2023/06/chinas-state-administration-for-market-regulation-releases-provisions-prohibiting-abuse-of-intellectual-property-rights-to-exclude-and-restrict-competition/.

Wininger, Aaron, *China's Supreme People's Court Releases Summaries of 43 Legal Application Issues from 2022 Intellectual Property Cases*, China IP Law Update, Apr. 27, 2023, https://www.chinaiplawupdate.com/2023/04/chinas-supreme-peoples-court-releases-summaries-of-43-legal-application-issues-from-2022-intellectual-property-cases/.

Wininger, Aaron, *China's Supreme People's Court Sets Low FRAND Rate in Another OPPO Case*, China IP Law Update, Jan. 15, 2024, https://www.chinaiplawupdate.com/2024/01/chinas-supreme-peoples-court-sets-low-frand-rate-in-another-oppo-case/.

Wininger, Aaron, *Chongqing No. 1 Intermediate People's Court Sets Global FRAND Rate for 5G SPEs at $0.707 in Nokia/OPPO Case*, China IP Law Update, Dec. 16, 2023, https://www.chinaiplawupdate.com/2023/12/chongqing-no-1-intermediate-peoples-court-sets-global-frand-rate-for-5g-seps-at-0-707-unit-in-nokia-oppo-case/.

Winnett, David, *Legal Malpractice: Proving the Case-Within-a-Case*, Plaintiff, Nov. 2015.

Wood, Lisa, *Hot Tub Redux*, Antitrust (Spring 2018).

Wu, Tim, The Curse of Bigness: Antitrust in the New Gilded Age (Columbia Global Reports, New York, 2018).

Xin, Nie, *The Regulation Framework of Antitrust Law on Patent Malicious Litigation*, 21 J. Shanghai U. Fin. & Econ., no. 3, 2019, at 107.

Yan, Yueming, *Corruption and the (Un)Clean Hands Doctrine in Investor-State Arbitration: Definitional and Reciprocity Challenges*, 38 ICSID Rev. – Foreign Investment L.J. 1 (2024).

Yang, Yi, Yong Bai & Ling Ho, *Antitrust Review of Reverse Payment Agreements to Settle Patent Disputes—The Emerging Legal Landscape in Mainland China*, Antitrust Intell. Prop. Healthcare & Life Sciences, Nov. 27, 2023, https://www.cliffordchance.com/insights/resources/blogs/talking-tech/en/articles/2023/11/antitrust-review-of-reverse-payment-agreements-to-settle-patent-disputes.html.

Ye, Fang, & Shi Shuwen, *SPC Allowed Invalidity Defense in a Patent Infringement Action*, Mondaq, Nov. 8, 2022, https://www.mondaq.com/china/patent/1248642/spc-allowed-invalidity-defense-in-a-patent-infringement-action.

Yelderman, Stephen, *Prior Art in the District Court*, 95 Notre Dame L. Rev. 837 (2019).

Yu, Xiang, & Di Lu, *Mainland China*, *in* The Enforcement of Patents 89 (Kung-Chung Liu & Reto M. Hilty eds., Kluwer Law International, Alphen aan den Rijn, 2012).

Yu, Yang, & Jorge L. Contreras, *Will China's New Anti-Suit Injunctions Shift the Balance of Global FRAND Litigation?*, Patently-O Blog, Oct. 22, 2020, https://patentlyo.com/patent/2020/10/contreras-injunctions-litigation.html.

Zhang, Guangliang, *Determination of the Global Royalty Rate of Standard Essential Patents: Judicial Jurisdiction and Determination Method from Chinese Law Perspective*, *in* FRAND: German Case Law and Global Perspectives 234 (Peter Georg Picht, Thomas F. Cotter & Erik Habich eds., Edward Elgar Publishing, Cheltenham, UK, 2024).

Zhang, Hui, *China: Comments on the New Rules on Preliminary Injunction and Representative Precedents*, Kluwer Patent Blog, Feb. 19, 2019, https://patentblog.kluweriplaw.com/2019/02/19/china-comments-on-the-new-rules-on-preliminary-injunction-and-representative-precedents/.

Zhang, Yazhou, AIPPI Question Q292-SR-G-2024: Unjustified Allegations of Infringement of IP Rights (China) (July 10, 2024).

Zheng, Minyu, Legal Responses to Unjustified Threats of Patent Infringement – Intellectual Property Approach or Unfair Competition Approach? (Edward Elgar Publishing, Cheltenham, UK, 2024).

Zheng, Wenton, *Competition Law in China: An Overview*, *in* Comparative Competition Law 415 (John Duns, Arlen Duke & Brendan Sweeney eds., Edward Elgar Publishing, Cheltenham, UK, 2015).

Zigann, Mattias, & Hubertus Schacht, *Anti-Antisuit Injunctions*, *in* FRAND: German Case Law and Global Perspectives 308 (Peter Georg Picht, Thomas F. Cotter & Erik Habich eds., Edward Elgar Publishing, Cheltenham, UK, 2024).

Zycher, Benjamin, et al., *Private Sector Contributions to Pharmaceutical Science: Thirty-Five Summary Case Histories*, 17 Am. J. Therapeutics 101 (2010).

Documents—Asia

China State Administration for Market Regulation, Provisions Prohibiting Abuse of Dominant Market Positions (Apr. 15, 2023).

China State Administration for Market Regulation, Provisions Prohibiting Abuse of Intellectual Property Rights to Exclude and Restrict Competition (Aug. 1, 2023).

China State Administration for Market Regulation, State Council Anti-Monopoly Committee Anti-Monopoly Guidelines in the Field of Intellectual Property Rights (Aug. 6, 2020).

China State Administration for Market Regulation, Anti-Monopoly Guidelines in the Field of SEPs (Nov. 8, 2024), *translated and quoted in* Aaron Wininger, *China's State Administration for Market Regulation Releases Anti-monopoly Guidelines in the Field of Standard Essential Patents*, China IP Law Update, Nov. 11, 2024, https://www.chinaiplawupdate.com/2024/11/chinas-state-administration-for-market-regulation-releases-anti-monopoly-guidelines-in-the-field-of-standard-essential-patents/.

Interpretation of the Supreme People's Court on Several Issues Concerning the Application of Law in the Trial of Civil Disputes over Monopoly (June 2024), *translated and quoted in* Aaron Wininger, *China's Supreme People's Court: Drug Patent Reverse Payment Agreements May Violate the Anti-Monopoly Law*, China IP Law Update, June 24, 2024, https://www.chinaiplawupdate.com/2024/06/chinas-supreme-peoples-court-drug-patent-reverse-payment-agreements-may-violate-the-anti-monopoly-law/.

Japan Fair Trade Commission, Guidelines Concerning Abuse of Superior Bargaining Position under the Antimonopoly Act (Nov. 30, 2010).

Provisions of The Supreme People's Court on Several Issues Concerning the Application of Laws in Adjudication of Action Preservation Cases Involving IP Disputes (Jan. 1, 2019), *English language translation available at* https://www.lindapatent.com/en/law_patent/803.html.

Supreme People's Court, Interpretation of Several Issues Concerning the Application of the General Provisions of the Civil Code of the PRC (Feb. 22, 2022), *English language translation available at* https://www.chinalawtranslate.com/en/%E5%85%B3%E4%BA%8E%E9%80%82%E7%94%A8%E3%80%8A%E4%B8%AD%E5%8D%8E%E4%BA%BA%E6%B0%91%E5%85%B1%E5%92%8C%E5%9B%BD%E6%B0%91%E6%B3%95%E5%85%B8%E3%80%8B%E6%80%BB%E5%88%99%E7%BC%96%E8%8B%A5%E5%B9%B2%E9%97%AE/.

Documents—Australia

Fed. Ct. Australia, Usual Undertaking as to Damages Practice Note (GPN-UNDR) (Oct. 25, 2016).

Documents—European Union

Brief of the European Commission as Amicus Curiae, Munich Higher Regional Court, 6 U 3824/22, *HMD Global Oy v. VoiceAge EVS GmbH & Co KG* (filed Apr. 15, 2024), *available at* https://competition-policy.ec.europa.eu/document/download/66e0bd63-36da-4b27-9eef-70602a8c7be2_en?filename=2024_Amicus_Curiae_6U3824_22Kart_de.pdf.

ETSI Rules of Procedure, Annex 6 Rules 4.1, 6.1, 6bis (Nov. 29–30, 2022), https://www.etsi.org/images/files/IPR/etsi-ipr-policy.pdf.

European Commission, *Press Release, Antitrust: Commission accepts commitments from Rambus lowering memory chip royalty rates - frequently asked questions* (Dec. 9, 2009), https://ec.europa.eu/commission/presscorner/detail/en/memo_09_544.

European Commission, SME Definition, https://single-market-economy.ec.europa.eu/smes/sme-definition_en.

European Medicines Agency, *National competent authorities (human)*, https://www.ema.europa.eu/en/partners-networks/eu-partners/eu-member-states/national-competent-authorities-human#list-of-national-competent-authorities-in-the-eea-11541.

European Medicines Agency, *What we do*, https://www.ema.europa.eu/en/about-us/what-we-do#evaluate-applications-for-marketing-authorisation-12355.

European Union, Principle of Proportionality, https://eur-lex.europa.eu/EN/legal-content/glossary/principle-of-proportionality.html.

Opinion of Advocate General Inghels, C.23.0375.F-C.24.0002.F.

Documents—United Kingdom

2025 Patents Court Guide.

U.K. Courts and Tribunals Judiciary, Intellectual Property Enterprise Court Guide (updated Oct. 2022).

U.K. Law Commission, Patents, Trade Marks, and Designs: Unjustified Threats, Law Com No 360 (Oct. 12, 2015).

Documents—United States

Antitrust Modernization Commission, Report and Recommendations (Apr. 2007), https://govinfo.library.unt.edu/amc/report_recommendation/amc_final_report.pdf.

Approved Drug Products with Therapeutic Equivalence Evaluations (Orange Book), U.S. Food & Drug Admin., https://www.fda.gov/drugs/drug-approvals-and-databases/approved-drug-products-therapeutic-equivalence-evaluations-orange-book.

Brief for the Respondents, Professional Real Estate Investors, Inc. v. Columbia Pictures Industries, Inc., 508 U.S. 49 (1993), No. 91-1043, 1992 WL 541278.

Chief Judge Colm F. Connolly, United States District Court for the District of Delaware, Standing Order Regarding Disclosure Statements Required by Federal Rule of Civil Procedure 7.1 (Apr. 18, 2022), https://www.ded.uscourts.gov/sites/ded/files/Standing%20Order%20Regarding%20Disclosure%20Statements.pdf.

Chief Judge Colm F. Connolly, United States District Court for the District of Delaware, Standing Order Regarding Third-Party Litigation Funding Arrangements (Apr. 18, 2022), https://www.ded.uscourts.gov/sites/ded/files/Standing%20Order%20Regarding%20Third-Party%20Litigation%20Funding.pdf.

Complaint, In the Matter of MPHJ Tech. Invs., LLC, 142 F.T.C. 3003 (Mar. 17, 2015) (No. C-4513), https://www.ftc.gov/system/files/documents/cases/150317mphjtechcmpt.pdf.

Congressional Research Service, *FTC Revives Enforcement of the Robinson-Patman Act*, Jan. 6, 2025, https://crsreports.congress.gov/product/pdf/LSB/LSB11257.

Equal Access to Justice Act Reporting, https://eaja.acus.gov.

FDA, *Review and Approval*, https://www.fda.gov/drugs/biosimilars/review-and-approval.

Fed. Trade Comm'n, Patent Assertion Entity Activity: An FTC Study 1 (Oct. 2016).

Fed. Trade Comm'n, Pay-for-Delay: How Drug Company Pay-Offs Cost Consumers Billions (Jan. 2010).

U.S. Dep't of Commerce, U.S. Pat. & Trademark Off., Proposed Rules: Changes to Require Identification of Attributable Owner, 79 Fed. Reg. 4105 (Jan. 24, 2014).

U.S. Dep't of Health & Human Servs. et al., Guidance of Industry: 180-Day Exclusivity: Questions and Answers (Jan. 2017 draft).

U.S. Dep't of Justice & Fed. Trade Comm'n, Antitrust Guidelines for the Licensing of Intellectual Property (Jan. 12, 2017), https://www.justice.gov/atr/IPguidelines/download.

U.S. Dep't of Justice & Fed. Trade Comm'n, Merger Guidelines (Dec. 18, 2023), https://www.ftc.gov/system/files/ftc_gov/pdf/2023_merger_guidelines_final_12.18.2023.pdf.

U.S. Government Accountability Office, Intellectual Property: Patent Office Should Strengthen Its Efforts to Address Persistent Examination and Quality Challenges (April 30, 2025).

U.S. Pat. & Trademark Off., PTAB Trial Statistics FY24 End of Year Outcome Roundup IPR, PGR (2024), https://www.uspto.gov/sites/default/files/documents/ptab_aia_fy2024__roundup.pdf.

USPTO, Patents Pendency Data July 2024, https://www.uspto.gov/dashboard/patents/pendency.html.

USPTO, *USPTO rescinds memorandum addressing discretionary denial procedures*, Feb. 28, 2025, https://www.uspto.gov/about-us/news-updates/uspto-rescinds-memorandum-addressing-discretionary-denial-procedures.

USPTO Office of Patent Quality Assurance, Summary FY 2024: Annual Review of Sampled Office Actions, https://www.uspto.gov/sites/default/files/documents/mrf-data-fy24.xlsx.

Documents—Other

IP5 Statistics Report 2021, https://link.epo.org/ip5/IP5%20Statistics%20Report%202021_1.pdf.
World Intellectual Property Organization (WIPO), Intellectual property statistical country profile 2024: China, https://www.wipo.int/edocs/statistics-country-profile/en/cn.pdf.
WIPO, Intellectual property statistical country profile 2024: United States, https://www.wipo.int/edocs/statistics-country-profile/en/us.pdf.
WIPO, International Case Management Guide for Judges (2023).
World Intell. Prop. Org. Comm. on Dev. & Intell. Prop., *Study on the Anti-Competitive Enforcement of Intellectual Property (IP) Rights: Sham Litigation*, U.N. Doc. CDIP/9/INF/6 REV, annex 64 (July 30, 2012).

Legislation and Conventions—Asia

Act on Prohibition of Private Monopolization and Maintenance of Fair Trade, art. 2(9) (Japan).
Anti-Monopoly Law (China), arts. 22-24 (2022 rev.), *English language translation available at* https://www.chinalawtranslate.com/en/anti-monopoly-law-2022/.
China Civil Procedure Law art. 108, *English language translation available in* Yang Li, *China, in* Preliminary Injunctions: What approach to liability is taken across the globe? 13 (Bird & Bird LLP, Apr. 2024).
Competition Act, 2002, art. 4(2) (India).
Monopoly Regulation and Fair Trade Act, art. 45(1)(6) (Feb. 6, 2024) (S. Korea).
Patent Act, art. 39 (Japan).
Patent Act, arts. 9, 22, 47 (China).
Patents Act §§ 18(b), 18A (Isr.).

Legislation and Conventions—Australia

Patents Act 1990 (Cth) §§ 128–32.

Legislation and Conventions—Canada

Patent Act § 36(1).
R. Civ. P. 40.03.
Regulations Respecting a Notice of Compliance Pertaining to Patented Medicines, SOR/93-133.
Trademarks Act, R.S.C., 1985, c. T-13, § 7(a).

Legislation and Conventions—European Union/Continental Europe

2d Patent Law Modernization Act (Patentrechtmodernisierungsgesetz, 2.PatMoG), art. 36.
Agreement on a Unified Patent Court, 2013/C 175/01, arts. 27(a), 33(b)(3), 69(4).

Charter of Fundamental Rights of the European Union, OJ C 364/1, Dec. 18, 2000, art. 17(2).
Code de Commerce (Fr.), art. L420-2.
Code of Economic Law, art. IV.2/1 (Bel.).
Competition Act (Ger.), art. 20 (as amended, 2020).
Consolidated Version of the Treaty on European Union art. 5(1), Oct. 26, 2012, 2012 O.J. (C 326) 18.
Council Regulation (EC) No. 1/2003 of 16 December 2002 on the implementation of the rules on competition laid down in Articles 81 and 82 of the Treaty, O.J. L 001, 04/01/2003, art. 23(2).
Directive 2004/48/EC of the European Parliament and of the Council of 29 April 2004 on the Enforcement of Intellectual Property Rights, 2004 O.J. (L 195) 16, arts. 1, 3(2), 6(2), 8(1), 10, 14, recitals 22, 25.
Directive (EU) 2024/1069 of the European Parliament and of the Council of 11 April 2024 on protecting persons who engage in public participation from manifestly unfounded claims of abusive court proceedings ('Strategic lawsuits against public participation'), OJ L., 16.4.2024.
EPC art. 104(1).
EPC Implementing Regulations R.88.
Guidelines on the method of setting fines imposed pursuant to Article 23(2)(a) of Regulation No. 1/2003, 2006/C 210/02, arts. 13, 19, 21.
Protocol (No 2) on the Application of the Principles of Subsidiarity and Proportionality.
Regulation (EC) No. 141/2000 of the European Parliament and of the Council of 16 December 1999 on orphan medicinal products, L 18/1, art. 8.
Regulation (EC) No. 1610/96 of the European Parliament and of the Council of 23 July 1996 concerning the creation of a supplementary protection certificate for plant protection products, L 198/30.
Regulation (EC) No. 1901/2006 of the European Parliament and of the Council of 12 December 2006 on medicinal products for paediatric use and amending Regulation (EEC) No. 1768/92, Directive 2001/20/EC, Directive 2001/83/EC and Regulation (EC) No. 726/2004, L 378/1, art. 36.
Regulation (EC) No. 469/2009 of the European Parliament and of the Council of 6 May 2009 concerning the supplementary protection certificate for medicinal products, L 152/1.
Regulation (EC) No. 726/2004 of the European Parliament and of the Council of 31 March 2004 laying down Community procedures for the authorisation and supervision of medicinal products for human and veterinary use and establishing a European Medicines Agency, L 136/1, art. 14(11).
Regulation (EU) No. 1215/2012 of the European Parliament and of the Council of 12 December 2012 on jurisdiction and the recognition and enforcement of judgments in civil and commercial matters (recast), L 351/1.
Treaty on the Functioning of the European Union, art. 102.
Unified Patent Court Administrative Committee, Decision on scale of ceilings, D AC/10/24042023_E (Apr. 24, 2023).

Legislation and Conventions—United Kingdom

Civ. Proc. Rules 25.9(3)(a), (5).
Patents Act 1977, c. 37, §§ 70(1), 70A(1)–(4), 70B, 70C(1), (3), (4), 70D(3).

Legislation and Conventions—United States

5 U.S.C. § 504.
15 U.S.C. §§ 2, 15(a), 15a, 15c(a)(2), 1117(a).
21 U.S.C. §§ 355(j)(2), (5)(B)(iii)–(iv), (F)(ii).
28 U.S.C. § 2412.
35 U.S.C. §§ 101, 156(c)(3), (g)(6), 271(d)–(e)(1), 285, 292(b).
37 C.F.R. §§ 1.321(c), 1.56, 11.18(b)(2), 42.11(a), (c), 42.51(b)(1)(iii).
42 U.S.C. § 262(k)(7)(A).
Cal. Civ. Proc. Code § 425.16.
Fed. R. Civ. P. 7.1(a), 11, 26(a)(1)(A)(iv), 65(c).
H.R. 1896, 114th Cong. § 2 (as reported by H. Comm. on the Judiciary, Apr. 20, 2015), https://www.congress.gov/bill/114th-congress/house-bill/1896/text.
H.R. 9, 114th Cong. § 4 (as reported by H. Comm. on the Judiciary, July 29, 2015), https://www.congress.gov/bill/114th-congress/house-bill/9/text#toc-H7E6F9EAE8263402492511BD54A562B0B.
H. Rep. 113-279, 113th Cong., 1st Sess., at 108 n.55 (Dec. 2, 2013), https://www.congress.gov/113/crpt/hrpt279/CRPT-113hrpt279.pdf.
Innovation Act, H.R. 3309, § 3(b)(1) 113th Cong., 1st Sess., https://www.congress.gov/113/cprt/HPRT85655/CPRT-113HPRT85655.pdf.
Robinson-Patman Act, 15 U.S.C. §§ 13a-13c, 21a.
Saving High-Tech Innovators from Egregious Legal Disputes Act of 2013 (SHIELD Act), H.R. 845, 113th Cong., § 2 (2013).
U.S. Const. amend. I.
Vt. Stat. Ann. tit. 9, §§ 4196(1)–(2), 4197(a)–(c), 4199 (2023).

International, Multilateral, and Bilateral Treaties

Agreement on Trade-Related Aspects of Intellectual Property Rights, Apr. 15, 1994, Marrakesh Agreement Establishing the World Trade Organization, Annex 1C, Legal Instruments-Results of the Uruguay Round vol. 31, 33 I.L.M. 1197 (1994), arts. 4(1), 8(2), 27(1), 33, 41(1), 45(2), 48, 50(3).
Paris Convention for the Protection of Industrial Property, Sept. 28, 1979, 828 U.N.T.S. 305, art. 5(2).

Table of Cases

A.C. Aukerman Co. v. R.L. Chaides Constr. Co., 960 F.2d 1020 (Fed. Cir. 1992) (en banc), *abrogated in part on other grounds by* SCA Hygiene Prods. Aktiebolag v. First Quality Baby Prods., LLC, 580 U.S. 328 (2017).
ABB Tech. AG v. Hyundai Heavy Indus. Co., 2013 FC 1050 (Can.).
Abbey Forwarding Ltd. v. Hone (No.3) [2014] EWCA Civ. 711, [2015] Ch. 309 (Eng.).
Acer Inc. v. Nokia Techs. Oy, [2025] EWHC 3331 (Pat.) (Eng.).
Advanced Codec Techs. v. OPPO, 2022 Zuigaofa ZhiMinZhong, Nos. 907, 910, 911, 916, 917, and 918 (Dec. 12, 2023).

Agria Polska sp. z o.o. v. European Commission, Case C-373/17 P, ECLI:EU:C:2018:756 (CJEU 2018).
Air Express Ltd. v. Ansett Transport Indus. (Operations) Proprietary Ltd. (1979) 146 CLR 249 (High Ct.) (Austl.).
Alain B. v. Thiérart SARL, PIBD No. 1068, III, 202, Trib. de la grande instance de Paris, Jan. 12, 2017 (Fr.).
Alice Corp. Pty. Ltd. v. CLS Bank Int'l, 573 U.S. 208 (2014).
Allergan USA, Inc. v. MSN Lab'ys Priv. Ltd., 111 F.4th 1358 (Fed. Cir. 2024).
Am. Hosp. Supply Corp. v. Hosp. Prods., 780 F.2d 589 (7th Cir. 1986).
Amazon.com, Inc. v. InterDigital VC Holdings, Inc., [2025] EWHC 3334 (Pat.) (Eng.).
American Cyanamid Co. v. Ethicon Ltd., [1975] A.C. 396 (H.L.) (U.K.).
AMC Capital Mgt., LLC v. FTC, 141 S. Ct. 1341 (2021).
Amgen Inc. v. Sanofi, 143 S. Ct. 1243 (2023).
Apotex, Inc. v. Cephalon, Inc., 255 F. Supp. 3d 604 (E.D. Pa. 2017).
Apotex Inc. v. Eli Lilly & Co., [2015] ONCA 305 (Can.).
Application of Braithwaite, 379 F.2d 594 (C.C.P.A. 1967).
Application of Vogel, 422 F.2d 438 (C.C.P.A. 1970).
Arrowhead Indus. Water, Inc. v. Ecolochem, Inc., 846 F.2d 731 (Fed. Cir. 1988).
Asahi Glass Co. v. Pentech Pharms., Inc., 289 F. Supp. 2d 986 (N.D. Ill. 2003).
Aspen Skiing Co. v. Aspen Highlands Skiing Corp., 472 U.S. 585 (1985).
Associated Press v. United States, 326 U.S. 1 (1945).
AstraZeneca AB v. European Commission, Case C-457/10 P, ECLI:EU:C:2012:770 (CJEU 2012).
AstraZeneca AB v. European Commission, Case T-321/05, ECLI:EU:T:2010:266, (Gen. Ct. 2010).
AstraZeneca AB v. Jiangsu Aisaikang Pharm. Co., (2021) SPX Zhi Civil Final No. 388.
AstraZeneca AB v KRKA, d.d. Novo Mesto, [2014] EWHC 84 (Pat) (Eng.).
AstraZeneca LP v. Breath Ltd., 542 Fed. Appx. 971 (Fed. Cir. 2013), *as amended on reh'g* (Dec. 12, 2013).
Atlantic Richfield Co. v. USA Petroleum Co., 495 U.S. 328 (1990).
Automatic Radio Mfg. Co. v. Hazeltine Rsch., Inc., 339 U.S. 827 (1950).
B.B. Chem. Co. v. Ellis, 314 U.S. 495 (1942).
Baxalta Inc. v. Bayer Healthcare LLC, No. 17-1316-RGA, 2020 WL 5445375 (D. Del. July 13, 2020).
Bayer Pharma AG v. Richter Gedeon Vegyészeti Gyár Nyrt, Case C-688/17, ECLI:EU:C:2019:722 (CJEU 2019).
BE & K Constr. Co. v. NLRB, 536 U.S. 516 (2002).
BGH, Judgment of 10 May 2016, X ZR 114/13—*Wärmetauscher*.
BGH, Judgment of May 5, 2020, KZR 36/17–*FRAND-Einwand I* (Ger.).
BGH, Judgment of Nov. 24, 2020, KZR 35/17– *FRAND-Einwand II* (Ger.).
Blonder-Tongue Lab., Inc. v. University of Ill. Found., 402 U.S. 313 (1971).
Borough of Duryea v. Guarnieri, 564 U.S. 379 (2011).
Brain v. Ingledew Brown Bennison & Garrett (No. 3) [1997] F.S.R. 511 (Ch) (Eng.).
Bristol Myers Squibb Holdings Ireland Unltd. v. Norton (Waterford) Ltd. t/a Teva Pharms. Ireland, [2024] IECA 49 (Ire.).
Broadcast Music, Inc. v. Columbia Broadcasting Systems, Inc., 441 U.S. 1 (1979).
Broadcom Corp. v. Qualcomm Inc., 501 F.3d 297, 314 (3d Cir. 2007).
Brulotte v. Thys Co., 379 U.S. 29 (1964).

BSH Haugeräte GmbH v. Electrolux AB, Case C-339/22, ECLI:EU:C:2025:108 (CJEU 2025).
C.R. Bard, Inc. v. M3 Sys., Inc., 157 F.3d 1340 (Fed. Cir. 1998).
California Motor Transport Co. v. Trucking Unltd., 404 U.S. 508 (1972).
Cancer Rsch. Tech. Ltd. v. Barr Lab'ys, Inc., 625 F.3d 724 (Fed Cir. 2010).
Case AT.40588—Teva Copaxone (Eur. Comm'n 2024).
Chambers v. NASCO, Inc., 501 U.S. 32 (1991).
City of Columbia v. Omni Outdoor Advert., Inc., 499 U.S. 365 (1991).
Cour de cassation, Judgment of June 12, 2007 (Fr.), 39 Int'l Rev. Intell. Prop. & Competition L. 354 (2008)—*False Ceiling* (Fr.).
Cour de cassation, Judgment of May 12, 2004, Case 02-16623 (Fr.).
Data Gen. Corp. v. Grumman Sys. Support Corp., 36 F.3d 1147 (1st Cir. 1994).
Dawson Chem. Co. v. Rohm & Haas Co., 448 U.S. 176 (1980).
Decision and Order, In the Matter of MPHJ Tech. Invs., LLC, 142 F.T.C. 3003 (Mar. 17, 2015) (No. C-4513), https://www.ftc.gov/system/files/documents/cases/150317mphjtechdo.pdf.
Dippin' Dots, Inc. v. Mosey, 476 F.3d 1337 (Fed. Cir. 2007).
Dr. Reddy's Labs. (UK) Ltd. v. Warner-Lambert Co. LLC, [2023] EWCA Civ. 73 (Eng.).
Düsseldorf Regional Court, Judgment of Sept. 29, 2022, 2023 GRUR 957 (Ger.).
Eastern R.R. Presidents Conf. v. Noerr Motor Freight, Inc., 365 U.S. 127 (1961).
eBay Inc. v. MercExchange, LLC., 547 U.S. 388 (2006).
Ericsson Inc. v. Samsung Elecs. Co., Ltd., No. 2:20-CV-00380, 2021 WL 89980 (E.D. Tex. Jan. 11, 2021).
Exergen Corp. v. Wal-Mart Stores, Inc., 575 F.3d 1312 (Fed. Cir. 2009).
Festo Corp. v. Skoketsu Kinzoku Kogyo Kabushiki Co., Ltd., 535 U.S. 722 (2002).
Flexiteek Ams., Inc. v. PlasTEAK, Inc., No. 08-60996-CIV-COHN/SELTZER, 2012 WL 5364247, (S.D. Fla. Oct. 31, 2012).
Flo-Con Sys., Inc. v. Leco Corp., 845 F. Supp. 1576 (S.D. Ga. 1993).
Fresenius Kabi USA, LLC v. Par Sterile Prods., LLC, Case No. 16-4544 (SDW) (LDW), 2020 WL 901967 (D.N.J. Feb. 25, 2020), *vacated and remanded on other grounds*, 841 Fed. Appx. 399 (3d Cir. 2021).
FTC v. AbbVie Inc., 329 F. Supp. 3d 98 (E.D. Pa. 2018), *aff'd in part, rev'd in part on other grounds*, 976 F.3d 327 (3d Cir. 2020).
FTC v. AbbVie Inc., 976 F.3d 327 (3d Cir. 2020).
FTC v. Actavis Inc., 570 U.S. 136 (2013).
FTC v. Qualcomm Inc., 411 F. Supp. 3d 658, 669-80 (N.D. Cal. 2019), *rev'd*, 969 F.3d 974 (9th Cir. 2020).
FTC v. Watson Pharms., Inc., 677 F.3d 1298 (11th Cir. 2012), *rev'd and remanded*, 570 U.S. 136 (2013).
G 0004/19 (Double patenting) 22-06-2021, ECLI:EP:BA:2021:G000419.20210622 (Société des Produits Nestlé S.A.).
Genentech Inc. v. Hoechst GmbH, Case C-567/14, ECLI:EU:C:2016:526, (CJEU 2017).
Generics (UK) Ltd. v. Competition and Markets Authority, Case C-307/18, ECLI:EU:C:2020:52 (CJEU 2020).
Gilead Sciences, Inc. v. Merck & Co., Inc., 888 F.3d 1231 (Fed. Cir. 2018).
GlaxoSmithKline Servs. Unltd. v. Comm'n of the European Communities, Cases C-501/06 P, C-501/06 P, C-513/06 P, C-515/06 P and C-519/06 P, ECLI:EU:C:2009:610 (CJEU 2009).

Golan v. Pingel Enter. Inc., 310 F.3d 1360 (Fed. Cir. 2002).
Goodyear Tire & Rubber Co. v. Haeger, 581 U.S. 101 (2017).
Google LLC v. Sonos, Inc., No. 2024-1097, 2025 WL 2473258 (Fed. Cir. Aug. 27, 2025).
Grip-Pak, Inc. v. Illinois Tool Works, Inc., 694 F.2d 466 (7th Cir. 1982).
Grobelaar v. Newsgroup Newspapers Ltd., [2002] UKHL 40.
Groupement des cartes bancaires (CB) v. European Commission, Case C 67/13 P (CJEU 2009).
Grupo Mexicano de Desarrollo S.A. v. Alliance Bond Fund, Inc., 527 U.S. 308 (1999).
GS Cleantech Corp. v. Adkins Energy LLC, 951 F.3d 1310 (Fed. Cir. 2020).
Guangdong OPPO Mobile Telecomm. Corp., Ltd. v. Sharp Corp., Yue 03 Min Chu No. 689 (Shenzhen Intermediate People's Ct. Oct. 16, 2020) (China).
Gunn v. Minton, 568 U.S. 251 (2013).
H. Lundbeck A/S v. European Commission, Case C-591/16 P, ECLI:EU:C:2021:243 (CJEU 2021).
Handgards, Inc. v. Ethicon, Inc., 601 F.2d 986 (9th Cir. 1979).
Hanover 3201 Realty, LLC v. Village Supermarkets, Inc., 806 F.3d 162 (3d Cir. 2015).
Hazel-Atlas Glass Co. v. Hartford-Empire Co., 322 U.S. 238 (1944).
Hewlett-Packard Co. v. Acceleron LLC, 587 F.3d 1358 (Fed. Cir. 2009).
High Concrete Structures, Inc. v. Nat'l Union Fire Ins. Co., No. 1264, 2004 WL 213235 (Pa. Ct. Com. Pl. Feb. 3, 2004).
Hilton v. Guyot, 159 U.S. 113 (1895).
Hoffmann-La Roche & Co. AG v. Secretary of State, [1975] AC 295 (H.L.) (U.K.).
Hollister Inc. v. Medik Ostomy Supplies Ltd., [2012] EWCA Civ 1419 (Eng.).
HTC Corp. v. Nokia Corp., [2013] EWHC 3778 (Pat.) (Eng.).
Huawei Technologies. Co. Ltd. v. Netgear Deutschland GmbH, UPC_CFI_9/2023 (Munich Local Division Dec. 18, 2024).
Huawei Technologies Co. Ltd. v. ZTE Corp., Case C-170/13, ECLI:EU:C:2015:477 (CJEU 2015).
Huawei v. Conversant, (2019) Zui Gao Fa Zhi Min Zhong 732, 733 & 734 No. 1 (SPC Aug. 20, 2020) (China).
Hurlbut v. Gulf Atl. Life Ins. Co., 749 S.W.2d 762 (Tex. 1987).
Hyatt v. Hirshfeld, 998 F.3d 1347 (Fed. Cir. 2021).
Hydranautics v. FilmTec Corp., 70 F.3d 533 (9th Cir. 1995).
Hydril Co. LP v. Grant Prideco LP, 474 F.3d 1344 (Fed. Cir. 2007).
Illinois Tool Works Inc. v. Independent Ink, Inc., 547 U.S. 28 (2006).
Image Tech. Servs., Inc. v. Eastman Kodak Co., 125 F.3d 1195 (9th Cir. 1997).
Imation Corp. Japan v. One-Blue LLC, Tokyo Dist. Ct., Feb. 18, 2015, Case No. 2013 (Wa) 21383.
Immunex Corp. v. Sandoz, Inc., 964 F.3d 1049 (Fed. Cir. 2020).
Impax Labs., Inc. v. FTC, 994 F.3d 464 (5th Cir. 2021).
Impression Prods., Inc. v. Lexmark Int'l, Inc., 581 U.S. 360 (2017).
IMS Health GmbH & Co. OHG v. NDC Health GmbH & Co. KG, Case C-418/01, ECLI:EU:C:2004:257 (CJEU 2004).
In re Berg, 140 F.3d 1428 (Fed. Cir. 1998).
In re Cardizem Antitrust Litig., 332 F.3d 896 (6th Cir. 2003).
In re Cellect, LLC, 81 F.4th 1216 (Fed. Cir. 2023).
In re Cipro Cases I & II, 348 P.3d 835 (Cal. 2015).
In re Indep. Serv. Orgs. Antitrust Litig., 203 F.3d 1322 (Fed. Cir. 2000).

In re Intuniv Antitrust Litig., Civil Action Nos. 1:16-cv-12653-ADB, 1:16-cv-12396-ADB, 2020 WL 5995326 (D. Mass. Oct. 10, 2020).
In re K-Dur Antitrust Litig., 686 F.3d 197 (3d Cir. 2012), *vacated and remanded*, 570 U.S. 913 (2013).
In re Loestrin 24 Fe Antitrust Litigation, 814 F.3d 538 (1st Cir. 2016).
In re Namenda Direct-Purchaser Antitrust Litig., 331 F. Supp. 3d 152 (S.D.N.Y. 2018).
In re Nexium (Esomeprazole) Antitrust Litig., 842 F.3d 34 (1st Cir. 2016).
In re R.M.J., 455 U.S. 191 (1982).
In re Solodyn (Minocycline Hydrochloride) Antitrust Litig., No. CV 14-MD-02503, 2018 WL 563144 (D. Mass. Jan. 25, 2018).
In re Summit Tech., Inc., No. 9286, Decision and Order (FTC Feb. 23, 1999), https://www.ftc.gov/sites/default/files/documents/cases/1999/03/ftc.gov-d09286visx.do_.htm.
In re Wellbutrin XL Antitrust Litig., 133 F.Supp.3d 734 (E.D. Pa. 2015), *aff'd*, 868 F.3d 132 (3d Cir. 2017).
In re Wellbutrin XL Antitrust Litig. Indirect Purchaser Class, 868 F.3d 132 (3d Cir. 2017).
In re Zetia (Ezetimibe) Antitrust Litig., MDL No. 2:18-md-2836, 2022 WL 3344191 (E.D. Va. Aug. 3, 2022).
Indium Corp. of Am. v. Semi-Alloys, Inc., 566 F. Supp. 1344 (N.D.N.Y. 1983).
Int'l Game Tech. v. WMS Gaming, Inc., 217 F.3d 850 (Fed. Cir. 1999).
Int'l Motor Contest Ass'n v. Staley, 434 F. Supp. 2d 650 (N.D. Iowa 2006).
Intamin, Ltd. v. Magnetar Techs. Corp., 623 F. Supp. 2d 1055 (C.D. Cal. 2009).
InterDigital, Inc. v. Xiaomi Commc'n Tech. Co., Ltd., Delhi High Court, IA 8772/2020, (Delhi High Ct. Oct. 9, 2020) (India).
InterDigital Tech. Corp. v. Lenovo Group Ltd., [2023] EWHC 539 (Pat.) (Eng.), *modified*, [2024] EWCA Civ. 743.
Intergraph Corp. v. Intel Corp., 195 F.3d 1346 (Fed. Cir. 1999).
International Salt Co., Inc. v. United States, 332 U.S. 392 (1947).
Intex Techs. (India) Ltd. v. Telefonaktiebolaget LM Ericsson, 2023:DHC:2243-DB (Delhi High Ct. Mar. 29, 2023) (India).
ITT Promedia NV v. Commission of the European Communities, Case T-111/96, ECLI:EU:T:1998:183 (CJEU 1998).
J.R. Simplot Co. v. McCain Foods USA, Inc., Case No. 1:16-cv-00449, 2024 WL 3796737 (D. Idaho Aug. 13, 2024).
Jiangsu Huari Webbing Leather Co., Ltd. v. Joes Identified in Schedule A, No. 1:23-cv-02605 (S.D.N.Y. Jan. 2, 2024).
Judgment of Aug. 29, 2022, 2001 (ne) 5555 (Tokyo High Ct.) (Japan), 37 Int'l Rev. Intell. Prop. & Competition L. 758 (2006)—*Warning Letter/Metallic Powder*.
Judgment of Dec. 24, 1968, 22 Minshū 3428 (S. Ct.) (Japan).
Judgment of Jan. 26, 1988, 1985 (o) 122 (S. Ct.) (Japan).
Katana Silicon Techs. v. Micron Techs., Inc., 671 F. Supp. 3d 1138 (D. Idaho 2023).
Keystone Driller Co. v. General Excavator Co., 290 U.S. 245 (1933).
Kimble v. Marvel Ent., LLC, 576 U.S. 446 (2015).
King Drug Co. v. SmithKline Beecham, 791 F.3d 388 (3d Cir. 2015).
Kingsdown Med. Consultants, Ltd. v. Hollister Inc., 863 F.2d 867 (Fed. Cir. 1988) (en banc).
Kofoed v. Statteministeriet, Case C-321/05, ECLI:EU:C:2007:408 (CJEU 2007).
KSR Int'l Co. v. Telefex Inc., 550 U.S. 398 (2007).
Laboratoires Negma SAS v. Biogaran SAS, Cour d'appel de Paris, Jan. 27, 2014.
Larson Mfg. Co. of S.D., Inc. v. Aluminart Prods. Ltd., 559 F.3d 1317 (Fed. Cir. 2009).

Lear, Inc. v. Adkins, 395 U.S. 653 (1969).
Leegin Creative Leather Prods., Inc. v. PSKS, Inc., 551 U.S. 877 (2007).
Lenovo Group Ltd. v. Telefonaktiebolaget LM Ericsson (Publ), [2025] EWCA Civ 182 (Eng.).
LePage's, Inc. v. 3M, 277 F.3d 365 (3d Cir. 2002).
Lexmark Int'l, Inc. v. Static Control Components, Inc., 572 U.S. 118 (2014).
LG Elecs., Inc. v. Daewoo Elecs., Inc., 2010da95390 (S. Ct. Jan. 19, 2012) (S. Kor.).
LG Munich, Judgment of Sept. 19, 2024, 7 O 14174/23 (Ger.).
Lite-Netics, LLC v. Nu Tsai Cap. LLC, 60 F.4th 1335 (Fed. Cir. 2023).
Low v. Pfizer Canada, Inc., [2015] BCCA 506 (Can.).
Lupin Ltd. v. European Commission, Case C-144/19 P, ECLI:EU:C:2024:545 (CJEU 2024).
Madey v. Duke Univ., 307 F.3d 1351 (Fed. Cir. 2002).
Mallinckrodt, Inc. v. Medipart, Inc., 976 F.2d 700 (Fed. Cir. 1992).
Mareva Compania Naviera SA v. Int'l Carriers SA (The Mareva), [1980] 1 All E.R. 213 (Ct. App. 1975).
Markman v. Westview Instruments, Inc., 517 U.S. 370 (1996).
Maslowski v. Prospect Funding Partners LLC, 944 N.W.2d 235 (Minn. 2020).
Mayor & City Council of Baltimore v. AbbVie Inc., 42 F.4th 709 (7th Cir. 2022).
MCI Commc'ns Corp. v. Am. Tel. & Tel. Co., 708 F.2d 1081 (7th Cir. 1983).
MedImmune, Inc. v. Genentech, Inc. 549 U.S. 118 (2007).
Medtronic, Inc. v. Mirowski Family Ventures, LLC, 571 U.S. 191 (2014).
Menzis Zorgversekeraar N.V. v. AstraZeneca B.V., Case No. 22/01071, ECLI:NL:HR:2023:1513 (S. Ct. 2023) (Neth.).
Merck Sharp Dohme S.A. v. Human Health Holdings, B.V., S/0026/19 (CNMC 2022) (Sp.).
Mercoid Corp. v. Mid-Continent Inv. Co., 320 U.S. 661 (1944).
Mercoid Corp. v. Minneapolis-Honeywell Regul. Co., 320 U.S. 680 (1944).
Microsoft Corp. v. Comm'n of Eur. Cmtys., Case T-201/04, ECLI:EU:T:2007:289 (Court of First Instance, Grand Chamber, 2007).
Microsoft Corp. v. Motorola, Inc., 696 F.3d 872 (9th Cir. 2012).
Microsoft Corp. v. Motorola, Inc., 795 F.3d 1024 (9th Cir. 2015).
Microsoft Corp. v. Motorola, Inc., 871 F. Supp. 2d 1089 (W.D. Wash. 2012), *aff'd*, 696 F.3d 872 (9th Cir. 2012).
Miller Pipeline Corp. v. British Gas PLC, 69 F. Supp. 2d 1129 (S.D. Ind. 1999).
Monsanto Co. v. Scruggs, 459 F.3d 1328 (Fed. Cir. 2006).
Morton Salt Co. v. G.S. Suppiger Co., 314 U.S. 488 (1942).
MPHJ Tech. Investments, LLC v. Ricoh Ams. Corp., 847 F.3d 1363 (Fed. Cir. 2017).
Mylan AB v. Gilead Sciences Finland Oy, Case C-473/22, ECLI:EU:C:2024:8 (CJEU 2024).
MyPort, Inc. v. Samsung Elecs. Co. Ltd., No. 2:22-CV-00114, 2023 WL 5612445 (E.D. Tex. Aug. 30, 2023).
Nader v. Democratic Nat'l Ctee., 567 F.3d 692 (D. C. Cir. 2009).
Nat'l Collegiate Athletic Ass'n v. Governor of New Jersey, 939 F.3d 597 (3d Cir. 2019).
Nat'l Collegiate Athletic Ass'n v. Murphy, Civ. Action No. 14-06450 (FLW), 2020 WL 7074398 (D.N.J. Dec. 3, 2020).
Nat'l Collegiate Athletic Ass'n v. Alston, 141 S. Ct. 2141 (2021).
Nintendo of Am. Inc. v. Lewis Galoob Toys, Inc., 16 F.3d 1032 (9th Cir. 1994).
Nobelpharma AB v. Implant Innovations, Inc., 141 F.3d 1059 (Fed. Cir. 1998).
Noco Co. v. Shenzhen Carku Tech. Co. Ltd., [2023] EWCA Civ 1502 (Eng.).
Nokia Techs. v. OPPO, Case No. (2021) Yu Min Chu 1232 (Chongqing Intermed. People's Ct. Dec. 13, 2023).

Nomadix, Inc. v. Hosp. Core Servs. LLC, No. CV 14-08256, 2015 WL 3948804 (C.D. Cal. June 29, 2015).
Nova Chems. Corp. v. Dow Chem. Co., [2022] SCC 43 (Can.).
NYNEX Corp. v. Discon, Inc., 525 U.S. 128 (1998).
Octane Fitness, LLC v. ICON Health & Fitness, Inc., 572 U.S. 545 (2014).
OLG Munich, Case 6 U 3824/22 Kart (Mar. 20, 2025) (Ger.).
Optis Cellular Tech. LLC v Apple Retail UK Ltd., [2021] EWHC 2564 (Pat.) (Eng.).
Optis Cellular Tech. LLC v. Apple Retail UK Ltd., [2025] EWCA Civ 552 (Eng.).
Optis Cellular Tech. LLC v. Apple Retail UK Ltd. (Trial B), [2021] EWHC 1739 (Pat.) (Eng.).
Order Modifying Entered Sanctions on Unopposed Remand and *Sua Sponte* Reconsideration, Spectrum Solutions, IILC v. Longhorn Vaccines & Diagnostics, LLC, IPR2021-00847 (Patent 8,084,443 B2), IPR2021-00850 (Patent 8,293,467 B2), IPR2021-00854 (Patent 8,669,240 B2), IPR2021-00857 (Patent 9,212,399 B2), IPR2021-00860 (Patent 9,683,256 B2) (June 5, 2025).
Otter Tail Power Co. v. United States, 410 U.S. 366 (1973).
P&O Nedlloyd B.V. v. Arab Metals Co, Stena Trading A.B., [2006] EWCA Civ 1717 (Eng.).
Pac. Bell Tel. Co. v. linkLine Commc'ns, Inc., 555 U.S. 438 (2009).
Paidar v. Hughes, 615 N.W.2d 276 (Minn. 2000).
Palimport Ltd. v. Ciba-Geigy Ltd., P.D. 29(1) 597 (S. Ct. 1975) (Isr.).
Panasonic Holdings Corp. v. Guangdong OPPO Mobile Telecommunications Corp. Ltd., UPC_CFI_ 210/2023, (Mannheim Local Division, Nov. 22, 2024).
Panasonic Holdings Corp. v. Xiaomi Tech. UK Ltd., [2024] EWCA Civ 1143 (Eng.).
Perma Life Mufflers, Inc. v. Int'l Parts Corp., 392 U.S. 134 (1968).
Petrella v. Metro-Goldwyn-Mayer, Inc., 572 U.S. 663 (2014).
Precision Instrument Manufacturing. Co. v. Automotive Maintenance Machinery Co., 324 U.S. 806 (1945).
Primetime 24 Joint Venture v. Nat'l Broadcasting Co., 219 F.3d 92 (2d Cir. 2000).
Princo Corp. v. ITC., 616 F.3d 1318 (Fed. Cir. 2010) (en banc).
Professional Real Estate Inventors, Inc. v. Columbia Pictures Industries, Inc., 508 U.S. 49 (1993).
Protégé Int'l Ltd. v. Commission européenne, Case T-119/09 (CJEU 2012).
PSC Comput. Prods., Inc. v. Foxconn Int'l, Inc., 355 F.3d 1353 (Fed. Cir. 2004).
Puerto Rico Tel. Co. v. San Juan Cable LLC, 874 F.3d 767 (1st Cir. 2017).
Qualcomm Inc. v. Broadcom Corp., 548 F.3d 1004 (Fed. Cir. 2008).
Radio Telefis Eireann (RTE) v. Comm'n of Eur. Cmtys. (Magill II), Case C-241/91, ECLI:EU:C:1995:98 (CJEU 1995).
Rambus Inc. v. FTC., 522 F.3d 456 (D.C. Cir. 2008).
Riles v. Shell Expl. & Prod. Co., 298 F.3d 1302 (Fed. Cir. 2002).
Rite Aid Corp. v. Lake Shore Invs., 471 A.2d 735 (Md. 1984).
Ritz Camera & Image, LLC v. SanDisk Corp., 700 F.3d 503 (Fed. Cir. 2012).
Samsung Elecs. Co. v. Apple Inc., Rb.'s-Gravenhage, HA ZA 11-2215, HA ZA 11-2213 (June 20, 2012), and HA ZA 11-2212, HA ZA 11-2213, and HA ZA 11-2215 (Mar. 14, 2012).
Samsung Elecs. Co., Ltd. v. Apple Japan Godo Kaisha, Judgment of May 16, 2014, 2013 (Ne) 10043 (IP High Court, Grand Panel) (Japan), *translated at* https://www.courts.go.jp/ip/eng/vc-files/eng/file/25ne10043full.pdf.
Samsung Elecs. Co., Ltd. v. Telefonaktiebolaget LM Ericsson (Wuhan Intermediate People's Ct. Dec. 25, 2020) (China).
Samsung Elecs. Co. v. ZTE Corp., [2025] EWCA Civ 1383 (Eng.).

San-Ei Gen FFI v. Nexira SASU, Cour de Cassation, Jan. 26, 2022, PIBD 179-III-1 (Fr.).
SanDisk Corp. v. STMicroelectronics, Inc., 480 F.3d 1372 (Fed. Cir. 2007).
Sandoz, Inc. v. Amgen, Inc., 582 U.S. 1 (2017).
Sandoz AG v. Bayer Intellectual Property GmbH, [2025] EWHC 2201 (Pat.) (Eng.).
Sanofi-Synthelabo v. Apotex, Inc., 470 F.3d 1368 (Fed. Cir. 2006).
SCA Hygiene Prods. Aktiebolag v. First Quality Baby Prods., LLC, 580 U.S. 328 (2017).
Scherer v. Newmat, Cour de Cassation, June 12, 2007 (Fr.), *English language translation published in* 39 IIC 354 (2008).
Sec'y of State for Health v. Servier Labs. Ltd. [2021] UKSC 24.
Semiconductor Energy Lab'y Co. v. Samsung Elecs. Co., 204 F.3d 1368 (Fed. Cir. 2000).
Seoul District Court [Dist. Ct.], 2011Kahap39552, Aug. 24, 2012 (S. Kor.).
Servier v. European Commission, Case C-201/19 P, ECLI:EU:C:2024:552 (CJEU 2024).
Shenzhen Libang Precision Instr. Co. v. Shenzhen Mairui Biomed. Elecs. Co., Case No. (2015) Min Shen I No. 191 (Supreme People's Ct. 2015) (China).
Shijiazhuang Shuanghuan Automobile Co. v. Honda Motor Co., Case No. (2014) Min San Zhong Zi No. 7 (Supreme People's Ct. 2015) (China), https://enipc.court.gov.cn/zh-cn/news/view-35.html.
Silbersher v. Valeant Pharms. Int'l, Inc., 89 F.4th 1154 (9th Cir.), *cert. denied*, 145 S. Ct.140 (2024).
SiOnyx LLC v. Hamamatsu Photonics K.K., 981 F.3d 1339 (Fed. Cir. 2020).
SmithKline Beecham plc v. Apotex Europe Ltd., [2006] EWCA Civ 658 (Eng.).
Sonos, Inc. v. Google LLC, No. C 20-06754, No. C 21-07559, 2023 WL 6542320 (N.D. Cal. Oct. 6, 2023), *aff'd in part, rev'd in part*, No. 2024-1097, 2025 WL 2473258 (Fed. Cir. Aug. 27, 2025).
Spectrum Solutions, LLC v. Longhorn Vaccines & Diagnostics, LLC, IPR2021-00847 (Patent 8,084,443 B2), IPR2021-00850 (Patent 8,293,467 B2), IPR2021-00854 (Patent 8,669,240 B2), IPR2021-00857 (Patent 9,212,399 B2), IPR2021-00860 (Patent 9,683,256 B2), 2024 WL3561972 (July 11, 2024).
Spectrum Sports, Inc. v. McQuillan, 506 U.S. 447 (1993).
SSI Techs., LLC v. Dongguan Zhengyang Elec. Mech. Ltd., 59 F.4th 1328 (Fed. Cir. 2023).
Standard Oil Co. (Ind.) v. United States, 283 U.S. 163 (1931).
Stowarzyszenie 'Oławska Telewizja Kablowa' v. Stowarzyszenie 'OłStowarzyszenie. Stowarzyszenie Filmowców Polskich, Case C-367/15, ECLI:EU:C:2017:36 (CJEU 2017).
Symbol Techs., Inc. v. Lemelson Med., Educ. & Rsch. Found., 422 F.3d 1378 (Fed. Cir. 2005).
Synteco SpA v. Laboratoires Negma SAS, Cour de cassation, Judgment of Feb. 10, 2015, PIBD No. 1025, III-260 (Fr.).
Taurus IP v. DaimlerChrysler, 726 F.3d 1306 (Fed. Cir. 2013).
TC Heartland LLC v. Kraft Foods Group Brands LLC, 581 U.S. 258 (2017).
TCL Commc'n Tech. Holdings, Ltd. v. Telefonaktiebolaget LM Ericsson, No. SACV 14-341, 2018 WL 4488286 (C.D. Cal. Sept. 14, 2018), *vacated in part, rev'd in part, and remanded on other grounds*, 943 F.3d 1360 (Fed Cir. 2019).
Telefonaktiebolaget Ericsson AG (Publ) v. Competition Commission of India, LPA 247/2016 (Delhi High Court July 13, 2023).
Telefonaktiebolaget LM Ericsson v. Lenovo (U.S.), Inc., 120 F.4th 864 (Fed. Cir. 2024).
Teva Branded Pharm. Prods. R&D, Inc. v. Amneal Pharms., LLC, 124 F.4th 898 (Fed. Cir. 2024).
Teva Branded Pharm. Prods. R&D, Inc. v. Amneal Pharms., LLC, 736 F. Supp. 3d 227 (D.N.J. 2024).

Teva Pharm. Indus. Ltd. v. Eur. Comm'n, Case C-2/24 P, ECLI:EU:C:2025:825 (CJEU 2025).
Texas Instruments v. Fujitsu, Case No. Hei 10(O) 364 (S. Ct. Apr. 11, 2000) (Japan).
Therasense, Inc. v. Becton, Dickinson & Co., 649 F.3d 1276 (Fed. Cir. 2011) (en banc).
Tongfa Pneumatic Valve Actuators Plant v. Yuan Li, Ning Min San Chu Zi No. 188 (Nanjing Intermediate People's Ct. 2006).
Tribunal de la Seine, Judgment of March 18, 1932, 1933 Annales 14 (Fr.).
Trucking Unltd. v. Cal. Motor Transp. Co. 1967 Trade Cas. (CCH) ¶ 72,298 (N.D. Cal.), *rev'd on other grounds*, 432 F.2d 755 (9th Cir. 1970), *aff'd*, 404 U.S. 508 U.S. (1972).
Trucking Unltd. v. Cal. Motor Transp. Co., 432 F.2d 755 (9th Cir. 1970), *aff'd*, 404 U.S. 508 (1972).
Tucker v. Comm'r, 676 F.3d 1129 (D.C. Cir. 2012).
Tunstall Grp. Holdings Ltd. v. Victrix Socsan, Cour d'appel de Bruxelles, June 8, 2023, ICIP 2023, 507.
Tunstall Grp. Holdings Ltd. v. Victrix Socsan, Trib. Entr. Bruxelles, July 26, 2022, ICIP 2022, 637, *aff'd in part, rev'd in part*, Tunstall Integrated Health & Care Ltd. v. Victrix Socsan SL, Cour d'appel de Bruxelles, June 8, 2023, ICIP 2023, 507, *rev'd*, Cour de cassation de Belgique, Feb. 20, 2025 (Belg.).
U.S. Futures Exch., LLC v. Bd. Of Trade of City of Chicago, 953 F.3d 955 (7th Cir. 2020).
U.S. Philips Corp. v. ITC, 424 F.3d 1179 (Fed. Cir. 2005).
Unipharm Ltd. v. Sanofi, Case Nos. DNA 5679/21, DNA 5886/21 (S. Ct. Dec. 26, 2023) (Isr.).
United Food & Comm. Workers Loc. 1776 & Participating Emps. Health & Welfare Fund v. Teikoku Pharma USA, 296 F. Supp. 3d 1142 (N.D. Cal. 2017).
United Mine Workers of Am. v. Pennington, 381 U.S. 657 (1965).
United Parcel Service v. Commission, Case T-194/13, EU:T: 2017:144 (Gen. Ct. 2020).
United States v. Grinnell Corp., 384 U.S. 563 (1966).
United States v. Loew's, Inc., 371 U.S. 38 (1962).
United States v. Paramount Pictures, Inc., 334 U.S. 131 (1948).
United States v. Singer Mfg. Co., 374 U.S. 174 (1963).
United States v. Terminal R.R. Ass'n of St. Louis, 224 U.S. 383 (1912).
United States v. Yemec, 2013 ONSC 50 (Can.).
United Therapeutics Corp. v. Liquidia Techs., Inc., 74 F.4th 1360 (Fed. Cir. 2023), *cert. denied*, 144 S. Ct. 873 (2024).
United Video Properties, Inc. v. Telenet NV, Case C-57/15, ECLI:EU:C:2016:611 (CJEU 2016).
Unitherm Food Systems, Inc. v. Swift-Eckrich, Inc., 375 F.3d 1341 (Fed. Cir. 2004), *rev'd on other grounds*, 546 U.S. 394 (2006).
Unwired Planet Int'l Ltd. v. Huawei Techs. Co. Ltd., [2017] EWHC (Pat) 711 (Eng.), *aff'd*, [2020] UKSC 37.
Unwired Planet Int'l Ltd. v. Huawei Techs. Co. Ltd., (UK) Co. Ltd., [2020] UKSC 37.
Uponor AB v. Heatlink Group Inc., [2016] FC 320 (Can.).
USS-POSCO Indus. v. Contra Costa County Bldg. & Constr. Trade Council, 31 F.3d 800 (9th Cir. 1994).
Va. Panel Corp. v. MAC Panel Co., 133 F.3d 860 (Fed. Cir. 1997).
Vanguard Rsch., Inc. v. PEAT, Inc., 304 F.3d 1249 (Fed. Cir. 2002).
Verizon Commc'ns Inc. v. Law Offices of Curtis V. Trinko, LLP, 540 U.S. 398 (2004).
Victrix Socsan S.L. v. Tunstall Group Holdings Ltd., Cour de cassation de Belgique, Feb. 20, 2025 (Belg.).
Villa Crop Prot. (Pty) Ltd v. Bayer Intell. Prop. GmbH, 2022 (4) BCLR 461 (CC) (S. Afr.).
Virgin Atlantic Airways Ltd. v. Zodiac Seats UK Ltd., [2013] UKSC 46 (Eng.).

Volkswagen AG v. Network Sys. Techs. LLC, UPC_CFI_514/2023, Application Nos. 11434/2024, 11453/2024, 11833/2024 (L.D. Munich Apr. 23, 2024).
Walker Process Equipment, Inc. v. Food Machinery and Chemical Corp., 382 U.S. 172 (1965).
Wang Lab'ys, Inc. v. Mitsubishi Elecs. Am., Inc., 103 F.3d 1571 (Fed. Cir. 1997).
Waugh Chapel v. United Food & Comm'l Workers, 728 F.3d 354 (4th Cir. 2013).
Wehrkamp-Richter v. Guitay, Cour de Cassation, Feb. 17, 2012 (Fr.).
WesternGeco LLC v. ION Geophysical Corp., 913 F.3d 1067 (Fed. Cir. 2019).
Whirlpool Corp. v. Camco Inc., 2000 SCC 67 (Can.).
Windsurfing Int'l, Inc. v. AMF, Inc., 782 F.2d 995 (Fed. Cir. 1986).
Winter v. Natural Resources Defense Council, Inc., 555 U.S. 7 (2008).
Wolverhampton City Council v. London Gypsies and Travellers, [2023] UKSC 47.
WT/DS611—China—Enforcement of Intellectual Property Rights, https://policy.trade.ec.europa.eu/enforcement-and-protection/dispute-settlement/wto-dispute-settlement/wto-disputes-cases-involving-eu/wtds611-china-enforcement-intellectual-property-rights_en.
WT/DS632-1—China—Measures Concerning Patent Licensing Terms: Request for Consultations by the European Union, Jan. 22, 2025, https://docs.wto.org/dol2fe/Pages/SS/directdoc.aspx?filename=q:/WT/DS/632-1.pdf&Open=True.
X v. SPRL Green & Co., 2012/RG/1003 (Mons Ct. App. Dec. 2, 2013) (Belg.).
Xiaomi Commc'n Tech. Co., Ltd. v. InterDigital, Inc., E 01 Zhi Min Chu No. 169 (Wuhan Intermediate People's Ct. Sept. 23, 2020) (China).
Xitronix Corp. v. KLA-Tencor Corp., No. A–14–CA–1113, 2015 WL 5037387 (W.D. Tex. Aug. 24, 2015).
Yue Gao Fa Min San Zhong Zi No. 306 (Guangdong High Ct. 2013) (China).
Zenith Elecs. Corp. v. Exzec, Inc., 183 F.3d 1340 (Fed. Cir. 1999).
Zenith Radio Corp. v. Hazeltine Rsch., Inc., 395 U.S. 100 (1969).
Zila, Inc. v. Tinnell, 502 F.3d 1014 (9th Cir. 2007).
Zorro Productions, Inc. v. The Individuals, Corporations, Limited Liability Companies, Partnerships, and Unincorporated Associations Identified on Schedule A Hereto, Case No. 23-cv-5761, 2023 WL 8807254 (N.D. Ill. Dec. 20, 2023).
ZTE Corp. v. Conversant Wireless Licensing Co., (2018) Yue 03 Min Chu No. 335-1 (Shenzhen Intermediate People's Ct. Sept. 28, 2020) (China).
Zudian Intelligent Technology Co., Ltd. v. Simsukian Electronic Technology Co., Ltd., (2022) 高法知民终124号.

Index

For the benefit of digital users, indexed terms that span two pages (e.g., 52–53) may, on occasion, appear on only one of those pages.